My Heart's Quest

Collected Writings of Eric Doyle,
Friar Minor, Theologian

Edited by
Josef Raischl SFO
and
André Cirino OFM

Franciscan International Study Centre
Canterbury, England
2005

Cover artists: Christine Cavalier and Marc Lisle
Cavalier Lisle Art & Design
www.cavalierlisle.com
Photographs from archives of the Province of Immaculate Conception,
England, except photo 13, used with permission of Rev. Alan Webster.

ISBN 0-9549272-0-6

Published by the Franciscan International Study Centre
www.franciscans.ac.uk
Printed in England

Contents

On Various Franciscan Themes

On Saint Bonaventure

On Blessed John Duns Scotus

On Teilhard de Chardin

On Various Themes

Two Recorded Talks

St. Francis—St. Clare and Spiritual Motherhood
Universal Call To Holiness

Preface

May I first express my gratitude to André and Josef for undertaking this monumental task of trying to compile a hands-on resource of the thoughts, words and prayers of a friar who was so catholic in his enthusiasm as to defy even the compilation of anything like an index of his interests. I am particularly grateful to accept this invitation to preface this volume on behalf of our Province of the Immaculate Conception.

In the elective Chapter of 1984, under the wise and fraternal guidance of our General Visitator, Charles Finnegan, Eric Doyle was re-elected to serve as Definitor, with special responsibility for formation and studies, and I was appointed as Guardian of our fraternity in Canterbury, with Eric as Vicar to the fraternity. More of this anon.

I am a friar who began and completed his *initial* formation and studies at a time prior to Vatican II. In those days teaching was done through the medium of the various manuals. Names that spring to mind are—Reinstaedler (Philosophy), Tanquerey (Theology), Noldin (Moral).

Part of my current ministry is helping with retreats and spiritual direction, and as my approach owes practically everything to Scripture, St. Francis, Bonaventure, Scotus, it not infrequently evokes comment, especially from clergy: "Why were we not taught this in seminary?" It is with a sense of embarrassment that I have to align myself with them and ask—"Why was I not taught this in seminary?" Mention of Bonaventure and Scotus was relegated to footnotes in the manuals, and in the case of Scotus, words advising caution appeared.

For me, this was Eric's most precious gift to our Province. He alerted us to the wealth of spiritual living, prayer, devotion, philosophy, theology that saturates our Franciscan heritage; and also to the more than significant contribution made in this by friars from what is now this Province. He did this in the only real way—not just by talking about it—but by his personal effort and commitment to try, daily, to become what he was first receiving—friar minor.

Like others before him, Eric had a dream, and part of this dream was about returning some day to Canterbury, the place where the Franciscan story began in this land, there to set-up a Franciscan Centre for study and formation in the Franciscan Charism. He was in the vanguard of this return when he moved from the Suffolk countryside, back to the place of our beginnings with a similar number of friars that formed that first arrival in 1224. Eric is rightly described as a *founding father* of what is now the Franciscan International Study Centre, which had its official opening in September 1974, commemorating the 750th anniversary of the coming of the Friars Minor to England.

This volume presents a cross-section of his vast interests, and for those who knew Eric, they will recognise a consonance between what he said and wrote and how he related to them individually.

In the days of renewal, consequent on Vatican II, Eric urged and led from the front in showing how the vision of Francis of Assisi has a perennial relevance in all matters relating to Church and World. His enthusiasm was infectious. It certainly infected me, to the extent that I began to hold out the hope that one day I might be able to work and live our Franciscan life more closely with Eric. Such was my dream, and what good fortune to receive from the Chapter Congressus of 1984 the opportunity to do just that.

My first task as Guardian of Canterbury, in July 1984, was to take Eric to hospital, in the care of our Sisters—Franciscan Missionaries of the Divine Motherhood—at Mount Alvernia, Guildford. Eric never returned to Canterbury, he died 25th August 1984.

His gift of himself to us remains with us in many ways. Whatever we might think of Eric being taken from us at such an early age, in his 46th year—like Francis—he would tell us that no matter how we might feel about this, his work is done; and I am sure I can hear him reminding us of what St. Francis said about this: "As the Lord has shown me what it was mine to do, may the Lord show you what it is yours to do".

So it is with real gratitude that I endorse what André and Josef have produced. It reminds us all that what Eric so passionately strove for in his life, he too had first to receive as gift—the gift that is on offer to each one of us.

To Eric, who helped show us just what a treasure we have in our hands, and to our editors who have made so much of this now accessible in one place, our thanks and appreciation. Such an opus as this cannot happen without being resourced. To our brothers especially in the Provinces of Immaculate Conception, New York; Holy Name, New York; John the Baptist, Cincinnati, and to so many others, brothers and sisters, who have rallied round, our grateful thanks for your fraternal generosity, affirmation and support.

Those who have died have not gone very far,
they have gone to God,
and God is very near.

Eric Doyle, Friar Minor.

Austin McCormack OFM
Provincial Minister
Province of Immaculate Conception
England

Introduction

In autumn 1981, Josef Raischl arrived in Canterbury for a year of theological studies in conjunction with the Catholic University of Eichstätt, Germany. Exposure to Eric Doyle's person and teaching helped to guide the work on his thesis back in Germany: *The Motive for the Incarnation in the Writings of St. Lawrence of Brindisi.*[1] Eric, a passionate man, was deeply reflecting on the incarnational question when Josef first met him. Two memories demonstrate the effect this man had on Josef as well as on other people:

> The more I think about Eric, the more I feel I owe a great deal to him. . . .I think his constant concern over TV to evolve a good popular theology, genuinely coping with the depths and mysteries both about God and about human life was extremely important and I sensed that in the years ahead, he would have made a major contribution of value to us all.[2]

> It's the Rev. Eric Doyle, a Franciscan friar, who comes on strongest, not only as a theological elucidator, but as a telly-character so unselfconscious that you're constantly aware of him. He's bespectacled and neat in his religious habit but he comes out with some startling things such as that he once fell asleep while praying. Then he says with utter simplicity: "In praying you are trying to listen with your heart". He takes even Swingfield's suggestion, that prayer is another version of the psychiatrist's couch, very seriously, but with a glint of irony in his answer: "Oh, yes, prayer is much cheaper than Harley Street".[3]

Hearing about his early death two years later, Josef, now back in Germany, deeply felt the loss of this great Franciscan scholar. And as a former

---

[1] See Doyle' article *John Duns Scotus and the Place of Christ* in this anthology.
[2] Alan Webster, former Dean of St. Paul's Cathedral, London, and colleague on a weekly television programme, in a letter to Doyle's Provincial, 17 September 1984.
[3] *Tom Hutchinson's Weekend View* in EVENING STANDARD, 25 November 1972.

student of Doyle, Josef was very much aware of his prolific writings scattered in many different journals and periodicals.

In 1987 we, André and Josef, first met in Rome where our friendship and cooperation on many Franciscan projects began—the most consistent being our retreat work with St. Bonaventure's "Journey into God".[4] Doing this work, we connected more and more with Doyle's ideas through his writings. And in 2000, when André arrived to teach at the Franciscan International Study Centre at Canterbury, he too discovered what Eric meant for this Centre, for the Franciscan Order and for the Church. So the idea began to take flesh, the same idea Eric himself had expressed in a letter from 13 October 1980 to his provincial minister:

> At the moment I am finishing an edition of St. Bonaventure's sermons on St. Francis for Chicago. Mark Hegener OFM is the authorised Censor. . . .He has asked me to put together all my articles on Religious Life and Franciscan Life and to add three chapters to make a book under some such title as *Following Christ in Religious and Franciscan Life*. . . .G. Chapman of Cassells now have asked me to write a book on Christology along the lines of Christ's uniqueness. That is now about half finished in my own hand.

We are very happy to present this anthology of Eric Doyle's writings for publication exactly 20 years after his death. We altered neither the author's language nor his style of writing, being very much aware of the fact that Eric would have expressed himself quite differently in this day and age. Moreover, when you read the articles we have chosen, you will occasionally encounter some repetition, such as the biographical facts of Blessed John Duns Scotus. We included the repetitions cognisant of the fact that anthologies are read sometimes by choice of topic and not from cover to cover.

Our anthology is somewhat atypical. We have woven many poignant memories about Eric Doyle throughout this collection of his writings because we feel that his life and writings are intertwined. To make it "user-friendly", we have highlighted the memorial sections in the table of contents. Also, the extensive use of photos and CDs of his voice allows him, so to speak, to "come alive" for the reader and listener in spite of the fact that some of the originals were not the best quality.

Being aware of the fact that Doyle's final writings were done in 1984, there is not a single article that we chose for this collection that does not have

---

[4] A. Cirino and J. Raischl, *The Journey into God. A Forty-Day Retreat with Bonaventure, Francis and Clare,* St. Anthony Messenger Press, Cincinnati OH 2002.

value for the reader today. This became clear to André when he was proof-reading the entire text for the first time in Italy. Sitting on a patio in Rome reading Doyle's article on *The Future of the Papacy* he looked up from the text at the dome of St. Peter's Basilica after reading Doyle's suggestion: "It would be a venture of tremendous significance if the pope were to invite the youth of the world to come to Rome to spend, say, three days with him reflecting and praying".[5] This suggestion became a reality on 20 December 1985 when Pope John Paul II announced the institution of 'World Youth Day', with the first international gathering in 1987.

Proof-reading *Reflections on the Theology of Preaching* on 10 June 2004—the 37th anniversary of his ordination—André heard Doyle's challenge:

> On his ordination day God says to every priest what once He said long ago to His prophet Jeremiah: "There! I am putting my words into your mouth" [Hebrews 1:9]. On that day every priest commits his entire and unknown future into the hands of God. From that moment, as a minister of the Word, every word the priest speaks and reads must be drawn into the service of the Word which remains forever. In particular, his private reading and study of the Scriptures is a proximate preparation for the Liturgy of the Word at Mass and especially for the proclamation of the gospel and the breaking of the bread of the Word which is the homily.

There were many such proof-reading moments of connection and integration. We hope for the same for each of you.

We would like to express our deep gratitude to the many people who made this book possible. First, the enthusiastic initial response and continued support of the Provincial Minister, Austin McCormack OFM strongly encouraged the editors in the development of this anthology.

To Philippe Yates OFM, Principal of the Franciscan International Study Centre, we give thanks for risking a new publishing venture at the Centre and for posting letters to many publishers for permission to reprint Doyle's writings.

We want to recognize Clare Knowles FMSL who monitored the mailing of the lengthy list of reprint permissions.

---

[5] See the conclusion of this article for the great detail Doyle delineates in his suggestion.

And we offer our gratitude further to all the publishers who so generously responded to our request to reprint articles Doyle initially published with them.

To Richard Caraccio, bursar of the Centre, we owe a special debt of gratitude for the many and varied tasks he supervised—caring for our funds, meeting with publishers and CD companies, and for basically keeping us focused on this project.

We thank Ann Moynihan, Centre Librarian, for finding so many esoteric articles included in this work and for procuring names and addresses of many publishing houses.

And we are likewise grateful to Ninian Arbuckle OFM, archivist of Doyle's Franciscan Province, for combing the provincial archives for many of the treasures we have been able to print in this book.

We acknowledge Christopher Dyczek OFM and George Smulski OFM for their generosity in surrendering to us their collection of Doyle's articles. We likewise thank Margaret McGrath FMSJ for her encouragement and for making video footage of Doyle available to us, and Brenda Abbott who gave us a cassette of one of his talks that we were able to convert into a CD.

We are grateful for the expertise of Marc Lisle and Christine Cavalier for the cover so artistically melded together from several different perspectives.

Our gratitude extends to Murray Bodo OFM and Joseph Schwab OFM for their helpful advice, especially in choosing a title for this anthology.

And it was the indefatigable scanning skills of Alvydas Virbalis OFM and Antanas Bluzas OFM, and the proof-reading of Anthony Cho OFM, that launched us on this publishing journey.

We acknowledge with deep gratitude the financial assistance from three provinces of the Friars Minor in the United States—the Province of the Immaculate Conception, New York; the Province of St. John the Baptist, Ohio; and the Province of Holy Name, New York—for helping us make this dream a reality.

And because of the great volume of Doyle's writings that we discovered, it was a final grant from Paul Perkins SFO, that gave us the elasticity we needed in the last months of editing.

We express our hope and dream that the spirituality and theology taught by Eric Doyle may bear fruit in the hearts of Franciscans all over the world as we still uncover the richness of this gift.

In Eric's diary we found these touching words of the thirty-year-old friar:

> *I feel very glad to be alive,*
> *to be a member of this race,*
> *to live on this earth.*
> *I want to be a student;*
> *I would like to study philosophy very deeply;*
> *I would like to write.*

May this anthology foster his *heart's quest* for each one of you!
Peace and all good!

Josef Raischl SFO and André Cirino OFM
Dachau/New York
25th August 2004
20th Anniversary of Eric Doyle's death

Chronology of Eric Doyle

13 July 1938	➤	Born in Bolton, Lancashire,
	➤	Baptized William Martin
	➤	St. Joseph's Primary school
	➤	Thornleigh Salesian College
1954	➤	Enters Order of Friars Minor Immaculate Conception Province in England
1955 to 1961	➤	Studies at East Bergholt, Suffolk
23 July 1961	➤	Ordination to priesthood at East Bergholt
15 October 1961	➤	Pontificium Atheneum Antonianum, Rome
28 June 1962	➤	Licentiate in Sacred Theology
25 November 1964	➤	Doctorate in Church History *Summa cum laude*
1964	➤	Franciscan House of Studies, East Bergholt, Suffolk
Summer 1971	➤	Residence at Canterbury
4 October 1973	➤	One of the founding friars of the Franciscan Study Centre
10 September 1974	➤	Official Opening of the Franciscan Study Centre

1970 to 1982	➢ Graduate Theology Summer Sessions at St. Bonaventure University, New York, USA
	➢ Teaching at the University of Kent at
Canterbury	
	➢ Member and one time Vice-President of the Teilhard de Chardin Society of Great Britain
1971 to 1984	➢ "The Big Question": a weekly talk-show on television; more than 500 broadcasts
	➢ Anglican-Roman Catholic Working Group on the ordination of women
	➢ Anglican-Roman Catholic Consultation on the ordination of women at Versailles
1984	➢ Member of the visiting team and theological commission for the renewal of the Antonianum, the Franciscan University in Rome
25 August 1984	➢ Sister death meets him 1.15 AM at Mt. Alvernia Nursing Home, Guildford, where he spent the last two weeks of his life. He died of cancer.
31 August 1984	➢ Burial at Franciscan Friary, Chilworth.

Doyle's Last Homily
Pentecost Sunday, 10th June 1984[1]

Jesus breathed on them and said: "Receive the Holy Spirit".
[John 20:22]

The Holy Spirit of God who dwells in the mystery of God's existence
for ever and ever, as the bonding between the Father and the Son, is probably
the most mysterious of the persons of the Blessed Trinity. For the Word of God
took our way of life and our existence to Himself. And so ever since, from the
time of Jesus, humanity can never be separated from God. and to think of the
best and the kindest, the most mature, the most integrated of people, which is
to think of Him, is now to think of God. For Jesus is Emmanuel, God with us.

And he used, during his earthly life, terms of intimacy and
indescribable familiarity when he spoke about the One whom we call the
Father. Not that we can really get an idea of God from an earthly father, but we
have to get to this man Jesus to understand something of what he means by that
word, that word used of the One who is Creator, from whom all is derived and
from whom for all eternity there wells up the truth of the Son and the love of
the Spirit.

But when we come to the Holy Spirit, then there is a little difference.
For we have to use so often analogies which say a little about Him but seem in
the end rather limp. And certainly however beautifully he may be depicted as
a dove, it does really little to understand the inner workings of the Holy Spirit.
If however there is a way to understand a little of the Holy Spirit, then it surely
must be through His workings. How something works will give you a little clue
as to what it is made of—what makes it tick, so to say.

The Holy Scripture associates the Spirit of God first of all with
someone who brings order from chaos. The primeval chaos over which the
Spirit broods, brought from it the order that we call cosmos. But then we meet
it so beautifully in the episode of the Annunciation. The Holy Spirit is not only

---

[1] Handwritten manuscript published with permission from the Province of Immaculate
Conception, England.

responsible for order but He is responsible for the real, true, historical Presence of the Word in our world. "How can this come to be since I know not a man?" said our Lady. "The Holy Spirit will come upon you" and there from the Holy Spirit we have that tiny, vulnerable adorably attractive little child and that is God.

And then the Holy Spirit is the principal author of Holy Scripture. And anyone, even with the most cursory acquaintance with the Holy Scripture, knows this is the hand of a poet, knows this is the hand of creativity, knows this is an eminent litterateur. Let us consider the psalms, consider the prologue of Saint John's gospel, consider the end of the book of Revelation: all that is rich and beautiful; never have words been used so beautifully for such a purpose.

And if this is not enough, He creates the power in the Church so that what came forth from the side of Christ on the Cross, the Church, the Blood and Water was now made manifest by a power that one could not believe possible. Not only were they bonded together, but they were bonded together without fear. And they could proclaim a presence because they were it. And that selfsame Presence continues until now.

And as if this was not enough, then we will hear the priest at Mass call down upon the elements of the Bread and Wine the Holy Spirit, so that he should now make the Risen and Glorified Saviour really and truly in his very Being, present in our midst under the tiny form of the little Host and the few drops of Wine in the chalice.

Everything that is beautiful, all our desire for unity, all our desire for identity with the world of our experience, all words we say about Almighty God, all poetry with art, all of it, has its source in the creative Spirit of God, and there is none other. That is the font whence it all is derived; that tells us what the Holy Spirit of God must be like. And then, floundering, we find ourselves coming upon such words as the Creative One, the Original, the Sustainer, the Tender, The Eternal Feminine in God, all that is creative and tender and caring and motherly which opposes all violence. And all that is destructive: the antipodes, the opposite of all this, which comes from the Father of Lies, the Destroyer and Murderer from the beginning.

He is then certainly the Soul of the Church. He is our common soul so to speak. And it is because of the Holy Spirit that we are here, and this real true presence of the Holy Spirit which is ourselves, is the proof that there is a holy Spirit and that there is the on-going Pentecost.

Notice in that reading, they were in the Upper Room, they were afraid. What is the first result of love according to Holy Scripture? It drives out fear. Where love is, there is no fear. Where love rules, there is no will to power. And there we see the doors smashed open as Christ himself had broken down the gates of Hell in his descent to the lower regions, so the Holy Spirit broke open the gates of fear in the hearts of the disciples. And that which was there among them was now shared—so much so—that they were thought to be sozzled; in which case you think you had it all. Not the way, of course, I suppose, let us say, if we all sat in a tea-chest. Locked away in a box, you know at least where you are, but it is highly doubtful if you know who you are. You need the others to attempt that. And that is why the Holy Spirit is the one who makes the Church a people by the unity of the Father, the Son an the Holy Spirit. God is not, so to speak, alone in the tea chest. He is always related to the Son, and the Son always related to Him and vice-versa through the Holy Spirit. Everything is possible to the Holy Spirit of God.

First of all, He will teach us to pray. That is the first act of the true disciple to worship Almighty God. To reverence His Holy Name and to worship Him, that is the essence of the mission, it is the essence of the Gospel. And the Holy Spirit is the one who teaches how to worship.

St. Paul describes Him as "dwelling in temples", the temple that is ourselves. And it is in the temple that we learn to contemplate, to be with our own temple. And in the temple in Jerusalem, the Holy of Holies which the High Priest enters but once a year on the day of atonement, in that Holy of Holies dwelt the presence of the living God. In this temple he dwells at the core of who we are; he now dwells and makes us holy.

Then if we speak of the Church, we have of course through the Holy Spirit a great image created for us in Our Lady. And our Lady has been described as the Spouse of the Holy Spirit. She is the Mother of God through the Holy Spirit. If she is an image in this regard to each of us as well as to the Holy Church, then we may take up the point made 700 years ago by St. Bonaventure that we can also be his mother:

> that He wishes to be conceived in us through the Holy Spirit. And by a change of heart and a radical conversion –to grow in us as the child grows in the womb of its mother. And then, mystically, to bring forth this child by a holy life and by words that edify; and by example that spurs people on to what is better and holier and nobler; to name Him. And what name shall we give this child? The name is Jesus. To say the name over and over again, for it is the Gospel of the name that we preach. And this name was given Him from God the Father, the

saviour. And there is no name more holy in heaven or on earth or under it. Jesus, so we name Him.

And then when it seems that He recedes, and He does not hear us in prayer, and we feel we have lost Him, then to go with the Magi looking for him. For he will then be found in all the places that we never thought He would be. We thought He might only be in Church. Oh, that is a vulgar error. He is found everywhere, lifting the stones, looking to the nooks and crannies, the little corners, under the cobwebs, in a tiny word, in somebody's wink, ass distinct from a blink. We find Him by looking for Him with the Magi and we ask, so often:

> Where is He who has been born King of the Jews?
> We have seen his star in the East.
> We have seen his splendour shining in the mind.
> We have caught his fragrance and it is alluring.
> We have heard his voice and it is soft and tender.
> We have felt his embrace and it is irresistible.
> Where is He? And looking He is found.
> And then we can kneel down and
> offer Him the gold of our prayer.
> And the frankincense of our devotion.
> And the myrrh of our sorrow for our sins.
> And then led by the Spirit we can take Him in the temple,
> The temple of the heart to present Him to God the Father.
> And there standing before the throne of God
> to offer Him the only gift—in any case there is—
> the gift that makes all of us a gift.

Finally by the Holy Spirit we are made Apostles. The Church is apostolic not simply because there are twelve Apostles but first, because God sent an Apostle to us from the distant nearness of His eternal life: the Apostle Jesus. And when Jesus was glorified and sat down at the right hand of God the Father in His Lordship, then did He sent the Holy Spirit, which is the second Apostle. And this second apostle is the one who gave the twelve their courage to go out and to proclaim what they themselves had received. An that selfsame Apostle is the one who gives us the power to do the same.

Saying to us: there is nobody who has not a talent and a gift in Christ. There is nobody who is not an Apostle. There is nobody who is exempted from proclaiming the word of God. Everyone receives the Holy Spirit. He has been poured upon us. And everyone is obliged because of that gift to share what was so generously received.

It is common place in accidents, when one hears of people collapsing, to give them the kiss of life. That is the image that came into my mind as I heard the words of the holy gospel earlier this morning. He breathed on them and in that breathing He brought back to life forever the heart of the whole Church. In the name of the Father and the Son and the Holy Spirit. Amen.

Homily Preached on 7th November 1984 at the Memorial Mass[1]
Ninian Arbuckle OFM

Since our brother, Eric Doyle, died on 25th August of this year a great number of people have written to us testifying to the wonderful work that Eric had done and sympathising with us at our loss of such a great man. However, the writers go further: they speak of what Eric meant to them personally, of the kind of person he was, of his joy, enthusiasm, and often simply of the pleasure and privilege they felt at having met him. A good number of these people recount little incidents of their encounter with Eric—there is a lot of anecdote surrounding his activity, memories that are recounted with love and affection: almost the beginning of a legend.

I am going to take my lead from such people and begin with an anecdote from Eric's life. It is my conviction that anecdote and legend retain and express in a more lasting way the character and truth about people much more than do abstract adjectives many of which are greatly overworked in our society. The great characters of the past, whether they be found in the Bible or in our own folklore are kept alive for us by the fact that stories about them have been preserved and handed down from age to age—stories that embody and give flesh to the qualities for which such people are remembered.

So, I want to recount a story about Eric which, for me, illustrates the kind of man I got to know over a period of 29 years. Eric liked to eat the little sweets called 'Smarties'. And he told us that there was only one way to eat Smarties. As he sat at his desk working, he would line the Smarties in a row on the desk beside him, not in any old way, but always in the same order of colour and flavour. And they had to be eaten in that order. In this way, Eric maintained, you progressed from one flavour to the other and so found full enjoyment in each small sweet. He knew. Because he had eaten Smarties in this way since he was a boy!

---

[1] THE TEILHARD REVIEW AND JOURNAL OF CREATIVE EVOLUTION 20.1 (Spring 1985) pp. 24-26. Published with permission from the British Teilhard Association.

Around the year 1977, however, Eric discovered that he could no longer detect the particular flavour of each individual Smartie. Only the orange flavoured one could be detected. The others all tasted the same. So Eric wrote a letter to the Production Manager of Rowntrees, who apparently make Smarties, complaining about this drop in standards. Eric told us that he received a very unsatisfactory answer that waffled on about the difficulty of keeping standards up and about wanting to meet the demands of the customer and low cost—along with two complimentary boxes of Smarties! And as Eric himself would finish the tale, his face would be transformed by that radiant and mischievous smile of his.

For me, there is so much in that account that is Eric. First there is that honest, unpretentious pleasure in simple things, even simple things retained from childhood, of which many of us have been robbed by the inhibitions and sophistication of adult life. But in Eric we were able to recapture, if only for a moment and vicariously, some of the joys of our own youth. Eric could inspire and refresh because he himself had not lost the capability of being inspired by the wonder of things whether great or small, the expanse of the vision of Teilhard de Chardin, or the distinctive taste of a strawberry-coated Smartie.

We see there, too, the method and orderliness of thought and work that manifested itself in his study, his methodology, in the tidiness of his mind. We see an awareness and an interest in little things, but for Eric, none of them unimportant. It isn't simply that Eric could relate to children and adults alike, could be at home talking to children and equally at home lecturing before the learned. No. People whom our society might consider unimportant or of no significance, for Eric were important and he dedicated a lot of his time to them in an unfailing fidelity, for example, in visiting the dying and consoling the bereaved. A number of the testimonies that we have received are written by those who clearly are not used to expressing themselves in writing, but who felt that they had to testify to Eric's care for them and the help and encouragement that they had received from him.

Eric didn't simply observe things or become aware. He became involved. It wasn't sufficient that he should note the decline in the quality of Smarties. Eric had to write and protest. He didn't dabble in things; he entered into them heart and soul. Many might lament the divisions within the Christian Church, the inequality in society, in particular the position of women in the Church. But Eric championed the ecumenical movement and the inter-church dialogue. He championed the cause that sought to investigate the ordination of women in the Church, he was a strong advocate for the permanent diaconate. He was concerned that the Franciscan Order in particular should be occupied with the marginalized in the Church (as they are styled)—the divorced, the homosexual, and so on. It wasn't for Eric to sit in judgment of these people. No, he recognised their plight within the Church, and from within the Church tried to help them.

Perhaps Eric was ahead of his time. He certainly was a man of vision—but not his own vision. Eric would be the first to repudiate that suggestion. Eric's vision was of Christ, and as far as he could do so, Christ seen through the eyes of St Francis of Assisi. This vision brought a unity and a dignity to all creation, a connection that creation was a brotherhood, with Christ the first brother of all men, and then the sun and the moon, the fire and the water and mother earth as all members of the family of God, all groaning together awaiting the revelation of the children of God. It was this, I am convinced, that led Eric to his fascination with Teilhard on the one hand and his regard for "mother earth" and interest in ecology on the other. Without his Christian faith and apart from St Francis, Eric would be totally incomprehensible. It was because of the strength of his faith that he was able to bring so many new and challenging aspects of Christ to the fore—in his writings, his lectures, and in the talks and conferences that gave so much inspiration and delight to so may of those who were privileged to hear him.

I do not say that Eric had no faults. No doubt many of the things that endeared him to all of us here were the very things that caused annoyance to others. So be it. That is their concern. Our concern at the moment is to recall with gratitude and friendship the pleasure and the great enrichment that Eric was to us and to so many others.

To many it must seem a terrible tragedy that such a person should die so young with, apparently, so much yet to give. All we can say is that Eric had run his course and completed the work God asked of him. His old age, as tonight's Scripture says, and his grey hairs were not to be counted in years or colour, but in his wisdom and understanding. St Paul advises his readers that we should not grieve as others do who have no hope. Nevertheless we can grieve at our loss, with that grief that is but another aspect of love and does not deny hope. Our grief is that we can no longer see and hear and touch and communicate with someone we loved and appreciated in the only ways that God has granted us in this mode of our existence. We can communicate through prayer—and that is why we are here tonight. Our grief is a recognition of our loss, and it is natural that we should grieve. But Eric lives on. His death, like the death of every Christian, is no more than the sowing of the seed that springs to new life in something more glorious than we can possibly imagine— any more than we could imagine the flower had we only known the seed. Those of us who were with him during the last weeks of his life know that Eric was watching and waiting for the coming of the Bridegroom, ready to welcome Him when He came. And we know that that restless search for knowledge, that capacity for wonder and that irrepressible gift of joy are now fully and eternally satisfied in the presence of the all holy God.

We know from records that Eric himself kept, that the first sermon he preached on his return to this country in 1964 was entitled "The Sleeping God". I feel that the last sermon of his life might be "The Impatient God", the God who could not delay to bestow on Eric the glory and happiness of His own divine presence, in a way that might seem to us to have been premature, but to God fulfilled his eternally determined plan for Eric.

It is not for us to begrudge either God or Eric the fulfilment of this divine plan, but to thank God from the bottom of our hearts for the great gift that He gave us when He gave us Eric.

A Bio-Bibliography[1]
Peter Hooper OFM

Eric Doyle was born on 13th July 1938, baptised William Martin, brought up and received his primary and secondary education in his home town, Lancashire, a very Catholic part of Northwestern England.

He began his education at St. Joseph's Primary school, moving from there to Thornleigh Salesian College, for secondary education. He joined the Order of Friars Minor at an early age, 16, and was formed in the pre-Vatican-II-way, strict and hidden, deep in the Suffolk countryside, until he was ordained at the age of 23 in July 1961. Because he had a talent for study and a keenness to explore further and develop his appreciation of the Franciscan Charism he was sent to read Church History at the Pontificium Atheneum Antonianum, Rome, from September 1961 to November 1964. His doctoral thesis had a Franciscan flavour, and was based on the life and writings of friar William of Woodford OFM (c. 1330-1400), with special reference to his replies to Wyclif and the Lollards. He was awarded maximum approval with a *summa cum laude.*

On his return from Rome, he returned to the Franciscan House of Studies, East Bergholt, in the beautiful countryside of Suffolk, immortalised in the pastoral landscapes of the famous English artist, John Constable, a native of that place. Eric loved the "green and pleasant land" surrounding him and indulged his passion for created beauty in that hallowed place.

He soon branched out from the generalities of Church History into the specifics of the Franciscan story, with special reference to the ancient Province of England, established during the life-time of St. Francis, 1224. Indeed, Eric was responsible for the revival of interest in things Franciscan in the English Province at that time.

In the summer of 1971 the first stages of the move of the House of Studies, from East Bergholt to Canterbury, began. Eric took up residence in a family house in that city, rejoicing that he was in the forefront of the friars

---

[1] Excerpts of an Integration Seminar Paper April 1999 focusing on Doyle's Franciscan Spirituality and his thoughts on the formation system in the English Province of the Immaculate Conception of the Blessed Virgin Mary. Published with permission.

return to Canterbury, the locus of the first Franciscan friary in England. There still are the substantial remains of that friary, straddling the river Stour in the heart of the old city. Eric enjoyed guiding visitors and enthralling them with the stories of that place and of the friars who lived there, as narrated in the Chronicle of Thomas of Eccleston, who tells of the coming of the friars to England.

Eric is rightly described as a 'founding father' of the Franciscan Study Centre, which had its official opening in September 1974, commemorating the 750th anniversary of the coming of the Friars Minor to England. It was ever his dream and abiding passion to establish a Franciscan International Study Centre, in Canterbury.

Such was his transparent enthusiasm for Jesus Christ, most especially in the incarnation as appreciated and celebrated by St. Francis, that Eric predictably was sought out as preacher, broadcaster, director, as well as lecturer and author. From 1970 to 1982 he was a lecturer in the Graduate Theology Summer Sessions at the Franciscan Institute, St. Bonaventure University in New York State, USA. During the academic year he not only taught Franciscan History and Spirituality, and courses on Ecumenism at the Franciscan Study Centre, but used to teach medieval ecclesiastical history at the University of Kent at Canterbury. He was a member and one time vice-President of the Teilhard de Chardin Society of Great Britain, and presented papers at national and international meetings. Rome appointed him to sit on the Anglican-Roman Catholic Working Group on the ordination of women meeting in Assisi in 1975. Three years later, in 1978, he was appointed again as a member of the Anglican-Roman Catholic Consultation on the ordination of women held at Versailles.

His interests were wide-ranging and he wrote many articles on his favourite subjects, though most of them centred on the Franciscan charism. He wrote only two books: *St. Francis and the Song of Brotherhood*, and *The Disciple and the Master*, a translation of St. Bonaventure's sermons on St. Francis. But he will be remembered most of all by those who saw him on television, or heard him on radio. He took part in more than 500 radio and television broadcasts, not just the learned presentations and informed discussions, but also the devotional and meditative "Prayer for the Day". He became a legend in East Anglia with his 'perky' and lively appearances on "The Big Question", a religious panel chat show which was broadcast weekly, almost without interruption, from March 1971 to March 1984 by Anglia Television. This was a serious question-and-answer programme, involving a Roman Catholic priest (Eric), an Anglican clergyman, and a

Methodist minister, all fielding written questions sent in by the public. Eric's vivacity, humour and depth of insight in the answers he gave, evoked many a comment.

Eric devoured books, especially those that would lead him into new, creative trains of thought, like Teilhard de Chardin, about whom some friars would tease him. Eric could joke with the best of them but he could be serious too, especially about life-and-death issues such as the abusive way humanity treats creation. He had a remarkable memory in reading, once admitting that he could remember most of what he had ever read. This photographic memory, combined with methodological rigour, made of him a formidable—yet courteous—member of any debating panel.

Eric would refer to the Incarnate Christ quite familiarly as "the first friar", and would call St. Francis, the "elder brother". It was he who introduced the programme of Franciscan studies in the student-house to encourage all the students to learn the ways of Franciscan theology because it would lead back always directly to friar Christ, the God-Man, who humbled himself and became poor in this world for our sake.

Writing in appreciation and celebration of the 750th anniversary of the death of St. Francis, he revealed some of the most important aspects of Franciscanism that have emerged over the years.[2] He asserted very strongly in this article the relativity of the original charism and the way that a romantic view of the early years had caused some sort of guilt about those halcyon days, as if one had to be sad about what was lost. He argued in this article that the transformation which the Order went through over the course of the first century was more authentic than harking back to the primitive days. To his mind it was more important to locate the fullness of the charism within the whole century of development : 1209–1308, and place the *locus* of the original charism in that period of development of the first hundred years, where history notes growth and change in form of life and Christocentric focus.

The form of life envisaged by Francis and the early friars had been changed and lost during the first hundred years through pressure from the Church and some elements among the friars who sought a more established order. The brotherhood of itinerant apostles was sent far and wide, first to worship "he God who was there before they came", and then to proclaim the gospel of peace and reconciliation: this, Eric seems to be saying that, because

---

[2] See *Seven-hundred-and-fifty Years Later: Reflections on the Franciscan Charism* in: REVIEW FOR RELIGIOUS 36 (Jun. 1977) pp. 12-35. Editors´ note: This article is reprinted in this volume: pp. 81 ff.

of the gradual onset of declericalisation and the successful growth of small communities with more experimental living. This could be the model for our recovering the original charism. We should be living among people, alongside them, preaching the Word and exercising an apostolate of presence.

His experience of the small group living helped him acknowledge the success of this phenomenon within the wider Order. He recognised change which suggests a deeper acceptance of the original charism: e.g. the true fraternal character showing through with fewer priests and a mix of brothers working with their hands both within community and beyond, working professionally with and for ordinary people and, where appropriate, getting due recompense for their labour. There is a greater sense of fraternal respect and acceptance of everyone's special gifts. He acknowledges that:

> The local fraternity is where individual uniqueness should flourish, allowing for true communion to differentiate. It is from there that the friar is to be led into ever deeper intimacy with the Trinitarian life of God. Life in the local fraternity helps reach that fine balance between *animus* and *anima*, between the masculine and feminine components of his nature which St. Francis attained so successfully and attractively.[3]

In and through renewal Eric sees friars becoming more deeply aware of what *being Franciscan* means. He responds: "There is no place for an elite or a caste system in the Franciscan Order".[4] This is crucial for him; he loved his priesthood, and even dressed often in a clerical collar to travel. This was not clericalism in his thinking. Ministry, for him, was always service; "the washing of feet; in the minority of Francis' following the Lord". He never wanted to be in charge, or placed over anyone; indeed he exercised the fraternal ministry of Guardian. All responsibilities, and there were many, he accepted humbly as a ministry of "being the first servant of the brethren".

The fraternal character of the Order was symbolised for him by life in small communities. When he pioneered the return to Canterbury, that initial group numbered five and lived there together for three years (1971-73). It demanded a level of both human and Christian maturity. This small group living was fruitful, educative, and became normative for future developments

---

[3] *Franciscan Life and the Evangelical Counsels* in: THE CORD 30.5 (1980) pp. 132-141. Editors´ note: This article is reprinted in this volume.

[4] *Seven-hundred-and-fifty Years Later: Reflections on the Franciscan Charism*, op.cit., p. 19.

Eric shared his experiences of this in his various writings on religious life. "Subsidiarity" and "co-responsibility" are terms he uses in speaking about the mystery of consecrated obedience:

> I have been outlining a theology of religious obedience which has its origin in the Word of God and which takes cognisance of personal freedom and co-responsibility. It is, therefore, something entirely other than power or coercion. Authority discerns, co-ordinates, and persuades. Its purpose is to ensure the unity of the community and to safeguard its diversity.[5]

The other aspect of this small-group experience which Eric found helpful and productive was the context, situation or place of small group living. Eric and his group (myself included) lived by the railway station in the middle of a housing estate, in the midst of the realities of modern living, just like the early friars settling in the centre of towns and cities: they were brought face to face with the realities of life; they got involved with the yin the local parish, an expression of what he referred to as a "modern form of the apostolate of presence",[6] living cheek by jowl with the non-ecclesiastical. There is no such thing as secular for Francis, and that was the same for Eric. For him this was now our human world, our responsibility to conserve and make fruitful, to build and renew, to support and enhance for the greater glory of God. The way forward for Eric was the apostolate of presence in the midst of urban life, banishing the distinction between sacred and profane, accepting all as created in the image of God.

The discovery of the image of God, Christ as centre, is emphasized by Eric as available to all through acquaintance and familiarity with the Franciscan school of theology. Francis' spirituality is Jesus Christ, pure and simple. Francis loved the God-Man deeply, to the core of his being. He loved him absolutely, without qualification. Through his understanding and identification with the love in Francis, Eric too was drawn into this ardour. When Eric preached he inspired people; he drew them in with the fire of his love. He spoke of Francis' tenderness with understanding and empathy, drawing his listeners in to feel and taste that love. Through all this renewal and recovery of the original charism Eric points out that tensions still exist. In his experience there was a time when things polarised around reactionary and

---

[5] *Response to the Word of God and the Mystery of Consecrated Obedience* in: SUPPLEMENT TO DOCTRINE AND LIFE 17 (Sept.-Oct. 1977) pp. 267-275. Editors' note: This article is reprinted in this volume: pp. 533 ff.

[6] *Seven-hundred-and-fifty Years Later: Reflections on the Franciscan Charism*, op.cit., p. 20.

progressive views, especially in the English Province with regard to the mode of presence and apostolate in friaries. The question was do we maintain a parish-based apostolate, given by the institutional Church, who tells us that priestly work is a paradigm of the Franciscan apostolate; or do we relinquish our parishes and maintain that our presence in the world is sufficient and that our apostolate need not be priestly nor connected with ecclesiastical institutions. This reflects the ongoing debate within the English Province for several years.

Eric's love for St. Francis and the Franciscan Charism was the basis of his great energy in studying and spreading the Franciscan message. It also prompted him to search for answers to such human and contemporary issues as ecology, liberation theology, ecumenism and the place of women in the Church. For us, his brethren, our life was enriched by Eric's love of the brethren, his community spirit and his great zeal and leadership in our struggles for renewal. Eric died peacefully. In welcoming Sister Death "from whose embrace no mortal can escape", Eric followed in death, as in life, St. Francis of Assisi.

Franciscan Friar: Devoted Disciple, Faithful Witness

As far as his life goes, he joined at a young age and also died young, but he spent most of his adult life ministering to young (and not so young) men in formation. His first posting was to the Study House; his days were filled with books and reading. He loved the friars, loved being a friar, and grew naturally into the humility and joy of Franciscan living. He wore the brown habit a great deal, even walking out with it on his travels. He was short, had a slight stoop to his step, which made him look like he always had his ear to the ground, listening to another voice.

As a friar he could be 'jolly' or serious, but never down-hearted. He was optimistic about the world, but wide-eyed and aware of what was going on, so that he was never distant or impenetrable, and always interested in new things. That may be why he was involved with so many and diverse publications, ranging from CLERGY REVIEW, JOURNAL OF ECUMENICAL STUDIES, NEW BLACKFRIARS, REVIEW FOR RELIGIOUS, THE TABLET—these were the varied interests he showed. He was an evangeliser and populariser of the committed life. There was clearly a deep-seated conviction and hope in the Lord, which he felt that others should know about. This mission was his through his personality, which shone through the media, both TV and Radio, and in public appearances. He was self-effacing like the Friar Minor he was, and his vulnerability made him easily approachable.

As a disciple of the Lord he loved the Scriptures and treated all liturgical things with reverence and appreciation. It was he who reminded his community and his group that they had to provide a special place in their rooms for the enthronement of the Scriptures, and we have that practice in all public and personal places still in Canterbury. Discipleship was important for him; that is why he was so good in formation work. He was often approached for spiritual direction, both at the Centre and in the locality. His regular reviews appeared in REVIEW FOR RELIGIOUS, DOCTRINE AND LIFE, THE CORD, THE TABLET and other religious publications; his compelling originality made him sought after by a variety of publishers. Though he was often quite busy with writing by hand, he maintained the "spirit of holy prayer and devotion, to which all created things are meant to contribute" (*Later Rule* 5:2). It made his preaching and teaching profound and lyrical. He was a popular preacher and received numerous speaking invitations both at home and abroad.

He was never one to draw attention to himself, but he would generally be at the forefront when anything was going on. I remember vividly one time when brethren and friends were parading down the High Street of Canterbury dressed in our habits for a major public celebration. I think it was for the 750th anniversary of the coming of Franciscans to the city (1274-1974). That was a tremendous gathering; friars came from all parts of the world and the city was a sea of brown, grey and white. Eric gave one of the public lectures during that week, while the Cathedral and grounds were filled to overflowing at the main Ecumenical Service: numbers mounted into tens of thousands.

The public witness that the friars give continues to encourage. When he visited *Greyfriars*, the remains of the first Franciscan building in Canterbury (1227), to show guests around, he would travel in his habit. It was difficult to walk down the High Street without being stopped when Eric was accompanying! But, of course, that does not say the half of it. Eric's face was on TV and he was a very popular and effective face, not just a 'pretty-face' but a good speaker with an infectious manner. He knew how to use the media. What he said was good and in language that people could understand and find some message to light their way. He was a regular on BBC's "Thought for the Day". That was quite an art to prepare: it had to be short, punchy and to the point. He worked hard at it, because he knew how important it was to preach and communicate to others, in ways that made them think and helped them see their lives in a different way. In this he followed many Franciscan traditions of preaching *metanoia* in season and out of season. The aim of his message was always: change and trust, look to fashioning a new world through fraternity in minority.

That was the major theme of his original book, the brotherhood and sisterhood of all creation, all persons, the whole universe. He learnt this, not only from Friar Christ, nor even from Friar Francis alone; no, Eric speaks often about fraternity and about the experience of sharing together in fraternal company, with all the give-and-take of communal living. This was his real experience which he learnt from small realities of life. It is what he called "brotherhood-without-boundaries" and it has to do with a breadth of vision: Like Francis he saw brotherhood/sisterhood as human, animal, mineral, and cosmic. In a word, it was literally universal.

That is why Eric can become a model for all of a Friar Minor who is humble, devoted, faithful; he advocated this experience in his life, his teaching, his prayer and devotion. And his witness still speaks loudly to those who have met him. Eric Doyle, friar minor!

**Photo 1 and 2
above**
At East Bergholt
Friary

Photo 3
Ordination on 16
July 1961 with
Bishop Leo Parker of
Northhampton, at
East Bergholt Friary

Photo 4

Student enrolment
booklet—*Libellus*—
from the
Antonianum, Rome

Photo 5

With friars at
St. Peter's, Rome,
for the Canonization of
the English martyrs,
25 October 1970

Photo 6

Concelebrating with
Antony Rickards OFM
at Porziuncola Chapel
in Assisi, 1970

On Various
Franciscan Themes

Francis of Assisi[1]

Francis of Assisi (1181/2-1226) was the founder of the Franciscan Order of Friars, the Poor Clares and an Order of Penance for laypeople, called today the Secular Franciscan Order. His father, Pietro Bernadone, was a wealthy cloth merchant. At about the age of twenty-three, after a dissipated youth, he underwent a radical conversion of life. It was connected with a number of mystical experiences among which a leper and the crucifix at San Damiano had crucial significance.

On hearing the text of Matthew 10:7ff. at Mass on the feast of St. Matthias 1209, he embraced a life of total poverty in literal obedience to Christ's words. From that moment the gospel became an absolute in his life, and his life unfolded as a kind of exegesis of the gospel. He founded an evangelical movement whose inspiration was not only the synoptic gospels but the good news contained in the *New Testament* as a whole. As a reform movement his observance of Christ's teaching was coupled with a deep love of the church, for it was in and through the church that he had come to know the gospel. His writings, and especially the prayers he composed, are full of adoration of the Triune God and a burning love of Christ our Brother. He writes "How glorious. . .it is to have a Father in heaven. . . .How holy and beloved. . .it is to have a Brother like this who laid down his life for his sheep".

His radical poverty was not primarily ascetical; it was evangelical and christological. Christ's freely-chosen poverty was for him a revelation of the humility of God. Hence he loved Jesus above all in the crib, on the cross and in the Eucharist as manifestations of God's powerlessness, vulnerability and littleness. His first biographer, Thomas of Celano, says of him: "He was always thinking about Jesus; Jesus was in his mouth, in his ears, in his eyes, in his lands; Jesus was in his whole being".

His evangelical movement was committed to brotherhood and poverty and pledged to preaching peace. After some hesitation Pope Innocent III gave

---

[1] *A Dictionary of Christian Spirituality*, Ed. G.S. Wakefield, London: SCM Press Ltd., 1983, pp. 157f. Published with permission.

oral approval to his way of life. Later in the *Rule* of 1223 St. Francis identified the rule and life of his friars with observing the gospel.

Poverty and brotherhood are dominant themes in his writings, especially the non-approved *Rule of 1221* and the *Admonitions.* To live a life of freely-chosen material poverty coupled with humility, its spiritual counterpart, involves a mystical death to self in order to be made alive again through the gifts of God's Spirit. Without possessions it is not necessary to have weapons to defend them and so by poverty we become instruments of God's peace. To be a brother is to be related in Christ to all creatures and to observe meekness towards them all. He called every creature his brother or sister, even death was his sister. This was no mere nature mysticism, but an expression of belief in the fatherhood of God the Creator and in the gift of unity in Christ.

In September 1224 while at prayer on Mt. La Verna the marks of Christ's stigmata appeared on his body, which he bore until death. It was the final configuration of his life, prior to death, to Jesus Christ. According to St. Francis the destination of the soul's journey to God is total conformity to Christ by following in his footsteps a life of poverty, humility and meekness, whereby the disciple becomes a living symbol of the master.

Franciscan Spirituality[1]

St. Francis of Assisi did not found a school of Spirituality, nor is there a systematic Franciscan Spirituality. He was keenly aware of the uniqueness of each individual's call to union with God, as his *Letter to Brother Leo* shows. Franciscan Spirituality covers a wide spectrum of approaches to the Christian mystery. It has been called christocentric, evangelical, existential, tender, devotional and practical. All these descriptions are justified from its origins in the faith and holiness of St. Francis.

He had a profound sense of God as transcendent mystery and holy love. Out of that, sprang his passionate love of the Saviour. He was filled with awe that God, exalted in his majesty, should come among us in humility. His one desire was to follow "the teaching and the footsteps of our Lord Jesus Christ". Everything centred on Christ, the poor, humble, obedient, suffering Servant who died and rose for us. Scripture and the liturgy were his sole guides on the journey to God and he sought to observe the gospel literally. That was no form of fundamentalism or legalistic literalism. Literal observance meant a total commitment to the spiritual values the gospel proclaims.

This simple and direct approach influenced and shaped Franciscan theology and piety. St. Bonaventure teaches that Christ is our metaphysics and logic, holding the central position in everything, because he is mediator between God and humanity. All intellectual activity has to begin at that centre *(medium)* in order to arrive at wisdom, not just knowledge. Reason has its place in the *Soul's Journey into God*, but it remains subject to faith. There comes a point where reason reaches its limits and then the will passes over into God. St. Bonaventure presents his master, St. Francis, as the perfect exemplar of Christian action and contemplation, and of the latter especially in his configuration to the Crucified on La Verna. Theology according to St. Bonaventure is primarily the study of scripture, which led him to consider

---

human beings, not in the abstract, but in their historical condition as fallen and redeemed.

The place of Christ is taken a step further by Duns Scotus in the doctrine of the absolute predestination of Christ, which became a distinguishing feature of Franciscan spirituality and theology. It was resumed later by the great Capuchin Doctor of the Church, St. Lawrence of Brindisi, who demonstrates its scriptural origin. Christ is first in the plan of God, the incarnation is not decreed because of sin. God's love alone is the reason because "God is formally love" and sovereignly free. Redemption is the way his love overcomes the powers of evil. This teaching is taken directly from scripture [cf. e.g. Colossians, Ephesians] and it has seminal expression in the writings of St. Francis. The incarnation is decreed because God wills to have co-lovers in his love.

Love of the incarnate Lord found form in a variety of devotions. St. Francis' crib at Greccio may have influenced crib-building at Christmastide. In any case, devotion to the Child Jesus is a theme found in most Franciscan spiritual writers. St. Clare wrote to St. Agnes of Prague[2] that she should meditate daily on the King of angels lying in a manger. St. Bonaventure composed a beautiful little treatise *On the Five Feasts of the Child Jesus* which explains how the Child is spiritually conceived, born, named, sought and adored with the Magi and presented in the Temple, by the devout soul. St. Francis' devotion to the passion and his *Office of the Passion of the Lord* inspired a wealth of literature on the sufferings of Christ. The devotion greatly influenced the practice of the Way of the Cross whose most ardent advocate, in the form we now have it, was the Franciscan, St. Leonard of Port Maurice. St. Francis' love of the Risen Lord present in the littleness and silence of the eucharist, made eucharistic devotion a pillar of Franciscan spirituality. He also revered the names of God and cherished above all the holy name of Jesus. Devotion to the name of Jesus was encouraged by Franciscans in the thirteenth and fourteenth centuries, but its most staunch defender was the Franciscan Observant, St. Bernadine of Siena, in the fifteenth Century. He preached the name of Jesus as the summary of the gospel of salvation [cf. Acts 8:12]. Love of the humanity of Jesus in the Franciscan tradition also encouraged devotion to the Sacred Heart. It is the theme of a number of St. Bonaventure's mystical writings.

---

[2] Editors' note: Since Agnes of Prague was canonised on 12 November 1989, we amended the text to indicate this.

St. Francis had a tender devotion to the mother of Jesus which never degenerated into sentimentality. His biographer, Celano, writes: "Towards the Mother of Jesus he was filled with inexpressible love, because it was she who made the Lord of Majesty our brother". He seems to have been the first to have called Mary "spouse of the Holy Spirit". She is presented as model of the spiritual life: "We are mothers to (our Lord Jesus Christ) when we enthrone him in our hearts and souls by love with a pure and sincere conscience and give birth to him by doing good". Spiritual motherhood and the tenderness which accompanies it should be a mark of every Christian disciple. Maturity in the spiritual life for St. Francis requires one to arrive at a balance of the feminine and masculine elements in human nature. The Franciscan Order held to the doctrine of the Immaculate Conception for centuries before it was officially defined. Duns Scotus received the title Marian Doctor for his defence of the doctrine which must always be understood in the light of his teaching on the absolute predestination of Christ. Mary's redemption took place through the foreseen merits of Christ. On the devotional side the Order introduced the feasts of the Visitation and Espousals of the Virgin Mary. The crown rosary in honour of the seven joys of Mary became established in the Order in the early fifteenth Century.

St. Francis looked on all creatures as brothers and sisters united in the vast friary of the universe: he called even the Stars his sisters. He gave mystical expression to this vision in *The Canticle of Brother Sun.* So far from being distractions, all creatures are revelations of the infinite richness of God. There is therefore a definite ecological element in his spirituality. This attitude to creatures took theological form in St. Bonaventure's doctrine of exemplarism, according to which all creation is seen as God's sacrament.

The Franciscan Order has been described as contemplative-active. It is an accurate description not only in the sense that apostolic works should flow from and lead back to prayer, but also because St. Francis made provision for the eremitical life in the Order. He wrote a short *Rule for Hermitages* which marks a new development in the history of this form of life. Those who feel called to it must live in small hermitages, numbering not more than four friars. Two of them are to be 'mothers' whose duty it is to take care of their 'sons', that is, those who are given completely to prayer. Thus, in his notion of the eremitical life St. Francis combines fraternity and prayer. He inspired St. Clare and her sisters to lead an enclosed life of contemplative prayer after the model of the hidden life of Jesus at Nazareth. St. Francis also founded a successful lay movement which was called the Order of Penance. The members pledged themselves to do penance and lead simple lives. The movement had important social consequences. The brothers and sisters undertook every kind of charitable work and they set up a common fund to help brethren who were in need. They did not take up arms, nor would they hold public office. St. Francis wrote a Rule for this Order. No copy of it survives but the shorter text of his *Letter to the Faithful* may well be a version of it. It contains a genuine lay spirituality.

The virtues cultivated in Franciscan spirituality are wisdom, poverty, humility and love. Wisdom, which is surrender to the truth as personal, is mentioned first by St. Francis in his *Praises of the Virtues,* and it is, as has been said, the aim of all theological study and spiritual endeavour. To embrace poverty is the highest wisdom because it demands a self-emptying which conforms one to Christ and allows the mind and heart to be filled with divine gifts. 'Lady Poverty', as St. Francis called the virtue, has been the topic of heated and often acrimonious arguments in the history of the Order and, ironically, the cause of division. It is of course multi-faceted, and while Franciscan spirituality has had to accommodate itself over the centuries to influences and developments which make the observance of St. Francis' radical poverty well-nigh impossible, it has always insisted on detachment, powerlessness and sharing, without which mere material poverty becomes an idol or a tyrant. Humility is, as it were, the inner side of material poverty. It is basically recognition of the truth, as St. Francis writes "What a man is before God, that he is and no more". In that truth St. Francis discovered that we are all brothers and sisters in Christ, little brothers and sisters. Our first duty is to love in Christ the most high God and one another, and love is a free act of the will. Franciscan spirituality has always taught the primacy of the will and the primacy of love, and nothing could summarize it better.

The Witness of Saint Clare[1]

St. Clare of Assisi stood at the dawning of the Franciscan movement and she herself brought to it a light, as strong as it was unique, which radiated from her serene and valiant soul. That light gave new and subtle colours to the Franciscan dawn. Clare inaugurated a new form of religious life for women, unheard of till then, that they should live in total poverty without the security of income or endowments. And she called this the privilege of poverty.

Clare then is part of the glorious heritage which has formed all of us, men and women, who belong to the Franciscan Order. With Francis she is the source of a living tradition that carries the Order into the future, as a river flows on to the sea. It is both a blessing and joy for us that this courageous and holy woman was there at the Franciscan springtime to create so beautiful a version of the Franciscan vision of God and the world he created.

I have called her courageous. That word together with 'tender' describes her perfectly. Though she embraced the ideals of St. Francis with all her heart and soul, she was no mere pale reflection of him. For two years before she took up his way of life she met with Francis to discuss and question his vision, his hopes and ideals. Then and only then, having understood all that he intended, did she join him. That was her decision entirely. And not all the threats and harsh treatment from her relatives could weaken her resolve. She was a liberated woman.

It was her steadfastness that led Pope Innocent III to confirm her decision to live in complete poverty. Monks and nuns for centuries had lived the vow of personal poverty. But here was something entirely new. Clare and her sisters lived in total communal poverty. Once she had the pope's approval she never wavered in her decision, nor did she allow anyone, not even subsequent popes, to change her mind. Pope Gregory IX tried to compel her to accept some possessions at least, for prudence's sake. She remained so resolute

---

[1] TROUBADOUR 33.1 (Christmas 1983) pp. 8f. Published with permission from the Province of Immaculate Conception, England.

that the pope ended up re-confirming her privilege of poverty! In that lay her understanding of the gospel life in imitation of the poor Christ.

On her deathbed she spoke softly to her own soul: "Go forward, for he who created you, sanctified you. He protected you always as a mother does her child and he loved you with a tender love". These simple words speak volumes about Clare's relationship with God. It had ever been a distinguishing feature of Franciscan teaching to proclaim God's tenderness in himself and to us. St. Francis wanted all his followers, men and women, to be tender and motherly towards everyone, just as God is to us all. Clare fulfilled this to the letter and in her dying words she witnessed so delicately to the 'mother-ness' of God.

Both Francis and Clare took Our Lady as a model of the Christian life. As she had conceived and given birth to God's Son, so we should conceive him spiritually in faith and bring him forth by holiness before God and through love for one another.

Christmas will soon be upon us. And that feast reveals God's tenderness more than all else. Let us then mark well this aspect of Clare's limpid sanctity and ask God to make us tender and give us the grace to conceive his Son in our soul, to give birth to him, to whisper his name and to present him in the temple of our heart to God our gracious Father and Mother.

Saint Francis and a Theology of Creation[1]

In a world where man makes himself through science and technology, and at a time when there is increasing reference to biological engineering, life in test-tubes and cybernetics, it might seem just a little quaint to be talking and writing about a thirteenth century mystic who called the worm his brother. Of course it is rather quaint, if all we have is the romantic picture of a gay troubadour skipping along the road singing at the sun, talking to the trees and preaching to the birds. In that guise St. Francis, attractive and appealing in his freshness, belongs to another world altogether, a world which we may legitimately sigh for, but one gone forever, lost in the twilight of fantasy.

To begin and end with "Francis the Nature-lover" is to miss the whole point about him, even to misrepresent him entirely. For all his joy and lightheartedness there was about him a seriousness which came out best of all, perhaps, when he preached to the swallows and praised God at vespers with a nightingale. His seriousness has a message for us which we need badly in order to evaluate the present critical point in man's scientific and technological evolution. However, before we try to discern what lay beneath his extraordinary relationship with nature, we want to indicate some of the problems that arise when we, some seven centuries later, begin to reflect on his love of every creature.

Granting that he has a message for us, we still have to admit that St. Francis belonged to an age whose world-view was completely different from ours. The world was seen as static, mechanistic and limited. We today, after Galileo, Copernicus and Darwin, have grown accustomed to a world in process, a world becoming, which is dynamic, organic and unlimited. Now, once that basic distinction is made, questions come teeming into the mind: How are we to see God in the cosmos today? Is it really true to say God made the country and man the city? What is the foundation of the distinction between 'natural' and 'artificial'? Is there any distinction at all? Is it, in fact, easier to see God in a range of mountains than in a line of skyscrapers? Is God as concerned with the jumbo jet as He is with the little sparrows? In science and

---

[1] THE FRANSISCAN 12 (13 Dec. 1970) pp. 31-34. Published with permission.

technology are we trying to dominate and conquer nature rather than co-operate with it? Why is it, that while we poison our lakes and waterways, pollute the atmosphere and gobble up the countryside for power stations and runways, we build new (artificial?) lakes, construct air-conditioned buildings and lay out parks where we may sit to contemplate the riches and beauty of the earth? Is it, perhaps, that we feel a natural kinship with nature which will never be outgrown no matter whither science and technology may lead us?

Even faced with these questions and the very different world we live in, the fact is that St. Francis' love of creatures still has a strong pull on man's heart in a technocratic age. Our concern here is to discover the message at the heart of the romantic picture of St. Francis, for God uses all kinds of devices to make us understand. For St. Francis the gospel was an absolute in his life, as Yves Congar has said. And it was absolute with the absoluteness of God Himself. Anyone who has read the life and writings of St. Francis cannot have failed to notice the strange, almost intangible, quality about him that runs as a thread through the years from his sickness after the Perugia imprisonment to his holy encounter with Sister Death in 1226. From the time of his conversion (the gentle touch of God's hand) he carried within him a sense of wonderment and awe before the Primordial Mystery that is God. Through the years his sense of the Mystery grew, bringing him finally to the mystical heights that caused him to compose those most beautiful lines in chapter 23 of the Rule of 1221:

> Almighty, most high and supreme God. . .Three and One, Father, Son and Holy Spirit. . .without beginning and without end, he is unchangeable, invisible, indescribable and ineffable, incompre-hensible, unfathomable, blessed and worthy of all praise, glorious, exalted, sublime, most high, kind, loveable, delightful and utterly desirable beyond all else, forever and ever. . . .

It led him to cry out in the anguish of grace-filled joy at the beginning of *The Canticle of the Sun*: "No mortal lips are worthy to pronounce Your Name". St. Francis lived always in the presence of the Unutterable Mystery, a contemplative absorbed by the vision of God; and in contemplating the All-Holy and All-Other, he was made like God in seeing that all that has been made is very good. Here we have our first insight into the meaning of his love of creatures: If there is such beauty, attraction, power and alluring sweetness in the world, what must He be like Who is the origin, ground and source of all that is? This is why St. Francis could never have been a pantheist: The world always made him love and think about *Someone*

Whose glory and sovereign power is reflected and made manifest in and through the whole created cosmos.

From his sense of awe before the Mystery of God came his love of the Incarnate Word in Whom the Mystery of God was made the Mystery of Man. The almost incredible closeness of the All-Other in Jesus so overpowered his heart and mind that he was constrained to build the crib at Greccio, to re-enact literally the Last Supper and fast for forty days on an island in Lake Trasimene; this also gives us the key to his love of the Holy Eucharist (bread and wine of our world) and of the Word of God—all presences in their own way of the Mystery of God in the most human of things at the heart of the world. St. Francis lived out his life in imitation of Him Who walked our earth so humanly and hence Francis is the most human of all the Saints. His life is such clear proof that the nearer we draw to Christ (the *eikon* of God) the more like God and the more truly human we become. He loved to call Christ a Friar, his Brother: "How desirable it is above all things to have a Brother like this Who laid down His life for His sheep" *(Letter to All the Faithful).* When you say "brother", you have to say "Our Father". Here, then, we have the second insight into the meaning of his love of creatures: that God came so close to us in our world, in space-time, immersed in human history, made part of the earth He loves, *became* man in a truly human *becoming.*

His awareness of the Mystery of God, Source of all being and his burning love for the Lord Christ gave him that reverence of persons and things that is the hallmark of the true mystic. He addressed everyone and everything by the most sacred name of *Brother or Sister.* He saw, in the words of Saint-Exupéry, with his heart what is invisible to the eye: "the meaning of things in themselves, the inherent value of things" which precedes by absolute priority the purpose of things for us. Beginning with brotherhood in Christ, he saw the uniqueness, the originality, the never-to-be-repeated identity of every person he met. Animate and inanimate creatures he called brother and sister (Duns Scotus later said *haecceitas,* "thisness" and Hopkins afterwards "inscape") to express their unique identity, their value and intrinsic dignity. The fox in *The Little Prince* was absolutely right when he ordered: "Go and look again at the roses. You will understand now that yours is unique in all the world". If, therefore, our first reaction to persons and things is what purpose will they serve, then we must remain for ever imprisoned in ourselves; if purpose-for-us is paramount and not meaning-in-things, then we are cursed with greed and will end up with the worst greed of all: thinking we are for ourselves alone. St. Francis' reverence for all things evoked a response from every creature. Celano writes: "It is indeed wonderful how even irrational creatures recognised his affection for them and felt his tender love for them" (I:59). Love is the power that drove him to seek out all else for its own sake. It is not really so miraculous that the swallows became silent to listen to him or that the hare refused to leave him— it is the most natural thing in the world. If we, unprofitable as we are, can eventually show a horse or a dog that we love them (and that is a grace to be cherished), then what must be possible for someone like St. Francis? The contemplative has a sense of wonderment. In wonderment a man becomes a child again and the world becomes transparent. Here, then, we have the third insight into St. Francis' love of creatures: a reverence for the mystery of being, the mystery of their given-ness—that things are—through which, as they are, they glorify the Lord Who sees them good.

These three insights may be taken as the basis of a Franciscan theology of creation and a theology of ecology. But now we ask: What is the message here for us?

If you compare the *Benedicite* in the Bible, *The Canticle of the Sun* of St. Francis and the *Hymn of the Universe* by Teilhard de Chardin (linking, as it were, Ancient, Medieval and Modern Times), you will find common to all three the same sense of mystery and the same reverence for the meaning and inherent value of all being. And there, beyond doubt, is the message for us. Unless we recover our sense of mystery and approach nature with reverence for what it is and not primarily for its purpose-for-us, we cannot but expect it to take from us an even greater toll yet. Without reverence there can be no response from nature but only rebellion. Reverence will give the vision of reality wherein all true power lies. One often wonders if the pollution problem and the horrors caused by the senseless destruction of so much precious life and matter are not nature's own way of bringing us to our senses, above all to the sixth sense of *heartsight* or *eyes of the spirit* as St. Francis calls it in his *First Admonition*. Perhaps nature, maltreated though it has been, will bring us back through its own meaning to the Mystery of God, the Ground of all meaning. *Utinam!* For, unless we trace back all our science and technology to Christ and the Holy Eucharist, we will never grasp the inherent meaning of what we are doing, let alone the intrinsic meaning of nature. In the meantime we must pray that the present critical point of realisation will prove to be a turning point and then the start of a return with nature to the Source and Ground of all that is.

Ecology and the Canticle of Brother Sun[1]

In an article published in March 1967, Professor Lynn White of the University of California, argued that the historical roots of the ecological crisis can be traced to the traditional Christian view of man's dominion over nature.[2] Professor White maintained that because the roots of the trouble are largely religious, the remedy must be essentially religious. He suggested that "the profoundly religious, but heretical sense of the primitive Franciscans for the spiritual autonomy of all parts of nature may point a direction" and he proposed "Francis as a patron saint for ecologists".[3] The article sparked off a good deal of interest. Richard Means, Associate Professor of Sociology at Kalamazoo College, Michigan, took up the point and expressing fundamental agreement with White on the religious aspect of the crisis, put forward pantheism as the basis of a solution.[4] While there is a superficial attraction in pantheism as a foundation of the unity of reality,[5] ultimately it destroys the diversity of creatures through a fusion in the All and it makes change, finitude and even evil, intrinsic to God Himself. Francis A. Schaeffer, Director of L'Abri Fellowship in Huemoz, Switzerland, submitted the proposals of White and Means to a detailed analysis.[6] In conclusion he rejected both: "So pantheism is not going to solve our international ecological problem. St. Francis's concept, as presented by Lynn White, is not going to solve it—the concept that everything is equal and everything is spiritually autonomous".[7]

---

[1] NEW BLACKFRIARS 55 (Sept. 1972) pp. 392-402. Published with permission.

[2] Lynn While, Jr., *The Historical Roots of Our Ecologic Crisis*, in: SCIENCE MAGAZINE (March 19th, 1967); also in Francis A. Schaeffer, *Pollution and the Death of Man. The Christian View of Ecology*, Hodder and Stoughton, London 1972, Appendix I, pp. 70-85.

[3] Ibid., p. 85.

[4] R.L. Means, *Why Worry About Nature?* in: SATURDAY REVIEW, December 2nd, 1967; also in Schaeffer, *Pollution and the Death of Man*, Appendix II, pp. 86-93.

[5] For example, Pierre Teilhard de Chardin felt the temptation of pantheism. However, he contrasts "the Christian solution" and "the pantheist solution" and appears to hold an orthodox 'panentheism'; see *Writings in Time of War*, trans. by R. Hague, Collins, London 1968, pp. 121f; *The Phenomenon of Man*, Collins, Fontana Books 1966, p. 338; *Christianity and Evolution*, Collins, London 1971, pp. 56-75.

[6] *Pollution and the Death of Man*, pp. 1-27.

[7] Ibid., p. 32.

Romanticism is no solution because "firstly, nature, as it now is, is not always benevolent; and secondly, to project our feelings and thoughts into a tree would mean that we would have no base upon which to justify cutting down and using the tree as a shelter for man".[8]

Schaeffer rejects the 'spiritual autonomy' of nature put forward by Lynn White as the concept of St. Francis. I am not sure what White means by spiritual autonomy. He maintains that St. Francis's view of nature and of man "rested on a unique sort of pan-psychism of all things animate and inanimate, designed for the glorification of their transcendent Creator".[9] Perhaps pan-psychism is what he means by spiritual autonomy. In any case, whatever it may mean in this context for White, there is no evidence in the sources for his life that St. Francis held any sort of pan-psychism. He was indeed a Christian nature mystic, that is "one whose mystical experience, whatever form it may take, is based on Christian beliefs and involves an appreciation of Creation as God's handiwork".[10] My quibble, however, is not with White (though the primitive Franciscan view was not heretical!) but with Schaeffer. After rejecting all these views, he proceeds to give the genuine biblical view, *the* Christian view, that will serve as a sufficient basis for solving the ecological problem. The view he presents as the authentic biblical and Christian view[11] is, in fact, substantially that of St. Francis of Assisi, as a study of his writings and the early Franciscan tradition, as channelled, for example, through the works of St. Bonaventure, makes abundantly clear. Schaeffer's approval of the quotation from The Doors: "What have they done to the earth, What have they done to our fair sister", brings him closer to St. Francis than he realised.[12] It is a pity that he did not take more care to examine what St. Francis's attitude actually was.[13] Had he done so, he would have agreed that St. Francis ought to be declared the Patron of Ecology!

---

[8]   Ibid., p. 15.

[9]   Ibid., p. 84.

[10]   E.A. Armstrong, *St. Francis: Nature Mystic. The Derivation and Significance of the Nature Stories in the Franciscan Legend*, University of California Press, 1973, pp. 9,16f.

[11]   *Pollution and the Death of Man*, pp. 34-69.

[12]   Ibid., p. 9.

[13]   He makes one very positive reference to St. Francis: "In this sense St. Francis's use of the term 'brothers' to the birds (he actually calls them 'sisters') is not only theologically correct but a thing to be intellectually thought of and practically practised. More, it is to be psychologically felt as I face the tree, the bird, the ant. If this was what THE DOORS had meant when they spoke of 'Our Fair Sister', it would be beautiful. Why have orthodox evangelical Christians produced no hymns putting such a beautiful concept in a proper theological setting"—see ibid., p. 55.

The Religious Basis of the Crisis

The ecological crisis cannot he solved merely by a further employment of science and technology. The crisis is a symptom of human selfishness which lurks behind man's every endeavour and achievement. No amount of discussion alone about cybernetics and the future of man can come to terms with the moral issue involved, which concerns the meaning of man and nature and the relation of one to the other. Any effort to prevent further environmental damage on the sole grounds that we humans are in danger of extinction, without asking ourselves at the same time why it is that nature in itself should be respected and revered, is only a new brand of the very selfishness which has brought us to our present unhappy condition. For this reason, the basic agreement among the authors mentioned on the religious dimension of the ecological crisis, is of far greater import than their disagreement about how it ought to be tackled. Western science and technology are the product of Christian civilisation, which was formed by the Word of God. This has determined our history, our outlook and our thought patterns. Any attempt to answer adequately the question 'What is man?' and to discern the mutual relationship between man and nature (that is, to construct an integral anthropology) will have to include, on the one hand, biological, psychological, sociological, philosophical, artistic and religious-theological dimensions and, on the other, undertake a thorough analysis of what actually happened in the history of the relationship of man and nature, in order to discover whether it is the essence of Christianity that has brought us to the present impasse, or rather, the misuse of the world and a misunderstanding (whether conscious or not) of man's place in nature by Christian men due to human selfishness, which the Christian Gospel is pledged to root out. Such a project cannot be attempted here. It may be asserted, however, without fear of contradiction, that the doctrines of Creation (that all reality originates in a most sovereignly free act of an all-loving God) and incarnation (that this God became part of created reality which manifests that, from the beginning, matter has had the potentiality of thus expressing God) point to the truth that it is not the essence of Christianity which has brought us to the crisis, but the blind selfishness of Christians, caused by sin, which has prevented them from understanding the full implications of these doctrines and from determining their relationship to nature.

The word 'dominion' in Genesis 1:27 is unfortunate, I think, but we should also notice that it does not mean that nature has no other reason to exist except to serve man. Commenting on this verse, Gerhard von Rad explains:

"Because of man's dominion it (the creature) receives again the dignity of belonging to a special domain of God's sovereignty".[14] God's sovereignty is one of love for all He has made and therefore even though "the expressions for the exercise of this dominion are remarkably strong",[15] man is created in His Image and so has a vice-regency[16] of love under God, which must not be identified with domination.

Our contention is that it is not the essence of Christianity nor Christian teaching that has brought us to the ecological crisis, but the sinfulness of men (be they Christian or post-Christian) who by misusing their God-given stewardship, have arrogated to themselves the sovereign rights of God's dominion over the world. The authentic Christian attitude to nature is exemplified par excellence in St. Francis of Assisi who, though not its only representative, is certainly its most famous one. We are not referring to the romantic picture of the Saint, so deeply imprinted in the popular mind, as the Saint who preached to the birds, nor to the image of him projected by such films as *Brother Sun and Sister Moon.* However much he loved nature, St. Francis was no innocent, natural mystic who restored the primordial order and peace of paradise. His fundamentally Christian attitude to nature is to be found, not in the *Fioretti,* but in the verses of *The Canticle of Brother Sun.*

Il Cantico di Frate Sole

The authorship and authenticity of *The Canticle* are beyond doubt.[17] Verses 1-22 and 32-33 were composed by St. Francis at San Damiano between April and May, 1225 on the occasion of a visit to St. Clare. During the visit his eye illness, which he had suffered for a number of years, grew worse and he was reduced to almost total blindness. His body was already weak from the Stigmata which he had received on La Verna in September, 1224, and he was suffering terribly from mental agonies. After a mystical experience in which it

---

[14] *Genesis—A Commentary*, trans. by J.H. Marks, SCM Press Ltd., 1961, p. 58.

[15] Ibid., 58

[16] A.R. Peacocke, *Science and the Christian Experiment*, Oxford University Press, 1971, p. 193: "It is the exercise of man's powers under God which is the proper destiny of man vis-à-vis his environment. Anything else is disaster and leads to the wholesale plunder of natural resources by means of man's enhanced powers for the benefit of a myopic generation. . . .Man should be vicegerent not dictator".

[17] It is found in all the important primitive sources. See the excellent presentation of the state of scholarship on *The Canticle* in O. Englebert, *St. Francis of Assisi. A Biography*, new translation by E.M. Cooper, Second English Edition revised and augmented, Franciscan Herald Press, Chicago Illinois 1965, Appendix VIII: *The Canticle of Brother Sun*, pp. 441-458, cf. also pp. 316-329, 490-491, 542-544.

was promised him that he would attain eternal life, he composed *The Canticle of Brother Sun* and had it sung by brother Pacificus.[18] Some weeks later, on hearing of a feud between the religious and civil authorities of Assisi, he added the verses on forgiveness and suffering (23-26) and ordered *The Canticle* to be sung at a meeting he arranged between the bishop and the *podestà,* together with their followers. The result of his initiative was that they resolved to put aside their grievances when they heard *The Canticle* sung and so Assisi was restored to peace. Verses 27-31 were written shortly before his death which occurred in October, 1226.

Text of *The Canticle of Brother Sun:*[19]

---

[18] It is also recorded that St. Francis composed a melody for The Canticle, see ibid., p. 321.

[19] The translation of *The Canticle* here given is that of the present author. See the thorough textual and literary study by V. Branca, *Il Cantico di Frate Sole. Studio delle fonti a testo critico* in: ARCHIVUM FRANCISCANUM HISTORICUM 41 (1948) pp. 3-87. I have followed Branca's presentation of the Italian text (ibid., pp. 82-87) which is as follows:

I.	Altissimo, onnipotente, bon Signore,	
	tue so le laude, la gloria e l'onore e onne benedizione.	
II.	A te solo, Altissimo, se confano e nullo omo è digno te mentovare.	
III.	Laudato sie, mi Signore, cun tutte le tue creature,	5
	spezialmente messer lo frate Sole, lo qual è iorno, e allumini noi per lui.	
IV.	Ed ello e bello e radiante cun grande splendore:	
	de te Altissimo, porta significazione.	
	V. Laudato si, mi Signore, per sora Luna e le Stelle:	10
	in cielo l'hai formate clarite e preziosc e belle.	
	VI. Laudato si, mi Signore, per frate Vento,	
	e per Aere e Nubilo e Sereno e onne tempo	
	per lo qual a le tue creature dai sustentamento.	
VII.	Laudato si, mi Signore, per sor Aqua,	15
	la quale e molto utile e umile e preziosa e casta.	
VIII.	Laudato si, mi Signore, per frate Foco,	
	per lo quale enn'allumini la nocte:	
	ed ello è bello e iocundo e robusto e forte.	
IX.	Laudato si. mi Signore, per sora nostra matre Terra.	20
	la quale ne sostenta e governa,	
	e produce diversi fructi con coloriti flori ed erba.	
X.	Laudato si, mi Signore, per quelli che perdonano per lo tuo amore	
	e sostengo infirmitate e tribulazione.	
XI.	Beati quelli che'l sosterrano in pace,	25
	ca da te, Altissimo, sirano incornati.	
XII.	Laudato si, mi Signore, per sora nostra Morte corporale,	
	de la quale nullo omo vivente po' scampare.	
XIII.	Guai a quelli che morrano ne le peccata mortali!	
	Beati quelli che trovarà ne le tue sanctissime voluntati.	30
	ca la morte seconda no li farrà male.	

I	1	Most high, all-powerful, good Lord.
	2	Thine are the praise, the glory and the honour and every blessing.
II	3	To Thee alone, Most High, they are due,
	4	and no man is worthy to mention Thee.
III	5	Be praised, my Lord, with all Thy creatures,
	6	above all Sir Brother Sun,
	7	who is day and by him Thou sheddest light upon us.
IV	8	And he is beautiful and radiant with great splendour,
	9	of Thee, Most High, he bears the likeness.
V	10	Be praised, my Lord, through Sister Moon and the Stars,
	11	in the heavens Thou hast formed them,
		clear and precious and beautiful.
VI	12	Be praised, my Lord, through Brother Wind,
	13	and through Air and Cloud and fair and all Weather,
	14	by which Thou givest nourishment to Thy creatures.
VII	15	Be praised, my Lord, through Sister Water,
	16	who is very useful and humble and precious and pure.
VIII	17	Be praised, my Lord, through Brother Fire,
	18	by whom Thou lightest up the night,
	19	and he is beautiful and merry and vigorous and strong.
IX	20	Be praised, my Lord, through our Sister Mother Earth,
	21	who sustains and directs us,
	22	and produces diverse fruits with coloured flowers and herbs.
X	23	Be praised, my Lord, by those who pardon for Thy love,
	24	and endure sickness and trials.
XI	25	Blessed are they who shall endure them in peace,
	26	for by Thee, Most High, they shall be crowned
XII	27	Be praised, my Lord, through our Sister Bodily Death,
	28	from whom no man living can escape.

XIV.   Laudate e benedicite mi Signore,
   e rengraziate e serviteli cun grande umilitate.

The meaning of *per* in lines 10. 12, 15, 17, 20, 23, 27, is hotly disputed among scholars. *Per* may be translated 'for'; 'on account of' (cause); 'by' (agent); 'through' (instrument). Thomas of Celano, the Saint's most famous biographer, is the chief source and authority for the 'per-by' thesis: the sources which emanate from Brother Leo and his companions support the 'per-for' thesis—see Englebert, *St. Francis*, pp. 442-445. We cannot here enter into the niceties of this controversy. We have translated *per* by the word 'through' in the instrumental sense. One of our reasons for this is the use of *cun (con)* in line 5: 'cun tutte le tue creature' which seems to us to be in the instrumental sense.

XIII	29	Woe to those who die in mortal sin.
	30	Blessed are those whom she will find in Thy most holy will,
	31	for the second death will do them no harm.
XIV	32	Praise and bless my Lord,
	33	and give Him thanks and serve Him with great humility.

The hymn *All Creatures of Our God and King*—W.H. Draper's translation of *Il Cantico di Frate Sole,* while undoubtedly well known and very popular, does not do full justice to the intentions of St. Francis.[20] The vernacular of *The Canticle* contains many elements proper to the Umbrian dialect, though it cannot be identified with the daily spoken form of this dialect. Its language is more accurately described as a polished and ennobled Umbrian dialect due to the influence of the Latin with which St. Francis was familiar, namely that of the Bible and the Liturgy.[21] It is at once a beautiful piece of poetry and a prayer of praise to God the Creator. It expresses an essentially religious attitude to nature and contains the authentic Christian outlook on nature. St. Francis does not romanticise nature by reading human reactions and qualities into non-rational creatures, precisely because this would be to destroy the value of creatures in themselves by ignoring what they actually are. St. Francis loved nature and creatures, that is, he let them be exactly what they are. It is interesting to note that *The Mirror of Perfection* gives another reason why St. Francis composed *The Canticle:*

> Whence I wish to make to His praise and to our consolation and to the edification of our neighbour a new Praise of the Creatures of the Lord, which we daily use and without which we cannot live, and in whom the human race much offends their Creator; and we are continually ungrateful for so much grace and benefit, not praising God, the Creator and Giver of all things, as we ought.[22]

Apart from his sense of gratitude to God for creation, it was also his sadness at man's misuse of creatures that moved him to write *The Canticle.* I will be forgiven the rather gross anachronism in saying that the ecological problem had its influence on the composition of *The Canticle of Brother Sun!* Perhaps the way in which we treat nature reflects our fundamental attitude to one another and vice versa. In any case it is worth noting that St. Francis added

---

[20] See *New Catholic Hymnal,* Faber Music Ltd., London 1971, n. 2, pp. 2f.
[21] Branca, *Il Cantico,* p. 79.
[22] *The Mirror of Perfection, chap.* C in: *The Little Flowers of St. Francis,* Everyman's Library 1973, p. 274.

his lines on forgiveness and suffering to *The Canticle* (he did not write another one) which originally concerned only inanimate creatures.

The poem is deeply mystical in which the author's prime concern is to praise God the Creator; there is no question of worshipping creatures, however we may be inclined to translate *per.*[23] The key to the piece lies in the use of the words 'brother' and 'sister'. For St. Francis the word 'friar' (brother) is certainly among the most sacred in his vocabulary; one might even say that for St. Francis this was a primordial word.[24] Through Brother Christ (he calls Christ a Friar[25]), the son of Pietro Bernadone was transformed into Little Brother Francis. His love of Christ and his deep reverence for God the Father soon attracted his first companions: Friar Bernard, Friar Giles, Friar Juniper, Friar Leo. Without one word of criticism of the institutions of Church or State, Francis struck at the root of the whole feudal system in providing a viable alternative to medieval privilege by establishing his Gospel Brotherhood. He lays it down that "they are all to be known as 'Friars Minor' (Little Brothers) without distinction, and they should be prepared to wash one another's feet".[26] From Friar Christ through his human brethren he was led to love Brother Wolf and his sisters the swallows and the hooded larks. His love extended to embrace Brother Fire—who is so strong and lights up the night and Sister Water—-so humble and pure and very useful, Sister Moon and Brother Sun. Thus, he was brought back to Him, the Elder Brother and Firstborn of all creation, Who came to cast fire on the earth and to give us waters that well up into springs of eternal life, the Unconquered Sun of justice and only-Begotten of the one Father of heaven and earth. St. Francis conceived the whole world as *one* vast Friary ('Brother'/ 'Sister') in which each brother and sister holds a unique and indispensable place. This is no mere romanticism, but a lovely poetic expression of the individuality, the originality, the never-to-be-repeated identity of every creature in nature. It is akin to 'thisness' *(haecceitas)* as Duns Scotus philosophises it[27] and to Gerard Manley Hopkins's description of the

---

[23] See footnote 19 above.

[24] As understood, e.g. by Karl Rahner, *Priest and Poet* in: *Theological Investigations III*, trans. by K.-H. and B. Kruger, Baltimore and London 1967, pp. 296-302.

[25] *O quam sanctum et quam dilectum. . .habere talem fratrem qui posuit animam suam pro ovibus suis et oravit Patrem pro nobis. . . .*
Epistola I. Litterae quas misit omnibus fidelibus in: *Opuscula Sancti Patris Francisci Assisiensis*, Ad Claras Aquas 1949, p. 94.

[26] *The Rule of 1221 (Regula non-bullata)* chap. 6 in: *The Writings of St. Francis of Assisi*, trans. by B. Fahy OFM with introduction and notes by P. Hermann OFM, London 1964, p. 37.

[27] *Reportata Parisiensia* II, d. 12, q. 5, nn. l, 8. 12, 14 (ed. Vivés XXlll 2S 29, 31, 32).

distinctiveness of things 'inscape'.[28] Moreover, St. Francis emphasises the activity and usefulness of creatures: Brother Sun is the day and gives us light, Sister Moon and the Stars make the heavens fair; God cherishes all creation through Brother Wind, Air and all kinds of weather. Sister Water is not only humble and pure, but precious and useful; Brother Fire is not only beautiful and merry, but he lights up the night and is vigorous and strong. Our Sister, Mother Earth, not only produces lovely flowers, but sustains and guides us. We are in nature's debt, a debt we must acknowledge in order to cooperate with her and to be able to recognise the inherent value of all creatures, animate and inanimate, which have come into being through God's freedom and love. There is not even a hint at forbidding the human use of nature in terms of pan-psychism or animism. Nature has a meaning-in-itself because it is created by God, it does not have its value or meaning purely from man. Man has a duty to respect it and the right to use it by working with it, not by dominating and exploiting it.

Sources and Comparisons

The biblical and liturgical sources of *The Canticle* are obvious. Thomas of Celano already in his *First Life* of St. Francis drew attention to its similarity to *The Song of the Three Young Men* in the Book of Daniel and Psalm 148 is a close model.[29] Raphael Brown has pointed to an eleventh Century hymn, *Jubilemus omnes,* taken from the ancient Roman-French missals, as a possible indirect liturgical source of *The Canticle*.[30] This hymn mentions the firmament, the stars, sun, moon, sea, land, hills, plains, deep rivers, air, winds and rain.[31] Comparative study manifests that *The Canticle of Brother Sun* is modelled on the rhythm of the Psalms and Canticles with which St. Francis was familiar in the liturgical offices of the Church.[32]

---

[28] W.A.M. Peters, *Gerard Manley Hopkins. A Critical Essay towards the understanding of his poetry*, Oxford 1948, pp. 21-28; *Poems and Prose of Gerard Manley Hopkins*, selected with an introduction and notes by W.H. Gardner, Penguin Books xxiii-xxiv, pp. 224-226.

[29] See Engelbert, *St. Francis*, p. 441, for further biblical references.

[30] 1 Celano 80 in: *The Lives of St. Francis of Assisi by Brother Thomas of Celano*, trans. by A.G. Ferrers Howell, Methuen & Co., London 1908, pp. 78f.: "For as of old the three children placed in the burning fiery furnace invited all the elements to praise and glorify the Creator of the universe, so this man also, full of the spirit of God, ceased not to glorify, praise, and bless in all the elements and creatures, the Creator and Governor of them all".

[31] The text is found in Latin and English in *The Liturgical Year* by A. Gueranger OSB, trans. from the French by Dom Laurence Shepherd OSB Advent, London 1931, p. 208.

[32] Branca, *Il Cantico*, p. 79.

If we compare three texts taken respectively from *The Song of the Three Young Men, The Canticle of Brother Sun* and the *Hymn to Matter* by Teilhard de Chardin, we find that each expresses a basically identical attitude to nature:

1. All things the Lord has made, bless the Lord. . .
    Sun and moon! bless the Lord. . .
    Stars of heaven! bless the Lord. . .
    Winds! all bless the Lord. . .
    Everything that grows on the earth! bless the Lord.[33]

2. Be praised, my Lord with all Thy creatures
    above all Sir Brother Sun . . .
    Be praised, my Lord, through our Sister Mother Earth.[34]

3. Blessed be you, universal matter, immeasurable time,
    boundless ether, triple abyss of stars and atoms
    and generations: you who by overflowing and
    dissolving our narrow standards of measurement
    reveal to us the dimensions of God. . .
    Without you, without your onslaughts, without
    your uprootings of us, we should remain
    all our lives inert, stagnant, puerile,
    ignorant both of ourselves and of God. . .[35]

Each of these cosmic hymns contains a sense of reverence and love for nature and non-rational creatures, as they are and for what they are in themselves. The authors—the first representing the ancient biblical tradition; the second a medieval Christian, a contemplative and poet; the third, a modern Christian, both priest and scientist—are mystics who are able to acknowledge the inherent value and meaning of nature; through their love of God and by their recognition of His sovereign rights over nature as the Lord Creator. Nature is not the product of Fate nor the result of Chance, but the eternally-willed object of God's creative love. The unity of origin in creation gives to all creatures—including man—a certain equality in virtue of which man can invite all creation to praise and bless the one Creator. Even though Teilhard's *Hymn to Matter* comes as a surprise at first (it is perhaps the most mystical of the three pieces), one realises eventually that the entire *Hymn* is conceivable only

---

[33] Daniel 3:57,62,63,65,76.
[34] See above, lines 5-6, 20.
[35] P.T. de Chardin, *Hymn of the Universe*, Collins London 1965, pp. 68-71.

in terms of God the Creator, a conclusion based on the explicit references to God and the incarnation in the *Hymn* itself and on the content of the author's other works, especially *Writings in Time of War*.[36] Man, of course, stands at a mid-point in nature, at once immersed in it and beyond it. Through his transcendence man comes to know his own meaning and value and discovers the responsibility he bears to treat nature as nature, no more and no less than that. He is made in the image of God. God knows and loves the animal as an animal, the flower as a flower and the stone as a stone. Man's obligation is to do precisely the same.

Concluding Remarks

In the end there remains the practical question: What is to be done in the face of the present state of the ecological crisis? Indeed, can anything be done at all? Although the situation is desperate, it is not too late to take more practical measures to control the destruction of the environment, nor are the measures at present being taken useless. Our suggestions here are based on the conviction that we must have a religious world view as the motive force of our practical efforts. Any suggestions to help solve the ecological crisis cannot he considered in isolation, because this crisis is linked intimately to political, economic and social questions over a very wide area. Whatever suggestions are made, however, they will have repercussions at many other levels.

In the first place, someone has to have the courage to tell us and show us as graphically as possible that we must be prepared to make sacrifices, to say 'No' to ourselves, as the only way to combat the greed and selfishness that is at the root of the crisis. Self-denial is an essential part of Christian discipleship and Christians ought to take the leadership in teaching and practising it in its obvious connections with ecology.

Secondly, theologians ought to formulate a theology of creation which includes aesthetic categories in its essential structure, along the lines suggested by Jürgen Moltmann.[37] The religious roots of the ecological crisis are tied up as much with our idea of God as they are with our concept of nature. This will involve Christian theology in a much more serious and extensive dialogue with Hinduism and the philosophies of India.[38]

---

[36] Ibid., pp. 93-114, 151-176.

[37] *Theology and Joy*, SCM Ltd. 1973, pp. 39-64.

[38] B. Walker, *The Hindu World*, London 1968, pp. 214-216; R.C. Zaehner, *Hinduism*. London 1966, pp. 98-101; H. Zimmer. *Philosophies of India*, Princeton 1951, pp. 570f., 596-599.

Thirdly, it is the duty of theologians to work out, with all the resources at their disposal, a theology of the environment as a logical corollary of the theologies of Creation, the incarnation and the Eucharist and in close liaison with the theologies of aesthetics and leisure.

Fourthly, Christian catechetical instruction from the earliest years should include teaching on the meaning and inherent value of matter and life in all its forms and at every level. This could be achieved most successfully by familiarising the pupils with the authentic Christian attitude to nature as found, for example, in *The Canticle of Brother Sun.*

Fifthly, education at every level—primary, secondary and tertiary — should make it one of its basic aims to restore the sense of wonder at the beauty, mystery and fascinating intricacy of nature. This will require, firstly, a correction of that fundamentally warped attitude of mind which imagines that understanding comes uniquely through knowledge of practical purposes! Secondly, it will require, communication by shared experiences of the pure enjoyment of nature. This means that school outings, for example, will not be restricted to visits to the British Museum, science exhibitions and art galleries, but will also include visits to lakes, woodlands, farms, hills, moors and rivers and occasional outings to see the sunset.

62

St. Francis—Patron of the Environment[1]

Earlier this year Pope John Paul declared St. Francis the Patron of the Environment. Of course everybody knows St. Francis loved animals, birds and flowers, so perhaps nobody was really surprised at what the Pope did. Yet it may turn out to be one of the most significant gestures this century.

The Pope has alerted us to a very grave problem: *the destruction of the environment*. The environment is the home of elements, plants, animals and humans. The world belongs to God because he made it. He handed it over to us to develop, not to destroy; to take care of lovingly, not to misuse selfishly and thoughtlessly.

We are acting as if we were gods. We assemble bits of creation and shoot them at one another as bullets or drop them on towns and cities as bombs. We have developed the repulsive neutron bomb which kills people but leaves buildings standing. We have poisoned rivers and seas and polluted the atmosphere. We maltreat God's creatures with unspeakable cruelty.

In vivisection laboratories animals are subjected to unimaginable horrors to find out what cigarette smoking can do to us or to get a better brand of nail varnish. To produce pâté that will titillate our palates, geese are strapped down to boards and an electric force feeder is used to stuff them with grain. A nice refinement of cruelty that is! The Japanese are killing dolphins because they eat fish. In one year, the governments of the world devote more than £200,000 million to military expenditure, that's over £2 for every star in our galaxy! What are we doing to the earth? Our attitude to the environment is a serious moral issue.

Why, then, did the Pope make St. Francis Patron of the Environment? The answer is really very simple: because St. Francis considered all creatures his brothers and sisters. He wrote *The Song of Brother Sun* precisely because people in his time were misusing creatures for selfish ends and he saw this as a great offence to the Creator. My word, how much more guilty we are of the same offence.

[1] THE TROUBADOUR 29.4 (Oct. 1980) pp. 56f. Published with permission from the Province of Immaculate Conception, England.

Francis loved and revered God as the Holy Father in heaven. He is holy because he is far beyond us; he is Father because he is close to us, closer in fact than our very selves. He gave his only Son because he loves the universe. And his only Son became our Brother. That's what *friar* means -a brother. St. Francis knew in his deepest heart that Jesus Christ is the Brother of us all. For Francis he was Friar Jesus Christ. Jesus said that God takes care of sparrows and clothes the lilies with splendour.

Friar Jesus transformed John Bernardone into Friar Francis. Francis attracted Friars Leo, Rufino, Angelo, Philip and Sister Clare. The brotherhood spread to include Friar Wolf, Sister Lark, Brother Rabbit and Sister Nightingale. Out further it went to embrace Brother Fire, Sister Water and Brother Air; then on to Sisters Moon and Stars and Brother Sun. From these it returned to Friar Christ and so to God the Holy Father. At peace with all creatures, Friar Francis stood before God and together with them prayed *Our Father* because God is the Father of heaven and earth, that is, the Father of everything.

If all creatures are our brothers and sisters how can we maltreat any of them? If, for instance, water is our sister, isn't it rather odd to pour poisonous chemicals into her? We wouldn't do that to our little sister at home.

From our point of view by calling the stars his sisters St. Francis included the distant galaxies in the brotherhood. The whole universe is the environment. For a Franciscan today the universe is the friary. And the extent of the observable universe is 25 billion light years. Light travels at a speed of 186,000 miles per second. So if we wanted to know the extent of the observable universe in miles we would have to multiply 186,000 x 60 x 60 x 365 x 25,000,000,000,000. If there is intelligent life elsewhere, those beings are already our brothers and sisters.

Yes, in proclaiming St. Francis the Patron of the Environment the Pope did something of incalculable importance for the future of this planet. If we take it seriously and act on it, we will be helping to build a future that is worth building and at the same time honouring God the Father of us all.

St. Francis on Praying and Being a Creature[1]

Twice a year I give a lecture on St. Francis in London as part of a course for yoga teachers. The group is a very mixed one, representing a wide variety of backgrounds. On one occasion just before I gave the lecture a man came up to me and said: 'I believe you're going to speak to us about St. Francis'. 'Yes, that's right', I replied. 'O good', he answered radiantly, 'I love St. Francis because he loved birds and I'm a keen ornithologist'.

Everyone who has heard about St. Francis usually knows he preached to birds and lifted worms from the roadway to save them from being trampled under foot. But this is only the surface splendour. There are depths upon depths beneath. His attitude to creatures reveals an exquisite sensitivity which is well nigh unparalleled in western history. But were we to stop at this, our view of him would be just a little too romantic. His sensitivity came from a source deep within him: his sense of the holiness of God and the recognition of his own creaturehood.

To be a Creature is to be a Prayer

What strikes one most about his writings is the number of times he gives thanks to God (see, for example, *1ˢᵗ Rule,* cc. 17,21, 23; *The Canticle*). And loveliest of all, he thanks God for being God: "We give you thanks for yourself" (*1ˢᵗ Rule,* c. 23). That's something like one reads on those delightful greeting cards: "Thank you for being you".

Then he thanks God for his goodness to us. God has given us everything. To him belongs all good and we must thank him without ceasing. Francis thanks him for creation, for redemption and holiness, for the second coming of Christ and even for sickness and insults. All is gift and the only really gracious response to a gift is to accept it and give thanks.

His awareness of God then, led him to acknowledge with sweet humility that the world has its meaning in divine love. Every creature emanates from the same source. He loved creatures because he accepted creaturehood.

---

[1] *Plan for Franciscan Living Committee*, Eighth Centenary Project 1982. Published with permission from the English Speaking Conference of Friars Minor.

And so creation is endowed with the sublime quality of brotherhood or sisterhood. Praying and being God's creature were for Francis interchangeable. Indeed, to the extent, that Celano could write those profoundly mysterious words about how Francis when praying, centred himself on God in such a way, that he was "not so much praying as having become a prayer" (2 Celano 95). The prayer and the prayer were one. Thus to be a creature is to be a prayer.

We All Need to be Brought to Wholeness

We have nothing of our own except our vices and sins, in fact we are wretched and pitiable (*Earlier Rule*, cc. 17 and 23). We should not let Francis rather excessive language about our human condition offend us. He expresses a truth it would be foolish to ignore. This is not grim pessimism, but utter realism. We are not only limited, finite creatures, there is also about us all an unintelligible selfishness which puts us in dire need of God's grace and love. Yet none of this turned Francis into a killjoy nor did it stop him singing.

Francis serenely accepted his creaturehood. It is the equivalent of self-acceptance and the outcome is gratitude. After all, to be a creature is to have been loved and willed for all eternity (see *Earlier Rule,* c. 23). In specific terms that means I have been loved and wanted forever by the most high and supreme God. To accept myself as this creature of God, limited, finite and loved, leads me to say Amen to God's affirmation of us all in the human of Christ who is the Yes made flesh [cf. 2 Corinthians 1:20].

Francis acknowledged willingly his need of God's grace and love. We all need to be delivered from the unintelligible power of sin and brought to wholeness. Otherwise we make gods of ourselves and idols out of money, ambition and power. Only the active acceptance of God's reign in our hearts can set us free to be true creatures, servants of one another and heralds of the great King. In this way we can accept our past and put aside the worries it causes us, be committed to the future and rid ourselves of the spectres and anxieties it conjures up before us, and so live in the present "in the love which is God" (*Earlier Rule*, c. 17).

To be Without Power is to Pray

By his extraordinary humility Francis recognized God's sovereign rights and our need of his grace. This produced in him the total surrender which in the psalms is poverty of spirit, forbade him to call anything his own because every creature is a brother or sister, led him to give away the only copy of the

New Testament they had at the Portiuncula and made him a man utterly devoid of power. Nothing shows more limpidly that he was a man without power, than his understanding of authority as service (see *Earlier Rule*, c. 6; *Rule of 1223, c.* 10), and his evangelical attitude to the sins and weaknesses of his friars *(Earlier Rule,* c. 5; *Rule of 1223,* cc. 7 and 10; *Admonition* 9). To be without power is to be a creature who prays.

Saint Francis: Prayer, Brotherhood, Littleness[1]

St. Francis was a man of prayer. His first biographer, a friar called Thomas of Celano, tells us that when St. Francis prayed he fixed his whole attention on God in such a way that he was not so much praying, as having become himself a prayer. Praying and being in love reveal *one* of our characteristic qualities as human beings: creativity. They both bring from the inmost depths of the heart what is most authentic and unique about us as individual persons; they have close resemblances. Words of love between human beings so often seem like words of prayer, words of surrender, thankfulness, wonder, praise and humility. Words of prayer are always words of love, because prayer is an encounter between lovers, made possible by God's gracious gift of his love to us.

No words about his prayer can reveal what the prayers themselves contain.[2] St. Francis was a man of prayer and a man in love. As a man of prayer he was patently a man of God; as a man in love with Jesus Christ, he stands as living proof that the closer we draw to God, the more truly and authentically human we become.

The most significant word in St. Francis' life and writings is friar. It is a translation of the Latin word for 'brother', friar. It was for him a primordial word, a word of mystery, that told him something about everything St. Francis loved Jesus Christ as the First Brother of us all. He actually calls Christ a friar: "How lovely it is to have a, friar like this who laid down his life for his sheep". (*Letter to the Faithful*)

Jesus Christ made the whole human race and all creation into a vast friary or brotherhood. Not only are human beings brothers and sisters *in* Christ, but also all creatures "animate and inanimate" are brothers and sisters. God created the whole universe and what he created he saw was very good.

---

[1] SCHOOLS OF PRAYER 1 (Autumn 1982) pp. 8-15. Published with permission.
[2] Editors' note: For a sample of his prayers, see *Francis of Assisi: Early Documents—The Saint,* R. Armstrong OFM Cap, W. Hellmann OFM Conv, W. Short OFM, New City Press, New York 1999, pp. 35-167.

And he so loved the world (John's Gospel says *kosmos* that is "the whole of created reality"), that he sent the only Son.

The world, indeed, the whole universe, was for St. Francis a vast friary. In the *Canticle of Brother Sun* he calls the moon and the stars his sisters. Though he did not know it that means we have 100,000 million sisters in this galaxy; and goodness knows how many more in the twenty-five billion light years of the observable universe. In calling the stars his sisters, St. Francis laid the foundation of an intergalactic brotherhood. That has enormous consequences in the event of there being intelligent life elsewhere in the universe. According to the principle laid down by St. Francis we will be obliged—should we ever get into contact with other intelligent beings, to treat them as brothers and sisters and not as aliens and enemies.

In calling all creatures his brothers and sisters, St. Francis gave us a vital directive for the preservation of the environment. If for example, water is our sister, then to pour toxic acids into her is a very strange way to act! It is hardly the normal way to treat one's sister. Further, if animals are our brothers and sisters, then how can we be so cruel in the way we treat them? It makes me shudder to read of what goes on in vivisection laboratories. Destruction of the environment is one of the gravest moral issues of the present time. It goes to prove that St. Francis' view of the universal brotherhood of creation *is* not a piece of cosy romanticism, but a message of vital urgency for the future of the planet.

The way we treat the environment and other creatures is a reflection of how we treat one another. We assemble bits of matter and shoot them at one another as bullets. We manufacture neutron warheads which kill people, while leaving buildings standing. According to the present statistics, the stockpile of nuclear weapons is equivalent to two tons of TNT for every person on the globe.

We are desperately lacking in humility. People often think that humility is weakness. In truth, humility is one of the strongest virtues. To be humble, a person needs great great courage, St. Francis learned humility from God himself. He loved the Infant Jesus who was powerless. A little child can do us no harm. He was always thinking about the Crucified Lord, and a dying man is always defenceless.

He treasured the Holy Eucharist, where Christ is truly present in a tiny host and is so silent in our midst, just as he was before Pontius Pilate. Francis learned about the God of love and tenderness from Bethlehem, Calvary and the Mass. God the Son came among us not asserting his rights, not manifesting his divine prerogatives, but in humility as one who serves.

So it is that Francis not only imitated Christ, but he put Christ on, clothed himself with Christ. And that made him a man of peace.

His biographer tells us that he was always speaking about peace and he created peace wherever he went by sharing the peace of God which the world of *itself* does not have. Our earth needs men and women of peace as it has never needed them before. If we strive to acquire that humility which respects others for what they really are our—brothers and sisters, irrespective of race, colour and creed—then we will be instruments of God's peace. And where there is hatred, we will sow love, where there is injury, pardon, and where there is doubt, hope.

Franciscan Spirituality[1]

Fundamentally there is only one spirituality in the Church. It derives uniquely from the New Testament and concerns our relationship with God the Father through Jesus Christ in the Holy Spirit, and our relationships with one another and all creation. The life of the spirit develops from the gift of grace gained for us by the life, death and glorification of the Lord Jesus. It is at once both evangelical and ecclesial. Every further specification of this one Christian spirituality, be it Benedictine, Victorine, Dominican, Franciscan, Carmelite or Jesuit, is but a variation on a theme. It is no more than an approach to the mystery of God already mapped out somewhere in the teaching of the gospel. The different traditions of spirituality which have emerged in the Church's history are testimonies to the "infinite treasure of Christ" [Ephesians 3:8]. It is also true that this one spirituality, even when channelled into a specific Tradition, finds as many expressions as there are disciples of Christ: "Each one of us, however, has been given his own share of grace, given as Christ allotted it" [Ephesians 4:7].

In this article I want to treat primarily the evangelical foundation of Franciscan spirituality and then say a little about its theological expression and devotional forms.

The Evangelical Foundation

Although St. Francis of Assisi (1181/2-1226) did not develop a system of spirituality which he then bequeathed to his Order, nevertheless, Franciscan spirituality is inseparably linked to his faith and holiness. He wanted nothing but to follow "the teaching and the footsteps of Our Lord Jesus Christ".[2] Everything centred on, began with and led back to the Christ of the New

[1] RELIGIOUS LIFE REVIEW 21 (Sept.-Oct. 1982) pp. 250-259. Published with permission.
[2] *Rule of 1221*, cc. 1:22 in: *St. Francis of Assisi. Writings and Early Biographies. English Omnibus of the Sources for the Life of St. Francis*, ed. by M.A. Habig, Chicago 1973 (*=Omnibus*) pp. 31, 49. The critical edition of the writings of Francis of Assisi was published by K. Esser OFM, *Opuscula Sancti Patris Francisci Assiensis*, Grottaferrata, Roma 1978. In this article I refer to the *Omnibus* edition of the writings of Francis. While occasionally I give my own translation—which is always indicated—I refer to the relevant place in the *Omnibus*.

Testament, the poor, humble, obedient, suffering Servant who died and rose for us. His first biographer, Thomas of Celano, says of him: "He was always thinking about Jesus; Jesus was in his mouth, in his, ears, in his eyes, in his hands; Jesus was in his whole being".[3]

He founded an evangelical movement. It has to be stressed, however, that its inspiration was not only the synoptic gospels, but the good news contained in the New Testament as a whole. Moreover, his literal observance of the gospel was no form of fundamentalism or legalistic literalism. Literal observance meant a total commitment to the spiritual values the gospel proclaims.[4] As a reform movement his observance of the gospel was coupled with a deep love of the Church, for it was in and through the Church that he had come to know the gospel. Not only did he refrain from criticizing the Church, he insisted on reverence for its institutions—the papacy, the priesthood, the sacraments—and on adherence to its teaching. Orthodoxy, however had to find expression in orthopraxy, the believer must do the truth in love.

On hearing the text of Matthew 10:7-14 on the feast of St. Matthias 1208, in which the Lord bids his disciples provide themselves with no gold or silver, he embraced a life of poverty in literal obedience to Christ's words. From that moment the gospel became an absolute in his life and his life began to unfold as a kind of exegesis of the gospel. For the remainder of his life he always consulted the scriptures prior to any major decision. In the *Rule* he identifies the Christian life of his friars with following the gospel: "The Rule and life of the Friars Minor is this, to observe the holy gospel of our Lord Jesus Christ, by living in obedience, without ownership and in chastity".[5]

The Humility of God

The prayers he composed reveal his profound sense of the transcendent mystery of the Triune God, and he received the title *cultor Trinitatis.*[6] From that sprang his passionate love of the Saviour as our Brother. Francis was filled with awe that God, infinitely exalted in his majesty, had freely chosen to be one of us and to live among us in powerlessness, vulnerability and littleness. Bethlehem, Calvary and the eucharist—a baby, a

---

[3] 1 Celano 115, *Omnibus*, p. 329.

[4] See A. Rotzetter OFM Cap, *Mysticism and Literal observance of the Gospel in: Francis of Assisi* in: CONCILIUM 149, pp. 56-64.

[5] *Rule of 1223*, c. 1, my translation, *Omnibus*, p. 57.

[6] See W. Lampen OFM, *S. Franciscus, cultor Trinitatis* in: ARCHIVUM FRANCISCANUM HISTORICUM 21 (1928) pp. 449-467.

crucified naked criminal, a tiny piece of bread—these for him were the high points of God's self-revelation.

Celano tells us that he loved Christmas and used to say it was "the feast of feasts on which God, having become a tiny infant, clung to human breasts"; and in an earlier account the same biographer describes how Francis built a crib at Greccio to "recall to memory the little Child. . .and set before our bodily eyes in some way the inconveniences of his infant needs".[7] After his experience at San Damiano, when he heard the figure on the cross tell him to repair the church, "compassion for the crucified was rooted in his holy soul".[8] Often his songs of gladness about the Lord would end in tears and "be dissolved in compassion for the passion of Christ".[9] The frequency and intensity with which he meditated on Christ's sufferings, lead one to conclude that he was marked interiorly with the stigmata long before they appeared visibly on his body in September 1224, a little over two years before he died. In his *Letter to All the Friars* he writes of the eucharist: "O sublime humility! O humble sublimity! That the Lord of the whole universe, God and the Son of God, should humble himself like this and hide under the form of a little bread for our salvation".[10] God in his majesty came into the world as a helpless baby, he left it by death on a cross, and after his glorious resurrection chooses to remain with us in the little, silent form of the eucharist.

Lady Poverty

It is against this background that we can understand the place of the virtue of poverty in Franciscan spirituality. The poverty of Francis, no matter how radical, was not primarily ascetical. It was evangelical and christological. He espoused 'Lady Poverty' because Christ and his mother had been poor. Christ's freely chosen poverty was part of the good news and it revealed the humility of God. It was the symbol of divine powerlessness in the world.

Francis discovered Christ in the poor, in the most wretched of the poor in medieval society, the lepers. It is not easy for us to appreciate the terrible plight of lepers in the middle ages. Once a leper was discovered, he or she was taken to the church and in a liturgical rite (which appears as a combination of

---

[7]   2 Celano 199; 1Celano 84, *Omnibus*, pp. 521f., 299.
[8]   2 Celano 10, *Omnibus*, pp. 370f.
[9]   2 Celano 127, *Omnibus*, p. 467.
[10] *Omnibus*, p. 103.

a funeral service and a religious profession) was permanently excluded from society.[11]

In his youth Francis had feared and loathed lepers. A few days before he died he dictated a short account of how God had entered his life and set it in a new direction. It is known as *The Testament of Blessed Francis.* He looked back across the years and in his gaze he saw the lepers.

> This is how the Lord granted to me, Brother Francis, to start out on a life of penance. When I was in sin I found it an exceedingly bitter sight to see lepers. Then the Lord himself brought me among them and I treated them with compassion. When I came away from them what I had found bitter was changed to sweetness of soul and body. After this I waited a little and then left the world.[12]

It was no theory, therefore, not even about poverty, that brought Francis to follow the poor Christ. It was a vivid experience of Christ still suffering in the poor and marginated of society. The lepers evangelised Francis and showed him that if he was ever to possess and be possessed by Christ, he would have to be poor.

In emphasizing the christological nature of his poverty, I do not mean to ignore its stark reality in his life. Francis was really poor. He renounced, as did his first followers, all possessions, individually and collectively, and every legal right of ownership. They were a band of poor men with no status in society and no social power or influence. Francis proved that human beings need very little, not only to survive, but to thrive and flourish. The world Francis left behind him was the world of mammon which cheats people into thinking that wealth gives security. Francis' security lay in the world of love created by the poverty of Christ, and though he owned nothing, the world was his and he was so happy to be in it. There is a great mystery about Francis' poverty which has left a feeling of unease in the Franciscan Order, even when it argues that it finds itself in circumstances different from his time.

Other Distinguishing Features

Humility is as it were the inner side of material poverty. It is basically recognition of the truth, as Francis writes, "What a man is before God, that he is and no more".[13] But in the truth Francis also grasped that before God we are

---

[11] See A Fortini, *Francis of Assisi. A new translation of Nova Vita di San Francesco* by H. Moak, New York 1981, pp. 206-212.

[12] My translation; *Omnibus*, p. 67.

[13] *Admonition 20* in: *Omnibus*, p. 84.

all brothers and sisters in Christ, little brothers and sisters. As little we must be humble before God, and as brothers and sisters in Christ, meek with one another. That is for Francis the sum total of gospel perfection and the source of true joy.[14] Meekness has no boundaries, it embraces all creatures and stretches to the stars, making of all creation one vast friary as he shows so beautifully in *The Canticle of Brother Sun*.[15]

Meekness leads directly into the virtue of obedience, which is as radical and total as poverty. According to Celano Francis taught the friars that the Holy Spirit is the minister general of the Order who "rests equally upon the poor and the simple".[16] In *The Praises of the Virtues* he writes that obedience subjects us not only to men "but to all the beasts as well and to the wild animals".[17] God speaks his word in creation, incarnation and inspiration. If we are to hear that word and respond to it with alacrity, we must renounce our own wills for God's sake.[18] No one can observe evangelical obedience or have any of the virtues "without first dying to himself".[19] We undergo a mystical death by emptying ourselves in order to be made alive again and be filled with the gifts of God's Spirit: "Keep nothing for yourselves, so that he who has given himself totally to you may receive you totally".[20]

Self-renunciation allows us to hear the Holy Spirit in our conscience, in the brethren, in the ministers and in all creation. Francis heard the words *brother and sister* in every creature and with love and obedience responded: Brother Wolf, Sister Water, and to the lepers, Brother Christians.

Authority according to Francis is a privileged form of service, the only way in which it can be creative. He writes: "The man who is in authority and is regarded as the superior should become the least of all and serve his brothers"; and he goes on to give the salutary warning: "We should not want to be in charge of others, we are to be servants".[21] Where love rules, as Carl Jung points out, there is no will to power. To want authority is to place oneself in a superior position, to judge oneself better than the others, and that turns

---

[14] On the use of true joy rather than *perfect joy* in the dialogue with Leo, see A. Jansen, *The Story of True Joy* in: FRANZISKANISCHE STUDIEN 63 (1981) pp. 271-288.
[15] See E. Doyle OFM, *St. Francis and the Song of Brotherhood*, London, 1980.
[16] 2 Celano 193, *Omnibus*, p. 517.
[17] *Omnibus*, p. 134.
[18] Cf. *Rule of 1223*, ch. 10 in: *Omnibus*, p. 63.
[19] *The Praises of the Virtue* in: *Omnibus*, p. 133.
[20] *Letter to All the Friars* in: *Omnibus*, p. 106.
[21] *Letter to All the Faithful* in: *Omnibus*, p. 96.

authority into power. Consequently, the ministers who possess authority must not want it, and that will ensure it remains authentic.[22]

His writings show a deep respect for individual freedom especially in all that concerns relationships with God. It was not empty rhetoric when he said the Holy Spirit is the minister general of the Order. He knew from his own experience that God is the supreme spiritual director. In *The Testament* he recalls: "After the Lord gave me some friars, no one showed me what I should do, but the Most High himself revealed to me that I should live according to the gospel".[23] *The Rule for Hermitages,* which marks a new development in the eremitical life, begins with the words: "Those who wish to live the religious life in hermitages",[24] thus indicating at the outset that divine inspiration, not human legislation, is the source of this vocation in the Order. But nowhere does he express his respect for freedom in the spiritual life more clearly than in the *Letter to Brother Leo,* his companion and confessor: "And in case you consider it necessary to come to me afterwards, this is my advice. In whatever way it seems best to you that you can please the Lord God and follow in his footsteps and poverty, do that with the blessing of the Lord God and my obedience. And if it is needful for you on account of your soul or for some comfort, to come to me, and you want to, then Leo, come".[25] Those are the words of a wise director of souls.

The Mother of Jesus

Francis had a tender devotion to the Virgin Mary which never degenerated into sentimentality. On the contrary, it had firm ecclesiological and christological roots. Celano writes: "Toward the Mother of Jesus he was filled with an inexpressible love, because it was she who made the Lord of majesty our brother".[26] Her place in the plan of God is expressed with admirable precision in the little work *Greetings to the Blessed Virgin Mary:* "Hail Lady, holy Queen, holy Mother of God, who are the Church made Virgin; chosen by the most holy Father in heaven, consecrated by him, with his most holy, beloved Son and the Holy Spirit, the Paraclete".[27] Among the tiles he gives to our Lady, it seems he was the first to call her "Spouse of the Holy

---

[22] *See Admonitions 4 and 20* in: *Omnibus*, pp. 80, 84.
[23] My translation, *Omnibus*, p. 68.
[24] My translation, *Omnibus*, p. 72.
[25] My translation, *Omnibus*, pp. 118f.
[26] 2 Celano 198, *Omnibus*, p. 521.
[27] My translation; in: *Omnibus*, pp. 135f.

Spirit".[28] She is presented as model of the spiritual life: "We are mothers to (our Lord Jesus Christ) when we enthrone him in our hearts and souls by love with a pure and sincere conscience, and give him birth by doing good".[29]

Spiritual motherhood and the tenderness which accompanies it, should be a quality of every friar: "If a mother nourishes and loves the child that is born to her, with what greater care should a friar love and nourish his spiritual brother?"[30] Maturity in the spiritual life requires of all of us a balance of the two aspects of human nature, feminine and masculine. There is good evidence that Francis himself arrived at this balance;[31] one could argue that it is vitally necessary for the spiritual development of celibates.

It is interesting that in *The Praises of the Virtues* Francis does not mention the word chastity. He speaks rather of *sancta caritas*: "Holy love confounds all the temptations of the devil and flesh and all carnal fears".[32] Holy love on the one hand excludes self-seeking and delusion, and on the other, fear of involvement and commitment. Consequently, the context in which chastity mentioned in the Rule is to be understood, is holy love and the tenderness of spiritual motherhood. It is the vow of fraternal love.

The Theological Expression

It is often repeated that Francis was opposed to study. That is a gross oversimplification born of romanticism. His attitude to study—as a category of work—can only be judged after an analysis of the seminal theology of work scattered throughout his writings. Then it will be found that study has to be pursued under the same conditions as manual work—another category of work—namely, as not to extinguish the spirit of prayer and devotion. All work must be an exercise in self-transcendence.[33]

It is most probable that Francis never read a learned book in his life, yet he inspired some of the most profound doctrines in the history of theology

---

[28] See W. Lampen OFM, *De S. P. Francisci cultu angelorum et sanctorum* in: ARCHIVUM FRANCISCANUM HISTORICUM 20 (1927) p. 15.

[29] *Letter to All the Faithful* in: *Omnibus*, p. 96.

[30] *Rule of 1223*, ch. 6, my translation; *Omnibus*, pp. 61f.

[31] See M. Daniels CSSF, *The Synthesis of Masculine and Feminine Elements in St. Francis' Personality* in: THE CORD 27 (1977) pp. 36-49; M.T. Archambault OSF, *Francis a Man of Tenderness* in: THE CORD 27 (1977) pp. 185-187.

[32] My translation; *Omnibus*, p. 133.

[33] See *Admonition* 7 in: *Omnibus*, p. 81: "On the other hand those have received life from the spirit of Sacred Scripture who, by their words and example, refer to the most high God, to whom belongs all good. all that they know or wish to know, and do not allow their knowledge to become a source of self-complacency".

and he became for Bonaventure a source of theology, along with St. Augustine and the Pseudo-Dionysius.[34] The theological approach to God, humanity and all creation, which grew out of Francis' evangelical movement, has significantly enough, always been described by medievalists as the Franciscan School. In the writings of its best representatives systematic and spiritual theology flow one into the other so that, though distinct, they may not be separated. Franciscan theologians have always been concerned to provide some interpretation of the spiritual tradition which originated in Francis himself.

Franciscan theology can be described comprehensively as christocentric. This characteristic, already present in St. Anthony of Padua, blossomed in Bonaventure and was crowned by Blessed John Duns Scotus.

Bonaventure summarized the chief concern of Franciscan theology when he explained that Christ is our metaphysics and logic.[35] According to him Christ holds the central position in everything, for he is *mediator* between God and humanity. All intellectual activity has to begin at that centre *(medium)* in order to arrive at wisdom.[36] He considered the entire theological enterprise as a quest for wisdom, not learning which is only a stage on the journey to union with God, where the intellect reaches the limits of its powers and the will passes over into God. It is not without interest in this regard that wisdom is mentioned first by Francis in *The Praises of the Virtues:* "Hail Queen Wisdom. May the Lord preserve you with your sister holy, pure Simplicity".[37]

Francis' love of creation, always experienced in relation to concrete, particular persons, animals and things, found beautiful theological expression in Bonaventure's doctrine of exemplarism in which he articulated "the Franciscan vision of the whole world as internally related, a vision of the universe itself as God's own sacrament".[38] Both Anthony and Bonaventure considered scripture as the heart of theology. Anthony defines it as the science of holy scripture, its sources being the book of revelation and the book of

---

[34] This is found in many of his works, but see especially *The Soul's Journey into God* in: *Bonaventure. . . .*Translation and Introduction by E. Cousins, New York 1978, pp. 53-116.

[35] *The Works of St. Bonaventure. . .*Translated from the Latin by J. de Vinck, *V: Collations on the Six Days*, 1:17, 30, Paterson N.J. 1970, pp. 10, 16.

[36] *Collations on the Six Days*, 1:10, 5-6.

[37] My translation; *Omnibus*, p. 132.

[38] D. Tracy, *The Analogical Imagination. Christian Theology and the Culture of Pluralism*, New York 1981, p. 381.

creation.[39] In his *summa* of theology, the *Breviloquium,* Bonaventure begins with the text of Ephesians 3:14-19 in which he discovers "the origin, progress and crowning point of holy scripture which is called theology".[40]

God is conceived by Duns Scotus primarily as holy love: "God is formally love, formally charity".[41] From this he derived his doctrine of the primacy of Christ. He changed the hypothetical question about the motive of the incarnation into the thesis of the absolute predestination of Christ, which is firmly based on scripture. Sin is not the explanation of the enfleshment of Christ; that is to be found in God's love alone and redemption is the way God's love overcomes the powers of evil. Scotus, therefore, taught a theology of the cosmic Christ.[42]

The place of Mary in Franciscan spirituality has its greatest exponent in Scotus. His defence of the Immaculate Conception must always be understood in the light of his teaching on the absolute predestination of Christ. Mary's redemption took place through the foreseen merits of Christ. We know for certain therefore in one case that Christ's grace was effective before he was incarnate. The consequences of this in respect of Mary's being model of the Church, "the universal sacrament of salvation" have yet to be fully drawn by theology.

The Devotional Forms

Over the centuries Franciscan spirituality has found expression in a variety of devotions and practices of piety which highlight its christocentric, existential and tender character.[43]

The crib at Greccio may have had some influence on the popular practice of building cribs at Christmastide.[44] In any case, devotion to the Child Jesus is a theme found in almost all Franciscan spiritual writers. St. Clare wrote to St. Agnes of Prague that she should meditate daily on "the king of angels,

---

[39] See T. Plassman OFM, *St. Anthony The Theologian* in: *St. Anthony of Padua. Doctor of the Universal Church*, Washington 1947, pp. 49-70.

[40] *The Works of Bonaventure II: The Breviloquium*, Paterson N.J. 1963, p. 1.

[41] *Ordinatio 1*, d.17, n.173, Vivés V, p. 222.

[42] Of course Scotus does not use the term 'cosmic Christ' but this is clearly implied in his teaching; see J.A. Lyons, *The Cosmic Christ in Origen and Teilhard de Chardin*, Oxford 1982, 2 n. 2, pp. 15, 17.

[43] See H. Holzapfel, *Handbuch des Geschichte des Franziskanerordens*, Freiburg i.B. 1909, pp. 226-228; A. Blasucci, *Spiritualité Franciscaine: 1226-1517* in: *Dictionnaire de Spiritualité* V, col. 1323-1325.

[44] But see C. van Hulst, 'Criche' in: *Dictionnaire de Spiritualité* 2, col. 2522.

the Lord of heaven and earth, lying in a manger".[45] Bonaventure composed a beautiful little treatise *On the Five Feasts of the Child Jesus* which explains how the Child is spiritually conceived, born, named, sought and adored with the Magi and presented in the Temple by the devout soul.[46] Francis' devotion to the passion and his *Office of the Passion of the Lord* inspired a wealth of writings on the sufferings of Christ. Clare learned the *Office of the Passion* by heart and prayed it often. This devotion gave great impetus to *The Way of the Cross* whose most ardent advocate, in the form we now have it, was the Franciscan, St. Leonard of Port Maurice (1676-1751). In his *Letter to All the Friars* Francis wrote: "Kissing your feet with all the love I am capable of, I beg you to show the greatest possible reverence and honour for the most holy Body and Blood of our Lord Jesus Christ".[47] Devotion to the Eucharist is one of the pillars of Franciscan spirituality. It is found in all the mystics of the Order and it was a theme often on the lips of the famous preachers of the Order. Franciscans promoted eucharistic confraternities in the fifteenth century. St. Paschal Baylon (1540-1592) a Spanish lay brother of the Order, because of his great reverence for the eucharist, was proclaimed heavenly patron of all eucharistic associations by Leo XIII in 1897.

Francis revered the names of God and cherished above all the holy name of Jesus.[48] Devotion to the name of Jesus was encouraged to a certain extent by Franciscans in the thirteenth and fourteenth centuries. It found its greatest advocate, however, in the fifteenth century in the Franciscan Observant, St. Bernadine of Siena (1380-1444). He preached the name of Jesus as the summary of the gospel of salvation [cf. Acts 8:12]. He devised a monogram made up of the letters YHS set in a golden sun with twelve rays, against a blue background with the text of Phil 2:10 surrounding the whole.[49] The feast of the holy name of Jesus was extended to the whole Church in 1721. Love of the sacred humanity of Jesus centred naturally in the Franciscan tradition on the symbol of the heart. Devotion to the Sacred Heart is the theme of a number of Bonaventure's mystical writings. These greatly influenced the

---

[45] *The Fourth Letter to Saint Agnes* in: E. Doyle OFM, *Discipleship of Christ in St. Clare's Letters to Saint Agnes of Prague* in: *Franciscan Christology. Selected Texts, Translations and Introductory Essays*, ed. by D. McElrath, St. Bonaventure N.Y. 1980, p. 37.

[46] *The Works of Bonaventure III: Opuscula Second Series*, Paterson N.J. 1966, pp. 199-214.

[47] *Omnibus*, p. 104.

[48] See especially the *Letter to Clerics* and *The Testament* in: *Omnibus*, pp. 101, 67.

[49] Eric Doyle OFM, *St. Bernadine of Siena and the Devotion to the Name of Jesus* in: *Franciscan Christology*, pp. 202-226.

spread of the devotion in the Order, and it became a favourite of many of the Order's saints and mystics.[50]

Devotion to the Mother of God led to the Order's establishing the feast of the Visitation and the Espousals of the Blessed Virgin Mary, both of which were later extended to the universal Church. The crown rosary in honour of the seven joys of Our Lady was introduced in the Order in the early fifteenth century. Bernadine of Siena added the words to the *Hail Mary:* "Holy Mary pray for us sinners" and Franciscans had some influence on the practice of ringing the *Angelus* bell.[51] Devotion to the Mother of Jesus extended to his foster father, St. Joseph and to his grandparents, Saints Joachim and Anne.[52] Finally, during the generalate of Bonaventure the Order introduced the feast of the Blessed Trinity and John Pecham, the Franciscan Archbishop of Canterbury in the late thirteenth century, is credited with having composed the Office of the Trinity.[53] Every spirituality concerns the whole of human life in this world. Though Francis of Assisi drew the inspiration of his spiritual movement from the life and teaching of Christ, that movement had direct and intended social and, in the most primitive and best sense of the word, political consequences. As Leonardo Boff, OFM has argued, Francis was a liberated and a liberating man.[54]

---

[50] See H. Eiler OFM, *James of Milan and the Stimulus Amoris* in: *Franciscan Christology*, pp. 89-107.

[51] See H. Thurston, *Ave Maria* and *Angelus* in: *Dictionnaire de Spiritualité* 1, 1161-1165.

[52] Holzapfel, *Handbuch*, p. 228.

[53] Blasucci, *Spiritualité*, col. 1323.

[54] *San Francisco: La Liberacion por la Bondad* in: CUADERNONS FRANCISCANOS 14 (1982) pp. 3-15.

Reflections on the Franciscan Charism[1]

This year marks the seven-hundred-and-fiftieth anniversary of the death of Francis of Assisi at the Portiuncula on October 3rd 1226. The sources for his life record that larks gathered on the roof above where he lay dying and sang sweetly as he welcomed Sister Death into his life.[2] No one would deny that on that Saturday evening in 1226 a most holy man, a truly human man and a faithful disciple of Christ Crucified passed over to God. And the earth was made the poorer for that passing.

Already in various parts of the world there have been courses of lectures and celebrations to mark the event and there will be quite a few more before the year has ended. Eulogies will be made in many languages and no doubt St. Francis from his place in heaven will hear himself hailed again as "Patron of the Environment" and "Patron of Ecumenism".

The anniversary provides a good opportunity for a Franciscan to reflect on the order's efforts to come to terms with the demands to rediscover its own charism made over the last decade or so since the Second Vatican Council. Though my primary concern is the First Order of Franciscans, and specifically the Order of Friars Minor, I think these reflections will have some relevance for the Conventuals, the Capuchins and the various branches of the Third Order Regular as well, for it is the same charism which ultimately inspires them all. These reflections may have even wider relevance. Orders which lead the so-called 'mixed' life share many of the same problems in facing the demands of renewal.

The Question of Poverty

These pages contain no detailed analysis of poverty. In the case of an order which has been so intimately associated with the, profession of poverty, this calls for a word of explanation. For the Franciscan Order the question of poverty is ambiguous. It can be a very complicated question and it can be a very simple question, according to the approach one takes to it. For the order

---

[1] REVIEW FOR RELIGIOUS 36 (June 1977) pp. 12-35. Published with permission.
[2] See *Legend of Perugia*, 110 in: *Omnibus*, pp. 1085f.

as it is *de facto* organized in the world, poverty is a complicated question. It cannot be examined or discussed in any realistic or satisfactory way if it is isolated from the findings of biblical exegesis and the understanding of poverty in the bible, from a study of all the elements contained in the idea of evangelical perfection which relativize the place of poverty in the life and writings of St. Francis, from the question about the extent and effectiveness of apostolic activity, and from the demands made on the Order to find resources to cope with and provide for the numbers who seek to enter it.

No one would deny that the Franciscan Order should be involved in work among the poor. At the theoretical level this is almost a truism for the Franciscan. At the practical level, however, it is no easy matter to determine who precisely are the poor today. While the term certainly covers the homeless, the destitute, the oppressed and the exploited, it may also be used to describe countless millions all over the globe who are spiritually impoverished.

But even when we have arrived at a moderately satisfactory answer to the question—who are the poor?—we find at once that there are required no mean resources, for example, to have a friar trained to be a competent and reliable apostle among social outcasts. For the Order to provide resources to train a friar as a professional social worker is a deeply Christian work and a tremendous act of service to the world.

On the other hand, the question of poverty can be very simple. If a person reads the accounts of the early history of the Order and is convinced that the poverty which St. Francis and his first companions embraced is the *unique* charism of the Order, and feels assured that he is called to do the same, then that person must go and do likewise and thus institute a new branch of the Franciscan Order in the world.

The same obligation, it seems, would rest upon a professed friar who became conscientiously convinced that the Order has sacrificed an essential element of its charism and mission to the world in abandoning the poverty of St. Francis. He would be bound quite simply to leave the Order as it is and to establish another form of the Franciscan life. It would be pointless to ask him where he would go, because, from that moment onward, total abandonment to divine providence would be of the structure of his vocation, and he would literally have to wait for something to turn up. What he certainly could not do would be to stay in the Order as it is now constituted, passing away his days in criticising it and growing old in bitterness, while living by its resources and in its security. Perhaps at the very outset he ought to familiarise with these difficulties all who seek to join us. They would then be able to make such considerations a conscious factor in their decision to join us or not. We should also make sure they know by experience that the gospel spirit of St. Francis does live on in the Order, despite the fact that his poverty is not observed.

I do not wish to suggest that the Order as it now finds itself can simply ignore the question of poverty. In fact it has not ignored it over the last decade. There have been many attempts to come to terms with it at the practical level. But it remains problematic.[3] However, the issue cannot be discussed in these pages, nor can any assessment be made of the attempts to come to terms with poverty, firstly, because it would take far too long and, secondly, because while it is undoubtedly an important issue, it is not, in our opinion, the most important issue for the life and mission of the order. There are more vital matters to be considered to which we now shall turn.

Rediscovery of the Original Charism

The Second Vatican Council called all religious to rediscover the particular charism given to the Church in the grace of their origins and to renew and adapt their life according to its form. By a process of discernment in the light of the gospel and according to the signs of the times—that is by Word and world—religious were required to define the specific and permanent acquisition made by the Church in the life and work of their particular Order.

The Franciscan Order, like every Order, belongs to the Church. Only in virtue of its ecclesial character can it be understood in its specific genius at any moment of its history and as a renewal movement at its origins. Apart from the Church, the Franciscan Order is ultimately meaningless. St. Francis himself was not only a man of the gospel, but also and by that very fact, he was a man of the Church. Therefore, the attempt by any Order or congregation to discover its own particular grace is not an exercise in self-analysis, but a profound act of service to the Church.

The call to rediscover the original charism raised at once a question for the Franciscan Order which has not yet been satisfactorily treated. The question is this: Is the original charism to be sought uniquely in the periods between the oral approval of the *Rule* by Pope Innocent and the death of St. Francis (1209-1226), or is it to be sought throughout the first century of the order's history from the approval of the *Rule* to the death of John Duns Scotus (1209-1308)? This is not just an academic question, but a matter of some

---

[3]   We have touched on some of these problems in *Reflections on the Theology of Religious Life*. Editors´ note: This article is reprinted in this volume: pp. 504 ff.

concern to any Franciscan conscious of the profound contribution made to the development of Christology by the Franciscan School in the first century of its history. The order has been far too preoccupied in its renewal program with the period up to the death of St. Francis. This is an unjust and uncritical restriction of the content of the Franciscan charism. Of course, the call to rediscover the charism required of us to return to St. Francis himself. About that there is no argument. The complaint being made here concerns the well-nigh exclusive preoccupation with the early years of the Order's life, which drastically truncates the Order's charism.

Many reasons might be suggested to explain this restrictive version of the charism. I wish to single out the one which bears most responsibility. It is *romanticism*. Romanticism has exercised far too much influence on judgments of the Order's history since the death of St. Francis. It has given the Order a bad conscience, especially over the last eighty years or so since Paul Sabatier's views became common patrimony.[4] What we can describe in general terms as the 'Fioretti-picture' of the early years, has exercised inordinate influence over the general public and over the scholarly fraternity, particularly its non-Catholic representatives. We need to be on our guard in the presence of romantics. Their understandable sadness at the way the Order developed can have the most extraordinary effect on how they read the sources.

When the Franciscan Order, for example, in late fourteenth-century English history is described by students of Wyclif, Chaucer and Langland as "decadent" I have often concluded that we really ought to read in many cases not "decadent' but "different"—that is, different from the little band of beggars which landed at Dover in September 1224 and different from the early days at Rivo Torto.

Disappointed and sad romantics are a dangerous breed. The "romantic myth" has had profound though subconscious influence on the Order. It has subtly brainwashed us into believing that if only we could repeat as closely as possible the form of life which St. Francis led, if only we could do away with the whole intellectual edifice which the Order constructed for itself, then we would be true and authentic Franciscans.

From these remarks it will be clear where we intend to place the *locus* of the original Franciscan charism. According to our view the original charism is to be sought in the period from the approval of the *Rule* in 1209 up to the death of John Duns Scotus in 1308. To return to the sources means, for a

---

[4]   *Vie de S. Francois d'Assise*, edition definitive, Fischbacher, Paris 1931.

Franciscan, a return to the first hundred years of development in doctrine and life. The fullness of the charism is to be found there and not exclusively in the life and teaching of St. Francis. It is quite legitimate, in function of this, to consider the Franciscan charism under two headings: form of life and christological doctrine. The first concerns the evolution of the Order's life in the thirteenth century. The second concerns the development of the Christology in the Franciscan School in the thirteenth century. The results of historical analysis show that the form of Franciscan life changed radically from what St. Francis had intended and that the christological doctrine of the Franciscan School remained totally faithful to his original Christocentric inspiration.

The Form of Life

The foundation of the Franciscan Order in the thirteenth century marked a new stage in the history of the religious life in the Western Church. While it is clearly the case that St. Francis intended to establish an Order in the commonly accepted sense of that term, it is equally clear that he was conscious of its radical newness. According to his intention, the Order was to be a brotherhood of itinerant apostles—whether priests or manual workers, or, as we should say today, professional men—who would go into a society that was still Christian and also go out to foreign lands among the Saracens, to spread the gospel of peace and reconciliation by the ministry of the Word and the apostolate of presence.

For a period of time that intention was realized. Whenever the friars met they showed that they were members of the same fraternity and they offered one another mutual help and support. At the end of their day's work they returned to their small communities to be refreshed bodily and spiritually, to pray together, and to draw strength from their fraternal celebration of the Eucharist. Thus renewed and restored, they were able to return to their mission of sharing with others what they themselves had received so generously from being together in the 'local church' of their own community.

As is universally recognized, this did not remain for very long the pattern of life of the Order. Due to internal tensions and from external pressures from the demands of the apostolate at the time and from the wishes of the Holy See, the Order was compelled to take a line of development which radically changed what St. Francis had intended and what the original form of life had been. There are those who look upon this as a salutary development, precisely because it took place ultimately under the authority and guidance of the Holy

See. While this attitude demands some respect, it also creates difficulties in deciding which has priority between the poles of institution and charism.

In responding to the call to rediscover its original charism (and it was the institution which gave the call) the Franciscan Order found itself in a slightly embarrassing position. As it retraced the steps of its development through a very chequered history back to the thirteenth century, it discovered that it was largely due to the institution that an important element in its charism had been lost. The loose structure of its form of life had been heavily institutionalised and the fraternity had been "monastified" and "hierarchized" almost beyond recognition.

Institution and Charism

From the outset there has been tension in the Franciscan Order between charism and institution. St. Francis himself, who is always proclaimed as a most obedient son of the Holy Roman Church, managed to get his own way with the wily and astute Pope Innocent III. One wonders what would have been the outcome if the pope had refused him permission to live his very distinctive interpretation of the gospel. Perhaps he would have become a hermit. To the end of his days, in any case, he remained convinced that what he desired his Order to be was completely at one with the will of God.

The turn of events in the thirteenth century gave the Order a very different character from that which it possessed in its early decades. The constitutional development from the late 1230's up to the Chapter of Narbonne in 1260 is the history of a gradual "monastification" of the Order. This cannot in justice be laid exclusively at the door of St. Bonaventure, for the winds of change had already been blowing for nearly thirty years when he was elected Minister General.[5] By the end of the thirteenth century the Order had been

---

[5]   See L.C. Landini, *The Causes of the Clericalization of the Order of Friars Minor 1209-1260 in the Light of Early Franciscan Sources*, Chicago: Franciscan Herald Press 1968. We have given no consideration here to St. Bonaventure's theology of history nor to his eschatological interpretation of the life of St. Francis. These highly developed aspects of St. Bonaventure's thought played no significant part in the Order's self-understanding and program of renewal during the past decade. For this reason we have not touched on his solution of the "Franciscan Question". This omission, therefore, should not be understood as a value judgment. Our concern is with those aspects of the original charism which have been re-discovered and, with varying degrees of success, reduced to practice, and with other aspects which deserve further consideration, which ought to influence the Order's continuing renewal. St. Bonaventure's eschatological interpretation of St. Francis is, in our view, the most satisfactory solution to the problem about the Order's relation to St. Francis. It is, however, not only satisfactory; it is

substantially altered, due in large measure to the institutional Church, for what were undoubtedly the most laudable ends.

Of course, there were also internal reasons for the change and it would be unhistorical to place responsibility entirely on the Holy See. It is no idle speculation to ponder what the Order might have been, had it not experienced the process of clericalization in the thirteenth century and had Friar Elias not alienated so many while he held office. But in the final analysis, one is compelled to conclude that the Holy See can hardly be said to have done all in its power to preserve what St. Francis so plainly intended. This was the result of tension between charism and institution.

The Church has known this tension in varying degrees of intensity ever since the New Testament, and perhaps never so acutely as over the last two decades. Tension arises precisely because both institution and charism proceed from the grace of God. Charisms are given to the Church for the sake of the institution; the prophet is always sent to renew the institution. The sad story is, however, that so often the institution resists the charism because it threatens the established Order; it leads out into the unknown and the uncharted. The temptation for the institution is always to neutralize charism by institutionalising it. This is not done maliciously or even consciously. But it *is* done and it is done effectively.

The intentions of St. Francis could not easily be categorized. They were not neat and tidy, cut and dried, but on the contrary, like himself, paradoxical and a fraction complicated. I have never believed that this passionate, romantic and ambitious young man was ever as simple as some of his biographers have made out. Of course, he did not have a legal mind; he had the soul of a poet and poets are notoriously difficult to pin down. In his own head (or perhaps better, in his own heart) everything was crystal clear: He wanted to live the life of the gospel according to the form that God had revealed to him. One can sympathize with Rome, therefore, whose genius has always been principally of the legal order. How does one categorize an intention that expresses itself in a *Rule* for itinerant apostles which is identified

---

also fully consonant with the way the early sources present him and the primitive community. It has most relevance in any discussion of Franciscan poverty, for it raises the question not only whether the Order can or cannot observe St. Francis' poverty, but whether or not it is even *meant* to observe it. To assess St. Bonaventure's place in the development of the order in the thirteenth century, without taking into serious account his theology of history and his eschatological interpretation of St. Francis, leads to profound misunderstanding of that development and commits injustice against St. Bonaventure.

with the gospel, and in another for hermitages that allows for a change of roles between Martha and Mary according to what seems best for the moment?

Aspects of the Charism Rediscovered

In going back to its original inspiration, the Franciscan Order knew in its heart that it simply could not recreate in our time the full intentions of St. Francis. However, it has managed to reintroduce some of the essential elements of his charism, and what it has done is a splendid achievement.

1. Over the last ten years the Order has "de-monastified" itself and restored in principle its truly fraternal character. It is now more obviously an *Order* of Friars, some of whom are engaged in priestly work, others in manual work inside and outside the Order and still others who are engaged in professional work. There is a deep consciousness of what it means existentially to be a Franciscan friar. This consciousness is growing apace and it will ultimately be in complete possession.

2. There has also been a gradual "de-clericalization" of the Order. This does not *necessarily* mean a reduction in the number of priests (though this will happen, I think) nor does it imply, nor should it ever have implied, an anti-priest complex. The order was unfortunately plagued with that complex for a period after the Council. To be a priest does not necessarily mean to be clericalized. There are many young priests, middle-aged priests and elderly priests in the Order who are most certainly not clericalized; but then there *are* some who are. Clericalization creates an elite and a caste system. There is no true place for an elite or a caste system in the Franciscan Order, nor, for that, matter, in the Church at large. The Church knows no hierarchy of persons but acknowledges only a hierarchy of functions, and at its pinnacle is service. Moreover, authority has been restored to its original role, according to the understanding of St. Francis, as a ministry and service to the friars. This has had its influence also on the gradual abolition of hierarchical structures from the Order.

3. Experiments of living the Franciscan life in small communities have proved in the main successful and have undoubtedly enriched the quality of community life. This has been one of the most significant contributions of all our efforts to restore the fraternal character of the Order. There have been losses, excesses and mistakes. But these are negligible when compared with the gains, the openness and the insights we have harvested. Franciscan life in small communities or groups has proved to be far more demanding on the individual friar than it ever was in the heavily structured

forms of life we knew for so long. Our experiences have taught us that life in small communities requires a high degree of human and Christian maturity. For life thus lived is a creative process, not a structured, unchanging pattern into which one is fitted.

4. Many of these small communities have been established in the centre of towns and cities where the realities of modern living, its pressures and demands may be witnessed and experienced at first hand. A number of friars in such communities have taken up work in social organizations often not instituted by the Church nor directly connected with it. These developments have given concrete expression to other aspects of the original charism and primitive form of life. Unlike the older monastic orders, the friars settled in the heart of towns and cities where they were brought face-to-face with the social evils of the time. As a result, the Franciscans were closely connected with the foundation of medieval guilds, the distant ancestors of the modern trade unions. They supported the organization of workers into guilds which protected the legitimate material interests of the workers and furthered their spiritual lives. Some of the charters of these guilds were drawn up in the refectories of the friars or on the altars of their churches. Later on, in the fifteenth century, the iniquities of usury led the Franciscans to establish the *Montes Pietatis*—an institution which guarantees them a place for all time in social history. All these developments may be traced back to St. Francis himself who, from the outset of his conversion, was involved in caring for lepers, one of the greatest social evils of the Middle Ages.

The modern form of the apostolate of presence: living at the heart of urban life and working from within non-ecclesiastical social structures, is really a reduction to practice of *The Canticle of Brother Sun* and of St. Bonaventure's beautiful work *On Retracing the Arts to Theology*. For the Franciscan there is no distinction between the sacred and the profane. The problems of what is described as *secularisation* prove for a Franciscan to be false problems. This is now simply man's world and man is made in the image of Christ and Christ is the image of the Father we cannot see.

The Spirituality of St. Francis

The rediscovery of the basic elements of Franciscan spirituality has been the most rewarding of all. A comparative study of the spirituality of the Conciliar documents and the writings of St. Francis shows how incredibly modern this very medieval man turns out to be. His spirituality is simply Jesus Christ.

The thoroughly biblical and sacramental, above all eucharistic, character of his piety and holiness make it clear that it was our spirituality and practices of piety that had to be brought up to date, renewed and reformed, not his! There is nothing nauseating about his spirituality, nothing repulsive about his piety. There is not one line, not one word, in the expressions of his evangelical holiness that need be changed, corrected or expunged. He loved the God-Man in all his poverty and humanity, in all his kindness and suffering. He loved him absolutely, without qualification. He loved Christ not only with his whole heart, but with his whole soul and mind and strength. His conversion was complete because it was born of love. Everything he said and sang, everything he desired and longed for, his every thought and deed, came from and led back directly to his love of Jesus Christ. The most distinctive feature of his holiness is its *tenderness.* And it bears that feature because he was a passionate man. He did not extinguish in himself the fire of passion; he redirected it by grace into the love of Christ, where it burned more ardently in the all-consuming flame of the love of Christ's heart for the Father and for all creation.

Our renewed understanding of the totally Christocentric spirituality of St. Francis has shown the Order that in its common life of prayer it does not need a multiplication of devotions and practices of piety. To be faithful to the spirituality of St. Francis requires of the friars to live and work, to think and pray, after the example of the life Jesus led on earth, by the power of his glorified existence with the Father, in the beauty of his vestiges and images in creation, according to the message of his Word, through his selfless love in the Blessed Eucharist and together with his brethren in the Church. All of which may be summarized by saying that we must live by his threefold presence in our midst; his *verbal* presence (the proclamation of the gospel among us); his *sacramental* presence, (preeminently the eucharistic celebration); his *mystical* presence (the community of believers which gathers to proclaim and celebrate his victory over death and his faithful witness to love).

The Tension That Remains

None of these changes according to the form of the original charism has been achieved without suffering and bitterness. This is the sad side to the history of renewal and reform in the Church generally. However, it was an inevitable and predictable concomitant to the renewal from the beginning and it is rooted in the tension between institution and charism. The movement for reform initiated by the Council brought to the surface two diametrically opposed views of the Church which have been labelled, not satisfactorily though not unjustly, as reactionary-conservative and liberal-progressive. The fears of the former soon turned to suspicion; the enthusiasm of the latter speedily became intolerant. And for a time the result was deadlock and suffering on both sides.

Tension between institution and charism can be healthy and constructive. It can also be deadly and destructive if attitudes polarize. As an outcome of the changes in the Order's form of life there was a polarization of attitudes. Two basic attitudes emerged which differed radically about what had taken place and what were being predicted as the lines of future development. The attitudes correspond to the labels *reactionary and liberal.* The tension between these polarized attitudes is by no means as acute now as it was five years ago, but it is still present. From a state of complete inability to communicate, a *modus vivendi* was eventually found, based on an unspoken and precarious truce to steer clear of all that might open the wounds. Now, thanks to more openness on the one side and greater tolerance on the other, the truce has given place to a willingness to dialogue and the signs are that the tension will become creative. Up to the present, however, while having had some creative and productive effect, it has been largely negative and counter-productive. Two "Orders" have been existing side by side in the one Order. But now the signs are that they are growing towards unity once more.

This tension continues to exist in varying degrees of intensity throughout all the provinces of the Order. To a greater or less extent it concerns every aspect of the charism in relation to our form of life and every attempt to reduce it to practice. But the deepest tension has been caused by the opposing views on what may be described as the Order's *apostolate of presence.*

The one view maintains that it is our vocation to engage in priestly ministerial work, in charitable works centred upon our friaries and in domestic works within the friaries, which latter ensure that they remain habitable and in good condition, so that the former works may be carried on with competence and efficiency. To these works the major part of the Order is now committed and this commitment has come to pass by the demands made upon us and the indications given to us by the institutional Church, whether the Holy See or the diocesan bishops. These works, it is argued, have been assigned to us by the authority of the Church and therefore they are clearly what we are meant to do under God. Furthermore, they put us in direct contact with the evolution of the Order as this took place under the guidance of the Holy See in the thirteenth century. This is a version of the adage, *Roma locuta est;* it gives priority to the institution. It maintains that priestly work is the paradigm of the Franciscan apostolate. This view is prepared to admit that *some* friars might well work in other forms of the apostolate which are neither priestly nor ministerial nor centred upon a friary. These forms of the apostolate, however, have significance only insofar as they proceed ultimately from the priestly ministry and eventually lead back to it.

The other view maintains that it is our vocation to spread the gospel message by our presence in the world. This can be fulfilled in a large variety of ways; by priestly ministerial work and charitable works centred upon our friaries; by domestic work inside and outside our friaries; by professional work outside the friaries in ecclesiastical institutions or non-ecclesiastical institutions; by taking up salaried trades and professions outside ecclesiastical institutions. This view, it is argued, is in direct continuity with the earliest years of the Order's history and is a version of the saying of St. Francis that the Holy Spirit is the Minister General of the Order; it gives priority to the original charism. It holds that there is no special paradigm for the Franciscan apostolate and that the Order must balance the demands made by the institution with the clear requirements of the charism, even if this means that we may have to sacrifice some of the areas in which we are exclusively committed to priestly ministerial work.

Due to circumstances we could neither foresee nor control, these two views eventually reached the compromise of co-existence and then entered into dialogue. The circumstances which brought them together were the overall decrease in numbers of those entering the Order, the high figure of those who left the Order and an extraordinary awareness of the original charism among the majority of those who seek to enter the Order. This last phenomenon is remarkable. Its major effect has been that entrants to the Order express their vocation simply in terms of wanting *to be friar* without further qualification. This is a reliable sign of how the future of the Order will evolve.

Christology and the Franciscan School

Earlier in this paper we insisted that the original charism of the Order is to be sought not exclusively in the life and teaching of St. Francis but in the whole period that extends to the death of Duns Scotus, the last of the major representatives of the Franciscan School of Theology. We must examine the reasons which justify this position.

During the period up to the death of Duns Scotus, theologians of the Order worked out a doctrine of the person and work of Christ and of his place in the *oikumene* and cosmos that is as beautiful as it is original and as inspiring as it is profound. It stands out as a remarkable contribution to the development of Christology in the Church. Any study or presentation of the original Franciscan charism that limits itself to the life of St. Francis not only misrepresents that charism, but also does disservice and injustice to the Church by depriving her of what belongs to her by right. The christological teaching of the Franciscan School is as much an essential element of the Franciscan charism as is the fraternal character of the early Order, the apostolate of presence, the *Rule of 1221,* the *Rule for Hermitages, The Canticle of Brother Sun* and the *Rule of 1223.* What Fr. Zachary Hayes OFM has written about the philosophy of education in the spirit of St. Bonaventure, may be applied without qualification to the christological doctrine of the whole Franciscan School.

Those of us who stand heirs to that Tradition have a weighty obligation to see that such a Tradition be not lost and that it be brought to bear in our world today. That it should have come to be deposited with such clarity and power in the Order that claims the poor, simple man of Assisi as its founder will no doubt puzzle those who tend to limit the meaning of that Order in an unhistorical and arbitrary way. That its outstanding spokesman should be a Franciscan does not make it the private possession of the Order. For what the order carries here as in an earthen vessel is a treasure for the whole of the Church and a heritage for mankind as such.

Certainly the Order would be unfaithful to its Tradition and remiss in its obligation to the Church and the world if it were not to take up this Tradition anew, in a creative way, in a world for which one of the most pervasive and potentially destructive idols is the ideal of rational control.[6]

The Constitutions of the Order

The General Constitutions of the Order published in 1953 state in Article 238, par. 6: "In the philosophical and theological faculties the lectors shall earnestly endeavour to follow the Franciscan School; they shall hold in high regard the other Scholastics, especially the Angelic Doctor, St. Thomas,

---

[6] *Toward a Philosophy of Education in the Spirit of St. Bonaventure, Proceedings of the Seventh Centenary Celebration of the Death of Saint Bonaventure,* The Franciscan Institute, St. Bonaventure N.Y. 1975, pp. 26f.

the Heavenly, Patron of Catholic Schools".[7] Despite this exhortation, however, the Order as a whole has not endeavoured as earnestly as it might have done to follow its own school. The manuals of philosophy and theology, which were the staple intellectual diet of most of the houses of study in the Order, were composed chiefly by authors of the Thomistic tradition (not always the same as the Tradition of St. Thomas!), who tended to reduce the contents of the Franciscan Tradition at best to footnotes and *scholia,* at worst, to being adverse to the thesis advanced. The high place accorded to St. Thomas in Catholic theology and the fact that he received honourable mention in the *Code of Canon Law* made him the touchstone of orthodoxy and the gauge of true Catholic doctrine. The second title given to him—the Common Doctor—resulted in every other doctor becoming for the most part decidedly uncommon. In comparing the Dominican and Franciscan Orders we find that the former exalted St. Thomas and tended to forget St. Dominic; the latter exalted St. Francis and tended to forget St. Bonaventure. Thus it is that we speak of the Thomistic School, not the Dominican School; of the Franciscan School, not the Bonaventurian School. This latter designation has further significance, as will be seen below.

In the *Revised General Constitutions* promulgated by the Minister General in December 1973, it is stated in Article 20, par. 1: "Mental prayer should be based on the writings and example of Francis and on the teaching of the Franciscan masters. Nevertheless, each friar is free to choose the method of prayer that suits him"[8]; in Article 170, par. 2: "Theological education should be encouraged in the Order with special care. The greatest attention should be given to the preparation of expert teachers of theology who will administer spirit and life after the intent of Francis and the other masters of the Order"; ibid., par. 4: "Where there are no houses of study of the Order, students should be given lectures on the history and teaching of the Franciscan School"[9]; in the *Introduction* to Chapter Six: *Formation to Franciscan Life:* "Franciscan pedagogy, according to a thought-plan (dialectic) which continually renews itself, takes as its greater and most difficult task to bring together the divine with the human—a process begun by St. Francis and set in logical order by the

---

[7] *The Rule and Constitutions of the Order of Friars Minor*, Rome 1953, p. 100.

[8] *The Plan for Franciscan Living. The Rule and General Constitutions of the Order of Friars Minor*, English-Speaking Conf. of Provincials: Pulaski, Wisconsin 1974, p. 70.

[9] Ibid., pp. 147f.

Masters of the Franciscan School, a process rightly styled 'thought in acting'— in other words, love"[10].

It is to be hoped that the spirit behind these statements in the new *Constitutions* will prevail over the strange indifference to the Franciscan theological Tradition that has characterised the Order in modern times and that it will eradicate the dull anti-intellectual element in the Order which resulted from that fatal romanticism mentioned earlier. This anti-intellectual element has been making itself felt in various parts of the Order over the past few years. Its root lies in a subconscious belief that there is something not quite authentic about a learned Franciscan or a Franciscan who wishes to devote his life to study. The popular picture of the Franciscan friar has had a surreptitious influence on the Order. The Franciscan is expected to be a jolly friar, simple to the point of lunacy, preferably rotund in shape and bald into the bargain, ruddy-faced and definitely not learned, who trips through the world hoping to get a good dinner, but happy to sing to the sun if he does not. This picture is reproduced each year on hundreds of Christmas cards all over the world. (I have made a collection of the more amusing ones!) The irony of the popular picture is that it bears no resemblance whatever to the first Franciscan. St. Francis himself was a man of joy, but in no sense could he be called jolly; he had the simplicity of the dove but also the cunning of the serpent, just as the gospel says; he was a small man, thin and emaciated; not bald, but shaven-headed; his skin was delicate and his flesh very spare;[11] though not learned in a bookish sense, he knew French, wrote tolerably good Latin, composed a very beautiful song and was acquainted with the intricacies of the cloth trade and he had some idea about building. His attitude to learning is at best ambiguous. In any case he advocated reverence for theologians and Scripture scholars and he warned even those who work with their hands not to allow their work to extinguish the spirit of prayer and devotion. Despite Masseron's fear that if St. Francis were to return to earth today, he would probably consign a Franciscan bibliography to Brother Fire,[12] I am convinced that he would not destroy the sermons of St. Anthony, the works of St. Bonaventure nor the third book of Duns Scotus' *Commentary on the Sentences*.

---

[10] Ibid., pp. 129f.

[11] See the description of St. Francis given in 1Celano 83 in: *Omnibus*, pp. 298f.

[12] A. Masseron, *The Franciscans*, Translation by W.B. Wells, New York 1932, p. 4: "What would St. Francis, if he returned to earth today, have to say to anyone who was rash enough to show him a Franciscan bibliography? Is it not to be feared that 'our Brother Fire' would be charged with settling the fate of a work of such unwieldy uselessness?"

The Development of Christology

It is noteworthy and encouraging that the *Renewed Constitutions* explicitly link the teaching of the Franciscan masters to St. Francis himself. Specifically, the christological doctrine of the Franciscan School took its origin from the insight of St. Francis into the, absolute centrality of the Word-made-flesh. His spirituality was centred totally on Christ. He gave concrete expression to it in devotion to the Crib, to our Blessed Lady precisely because she made the Lord of Majesty our brother, to the Passion and Cross, to the Word of God in Scripture and to the Blessed Eucharist. To read of the imprinting of the stigmata on his poor body comes hardly as a surprise after a life spent in total conformity to the Gospel Christ.

His initial encounter with Christ issued in a desire to imitate the life of Christ in its every detail, to follow in the very footsteps of Christ. To follow the footsteps of Christ was for Francis to take the Way that leads back to the Father. Though his heart and soul were centred on the poverty and humility of Jesus in the New Testament, whereby the *Rule* and life of his order became synonymous with observing the gospel, there is no exclusive concern with the so-called "simple" Jesus of history in the life and writings of St. Francis. He embraced a life of poverty in imitation of Christ who "is the glorious Word of the Father, so holy and exalted, whose coming the Father made known by St. Gabriel the Archangel to the glorious and blessed Virgin Mary, in whose womb he took on our weak human nature. He was rich beyond measure and yet he and his holy Mother chose poverty".[13] This humiliation which the Word of the Father freely chose for our sake, is daily renewed on our altars: "Every day he humbles himself just as he did when he came from his heavenly throne [Wisdom 18:15] into the Virgin's womb; every day he comes to us and lets us see him in abjection, when he descends from the bosom of the Father into the hands of the priest at the altar".[14]

There are three texts in the writings of St. Francis which in our opinion contain the seeds of the future development of Christology in the Franciscan School. If these were all he had left us, they would be more than sufficient as the foundation of the Franciscan School. The first is to be found in the fifth *Admonition:* "Try to realise the dignity God has conferred on you. He created and formed your body in the image of his beloved Son and your soul in his own likeness" [see Genesis 1:26].[15] The second is in the first paragraph of his *Letter*

---

[13] *Letter to all the Faithful* in: *Omnibus*, p. 93.
[14] *Admonition 1* in: ibid., p. 78.
[15] Ibid., p. 80.

to All Clerics: "Indeed in this world there is nothing of the Most High himself that we can possess and contemplate with our eyes, except his Body and Blood, his name and his words, by which we were created and by which we have been brought back from death to life".[16] The third is found in the *Letter to a General Chapter:* "Kissing your feet with all the love I am capable of, I beg you to show the greatest possible reverence and honour for the most holy Body and Blood of our Lord Jesus Christ through whom *all things, whether on the earth or in the heavens,* have been brought to peace and reconciled with Almighty God" [see Colossians 1:20].[17] There is a fair amount of deep theology in the writings of St. Francis, but nowhere is this more clearly attested than in these texts. Their depths and the implications they contain will be obvious to any student of St. Bonaventure or Duns Scotus. With regard to the first text, we may ask if St. Francis meant to say that the body of the Word Incarnate was the blueprint used by God in the creation of Adam? He states explicitly: "He created and formed your body in the image of his beloved Son". The Son as Son has no body; it is the Son as Word-Incarnate who possesses a body. Whether or not St. Francis was aware of the implications of what he wrote, these lines evoke at once Duns Scotus' doctrine of the absolute primacy of Christ. Furthermore it would not be difficult at all to trace St. Bonaventure's entire theology of creation and incarnation back to the two latter texts we quoted.

St. Anthony, St. Bonaventure and Duns Scotus

1. The christological teaching of the Franciscan School found its earliest expression in the sermons of St. Anthony of Padua. Already therein we find contained the doctrine of the primacy of Christ, for which Scotus is so justly acclaimed. St. Anthony shows a preference for the symbol of the circle of egression and return of which St. Bonaventure made such profound and superb use in his theology of the Word and creation.[18]

2. It is, however, St. Bonaventure himself who gave the most complete theological formulation to the christological insights of St. Francis. He is the mystical theologian par excellence of the Franciscan Order and in him the

---

[16] Ibid., p. 101.
[17] Ibid., p. 104.
[18] See V. Schaaf OFM, *Saint-Antoine de Padoue. Docteur de l'Eglise*, Montreal: Editions Franciscaines 1946; T. Plassmann OFM, *St. Anthony the Theologian. St. Anthony of Padua, Doctor of the Church: Universal Souvenir of the Commemorative Ceremonies*, Washington D.C. 1946, pp. 49-70; J. Heerinckx OFM, *Antoine de Padoue* in: *Dictionnaire de Spiritualité*, I, 714-717.

School reached the high point of its development. He belongs to the Tradition in the Church which has its origin in the Greek and Latin Fathers, according to which the work of the theologian and the ministry of preaching are understood to be no more than different modalities of one and the selfsame service of the Word of God.

Every concrete form in which St. Francis expressed his devotion to the poor and humble Christ, is paralleled by a mystical work in the Bonaventurian *corpus*. For example, to the crib at Greccio corresponds the beautiful work *On the Five Feasts of the Child Jesus*; to St. Francis's reverence for the Blessed Eucharist corresponds the work *On How to Prepare for the Celebration of Mass*[19]; to his devotion to the Passion and Cross of Christ correspond St. Bonaventure's *The Tree of Life* and *The Mystical Vine*.[20]

St. Bonaventure's theology of the Word may be summarized as follows: the Word is the inner expression of the Father and the world is the outer expression of the Son. Creation gives outward expression to the inner Word of the Father. With the advent of man, the Word of God is spoken in a radically new way, for it now opens the possibility of the most perfect outward expression of God's inner Word in the incarnation of the Word: the Man, Jesus of Nazareth. By the enfleshment of the Word, the words already spoken by God in every creature throughout all creation can be heard unambiguously for what they are—revelations of God. As the Eternal Word is the Centre of the Trinity, so the Incarnate Word is the Centre of everything outside the Trinity. Nothing can be known unless it is known through Christ. At every level and in all orders of reality Jesus Christ is Mediator. To have true knowledge of God, man and the cosmos we must take faith as our starting point. From this we may then proceed to reason in order to know what it may discover about God, man and the cosmos.[21] This latter aspect of St. Bonaventure's world view has a relevance

---

[19] *The Works of Bonaventure*, Translation by José de Vinck. III: *Opuscula, Second Series*, Paterson N.J.: St. Anthony Guild Press 1966, pp. 197-214; 215-238.

[20] Ibid., I: *Mystical Opuscula*, Paterson N.J.: St. Anthony Guild Press 1960, pp. 95-144; 145-205.

[21] For recent presentations of the Christology of St. Bonaventure see the important studies by Z. Hayes OFM, *Revelation in Christ. Proceedings of the of Seventh Centenary Celebration of the Death of St. Bonaventure*, The Franciscan Institute: St. Bonaventure N.Y. 1975, pp. 29-43; *The Meaning of Convenientia in the Metaphysics of St. Bonaventure* in: FRANCISCAN STUDIES vol. 34, Annual XII, 1974, pp. 74-100; *Incarnation and Creation in the Theology of St. Bonaventure, Studies Honoring Ignatius Brady, Friar Minor*, ed. by R.S. Almagno OFM and C.L. Harkins OFM, The Franciscan Institute: St. Bonaventure N.Y. 1976, pp. 309-329. See also I. Brady OFM, *St. Bonaventure's Theology of the Imitation of Christ. Proceedings of the of Seventh Centenary Celebration of the Death of St. Bonaventure*, The Franciscan Institute: St. Bonaventure N.Y. 1975, pp. 61-72.

today which it would be difficult to overestimate. It concerns particularly the separation between philosophy of God and theology in Catholic institutes of education which has had deplorable effects on intellectual formation.[135] A return to the concreteness of St. Bonaventure's method will teach us to distinguish, but not separate, a philosophy of God from theology. The correct method is to treat the theology of God first.

After St. Clare I know of no one who loved St. Francis more than St. Bonaventure did. His sermons on St. Francis show him to have agonized in loving astonishment at what God had done in the person and life of the poor Francis of Assisi.[23] Everything St. Bonaventure strove after in his study of the Word of God he found realized in St. Francis. Of all the virtues which St. Francis possessed, St. Bonaventure avowed that he admired most his poverty and humility. He laid down at the feet of St. Francis the powers of his brilliant mind and the rich treasures of his wide and deep learning. Thus it was in his own act of humility that St. Bonaventure proved that after all a learned man can be holy and be saved!

3. In the teaching on the absolute primacy of Christ, Duns Scotus put the final touches to the christological doctrine of the Franciscan School. The incarnation is not occasioned by sin, though sin affected its modality. Scotus is not indifferent to evil and sin in the world, nor does he merely juggle with hypotheses. But the destruction of sin and evil is no more than a moment in God's movement out of himself towards the world, to unite all creation in the Love that is forever. The most recent and famous formulation of this doctrine has been made by Teilhard de Chardin in terms of an evolving cosmos. Speaking of the Scotistic doctrine with Padre Allegra, Teilhard exclaimed: "Voilà, la theologie cosmique; voilà, la theologie de l'avenir"—a cosmic theology, a theology of the future. Because of the unambiguous value it places on creation, one can readily understand why this doctrine is so attractive to the French Communist philosopher, Roger Garaudy.[24]

These brief reflections on the development of Christology from St. Francis himself to the School which has from him its name, make it clear that Franciscan Christology is a structural element in the original Franciscan charism. If it is ignored or neglected, then the charism itself is impaired.

---

[22] See: B.J.F. Lonergan SJ, *Philosophy of God and Theology*, The Westminster Press: Philadelphia 1973.

[23] See his five sermons on St. Francis in: *Opera Omnia* IX, Ad Claras Aquas 1901, pp. 573-597.

[24] See Eric Doyle OFM, *John Duns Scotus and the Place of Christ*, THE CLERGY REVIEW, vol. LVII (Sept. 1972) 667-675; (Oct. 1972) 774-785; (Nov. 1972) 860-868. Editors' note: These articles are reprinted in this anthology: pp. 282 ff.

Charism and Ongoing Renewal

As the Order moves on towards the beginning of the third millennium of the Church's history, it will continue to adapt and renew itself according to the spirit of its original charism. In the process of ongoing renewal the following aspects of the charism will need to be given more serious consideration:

1. Public witness—minimum structure: The 'monastification' of the Order was an undesirable development, not merely because it led to a dull uniformity and reduced individuality to a minimum, but also because it imposed a superstructure of organization on the Order's life which virtually abolished one of the most characteristic aspects of the Franciscan charism. This is the genius of living a public religious life in the Church (St. Francis founded an Order) with a minimum amount of structure (St. Francis was conscious of its original newness). It is among the Order's most attractive and, at the same time, most demanding characteristics. It is attractive because it manifests the freedom won for us in Christ Jesus; it is for the Order a sacrament of freedom from the burden of the Law. It is demanding because it places firmly on the shoulders of each member of a community full responsibility for every facet of communal life. Community life is an ongoing process, created by the uniqueness and originality of its several members and it issues in a unity which is something more than the mere sum total of the individuals. In such a process no one can shirk responsibility without setting back this process and thus injuring community life.

An important area in which this aspect of the charism should exercise maximum influence is formation. The whole process of formation must have as its chief aim the active reception by each friar of total responsibility for our way of life, where the duty of each is to help the others to grow in wisdom and maturity before God and man. The capacity and willingness to accept this responsibility may be taken as the touchstone of suitability for this way of life.

2. The Rule for Hermitages:[25] Thomas of Celano in his *Second Life* tells us that St. Francis "wanted his brothers to live not only in the cities, but also in hermitages". This element of the charism has had effect in some provinces and it is recommended and encouraged in the *Renewed Constitutions.*[26] It is clear from the short *Rule for Hermitages* that St. Francis wished his Order to lead not only a "mixed" life—that is, one devoted to prayer

---

[25] *Omnibus*, pp. 72f.
[26] *The Plan for Franciscan Living*, Articles 28-31.

and the apostolate—but to hold within itself at one and the same time the two distinct expressions of the religious life: the active and the contemplative. The contemplative life he intended as a permanent feature of the Order's existence in the world. It is interesting to recall in this context that both the *Rule* of the Friars Minor (for itinerant apostles) and the *Rule* of St. Clare (for enclosed contemplatives) are identified with life according to the Holy Gospel.

In our opinion the notion of a 'hermitage' should not be confused with a 'house of prayer'. Houses of prayer, to which friars may resort for shorter or longer periods of recollection, do not fulfil adequately what St. Francis appears to have intended. It seems that he wanted the contemplative life to be a permanent feature of the life of the First Order. If our view here is correct, then there should be a place in the Order for the exclusively contemplative life. On this understanding a 'hermitage' and a 'house of prayer' are quite distinct notions. The former should be employed uniquely to describe a community of friars dedicated exclusively to the contemplative life. The features that would distinguish a Franciscan contemplative community from the older monastic forms of the contemplative life would be precisely the minimum structure and the far smaller number in the community. Whether the number would have to be restricted to three or four, as is mentioned in the *Rule for Hermitages,* is a matter that calls for further discussion.

It may not be possible for every province of the Order to have a hermitage (or hermitages) as a permanent feature of its life. Perhaps, therefore, hermitages could be instituted at the inter-provincial level and be made open to international membership. Such contemplative communities in the Order would give fine expression to this element of the Franciscan charism.

The reference made above to the *Rule* of the Poor Clares recalls what St. Francis wrote down in the *Form of Life* for St. Clare: "I desire and promise you personally and in the name of my friars that I will always have the same loving care and solicitude for you as for them". Their way of life was very dear to St. Francis both because he loved St. Clare and because he himself was strongly attracted to the contemplative life. The First Order today should show the same loving care for the Poor Clares and there ought to be more frequent and closer contact between the first and second branches of the Order. By so doing we would be more faithful to St. Francis and we would be helped considerably to discern our own charism more clearly.

3. The Rule of 1221:[27] Although the *Rule* of 1223, which gave the Franciscan Order its legal basis, and the *Rule* of 1221, which never received papal approval, both contain the spirit of St. Francis, it could be argued that the latter is a finer expression of that spirit than the former. This is not to deny that the *Rule* of 1223 is more a spiritual document than legal code. Nevertheless, it is just that one step removed from the earliest expression of the form of life and, therefore, just that little further from the original charism.

In terms of continuing renewal, the directives of the seventh chapter of the *Rule* of 1221 raise important questions for the future development of the Order. The chapter is titled: "Work and the Service of Others". It concerns the friars who are engaged in the service of lay people and those who already have a trade when they join the order. The chapter lays down: "Everyone should remain at the trade and in the position in which he was called". This one sentence alone gives rise to a serious question about what attitude the Order ought to adopt to a person seeking admission to it who is already qualified in a trade or profession. It is not a question about whether the Order should *allow* a plumber or a doctor to continue as a plumber or doctor after an initial period of formation; it is rather a question of whether or not the Order is *obliged* to allow a plumber or a doctor to return at least for a certain time, to his previous work, after the period of formation. Priests who have joined the Order in the past have continued to exercise their priestly ministry to a limited extent during the period of formation and it has always been assumed that they will go back to its full exercise after formation. There are many, many more professions and trades which are as equally compatible with the vocation of being a Franciscan friar as is the ministerial priesthood.

Before the oral approval of the *Rule* in 1209, St. Francis had already assured the Bishop of Assisi that he and his companions would earn their living and have recourse to begging only when it was absolutely necessary. Some of them worked as labourers in monasteries and private houses; others took care of lepers in the lazar houses; others helped farmers in the fields. In the early years after the approval of the *Rule* the friars were given to preaching, praying and manual work.

The statement made at the Madrid Chapter in 1973 concerning the vocation of the Order today, gave definite approval to this aspect of the original charism as contained in the *Rule* of 1221. The statement emphasizes:

---

[27] *Omnibus*, pp. 31-53.

For recent times, our participation in the general evolution of religious life and the influence of certain other communities have led us to the rediscovery of an aspect of work as it was understood by Francis. New forms of work and a variety of occupations are now being undertaken by our friars. Ministry, our own works, and domestic tasks within our friaries legitimately occupy the majority of our friars, but it is becoming more frequent to find friars engaged in salaried trades and professions within enterprises and institutions which belong neither to the Order nor to the Church. An orientation of this kind appears to us to be in line with our vocation; by it we are a part of society in a special way, working for its upbuilding and we are brought closer to those who live by their work. While placing us squarely on the road to the future it brings us back to one of the institutions of our origins.[28]

This new type of work is itself the apostolate: the apostolate of presence by silent witness. We must not forget, however, that this form of the apostolate is not easy. It demands that a friar put into practice the unsystematic though profound theology of work scattered throughout the writings of St. Francis. Thus, pay is not to be the motive of work, nor should the friars become the slaves of work or of gain. Work is to be undertaken as a contribution to the final form of creation, carried out under the supreme lordship of God; it is to be sanctified by being brought back to its right relationship with God. It is not, nor can it be, for the friar an end in itself; it is a means of exercising the apostolate of peace and reconciliation in the midst of the world. It requires above all of those who engage in it, that they be contemplatives. Before action there has to be what St. Bonaventure calls *sursumactio*—that uplifting activity which is contemplative prayer.

Further developments of this kind of work may well bring about a decrease in the number of priests in the Order. At the same time it must not be ignored that those engaged in the apostolate who are not priests (for example, nuns and brothers) often find that there are circumstances where it would be a definite advantage to be a priest. In fact, experiences of this kind have often led non-ordained apostles to seek ordination to the priesthood.

4. St. Francis the Deacon:[29] St. Francis never became a priest. One often bears that the reason for this was his deep humility; he felt himself

---

[28] *General Chapter Documents*, Madrid 1973, The English-Speaking Conf. of the Order of Friars Minor 1974, p. 68.

[29] See 1 Celano 86 in: *Omnibus*, p. 301: "The saint of God was clothed with the vestments of a deacon, and he sang the holy Gospel in a sonorous voice".

unworthy of so sublime a dignity. This explanation, however, is not to be found in the sources; in fact there appears to be no mention of the matter at all. In any case our concern here is not with the reason why he did not become a priest, but with the *fact* that he was a deacon.

The re-institution of the order of permanent diaconate is one of the most encouraging results of Church renewal. The diaconate in the Church is directly derived from, and immediately related to, the episcopal office. It concerns the Church's mission to the world in the very concrete form of the corporal and spiritual works of mercy and of work for reconciliation, justice and peace. These works pertain to the essence of the apostolic office. It is, therefore, theologically incorrect and quite unsound to understand the diaconate merely in terms of assistance to the priestly ministry; nor is the diaconate adequately presented exclusively in terms of liturgical functions.

In practice at the moment, however, the actual form of ministry exercised by permanent deacons is, in the vast majority of cases, only a lesser form of the priestly ministry. This is true throughout the Western Church. On the missions it has been made a substitute for the priesthood, and the permanent deacon is in fact a "mini-priest". With the exception of saying Mass and administering absolution, he does everything that the priest does. The diaconate has become also a substitute for a married priesthood. In many of our city and town parishes in the Western world, the ministry of the permanent deacon is in fact no more than that of assistant to the local priests. In all these cases, therefore, the priesthood is the determining factor in the performance of the office of deacon. It would be a pity if this were to become the exclusive form of the diaconal ministry.

The permanent diaconate in the Church proclaims that the corporal and spiritual works of mercy and work for reconciliation, justice and peace are not merely the special concern of individuals who may feel called to perform them. They belong to the episcopal office, because the bishops must have anxious care not only for all the churches but also for the whole world. Ordination to the permanent diaconate graces the man called to this work with the authority and power of the apostolic mission to the world. In virtue of this sacrament the deacon is sent by the bishop publicly in the name of Christ to work, for example, in the field of communications, as a counsellor, a welfare officer, a doctor or a nurse.

The Franciscan Order is committed by its very existence to work for reconciliation, justice and peace. It would be most fitting for the Order to incorporate the permanent diaconate, as here understood, into its life and mission and to offer this as an option to those wishing to join the Order. It would manifest that work other than priestly ministry is not merely the hobby or particular preference of an individual, but a part of the Church's mission to the world. It would contribute also towards restoring the diaconate to its fuller ministry.

5. *Christology of the Franciscan School:* Every friar should receive a thorough grounding in the doctrine of the Franciscan School. Christology is at the heart of that doctrine from which has developed a distinctive anthropology, the values of which centre on freedom, the primacy of the will and charity, and the dignity of the individual person. In order that this rich heritage be not lost, it is of paramount importance that studies be encouraged ever more keenly in the Order. One acknowledges with gratitude the renewed interest in Franciscan studies brought about by the establishment of the Franciscan Institute at St. Bonaventure University, New York.[143] More friars should be encouraged to devote their lives to the production of good texts and critical editions of the authors of the Franciscan School. It must be impressed on them that this is not a waste of time nor merely the private interest of the scholarly 'types' which the Order can tolerate, but a splendid contribution to the understanding of a Tradition which belongs to the Church and mankind at large.

The Future of the Order and Its Vocation

The future will see a more balanced proportion between the number of priests and non-priests in the Franciscan Order. The indications are that throughout the world the Order as a whole will continue to decrease in numbers. There will be many more small communities.

In fidelity to its many-faceted charism the Order will have to learn to hold within itself a great pluriformity of life-styles and work. The former will have to contain the widest variety from the contemplative to the active life. The latter will have to embrace every form from strictly priestly work to the apostolate of presence and silent witness in salaried trades and professions. Every friar on the apostolate will have to be prepared to preach, teach or share with others, in whatever ways are opened up, the riches of the Order's christological tradition, particularly the teaching on the centrality of the Word and the absolute primacy of Christ. By so doing, the Order will contribute to the fruitfulness of the encounter and dialogue between East and West, from

---

[30] Editors's note: By 1977, the date this article was written, the Franciscan International Study Centre had already been in existence for three years, and today offers a full curriculum of courses in Franciscan Studies, a realisation of Doyle's dream.

which will result a spirituality for the post-modern world. The East has developed towards an extreme spiritualistic interpretation of man and the world; the West towards an extreme materialistic interpretation of man and the world. There are, however, strands in the Tradition of both East and West, which point the way to a real unity and balance between these extremes. It is not too much to suggest that the theology of the Franciscan School and the spirituality of St. Francis belong to these strands in the West. This theology and spirituality lead one to a material spiritualism or spiritual materialism, to a holy worldliness or worldly holiness. It is along these lines that spirituality in the future will develop.

In conclusion we wish to make a brief comment about a very important matter. It concerns a fair number of those friars who have left the Order and have taken up other walks of life. In travelling around one frequently comes across ex-friars who long to share again the spirituality and atmosphere which formed them and left a deep impression on their minds and hearts, and who desire to participate once more in some way directly in the Order's mission to the world. It is not that they are unhappy in their new way of life or regret having married. These longings and desires are the outcome of a renewed and deeper appreciation of Franciscan values which their new life has brought home to them. Specifically, it is married life which is most frequently mentioned as the cause of this. There is a very positive impulse behind these desires which one discerns as the Holy Spirit of God. Serious thought and prayer must be given to working out how these desires might be fulfilled. It must not be presumed *a priori* that we can do nothing for them. One suggestion would be the institution of a *new form* of the Third Order which could be so established as to meet both desires mentioned. It could exist in very close liaison and cooperation with the work of the First Order, for this latter is mature enough to embrace an added element in its pluriformity. In this way the Order would be helping to prepare for the eventual re-deployment of so much energy, goodwill and holiness in the apostolic mission of the Church.

An Instrument of God's Peace[1]

In October 1981 celebrations will be held all over the world to mark the eighth centenary of the birth of St. Francis. Of course nobody knew eight centuries ago that in 1981 the world would be remembering him as a holy and very human man and as Patron of the Environment. But we know now that in the life of this poor little man God's grace was so radiantly victorious that humanity, indeed creation itself, reached one of its most authentic and beautiful expressions.

Yet St. Francis himself wanted nothing other than to follow in the footsteps of Christ. He didn't want to do anything novel or unheard of or initiate a new movement. In fact, all he set out to do and then achieved so gloriously, was something very old and well-tried for more than a thousand years before him: to be a faithful and humble disciple of the gospel Christ. And paradox though it be, his life of literal and even slavish imitation of Christ produced this breathtakingly original man we call St. Francis of Assisi. His life is graphic proof that the truths of the gospel are living and fresh, always open to new discovery, ever ancient and ever new.

St. Francis was a man in love, unconditionally unreservedly, madly in love with Jesus Christ. He grasped with unparalleled clarity that in Jesus Christ God the Son became a friar, the brother of all creatures. And so profound was this realization, that in his life and little sermons people saw and heard again the Jesus of the gospels lying in a manger, walking through the streets, serving and healing the sick, talking to children and Mary Magdalene, consoling the widow of Naim, proclaiming the beatitudes, stumbling up Calvary Hill and crucified on the cross. No longer was he merely the distant figure in heaven who had left our earth or the majestic judge enthroned on high in cathedral apses. Yes, the life of St. Francis was a representation, a re-enactment of the life of the gospel Jesus.

So it was that Francis loved God in his powerlessness and infinite goodness at Bethlehem, in his utter defencelessness and boundless mercy on

---

[1] THE FRANCISCAN MISSIONARY HERALD 46 (1981) pp. 1-3. Published with permission.

Calvary and in his silence and divine humility in the Eucharist. The crib, the cross and the Mass—these were the realities for Francis that spoke most eloquently of God. These divine characteristics, which bring tumbling down all our proud human ideas of what God ought to be like. St. Francis expressed in the lovely words: Friar Jesus Christ. Friar Christ brought Francis to accept himself as Christ's brother and so he was at peace with himself by the gift of God's limitless love.

It was through Friar Christ—one could say Brother Christ—that he knew everyone was part of him as a brother or sister, and especially the lepers. God drew him among the lepers as he himself tells us. What had once been for him a bitter sight was now a source of sweetness, for he had learned to love the lepers with Christ's own compassion. His love of everyone was the drive behind his mission to establish peace wherever he went. The early accounts of his life tell us that he was always speaking about peace.

Friar Jesus Christ made the whole world and all creation a friary. No building—not even the most serene monastery—can really symbolize or give expression to his sublime vision of the universal friary. In an enchanting allegory written not long after he died we read how St. Francis and some of his companions went in search of Lady Poverty. When asked by her to be shown the cloister, they took her to a hill, pointed to the whole world in front of her and said: "This, Lady, is our cloister".

Everyone and everything bore the sacred name of brother or sister. Though no one ever loved poverty like St. Francis, and he called nothing in the world his own, no one was ever more at home in the world and more at peace with it. That is the reason why Pope John Paul II made St. Francis Patron of the Environment. As the first Adam is recorded in the Book of Genesis to have given the animals what we may call their earthly names, so St. Francis, a living image of the second Adam, gave them their heavenly name: brother or sister. Brother Fox and Brother Rabbit found at last a friend in Francis. I have sometimes wondered if St. Francis, because of his exquisitely sensitive love of all creatures as brothers and sisters of Christ, is not now weeping before the throne of God at our wars and weapons of destruction, at our foul cruelty to animals and at the way we choke and smother Sister Water and Brother Air.

He loved the poor Christ because his poverty, above all on the cross, proved that Christ was without power. St. Francis too was a man without power. He saw the dangers in riches, ambition and learning. They have a terrible power which causes disunity and division. As he once pointed out with devastating simplicity: when you have riches, you need weapons to defend them. Therefore his poverty was not an end in itself, it was a protest against the organized evil powers of the world that bring injustice, exploitation and oppression. He used the most effective non-violent means to oppose those powers. He chose freely to be poor and so identified himself with the marginated and the outcasts of his society, and thus with the still-suffering Christ.

His free acceptance of poverty for the sake of the gospel did not mean indifference to the plight of the poor. We read in one account of his life that once a poor old lady, who had two sons in the Order, came to the little huts at the Portiuncula seeking alms from St. Francis. He called her "mother" because he considered any friar's mother his mother and the mother of all the friars. Finding there was nothing else to give her, he told one of the friars to give her the only copy of the New Testament they had, so that she could sell it. "Give our mother the New Testament", he said, "so that she can sell it for her needs. I firmly believe that it will please God more and the blessed Virgin, his mother, than if you read it". What a remarkable story that is. Even the most sacred book was subject to a higher principle, the needs of a poor member of Christ. One feels that St. Francis, faced with the oppressed poor, would have little hesitation about what to do with cherished surplus church plate.

His early companions bear witness that he often said if he could speak with the emperor he would implore him to command the authorities of cities and the lords of towns and villages, to compel their subjects to scatter corn on the roads outside the cities and towns on Christmas Day, so that the birds would have something to eat on the great festival, to give extra food to every ox and ass on the birthday of the Infant Jesus because he lay between them in the stable, and to oblige the rich to give the poor their fill on the day when God became the brother of us all. It is noteworthy that St. Francis refers to those with the authority and means in the world to achieve this gracious sharing. Given the opportunity he would appeal to them to destroy for one day at least the evils of oppressive poverty, suffered not only by human beings, but also by birds and animals.

If they could do it on one day, they could do it every day. Is it too romantic to speculate on what the governments of the world could do for the oppressed poor today with one day's expenditure on arms—more than six hundred million pounds. Seeing the results they just might be moved to do it more often, perhaps even every day.

The keys to the mystery of the life of St. Francis are brotherhood and poverty. Let us hope that through the celebration of the eighth centenary of his birth, those keys will open the hearts of all of us to the riches of God's love for us in Christ, and so bring peace to our lovely, but sad and troubled world. That would please St. Francis more than any mere memorial of his birth.

St. Francis and the Benedictines[1]

The year 1976 sees the 750th anniversary of the death of St. Francis in the chapel of the Portiuncula in Assisi on 3rd October 1226. Because St. Francis and his Order up to the present day owe a considerable debt of gratitude to the Benedictines, it is so very fitting to have the opportunity to express our gratitude and to explain the reasons for it in a Benedictine publication.

After he broke with his father and turned from his former life of revelling and parties St. Francis worked for a time in the Abbey of San Verecundo. Then when St. Clare joined him in 1212 he placed her with the Benedictine nuns in the Abbey of San Paolo about two miles from Assisi. A little later Clare was followed by her sister Agnes and St. Francis moved them to the Abbey of Sant' Angelo on the slopes of Monte Subasio, where they stayed for about four months before making their permanent settlement at San Damiano. Though St. Francis did not found a monastic order, nevertheless, critical studies of his writings and particularly of the *Rule,* show that he knew and used the *Rule* of St. Benedict.

There are, however, far greater reasons for gratitude than hospitality and some literary influence. In the spring of 1209 St. Francis set out for Rome with eleven companions to obtain papal approval for his way of life in absolute poverty "according to the form of the holy Gospel". At first Pope Innocent III expressed great reluctance to approve a way of life that seemed to him so austere as to be impossible. On seeing the Pope's reaction the Benedictine Cardinal John of St. Paul pointed out to him that if they were to reject this poor man's request, it would be a declaration that the gospel cannot be observed and this would be to blaspheme its author, Christ. These words so impressed the Pope that he promised to consider the request. The outcome was that he gave oral approval to the *Rule* and granted permission to St. Francis and his followers to preach penance, peace and the coming of the kingdom. It is no

---

[1] *A commemorative article, 1226-1976* in: THE AMPLEFORTH JOURNAL 881, Part III (Autumn 1976) pp. 18-20. E. Doyle was a friend of Ampleforth, having given the Community its annual retreat. Published with permission.

exaggeration therefore to say that the Franciscan Order owes its existence in the Church to a Benedictine.

Shortly after his conversion Francis began to restore abandoned churches around Assisi. Among these was the little chapel of St. Mary of the Angels, known locally as the Portiuncula, which belonged to the Benedictine monks of Monte Subasio. After its restoration mass began once more to be celebrated in the chapel. On the feast of St. Matthias, 24th February 1208, St. Francis received from God the revelation of his true vocation. When mass was finished he asked the Benedictine priest to explain to him the words of the gospel [Matthew 10:7-10]. The priest told him that Christ had commanded his disciples to preach that the kingdom of God is at hand, to take nothing on their journey and to have absolute trust in divine providence. St. Francis exclaimed: "This is what I want, this is what I am looking for, this is what I am longing in my inmost heart to do". And so was born the Order of the Poor Brothers of St. Francis. A little later when St. Francis was looking for a suitable chapel and dwelling place for himself and his followers, the Abbot of Monte Subasio offered him the chapel of St. Mary of the Angels and the plot of earth around it. St. Francis would not accept it as a gift for this would be against his total poverty. So he rented it and arranged to pay the monks a basket of loaches every year. St. Francis loved this little chapel more than any other place on earth. *The Mirror of Perfection,* written at the beginning of the 14th century, praises the Portiuncula in these beautiful words:

Holy of Holies is this place of places. . . .
This holy temple God chose as the birthplace
Of the Friars Minor, humble, poor and joyful. . . .
Here was the Holy Rule to guide the Order written by Francis. . . .
Here, too, was granted to the holy Father
All that he asked for in his intercession.[2]

So it is that the Franciscan Order owes its most cherished and hallowed spot to the kindness and generosity of the Benedictines.

The Friars of the English Province owe a special word of thanks to the Benedictines. When St. Francis sent his friars to England in 1224, it was the Benedictines of Fecamp in Normandy who conveyed them across the Channel. On arriving in Canterbury in September that year they received hospitality from the monks of the Priory of the Holy Trinity before they made their permanent settlement in Stour Street.

---

[2] *The Mirror of Perfection* 84 in: Omnibus, p. 1217.

For all this the Franciscan Order expresses its deep gratitude to the Benedictines.

Although blessed Francis was in greater pain from his diseases than usual, when he heard that Sister Death was fast approaching, he was filled with fresh joy, and praised the Lord in great fervour of spirit, saying, "If it be my Lord's pleasure that I should die soon, call me Brother Angelo and Brother Leo, and let them sing to me of Sister Death". And when these two friars, filled with sorrow and grief, had come to him, they sang with many tears the Song of Brother Sun and the other creatures which the Saint had written. And before the last verse of the Song, he added these lines on Sister Death: "Praised be Thou, my Lord, for Sister Bodily Death From whom no man living may escape".[3]

---

[3] *The Mirror of Perfection* c. 124 in: ibid., p. 1263.

The Men St. Francis Sent Us[1]

On September 10, 1974 the Franciscan Order celebrated the 750th anniversary of the coming of the first Franciscans to England on Tuesday, September 10, 1224.

The group of nine friars, which included three Englishmen, was sent to England by St. Francis himself at the Chapter of the Order held at Assisi in June of that year. The leader of the little band was Blessed Agnellus of Pisa, the first Provincial of the Order in England. Only a few days after they arrived to lay the foundations of his Order in England, St. Francis reached the crowning point of his life in imitation of the Poor Christ by receiving the marks of the Sacred Stigmata on his frail body while at prayer on Mount La Verna in Tuscany.

The celebrations of the anniversary are taking place in Canterbury where the first Franciscans first settled after their arrival in England.

Little House

Their permanent friary, however, was not built until about 1267. All that remains of the friary now is the beautiful little house which stands serenely over the River Stour in the Franciscan Gardens off Stour Street. Legend has it that the Brother Cook used to fish from a trap-door in the kitchen for the community's dinner on abstinence days! The house has not been inhabited by Franciscans since the Dissolution of the Monasteries in 1538.

In 1909 the then owner, Major H.G. James, had considerable work done on the building to restore it, as far as was possible, to its original condition. The house is open to the public from Easter until September each year. But even outside the season every visitor to Canterbury ought to spend a little time at the Franciscan Gardens to experience the peace of St. Francis that still surrounds this beautiful 13th century building.

As well as commemorating the arrival of the Franciscans, the

---

[1] THE UNIVERSE (September 6, 1974) p. 10. 1974 the Franciscan Order was celebrating the 750th anniversary of the coming of the first Franciscans to England on Tuesday, September 10, 1224. Published with permission.

celebrations also recall the fact of 750 years of unbroken Franciscan presence in England. Towards the end of the 15th century the Observant Franciscans were introduced into England. These were a reform movement in the one Franciscan Order until Pope Leo X divided the Order into Observants and Conventuals in 1517.

The Observants were suppressed in England in 1534. They had been the first to challenge Henry VIII and they refused almost to a man to subscribe to his supremacy over the Church in England. Suppression, however, did not mean their extinction. The Observant friary at Greenwich was restored in 1555 under Mary, then finally suppressed in 1559 under Elizabeth I.

The Observants managed to preserve the Greenwich seal and St. John Jones (+1598)—canonised among the Forty Martyrs by Pope Paul—passed on this seal to Fr. William Stanney when both were in the Matshalsea Prison in London.

Fr. Stanney in turn passed it on to Fr. John Gennings who played the most prominent part in the restoration of the Observant Province in England in the early 17th century. This seal of the Greenwich friary is now in the archives of the English Province of Friars Minor at the Franciscan International Study Centre at Canterbury.

It is a most treasured possession because it forms a link in direct continuity with the pre-Reformation friars. The Observants, who today are called Friars Minor, flourished throughout the 17th and 18th centuries. Numbers dwindled in the early 19th century. But due to help from the Friars Minor in Belgium, the Province was once more established before the end of the century.

Despite every vicissitude, therefore, there has never been a time since their arrival in 1224 that there were no Franciscans in England.

The Return

The Franciscans returned to Canterbury in 1969. This resulted from a decision by the Friars Minor and the Friars Minor Conventual to establish a joint House of Studies there. At first friars from both Orders lived at St. Augustine's College where ordinands are trained for the ministry in the Anglican Communion.

During the next two years the Friars Minor set up two small communities in the city. Building began on the Franciscan Study Centre in October 1971. Two years later friars from both Orders took up residence in their respective friaries at the Franciscan Study Centre in Giles Lane. Thus was established the second permanent home of the Franciscans in England after an absence of well over 400 years. By an exchange of letters the University of Kent and the Franciscan Study Centre acknowledge a mutual relationship and association directed towards the advancement of learning in the field of theology and related disciplines.

The Franciscan Study Centre is established and maintained jointly by the English Province of the Friars Minor and the Friars Minor Conventual for the training of students for the pastoral ministry in the Franciscan tradition.

Brothers All

This tradition, as the name indicates, is traced back to St. Francis of Assisi, perhaps the best known and most loved of all the Saints. St. Francis grasped with incredible clarity what it means to call Christ our Brother. His awareness and love of Brother Christ transformed him from John Bernardone into Brother Francis of Assisi. He opted out of the medieval rat-race—without, however, a word of criticism of Church or State—and found himself in the Friary or 'Brothery' of the world, where all men, animals, plants, the elements, the sun, the moon and the stars were united in one vast fraternity.

Priority

He says in the *Rule* that his friars are always to show that they are brothers. This is the aspect of the holiness of St. Francis that his Order is most conscious of today when there is so much loneliness in the world.

As an absolute priority it seeks to establish communities of brothers where there is unity in diversity, where each may be himself and form part of a reality greater than self and where each may grow in the love of Christ, of all men and of the entire world.

The Franciscan tradition has always understood learning to be subservient to wisdom, that is, to knowledge which edifies. The Franciscans at Canterbury strive to live by this tradition and to share its graces in whatever way God may inspire.

Franciscan Life and the Evangelical Counsels[1]

It is customary in the Church to speak of the various orders and congregations as constituting a uniform category which is distinct from the 'laity' and the priesthood. This is an acceptable canonical arrangement because there is a theology of religious life as such; there can be a legal approach to the 'vows' because there is a theology of the evangelical counsels. The theology of religious life emphasises such common elements as the 'taking of three vows' by religious, and then proceeds to explain their theological intelligibility; canon law draws out the common legal obligations involved in them and elucidates the 'rights' they confer.

People in the Church, however, do not actually become 'religious'. They become part of already existing groups of men and women which have a specific identity and are committed to a particular life-style. Out of this experience, I would contend, the theology of religious life as such emerges, and from this, in its turn, the canon law for religious comes into existence. To put it another way; the charism or genius of the particular orders and congregations has priority. This makes possible theological reflection on common elements, and from this is derived the general canonical approach.

The predominance until relatively recently of the canonical approach made it difficult, I think, to give sufficient attention to the distinctive character of the various orders and congregations in the Church. Yet their distinctiveness is crucial and of prior importance evangelically, ecclesiologically, and theologically. The Church is *in Christ,* and its various groups and individuals members manifest distinct aspects of the whole Christ.

In respect of this priority there is little to be gained from beginning with 'the religious state' or 'the religious life' as such, especially in formation programs. What needs to be stressed from the outset is that among the People of God there are groups of men and women living out their lives under the guidance of some aspect of gospel teaching, according to a quite specific love and understanding of the obedient, poor, and celibate Christ; and this love and understanding specify and mould what are called 'the evangelical counsels'.

---

[1] THE CORD 30.5 (1980) pp. 132-141.

Therefore, there are not three abstract vows which reduce religious to a uniform group, so that we are forced to search for what might be, for instance, the distinctive Franciscan spirit, at some other level or in some other area. On the contrary, there is first of all a spirit, an attitude, an outlook, born of an insight inspired by God's Spirit, which determines concretely all the elements that go to make up a way of life and which qualifies its every structure. According to this approach, for example, there is no reason why the poverty professed by one order should be the same as that professed by another.

What I want to attempt in the following reflections is to highlight the distinctive feature of St. Francis's gospel vocation and then to examine how this situates precisely our Order's understanding of 'the evangelical counsels'. I am concerned directly with the First Order, but what follows applies to all Franciscans.

On Being a Friar Minor

The words *friar minor* are not our title; they describe ideally our authentic existence. The *little brother* who belongs to the group that owes its origin to the insight and inspiration of Francis of Assisi, follows a life which is itself a 'rule', observing the gospel. He lives in obedience, without ownership, and in chastity; he proclaims peace, eats what is set before him, prays, works, takes care of the sick as he would like to be cared for himself, announces the gospel, and goes serenely among those who do not know the Lord Jesus Christ; he guides his life also by the *Rule of 1221*, the *Testament*, the *Rule for Hermitages* (it matters little from this point of view that these were never 'approved'), the *Canticle of Brother Sun*, and the teaching of St. Francis in his other writings.

The son of Pietro Bernardone was Friar Francis from the moment of his conversion—that is, from the reorientation of his life that marked the starting point of his inner integration and liberation. That process reached its summit on La Verna and was sealed irrevocably by Sister Bodily Death. Never was Francis more a friar minor than in the experience of his stigmatisation. At that moment he emptied himself, surrendered his humanity, to be divinized by grace.

Friar Jesus Christ

St. Francis's understanding of brotherhood or 'friarship' was derived uniquely from Jesus Christ, the Elder Brother of the human race. The Christian gospel introduced humanity to a unique concept of brotherhood. Expressed in its most radical and simple terms this is 'brotherhood-without-boundaries'. We have a Father in heaven, the Father of our Lord Jesus Christ, and Jesus is the first of many brethren, and we share, each in his own way, in their Spirit. Christianity proclaims unambiguously that God is 'God-with-us'. Brotherhood for Francis was human, animal, mineral, and cosmic; for it embraced not only Brother Leo and Sister Clare, but also Sister Crested Lark, Brother Fire, Sister Water, and Sisters Moon and Stars. In a word, it was literally universal.

The Poor Friar Jesus Christ

Friar Jesus was not born in Jerusalem, Athens, or Rome. If we take what it means to be a human being in purely ontological terms, we can make the following reflection. Had Jesus been born into some influential religious group in Israel, or emerged out of the great philosophical tradition of Greece, or identified himself with the powerful political machinery of the Roman Empire, it would still have been true to call him "humble". For had he come as High Priest, learned philosopher, or even as emperor, we would still have been able to say: "Though he was in the form of God [he] did not count equality with God a thing to be grasped, but [he] emptied himself, taking the form of a servant, being born in the likeness of men".[2] In the enfleshment of the Word, God became other, and for God to become other, is necessarily to become less than himself. He who is, is made he who becomes; the infinite is made finite; the immortal, mortal; the eternal, temporal.

Thomas of Celano tells us that Francis loved and revered Mary because she made "the Lord of Majesty our brother".[3] Whatever group or category might have been the *locus* of the incarnation of the Word, he would still have been ontologically a creature and a brother to humanity. The majesty of God is to be God, to be his own inner ontological perfection. Had he come, then, as king and been born in Herod's palace, it would still have been possible to celebrate Christmas in some sense, and contemplate in sheer admiration with Francis this feast "on which God, having become a tiny infant, clung to human breasts".[4]

But the staggering fact of the incarnation is its ordinariness, one might say without offence, its commonplace circumstance. This has to be considered in its full *historical* significance, for God became a man in history. A human

---

[2] Philippians 2:6-7.
[3] 2 Celano 198 in: *Omnibus*, p. 521.
[4] 2 Celano 199 in: ibid.

being can never be understood satisfactorily as an ontological reality in the abstract. A man or woman is always an ontological reality in history.

Had Jesus been born into an important pharisaic group, or been connected in some way with a philosophical school, or been identified with the imperial power, his mission would have to have started by his challenging the very existence of the immediate group to which he belonged. Otherwise he would have been one with the sin of the world. For it is by institutionalising religion, truth, and authority (= Jerusalem, Athens, Rome) that the powers of this world, born of the sin of the world, have their influence, construct idols, and exercise their oppression. It is therefore a priori improbable that Jesus would identify himself in any way with the powers of this world. He came because *God loved the world* and willed to deliver it from the power of evil.

Whether Jesus was poor in the sense of professing 'absolute poverty', of being totally without ownership, we may leave among the conundrums of the late 13th and early 14th centuries; whether Francis himself was entirely correct 'objectively' in considering Jesus to have been utterly poor, need not detain us. The fact is that Jesus cannot be counted among the rich of this world, nor can he be said to have had political power or philosophical Status; nor was he in the worldly sense a 'religious leader'.

The incarnation of the Word, therefore, in this context, is a revelation at two levels. First, it is the sacrament of God's humility; the Word emptied himself, he left everything; that is, he became a creature. Secondly, it reveals that in order to be fully and authentically human a person must be poor; that is, devoid of economic, philosophical, political, and religious power. His material poverty in that sense is a sacrament of his total dedication and surrender to God and the Symbol of his true humanity. This poverty led him to the final surrender in death as John's gospel beautifully records it: "For this reason the Father loves me, because I lay down my life, that I may take it again. No one takes it from me, but I lay it down of my own accord" [John 10:17-18]. Thus it can legitimately be said of Jesus: though he was in the form of humankind, he did not count equality with humankind a thing to be grasped, but he emptied himself, being born to eternal life in the likeness of God. And so the circle of the movement is completed in the Resurrection, wherein his humanity was divinized and therefore totally humanised. Without poverty as described here this would not have been possible.

Though without political power, Jesus was full of authority; without economic power, he possessed a treasure that not all the riches of the world can buy; without philosophical power, he had true wisdom; without religious power, he was the holiest and most integrated man ever to have lived. That Jesus had the security of a carpenter's life and the standard of living this provided, in no way militates against his poverty, nor indeed the fact that Judas kept a common purse for him and the Apostles. Thus, like Friar Jesus, Francis was dispossessed; yet the world was his.

St. Bonaventure on Being a Friar Minor

Speaking about our way of life in his beautiful fifth sermon on St. Francis, St. Bonaventure explains that just as the Christian learns from Christ to be "meek and humble", so the Franciscan learns from Francis to be a friar minor. Meekness is the virtue which rules and guides all our relationships with our brethren. It is to be a brother or a friar to them. Humility is the virtue that rules and guides our entire relationship with God. We are his creatures; we are brothers and sisters in Christ and so also sons and daughters of the Father; and we are dwelling places of the Spirit. Humility recognises and accepts those truths. To be humble is to be little or minor. To be meek and humble, therefore, is to be a friar minor. And Bonaventure concludes his thoughts on this with the profound reflection: "In this is contained the compendium of evangelical law and the teaching of St. Francis".[5] With this firmly fixed in our minds, we can now turn to the 'evangelical counsels'. I am concerned here with their positive meaning. We have heard sufficient of their negative side—the renunciation involved in professing them. Every choice entails of necessity some form of sacrifice.

The "Evangelical Counsels"

1. By living in obedience. . .

It is to be noted at once that St. Francis mentions obedience first: our rule and life is to observe the gospel by living in obedience. I know that the Decree on the up-to-date renewal of religious life, *Perfectae caritatis*, of Vatican II places chastity first.[6] But this is just another example of how unsatisfactory, albeit at times necessary, it is to treat "religious life" in general

---

[5] *St. Bonaventure, Opera Omnia* IX, Quaracchi 1901, col. 594a:. . .*esse ergo mitem et humilem corde, hoc est esse vere fratrem minorem. . .et in his consistit summa evangelicae legis et doctrinae beati Francisci.*

[6] Vatican Council II, *The Conciliar and Post Conciliar Documents*, ed. A. Flannery OP, Worse., England: Fowler Wright; Collegeville MN: Liturgical Press 1975, pp. 612, 617.

terms. If we are to search for the specific charism of our origins, we must accept the charism as we find it and not foist onto it an alien interpretation nor squeeze it into a priori categories. Of course we have to bring it up to date where that is required and appropriate, but this is never at the price of sacrificing what is a permanent acquisition by the Church in the grace of origins.

To understand the meaning of obedience for St. Francis we have to begin with two of his most original and characteristic utterances. First, Celano tells us that he taught the friars that the Holy Spirit is the Minister General of the Order who "rests equally upon the poor and the simple".[7] And secondly, he writes explicitly in *The Praises of the Virtues* that obedience subjects us not only to men "but to all the beasts as well and to the wild animals".[8] These texts create the atmosphere in which a Franciscan enters into the meaning of evangelical obedience A friar minor professes to listen to the Word spoken in creation and to the Word uttered in the recreation: Christ Jesus, and to respond totally to what he hears. A theology of obedience resolves itself into a theology of the Word. In creating the universe, God spoke a word about himself, and because it cannot exist without him, he is always creating, sustaining, and conserving by his word the being and becoming of all creatures. The universe as a totality and every being in it speak a word about God. Francis in total and authentic obedience always heard the word in creatures and responded to what he heard. They whispered to him: "We are creatures like you; we are your brethren, and we reflect Another's loveliness". And obediently he replied: "Brother, Sister". And so it was that he composed the *Canticle of Brother Sun.*

The Holy Spirit continues in us and in all creation the work of re-creation begun in Christ. Christ is the New Adam, and in him is the new creation. The Holy Spirit came upon Mary, and it is the Holy Spirit who renews the face of the earth. His work is to bring back to our minds all that Christ said. And because Christ is what he proclaimed: liberation and holiness, the Holy Spirit makes present who Christ is, and so we are made *to be in Christ.* The Church has an active and living memory of Christ because of the Holy Spirit cannot let her forget her Lord and Liberator. The Holy Spirit knows the secrets of God, and he discloses them as he wills.

Francis's 'vow' of obedience began at the moment of his conversion, and he responded unhesitatingly to the inspired Word up to the end. Similarly,

---

[7] 2 Celano 193 in: *Omnibus*, p. 517.
[8] *Omnibus*, p. 134.

our own public profession of obedience is itself an act of obedience to the highest and most sublime authority; that of God's Word spoken to us in the Holy Spirit. The only barrier to this is selfishness or self-seeking, and so the friar have to remember that "they have renounced their own will for God's sake" and "they should desire above all things to have the Spirit of the Lord and his holy grace".[9] This does not mean that they divest themselves of free will—that is simply not possible. Much less should the former text be construed as defence of 'blind obedience' or as a support for the once widespread, though weird, theory of 'hot-line' authority as service, but it loses nothing for being repeated. By thus understanding it, he was in fact summarising one of the clearest messages that comes from St. Mark's gospel: namely that true greatness consists in service of others. Christ Jesus was *the* Servant, the Suffering Servant of us all.

Taking his notion of authority together with his extraordinary respect for the individual person, we can appreciate how *friar minor* qualifies obedience. We are to search for God's will and listen to his Word together. We have a literally fraternal responsibility to the Word. We meet that responsibility by listening to the Word when we gather to celebrate the Eucharist and by coming together in chapters to hear what the Spirit is saying to our *ecclesiola*—the little church of our local fraternity within the great *Ekklesia* of God.

2. Without property. . .

As the Word did not consider the divinity something to be held onto, so Francis did not consider his humanity a thing to be grasped. Nothing belongs more to the Word, there is nothing more his own, than the divine nature; and there is nothing more our own than human nature. Yet it is this that must be surrendered if we are to be divinized. By recognising God's sovereign rights over us as our Creator-Father, we are led to hand over to him our very being. By stripping himself naked in public Francis symbolised his total surrender to God. His material poverty was the permanent sacrament of his self-donation to God. It was not therefore an end in itself, but the outward sign of a spiritual reality: his relationship with God. There is no way to proclaim more radically that we belong to God. In dispossessing himself of self Francis had literally nothing to lose, and so fears fell away and true and lasting peace pervaded his life.

---

[9] See the Latin text in: *Opuscula S.F.F. Assisiensis*, ed. K. Esser OFM, Collegio S. Bonaventura, Grottaferrata 1978, pp. 235f.

His material poverty manifested also his profound love of creation. Creatures not only belonged to God; they were intimately related to Francis as his sisters and brothers. He could not call any sister or brother—whether human, animal, or mineral—his possession, for that would have been to oppress and enslave them. He loved his fellow creatures as and for themselves; and his love, like God's, was an authentic letting-be. The inner meaning of poverty and its visible sacrament, material poverty, emerge from the core of being a friar minor.

A life of material poverty and total simplicity raises problems for a friar minor today in respect of the Order's visible structure. While I cannot enter into any detailed discussion of these problems here, I would like to make one or two comments about material poverty because it is a vital ingredient of the Franciscan charism.

There have been enormous economic and social changes over the centuries since St. Francis's time, and our world, in particular, is a vastly complex and, in many ways, terrifying economic system. These make it quite impossible for us to reproduce literally what St. Francis did. But we cannot be excused from striving at least gradually to release ourselves from the total security which life in the Order affords us today.

Moreover, while doing our utmost to embrace material poverty, as circumstances can be changed and will allow, and thus identifying ourselves with the real poor, we must not forget that the poor are our brothers and sisters. This unalterable truth demands that we work tirelessly by all the means available to us to establish social justice. The dignity of our brethren the poor makes it imperative that injustice be abolished, so that they may reach the standard of living where they too may freely embrace the poverty that liberates. It would be tragic for them to turn simply into idolaters of wealth. But to arrive at the poverty that liberates requires the elimination of the poverty that oppresses. The profession of evangelical poverty by a friar minor necessarily entails unqualified commitment to social justice.

3. In chastity

To profess evangelical chastity or celibacy as a friar minor is to profess universal fraternal love. It is a way of loving. When a man becomes a friar minor he proclaims not only that all men and women without distinction are his brothers and sisters, but also that the badger and the otter are his brothers and the swallows his sisters. In a word, he proclaims that creation is a brotherhood and the universe is his friary. He is committed to announcing peace and working to establish it between individuals and where possible among the nations of the earth. Besides this, in accordance with the original charism of St. Francis and the signs of the times as we journey towards the beginning of the third millennium, he accepts responsibility for respecting and loving the environment. A friar minor by his very calling is a friend of the earth because as a follower of St. Francis, he knows it to be at once his sister and his mother: "Be praised, my Lord, through our Sister Mother Earth".[10]

The profession of universal fraternal love is meant to have its most telling symbol in the life of the local fraternity. We came together not because we have the same background, not because we have the same gifts, not because we are physically attracted to one another, but because God brought us together in Christ under the inspiration of the life and teaching of St. Francis. We live together with Friar Christ in our midst. Our love has its source in our wills; we love one another because it is right to do so. God loves without distinction and without making comparisons. By professing universal fraternal love we pledge ourselves to the selfsame love. I do not mean to exclude natural attractions. What I am urging is that they cannot rule our community lives, for that would lead inexorably to injustice. And where there is injustice, there can be neither love nor peace.

The local fraternity is where the individual friar minor should grow in his uniqueness, for true union always differentiates. And it is there that he is to be led into ever more intimate union with the Trinitarian life of God through ever more authentic communion, communion with his friars. Life in the local fraternity should aid him to reach that fine balance between *animus* and *anima*, between the masculine and feminine components of his nature which St. Francis himself attained so successfully and attractively. Brother Pacificus, it will be remembered, once addressed Francis as "dearest mother".[11] Finally, fraternal life should nurture and encourage friendships both inside and outside the local fraternity for its own enrichment and edification.

Concluding Remark

The authentically Franciscan approach to the evangelical counsels which I have been considering is of paramount importance for the future of

---

[10] Ibid., pp. 85, 88.
[11] 2 Celano 137; 737 in: *Omnibus*, p. 473.

our Order because it concerns our very identity. Its relevance to formation programs requires no comment.

Select Bibliography
on the Life and Message of St. Francis[1]

St. Francis was born eight hundred years ago. Noone then had the faintest notion that in the person and life of this man, humanity would reach one of its finest and most authentic expressions. It is hardly surprising, therefore, that we should want to remember him. As our memory travels back over the eight centuries, it finds it cannot stop at St. Francis. It is compelled to keep going until it comes to the one who made St. Francis possible, Jesus Christ the Lord. St. Francis is a model of Christian discipleship and his life was a kind of exegesis of the gospel, an exegesis that has never gone out of date. It is as fresh and attractive now as it was when he was alive.

The memory of St. Francis stirs the heart. It tells us that individual efforts to make brotherhood and peace realities in our world are not futile, never lost. Individuals can change the course of history and renew the face of the earth. Our memory of St. Francis engenders hope for the future. St. Francis presents us now with a challenge to face the responsibilities we have to the centuries that are yet to come. The holiness of St. Francis was a gift to humanity. His life remains a mystery of God's enlightening and strengthening grace.

If we desire to enter this mystery we can do nothing better than begin with the Saint's own writings which put us in close contact with his experience of God in Jesus Christ. The best text is the critical edition by K. Esser OFM, *Opuscula Sancti Patris Assisiensis* (Grottaferrata, Rome 1978). It is available in an excellent German edition with introduction and commentaries by Lothar Hardick OFM and Engelbert Grau OFM, *Die Schriften des heiligen Franziskus von Assisi* (Werl/Westfalia, 1980).

There is a rich collection of sources on St. Francis himself and the early history of the Order. A good, brief and concise introduction is *Approccio Storico-Critico alle Fonti Francescane* (ed. Antonianum, Rome 1979). This

---

[1] CONCILIUM 149 (November 1981) pp. 73-77. Published with permission. Editors' note: This article was translated and published in Italian, Spanish, Dutch, German and French.

will introduce the Student to the fascinating and intricate questions about the relationship of the sources to one another, their provenance and authorship.

Among the early sources the writings of Thomas of Celano are indispensable. He entered the Order in 1215 and he knew St. Francis personally. He wrote *The First life of St. Francis* within some three years of the Saint's death. *The Second Life of St. Francis* was composed in the late 1240s for which he used additional material sent to the Minister General, Crescentius of Jesi, by close companions of St. Francis. A fine edition of these materials, drawn up by the early companions in 1246. has been published in a parallel Latin-English version by R.B. Brooke, *The Writings of Leo, Rufino and Angelo, Companions of St. Francis* (Oxford 1970). It gives first-hand knowledge by those who were with St. Francis.

The Major Life of St. Francis, composed by St. Bonaventure between 1260 and 1263, is a spiritual biography by his most illustrious follower. It has received harsh treatment from a number of modern historians, for instance, P. Sabatier. A.G. Little, J. Moorman and R.B. Brooke, as having had a 'political' motive, namely to reconcile the differing factions in the Order at that time. This is an unjust assessment. St. Bonaventure's work cannot be judged satisfactorily in exclusively historical terms. It is the work of a learned and creative theologian which presents St. Francis as a model of gospel perfection and an exemplar of the evangelical virtues of poverty, humility, obedience. meekness and purity of heart. Indeed. St. Francis is presented as an eschatological figure sent to the world in this final age, to renew the gospel life and to inflame people's hearts with the love of God. For St. Bonaventure the crucial fact about St. Francis was his mission, the new charism given to the Church by the Holy Spirit.

There are three other texts the popularity of which never seems to wane. They have been translated into many modern languages and published in various editions. The *Sacrum Commercium,* or as one English translation has it: *The Sacred Romance of St. Francis with Lady Poverty,* was written between 1227 and 1245, probably nearer the earlier date. It is an enchanting allegory which describes how St. Francis and a group of his friars sought out the Lady Poverty who had withdrawn to a high mountain. She instructs St. Francis and his companions, and the piece ends with a banquet at which they all share a meal of crusts of bread and cold water. The text tells us that Lady Poverty asked to be shown the cloister. They took her to a hill and, pointing to the whole world before her, said: "This, Lady, is our cloister". The word *commercium* in the Latin title of the allegory would be better translated 'pact' or even better still 'covenant', for St. Francis and his companions resolved to live the poverty of Christ, who is himself the New Covenant between God and humanity. *The Mirror of Perfection,* compiled from earlier sources in 1318, though somewhat polemical in character, gives an interesting picture of life at the Portiuncula, that blessed place where St. Francis heard the gospel message that changed his life, where he spent so much of his time and where finally he met Sister Death in 1226. The third of these popular writings is the *Fioretti* or *The Little Flowers of St. Francis.* It was written about 1330 and it presents a most faithful picture of the dynamic and attractive personality of St. Francis.

Besides the writings of St. Francis and the early written sources of his life and message, there remains still one more source: the city of Assisi itself. It is one of the holy places of the earth, of which Evelyn Underhill said: "Its soul is more manifest than any other city that I have ever known". It is a source in two senses. First, the spirit of St. Francis pervades its every inch. It is filled with an atmosphere of brotherhood, love and peace which no amount of commercialism ever manages to smother. Second, its medieval buildings, holy places and Giotto's frescoes reveal dimensions of St. Francis' person and life that no written source can possibly hope to communicate. All this is to suggest, I suppose, that anyone who wants to penetrate the mystery of St. Francis, really ought to visit Assisi. Where that is not possible, one can turn to the attractive publication *Assisi* (Narni-Terni, ed. Plurigraf, 1978), which takes one on an exciting pictorial tour of the city. Then there is R. Brown's *True Joy from Assisi. The Assisi Experience of Inner Peace and Joy* (Chicago 1978). It is a wonderful book which shows how Assisi can bring out the contemplative in all of us. The author has assembled a series of testimonies, from about fifty writers, to the Spiritual effect Assisi had on them. No one, I think, who reads this book will close it without a desire to go to Assisi.

Anyone who starts out on a study of St. Francis and his evangelical movement, sooner or later comes across the name of P. Sabatier. It is no exaggeration to say that he initiated a new era in Franciscan studies. His brilliant, passionate and provocative *Vie de St. Francois d'Assise* which went into many editions and translations, remains a classical study of the life of St. Francis. G.K. Chesterton's book *St. Francis of Assisi* reveals beyond doubt the heart of the Saint and what can only be called the utter genius of his holiness. Above all, Chesterton understood, as few have done, I think. St. Francis' love of particulars, of individual people, of animals, birds and stones. He writes with discernment and wisdom: "I have said that St. Francis deliberately did not see the wood for the trees. It is even more true that St. Francis deliberately did not see the mob for the men". For a penetrating analysis of St. Francis' spiritual journey and enlightening reflections on the virtues of poverty, humility and perfect joy, there is the admirable work by E. Longpré OFM, *Francois d'Assise et son experience spirituelle* (Paris 1966).

For those who would wish to pursue their interest in St. Francis, a convenient and comprehensive research bibliography is provided in the second, revised and augmented English edition of O. Engelbert *St. Francis of Assisi. A Bibliography* (Chicago 1965). The text of the life of St. Francis is followed by eight *Appendices* concerning various aspects of the life and writings of St. Francis, and extensive notes to the text. A comprehensive and detailed presentation of the topographical and social background is provided by A. Fortini *Nova Vita di San Francesco,* 4 vols. (Assisi 1959).

On the writings of St. Francis there are a number of very important scholarly works which are both instructive and edifying. D. Flood OFM published a careful and detailed study on the Rule of 1221, sometimes called *The First Rule*, which gives a critical edition and analysis of the text: *Die Regula non bullata der Minderbrüder* (Werl/Westf. 1967). This Rule was never approved for the Order. The English edition under the title *The Birth of a Movement: A Study of the First Rule of St. Francis* (Chicago 1975) is made up of three parts. The first by D. Flood, treats of the historical context and formation of the *Rule* and gives an analysis of the text. We are given a graphic picture of the development of the early fraternity and understand clearly the use of the word 'movement' to describe the first decade of the Order's history. This is followed, in the second part, by an English translation of the *Rule* by P. Schwartz OFM and P. Lachance OFM. The third part by T. Matura OFM examines the nature of the Franciscan charism and puts some searching questions to the Franciscan Order today. Matura's text was originally published in the French edition of the book: *La Naissance d'un Charisme* (Paris 1976).

The most scholarly modern works on the *Rule of 1223*, which the Order follows today, and the *Testament* of St. Francis, which he wrote shortly before he died in 1226, were written by K. Esser, *Die Endgültige Regel der Minderen Brüder im Lichte der Neuesten Forschung* (Werl/Westf. 1965) and *Das Testament des Heiligen Franziskus von Assisi. Eine Untersuchung über seine Echtheit und seine Bedeutung* (Münster 1949). These works are indispensable for any critical study of the *Rule* and *Testament* of St. Francis. Esser's study of the *Rule* is also an edifying presentation of the spirit of the *Rule* and its unique character. There is an English version of this, including a translation of Spiritual Conferences on the

Testament by Esser, which had not previously been published in any language: *Rule and Testament of St. Francis. Conferences to the Modern Followers of Francis* (Chicago 1977). A beautiful and deeply moving study of the *Testament* in the light of the biblical concept of the covenant, is the work by A. van Corstanje OFM, *Het Verbond van Gods Armen* (Brummen 1962). An augmented and revised French version was then published: *Un Peuple de Pelerins: Essai d'Interpretation biblique du Testament de Saint Francois* (Paris 1964), and subsequently an English version which added five chapters on the biblical background for covenant and poverty: *The Covenant with God's Poor. An Essay on the Biblical Interpretation of the Testament of St. Francis of Assisi* (Chicago 1966). Van Corstanje's study is undoubtedly one of the finest theological reflections on Franciscanism published for many years.

The *Canticle of Brother Sun* is perhaps the most famous, but certainly the most beautiful, of the writings of St. Francis. A remarkable study for depth of insight and originality, is the book by E. Leclerc OFM, *Le Cantique des Creatures ou les Symboles de l'Union* (Paris 1970). Leclerc interprets *The Canticle of Brother Sun* as a symbolic expression of an experience that unfolds in the night of the soul. He demonstrates that the interior and exterior cannot be separated in any satisfactory interpretation of St. Francis' mysticism. Leclerc discovered in the primary cosmic meaning of *The Canticle* another meaning that is of the interior order.

In November 1979 Pope John Paul II declared St. Francis the Patron of the Environment. St. Francis looked on the whole of creation as a vast fraternity with Brother Christ at its centre. He gave the name of sister or brother to every creature. It is instructive that one of the reasons why he composed *The Canticle of Brother Sun,* more than seven hundred years ago, was to protest at the misuse of creatures by human beings. How much more guilty we are today than they were in the middle ages. On the ecological significance of *The Canticle* E. Doyle OFM has published a useful book: *St. Francis and the Song of Brotherhood* (London 1980). The book was written for everyone who is concerned about the environment and the senseless destruction of so much precious life and matter. If water is our sister, as St. Francis said, then how can we put her to death as we do, by pouring toxic acids into our lakes and rivers?

It is not widely known that St. Francis wrote a *Rule for Hermitages.* He provided for a specific form of the eremitical life in the Franciscan Order in which three and not more than four friars may live together as hermits. The *Rule* begins with these words: "Let those friars who want to lead the religious life in hermitages, do so in groups of three or at most four. Two of these are to be mothers and they are to have two sons or at least one. The two who are mothers are to lead the life of Martha; the two who are sons the life of Mary". The best study of the *Rule for Hermitages*, which also gives a critical edition of the text, is K. Esser OFM, *Die Regula pro Eremitoriis data des Hl. Franziskus von Assisi* in: FRANZISKANISCHE STUDIEN 44 (1962) pp. 383-417.[2] T. Merton made some very interesting comments on this aspect of Franciscan life in *Contemplation in a World of Action* (London 1971) pp. 260-268.

For an inspiring introduction to the Franciscan vision of the world A. Gemelli's exciting and comprehensive study remains a classic: *Il Francescanesimo* (Milan 1932). This book went into its second edition after only six months from its initial publication. The first part presents the life of St. Francis and his spirituality. After this, one is led through the history of the Franciscan Order and its significance down to the nineteenth Century. The third part treats of the relevance of Franciscan thought to the problems and questions of the early twentieth Century.

Another excellent introduction to the significance and relevance of St. Francis is the book by von Galli SJ, *Gelebte Zukunft: Franz von Assisi* (Lucerne and Frankfurt 1970). Von Galli is concerned above all with the poverty of St. Francis. St. Francis stands before the world as a model of gospel poverty and he is an incentive to us to share what we have received so generously. In his love of poverty St. Francis shows us a pathway to the future. On the meaning of the Franciscan way of life in the world of our time, L. Iriarte de Aspurz OFM Cap presents a fine theological study: *Vocacion Franciscana* (Madrid 1971). He examines the fundamental principles of the Franciscan charism and shows both their relevance and attractiveness. The heart of this book lies in the chapter on fraternity in which the author insists that it is essential to understand that St. Francis first discovered his brother, that is, Jesus Christ, before he founded a brotherhood. In fact, in his discovery of Christ the Brother, St. Francis realised that all creatures are a brotherhood.

An original and very instructive study of St. Francis and his spirituality is the book by A. van Corstanje OFM, *Franciscus Bijbel der Armen* (Haarlem 1976). Reading this book convinces one that St. Francis belongs to all humanity, he is a man for all seasons. His life was a living gospel, a visible gospel, as L.A.M. Goosens OFM says in his introduction. Van Corstanje leads

---

[2] Editors' note: See translation in: A. Cirino and J. Raischl (eds.), *Franciscan Solitude*, The Franciscan Institute, St. Bonaventure University N.Y. 1995, pp. 147-194.

us into the secret and mystery of St. Francis, and his book bears witness that the evangelical virtues of voluntary poverty, obedience and humility are strong and courageous virtues and are the basis of hope for the future.

No bibliography that would seek to introduce St. Francis can possibly omit the novel by N. Kazantzakis, *God's Pauper—St. Francis of Assisi* (Oxford 1962). This is a translation from the original Greek, and it is found in a number of other translations. The book is not a historical biography; as the title says, it is a novel. As a novel it is a profound, inspiring and authentic interpretation of St. Francis. Let then Kazantzakis have the last word in this essay. I quote from the final paragraph of his prologue:

> For me Saint Francis is the model of the dutiful man, the man who by means of ceaseless, supremely cruel struggle succeeds in fulfilling our highest obligation, something higher even than morality or truth or beauty: the obligation to transubstantiate the matter which God entrusted to us, and turn it into spirit.

Saint Francis and Theology[1]

In these reflections I want to steer clear of the hoary question about Saint Francis' attitude to study. On this score let two remarks suffice. First, we can recall that he was quite happy for Saint Anthony to teach theology to the friars with the proviso that in doing so "he should not extinguish the spirit of prayer and devotion, as is contained in the Rule"; and that in the *Rule of 1223* he warns the friars not to let manual work extinguish the spirit of holy prayer and devotion (c. 5). There are snares lying in wait for those who do manual work, just as there are for those given to study. Secondly, Saint Francis explicitly stipulates that we are to honour and reverence all theologians and those who impart God's holy words to us because they administer spirit and life (*Testament* 13). We should note that these words in the *Testament* follow references to the Eucharist, the holy names of God, and the Scriptures. There is here, I believe, an embryonic theology of theologians!

It is a fascinating characteristic of the Franciscan Movement that it produced a Franciscan theology at all. Yet it is a fact of our history that there emerged quite quickly out of the primordial Franciscan experience a way of looking at God, humanity, and the world which medievalists have insisted on calling the Franciscan School. It says something of significance that in the academe the Dominicans have been identified as members of the Thomistic School, whereas we have been labelled followers of the Franciscan School. With us the founder predominated over the learned doctors; in the Dominican Order the learned doctor predominated over the founder.

The Franciscan School embraces a wide spectrum of thinkers. Though not technically in the School, Saint Anthony cannot be left out. He received some superb training in mystical theology which shows itself in his exposition of Scripture. No matter how far he travelled from the literal sense, Vigouroux still included him in the *Dictionnaire de le Bible*. There are the famous and not so famous names of friars to whom Paris, Oxford, and Cambridge will always owe a debt of gratitude: Haymo of Faversham, Simon of Sandwich (two places

---

[1] The Cord 32.4 (1982) pp. 108-111. Published with permission of The Franciscan Institute, St. Bonaventure University, New York.

not too far down the road from us here in Canterbury), Alexander of Hales, John de la Rochelle, Saint Bonaventure, John Duns Scotus, Adam Marsh, Roger Bacon, John Pecham (buried in Canterbury Cathedral), Vincent of Coventry, William of Poitou, Eustace of Normanville, William of Ockham.

The fact of the matter is that Saint Francis has a magnetic attraction for the human intellect, especially *fide illustrata,* the intellect suffused with the light of faith. And had it been otherwise, it would not only have been sad, but very disturbing. The intellect is also part of human nature, as much as the heart, the will, and the imagination. The life and writings of Saint Francis are far too rich to be ignored by the intellect. Anyone with the tiniest glimmer of theological acumen cannot fail to be impressed and inspired by the theological significance of his life and the theological content of his writings. The unity of orthodoxy and orthopraxy in his life is remarkable. Consider for a moment the effect Saint Francis' literal imitation of Christ had on Saint Bonaventure's theology. He saw that this was no mere moral or behavioristic patterning of his life on the model of Christ's, but an ontological conforming of his very existence to Jesus Christ whereby the divine activity becomes effective in the world.

His writings show he had a profound grasp of the meaning and import of all the great saving truths of revelation: the Trinity, incarnation, creation, grace, the virtues, and eschatology. And having grasped them, he communicated them in drama, poetry, and above all by imitating Jesus Christ. He was a superb exegete. He observed the gospel literally—there was no sacrificing of the literal sense for him. Then penetrating further, he drew from it the message it has for faith, the directions it gives for life, and the hope it holds out for eternal life.

He lived the four senses of Scripture that formed the framework of medieval exegesis: the literal, allegorical, tropological, and anagogical. It would, therefore, have been a truncated development if his inspiration had been restricted to artists and poets. As it is, he inspired a theology whose best representatives became artists and poets in their theology, and of none is that truer than Saint Bonaventure. Pervading his writings as an atmosphere pervades a room is the sublime theology of the centrality of Christ, which is the distinguishing feature of Saint Bonaventure's theology. In the most surprising contexts one finds the seeds of the great themes of Franciscan theology: the primacy of Christ, the meaning and value of creation, the primacy of charity, the unique dignity of every individual. Let us take one example. He writes in the *Admonitions*: "Consider with what great dignity the Lord God has endowed you. He created and fashioned your body in the image of his beloved Son and your soul in his own likeness" (5:1). Is this not a seminal expression of the doctrine of Christ's absolute primacy? His words recall a beautiful text in Tertullian, *On the Resurrection of the Flesh:*

> Imagine God wholly employed and absorbed in it—in his hand, his eye, his labour, his purpose, his wisdom, his providence, and above all, in his love, which was dictating the lineaments of this creation, Adam. For whatever was the form and expression which was then given to the clay, Christ was in his thoughts as one day to become man, because the Word, too, was to be both clay and flesh, even as the earth was then. . . .And God made man. . .after the image of God, in other words, of Christ, did he make him [c. 6].

Obviously, I am not maintaining that Duns Scotus' teaching was somehow in the mind of Saint Francis. But it seems reasonably certain that creation without Christ was inconceivable for Francis. It is the self-same love that redeems and heals, as perfects, fulfils, and sanctifies. To say Redeemer is a way of saying Divine Lover.

Saint Bonaventure had a unique understanding of the theological significance of Saint Francis. There is no doctor of the Church on whom the founder of an Order had greater influence. Bonaventure himself drew attention to the parallel between the early development of the Franciscan Order and the history of the ancient Church in his *Letter to an Unnamed Master*, 13 (*Opera Omnia* VIII, p. 336). And it is indeed striking that the Apologists presented the Crucified One of Calvary as the very wisdom the Greeks had sought for centuries. Saint Francis was a *locus theologicus* for Saint Bonaventure. It seems beyond question that Saint Francis was a source of Bonaventure's Christian philosophy wherein reason takes its honourable place under the guidance of faith from the outset. This places natural theology and all philosophical theology in the context of the actual knowledge of the Living God revealed in Jesus Christ. These therefore become a moment in the movement of the mind, illumined by divine light, towards contemplative union with God. It was through the gift of faith and the insights that accompany it, that Saint Francis penetrated the mystery of existence and the meaning of all creatures.

So far from being against study, I fancy Saint Francis is whispering to us in the midst of our celebrations of the eighth centenary of his birth, that we should immerse ourselves in our theological tradition and enter into fresh dialogue with it, until it becomes part of the very air we breathe and forms the structures of our vision of God, humanity, and the world. This tradition has never had more importance than at present.

In an article in The Tablet recently on a debate about freedom and authority the author, C.J. Hamson, one-time Professor of Comparative Law at Cambridge, makes a noteworthy comment. I intend no offence to Saint Thomas in quoting Professor Hamson's words. My purpose is to stress the obligation incumbent on us to do all in our power to appropriate and share the rich treasures of the tradition to which we are so often neglectful heirs. Professor Hamson writes:

> It is a pity that St. Thomas Aquinas, whom I greatly admire, was so powerful a mind and so destructive a theologian: the world we inhabit today would have been, I think, less ferocious if more of St. Bonaventure had managed to survive Aquinas—if some of the music of the spheres had survived Galileo and Newton.

St. Francis and the Papacy[1]

As this is the year of the Pope's visit to Britain, I am pleased to have been asked to write an article about St. Francis' love of the papacy.

In 1209, when the number of the first friars had grown to twelve, St. Francis decided to go to Rome to ask Pope Innocent to approve his way of life. Now this is interesting in the light of what we find in his *Testament,* a short text dictated in 1226, just a few days before he died.

Looking back over the years, he tells us: "After the Lord gave me some friars, there was no one to show me what I should do, but the Most High himself revealed to me that I should live according to the way of the holy gospel. I had this written down in a few words and simply, and the Lord Pope approved it for me". There is no other text which tells so plainly both the humility of St. Francis and his deep faith in the Church, represented by the Pope. Certain of what he had to do, indeed fully convinced that God had shown him the way, still he sought the Pope's approval, as the only sure guarantee that his call from God to live in poverty, as the gospel teaches, and to preach peace, was authentic.

St. Francis knew that the Church is the guardian of the scriptures, authorized by Christ himself to explain and interpret them. There was nothing of the proud fanatic about St. Francis, not a hint that he thought that private interpretation of the gospel was superior to the Church's approval. In humility he submitted his own inner convictions to the Pope. This alone, he realised, would keep him and his Order for all time within the Catholic unity of the Church. The Church embraces a vast and diverse number of peoples and outlooks. Christ's gift of the papacy holds the Church's great diversity in unity, and guarantees that it will not splinter into division.

When St. Francis was a boy there were a number of reform movements in the Church which advocated a return to a life of gospel simplicity. *But* through criticism and impatience with the papacy they separated themselves from the Church. That did not happen to St. Francis. Like St. Thomas More at

---

[1] THE TROUBADOUR (Easter 1982) pp. 24f. Published with permission from the Province of Immaculate Conception, England.

a later time, he saw through all the failings and weaknesses of the Church to the presence of God's guiding Spirit within. So it is that at the beginning of the *Rule* he promises obedience to the Pope for himself and on behalf of all the friars.

After he had written the first version of the *Rule* in 1221, St. Francis asked Pope Honorius to appoint one of the cardinals to take care of the Order. In his humility he thought it was too much to ask the Pope himself who was already burdened with the weighty affairs of the Church and State. The Pope appointed Cardinal Hugolino whom St. Francis considered the pro-Pope for the Order, by whom it would be linked to the life and guidance of the Church.

Cardinal Hugolino was a great friend of St. Francis and St. Francis foretold that he would be Pope. The year after St. Francis died he was elected Pope and he took the name Gregory IX. There is a beautiful story about Pope Gregory which shows what deep influence St. Francis had on him.

Because he loved St. Francis dearly, Pope Gregory wore the Franciscan habit under the papal robes and he kept a leper in his room, because St. Francis had loved lepers and taken care of them. Every evening when his work as Pope was done, he used to take off the papal robes and, in the habit of a friar, washed the leper and fed him. One evening when he was very tired after a heavy day, he was slower than usual in looking after the leper. As the sick sometimes understandably do, the leper got impatient, and snapped at Pope Gregory: "Has the Pope not got anybody besides an old man like you to look after me?" "No", replied the Pope, "he has nobody else". The leper never knew that it was the Pope Who took care of him.

The Franciscan Order and the Permanent Diaconate[1]

To mark the 750th anniversary in 1976 of the death of St. Francis I wrote an article in which I reflected at some length on the charism of our Order.[2] Among the aspects I emphasized is the fact that St. Francis was a permanent deacon.[3] Periodically since that article was published I have returned to this aspect of our charism in private reflection, fraternal dialogue, and public discussion. All this produced in me the unshakeable conviction that both fidelity to our origins as followers of Friar Deacon Francis and obedience to the signs of the times, made manifest by God's Spirit in the Church of the post-modern world, particularly in respect of the developing understanding of ministry, require our Order to incorporate the permanent diaconate into its life and world-wide mission, as an option open to candidates on an equal footing with the priesthood. In this way the Order would be constituted of friars, friar deacons, and friar priests. One may note in passing that it is indeed remarkable how several elements of the original charism of St. Francis have become more relevant in our time than they were in his and have assumed greater significance. And of these one may certainly instance his ecological awareness and his having been a permanent deacon.

It is now a cause of joy and some satisfaction to record that the General Chapter of the Order, held in Assisi in 1979, voted to petition the Holy See, in accordance with the norms laid down by Paul VI in *Sacrum Diaconatus Ordinem,* to institute the permanent diaconate in the Order of Friars Minor.[4]

---

[1] THE CORD 31.4 (1981) pp. 101-107 and THE CORD 31.5 (1981) pp 132-135. Published with permission from The Franciscan Institute, St. Bonaventure University, New York.
[2] Editors' note: The article *Seven-hundred-and-fifty Years Later: Reflections on the Franciscan Charism* is reprinted in this volume: pp. 81 ff.
[3] Ibid., pp. 32f.
[4] VII, p. 32: *Diaconatum permanentem constituere apud religiosos ius proprium Sanctae Sedis est, ad quam unice pertinet Capitulorum Generalium hac de re vota expendere atque probare;* p. 33: *Diaconi religiosi ministerium diaconale obeant sub episcopi suorumque antistitum auctoritate, secundum normas, quae in sacerdotes religiosos valent; tenetur quoque legibus, quibus eiusdem religionis sodales astringuntur*—cf. ACTA APOSTOLICAE SEDIS 59 (1967) pp. 703f.

In this article I want to explain the reasons why this decision of the General Chapter is singularly appropriate to the Franciscan Order. This explanation will, however, be given in the second half of the article. To present it effectively I must first, in the following pages, consider the theological character of the permanent diaconate.

Whenever I have begun to think about the permanent diaconate in recent months there has come first to my mind not theological doctrine but a cluster of four names: Stephen, Lawrence, Ephraem, and Francis.

St. Stephen the Protomartyr and six others were chosen out to receive the imposition of hands for the honourable task of serving at table. This allowed the Twelve to give themselves continually to the service of the Word.[5] St. Lawrence, Deacon and Martyr, served the Church at Rome. He took care of the poor and afflicted whom he considered the treasure of the Church. He was put to death during the persecution of Valerian in 258, a few days after the martyrdom of Pope St. Sixtus II and four deacons. St. Ephraem, Deacon and Doctor of the Church, founded a school of theology. He served God's Word by preaching and theological reflection. He died in 373. St. Francis of Assisi, Deacon and Founder of the Franciscan Order, served lepers, preached penance and peace, desired martyrdom, and sang the gospel.[6] The diaconate of these four saints embraces a wide spectrum of ministries.

For complex historical reasons in the Church it has become extremely difficult for us to assess and appreciate the true nature of this unique ministry. To begin my brief theological analysis of its place and significance I will compare two quite different approaches to it which can be represented in schematic form as follows.

scheme n.1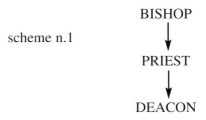

---

[5] Acts 6:1-6.

[6] The founder and first Provincial of the English Province, Blessed Agnellus of Pisa (c. 1194-1236), was almost a permanent deacon! After long being Provincial he was commanded by the General Chapter, against his wishes, to be ordained a priest. As Eccleston says, *Cum diu in ordine diaconatus fuisset minister Angliae*, I would hazard the guess that this took place at the General Chapter of 1230; See *Fratris Thomae vulgo dicti de Eccleston Tractatus de adventu Fratrum Minorum In Angliam*, ed. A.G. Little, Manchester 1951, col. XIV, p. 78.

In scheme n. 1 the diaconate is understood primarily as the lowest degree of the hierarchy. According to this approach the deacon is in a subordinate position to the priest. He can perform some of the functions of the priest, but not others: he cannot celebrate the Eucharist nor administer the sacrament of reconciliation. Though it is recognised in theory that he has a liturgical function directly related to the bishop, in practice he is almost always a liturgical assistant to the priest. In this scheme it is the notion of 'priestly power' rather than 'priestly ministry' which predominates.

The discipline requiring that a candidate for the priesthood shall first be ordained a deacon (the discipline of the temporary diaconate), has served to reduce our understanding of it to being primarily a stage on the way to the priesthood. It has no specific existential significance and little theological intelligibility as the *diaconal* ministry in these circumstances. It is a preparation for the priesthood, and during its exercise the temporary deacon learns some of the skills and techniques required in being a priest. He is in a sense a 'mini-priest'.

The restoration of the permanent diaconate has not yet counterbalanced this limited and restrictive understanding. Permanent deacons are in the main pastoral (and most generally parochial) assistants to the parish priests. There is of course ancient precedent for the deacon's being an assistant to the priest. But this did not circumscribe the deacon's function nor endow it with its primary definition. Moreover, the permanent deacon's well nigh exclusive association with the priestly ministry, which defines him for all practical purposes in liturgical terms, leads inevitably to the conclusion that his ministry is in fact priestly. Deacons often wear clerical dress, which serves to make them appear to be priests, and they are frequently addressed as 'Father'. One hears also that were the law of celibacy changed, many permanent deacons would offer themselves for ordination to the priesthood.

I do not mean to question the value of the temporary diaconate as a final period of preparation and training for the priesthood, nor to denigrate in any way the necessity and usefulness of permanent deacons acting as assistants to the parochial clergy. What I am advocating is that the diaconal ministry cannot be determined satisfactorily, in the light of the Tradition we have received, simply by its relation to the priesthood, neither as a stage towards it, nor as an assistance of it by relieving it of some of its tasks, responsibilities, and duties. Nor is there any question here of denying the hierarchical structure of the one sacrament of order. The point I am stressing is that the diaconate cannot be defined adequately merely by understanding this 'lowest' degree of the hierarchy as some thing less than the priesthood. That it is the 'lowest' degree of the hierarchy can be taken to mean that it is a distinct ministry within the sacrament of order.

scheme n.2:

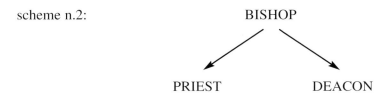

In scheme n. 2 the priest and deacon are related collaterally, deriving from the bishop. This represents the true nature of the permanent diaconate, which is a sharing in the episcopal ministry in a way specifically different from the priesthood.

In acknowledged dependence on the *Didascalia* the Constitution on the Church of Vatican II teaches that deacons "receive the imposition of hands 'not unto the priesthood, but unto the ministry'. . . ."[7] By sacramental grace "they are dedicated to the People of God, in conjunction with the bishop and his body of priests, in the service of the liturgy, of the gospel and of works of charity". The text then proceeds to explain at some length almost exclusively the liturgical function of the deacon:

> It pertains to the office of a deacon, in so far as it may be assigned to him by the competent authority, to administer Baptism solemnly, to be custodian and distributor of the Eucharist, in the name of the Church, to assist at and to bless marriages, to bring Viaticum to the dying, to read the sacred scripture to the faithful, to instruct and exhort the people, to preside over the worship and prayer of the faithful, to administer sacramentals, and to assist at funeral and burial services.

Then in no more than one sentence, the Constitution refers to the deacon's non-liturgical functions: "Dedicated to works of charity and functions of administration, deacons should recall the admonition of St. Polycarp: 'Let them be merciful'. . . ."[8]

It cannot be questioned that the deacon has a liturgical function, but it is a pity that this function was mentioned in first place by the Constitution. As the priest is meant to celebrate the liturgy and above all preside at the

---

[7] See c. 3, p. 129, in: *Vatican Council II. The Conciliar and Post-Conciliar Documents*, ed. by A. Flannery OP, Tenbury Wells, Worcs., England: Fowler Wright Books, Ltd.; Collegeville, MN: Liturgical Press, 1975, p. 387.

[8] Ibid.

Eucharist, and then to bring the grace of the Eucharist to the world, so the deacon is meant to serve the mystical body and the world, outside the liturgy, and to bring the life of Christians into the world, and the world itself to the Eucharist. From this follows his assistance of the bishop (priest) at the celebration of the Eucharist. In other words, it is first to the non-liturgical sphere of the Church's life and mission that the ministry of the diaconate belongs. Furthermore, while what pertains to the office of deacon "may be assigned to him by the competent authority", as the Constitution *Lumen Gentium* says, a ministry is committed to him by his receiving the imposition of hands. He is given a share in a particular ministry whose essential character is not *assigned* to him by the competent authority, but is *imparted* by the sacrament of order. The deacon is not only "dedicated to works of charity and functions of administration", he is commissioned in the sacrament to the ministry of performing them. This formally determines the diaconal ministry, and 1 want to consider now how this is the case.

The Ministry of the Permanent Deacon

The bishop, as head and leader of the local church, indeed as 'vicar of Christ' in his diocese, has the first and highest liturgical ministry, the first and highest ministry of the gospel, the first and highest ministry of the corporal and spiritual works of mercy. It is equally part of the sacred task committed to him, for instance, to preside at the Eucharist, to bring the word to those who do not know Jesus Christ, to take care of the sick and afflicted, to sanctify the world, to work for social justice.

As is obvious, no individual bishop can perform all these ministries or even one of them without the help of others. He is therefore assisted in his episcopal ministry by deacons and priests, who share the sacrament of order. The priest's sharing in the sacrament focuses on the liturgy and preeminently on the eucharistic celebration; the deacon's sharing in it focuses on works of charity, mercy, and justice, on evangelisation and the presence of the Church in the world.

It is crucial to realize that the ministries of charity, mercy, and justice, of evangelisation and of making the Church present in the world, belong essentially to the episcopal office. These are not mere appendages to his other ministries. The bishops have committed to them a ministry of the world as well as of the Church. Consequently, when a man is ordained to the permanent diaconate, the Church through the bishop makes a public proclamation that it is committed in obedience to Christ, to the diaconal ministry. It is not just a private concern or interest of the man being ordained. Nor is it merely a matter of publicly ratifying someone to do what he might otherwise be able to do if he were not ordained. The deacon is commissioned from within the sacrament of order to exercise a distinct aspect of the episcopal ministry. The deacon himself receives the grace of the sacrament directly related to this ministry.

The deacon's ministry of charity and mercy may be expressed succinctly in the seven corporal and seven spiritual works of mercy, whose form is to be determined by the signs of the times. These may direct that a deacon be in a church organization or, for example, in a counselling centre set up by a local government authority. The crucial point is that he is commissioned by the bishop once the latter is aware of the need of the specific ministry.

Since the sixteenth century the large number of congregations and institutes of sisters and brothers that have been established in the Western Church, dedicated to educational work, to caring for the sick, the deprived, and the outcast, have, for all practical purposes, exercised the Church's diaconal Ministry. It is no merely legal requirement that they had to receive authorization for their life and work from the local bishop, and in many instances also from Rome. The existence and apostolates of these vast numbers of men and women throughout the last four centuries originated, of course, in the charism of their founders, and not formally out of the sacrament of order. What may be the precise relationship of these two forms of the diaconal ministry in the Church, or the implications contained in the relationship for ordaining women to the diaconate, I do not wish to investigate here. The point is, the charism was discerned and preserved by episcopal and/or papal authorization. In the light of these considerations one could present a strong case for the view that the Brothers of St. John of God, for example, would qualify unquestionably to become an institute of permanent deacons.

With regard to work for social justice and evangelisation there is need for but little comment. The awareness of our collective responsibility in the First World for a great deal of the oppression and increasing poverty in the Third World, has placed heavy burdens on the shoulders of the bishops. There is no doubt that this could be borne nationally and internationally—and no more fittingly than—by permanent deacons.

In respect of administration at the diocesan level, it would be an immense contribution to our understanding of the diaconate if permanent deacons were appointed bishops' secretaries. Apart from its being a clear and unambiguous exercise of the diaconate, it would manifest to the diocese the direct relationship of the deacon to the bishop.

One of the chief tasks the Second Vatican Council set itself was to arrive at a deeper understanding of the Church's relationship to the world. As a fundamental, though not final, statement about this, the Council published its *Pastoral Constitution on the Church in the World of Our Time,* that is, the post-modern world. The relation of the Church to the World raises vast and intricate questions, whether it be considered as a general question or in some particular case. However, the diaconal ministry is directly concerned with its practical realization. It is well attested in the history of the Church, that at the point where the two meet, either in charity or in confrontation, deacons have played a significant role. The importance of this element of the diaconal ministry I have found expressed nowhere more accurately than in the following text by Père Joseph Lécuyer CSsP: ". . .it is by their (the deacons') means that the bishops accomplish their most difficult and delicate tasks, in which the hierarchy finds itself in closest contact with the world and its temporal concerns on the dangerous frontier between the purely spiritual and the material".[9]

It is not unusual in Church history to find deacons acting as ambassadors and legates. At present it is the practice of the Vatican to appoint nuncios where there are full diplomatic relations between the Holy See and national governments. The question of Vatican diplomacy is an involved theological issue and in any extensive consideration of it one could not ignore the attitude taken to it by the liberation theologians of Latin America. However, it would be to stray too far from our set purpose to pursue it here. If we accept it as practiced, it seems to me that this is an area to which the permanent diaconate is singularly appropriate. In this context it is not outlandish to suggest that for this task the office of Cardinal Deacon might be restored.[10]

The restoration of the permanent diaconate is a landmark in the Church's understanding of ministry. Its implications will be drawn for

---

[9] *What is a Priest?*, FAITH AND FACT BOOKS 53, London: Burns and Oates, 1959, p. 62.

[10] I realize that all Cardinals are now bishops. This goes back to a provision made by John XXIII shortly before the Second Vatican Council. My suggestion, however, is based on the responsibility in the diaconal ministry for the areas where the Church and world meet. This is nowhere more obvious than in the Holy See's relations with national governments. To appoint Cardinal Deacons as nuncios (I prescind altogether from Delegates), would manifest more clearly the pope's universal episcopal ministry.

decades, perhaps even for centuries, to come. It has already led to a new approach to the sacrament of order and in particular to the episcopal office.

Part Two: Permanent Deacons and the Franciscan Order

1. St. Francis the Deacon

We should be careful not to neutralize the importance of the historical fact that Francis was a permanent deacon, by thinking that he did not become a priest out of humility before so exalted an office. There is no evidence for this. That Francis had great reverence for priests issued from his deep love of the Church and the Eucharist; it tells us nothing about his personal attitude towards becoming a priest. He was a deacon, and that should be taken to mean that he wanted to be a deacon. As a possible interpretation of this I would suggest that being a deacon, for him, assimilated his life more closely to Friar Jesus Christ the Deacon, the *Servant* of all, who washed the feet of his disciples.

It is probable that Francis received the diaconate on the occasion of his visit to Rome in 1209 to obtain approval of his new way of life from Innocent III. Prior to the approval Francis and his first followers had preached penance and worked among lepers, and there is evidence that they continued in these ministries afterwards.

In the light of this it would be fully consonant with the Order's specific mission to receive a candidate who wished to be a deacon in imitation of St. Francis and to work, for instance, in a hospital for terminally sick patients.

2. Relevant Elements of the Original Charism

In becoming a Franciscan a man commits himself to a life according to the Order's charism. This charism is multi-faceted. Here I wish to select two facets which have immediate bearing on the diaconal ministry.

a. The Gospel of Peace

The Franciscan friar pledges himself in imitation of St. Francis to preach peace. Evangelical peace is personal and social, both of which are derivatives of justice.

There is a peace surpassing all understanding which the world cannot give. It proceeds from righteousness in regard to God, self, and others. The grace of righteousness or justification is the beginning of integration and liberation (that is, salvation), which involves the whole of our being, and not only our spirit. Acceptance and true love of oneself, the healing of memory, commitment to the future in the face of anxieties, awareness of the value of the now, are all intimately bound up with integration. The pace and pressure of life in the West have made it frighteningly clear that the meaning of *salvation* is considerably wider than the remission of sins and interior spiritual renewal. In so many cases it is intertwined with the need for counselling, psychotherapy, spiritual direction, and discernment. These are concerned precisely with self-acceptance and self-awareness, healing, and contemplative peace. Peace in this sense—as involving every level of human existence—is defined by the signs of the times, and it can be proclaimed effectively and with credibility only if we take seriously that grace is given to a human being as a totality. Counselling, psychotherapy, spiritual direction, and discernment are works of mercy and love. For this reason, as pathways to personal peace they may be numbered rightfully and most fittingly among the ministries of the permanent diaconate in the Franciscan Order.

Social peace is impossible without social justice. Peace is not the absence of war; it is the sacrament of integral liberation. Freedom, equality, and brotherhood are the pillars of justice. To proclaim peace in our world means to set people free. In the First World, to set free means to deliver ourselves from greed, from the aimlessness of consumerism, from the arms race, and from the idols of money and the craving for ever higher economic standards of living. In the Third World, to set free means to remove oppression, poverty, disease, and exploitation, so that men, women, and children may find dignity and have hope. The profession of poverty as freedom from economic and political power, obliges a Franciscan to work for social justice. Poverty freely chosen is the implacable enemy of the poverty that is enforced and destroys.

It would be an eloquent witness to the Order's charism for Franciscan deacons to be involved in work for social justice either at the local or at the national level, under the auspices of Church or government, or at the international level through the United Nations.

b. The Love of Creation

The ecological awareness of St. Francis is one of his most distinctive features. He formulated it beautifully in the stanzas of *The Canticle of Brother Sun*. In the poetry of that remarkable song there is a word of reproof to our selfishness. We, the Creator's image, are destroying the Creator's work, and thereby defacing his image in ourselves. Any participation in efforts to re-establish our fraternal relationships with all creatures and to lessen our malicious domination of Sister Water and Brother Air, is a sharing in Francis's attitude to creation.

The ecological crisis poses a particularly acute problem for those who believe in God the Creator and Sustainer of the universe. As a grave moral issue it places obligations on the Church to proclaim the authentically Christian attitude to creation, which is, in fact, fraternal, and to make this message credible by doing everything possible to solve the crisis.

As the Franciscan Order is committed to proclaiming that the earth is our sister and our mother, and that the stars are our sisters, the ecological awareness of our time is an eminently appropriate area for the ministry of Franciscan deacons.

3. Sanctification of the Structures of the World

St. Francis writes in his *First Rule* that the friars "should exercise the same skill which they already know, provided it is not contrary to the salvation of their souls and can be honestly pursued".[11] This provision may be applied to the arts, crafts, and professions. The text envisages that a man comes from the world with all his talents, gifts, and skills, to enter the brotherhood. Having become a friar he then returns to the world bringing with him a new kind of existence: his *friarship*. Moreover, the text introduces us to that area where Church and world meet and mutually influence one another.

What St. Francis says here can be linked in a given case with the permanent diaconate, dependent on the situation and the experience and call of the individual friar. The place of this form of the permanent diaconate in the Order should not be hastily dismissed, for it would be a most efficacious way of bringing the world to the Eucharist.

Concluding Remarks

It might be objected that the suggestions I have made about areas in which permanent deacons of the Franciscan Order may fittingly exercise their ministry, could be applied equally to the priests of the Order and, for that matter, to friars who have no desire to receive the sacrament of order. Then,

---

[11] D. Flood OFM and T. Matura OFM, *The Birth of a Movement: A Study of the First Rule of St. Francis*, trans. by P. Schwartz OFM, and P. Lachance OFM, Franciscan Herald Press, Chicago 1975, p. 75.

some might say that ordination to the permanent diaconate is not *necessary* for these apostolates.

To the first I would answer that my reflections have been written in the light of what I observe to be a new, wider, and developing appreciation of the meaning of ministry, and of an emerging outline of what the Church's presence will be in the world of the not-too-distant future. These have already influenced the Order's apostolate, and they will do so ever more radically as time passes. The Order has experienced a certain 'declericalization' over the past ten years. More and more candidates entering the Order have no desire to be priests. However, it should be noted that to be a priest does not necessarily mean to be clericalized, and in the Franciscan Order it should not mean this anyway. With fewer priests two results will follow. First, some exclusively priestly apostolates will be curtailed. Secondly, the priests of the Order will have to concern themselves more extensively with the Church's liturgical life and with all the ways in which that is developing, in particular with preaching the Word and celebrating the Eucharist. Concern with the Church's liturgical life can be a full-time apostolate, and indeed ought to be. In this way the quality of liturgical celebration will be enhanced. Yet I must agree that the areas specified are certainly open to priests of the Order and friars who have no wish to receive the sacrament of order. But these would not be exercising the *diaconal* ministry.

With regard to the second objection: I would concur that the diaconate is *not necessary* for the exercise of these apostolates. But then I would refer the objector to what I have written above about the character of the episcopal office in the Church. This objection derives from the restrictive understanding that the deacon has no specific *powers*. I have been arguing that the diaconate is a ministry to which the Church is committed. To say that ordination to the diaconate is not necessary for the exercise of these apostolates misses the whole point. It is necessary that the Church publicly manifest to the world that she has been pledged by her Lord to its service. Ordination to the permanent diaconate is the formal proclamation that service of the world is of the essence of Christ's mandate, and it is the official commissioning of men in the Church to fulfil it.

The Order in the World[1]

In these days of adaptation and change Religious Orders have had to do a lot of hard thinking about their place and purpose in the world. Cherished by the Church as belonging inseparably to her life and holiness, they have been assigned the tremendous task of recapturing the spirit of their Founder and of determining its precise and lasting value in the light of the gospel for the needs of our time.

St. Francis, Pilgrim and Stranger

Nobody ever loved the world more than St. Francis of Assisi, and nobody ever had less of what it has to offer. He considered himself a pilgrim and stranger in the world, yet he was on terms of the utmost intimacy with man and beast, bird and fish, sun and moon, earth, fire, and water. He called them all by the familiar names of brother and sister. He never felt too out of place to remind them all to give thanks and to glorify the Great King. Though a stranger, he had a word for everyone; though a pilgrim, he was at home everywhere. Pilgrim and stranger indeed he was, but who has ever loved more what for God's sake he had renounced?

Christ Our Brother

For St. Francis the first Friar was Christ. He grasped with clarity and realism excelled only by St. John and St. Paul, that the incarnation means the Son of God became our Brother, our Friar. In Friar Christ the son of Pietro Bernardone was transformed into Friar Francis, a brother of Him Who revealed to us that God is the Father of heaven and earth. Francis soon attracted Friar Bernard, Friar Peter, and Friar Giles to his new way of life. So was born the Order of the Little Brothers of St. Francis. Above all else the gospel meant brotherhood to St. Francis. That is why he says that the *Rule* of the Order is to observe the holy gospel. To observe the gospel is to be a Friar, a brother of Christ.

---

[1] THE NEW FRANCISCAN 1.11 (November 1968) pp. 258-261. Published with permission from the Province of Immaculate Conception, England.

The love of St. Francis stretched out from Christ to embrace Brother Wolf and Sister Swallow, Brother Fire "full of power and strength" and Sister Water "so limpid, pure, and useful".

Through these he was brought back to Him Who came to cast fire on the earth and to give water welling up to eternal life. In Christ he found the basic unity of all creation, and in that unity the universe became for him transparent. He saw God everywhere. This was the source of his love and respect for creatures which he expressed by the beautiful names of brother and sister. Love forbade him to call anything his own because owning things somehow seemed to belittle their value and dignity. The world became for him one vast Friary where men should live together in the love of Friar Christ. We can understand why St. Francis wanted no other *Rule* but the gospel and why he did not become a monk. He needed no monastery when he had the world. His vision extended to the dimensions of the universe, and what building on earth could contain that?

The Poor Christ

Christ became our Brother in poverty. As one of us in a sin-laden, death-ridden world, He learned obedience through suffering. He came from His Father to the world where His life was one long journey through suffering and death back to His Father. Littleness before God demanded real poverty and it forbade anything that might suggest even a hint of power, of greatness, of wealth, or of security in the world. Everything that littleness and poverty stand for is contained in the word 'Minor'. Francis called his followers "Friars Minor" because they were to be always poor little brothers on their way through the world to their Father. "Friar Minor", therefore, is not so much a title as a description of a way of life according to the gospel.

The Need for Renewal

Brotherhood in Christ and littleness in poverty are realities of the gospel that can never grow old, never become outmoded. The Church needs a constant reminder of those realities because they are essential to her mission in the world. The sublime and simple vocation of the Little Brothers of St. Francis is to bear witness to them in their life and work. The Franciscan Brotherhood is to embrace all men irrespective of colour, of race, and even of creed; Franciscan Littleness is to find its expression in real material poverty of life and work.

From the beginning St. Francis insisted on the newness and originality of his way of life. It is a sad fact, however, that as the years slipped by the little Brotherhood took on more and more the characteristics of a Monastic Order. It became enshrined, for example, in large monastic buildings which secured the Friars to a particular place, and which, as the centuries went by, tended to hamper the Order from apostolic works requiring freedom for movement and experiment. Perhaps all this was inevitable because of large numbers and the very newness of St. Francis' way of life. Whatever the reasons may be, the external appearance of the Franciscan Order has been more akin to a monastic, enclosed, established way of life than to that of an itinerant brotherhood preaching the gospel of peace in the midst of the world.

A Chapter in Renewal

I say "external appearance" advisedly. In the inner depths of the Order's life there has been always a longing to go back to earlier times, not to refashion Franciscan life after the pattern of a bygone age, but to recreate its message and spirit for the needs of a new one.

Last year (1967) the General Chapter of the Order met at the Portiuncula in Assisi. Inspired by that longing, Friars came from all over the world to initiate the renewal of the Order according to the gospel spirit of St. Francis. The Chapter cut across the developments, accretions, and compromises of seven centuries to get as clear a vision as possible of Franciscan life as St. Francis conceived it. For ten weeks the Chapter examined and discussed every aspect of the Order's life and work in the world. The guiding principle throughout it all was fidelity to the name the gospel gave us: "Friars Minor". This principle was responsible for far-reaching and courageous changes to restore the Order to its original mission. Looking over the centuries, I think the 1967 General Chapter is the most important since the Chapter of Mats in 1222 at which St. Francis adamantly refused to accept a monastic rule of life.

An Extraordinary Chapter

The General Chapter was able to deal only with the most general principles. The work of reducing theory to practice was left to the Provinces and individual Friars. To facilitate this each Province was asked to hold an Extraordinary Chapter to determine the best way of renewing the Order at the local level. The English Province held its Extraordinary Chapter at Forest Gate during September 1968 and I was privileged to attend it. As a fundamental principle fidelity to our calling and mission as Friars Minor was emphasized again and again. It was urged that we cannot be faithful to our calling unless we are thoroughly acquainted, in a spirit of openness and generosity, with the way of life, the needs, and the aspirations of the modern world.

Space does not permit me to cover all the practical decisions of the Chapter. I select two of them: one concerning our life as brothers; the other touching on our work as followers of the Poor Christ. Every effort is to be taken to ensure that Friary life is a true expression of Franciscan Brotherhood. A Friary is a sign of the brotherhood and equality of all men. It is part of our calling to work to make the world one Friary, one Brotherhood. We live together because we believe in one another. For a sign to be effective it has to be apparent. This means that our Friaries will have to be open to the needs of people everywhere. Once people know from first-hand experience that we live together as brothers, they will no longer ask how we are Friars but only why.

All work is Franciscan work. But nobody, I think, who knows the story of St. Francis and the Leper, would deny that the service of the misfits, the despised, and the outcasts of society, is preeminently Franciscan work. The Poor Christ went out of His way to identify Himself with the hungry, the naked, the sick, and the imprisoned. Accepting a wide definition of poverty, the Chapter affirmed unanimously that work with the poor holds prior place in the apostolate of a Friar Minor. It was very edifying to hear of so much work being done for the poor by Friars in a wide variety of fields. In this connexion the work being done on our Missions in India and South Africa made a profound impression on everyone. One would never have imagined that the word 'missionary' covered such an extensive area of activity and responsibility.

My most cherished memory of the Chapter is the spirit of brotherly charity that pervaded its every session. To have shared in it was grace in abundance. I came back to East Bergholt more firmly convinced that the world cannot do without the spirit of St. Francis. It needs it as it never did before. And it will not be disappointed.

The Secret Beauty of an Ugly Little Man[1]

Most people have a very romantic idea about St. Francis. They think of him as a dashing young gallant, poetic, ambitious and very passionate, who spent his youth and early manhood in luxury and sensuality. Then having heard heavenly voices he broke with his family, gave up all his riches and spent the rest of his life as a kind of Christian troubadour, carefree and secure in his love of the gospel of Christ, singing to the sun, preaching to the birds, talking to the animals and praising the virtues of Lady Poverty.

The trouble about the romantic picture of St. Francis is not so much that it is false, as that it manages, most effectively, to neutralise the real and deadly serious and very uncomfortable aspects of his life and message. It would be a terrible failure if the celebration of the 8th centenary of his birth were to achieve nothing more than a representation of that gloriously romantic but utterly irrelevant picture of St. Francis.

The fact of the matter is that St. Francis in his early years was attractive for his eccentricity rather than his good looks. From what we know of him from the written sources, the painting at Greccio and his mortal remains in Assisi he was ugly and short—about 5ft 2ins. He always had poor health and it seems was given to bouts of deep depression. The penances he inflicted on himself after his conversion eventually took their heavy toll and he suffered all the effects of malnutrition. There is some evidence that he may even have had cancer. He was a passionate man and that drove him to throw himself into the snow and on to stinging nettles to curb temptations of the flesh. Sometimes his reactions to things he didn't approve of were excessive and cruel. For a minor infringement he ordered a friar to take off his habit in public, then, repenting of his harsh treatment of the friar he took off his own habit and exposed himself to the public.

Yet strange though it seems all this makes him more attractive than any romantic picture. His journey to holiness following in the footsteps of Christ was a long and steep and arduous path. Saints are fashioned in the crucible of suffering, self-combat and failure, they are not ready made. This is encouraging

[1] CATHOLIC HERALD (2 Oct. 1981) p. 5. Published with permission.

and hopeful for the rest of us. God's grace manages to co-exist with weakness and sins, even in the lives of the saints.

The remarkable thing about Francis of Assisi is that he listened, really listened, to the word of God speaking to him in a leper and in the gospels. Like all medieval people he loathed lepers. They were the marginated of his society. One day he saw a leper lying in the road. His instinctive reaction was to ride on quickly. But something made him stop. He got down from his horse, went to the leper and kissed him on the lips. The unthinkable had happened. This was an encounter with Christ still suffering in the world, for Christ had identified himself literally with the outcast the suffering and the poor of the world. And so the leper had evangelised Francis; he had done nothing for the leper, the leper had done everything for him.

After he had broken with his father, Francis was at Mass one day in the little chapel at the Portiuncula. He heard the priest read the gospel about the sending of the Apostles on their mission: "As you go proclaim that the Kingdom of Heaven is close at hand. . .you received without charge, give without charge. Provide yourselves with no gold or silver not even a few coppers for your purses, with no haversack for the journey or spare tunic or footwear or a staff". He took these words as a direct revelation from God and immediately embraced a life of total poverty.

Poverty was an absolute for Francis. He owned nothing. But poverty was not an end in itself. It was both a protest against the inequalities of his own time and the scandalous riches of the medieval Church, and an indispensable condition of peace. As he said with devastating simplicity, once you have possessions you need arms to defend them. Riches breed envy and fear, they bring divisions and disunity. There is not a millionaire in the world who loves his possessions more than St. Francis loved poverty. People thought he was made for divesting himself of everything. In doing so he put himself among the outcasts and the marginated. He then attempted to create an alternative society based on the fundamental evangelical teaching of brotherhood in Christ.

Thus it was that he overturned the entire medieval system which divided the nobles from the commoners, the rich from the poor, the privileged from the unfortunate.

His poverty did not make him indifferent to the suffering of the poor. The early sources tell us that he often gave away his habit and his cloak. On one occasion he gave away the only copy of the psalter they had to an old lady who came seeking alms. He told the friars "it will please the Lord Jesus and his poor Mother more than if we recited". Francis would have had no difficulty about what to do with surplus church plate.

From the gospels he grasped with unparalleled clarity that the incarnation means that God's Son became our Brother, our Friar. Friar Christ was at the heart of everything he did and said. He wanted, like John the Baptist, to fade away, so that Christ might appear ever more graphically in his life and that was a life-long task. It reached its zenith two years before he died when the marks of Christ's stigmata appeared visibly on his hands, feet and side.

Friar Christ made him Friar Francis. He realised that because God had spoken his Word in the person and life of Jesus, he had also spoken a word in every creature. And that is why Francis gave them all the sacred name of brother and sister. His friary was not a building but the whole of creation stretching to the stars. It included for Francis Friar Christ, Friar Francis himself, Sister Clare, Brother Wolf, Sister Nightingale, Brother Fire, Sister Water, his Sisters the Moon and Stars and his Brother the Sun. And from these he came to God the Father of Heaven and Earth.

His vision of creation as a unity of brother and sisters explains why Pope John Paul made St. Francis patron of ecologists and environmentalists. Francis had the same concern as environmentalists have today. He was desperately worried about senseless waste and unnecessary cruelty. We know that one of the reasons why he wrote the *Canticle of Brother Sun* was that the human race greatly offends the Creator by misusing creatures.

The memory of St. Francis then, ought to make us all a little uncomfortable. If the celebration of the 8th centenary of his birth manages to do that it will teach us the necessity of sacrifice and ever of embracing poverty in order to create a world of justice and peace. It will also teach us that those who are concerned about the environment are concerned about nothing less than the future of the earth. Should it achieve this then it will have been worthwhile to recall the 8th centenary of St. Francis' birth.

St. Francis—and God's Humility[1]

A baby with tiny finger-nails, a man bleeding and thirsty nailed to rough wood, a small white wafer held high for veneration. Little, powerless, silent. Manger, cross, bread, Bethlehem, Calvary, Eucharist.

What paradox it is and too fantastic to be false that the Creator of heaven and earth, the Mighty Lord, the Immortal and Invisible One, was born and died, was seen and touched in this world. So finely did he entwine himself in the weft and warp of human existence, submitting to the rule of time and conforming to the limits of space, that one confesses quite simply: Emmanuel—God with us. There is no better way to say it:

After the stars and the rivers, the sea and the dry land, the delicate and lovely flowers, especially lilies of the valley that bow their heads before God's gaze like shy pretty girls, the whole gigantic universe—yes after all this—the Father's Eternal Word whom creation came to be was whispered softly, sweetly into the world, while gentle silence enveloped all things and night was halfway through. They were waiting for a Wonderful Counsellor, the Prince of Peace, upon whose shoulder would be the government. And there came a little child. They expected a Messiah and "Behold the Man". He is with us now till the close of the age: "This is my body".

Bethlehem, Calvary, Eucharist

To Francis of Assisi these said everything about God's love for us and they formed the axis of his holiness. He loved the Infant Jesus, he grieved and wept over the sufferings and death of Christ, he cherished the sacrament of Christ's Body and Blood with a special and deep devotion.

The exquisite tenderness of God's love is revealed in the helplessness of a baby, the defencelessness of a crucified man, the silence of the consecrated bread and wine on the altar. God approaches us with such humility and leaves himself open to rejection. With his whole heart. Francis understood that it is the manner of God's coming to us in Jesus Christ that tells us the extent of his love for us.

---

[1] THE TROUBADOUR 28.1 (Christmas 1978) pp. 8f. Published with permission from the Province of Immaculate Conception, England.

This insight so increased Francis' love of Jesus Christ that he became the Apostle of the incarnation. It was the all-consuming mission of Francis' life to proclaim the nature and extent of God's love revealed in God's humanity.

Humility liberates because it is a virtue that springs from truth and the truth sets us free. It has nothing in common with subservience or cringing. Humility acknowledges the inherent value and proper dignity of every being. In humility the Son of God respects our dignity as free creatures of God. He appeals to us in our freedom and he awaits our response. Indeed he waits until we are ready to surrender to his love. There is no compulsion, no constraint. Through Christ's humility Francis became a humble man. In humility he honoured and loved God as the Sovereign Lord of existence, he believed God's word, he accepted himself as a creature of God and he respected and valued every fellow creature in the universe, including our distant sisters, the stars.

No matter how learned or mystical we may be, we may never ignore or neglect the divine humility in God's humanity, whereby he became intimately involved in such day-to-day things as birth and death and bread. Through faith we have the humility which recognizes and loves God in a crying infant, a dying criminal and the breaking of bread. By the testimony of the gospels it is not only the man transfigured on the mountain that we confess as the Son of the living God, but also the man with sweaty matted hair and dust between his toes, who was so exhausted that he slept in a boat on Lake Galilee during a raging storm, and the man who crawled on the ground in fear in the Garden of Gethsemani.

St. Francis brought back to the Church, in the early thirteenth century the figure of Jesus of Nazareth in all his compassion, kindness and love. People knew again the Jesus who had walked with the downtrodden and oppressed, who had loved children, who had wept when he heard that his friend Lazarus was dead. A new emphasis was given to all that brings Jesus closer to us, all that unites us to him, rather than what separates him from us. And the closeness of Jesus is God's closeness to us.

For St. Francis everything was derived from and led back to Jesus Christ. That Christ was the focal point of his life and preaching had tremendous influence on his Order. Among Franciscans, devotion has always tended to highlight the tenderness of God's love towards us and to pick out concrete details from the life of Christ. And so it is totally in character that love of the Sacred Heart devotion, to the Infant Jesus and the Holy Name and the practice of the Stations of the Cross should be distinctive features of Franciscan piety. In imitation of Francis the Order has always had special reverence for the

Eucharist, because in this sacrament, Christ remains with us and stays close to us in his littleness and humility.

Comparative Faiths—Comparative Humilities

Mary heard the word, saw the baby, combed a small boy's hair, showed him the Temple, and kept all these things in her heart.

Peter walked with him, talked with him, ate with him, laughed with him, saw him praying and confessed: "You are the Christ, the Son of the living God".

We hear the words, see the bread, feel the bread, taste the bread, hear the words, see the wine, lift the cup, taste the wine and eat and drink the Body and Blood.

St. Francis: Contemplation and Hermitages[1]

St. Francis was a contemplative. His life was centred on the mystery of God revealed in Jesus Christ who is God's Word, God's Yes to the world, made flesh. He lived in the presence of God, that is, in the present moment in such a way that everything was unified towards and around a centre. A twelfth century scholar, Alan of Lille, described God as an intelligible sphere whose centre is everywhere and whose circumference is nowhere. St. Francis concentrated his will on God as the centre-point of existence. Attending to God in this way did not engender in him an indifference to created things, rather it brought him into deeper union with everything. Having found the still centre in himself, he then discovered the heart of everything else.

Thomas of Celano, St. Francis's first biographer, records that St. Francis used every moment as an opportunity to acquire wisdom of heart. The wisdom he acquired consisted above all in humility and obedience.

He had a very clear grasp of what it means to be a creature. No created thing has meaning in itself. Its significance is derived from the almighty Creator, who is, as St. Francis writes, supreme goodness, all goodness, eternal goodness, and without whom there is no goodness. In evangelical humility Francis acknowledged the gift-character of creation. To be created is to be a gift of God. This explains the sense of gratitude which pervaded his life and why he gives thanks so often in his writings. We find him thanking God for being God, for the gift of life, for every creature, for the love revealed and shared in Christ Jesus, for every grace and for the promise of glory. He gave thanks without ceasing and he knew that thanksgiving was also a gracious gift.

The simplicity, the balance of solitude and fraternity and the respect it has for individual freedom make the *Rule for Hermitages* of significance beyond the limits of the Franciscan Order. It would provide a ready and attractive basis for small groups wishing to lead an active-contemplative life. There would be nothing to prevent the friar-mothers from working outside the hermitage for the needs of the fraternity. Nor need the number be restricted to four. But in keeping with the wishes of St. Francis to preserve

[1] MOUNT CARMEL 30.4 (Winter 1982) pp. 193-199. Published with permission.

brotherhood/sisterhood and poverty, the number should not go into two figures. Adhering to this, a basic eremitical community would not become over-burdened with organisation nor become forbidding and powerful.

His evangelical humility brought him to a unique and original understanding of obedience. Celano tells us that St. Francis said the Holy Spirit is the minister general, or highest superior of the Order. Besides that he himself writes in the *Greetings to the Virtues* "obedience leads a man to submit and subject himself to everyone in the world, and not only to human beings, but also to all beasts and wild animals". He loved Jesus Christ above all else because he became our brother, our friar. As the Word of God enfleshed, 'enhumaned', Jesus Christ is God's own exegesis of himself to humanity. In him, as in no one else, God is unfolded, revealed, to the human race. Through his love of the Word enfleshed, St. Francis knew that God had uttered a word about himself in every atom, every star, every flower, every bird and animal and in every man and woman. So it is that through his obedience Francis became a perfect listener. He listened for a word from the Holy Spirit in every creature in the world. And each whispered to him: "We are creatures like you; we are your brothers and sisters. Our beauty reflects the loveliness of God himself". Francis responded in humble obedience: "Brother Sun, Sister Moon, Brother Fox, Friar Leo, Sister Clare". Enriched with evangelical humility and so original an understanding of obedience, it was the natural outcome that St. Francis was always at prayer in this precise sense, of living constantly in the presence of God and of centring his whole being on him. He writes in the *Rule of 1221*: "All over the world, in every place, at every hour, at every moment, every day and without ceasing, we should believe truly and humbly and cherish in our heart and love, reverence, adore, serve, praise and bless, glorify and exalt, magnify and thank, the most high and supreme eternal God" (c. 23). According to this text and from ample evidence in his life, it is clear that St. Francis saw prayer first of all as an intimate relationship with the Triune God and a way of being, and then as frequent communion with God in the liturgy and periods of personal recollection.

St. Francis saw no disparity between prayer and activity. Prayer was the soul of his activity and activity was the sharing of the fruits of his prayer with others. Celano again tells us that when anyone came to see him or some unexpected business needed his attention, he would interrupt his prayer at once, and return to it afterwards in his deepest heart.

He wanted his friars to be both contemplative and active. Celano records that Francis once said: "The preacher must first draw from solitary prayer what he will later proclaim in sermons; he must first be on fire within before he speaks words which in themselves are cold".

St. Francis knew from experience the value of solitude and silence and the need of them in those committed to the active apostolate. For this reason he composed a text which testifies to that value and provides for that need. It is known as *The Rule for Hermitages* and it is one of the most remarkable of his writings.

The Text of the *The Rule for Hermitages*

1. Those friars who wish to live a life of prayer in hermitages may do so in groups of three or at most four. Two of them are to be mothers, and these are to have two sons, or at least one.
2. The two who are mothers are to lead the life of Martha; the two who are sons, the life of Mary. The sons are to be given a secluded area where each is to have a little dwelling place in which to pray and sleep.
3. They are always to recite Compline of the day immediately after sunset. They should take care to observe the silence and to pray the breviary. They should get up at the time for Matins, and seek first the kingdom of God and his justice.
4. They are to recite Prime at the proper time. After Terce they may break the silence and go to their mothers. As they judge it opportune, they may ask them for alms for the love of God like poor, humble beggars. Afterwards they are to recite Sext and None, and then Vespers at the proper time.
5. They are not to allow anyone to enter the secluded area where they live or allow them to eat there.
6. The friars who are mothers should take care to stay away from outsiders and, in obedience to their minister, to protect their sons from outsiders so that no one disturbs them. The sons are to speak to no one except to their mothers and to the minister or custos, when these choose to visit them, with the blessing of the Lord God.
7. The sons may sometimes take their turn at the office of mothers, as seems best to them at the time. But they should strive to observe carefully and eagerly all that has been laid down in this Rule.

This simple document, written sometime between 1217 and 1221, marks a new development in the history of the eremitical life. Despite the use of the word 'rule', this is more a spiritual directive than a legal code. In no way was St. Francis a lawyer.

The text is infused with the spirit of brotherhood and poverty. The friars who want to lead the eremitical life must do so precisely as friars minor, that is, as poor, humble brothers. In the mind of St. Francis the hermit life cannot be separated from the life of fraternal love because fraternal love is the surest guarantee that the spirit of prayer and devotion is present in any community. By situating the eremitical life and the pursuit of contemplative union with God firmly in the context of a small fraternity, St. Francis excluded all individualistic and egocentric motives, such as the desire to get away from others, as reasons for embracing it. The fraternity has to be small—not more than four friars—in order to preserve poverty. As far as St. Francis was concerned, large communities of hermits living together would not have been in accordance with evangelical poverty. St. Francis wanted the eremitical life, just as much as the active apostolate, to be firmly established on the three pillars of fraternity, poverty and prayer. The *Rule for Hermitages* is the product of a vision of the Church as the poor, holy, pilgrim People of God.

The first paragraph reveals at once St. Francis' profound respect for the working of God's grace in the individual friar. It is certain, according to Celano, that St. Francis "wanted his friars to live not only in cities, but also in hermitages". Nevertheless, the decision as to which friars should live in hermitages depended entirely on the Holy Spirit.

There is no indication whether those who chose to live the eremitical life did so permanently or only for a time. That, therefore, has to remain an open question. But given the intrinsic value of solitude and silence in which the Holy Spirit reaches "even the depths of God" [1 Corinthians 2:10], it can be safely assumed that St. Francis would have welcomed lifelong hermits in his Order. In any case, it is clear that any friar who wished to withdraw for longer or shorter periods from active work, was free to do so.

The text says that the hermits are to live "in groups of three or at most four. Two of them are to be mothers, and these are to have two sons, or at least one". However, as the text always refers to both in the plural, we may conclude that St. Francis preferred them to live in groups of four.

Two of the friars are to be mothers. The idea of motherhood held a paramount place in St. Francis' spiritual vision. He himself was generously gifted with motherly tenderness. He had a finely developed *anima*. On one occasion Friar Pacificus addressed him as "dearest mother". He expected every friar to have a maternal love for his brethren: "Wherever friars are and meet one another, they should show that they are members of the same family. With confidence let them make their needs known to one another. For if a mother loves and provides for her natural child, with how much more care should a friar love and provide for his spiritual brother?" (*Rule of 1223*, c. 6). Spiritual motherhood, according to St. Francis, is a distinguishing feature of the true disciple of Christ: "We are mothers to him (Christ) when we carry him in our heart and body through divine love and by an honest and sincere conscience. We give birth to him by our good works, which should shine out as an example for others" (*Letter to the Faithful* I 1).

The chief duties of the friars who are mothers in the hermitage are to provide for the material needs of the sons, to take care of them with a mother's love and to protect them from disturbance in their life of prayer. Whether the mothers are superiors in a technical sense, is difficult to decide, first, because there are two of them and, second, because they are free, according to the seventh paragraph, to exchange places with the sons whenever that seems best to them.

According to the second paragraph the mothers are to lead the life of Martha and the sons the life of Mary. Here St. Francis is influenced by the traditional analogy, taken from St. Luke's gospel [10:38-42] of Martha as the prototype of the active life, and Mary as the prototype of the contemplative life.

The four friars are to pray the office together. The Eucharist is not mentioned, but can be taken for granted. Where one of the friars was a priest, he would have celebrated Mass for the fraternity. If there was no priest, then they would have attended a local church.

The purpose of the hermitage is clearly stated in paragraph 3: the friars are to seek above all else the kingdom of God and his justice. God's reign in the heart brings truth and life, love and peace. His justice gives holiness or integrity, whereby what we are and what we will, become one. No details are laid down about how this is to be achieved. Each is left complete freedom to discover his own road to God, in union with him who is the Way, the Truth and the Life.

After the silence the sons may speak to the mothers and, presumably, to one another. With humility and confidence they may ask for what they need from the mothers.

The stipulation that the mothers should stay away from outsiders can only have referred to unnecessary contact. There would obviously have been times when they had to go for alms. What St. Francis says in the *Rule of 1221* will also have applied to hermitages: "When necessary, let them go for alms" (c. 9). The sons were totally dependent on the mothers, which serves to emphasize the close link there is between fraternal charity and contemplation. We are all, in fact, dependent on one another in our search for God and his peace. On this question of contact with outsiders, there is another relevant text in the *Rule of 1221*: "Wherever they are, whether in a hermitage or in any other place, the friars should be on their guard not to have ownership of the place or to defend it against anyone. Whoever comes to them, friend or enemy, thief or villain, is to be received with kindness" (c. 7). The hermitage, therefore, is not completely cut off from the outside world, though the duty to look after visitors obviously rests on the mothers.

The simplicity, the balance of solitude and fraternity and the respect it has for individual freedom make the *Rule for Hermitages* of significance beyond the limits of the Franciscan Order. It would provide a ready and attractive basis for small groups wishing to lead an active-contemplative life. There would be nothing to prevent the friar-mothers from working outside the hermitage for the needs of the fraternity. Nor need the number be restricted to four. But in keeping with the wishes of St. Francis to preserve brotherhood/sisterhood and poverty, the number should not go into two figures. Adhering to this, a basic eremitical community would not become over-burdened with organization nor become forbidding and powerful.

Canterbury Friary Journal
August 1984[1]

It is right for our community to record the dedication of Fr. Eric over so many years to the life of St. Francis growing in each of the friars, his friendship and love for all of us, his joy and gift of himself wherever the brothers were in need of him. We can also say that what he has done to encourage friars from all over the Province was never clearer than in his work for the Provincial Chapter in July. Those who depended most heavily on him are not abandoned now through the shock of his sudden death: he is closer to us now than ever, as close as he always desired to be, but was unable to be through the limitations of human living. Now he is with God, nearer to us than we are to ourselves.

He had been elected to the Definitory at the Chapter but fell ill at their first meeting and when this finished, he returned to Canterbury on 21st July. He was admitted to Kent & Canterbury Hospital for examination of his stomach, which was distended. The observation of the consultation when fluid was found to be the cause, lying between the outside of the stomach and the wall of his abdomen was 'I do not think this is unconnected with the previous melanoma situation?'

On Monday 23rd July, he was transferred to Mount Alvernia Hospital in Guildford, where chemotherapy began on Friday. On the 2nd August, Eric went to Chilworth for a break, and returned to Canterbury on the 8th August. On the 12th, he was at Ladywell Convent and back in Mount Alvernia on the 13th.

During this illness, he went to keep a promise he had made to the St. John of God Brothers, to address their Chapter, which he did on Wednesday 8th August, and again on Thursday 9th.

During Mass on the 14th, he received the sacrament of healing, at which his mother was present.

---

[1] Published with permission from the Province of Immaculate Conception, England.

He accepted the second row of chemotherapy but on Friday 17th it was apparent that this was ineffective.

Secondaries affected Eric's brain to the extent that his right side was paralysed, though he retained his speech and understood what was said to him.

Eric died peacefully, with a full joyful acceptance of his death. It happened early in the morning (1:15 AM) of Saturday 25th August. Those who were present at his death were his mother, his sister Margaret, his niece Carmel, Sr. Maria, who nursed him with great love and care, Sr. Angela and Austin Linus.

At his Requiem Mass at Chilworth, many of Eric's friends filled the Church, including 105 priests, to whom so much of his work was devoted. Fr. Luke, the Provincial, who presided, spoke of the completeness of Eric's life and work, consoling us with this mystery of God's ways, his path of friendship. There was an extraordinary peace and openness among everyone present, just as there had been when Eric's body was first brought to the Church. The Mass itself was at midday, 12:00 on Friday 31st August, and Eric was buried, as he dearly wished, in the friary cemetery at Chilworth.

Poem

by Tracy Hansen[2]

Will the birds sing at Chilworth tomorrow, I wonder,
or will they be driven by windstorm and thunder
under the dying leaves
of the golden, tarnished trees?
Will the ending of summer be lingering still
or the first chill of winter creep over to fill
the hollow you've left behind
as a grieveprint on my mind?
Whatever the wildlife, whatever the weather,
you will not contemplate sunshine or feather,
but I shall be watching, and I will remember ,
and I shall remember you every September.

Your dying day; to me it seems
like all the days I saw—
the earth turned through the same degrees
of daylight as before—
Except there is a hollow in
the leafy, shaded place
you used to walk, and shadows on
my image of your face.

[2] THE TROUBADOUR (Christmas 1984). Published with permission from the Province of Immaculate Conception, England.

Photo 7

With provincial minister
Urban Judge OFM

Photo 8 below

With his patron
for his doctoral thesis,
Dr. Lucien Ceyssens OFM

**Photo 9
and 10** (next page)

1983 with
Alcuin Coyle OFM,
who invited him
to teach at
St. Bonaventure
University, New York,
USA

Photo 11 above
With general minister
John Vaughn OFM, Canterbury
1983

Photo 12
With original student fraternity at Ronton (San Damiano Friary),
1978

On Saint Bonaventure

St. Bonaventure's Prayer
for the Seven Gifts of the Holy Spirit[1]

We pray the most merciful Father,
through You, his only-begotten Son,
made man for us, crucified and glorified,
that he send us from his treasures the Spirit of sevenfold grace
who rested upon you in all fullness.

The spirit, that is, of wisdom,
that we may savour the life-giving taste
of the fruit of the Tree of Life, which you truly are;

the gift of understanding,
which enlightens the insights of our mind;

the gift of counsel,
whereby we may set out on our journey along right paths,
following in Your footsteps;

the gift of fortitude,
through which we may overcome
the violent assaults of the Enemy;

the gift of knowledge,
by which we may be filled
with the brilliance of your sacred teaching
to discern good from evil;

---

[1] Trans. by E. Doyle from St. Bonaventure's *Tree of Life* in: THE TABLET (8 July 1974) p. 567. Published with permission (www.thetablet.co.uk).

the gift of piety,
that we may clothe our hearts with mercy;
the gift of fear,
whereby, drawing away from all evil,
we may be at peace
in the reverential love of your eternal Majesty.

For You have willed us to ask for these things
in that holy prayer you taught us;
so now we implore them of you
through your holy cross and
to the praise of your most holy name.

To whom, with the Father and the Holy Spirit,
be all honour and glory, thanksgiving, splendour and power
for ever and ever.
Amen.

Saint Francis and Franciscan Theology[1]

The year 1981 sees the anniversary of three of the first four Ecumenical Councils: Constantinople I (381), Ephesus (431), and Chalcedon (451). They marked critical stages in the Church's early history as she sought to answer with increasing clarity the gospel question: "Who do you say I am?"

It is native to the Church's faith to recognize that any assertion about Jesus Christ necessarily involves fundamental issues about the meaning of life and death. Through the mystery of Christ the Church knows that all statements about God automatically say something about humanity, and all statements about the origin, purpose, and destiny of human beings say ultimately something about God. If we get it wrong about the one, we inevitably get it wrong about the other.

Since the 1500th anniversary of Chalcedon in 1951 thousands of books, articles, and studies have been written about the person, mission, and significance of Jesus Christ. In recent years we have had the stimulating and provocative books by H. Küng and E. Schillebeeckx, and the interesting and sometimes startling works from Cambridge by M. Wiles and lately D. Cupitt.

A study of developments in Christology over the past thirty years has convinced me that the Franciscan Order ought to enter into a more sustained and extensive dialog with its theological tradition, especially in the period from the conversion of Saint Francis to the death of Duns Scotus.

I believe we possess a treasure of inestimable riches. The Franciscan theological tradition has a distinctive, indeed unique approach to reality which has a relevance now greater than ever before.

We owe our origins to a poor unlettered man who sparked off an astounding spiritual and theological movement. Devoid of all preconceived ideas about what God is or should be like, he was drawn by the instinct of faith to imitate the life of the gospel Christ through which his own life became a dramatic and poetic exegesis of the person, mission, and teaching of Jesus Christ.

---

[1] THE CORD 31.8 (1981) pp. 226f. Published with permission from The Franciscan Institute, St. Bonaventure University, New York.

His life was the morning star of the Franciscan vision of the world. According to Saint Bonaventure Francis himself was a theological source, a *locus theologicus*. It is of course a truism to say that Franciscan theology is christocentric. The point about a truism is that it is true. This characteristic is the ground of its methodology where God and humanity, spirit and matter, faith and reason, imagination and intellect, mind and heart, image and word are taken simply and precisely in their historical unity.

To pursue very briefly one example, the relationship between faith and reason. Do we really have such sure evidence to assign them to quite separate compartments? The whole of human life and history is based on many tacit assumptions and surrounded by mysteries which make it extremely questionable whether there is such a thing as "pure reason". This is not to deny the powers of reason or its right to function—a study of the writings of Saint Bonaventure makes that clear—but to argue that reason is subject to truths and realities which it does not create but discovers as the condition of its own rationality. There are so many other areas, too: the primacy of charity, the primacy of Christ, the symbolic character of creatures; but they cannot be treated here.

My plea is therefore that we initiate a fresh dialog with our theological past. It will bring us speedily into fruitful dialog with our own time.

The Seraphic Doctor[1]

Earlier this year we commemorated the seventh centenary of the death of St Thomas Aquinas, the Angelic and Common Doctor. This month marks the same centenary of the death of St Bonaventure, the Seraphic Doctor, during the second Council of Lyons on 15 July 1274. The writings of these two saints brought thirteenth-century Scholasticism to its splendid climax. With St. Thomas, Christian Aristotelianism found its most perfect expression; with St. Bonaventure, medieval Augustinianism received its final synthesis.

St. Bonaventure is preeminently a doctor of mystical theology. One closes his works with a sense of sorrow that he has not been more widely read and studied. He ranks among—even towers above—those authors in the Tradition of western mysticism who hold out the very riches of contemplative peace which so many people set off to search for in the east, riches they had not found or been offered in the west.

St. Bonaventure was born in 1217 at Bagnorea, a little town in Italy, lying between Orvieto and Viterbo. In 1233 he went to Paris to study arts. By 1243 he was Master of Arts and in that year he joined the Franciscan Order. He came under the direct influence of Alexander of Hales, a learned clerk from Gloucestershire, who had entered the order in Paris in 1231. He said of St. Bonaventure that it seemed Adam had not sinned in him. St. Bonaventure obtained the doctorate in theology in 1254. Three years later he was elected Minister General of the Franciscan Order. This meant he had to relinquish the calm and serenity of his study in order to guide the young fraternity through some of its most critical years. In October 1259, he went up La Verna in Tuscany—the holy mount of the Franciscan Order—to meditate on the life of St Francis, at the very spot where he had received the sacred stigmata in September 1224—month and year the Franciscans first arrived in England. From his experiences on La Verna came St. Bonaventure's loveliest of mystical works *The Journey of the Mind to God,* in which he traces the soul's ascent to contemplative union with God. In 1265 he was nominated Archbishop of York by Pope Clement IV, but he managed to get the Pope to rescind the nomination.

---

[1] THE TABLET (13 July 1974) pp. 668-70. Published with permission (www.thetablet.co.uk).

In 1273 he was created Cardinal-Bishop of Albano and tradition has it that he was washing dishes when the news of the appointment was brought to him. After taking an active part in the deliberations of the Council of Lyons, he died in that city on the morning of 15 July 1274.

This would not be the place to enter again into the question of the character of St. Bonaventure's philosophy. That his works contain material that is undoubtedly philosophy will be obvious to all who have read them. Fr. Copleston's presentation is proof enough of this.[2] If, however, one understands by philosophy only the product of unaided human reason, then one will search in vain for this in the works of St Bonaventure. His writings contain the quintessence of medieval Augustinianism and it is only in the context of the synthesis of Augustinianism he created, that one can grasp the meaning of his Christian philosophy. His doctrinal synthesis may be summarized in the three ideas: emanation, exemplarity and consummation. All creation proceeds from God, all creatures reflect the divine exemplar according to which they were created and they return to God for whom they were created. One may not compare the philosophy of St. Bonaventure with that of St Thomas, for the simple reason that they begin from totally differing presuppositions. For St. Bonaventure there is no such entity as unaided human reason, in the sense in which St. Thomas takes it; philosophy cannot be separated from theology and indeed, there is no self-sufficient philosophy outside the faith. Philosophy is the result of the human mind's being illumined by God's light, which enables it to discover God's presence in the universe. Reason, in fact, is restored to itself by the light of God's revelation. There is no rejection of Aristotle as such in the works of St. Bonaventure; what he impugned to the end was a self-sufficient philosophy.

Echoes in Karl Barth

There is an extraordinary similarity between St Bonaventure and Karl Barth on the question of the relation of philosophy and theology. But the likeness goes much further. They hold identical positions on the epistemological foundation of theology, the special kind of knowledge that is faith-knowledge, the understanding of the 'ontological' argument of St. Anselm, the sovereignty of the Word of God. They are doctors of the adage *Credo ut intelligam.* Knowledge from faith is for St. Bonaventure, as it is for Karl Barth, super-eminently rational. Anyone looking for a thesis topic in

---

[2] *A History of Philosophy* in: *Medieval Philosophy—Augustine to Scotus*, London 1959, pp. 243-292.

theology would find a comparative study of Bonaventure and Barth a fascinating and worthwhile pursuit.

St. Bonaventure was a mystic who wrote works of mystical theology. Though influenced extensively by St Augustine, Dionysius, St Bernard and the Victorines, it is St Francis who was his principal inspiration and constant point of reference. No matter how far he travels in speculative genius, the link with St Francis is never lost. He loved St Francis in a very special way, as he himself avows quite unaffectedly in one of his sermons on the saint. It is no exaggeration to say that his mystical theology is a commentary on the holiness of St Francis.

For him the revelation of God is required in order that we may be able to read the book of creation. Through God's Word man is enabled to know the world as it really is: "The universe is like a book reflecting, representing and describing its Maker, the Trinity, at three different levels of expression: as a trace, an image and a likeness". By every creature in the world the soul rises gradually, till it reaches at last ecstatic union with God. This totally positive attitude to creation at every level of existence, as an intrinsic element in the soul's ascent to union with God, marks a sharp distinction between St. Bonaventure and the Pseudo-Dionysius and, for that matter, between St. Bonaventure and St. Bernard. The inspiration here is completely that of St. Francis. Every creature, every art, every science, including philosophy itself, always points beyond itself to the Ultimate Mystery of God wherein all is silence, rest and peace.

The ascent to contemplative union with God begins with prayer which is "the mother and source of all ecstasy".[3] The final aim of all prayer is to attain the mystical Passover with Christ on the cross where rest is given to the understanding and the affection of the will passes over entirely to God:

> In this passing over, if it is to be perfect,
> all intellectual activities ought to be relinquished
> and the most profound affection transported to God,
> and transformed into him.
> This, however, is mystical and most secret,
> 'which no one knows except him who receives it',

---

[3] *The Journey of the Mind to God* 1:1.

no one receives except him who desires it,
and no one desires except him
who is penetrated to the marrow by the fire of the Holy Spirit,
whom Christ sent into the world.
That is why the Apostle says that
this mystical wisdom is revealed
by the Holy Spirit.[4]

Reflecting further in the *Collationes in Hexaemeron* on this supreme union of love with God, St Bonaventure explains that love here transcends every intellect and every science. This wisdom—which surpasses all knowledge—is union, in which the mind is joined to God where, in one sense it sleeps, in another it keeps vigil. Only the affection of the will is awake, silence is imposed upon all the other powers of the soul: "In this union the power of the soul is recollected, and it becomes more unified, and enters in its intimate self, and consequently it rises up to its summit: for according to Augustine, the intimate self and the summit are the same".[5] These sections of the *Collationes in Hexaemeron* may be taken as a commentary on the final chapter of *The Journey of the Mind to God*. They describe, as it were, the other side of the Passover and they manifest that the proper act of the gift of wisdom is not cognitive but affective because wisdom and ecstasy are identical.

Infused contemplation and Christian perfection are interchangeable terms in St. Bonaventure's theology. Contemplation involves three elements: the silence of the intellect, the passivity of the will and the "taste" of God—this last in virtue of union with him, granting to the soul a knowledge which is inseparable from joy. Thought cannot attain this knowledge. Everyone is called to this union with God, it is not the prerogative of a few chosen ones. Infused contemplation—is St. Bonaventure's understanding of the gospel injunction: "Be perfect as your heavenly Father is perfect".

The theology of St. Bonaventure proceeds from prayer and it leads the student to its highest peak. All theological endeavour is directed to the holy mystery of God; theology, according to St Bonaventure, is indeed a *reductio in mysterium*. Among the indispensable elements of theology of the future must

---

[4] *The Journey of the Mind to God*, VII 4 in: *Works of Saint Bonaventure. . . .Saint Bonaventure's Itinerarium Mentis in Deum*, The Franciscan Institute, Saint Bonaventure, N.Y. 1956, p. 99.
[5] *2nd Collation*, 30-31, de Vinck, v, pp. 36-38.

be the conviction that theology is not and never can he a purely intellectual exercise if it is to remain theology, not merely in the sense that it must always have a message for the human condition, but above all in the sense that it already affects the human condition by changing the theologian through the wisdom it ultimately brings which surpasses all knowledge.

St. Bonaventure's Sermons on St. Francis
A Comparison of the Quaracchi Edition with Some Manuscripts[1]

Volume IX of the *Opera Omnia* of St. Bonaventure, published in 1901 at Quaracchi, contains six sermons on St Francis. There is one *De Translatione St. Francisci* (534a-535b) and five *De S. Patre nostro Francisco* (573a-597b). Of these, four are by St. Bonaventure: I, II, IV and V; the remaining one, III, is by an unnamed cardinal, probably Odo of Chatcauroux[2].

Since the publication of the Quaracchi edition new manuscripts have come to light[3]. During the course of translating these sermons into English[4], I decided it was necessary to consult the additional manuscripts for my translation to be reliable. Therefore I obtained microfilm copies of the following: Berlin, Staatsbibliothek, theol. lat. oct. 31, f. 47r-v; Bordeaux, Bibliotheque Municipale, 402, ff. 244ra-249va; Cambridge, Jesus College Library, Q.G.6. ff. 212r-214r; Munich, Staatsbibliothek, Clm 23372, ff. 119v—124r; Paris, Bibliotheque Nationale, lat. 14595, ff. 118r-v, 148r-150r; lat. 3747, ff. 356ra-361ra; Vendome, Bibliotheque Municipale, 218, ff. 125v-127v.

I examined these texts and compared them with the Quaracchi edition of the sermons. These are my findings[5].

Sermo I: MS Paris, Bibl. Nat., lat. 14595, f. l49v-150r. This is an abbreviated, though faithful, version of the sermon. It is of no more than confirmatory value.

Sermo II: MS Berlin, Staatsbibliothek, theol. lat. oct. 31, f. 47r-v. This is an abbreviated, though faithful, version of the sermon.

MS Cambridge, Jesus Coll. Lib., Q.G.6, ff. 212r-214r. This gives the full text of the sermon in a clear, legible hand. It is independent of the Troyes MS used for the Quaracchi edition.

[1] ARCHIVUM FRANCICANUM HISTORICUM 75 (1982) pp. 416-420. Published with permission.

[2] See I. Brady OFM, *St. Bonaventure's Sermons on Saint Francis* in: FRANZISKANISCHE STUDIEN 58 (1976) pp. 132-137.

[3] L.J. Bataillon OP, *Sur Quelques Sermons de Saint Bonaventure, in: St. Bonaventura 1274-1974. II. Studia de Vita, Mente, Fontibus et Operibus Sancti Bonaventurae*, Coll. St. Bonaventura, Grottaferrata Roma 1973, p. 514.

[4] Editors' note: Doyle's English edition of the Sermons was published by Franciscan Herald Press, Chicago. See bibliography.

[5] I give only the most significant variations and additions.

1. In place of "ut nec minus alte" (IX, 575b), it has "ut [nec] prolixe nec abbreviate loquitur" (f. 212r).

2. It confirms the use of "senex" (f. 212r) questioned by the Quaracchi editor (IX, 575b).

3. It has "per quam in Deum excessit" (f. 212r) in place of "per quam in Deum (se) erexit" (IX, 576a).

4. It reads "quia est simplex in intentione mentis; timens Deum in affectione; et recedens a malo in operatione, divino servitio fuit deputatus et cultor Dei magnificus" (f. 212r-212v) in place of "quia est simplex in intentione mentis; timens Deum in affectione; et recedens a malo, in operatione divina, servus fuit computatus et cultor Dei magnificus" (IX, 576b).

5. It has "et nudus venit coram toto populo dicens omnia temporalia dimisit. Postquam fuit vir eximiae sanctitatis fecit se nudum trahi per lutum. Non potuit audire quod laudaretur" (f. 213r) in place of "et nudus venit coram episcopo et omnia temporalia dimisit, postea fuit vir eximiae sanctitatis" (IX, 577b).

6. It gives "sicut etiam in novo testamento omnes se humiliabant" (f. 213r) in place of "sicut etiam in nomine tuo omnes (se) humiliabant" (IX, 578a).

7. It has "et tunc iuvenis non sentit carnis pruritum" (f. 213r) in place of "et in venis non sentit carnis pruritum" (IX, 578b).

8. It gives "servatur a sororibus Sancti Damiani" (f. 214v). The Quaracchi editor supplied the text "narratur, quod in ecclesia" (IX, 580b) and see the editor's n. 6: "Verba parenthesis supplevimus, pro quibus codex habet *servatur a* et deinde lacunam".

9. It specifies "in ecclesia beati Ruffini" (f. 215l); whereas the Quaracchi editor gave "in ecclesia (cathedrali)" (IX, 581a) and noted a lacuna in the codex, see the editor's n. 4.

10. It has "et quod abominetur creaturam praesentem, praeteritam et futuram" (f. 215r) in place of "et quod abominetur creaturam praesentem" (IX, 581b).

MS Paris, Bibl. Nat., lat. 3747, ff. 356ra-361ra. This gives the full text in a clear hand and is independent of MS Cambridge and MS Troyes.

1. In place of "ut nec minus alte" (IX, 575b), it has "ut nec nimis alte loquatur nec nimis infime" (f. 356ra).

2. It omits "senex" (f. 356ra).

3. F. 356va; as in MS Cambridge, see above, 3.

4. It gives "et nudus venit coram episcopo et omnia temporalia dimisit. Postquam fuit vir eximiae sanctitatis fecit se nudum trahi per lutum. Non potuit audire quod laudaretur" (f. 357rb) in place of the Quaracchi text given under MS Cambridge, 5.

5. It also gives "servatur a sororibus Sancti Damiani" (f. 359vb), see above under MS Cambridge, 8.

6. It has the same text (f. 360rb) as MS Cambridge, 10.

Sermo III: (Odo of Chateauroux) MS Bordeaux, Bibl. Mun., 402, ff. 244ra-246va. This is a complete, clear and reliable text.

1. It adds "et habui diu quia inveni illum" (f. 244rb) to the (Quaracchi text "quia habui eum propitium mihi" (IX, 583a).

2. It has "Dedit enim illi Dominus remissionem omnium peccatorum et de hoc habuit etiam responsionem et revelationem adhuc vivens in corpore" (f. 245va) in the place of "Dedit enim illi Dominus remissionem omnium peccatorum adhuc viventi in corpore" (IX, 584b).

Sermo IV : MS Bordeaux, Bibl. Mun., 402, ff. 246va-249va. This gives the full text of the sermon.

1. It adds "Et sicut voluit signum victoriae ponere in ipso Constantino, sic et voluit signum ponere poenitentiae in beato Francisco" (f. 247ra)—see IX, 587a.

2. It gives "In quo caelo libenter sederet Dominus?" (f. 247rb) in place of "In quo caelo libenter (habitat) Dominus?" (IX, 587a).

3. It reads „secundum veritatem" (f. 247rb) rather than „secundum virtutem" (IX, 587a).

4. It adds "quia in ea pauperrimus fuit, ita ut non [habuit] panniculum ad tegenda verenda sua micturarum, etiam beatus Franciscus altissimam paupertatem praeelegit" (f. 247va) after the words in IX, 587b "Si ergo crux Christi signum est paupertatis".

5. It adds "graviter affligendo et" (f. 247vb) after "carnem suam castigando et" (IX, 588a).

6. It adds "sic quod nullus labor est ibi, nulla inordinatio, nulla poena" (f. 248ra) to "trahit omnes alias" (IX, 588a).

7. It reads "quid sibi videretur de se ipso, quid de se sentiret" (f. 248rb) which is a preferable reading for it requires no editorial addition: "quaesivit ab eo, quid sibi videretur (et) de (se) ipso sentiret" (IX, 588b).

8. It adds "secundum quod sonat nomen eius. Iste bene fuit frater minor humillimus et modicus" (f. 248rb) after "summus" (IX, 588b). This, I think, is the only occasion where St. Bonaventure actually describes a biblical figure as a friar minor.

9. It reads "tunc ergo magis illuminatur secundum veritatem" (f. 249ra) rather than "secundum virtutem" (IX, 590a).

10. It supplies the lacuna noted by the editor (IX, 590a): "quattuor virtutes cardinales et tres theologicas" (f. 249va).

11. It supplies the lacuna noted by the editor (IX, 590b): "caloribus inflammans per suffragia devotae orationis, et fulgoribus coruscans per miracula sanctitatis et virtutis" (f. 249va).

Sermo V: MS Paris, Bibl. Nat., lat. 14595, ff. 148r-149v. This is an abbreviated, though faithful version of the sermon. It is of confirmatory value.

MS Vendome, Bibl. Mun., 218, ff. 125v-127v. This is a moderately long synopsis of the sermon in very small hand-writing, somewhat difficult to read. However, it was of confirmatory value.

Sermo De Translatione MS Munich, Staatsbibl., Clm 23372, ff. 119v-124r. Lerner's transcription is a faithful copy of the text[6] however, there are grounds for different interpretations of some of his dispositions of the text.

MS Paris, Bibl. Nat., lat. 14595, f. n8r-v. This is an abbreviated, though faithful, version of the sermon. It is of confirmatory value.

On the basis of this comparison it seems advisable that a new edition be made of Sermones II, III, and IV. I hope to undertake this task in the not-too-distant future.[7]

---

[6] R.E. Lerner, *A Collection of Sermons given in Paris c. 1267*, including a new text by St. Bonaventure on the life of Saint Francis in: SPECULUM 49 (1974) pp. 491-498.

[7] Editors' note: This new edition was realized in 1983 with the publication of Doyle's book *The Disciple and the Master—St. Bonaventure's Sermons on St. Francis of Assisi*, Chicago: Franciscan Herald Press, 1983.

St. Bonaventure on St. Dominic[1]

One medieval mystic preaches about another,
whom he greatly admired.

The lives of St. Dominic and St. Francis have been goldmines for iconographers and hagiographers through the centuries. The friendship between them and their alleged meetings have provided ready materials for both. Under the critical eye of the historian, however, these episodes are stripped of their romanticism and they appear extremely limp when hedged about with hypotheses and qualified by long and learned footnotes.[2] But it cannot be denied that the friendship between the two saints and their various meetings are among the episodes best known to readers of the lives of both. To the popular mind, indeed, the history of the relations between the two Orders is characterized precisely by the close friendship of the two founders at the beginning and by antagonism and petty squabbles between their followers ever since. The naivety and shallowness of this vulgar view need not detain us here. What is not quite so well known—if it is known at all outside a small circle of savants—is St. Bonaventure's love and understanding of St. Dominic and the place of St. Dominic and the Dominican Order in his theology of history. St. Bonaventure's theological reflections on these deserve a wider public, not least because they concern St. Dominic, who ranks among the most attractive and warm-hearted of medieval saints.

Among the sermons of St. Bonaventure published by the Quaracchi Editors, there is a profound and very beautiful meditation on the holiness and virtues of St. Dominic.[3] The text is based on two manuscripts. one from the beginning of the fourteenth century, conserved at Todi: the other from the

---

[1] SUPPLEMENT TO DOCTRINE AND LIFE 52 (July-August 1974) pp. 26-46. Published with permission.

[2] See M.H. Vicaire OP, *St. Dominic and His Times*, transl. by K. Pond, London 1964, pp. 201, 494, 500, 504, 515; W.A. Hinnebusch OP, *The History of the Dominican Order. Origin and Growth to 1500*, vol. One, Alba House, New York 1965, pp. 154f., 165f.; O. Englebert, *St. Francis of Assisi. A Biography*, second English edition, trans. by E.M. Cooper, Chicago 1965, pp. 474f.

[3] *Doctoris Seraphici St. Bonaventurae. . . .Opera Omnia. . . .Tomus IX. . . .Sermones de Tempore, de Sanctis, de Beata Virgine Maria et de Diversis*, Ad Claras Aquas 1901, pp. 562-565.

fifteenth century, conserved at Florence. The authenticity of the sermon is beyond any doubt—a conclusion based on internal evidence furnished by several sections of the sermon, which summarise or touch on specifically Bonaventurian themes. The attractiveness of the sermon lies in the account it gives of St. Dominic's holiness, zeal and kindness. It tells us also how much St. Bonaventure must have loved and revered St. Dominic. The importance of the sermon comes from the indications it contains of the place given to St. Dominic and his Order in St. Bonaventure's theology of history.

This year commemorates the seventh centenary of the death of St. Bonaventure at the Council of Lyons in July 1274—as it marks the same centenary of the death of St. Thomas Aquinas. It is fitting, therefore, to present these reflections on St. Dominic in a periodical published by the Order he founded.

St. Bonaventure's Metaphysics of Light[4]

To appreciate the content of the sermon we need to recall briefly St. Bonaventure's theory of divine illumination and to place the sermon against the background of least three of his major works: the *Itinerarium mentis in Deum,* the *De Reductione Artium ad Theologiam* and the *Collationes in Hexaemeron.*

In St. Bonaventure's theory of knowledge there is an essential relationship between light and truth and he adheres unswervingly to the doctrine of illumination. It is in his theory of knowledge one finds, perhaps most clearly of all, the fundamental unity of intellectual and spiritual life, that is, the unity of *lectio, speculatio* and *unctio.* Light and truth are interchangeable terms : "Divine Truth is itself Light".[5] "Truth is the light of the soul. This light never falls".[6] The human intellect is a light from God and the truth of all knowledge rests in God who is the light wherein we apprehend the unchanging and unchangeable truth of reality. All knowledge, in fact, comes about "by

---

[4] See B.A. Gendreau, *The Quest for Certainty in Bonaventure* in: FRANCISCAN STUDIES 21 (1961), pp. 104-227; E. Gilson, *The Philosophy of St Bonaventure,* trans. by Dom I. Trethowan and F.J. Sheed, St. Antony Guild Press, Paterson N.J. 1965, pp. 127-146, 245-264, 309-390; F. Copleston, *A History of Philosophy,* vol. II: *Medieval Philosophy. Augustine to Scotus,* London 1959, pp. 240-292; P.M. de Zamayon OFM Cap, *Teoria del conocimiento secun S. Buenaventura. La Illuminacion in St. Bonaventura* 1274-1974 III: *Philosophica,* Coll. St. Bonaventura, Grottaferrata Roma 1973, pp. 407-430; T. Crowley OFM, *Illumination and Certitude,* ibid., pp. 431-448.

[5] *Quaestiones Disputatae de Scientia Christi,* III, *conclusio Opera Omnia* V, 14a.

[6] *Collationes in Hexaemeron* IV, 1, *Opera Omnia* V, p. 394a.

reason of the uncreated light".[7] However, the Eternal Light which is God, is not directly perceived nor is it an object immediately known, because of itself the Eternal Light is inaccessible, though it is most close to the soul; it is unconfinable, though it is also supremely intimate.[8] To apprehend any truth at all it is required that there be immutability in object known and infallibility in the knowing subject.[9] On these two conditions depends all certain knowledge. God alone is immutable and therefore he must aid the human intellect in arriving at the certitude which, as a matter of experience, it undoubtedly possesses. Certain knowledge must in some way be established on the divine ideas; it must be related to the *ars superna,* the divine ideas (*rationes aeternae*) as to light and truth: light which gives infallibility to the knower and truth which gives immutability to the object of knowledge. The illumination of the human intellect by the divine ideas has a regulating and motive action in the process of arriving at certitude. However. the divine ideas do not have the sole influence in our acquisition of knowledge, nor are they known in their total clarity. They exercise their influence only through created reason and they are but dimly contuited by us in our pilgrim state here on earth.[10] There is, then, no question in his theory of knowledge of dispensing with sense data. nor with the process of abstraction. By divine illumination the human intellect grasps in the object known the reflection of the immutable, eternal idea and thus arrives at certain knowledge. Creatures are the *exemplata* of the divine exemplar—a truth which manifests the intimate connexion between St. Bonaventure's theory of divine illumination and his doctrine of exemplarism. The Eternal Ideas are one with the Word of God. Christ

> teaches interiorly, so that no truth is known except through him, not through speech as it is with us, but through inner enlightenment. Wherefore He must necessarily have within himself the most clear species, which He cannot possibly have received from another. He Himself, then, is intimate to every soul and he shines forth by means of his most clear species upon the obscure species of our understanding. And in this manner, these obscure species mixed with the darkness of images, are lit up in such a way that the intellect understands. If indeed to know a thing is to understand that it cannot be otherwise than it is,

---

[7] *I Sent., d.* III, p. I, art. unicus, q. 1. *Opera Omnia* I, p. 68b.
[8] *Collationes in Hex.,* XII, 11. *Opera Omnia* V, p. 386.
[9] *Quaes. Dis. de Scientia Christi,* IV, conclusio, *Opera Omnia* V, 23b.
[10] Ibid., IV, *Opera Omnia* V, 23b.

by necessity he alone will make it known who knows the truth and possesses the truth within himself.[11]

All bodies in creation possess light as a substantial form.[12] Now God is the Fount of Light and from him flow manifold rays. In the *De Reductione Artium ad Theologiam* (c. 1254/55),[13] St. Bonaventure distinguishes the various lights which descend from the Father of lights, by which the human mind arrives at truth at different levels of knowledge. There is the external light of mechanical art whereby the mind is enlightened in regard to the structure of artifacts; then there is the lower light of sense perception which illumines the mind in regard to natural forms; thirdly, there is the inner light, that is, the light of philosophical knowledge, which illumines the mind in regard to intellectual truth; finally, there is the higher light, that is, the light of grace and of the Scriptures which enlightens the mind in regard to saving truth. This last of the four lights makes known truths which are beyond reason and it is infused and inspired by God.[14] This fourfold light admits of four modifications or illuminations which are related to the six days of creation, leading to the seventh day of rest, the illumination of glory.[15] All illumination from God is directed ultimately to union with him through charity "without which all knowledge is vain".[16]

The *Itinerarium mentis in Deum*,[17] written in 1259/1260, was the result of his experiences on Mount La Verna in Tuscany during October 1259. This work traces the ascent of the soul to mystical union with God. The work begins with a contemplation of his vestiges in the visible world, passes on to consider the image of God imprinted in the soul at creation and the likeness to God impressed on the soul by grace in the recreation through Christ, from which it passes to a consideration of the Divine Unity as Being and the Blessed Trinity as the Supreme Good. Finally, St. Bonaventure describes the mystical transport

---

[11] *The Works of St. Bonaventure*, trans. I by José de Vinck, V: *Collations on the Six Days*, St. Antony Guild Press: Paterson N.J. 1970, 12th Collation, 5, pp. 174-175.

[12] See the extraordinarily profound reflection on light in: *II Sent.*, d XII, *Opera Omnia* II, pp. 310a-333b.

[13] *Opera Omnia* V, pp. 319a-325b.

[14] *De Reductione Artium*, I, *Opera Omnia* V, p. 319a; see also *On Retracing the Arts to Theology in The Works of St. Bonaventure. . . .*trans. by J. de Vinck, III: *Opuscula*. Second series (St. Anthony Guild Press, Paterson, N.J. 1966), pp. 13-32; *Works of St Bonaventure*, ed. by Ph. Boehner OFM and Sr. M.F. Laughlin SMIC, *St. Bonaventure's De Reductione Artium ad Theologiam*, commentary with an introduction and translation by Sr. E.T. Healy, The Franciscan Institute, St. Bonaventure NY 1955.

[15] *De Reductione Artium*, pp. 6-7; *Opera Omnia* V, pp. 321b-322a.

[16] Ibid., p. 26; *Opera Omnia* V, p. 325b.

[17] *Opera Omnia* V, pp. 295a-313b.

of the mind, wherein rest is given to the understanding, and affection of the will passes over completely to God. Throughout the entire work St. Bonaventure uses the term *speculatio,* which is synonymous with contemplation. The term is used in intimate connexion with its etymological root speculum, thus describing, the reflecting activity of a mirror. The mind is a mirror which reflects in image and similitude the truth and light of God.[18] The aim of the entire journey is to arrive at wisdom or ecstatic knowledge, which begins in knowledge and ends in love. This is the state of perfect contemplation of which, says St. Bonaventure, St. Francis is the perfect example. He reached this highest wisdom by a special vocation from God. The man of learning is also called to this mystical state, but he arrives at it through study, knowledge and thought. Intellectual activity is his proper way to reach mystical union with God.[19] In certain holy contemplatives mystical union sometimes reaches ecstasy and even rapture, though this only happens in rare cases.[20] The whole of St. Bonaventure's philosophical and theological writings are directed to one end : to lead the soul to mystical union with God. He is pre-eminently a doctor of mystical theology. Of this he gives us his own clear definition: the whole of mystical theology is concerned with arriving at ecstatic love of God according to the purgative, illuminative and perfective or unitive ways.[21]

The *Collationes in Hexaemeron* is St. Bonaventure's last and greatest work.[22] It was unfortunately left unfinished. He delivered it in sermon form at Paris between April 9 and May 28, 1273, on which latter date he was created cardinal together with, among others, Peter of Tarantasia, OP, the future Pope Innocent V[23] This work contains his profound reflections on the theology of history to which we will return after presenting the content of the sermon on St. Dominic.

---

[18] See *Works of St. Bonaventure*, ed. by Ph. Boehner OFM and M.F. Laughlin SMIC, *Saint Bonaventure's Itinerarium mentis in Deum*, with an Introduction, Translation and Commentary by Ph. Boehner OFM, The Franciscan Institute, St. Bonaventure NY 1956, pp. 23f., 107-109.

[19] Ibid., pp. 99, 130f.

[20] *III Sent., d.* XXXV, art. unicus, q. 1, *Opera Omnia* VII, p. 774b.

[21] *Commentarius in Evangelium S. Lucae,* c. XIII, n. 46, *Opera Omnia* VII. p. 349b.

[22] *Opera Omnia* V, pp. 329a-449b.

[23] *St. Bonaventura 1274-1974,* II: *Studia de Vita, Mente, Fontibus et Operibus Sancti Bonaventurae,* Collegio St. Bonaventura, Grottaferrata Roma 1973, p. 13.

St. Bonaventure's Sermon on St. Dominic

What strikes one immediately after reading this sermon is its consonance with ancient and modern biographies of the Saint. The theme of light is mentioned in the ancient sources and the virtues picked out by St. Bonaventure are highlighted in lives of the Saint and emphasized in the acts of his canonization.

In this section we are concerned to present the content of the sermon rather than to give a translation. We have added explanatory notes in the text and have given references where these were deemed necessary.

(I) Introduction

The sermon begins with the text of *Ecclesiastes* 8:1, quoted according to Jerome and the Vulgate: "The wisdom of a man shineth in his countenance and the most mighty will change his face". The two parts of the verse are applied to St. Dominic after a brief analysis of the nature of Christian perfection. St. Bonaventure explains that the height of Christian perfection consists in two elements, a clear understanding of truth and a faithful practice of virtue. The first of these refers to the contemplative life and concerns the very purpose of human existence in terms of the theological and speculative virtue. The second refers to the active life and concerns the means of reaching the purpose of our existence through the moral and cardinal virtue. These two elements of Christian perfection show in St. Dominic as in the brightest star. The text quoted at the beginning of the sermon applies to St. Dominic because he is to be praised as one in whom the eternal light was reflected ("the wisdom of a man shineth in his countenance") and for his constancy of virtue ("the most mighty will change his face").

(II) Reflection of Eternal Light

He is worthy of praise, firstly, because he was a true reflection of eternal light. To shine is an activity of light, as corporeal light shines to the eyes.[24] Light is understood here as wisdom and both uncreated and created wisdom may be compared to light. Uncreated Wisdom is light by essence and thus we say God is Light. Created wisdom is light by participation. As visible light has three functions: to dispel darkness, to manifest forms and to give joy to the cognitive powers, so spiritual light cleanses the mind, enlightens it and perfects it by wisdom. Man, endowed with reason, bears not only an image of eternal light impressed by nature, but also a likeness to eternal light infused by

---

[24] See *II Sent.*, d. XIII. *Opera Omnia* II, pp. 310a-33b.

grace. The words of *Wisdom* 1:26 "the brightness of eternal light" can be applied to the light of created wisdom, because it is purgative by dispelling darkness; created wisdom is a mirror without blemish, because it is illuminative by manifesting forms; it is an image of goodness, because it is perfective by giving joy to the cognitive powers. Now, the light of wisdom has a threefold shining effect in the face of a wise man: firstly, as the light of lively trust through faith, which is purgative by dispelling darkness; secondly, as the light of bright reasoning, which is illuminative by manifesting forms; thirdly, as the light of sweet contemplation, which is perfective, through the joy it brings to the cognitive powers. St. Bonaventure now applies this threefold effect of the light of wisdom to St. Dominic.

(1) Firstly, the light of wisdom shines in the face of a man as the light of lively trust through faith, which dispels darkness. The light of faith, however, not only dispels darkness, it also unites us to the Fount of life which is Christ; it unites us to the truth itself, the truth of light inaccessible. It is faith which first conforms us to that light which is the fount of life, that fount which has the power to give birth to sons of light. This light shone in the face of the blessed Dominic; it made him a son of light and through him it dispelled the darkness of error. His birth appeared under a twofold symbol: a star, which shines brightly in itself and a torch which brings light to others. St. Bonaventure is referring here to the dream which St. Dominic's mother had before his conception, in which she saw a little dog holding in its jaws a flaming torch and to the vision which his godmother had of a bright star appearing on the forehead of the child.[219]

(2) Secondly, the light of wisdom shines as the light of bright reasoning, which is illuminative by manifesting forms and by opening up to us knowledge of the sciences. Divine wisdom reveals to us the works of God which are twofold : creation and re-creation in Christ. Creation refers to nature which philosophy studies; re-creation refers to grace which theology studies. To know what Divine Wisdom reveals requires illumination from on high; it is impossible for anyone to arrive at an understanding of any truth other than through the infallible light of eternal truth. Divine wisdom reveals the truths of creation to the mind by ordinary illumination, but the truths of re-creation are revealed by spiritual enlightenment which is beyond the powers of reason and is grounded in necessary prophecy (revelation). God revealed the truths of

---

[25] Jordan of Saxony, *Libellus de principiis ordinis praedicatorum*, ed. by H. Chr. Scheeben, MOPH XVI, Romae 1935, nn. 5, 9; see Vicaire, *St. Dominic*, p. 21; Constantine of Orvieto, *Legenda S. Dominici*, ed. by H. Chr. Scheeben, MOPH XVI, Romae 1935, n. 6; see Hinnebusch, *The History of the Dominican Order* (I), pp. 17, 33.

creation and re-creation (nature and grace) to the blessed Dominic, because he was first of all learned in philosophy and then in sacred scripture or theology. He was especially learned in theology which is wisdom.[26]

We know from the details of his life that St. Dominic studied both philosophy and theology and that he gave himself above all to the study of sacred scripture.[27] When asked towards the end of his life in which book he had studied most, he answered : "In the Bock of Charity more than in the books of men".[28] He meditated continually on "the New Testament, especially on the gospel of St. Matthew and the epistles of St. Paul which he carried with him always and which he knew almost by heart".[29] Knowledge of the teaching of the New Testament and of the doctrine of the faith was absolutely necessary for the friars of his Order so that their preaching might be effective and fruitful. Study, according to the mind of St. Dominic, was not an end in itself but was subordinate and subservient to contemplation and the preaching apostolate. As Mandonnet succinctly expresses it: "For his own life and for that of his brethren, St. Dominic resolved the seeming contradiction of continual prayer and the apostolate by his admirable command 'Speak only of God or with God' "[30]

(3) Thirdly, says St. Bonaventure, the light in the face of the blessed Dominic was the light of sweet contemplation, which is perfective light by bringing satisfaction to the cognitive powers. Contemplative wisdom is the greatest of all lights from God. This final light is seen in heaven in the face of God revealed to us; here on earth it is seen by theophanies, that is by spiritual illumination which may be symbolic or mystical. Symbolic illumination, according to St. Bonaventure's understanding of symbolic theology is light from God given through a knowledge of the Scriptures in order to understand the symbolism of the world and creatures as reflections of God and to love and honour him through all that is in creation.[31] Mystical knowledge is the most

---

[26] The wisdom mentioned here by St. Bonaventure is clearly that *sapientia magis stricto* which is knowledge of God through holiness (*cognitio Dei secundum pietatem*), that is, knowledge of God in worshipping him by faith, hope and charity; see III *Sent., d.* XXXV. art, unicus. q. l, *Opera Omnia* III. p. 774b; *Itinerarium mentis in Deum*, ed. by Boehner, pp. 130f.

[27] Vicaire, *St. Dominic*, pp. 25-28; W.A. Hinnebusch, *The History of the Dominican Order I*, pp. 17f.

[28] P. Mandonnet OP, *St. Dominic and His Work*, trans. by M.B. Larkin OP, Herder Book Co., St. Louis and London 1948, p. 62.

[29] Ibid., p. 60.

[30] Ibid., pp. 317f., cf. pp. 172, 185. On St. Dominic's mind on studies see W.A. Hinnebusch OP, *The History of the Dominican Order. Intellectual and Cultural Life to 1500*, vol. II, Alba House, New York 1973, pp. 3-10.

[31] *Collationes in Hex.*, XIII, p. 12, *Opera* Omnia V, p. 390a.

sublime and the most hidden. It is granted only to the Saints and it comes about by ecstatic love, which is found only in the most fervent of men.[32] It is obviously the case that St. Bonaventure is speaking here of that mystical union wherein understanding is at rest and the affection of the will passes over entirely to God—the passing over into God in a transport of contemplation. This is the peace, the learned ignorance, the charity, the wisdom of mystical union with God.[33] *Amor plus se extendit quam visio.*[34] It appears, therefore, that St. Dominic was among the ecstatics.[35]

(III) Faithful Practice of Virtue

Man cannot progress towards truth without the practice of virtue. Thus it is said : "the most mighty will change his face", which means that virtue cannot be acquired without the almighty power of God. The face of St. Dominic was changed and this 'changed face' may be understood in terms of the four faces seen in the vision by Ezechiel the Prophet [1:10]. The first is "the face of a man" which St. Dominic had by the gentleness of mercy; the second "is the face of a lion" which St. Dominic had by the greatheartedness of courage: the third is "the face of an ox" which St. Dominic had by the humility of obedience; the fourth is "the face of an eagle" which St. Dominic had by the insight of prudence.[36]

(1) Firstly, he had "the face of a man", that is, he was endowed with the gentleness of mercy. Mercy is the noblest part of the virtue of justice and it pertains above all to man, because, as Aristotle says, it is proper to man "to be kind by nature". From mercy come *humanitas* and *benignitas*. This virtue was found in the blessed Father Dominic and in him the words of *Ecclesiasticus* 3:19 were fulfilled "My son, do thy works in meekness". To him applies also the description of Moses in *Numbers* 12:3 "For Moses was a man exceeding meek above all men that dwelt upon earth".

(2) Secondly, he had "the face of a lion" by his greatheartedness of courage. This is explained according to the words of *Proverbs* 30:30 "A lion,

---

[32] *Itinerarium*, VII, 3 (Boehner, p. 99): "In this passing over, if it is to be perfect, all intellectual activities ought to be relinquished and the most profound affection transported to God, and transformed into Him. This. however, is mystical and most secret, *which no one knows except him who receives it*".

[33] *Itinerarium*, Prol. 1; VII 1; Opera Omnia V, p. 259a; *Breviloquium* V, p. 6, ibid., p. 260a; *De Reductione*, 26, ibid., p. 325b.

[34] *II Sent.*, d. XXIII, q. 2, 3, ad 4, *Opera Omnia* II, p. 545b.

[35] On the significance of assigning St. Dominic to the order of ecstatics, see below.

[36] On the virtues and holiness of St. Dominic see Vicaire, *St. Dominic*, pp. 388-395; Mandonnet, *St. Dominic*, pp. 58-62.

the strongest of beasts who hath no fear of anything he meeteth". He had the courage of Eliseus: "in his days he feared not the prince" [Ecclesiastes 48:13]. St. Bonaventure quotes the reply St. Dominic gave when once threatened: "You may cut my whole body into pieces and leave them to steep in my own blood". This is most probably a reference to the answer St. Dominic gave to the knights who questioned him after the ambush, planned to take place very likely on the road between Fanjeaux and Prouille, had been called off.[37]

(3) Thirdly, he had "the face of an ox", that is, he possessed the humility of obedience. This is explained according to 1 Corinthians 9:9 "Thou shalt not muzzle the mouth of the ox that treadeth out the corn", which the Apostle means to be understood of preaching the truth. Preaching, it may be said, ploughs the ground and draws over it the ploughshare of the word of God. By the ploughshare it understood preaching and the ox cannot pull the ploughshare unless it bears the yoke. Therefore, the Lord says : "Take my yoke upon you" [Matthew 11:29], because no man is fitted to preach evangelical doctrine unless he is placed under the yoke of obedience. Since it is easier to pull the ploughshare with two oxen than with one, in these recent times, St. Bonaventure says, two Orders have been founded (the Dominicans and the Franciscans) whose mystery was prefigured in the two kine that took the ark of the Lord from the land of the Philistines : "And the kine took the straight way that leadeth to Bethsames and they went along the way, lowing as they went: and turned not aside to the right hand nor to the left" [1 Kings 6:12]. Thus, in order to draw the Lord's yoke, Paul is joined to Peter, Bernard to Benedict and Francis to Dominic.

(4) Fourthly, he had "the face of an eagle" through the insight of prudence, about which Job says: "Will the eagle mount up at thy command and make her nest in high places" [39:27] which describes prudence in conversation and "where so ever the carcass shall be, she is immediately there" [39:30], which may be applied to St. Dominic on account of the vigilance he exercised in order to convert sinners. This eagle "enticed her young to fly", that is, by the contemplation of truth and the practice of virtue, St. Dominic taught his sons to see the divine light and to taste the eternal peace.

Joachim of Flora and the Order of Preachers

To understand the place of the Dominicans and attempt to discover that of St. Dominic himself in St. Bonaventure's theology of history we must first

---

[37] Vicaire, *St. Dominic*, p. 156.

say something about Joachim of Flora's predictions about the third age of history.

The profound and widespread influence of Joachim of Flora on the world of the thirteenth century is one of the most fascinating topics in the history of the Middle Ages. His apocalyptic ideas made a deep impression on men who sought to renew the Church by a return to the apostolic life and by preaching the pure word of God. The extent and full story of this influence and the movements connected with it are obviously beyond the scope of these pages. Our interest lies in the links which were discerned between Joachim's predictions and the appearance in history of the Dominican Order.[38]

The term *ordo praedicatorum* which we use uniquely of the Order of St. Dominic, had a very different meaning from patristic times up to the twelfth century. In the writings of the Fathers the preacher was essentially the bishop to whom was committed by divine right the task of proclaiming the word of God. St. Gregory the Great, for example, uses the term exclusively in this sense and he also designates the bishops as the *ordo doctorum*. The word *ordo* here expresses a class or category of people in the Church, namely, those officially commissioned to preach the word of God and, it appears, St. Gregory was the first ever to designate the preachers of the Church as an *ordo* or category.[39]

As the centuries went by this concept began to undergo changes and very gradually it came to embrace the idea of a group of preachers no longer exclusively restricted to the bishops. However, it is principally in commentaries on the book of the Apocalypse, which appeared in abundance in the late twelfth century that the concept *ordo praedicatorum* takes on this wider connotation. Commentators such as Richard of St Victor, Anselm of Laon, Rupert of Deutz, identify the seven angels of the Apocalypse with the *ordo praedicatorum* of all ages. We find also that with the appearance of the sixth and seventh angel the *ordo praedicatorum* is described as the *ordo doctorum*.

Joachim of Flora wrote his commentary on the *Apocalypse* at the request of Pope Lucius III.[40] He divides the history of the world into three ages: that of the Father, that of the Son and that of the Holy Spirit. The first is the age of the married state, the second the age of priests/preachers and the third the

---

[38] Mandonnet, *St. Dominic*, pp. 156-174. Our remarks on the meaning and development of the term *ordo praedicatorum* are dependent on this scholarly and authoritative work.

[39] Ibid., pp. 158-160.

[40] *Expositio magni prophetae Abbatis Joachim in Apocalypsim* (Venice 1527); cf. Vicaire, *St. Dominic*, pp. 187-191; Mandonnet, *St. Dominic*, pp. 167-172.

age of the order of monks or the age of contemplatives. The third age will be the final age of the Eternal Gospel. Joachim divides the second age into seven periods and the time at which he was writing (towards the end of the twelfth century) he identified with the transition from the fifth to the sixth period. With the sixth period a new order would appear whose founder with his disciples would constitute the *ordo praedicatorum* in imitation of the poor life of Jesus and his apostles. The founder of this *ordo* is predicted to be a great preacher. Joachim calls the order that of the just and the perfect precisely because it will resemble closely the holy life of Jesus and the Apostles. He speaks at times of the rise of two orders in the near future, both of which will have the mission to preach the word of God. It is interesting to note that that Franciscans were also given the title 'Order of Preachers' at various times.[41] Thus, at the beginning of the thirteenth century, the concept *ordo praedicatorum* embraced two meanings. On the one hand it referred to the bishops and their delegates who in virtue of their apostolic office, were officially commissioned to preach the word of God; on the other hand, it referred to a group or groups of preachers to be founded who would form an *ordo* quite distinct from that of the bishops. This second meaning of the term was readily identified with the Dominican Friars who exercised the office of preaching quite apart from the episcopal office and the established *cura animarum*. Joachim's predictions were seen to be fulfilled in the order founded by St. Dominic.

The question of the fulfilment of Joachim's predictions in the appearance of the Dominican Order tends to be left at this point by Dominican historians. St. Bonaventure, however, goes much further in his reflections which were influenced quite extensively by Joachim's ideas.

St. Bonaventure and Joachim of Flora[42]

In the *Collationes in Hexaemeron* St. Bonaventure presents an overall theology of history in which both the Franciscan and Dominican Orders have an important and very definite place. There can be no doubt that his concern to find a solution to the 'Franciscan Question' (which involved among other matters the serious problem of studies in the Order) had great influence on his elaboration of a theology of history. This theology of history, in its turn,

---

[41] See C. Esser OFM, *Origins of the Franciscan Order*, Franciscan Herald Press, Chicago 1970, pp. 30, 47.
[42] Cf. Joseph Ratzinger, *The Theology of History in St. Bonaventure*, trans. by Z. Hayes OFM, Franciscan Herald Press, Chicago 1971, pp. 1-55. This presentation of St. Bonaventure's theology of history appears to us to be totally acceptable.

presented a solution to the 'Franciscan Question' that is as welcome to Franciscans today (whose lot it is to pursue studies) as it was ingenious in the circumstances of the order's history in which he propounded it.

St. Bonaventure did not totally reject the views of Joachim of Flora. He incorporated many elements of Joachim's theological analysis of history into his own theology of history.[43] St. Bonaventure divides both the history of the Old Testament and the times of the New Testament in seven periods: "The times of symbols were seven in number. . . .Likewise in the New Testament there are seven times".[44] There is a strict correspondence between the events of the seven periods of the Old Testament and the seven periods of the New Testament. In terms of this correspondence we are enabled to understand not only the past but also to know something of the future of New Testament times: "Thus it is clear how Scripture describes the succession of times; and they are not haphazard nor left to chance, but they contain a marvellous light and many spiritual meanings".[45] The seventh age of New Testament times is not outside history, but clearly historical and pre-eschatological.[46] This period is described in connexion with the prophecy of Ezechiel 40f.: "'Then will be fulfilled the prophecy of Ezechiel when the city will come down from heaven, not indeed that city which is above, but the one below that is the (Church) Militant: when it will be conformed to the (Church) Triumphant, as far as it is possible in the pilgrim way. And then there shall be peace. But how long this peace will last, God knows".[47]

The sixth period of New Testament times is understood by comparison with the sixth period of the Old Testament. Charlemagne, who loved the Church and was zealous for her good, corresponds to Ezechias or Ozias. Henry IV and Frederick I, who brought great tribulation to the Church correspond to Manasses. St. Bonaventure then predicts that only two great events separate the sixth from the seventh period (the sixth day from the seventh day of peace) another great ruler who will love the Church and work for her good, corresponding to Josias and a further great tribulation of the Church, corresponding to the Babylonian exile.[48] From this tribulation will come the new order.[49]

---

[43] Ibid., pp. 8, 23, 39-42, 48f.
[44] *Collations on the Six Days* (de Vinck), 16th Collation, 12-13, pp. 236-237.
[45] Ibid., 16th Collation, 31, p. 250.
[46] Ratzinger, *Theology of History*, pp. 22f.
[47] *Collations on the Six Days*, 16th Collation, 30, pp. 240-250.
[48] Ibid., 16th Collation, 29, p. 248.
[49] Ratzinger, *Theology of History*, p. 30.

In his theology of history St. Bonaventure draws a parallel between Elias and St. Francis in terms of Malachy's prophecy: "Behold I will send you Elias the prophet, before the coming of the great and dreadful day of the Lord" [Malachi 3:23]. There is an obvious influence here of Joachim of Flora who related the expectation of Elias to the prediction of the two witnesses in the Apocalypse: "But I shall send my two witnesses to prophesy for those twelve hundred and sixty days, wearing sackcloth" [11:3]. A new Elias and a new Henoch are predicted at the beginning of the third age by Joachim.[50] St. Bonaventure writes: "The fifth time, at the end, is that of the restoration of ruins, for 'Elias indeed is to come and to restore all things' and with him Henoch will come too".[51] Commenting on this text Ratzinger notes: "It was possible to see this prediction fulfilled in Francis and Dominic"—an identification that was made by the author of the pseudo-Joachimite *Commentary on Jeremias.*[52]

Joachim of Flora speaks of the order of contemplatives in the third age, that of the Holy Spirit. The two orders which will appear at the end of the sixth period of the second age will be only provisional to mark the transition from the sixth to the seventh period. The final order will be quite different from these as the order of pure contemplatives.[53] St. Bonaventure accepts this solution substantially and identifies these two orders with the Dominicans and the Franciscans. The order of the seventh period of New Testament times in his division of history will also be an order of contemplatives who will have true wisdom and restore the primitive apostolic life of the Church.[54]

In the course of his *Collationes* St. Bonaventure establishes parallels between the heavenly hierarchy of angels and the ecclesiastical hierarchy on earth. He writes: "It is fitting, then, that the Church militant have orders corresponding to the model hierarchy".[55] When he comes to speak of contemplatives in the Church who are found at the apex of the ecclesiastical hierarchy, he disposes them in three orders : "Now they tend to divine matters in a threefold way: some by means of supplications, others by means of speculations, others again by means of elevations".[56] To the first of these

---

[50] See the text of *Concordia veteris et novi testamenti*, 1, IV, c. 36, f. 57v, quoted in Ratzinger, *Theology of History*, p. 179, n. 28, and the text of *Expositio magni prophetae Abbatis Joachim in Apocalypsim*, f. 147rb in Mandonnet, *St. Dominic*, p. 169, n. 67.
[51] *Collations on the Six Days*, 15th Collation, 28, p. 230.
[52] J. Ratzinger, *Theology of History*, 33, pp. 40f.
[53] Ibid., p. 42.
[54] Ibid., pp. 44, 52.
[55] *Collations on the Six Days*, 22nd Collation, 2, p. 342.
[56] Ibid., 20, pp. 350f.

belong the Cistercians, Premonstratensians, the Carthusians and the Canons Regular, who devote themselves entirely to prayer, devotion and the praise of God, who do a certain amount of manual work to supply their needs and who pray for those who have given them estates and possessions. In the heavenly hierarchy the Thrones correspond to these.[57] The second are those who attend to divine things by speculation, that is the speculatives who devote themselves to a study of scripture, for which they must purify their minds because "one cannot grasp the words of Paul unless one has the spirit of Paul. . . .These are the Preachers and the Minors".[58] He identifies the speculatives, therefore, with the Dominicans and the Franciscans to whom the Cherubim in the heavenly hierarchy correspond. The Dominicans are concerned with speculation first and with piety, next; the Franciscans with piety first and then with speculation. St. Bonaventure adds that St. Francis wanted his Friars to study, but they were first to practice what they preached. It must be emphasized that St. Bonaventure is not making an odious comparison here between the Dominicans and the Franciscans; he is concerned merely to point out the different attitudes of these two orders based on their particular spirit. Both belong to the order of speculatives and both have a love of God which corresponds to the Cherubim. These are the two orders, he says in the sermon on St. Dominic, founded in recent times to preach the word of God. "The third manner", he says, "is concerned with those who attend to God by means of elevation and ecstasy".[59] This is the Seraphic Order in which St. Francis is placed by St. Bonaventure. "This order will not flourish, unless Christ appears and suffers in his Mystical Body".[60] St. Francis, therefore, belonged to a unique order which cannot be identified with the Franciscan order. All other Franciscans belong to the Order of Minors. This distinction is based on the unique charism which St. Francis received, a charism that cannot be repeated in the Franciscan Order. The conclusion drawn by St. Bonaventure is that the Minors must attain to contemplative union by speculation. At the practical level, therefore, St. Bonaventure had here his solution to the thorny problem of the order's relationship to St Francis. In terms of his theology of history, however, he places St Francis in the order of contemplatives of the final age because of his mystical love of God, his knowledge of the Scriptures given by divine illumination and his life of poverty in imitation of the Poor Christ and his Apostles. St. Bonaventure would never have agreed to calling the

---

[57] Ibid., 20, p. 351.
[58] Ibid., 21, p. 351.
[59] *Collationes in Hex.*, XXII, 22, *Opera Omnia* V, 440b-441a.
[60] *Collations on the Six Days*, 22nd Collation, 23, p. 352.

Franciscan Order the "Seraphic Order", for the simple reason that the latter is the order of the final age. He is extremely careful not to identify it with the Franciscans. Neither these nor the Dominicans are identified with it. Lastly, it should be noted that St. Bonaventure does not assign any date nor give details for this final order: "But what this order is to be, or already is, it is hard to know".[61]

St. Dominic and the Seraphic Order

The passage in the *Collationes in Hexaemeron* which has been analysed (XXII, 20-23), makes no mention of St. Dominic as belonging to this Seraphic Order or Order of contemplatives. I am convinced, however, that according to the signs given by St. Bonaventure when discussing St. Francis in this context, all indications point to the conclusion that St. Dominic also belonged to it. St. Bonaventure gives three signs which qualify St. Francis to be placed in it: his mystical love of God, his knowledge of the Scriptures through divine illumination and his apostolic poverty.

Firstly, mystical love of God. St. Bonaventure states in the sermon that St. Dominic possessed that mystical knowledge which comes about as a result of ecstatic love (*per amorem excessivum* are his words in the sermon; he describes the Seraphic Order as follows : *Tertius ordo est vacantium Deo secundum modum sursumactivum, scilicet ecstaticum seu excessivum).* Furthermore, he taught his sons to taste the eternal peace. This is that peace which surpasses all understanding, the peace which comes at "the end of the way of six contemplations. They are like six steps by which the mind arrives at peace as at the throne of the true Solomon, where the Man of Peace rests in the peaceful mind as in an inner Jerusalem".[62] St. Francis's reception of the Stigmata as a unique gift cannot be urged against our interpretation because, firstly, it is only a *sign* that he belonged to the Seraphic order and, secondly, because St. Francis was already in ecstasy before he took the habit.[63]

The Dominican Order has not laboured under the same difficulty with regard to its relation to St. Dominic as the Franciscan Order has in its relation to St. Francis. Perhaps this is one of the reasons why St. Bonaventure did not mention St. Dominic in this context. There was no apologetic reason, as far as he was concerned to do so. Fidelity to the intentions of St. Dominic, at least as regards the clear injunctions on preaching and the necessary studies to carry

---

[61] Ibid., 22, p. 352.
[62] *Itinerarium*, VII, l; cf. Prol. l in: Boehner, pp. 31, 97.
[63] *Collations on the Six Days*, 22nd Collation, 22, p. 352: "And he said that he (Francis) was in ecstasy before even receiving the habit, and was found near a certain hedge".

out this apostolate, admit of no ambiguity at all. Our concern here, in any case, is to try to place St. Dominic in St. Bonaventure's theology of history.

Secondly, knowledge of the Scriptures through divine illumination. It seems to me that the whole tenor of the first part of the sermon on St. Dominic is more than enough evidence here. St. Bonaventure says that the light of wisdom shone in the face of St. Dominic as the light of life-giving trust through faith, as the light of clear reasoning, and as the light of sweet contemplation given by spiritual illumination, both symbolic and mystical. "God revealed the truths of creation and re-creation to the blessed Dominic, because he was first of all learned in philosophy and then in Sacred Scripture and theology. He was especially learned in theology which is wisdom" (Sermon II, 2). All that has been noted above about his knowledge and love of Scripture is relevant here. Unlike St. Francis, of course, St. Dominic had studied philosophy and theology and therefore he had progressed from *speculatio* to mystical knowledge and union with God, which is wisdom. This is the path which men of learning are to travel in order to come to wisdom which surpasses knowledge. St. Dominic, in fact, was already, on the road to heroic sanctity—the means of passing from knowledge to wisdom[64]—in his student days, long before he founded the Order of Preachers, as the early sources of his life attest.[65]

Thirdly, apostolic poverty. I do not intend to introduce the question of whether St. Francis had any influence on St. Dominic in the matter of the observance of poverty.[66] There is no real evidence that St. Francis did so influence him. From the mid-twelfth century onwards the air had been full of ideas about apostolic poverty, and the apostolic life and these alone would explain St. Dominic's attitude to poverty. Neither he nor St. Francis came as an evangelical bolt from the blue. There is, of course, profound originality in them both and particularly in their observance of poverty, but they were not the first to take apostolic poverty seriously!

From the abundant evidence of his life it seems that we are quite justified in drawing sharp distinction between the mind and intentions of St. Dominic on absolute poverty and the subsequent attitude and practice of his

---

[64] Ibid., 19th Collation, 3, pp. 284f.: "Therefore passing from knowledge to wisdom is not assured: a means must be placed in between, that is, holiness. But passing over is an endeavour: the endeavour to pass from the study of the sciences to the study of holiness and from the study of holiness to that of wisdom".

[65] Hinnebusch, *The History of the Dominican Order 1*, pp. 19f., 27-32.

[66] Ibid., pp. 154-157.

order, even while he was still alive.[67] That he practised absolute poverty in his own life is beyond any doubt from the biographical details we have and we can agree, wholeheartedly with Fr. Hinnebusch's conclusion about St. Dominic's poverty: "With St. Francis he stands as a great lover of *Lady Poverty*".[68]

The observance of the strictest poverty gave to preaching its credibility at a time when the luxury of clerical life was in open contradiction to the poor life of Christ and his Apostles. But, as we have mentioned, there was more involved in the observance of apostolic poverty than its power to add efficacy to the preached word. The restoration of the apostolic life, in which absolute poverty was an essential element, was understood to be a sign of the new and final order of contemplatives. St. Bonaventure emphasizes the close link between contemplation and poverty and in this he had already been preceded by Joachim of Flora.[69] St. Bonaventure quotes St. Dominic in support of mendicancy in an earlier work concerning evangelical perfection. He singles out the story that St. Dominic called down a curse on all who would try to induce his order to have possessions, because it was his will that his followers live by alms as he had done.[70] In reading the life of St. Dominic one is struck by the similarities and parallels there are with the life of St. Francis, above all in this matter of the observance of poverty.

On the evidence, then, of St. Dominic's mystical love of God, his knowledge of the Scriptures by divine illumination and his absolute apostolic poverty, we are justified in placing him in the Seraphic order with St. Francis, according to St. Bonaventure's theology of history.

Conclusion

St. Bonaventure's sermon gives us an understanding of St. Dominic that is substantially the same as that contained in the primitive Dominican sources. Moreover, his reflections on St. Francis and St. Dominic and on the orders they founded are relevant to our attempts at renewal through rediscovery of the original inspiration of both orders. In the first place, it must be admitted

---

[67] See Madonnet, *St. Dominic*, pp. 4-6; Hinnebusch, *The History of the Dominican Order* I, pp. 145-168, esp. p. 149.

[68] Hinnebusch, *The History of the Dominican Order* I, p. 157.

[69] J. Ratzinger, *Theology of History*, pp. 52-53, 190, n. 1102. *Collations on the Six Days*, 20th Collation 30, p. 317: "Contemplation cannot come about except in the greatest simplicity; and the greatest simplicity cannot exist except in the greatest poverty. And this is proper to this Order. The intention of the Blessed Francis was to live in the greatest poverty".

[70] *Quaestiones Disputatae de Perfectione Evangelica*, q. 2: *De Paupertate*, art. 2,22, *Opera Omnia* V, 138b. See also Hinnebusch, *The History of the Dominican Order* 1, pp. 156-157.

that neither order can recapture or re-live the charism as such of its founder. Secondly, the message of the two founders to their orders is clear to strive to establish as far as possible and without oversimplification, in the circumstances of our time, the apostolic life in the Church by living in true poverty, by creating authentic communities and by restoring to pride of place that magnificent principle of Dominican life expressed by St. Thomas (which may be applied also to Franciscan life): *Contemplata aliis tradere.*[71]

Finally, I would like to make a personal comment. St. Bonaventure's sermon has been for me a discovery of St. Dominic. Any view that would present him as an 'intellectual' (a word which always appears to imply 'mind-over-heart' or even 'mind-and-heart') is a one-sided view and it fails to do justice to historic evidence. St. Dominic was in the first place a mystic. The blessed Father Dominic deserves to be known more widely as he really was, in all his warmth, ardour, courage, holiness, prudence and simplicity. The attractiveness of his character makes him the most fruitful source of vocations to the Dominican Order.

---

[71] *Summa Theol.*, IIa-IIae, q. 188, a. 6; cf. also q. 182, a. 1, ad 2um; IIIa, q. 40, a. 1, ad 2um. Cf. Mandonnet, *St. Dominic*, pp. 317-318. On renewal of the Dominican Order see V. Walgrave OP, *Essai d'Autocritique d'un Ordre Religieux. Les Dominicains en fin de Concile*, Deuxieme edition, editions du Cep, Bruxelles 1966, pp. 312-352.

St. Bonaventure 1274-1974
Some Aspects of His Life and Thought[1]

This year commemorates the seventh centenary of the death of St. Bonaventure as it marks the same centenary of the death of St. Thomas Aquinas. Of these two Princes among the Scholastics, St. Thomas is hailed as the *Doctor Communis*. We need not enter into discussion of why this is the case, but we must not allow it to overshadow for us the importance of the Seraphic Doctor.

1. Biographical Notes

My chief intention here is to give a concise account of the results of most recent research. St. Bonaventure was born in1217 in Bagnorea, a small town lying between Orvieto and Viterbo in northern Italy. He tells us that at an early age (when he was about twelve years old) he was cured of a fatal illness through the intercession of St. Francis. The debt of gratitude he felt towards the Saint for his life is what moved him to accept the decision of the General Chapter of Narbonne in 1260 to write the life of St. Francis.[2] In 1235 he went to Paris where he studied the arts. By 1243 he was Master of Arts and in that same year he joined the Franciscan Order and began his theological studies. The Franciscan tradition, above all the holiness of its founder, became now the chief factor and motive force in St. Bonaventure's theological and spiritual formation. In 1244 he made profession of vows in the Order and for the next decade he pursued his theological and biblical studies. He obtained the title of Doctor of Theology in 1254. In the midst of his academic career, while he was regent master in the Franciscan School at Paris, he was elected Minister General of the Order on February 2nd, 1257. He was now pulled away from the peace and calm of a life of study and thrown into the maelstrom of the Order's history, at a time when feelings were sharply divided on the interpretation of the *Rule* and the mind of St. Francis and when the ideas of Joachim of Flora were exercising a strong influence in some sections of the

---

[1] THE BULLETIN 37 (7 July 1974) pp. 16-33. Published with permission from the Province of Immaculate Conception, England.
[2] See *Legenda Maior* 3.

Order. Two years after his election he went to Mount La Verna in Tuscany to meditate on the life of St. Francis in the very place where the Saint had received the Stigmata some thirty years before. From his experiences on La Verna came one of his most beautiful and profound works: *The Journey of the Mind to God,* in which he traces the steps of the soul's ascent to contemplative union with God. For the greater part of two decades he served the Order as its Minister General, making incredible journeys in Italy and France to preach the word of God, to exhort the friars in their observance of poverty and to correct abuses against the *Rule.* In May, 1273 he was created a Cardinal. Tradition has it that he was washing dishes when the news was brought to him. Later that year he was consecrated Bishop of Albano. It is recorded that he had refused earlier to accept the Archbishopric of York.[3] He took an active and influential part in the Second Council of Lyons. He died in Lyons on July 15th, 1274, where he was buried. He was canonized in October 1482 by Pope Sixtus IV and placed among the Confessors-Bishops and Doctors of the Church[4] He was placed among the highest and most famous doctors of the Church by Pope Sixtus V in 1588.[5] He was already declared Doctor of the Church at his canonization; Pope Sixtus V included him among the greatest Doctors of the Church.

2. Remarks on Selected Works

To treat the whole contents of the ten volumes of St. Bonaventure's *Opera Omnia* published by the Quaracchi Editors would be a task obviously beyond the range of these pages. I will be forgiven if I select the three works that have made the deepest impression on me.

A. *Itinerarium mentis in Deum-The Journey of the Mind to God*

This was written, as we have already noted, in 1259 after St. Bonaventure had been Minister General of the Order for two years. In this work he traces the ascent of the soul to mystical union with God. The work begins with a contemplation of God's vestiges in the visible world, passes on to consider the image of God imprinted in the soul at creation and the likeness to God impressed on the soul by grace in the re-creation through Christ. From here the work passes on to a consideration of the Divine Unity as Being and

---

[3] See *Vita seraphici Doctoris. . . .*in: *Doctoris Seraphici St. Bonaventurae. . . .Operum Omnium Complementum,* Tomus X, Ad Claras Aquas, Quaracchi 1902, p. 58b.

[4] *See Superna caelestis patria of Sixtus IV* in *Doctoris Seraphici. . . .Opera Omnia. . . .*Tomus 1, Ad Claras 1882, pp. XXXIX-XLIV.

[5] See *Triumphantis Hierusalem* of Sixtus V, ibid., pp. XLV-LII.

the Blessed Trinity as the Supreme Good. Finally St. Bonaventure describes the mystical transport of the mind, wherein rest is given to the understanding and affection of the will passes over completely to God. Throughout the entire work St. Bonaventure uses the term *speculatio*–which is, in fact, synonymous with contemplation. The term is used in intimate connection with its etymological root *speculum,* thus describing the reflecting activity of a mirror. The mind is a mirror which reflects in image and similitude the truth and light of God. The aim of the entire journey is to arrive at wisdom or ecstatic knowledge which begins in knowledge and ends in love. This is the state of perfect contemplation of which St. Francis is the perfect example:

> This also was shown to the Blessed Francis, when, in a transport of contemplation (*in excessu contemplationis*) on the mountain height— where I pondered over the matter that is here written—there appeared to him the six-winged Seraph fastened to a cross, as I and many others have heard from the companion who was with him at that very place. Here he passed over into God in a transport of contemplation. He is set forth as an example of perfect contemplation, just as previously he had been of action, like a second Jacob-Israel. (*Itinerarium* VII 3)

St. Francis reached this highest wisdom by a special grace from God. The man of learning, however, is also called to this mystical state, but he arrives at it through study, knowledge and thought. Intellectual activity is his proper way to reach mystical union with God. This work must be studied in close connection with *De Triplici Via.* The *De Triplici Via* follows the traditional three ways to mystical union with God. It is a more acceptable opinion, in my view, on the evidence we have, to assign the *Itinerarium* to the illuminative way. In his mystical theology of this work is a protracted reflection on divine illumination leading to union with God in contemplative wisdom.

B. De Reductione Artium ad Theologiam—Retracing the Arts to Theology (1254-55)

In this work St. Bonaventure distinguishes the various lights which descend from the Father of lights by which the human mind arrives at truth at different levels of knowledge. There is the external light of mechanical art whereby the mind is enlightened in regard to the structure of artifacts; then there is the lower light of sense perception which illumines the mind in regard to natural forms; thirdly, there is the inner light that is the light of philosophical knowledge, which illumines the mind in regard to intellectual truth; finally, there is the higher light, that is the light of grace and of the Scriptures which enlightens the mind in regard to saving truth. This last of the four lights makes known truths which are beyond reason and it is infused and inspired by God. All illumination from God is directed ultimately to the union with Him through charity "without which all knowledge is vain" (*De Reductione Artium* 26). Without exaggeration one might call this work a commentary on the *Canticle of Brother Sun.*

C. Collationes in Hexaemeron—Sermon on the Six Days

This is St. Bonaventure's last and greatest work. It was, unfortunately, left unfinished. He delivered it in sermon form at Paris between April 9th and May 28th, 1273, on which latter date he was created cardinal. This work contains his profound reflections on the theology of history and it sets out to mark the limits of the human mind unaided by grace in its search for truth. We will return to this in the section concerning St. Francis.

In reading the works of St. Bonaventure one understands' very clearly Paul Tillich's remark about the Scholastics in general:

> The real intention of scholasticism was the theological interpretation of all problems of life. The meaning of mysticism has been misinterpreted by Protestant theology which began with Ritschl and is still alive in Barthian theology. It is misleading when people identify this mysticism with the Asiatic mysticism of the Vedanta type, or with Neo-Platonic mysticism (Plotinus). Forget about this when you approach the Middle Ages. Every medieval scholastic was a mystic; that is, he experienced what he was talking about as personal experience. This is what mysticism originally meant in the realm of scholasticism. There was no opposition between mysticism and scholasticism. Mysticism was the experience of the scholastic message. The basis of the dogma was unity with the divine in devotion, prayer, contemplation and ascetic practices. If you know this, it may be hoped that you will not fall into the trap of removing mysticism from Christianity, which would mean to reduce the latter to an intellectualised faith and a moralized love.[6]

Theology is a science that is at once both speculative and practical: its purpose is to lead to an understanding of God's Word through contemplation and to the practice of virtue. He says in the 19th Collation: "Therefore passing

---

[6] P. Tillich, *A History of Christian Thought*, ed. by C.E. Braeton, SCM Press Ltd., London 1968, pp. 135f.

from knowledge to wisdom is not assured: a means must be placed in between, that is, holiness. But this passing over is an endeavour: the endeavour to pass from the study of the sciences to the study of holiness and from the study of holiness to that of wisdom".[7] Perhaps one of the chief elements in the renewal of theology is precisely this conviction that it is not and never can be a purely intellectual exercise, not merely in the sense that it must always have a message for the human condition, but above all that it already affects the human condition by changing the person who devotes himself to it, through the wisdom it gives which surpasses all knowledge.

3. St. Bonaventure's Metaphysics of Light

There has always been debate about what place 'pure' philosophy held in St. Bonaventure's world view. It is beyond doubt that there is no purely philosophical system in his works. This must not be taken to mean however that he ignored philosophy. Because he maintained that the highest knowledge is revealed wisdom, then to remain with the findings of philosophy and to be satisfied with these, is to be confirmed finally in error. For example, to rest in the knowledge of God's unity and to know nothing of the Trinity-in-Unity, is not to know God as in fact He is.

In St. Bonaventure's theory of knowledge there is an essential relationship between light and truth and he adheres unswervingly to the doctrine of illumination. It is in his theory of knowledge that one finds, perhaps most clearly of all, the fundamental unity of the intellectual and spiritual life, that is, the unity of *lectio, speculatio* and *unctio*. Light and truth are interchangeable terms: "Divine Truth is itself Light".[8] "Truth is the light of the soul. This light never fails".[9] The human intellect is a light from God and the truth of all knowledge rests in God, Who is the Light wherein we apprehend, the unchanging and unchangeable truth of reality. All knowledge, in fact, comes about by reason of the Uncreated Light.[10] However, the Eternal Light which is God is not directly perceived in the act of knowledge, nor is it an object immediately known, because of itself the Eternal Light is inaccessible, though it is most close to the soul; it is unconfinable, though it is also supremely intimate.[11] To apprehend any truth at all it is required that there be

---

[7] *The Works of St. Bonaventure*, trans. by J. de Vinck, *V Collations on the Six Days, St.* Anthony Guild Press, Paterson N.J. 1970, pp. 284f.

[8] *Quaestiones Disputatae de Scientia Christi*, III, conclusio, *Opera Omnia* V, 14a.

[9] *Collationes in Hexaemeron*, IV,1, *Opera Omnia* V, p. 386.

[10] I Sent., d. II, p I, art. unicus, q. 1, *Opera Omnia* I, 68b.

[11] *Collationes in Hexaemeron* XII 11, *Opera Omnia* V, 386a.

immutability in the object known and infallibility in the knowing subject. On these two conditions depends all certain knowledge. God alone is immutable and therefore He must aid the human intellect in arriving at the certitude which, as a matter of experience, it undoubtedly possesses. Certain knowledge must in some way be established on the divine ideas; it must be related to the *ars superna,* the divine ideas *(rationes aeternae)*, as to light and truth: light which gives infallibility to the knower and truth which gives immutability to the object of knowledge. The illumination of the human intellect by the divine ideas has a regulating and motive action in the process of arriving at certitude. However, the divine ideas do not have the sole influence in our acquisition of knowledge, nor are they known in their total clarity. They exercise their influence only through created reason and they are but dimly contuited (not intuited) by us in our pilgrim state here on earth.[12] There is no question, then, in his theory of knowledge dispensing with sense data, nor with ignoring the process of abstraction. By divine illumination the human intellect grasps in the object known the reflection of the immutable, eternal idea and thus arrives at certain knowledge. Creatures are the *exemplata* of the divine exemplar—a truth which manifests the intimate connection between St. Bonaventure's theory of divine illumination and his doctrine of exemplarism. The Eternal Ideas are one with the Word of God. Christ, he says:

> teaches interiorly, so that no truth is known except through Him, not through speech as it is with us, but through inner enlightenment. Wherefore He must necessarily have within Himself the most clear species[13], which He cannot possibly have received from another. He Himself, then, is intimate to every soul and He shines forth by means of His most clear species upon the obscure species of our understanding. And in this manner, these obscure species mixed with the darkness of images, are lit up in such a way that the intellect understands. If indeed to know a thing is to understand that it cannot be otherwise than it is, by necessity He alone will make it known Who knows the truth and possesses the truth within Himself.[14]

4. St. Bonaventure on St. Francis

It is not only in the pages of the Fioretti and in the writings of Leo, Rufino and Angelo that we find the 'real' St. Francis. For all their freshness and simplicity, these have no exclusive claim to the authentic picture of St. Francis.

---

[12] *Quaestiones Disputatae de Scientia Christi* IV, conclusio, Opera Omnia V, 23b.

[13] *Species* here is almost exactly equivalent to the Platonic ideas—the only difference is that *species* here indicates individual rational representations within God's mind of all creatures.

[14] *Collations on the Six Days*, 12th Collation, 5, de Vinck, pp. 174f.

Were these, in fact, our only sources, we should have no more than a highly romantic or naively visionary picture of St. Francis. St. Bonaventure's theological and mystical reflections on the life and spirit of the Poverello, whom he considered a perfect contemplative, have given us a rich and precious understanding of the Saint through the eyes of a learned and saintly follower, who loved him above all for his humility and poverty.

His love of St. Francis pervades every page of his mystic writings and one reads these with a deep sense of admiration for the holiness and humility of their author. What seems to have attracted him to the Order at first was the similarity of its history to that of the early Church. Just as the Church began with a little band of fishermen and then later attracted some of the greatest minds of Christian Antiquity, so the Franciscan Order started with simple and unlettered men, but soon drew to itself learned masters and clerics from the Schools. When St. Bonaventure joined the Order he came under the direct influence of Alexander of Hales, a learned master from Gloucestershire who had himself entered the Order at Paris in 1231 much to the consternation of his contemporaries. In the works which date from his early years in the Order St. Bonaventure had little to say about St. Francis; for example, in his long Commentary on the sentences he makes no more than two brief references to St. Francis. But from the time of his visit to La Verna in October 1257 his works reveal a depth of knowledge and love of St. Francis and tremendous zeal for the observance of the *Rule* and they tell us much about his own discipleship of St. Francis.

There are some people who maintain that St. Bonaventure betrayed the ideals and attitudes of St. Francis, especially in the question of learning and studies. This, it must be said, does grave injustice to St. Bonaventure. At best St. Francis' attitude to learning was ambiguous. His ideals and charism were uniquely his own and cannot be emulated. Moreover, we can never get away from his injunction in the *Testament:* "All theologians and those who minister to us the most holy words of God we ought to honour and venerate as those who minister to us spirit and life". While he advised the unlettered not to strain after learning (*Rule* 1223, c. 10), he also exhorted those who worked with their hands to do so "faithfully and devotedly, yet in such wise that excluding idleness which is hurtful to the soul, they do not distinguish the spirit of holy prayer and devotion" (*Rule* 1223, c. 5). Both manual work and learning, evidently, can have their dangers for the soul. We should also note, that St. Francis never forbade learned men to enter the Order. The idea that there is something not quite authentic about a learned Franciscan, is a notion born of fantasy and romanticism, contradicted by the first century of the Order's history in general and most forcefully of all by St. Bonaventure himself. The learned to whom God has given the vocation to serve Him with the powers of the mind, also need God's grace in their longing for holiness and salvation. St. Bonaventure was deeply aware of this need. He submitted the entire treasure of his philosophical and theological knowledge to the spirit of St. Francis and in this lies his greatness and his humility as a true Franciscan.

A. The Five Sermons on St. Francis

In volume IX of the *Opera Omnia* are contained five sermons on St. Francis. These tell us a great deal about St. Bonaventure's understanding and love of his Seraphic Father. He avoids quite unselfconsciously in the first sermon that what moved him to preach it was obedience to the Pope and a very special love he bore St. Francis. What comes over strongest of all in these sermons is his love and admiration of the poverty and humility of St. Francis. Perhaps this is something we should expect from a man of learning who knows so well the terrible dangers of pride and vainglory that lurk in knowledge that is not yet true wisdom. Speaking of the excellence of the poverty of St. Francis he remarks that poverty makes a man heavenly, above all when it is poverty in which a man glories and finds joy. He goes on: "And you will not find anyone who ever professed poverty as St. Francis professed it or who gloried in it as he did". God confirmed his Order and the profession of most high poverty by His own bull of approval in impressing the seal of the Sacred Stigmata on his humble and poor servant, the blessed Francis.

St. Bonaventure gives us an interesting detail from the life of Pope Gregory IX. He tells us in the second sermon that Gregory IX, on account of the friendship he had for St. Francis, became an imitator of his humility. He kept a leper in his own room in the papal palace and, dressed in the Franciscan habit, served him and took care of him. One day the leper said to the Pope: "Has the Supreme Pontiff nobody other than an old men to look after me?" The Pope was extremely tired after his work for the Church and the leper had never recognised him. This episode should make us very wary of assuming too quickly that Hugolino had the predominant influence on St. Francis. This detail makes it look very much the other way round.

In a meditation on the fifth sermon on the text of Matthew 11:29: "Learn of me, for I am meek and humble of heart", St. Bonaventure applies these words to St. Francis as one who followed faithfully in the footsteps of Christ. To be meek, he says, means to be a brother of all; to be humble is to be least of all. The follower of Christ must be meek in his relationships with other men and humble before God. 'To be meek and humble is to be a poor little brother that is, a friar minor. This is the name St. Francis wished his followers to have: "They are all to be known as Friars Minor without distinction" (*Rule* 1221, c.6). In this—to be a friar minor—is contained the summary of the gospel life and the teaching of St. Francis.

B. The Collationes in Hexaemeron

In this work St. Bonaventure presents an overall theology of history in which both the Franciscan and Dominican Orders have an important and very definite place. There can be no doubt that his concern to find a solution to the "Franciscan Question" (which involved among other matters the serious problem of studies in the Order) had great influence on his elaboration of a theology of history. This theology of history in its turn, presented a solution to the "Franciscan Question" that is as welcome to Franciscans today (whose lot it is to pursue studies) as it was ingenious in the circumstances of the Order's history in which he propounded it.

St. Bonaventure did not totally reject the views of Joachim of Flora on the meaning of history. Joachim wrote a *Commentary on the Apocalypse* at the request of Pope Lucius III. Therein he divided the history of the world into three ages: that of the Father, that of the Son and that of the Holy Spirit. The first is the age of the married state, the second is the age of the priesthood and preaching and the third the age of the order of monks or the age of contemplatives. The third age will be the final age of the Eternal Gospel. Joachim divides the second age into seven periods and the time at which he was writing (towards the end of the twelfth century) he identified with the transition from the fifth to the sixth period. With the sixth period, a new order would appear whose founder with his disciples would constitute the order of preachers in imitation of the poor life: Jesus and His Apostles. He speaks at times of the rise of two orders in the near future, both of which will have the mission to preach.

St. Bonaventure incorporated many elements of Joachim's theological analysis of history into his own theology of history.[15] St. Bonaventure divides both the history of the Old Testament and the times of the New Testament into seven periods: "The times of symbols were seven in number. . . .Likewise in

---

[15] See J. Ratzinger, *The Theology of History in St. Bonaventure*, trans. by Z. Hayes OFM, Franciscan Herald Press, Chicago 1971, pp. 1-55.

the New Testament there are seven times".[16] There is a strict correspondence between the events of the seven periods of the Old Testament and the seven periods of the New Testament. In terms of this correspondence we are enabled to understand not only the past, but also to know something of the future of New Testament times: "Thus it is clear how Scripture describes the succession of times; and they are not haphazard nor left to chance, but they contain a marvellous light and many spiritual meanings".[17] The seventh age of the New Testament times is not outside history, however, but clearly historical and pre-eschatological. The period is described in connection with the prophecy of Ezechiel 40ff.: "Then will be fulfilled the prophecy of Ezechiel when the city will come down from heaven, not indeed that city which is above, but the one below that is the (Church) Militant: when it will be conformed to the (Church) Triumphant, as far as it is possible in the pilgrim way. . . .And then there shall be peace. But how long this peace will last, God knows".[18]

The sixth period of New Testament times is understood by comparison with the sixth period of the Old Testament. Charlemagne, who loved the Church and was zealous for her good, corresponds to Ezechias or Ozias. Henry IV and Frederick I, who brought great tribulation to the Church correspond to Manasses. St. Bonaventure then predicts that only two great events separate the sixth from the seventh period (the sixth day from the seventh day of peace): another great ruler who will love the Church and work for her good corresponding to Josias and a further great tribulation to the Church, corresponding to the Babylonian exile.[19] From this tribulation will come the new and final Order.

In his theology of history St. Bonaventure draws a parallel between Elias and St. Francis in terms of Malachi's prophecy: "Behold I will send you Elias the prophet, before the coming of the great and dreadful day of the Lord" [Malachi 3:23]. There is an obvious influence here to Joachim of Flora who related the expectation of Elias to the prediction of the two witnesses of the Apocalypse 11:3: "But I shall send my two witnesses to prophesy for those twelve hundred and sixty days, wearing sackcloth". A new Elias and a new Enoch are predicted at the beginning of the third age by Joachim. St. Bonaventure writes: "The fifth time, at the end, is that of the restoration of ruins, for 'Elias indeed is to come and to restore all things' and with him Enoch

---

[16] *16th Collation*, de Vinck, 12-13, pp. 236-237.
[17] Ibid., p. 250.
[18] Ibid., pp. 249f.
[19] Ibid., p. 248.

will come too".[20] Commenting on this text Ratzinger notes: "It was possible to see this prediction fulfilled in Francis and Dominic"—an identification, that was made by the author of the pseudo-Joachimite commentary on Jeremias.[21] Joachim of Flora speaks of the order of comtemplatives in the third age, that of the Holy Spirit. The two Orders which will appear at the end of the sixth period of the second age will be only provisional to mark the transition from the sixth to the seventh period. The final Order will be quite different from these as the Order of pure contemplatives. St. Bonaventure accepts this solution substantially and has identification of these two Orders with the Dominicans and the Franciscans. The Order of the seventh period of New Testament times in his division of history, will also be an order of contemplatives who will have true wisdom and who will restore the primitive apostolic zeal and life of the Church. St. Bonaventure, therefore, does not totally reject the doctrine of Joachim, though he does not admit any Gospel other than that of the New Testament, which is itself the eternal gospel.

In the course of his *Collationes* St. Bonaventure establishes parallels between the heavenly hierarchy of angels and the ecclesiastical hierarchy on earth. He writes: "It is fitting, then, that the Church Militant have orders corresponding to the model hierarchy".[22] When he comes to speak of the contemplatives in the Church who are found at the apex of the ecclesiastical hierarchy, he disposes them in three orders: "Now they tend to divine matters in a threefold way: some by means of supplications, others by means of speculations, others again by means of elevations".[23] To the first of these belong the Cistercians, Premonstratensians, the Carthusians and the Canons Regular, who devote themselves entirely to prayer, devotion and the praise of God, who do a certain amount of manual work to supply their needs and who pray for those who have given them estates and possessions. In the heavenly hierarchy, the Thrones correspond to these. The second are those, who attend to divine things by speculation, that is, the speculatives who devote themselves to a study of Scripture, for which they must purify their minds because "one cannot grasp the words of Paul unless he has the spirit of Paul. . . .These are the Preachers and the Minors". He identifies the speculatives, therefore, with the Dominicans and the Franciscans to whom the Cherubim in the heavenly hierarchy correspond. The Dominicans are concerned with speculation, first

---

[20] Ibid., p. 230.
[21] Ratzinger, *Theology of History*, pp. 33, 40f.
[22] *22nd Collation*, de Vinck, 2, p. 342.
[23] For this and subsequent quotations see *22nd Collation*, 22-23, pp. 350-352.

and with piety next; the Franciscans with piety first and then with speculation; St. Bonaventure adds that St. Francis wanted his Friars to study, but they were first to practise what they preached. It must be emphasized that St. Bonaventure is not making an odious comparison here between the Dominicans and the Franciscans, he is concerned merely to point out the different attitude of these two Orders based on their particular spirit. Both belong to the Order of speculatives and both have a love of God which corresponds to the Cherubim. "The third manner", he says, "is concerned with those who, attend to God by means of elevation and ecstasy" (*secundum modum sursumactivum, scilicet ecstaticum seu excessivum*). This is the Seraphic Order in which St. Francis is placed by St. Bonaventure. "This Order will not flourish, unless Christ appears and suffers in His Mystical Body". St. Francis, therefore, belonged to a unique Order which cannot be identified with the Franciscan Order. All other Franciscans belong to the Order of Minors. This destination is based on the unique charism which St. Francis received, a charism that cannot be repeated in the Franciscan Order. The conclusion drawn by St. Bonaventure is that the Minors must attain to contemplative union by speculation. At the practical level, therefore, St. Bonaventure had here his solution to the thorny problem of the Order's relationship to St. Francis. In terms of his theology of history, however, St. Francis is placed in the order of contemplatives of the final age because of his mystical love of God, this knowledge of the Scriptures given by divine illumination and his life of absolute poverty in imitation of the Poor Christ and His Apostles. St. Bonaventure would never have agreed to the Order being called the Seraphic Order for the simple reason that this is the Order of the final age to which St. Francis belonged by special gift of God. He would not have agreed either to the title 'Seraphic Doctor' which the Order has given him. The reception of the Stigmata as a unique gift is the external sign of his having belonged, while still on earth, to the Order of the Seraphim. St. Francis was already in fact in ecstasy before he founded the Order. St. Bonaventure writes:

> And he said that he (Francis) was in ecstasy before even receiving the habit, and was found near a certain hedge. This indeed, is the most difficult, that is, *elevatio in sursumactione*, for the whole body is shaken, and unless there be some consolation of the Holy Spirit, it could not survive. And in these things the Church is consummated. But what this order is to be, or already is, is hard to know.[24]

---

[24] *22nd Collation*, 22, p. 152.

This solution, of the difficult question of the relationship of the Franciscan Order to St. Francis commends itself, I think, to respectful and worthy consideration. It introduces of course the problem of what obligation and possibility an Order has of re-living the charism of its Founder. When the Second Vatican Council advised each religious Order to re-discover the sources of its original inspiration, it placed our Order in an unenviable position:

> The appropriate renewal of religious life involves two simultaneous processes: (1) a continuous return to the success of all Christian life and to the original inspiration behind a given community and (2) an adjustment of the community to the changed conditions of the times.[25]

Is it possible, in fact, to re-live or recapture an origin, inspiration which sprang from a charism? With regard to the absolute (and what does this mean?) poverty of St. Francis, I do not think the statement of M.D. Lambert can be gainsaid:

> The standard of poverty intended by St. Francis, if appallingly severe, was coherent and, just, observable. It could stand with a moral exhortation, *annuntiando eis vitia et virtutes, poenam et gloriam cum brevitate sermonis.* . .because this did not demand learning. But as I see it, it is incompatible with the regular pursuit of learning. The new entrants to the Order were bound to desire the practice of preaching, in the full, learned sense. If learning be adopted, then the full poverty must be mitigated.[26]

Allow me to quote here what I said about poverty in another context.[27] From this it will be clear that I do not consider the issue of poverty unimportant for the Franciscan Order. My point is, however, that we cannot reproduce the internal and external poverty of St. Francis which was a charismatic gift. St. Bonaventure understood this in establishing a *via media* between what may be described as the lax party in the Order and the Spirituals. Nor must it ever be forgotten that St. Bonaventure himself was extremely strict about the

---

[25] *Perfectae Caritatis*, 2, in: *The Documents of Vatican II*, ed. by W.M. Abbott SJ, Chapman, London-Dublin 1966, p. 468.

[26] *Franciscan Poverty. The Doctrine of the Absolute Poverty of Christ and the Apostles in the Franciscan Order 1210-1223*, London SPCK 1961, p. 68, n.1.

[27] Editors' note: Doyle refers here to *Reflections on the Theology of Religious Life*, reprinted in this volume (pp. 504 ff.): "There are a number of aspects. . . .Its charism concerns material poverty in a very real way".

observance of poverty in the life of the Order in the second half of the thirteenth century.[28]

Moreover, St. Bonaventure did not change this Mendicant Order into a Monastic Order—this view is based on the common assumption, that monastic life is the paradigm of the common life. This assumption, however, is false. There are many ways in which the common life may be realized: that of the Mendicant, Franciscan Order was one, just as the Monastic life was another and the Canons Regular still another. It must be recorded, however, that St. Bonaventure was aware that the Order had not remained faithful to St. Francis. He shows himself to have been preoccupied with this state of affairs, which the following text makes clear, a text which merits long meditation:

> Contemplation cannot come about except in the greatest simplicity and the greatest simplicity cannot exist except in the greatest poverty. And this is proper to this Order (the Seraphim). The intention of Blessed Francis was to live in the greatest poverty. And he said[29] we had receded a lot from our state, and therefore God permitted that we be afflicted so that by these means we may be led back to our state that must possess the promised land.[30]

5. The Doctor of Mystical Theology

The whole of St. Bonaventure's philosophical and theological writing is directed to but one end: to lead the soul to mystical union with God. He is pre-eminently a doctor of mystical theology. Of this he gives us his own clear definitions: the whole, of mystical theology is concerned with arriving at ecstatic love of God according to the purgative, illuminative and perfective or unitive ways. He describes these in detail in the *De Triplice Via*. The purgative way leads to peace, the illuminative way to truth and the unitive way to charity. Each of these has three exercises: meditation, prayer and contemplation.

Practically every theological doctrine of St. Bonaventure can be traced back ultimately to a source in the spirituality of St. Francis. His doctrine of exemplarism (every creature is a word of God), his Christocentric teaching, the primacy of charity, are all of them, in their own way theological expressions of

---

[28] See the injunctions of the *Constitutiones Narbonnenses* or the quality of the habit, footwear and the observance of poverty in *Opera Omnia* VIII, 449a-467b, esp. 451a-453a; see also the *Quaestiones de perfectione evangelica*, q.2: *De Paupertate* and the *Apologia Pauperum*. In both works St. Bonaventure emphasizes that Franciscan poverty is a poverty both communal and private. He never accepted the loose notion of the lax party.

[29] Often the text of the *Collationes in Hexaemeron* contains only the reporter's words, which makes it a work difficult at times to interpret.

[30] *20th Collation*, de Vinck, 30, p. 317.

the intuitions and insights which came from St. Francis' seraphic love of God. To end these pages I want now to say a little about his theology of Christ.

> Now since it is necessary to ascend before we can descend on Jacob's ladder, let us place our first step in the ascent at the bottom, setting the whole visible world before us as a mirror through which we may pass over to God, the Supreme Creative Artist. . . .The supreme power, wisdom and benevolence of the Creator shine forth in created things in so far as the bodily senses inform the interior senses.[31]

> The material world contains vestiges of the Blessed Trinity and we are able to contemplate God both through and in creatures. Christ is the expression of the Father and the exemplar of all creation. Every creature has come from God the Creator through the Eternal Word, bearing His vestige and image. All creation participates in Christ, the Incarnate Word, Who is present in all things. In fact all creation has a tendency that points to the incarnation, which is the most perfect of all God's works. Again, the natural tendency in matter is so ordained toward intellectual causes that the generation is in no way perfect unless the rational should be united to the material body. By similar reasoning therefore we come to the conclusion that the highest and noblest perfection can exist in this world only if a nature in which there are seminal causes, and a nature in which there are the intellectual causes, and a nature in which there are the ideal causes are simultaneously combined in the unity of one person, as was done in the incarnation of the Son God.[32]

In this text St. Bonaventure has all but reached the doctrine of Duns Scotus on the Primacy of Christ. There are scholars who have gone so far as to compare this text with passages from the writings of Teilhard de Chardin. The place of Christ in St. Bonaventure's theology is undoubtedly the foundation of his mystical teaching. His mystical writings: *The Journey of the Mind to God, On Retracing the Arts to Theology, The Tree of Life, The Five Feasts of the Child Jesus, The Treatise on Preparation for Mass, The Office of the Passion, The Mystical Vine* provide autobiographical hints about the character and

---

[31] *Itinerarium mentis in Deum* I 9, St. Bonaventure's *Itinerarium mentis in Deum* with an Introduction, Translation and Commentary by Ph. Boehner OFM, The Franciscan Institute, St. Bonaventure 1956, p. 45.

[32] *De Reductione ad Theologiam*, 20, in: *Reductione Artium ad Theologiam*. A Commentary with an Introduction and Translation by E.T. Healy, The Franciscan Institute, St. Bonaventure 1955, pp. 37f.

holiness of this extraordinary man, whose life in the main is hidden behind the pages of his works. No one could have written about the love of Christ as he did without having experienced the greater part of what he was writing. Christ in all His mysteries from His birth and infancy to His manhood, death on the Cross and Resurrection was the object of St. Bonaventure's ardent love of God and men. His entire system of theology is summarized in these most mystical words from the *Collationes in Hexaemeron:*

> It is not without reason that the scroll was sealed with seven seals. "Behold, said one of the Elders, the Lion of the tribe of Juda, the Root of David, has overcome to open the scroll and its seven seals". [Apocalypse 5] These are the seven Centres. By their significance, Christ opened the tomb, and this represents the opening of the scroll, and He removed the shroud, and this represents the manifestation of mysteries. This is our logic this is our reasoning which must be used against the devil who constantly argues with us.[33]

---

[33] *1st Collation*, de Vinck, 30, p.16.

Saint Bonaventure, Seraphic Doctor
1217-1274[1]

The year 1974 which marks the 750th anniversary since the Franciscan Friars first came to England, is also the 700th anniversary of the death of St. Bonaventure. While we are recalling the former with thankfulness to God, we ought not to forget the latter anniversary, nor allow it to slip by without record or remark. St. Bonaventure was precisely what posterity has given him as his proper title: *Seraphic Doctor*—an intellectual giant, burning with the love of God, who served the Lord with all his heart and mind as a follower of the Poor Little Man of Assisi. It is not only in the pages of the *Fioretti* and the writings of Leo, Rufino and Angelo that we find the 'real' St. Francis. For all their freshness and simplicity, these have no exclusive claim to the authentic picture of St. Francis. Were these, in fact, our only sources, we should have no more than a highly romantic or naively visionary picture of St. Francis. St. Bonaventure's theological and mystical reflections on the life and spirit of the Poverello, whom he considered a perfect contemplative, have given us a rich and precious understanding of the Saint through the eyes of a learned and saintly follower who loved him above all for his humility and poverty.

St. Bonaventure was born in 1217 in Bagnorea, a small town lying between Orvieto and Viterbo in northern Italy. He tells us that at an early age (when he was about twelve years old) he was cured of a fatal illness through the intercession of St. Francis. The debt of gratitude he felt towards the Saint for his life is what moved him to accept the decision of the General Chapter of Narbonne in 1260 to write the life of St. Francis. In 1235 he went to Paris where he studied the arts. By 1243 he was Master of Arts and in that same year he joined the Franciscan Order and began his theological studies. The Franciscan tradition, above all the holiness and spirit of its Founder, became now the chief factor in St. Bonaventure's theological and spiritual formation. In 1244 he made profession of vows in the Order and for the next decade he pursued his theological and biblical studies. He obtained the title of Doctor of Theology in 1254. In the midst of his academic career, while he was regent master in the Franciscan School at Paris, he was elected Minister General of

[1] THE FRANCISCAN 16 (September 4, 1974) pp. 176-179, 182. Published with permission.

the Order on 2 February, 1257. He was now pulled away from the peace and calm of a life of study and thrown into the maelstrom of the Order's history, at a time when feelings were sharply divided on the interpretation of the *Rule* and mind of St. Francis and when Joachimite ideas were exercising a strong influence in some sections of the Order. Shortly after his election he went to Mount La Verna in Tuscany to meditate on the life of St. Francis in the very place where the Saint had received the Stigmata some thirty years before. From his experiences on La Verna came one of his most beautiful and profound works: *The Journey of the Mind to God,* in which he traces the steps of the soul's ascent to contemplative union with God. For the greater part of two decades he served the Order as its General Minister, making incredible journeys in Italy and France to preach the word of God, to exhort the friars in their observance of poverty and to correct abuses against the *Rule*. In May, 1273 he was created a Cardinal (tradition has it that he was washing dishes when the news was brought to him) and later that year he was consecrated Bishop of Albano. It is recorded that he had refused earlier to accept the Archbishopric of York. He took an active and influential part in the proceedings of the Council of Lyons. He died in Lyons on 15 July, 1274 where he lies buried. He was canonized in October, 1482, by Pope Sixtus IV and declared a Doctor of the Church by Pope Sixtus V in 1588.

St. Bonaventure holds a unique place in the Golden Age of the Scholastics, among whom he adhered unswervingly to the teaching of St. Augustine. However, it is not this aspect of his thought that I want to mention here. Instead, I propose to meditate a little on his love of St. Francis and his mystical teaching.

His love of St. Francis pervades every page of his mystical writings and one reads these with a deep sense of admiration for the holiness and humility of their author. What seems to have attracted him to the Order at first was the similarity of its history to that of the early Church. Just as the Church began with a little band of fishermen and then later attracted some of the greatest minds of Christian Antiquity, so the Franciscan Order started with simple and unlettered men, but soon drew to itself learned masters and clerics from the Schools. When St. Bonaventure joined the Order he came under the direct influence of Alexander of Hales, a learned master from Gloucestershire, who had himself entered the Order at Paris in 1231, much to the consternation of many of his contemporaries. In the works which date from his early years in the Order, St. Bonaventure has little to say about St. Francis. For example, in his long *Commentary on the Sentences* he makes no more than two brief references to St. Francis. But from the time of his visit to La Verna in October,

1259, his works reveal a depth of knowledge and love of St. Francis, and tremendous zeal for the observance of the *Rule* and they tell us much about his own discipleship of St. Francis.

There are some people who maintain that St. Bonaventure betrayed the ideals and attitudes of St. Francis, especially in the question of learning and studies. This, it must be said, does grave injustice to St. Bonaventure. At best St. Francis's attitude to learning was ambiguous; his ideals and charism were uniquely his own and cannot be emulated. Moreover, we can never get away from his injunction in the *Testament:* "All theologians and those who minister to us the most holy words of God we ought to honour and venerate as those who minister to us spirit and life". While he advised the unlettered not to strain after learning *(Rule* 1223, c.10), he also exhorted those who worked with their hands, to do so "faithfully and devoutly, yet in such ways that, excluding idleness which is hurtful to the soul, they do not extinguish the spirit of holy prayer and devotion" *(Rule* 1223, c.5).

Both manual work and prayer, evidently, can have their dangers for the soul. We should also note that St. Francis never forbade learned men to enter his Order. The idea that there is something not quite authentic about a learned Franciscan, is a notion born of fantasy and romanticism, contradicted by the first century of the Order's history in general and most forcefully of all by St. Bonaventure himself. The learned to whom God has given the vocation to serve him with the powers of the mind, also need God's grace in their longing for holiness and salvation. St. Bonaventure was deeply aware of this need. He submitted the entire treasure of his philosophical and theological knowledge to the spirit of St. Francis and in this lies his greatness and humility as a true Franciscan.

There is not space to show in detail how St. Francis was the inspiration of so many of his works. It must suffice to say a brief word about his love of St. Francis which comes through a study of five sermons on the Saint contained in vol. IX of the *Opera Omnia.* He avows unselfconsciously in the first sermon that what moved him to give it was obedience to the Pope and a very special love he bore St. Francis. What comes over strongest of all in these sermons is his love and admiration of the poverty and humility of St. Francis. Perhaps this is something we would expect from a man of learning who knows so well the terrible dangers of pride and vainglory that lurk in knowledge that is not wisdom. Speaking of the excellence of the poverty of St. Francis he remarks that poverty makes a man heavenly, above all when it is poverty in which a man glories and finds joy. He goes on: "And you will not find anyone who has ever professed poverty as St. Francis professed it or who gloried in it as he did". God confirmed his Order and the profession of most high poverty by His own bull of approval in impressing the seal of the Stigmata on his humble and poor servant, blessed Francis.

In a meditation in the fifth sermon on the text of Matthew 11:29 "Learn of me, for I am meek and humble of heart", St. Bonaventure applies these words to St. Francis as one who followed faithfully in the footsteps of Christ. To be meek, he says, means to be brother of all; to be humble is to be least of all. The follower of Christ must be meek in his relationships with other men and humble before God. To be meek and humble is to be a poor little brother, that is, a friar minor. This is the name St. Francis wished his followers to have: "They are all to be known as Friars Minor without distinction" *(Rule 1221*, c. 6).

In this—to be a friar minor—is contained the summary of the Gospel life and the teaching of St. Francis. Every theological doctrine of St. Bonaventure can be traced back ultimately to a source in the spirituality of St. Francis. His doctrine of exemplarism (every creature is a word of God), his Christocentric teaching, the primacy of charity, are all theological expressions of the intuitions and insights which came from St. Francis's seraphic love of God.

It is not an oversimplification to say that St. Bonaventure's entire literary output had but one aim: to lead the reader to wisdom, which can never be attained by erudition alone, but ultimately only through holiness. The mystical way to union with God is not the privileged path of a few (be they learned or unlettered), but is open to all who have the will to follow the call of grace through its various stages to contemplative union. Recalling the Stigmata of St. Francis on La Verna, he writes in *The Journey of the Mind to God* (VII, 3):

> Here he passed over into God in a transport of contemplation. He is set forth as an example of perfect contemplation. . . .And thus, through him, more by example than by word, God would invite all truly spiritual men to this passing over and this transport of soul. In this passing over, if it is to be perfect, all intellectual activities ought to be relinquished and the most profound affection transported to God and transformed into Him.

St. Bonaventure:
Prologue to the First Book of Sentences[1]

The depths of rivers he has searched out and hidden things he has brought to light [Job 28:11].

After carefully analysing this text from the twenty-eighth chapter of the Book of Job, the way was opened up for us to know here at the outset the four kinds of cause in the Book of the Sentences: the material, formal, final, and efficient causes. The material cause is intimated by the word rivers; the formal cause, in the phrase searching out *the depths;* the final cause, in the revelation of *hidden things;* and the efficient cause is understood from what underlies the two verbs *he has searched out* and *he has brought to light.*

1. The Material Cause

The material cause is signified by the word rivers. It is in the plural and not the singular, because it refers not simply to the subject matter of the *Books of the Sentences* as a whole, but to the subject matter of each book taken separately. We should note that just as a river has four characteristics, so a "spiritual river" possesses four specific qualities. And in line with this fourfold distinction, there are four *Books of the Sentences.*

When I consider that a river goes on flowing, lastingness comes into my mind. As Saint Isidore says, "A river is an unending current".[2] When I reflect on the width of rivers, vast expanses come into my mind. In fact that is what distinguishes a river from a little brook. When I think about their

---

[1] THE CORD (March 1985) pp. 80-89. Published with permission from The Franciscan Institute, St. Bonaventure University, New York.

The publication of this *Prologue to the First Book of Commentary of the Sentences of Peter Lombard* that St. Bonaventure wrote at Paris c. 1248-1253, is the first of a series of four prologues. Since they provide us with basic outlines—in the form of poetic prose—they are beautiful works of medieval literature. Because they touch on many aspects of spiritual theology, however, such as the mystery of God, anthropology, the role of the sacraments, etc., they offer us invaluable tools with which we may attempt to penetrate the depths of Bonaventure's approach to Franciscan spirituality. E. Doyle, translator of this first Prologue, passed away before this, one of his last works, could be published.

[2] *Etymologiarum Liber XIII*, c. 21, n. 1, in: *PL* 82, p. 489: *Fluvius est perennis aquarum decursus.*

movement, I find myself reflecting on circularity. As it says in the Book of Ecclesiastes: "To the place from where the rivers come, they return to flow again" [1:7]. When I consider the usefulness of rivers, I find myself thinking about processes of purification. Because of the vast amount of water they contain, rivers purify the land through which they flow without getting polluted themselves.

Every analogy is based on some similarity.[3] Taking these four qualities metaphorically, therefore, we find that a river has a fourfold spiritual meaning, as we can gather from Holy Scripture.

1. First, then, in terms of lastingness, the emanation of the Persons in the Trinity is described as a river. This emanation uniquely is without beginning and without end. Of this river Daniel says: "The Ancient of days was seated and a swift, fiery river issued from his face" [7:9-10]. This Ancient of days is the Eternal Father, whose antiquity is his eternity. The Ancient One was seated because he is endowed not only with eternity, but also with immutability. The text says: From "the face of the Ancient One issued forth a swift, fiery river". That is to say, from the sublime nature of his Godhead there proceeded the fullness of love and the fullness of power. The fullness of power is the Son, and thus the river was swift; the fullness of love is the Holy Spirit, and thus the river was fiery.

2. Secondly, in terms of vast expanses, the created world is described as a river. In fact, because of its vastness, the Prophet in the Psalms calls this world not only a river, but also a sea: "So is this great sea which stretches wide its arms" [Psalms 103:25]. Ezechiel says about this river: "Behold I come against you, Pharaoh, king of Egypt, great dragon who lie in the midst of your rivers and say: 'The river is mine and I made myself'. But I will put a bridle in your jaws" [29:3-4]. This great dragon whom the Lord addresses and threatens in the figure and person of Pharaoh, king of Egypt, is the devil. He reigns over those whom he has blinded with the darkness of error, such as heretics, for instance, to whom he also says: "The river is mine and I made myself", as if he himself made this world and had not his own origin in another. It was the devil who framed this error and put it into the minds of the wicked Manichees, who maintain that the whole structure of the visible world was made by an evil god. The Lord will put a bridle on the jaws of this dragon when, having destroyed the power of spreading falsehood, he will manifest himself as the Creator of

---

[3] Aristotle, *Topica* VI, II, in: *The Loeb Classical Library* II, Cambridge MA 1976, p. 567: "For those who use metaphors always do so on account of some similarity".

this river. Thus it follows in the same text of Holy Scripture: "And all the inhabitants of Egypt shall know that I am Lord" [Ezechiel 29:6].

3. Thirdly, in terms of circularity, the incarnation of God's Son is called a river. For just as in a circle the end is joined to the beginning, so in the incarnation the highest is joined to the lowest, God to the dust of the earth, the first to the last, the eternal Son of God to human nature created on the sixth day. Of this river Sirach says: "I, like the River Dorix and like an aqueduct, came out of paradise" [24:41].[4] Dorix means a life-giving remedy. It is used here figuratively and may be understood conversely as the source of a life-giving remedy.[5] For the incarnation was none other than the source of life-giving remedy for us: "Surely he has borne our infirmities and carried our sorrows" [Isaiah 53:4]. Rightly, then, is the incarnation of the Son of God called the River Dorix. Christ says truly of himself: "I, as the River Dorix"—that is, a healing river—"and like an aqueduct, came out of paradise". Now it is of the nature of water that as high as it rises so far does it come down. Such was the going forth of the incarnation, as the Psalm says: "His going out is from the end of heaven and his circuit even to the end thereof" [18:7]. And in Saint John's gospel we read: "I came from the Father and have come into the world; again I am leaving the world and going to the Father" [16:28], and thus he completed a circle. A text contained in a dream which Mordecai had, can be applied to this river which is Christ, taking it to refer to his coming forth from his mother: "The tiny spring that became a river and was turned into a light and into the sun" [Esther 10:6]. Who, I ask you, is this tiny spring other than the most humble Virgin Mary? She became a river when she brought forth Christ who, on account of the abundance of grace he brings, is not only called a river, but also the light of wisdom and the sun of justice, as Saint John says of him: "He was the true light" [1:9].

4. Fourthly, in terms of processes of purification, the sacramental system is called a river. The sacraments cleanse us from the stain of our sins without getting polluted themselves. Of this river, the Book of Revelation says:

---

[4] *Dorix*: this reading (the Vulgate has *dioryx*) is taken from the Old Vulgate and does not appear in modern translations; see, e.g., Sirach 24:30. The editors of the Latin text refer the reader to commentaries on this text by Hugh of Saint-Cher OP (1200-1263), the first Dominican Cardinal (cf. C. Jerman, *Hugh of Saint-Cher*, DOMINICANA 44 (1959) pp. 338-347; J.P. Torrell, *Hugh de Saint Cher et Thomas d'Aquin* in: REVUE THOMISTE 82 (1974) pp. 5-22; and by Nicholas of Lyre OFM (1270-1349); cf. H. Labrosse, *Source de la biographie et oeuvres de Nicholas de Lyre* in: ETUDES FRANCISCAINES 16 (1906) pp. 383-404; 17 (1907) pp. 489-505, 593-608; 19 (1909) pp. 41-52, 153-175, 368-379; 35 (1923) pp. 171-187, 400-432.

[5] It is difficult to reproduce St. Bonaventure's play on words here: *generationis medicamentum, generatio medicamenti.*

"He showed me the river of the water of life, bright as crystal, flowing from the throne of God and of the Lamb" [22:1]. The sacramental system is described as a river bright as crystal because of the splendour and lustre the sacraments leave in the soul which has been purified in this river. It is called the river of the water of life because of the efficacy of grace which gives life to the soul. It flows from the throne of God and of the Lamb. Sacramental grace flows from God as from its author and efficient cause, and from Christ as from its mediator and meriting cause. That is why all the sacraments are said to have their efficacy from the Passion of Christ. Saint Augustine witnesses to this when he says: "From the side of Christ sleeping on the cross the sacraments came forth while the blood and water flowed out".[6]

There is a text in the Book of Genesis which refers to all these rivers, both taken together and considered separately, which reads: "A river flowed out of Eden to water the garden and there it divided and became four rivers. . . .The name of the first is Pishon. . . .The name of the second river is Gihon. . . .And the name of the third river is Tigris. . . .And the fourth river is the Euphrates" [2:10-14]. The river flowing out of Eden is the subject matter of the whole *Book of the Sentences*. The four rivers coming from it are the specific subject matter of each of the four books, as anyone can easily recognize who sets himself to explain carefully the meanings of the above mentioned names.

Pishon means "movement of the mouth", and for this reason it refers to the emanation of the Persons. As word and breath go forth from a physical mouth, so the Son and the Holy Spirit proceed from the mouth of the Father, as it says in Sirach: "I came out of the mouth of the Most High, the firstborn before all creatures" [24:5]. These are the words of the Son himself, who is the Word and Wisdom of the Father. And in the Psalms we read: "By the word the heavens were established and all the power of them by the spirit of his mouth" [Psalms 32:6].

Gihon means "the sands of the seashore", and it refers as such to the created universe. As the universe of creatures is likened to the sea because of its vast expanse, so it is compared to the sands of the seashore because of the multitude of beings it contains. As it is written in the Book of Sirach: "Who has numbered the sand of the sea and the drops of rain?" [1:2].

---

[6] *The Works of Aurelius Augustine*, ed. M. Dods, X: *Lectures or Tractates on the Gospel according to St. John*, vol. 1, Edinburgh 1873, p. 134: "When Christ is dead, the spear pierces his side, that the mysteries may flow forth whereby the Church is formed" (cf. *PL* 35, p. 1463).

Tigris means "an arrow", and in this it refers to the incarnation of the Son of God. For just as in an arrow iron is joined with wood, so in Christ the strength of divinity is united with the weakness of humanity. And as an arrow flies through the air from a wooden bow to smite the enemy, so Christ springing from the cross destroys the adversary. This is the arrow of which the Fourth Book of Kings speaks: "The Lord's arrow of victory, the arrow of victory over Syria" [4 Kings 13:17].

Euphrates means "fruit bearing", and this refers to the sacramental system which not only cleanses the soul of sin, but makes it fruitful in grace. This is indicated in the Book of Revelation where it says that on both sides of the crystal river "was the tree of life. . .and the leaves of the tree were for the healing of the nations" [22:2].

2. The Formal Cause

As there are four rivers, so there are four deep mysteries[7] corresponding to them.

1. There is the deep mystery of eternal emanation which is the sublime nature of the divine being, to which a text in Ecclesiastes may be taken as referring: "It is a great depth, who shall find it out?" [7:25]. Truly God is a great depth and a deep mystery. This is what brings Paul the Apostle to exclaim in Romans: "O the depth of the riches and wisdom and knowledge of God! How unsearchable are his judgments and how inscrutable his ways" [2:33]. God's judgments are indeed unsearchable because they are so deep. As the Psalm says, "Your judgements are a great deep" [35:7], and we read in Sirach: "Who has measured. . .the depth of the abyss?" [1:2]. This same depth is indicated in the Book of Job: "Can you find out the deep things of God? Can you find out the limit of the Almighty? It is higher than heaven-what can you do? Deeper than Sheol—what can you know?" [11:7f.]. All of which is to say, of yourself you can do nothing, you can know nothing. Thus, Paul advises us in the Letter to the Ephesians: "That you, being rooted and grounded in love, may have the power to comprehend with all the saints what is the breadth and length and height and depth" [3:17f.].

The Master searches out this deep mystery in the first *Book of the Sentences*. The sublime nature of the divine being consists in two things: the most awe-inspiring emanations, namely generation and procession; and the most noble qualities, which are the highest wisdom, omnipotence, and perfect

---

[7] Thus I translate *profunda*. It does not keep to *the depths of rivers (profunda fluviorum)* of the text from Job 28:11; but it makes for better and more intelligible English.

love. All this forms the subject matter of the first Book. In the first part he treats of the most holy Unity and Trinity of God, and in the second part, in a special treatise, he examines the three qualities just mentioned.

2. The deep mystery of creation is the impermanence of created being. The more a creature wastes away, whether because of sin or because of punishment, the deeper it goes into the depths. For this reason the Prophet, speaking in the place of a man who has faded away because of sin, says in the Psalm: "I stick fast in the mire of the deep and there is no sure standing" [68:2]. Again, the Prophet prays that he may not waste away through punishment: "Let not the tempest of water drown me, nor the deep swallow me up" [Psalms 68:16].

The Master searches out this deep mystery in the second Book. The impermanence of created being lies in two factors: the change from non-being to being, and the reversal once more to non-being. Now, although no creature of its nature tends to non-being, nevertheless, as Saint Augustine says, the sinner tends towards non-being because of sin.[307] These two factors form the subject matter of the second Book. In the first part he treats of the issuing forth of all things, and in the second part he deals with the fall, the temptation by the devil, original and actual sin, and so we reach the end of the Book.

3. The deep mystery of the incarnation is the value of Christ's humanity, which was so great that it can truly be described as deep, as having no limit, as inexhaustible. A text from Jonah may be applied to this deep mystery: "You did cast me into the deep, into the heart of the sea, and a flood encompassed me" [2:4]. This can be understood of Christ, for he was so humbled that he can truly be said to have been cast into the deep and degraded. We read in Isaiah: "We have seen him, and there is no sightliness that we should be desirous of him. Despised and the most abject of men, a man of sorrows, and acquainted with infirmity" [53:2-3]. Therefore, he describes himself accurately as cast forth. But where is he cast? Into the depths of the sea and the depths of a river. The passion of Christ may be likened to the sea because of the bitterness of his sufferings and likened to a river because of the sweetness of his love. For the heart of Jesus was so affected towards us by the tenderness of love, that it did not seem too much to him to undergo the worst and most bitter death for our sake.

---

[8] The exact text does not appear literally in the works of St. Augustine. But the sense of this passage will be found in the *Confessions* VIII, 16, in: *The Fathers of the Church* XXI, Washington 1973, pp. 185f.; PL 32, p. 744; *The City of God*, Bk. XIV, c. XIII, in: EVERYMAN'S LIBRARY, New York 1945, pp. 43f. (PL 41, pp. 420-422); *De vera religione Liber unus*, c. XI, *PL* 34, pp. 131f.

The Master searches out this deep mystery in the third Book. The value of Christ consists in two things: namely, his sufferings, by which he redeemed us; and his actions, by which he formed us and which consist in the works of the virtues, the gifts and the commandments. These form the subject matter of the third Book. The first part treats of the incarnation and passion in which is found our salvation; and the second part treats of the virtues, the gifts, and the commandments, in which is contained our formation.

4. The deep mystery of the sacramental system is the power of perfect healing. So great in fact is the efficacy of sacramental healing, that it is beyond the human mind to comprehend it, and so it may rightly be described as a deep mystery. Of this Isaiah says: "You made the depths of the sea a way for the redeemed to pass over" [51:10]. This depth in which the Egyptians were submerged and which the children of Israel, delivered from Egypt, passed over, is the efficacy of the sacraments, in which the works of darkness are destroyed and the armour of light and the gifts of grace conferred, through which we pass from the power of darkness into the kingdom of the children of God's love. The efficacy of the sacraments is compared to the depth of the sea and the depth of a river. Of the sea, because it first delivers us from sin and leads us to the bitterness of penance; of a river, because it delivers us from wretchedness and leads us to the delights of glory. This was graphically prefigured in the children of Israel, for whom, as they left Egypt, the sea dried up and they went across on "dry ground in the midst of the sea", as the Book of Exodus tells us [15:19]. When they entered the Promised Land, the river dried up and they passed over the Jordan, as is written in the Book of Joshua [4:22f.].

This deep mystery the Master searches out in the fourth Book. The power of perfect healing has two components: the curing of the diverse weaknesses that assail us, and liberation from all the miseries that plague us. These two components form the subject matter of the whole of the fourth Book. The first part treats of the various kinds of healing which the seven sacraments bring about. The second part deals with that perfect healing: the glory of the risen life, to which they come who truly and faithfully received the sacraments of the Church; and, on the other hand, it deals with the punishments of the wicked who despised the sacraments of the Church.

3. The Final Cause

After searching out the four deep mysteries in the four Books, there emerges the purpose or final cause, that is, the revelation of four hidden mysteries.

1. The first is the mystery of the divine nature, of which Isaiah says: Truly, "you are a hidden God, the God of Israel, the Saviour" [45:15]. The majesty of the divine nature is indeed hidden for us, as it is written in the Book of Job: "How small a whisper do we hear of him! But the thunder of his power who can understand?" [26:14]. For certain no one can understand this, except him with whom the wisdom of God dwells. This is the reason why that lover of wisdom, the author of the Book of Wisdom, made this prayer: "Send her forth from your holy heavens and from the throne of your glory send her" [9:10].

The Master, filled with wisdom from on high, brings this hidden mystery to light in the course of his investigations in the first Book. He examines and unfolds the most awe-inspiring emanations and the most noble qualities of the Godhead, and so he reveals to us, as far as it is possible while we are in this world, the majesty of the divine nature.

2. The second hidden mystery is the order of divine wisdom, of which Job speaks: "But where is wisdom to be found? And where is the place of understanding? It is hid from the eyes of all living" [28:12, 20f.]. Indeed wisdom is hidden, for as Job also says: "But wisdom is drawn out of secret places" [28:18]. To know wisdom it is necessary to search out its depths, not in itself, but in its works in which it shines forth. So it says in the Book of Sirach. "There is one most high Creator, and he poured her out upon all his works" [1:8, 10].

The Master reveals this hidden mystery in his analyses in the second Book. He examines the order of good and evil and makes known to us how the wisdom of God "was set up from all eternity and of old before the earth was made" [Proverbs 8:23].

3. The third hidden mystery is the strength of divine power, of which Habakuk says, "Horns are in his hands: there is his strength hid" [3:4]. He is speaking there about Christ hanging on the cross where the strength of his power was hidden under the veil of weakness. This "is the plan of the mystery hidden for ages of which Ephesians speaks: To me, grace was given to preach to the Gentiles the unsearchable riches of Christ and to make all men see what is the plan of the mystery hidden for ages in God" [3:8f.]. This is the hidden mystery, the sacred secret, that the mighty God was clothed with the protection of our weakness in order to overcome the enemy. This is unheard of since the world began.

The investigations of the third Book make known the strength of the divine power. It shows how Christ in his weakness overcomes the opposing power. If he was victorious by weakness, what would have happened if he had entered the fight with his power? And if "the weakness of God is stronger than men" [1 Corinthians 1:25], who shall "turn back" [Isaiah 14:27] the arm of God? It is abundantly clear that his power is indescribable whose weakness is so strong.

4. The fourth hidden mystery is the sweetness of the divine mercy, of which the Psalmist says: "How great is the abundance of your sweetness, O Lord, which you have hidden for those who fear you" [30:20]. Indeed, the sweetness of mercy is hidden and stored up for those who fear God because, as the Psalmist says, "the mercy of the Lord is from everlasting to everlasting upon those who fear him" [102:17], and "on those who hope in his mercy" [146:11].

This sweetness is revealed in the analyses contained in the fourth Book. He unfolds how God forgives our sins in the present, what cures he applies to our wounds, and what gifts he will grant us in the future. In this way the Master makes known to us the sweetness of divine mercy.

4. The Efficient Cause

The unveiling of these hidden mysteries is the aim of the four Books as a whole. With this intention in mind for himself and for his readers, the Master of the *Sentences* "searched out the depths of rivers" under the guidance of the Holy Spirit. The Holy Spirit himself is the chief searcher of secret things and of the depths, as Saint Paul tells us: "For the Spirit searches all things, even the depths of God" [1 Corinthians 2:10]. Inflamed with the love of this Spirit and enlightened by his radiance and splendour, the Master composed this work and "searched out the depths of rivers". By the aid of this same Spirit he became a revealer of hidden mysteries. It is he of whom the Book of Daniel says: "He reveals deep and hidden things and knows what is in darkness" [2:22].

This was the Master's aim and intention, as he himself explains in the Prologue: "Wishing to place the light of truth on the candlestand, we composed this volume with God's help and much work and effort, from the witnesses to truth who are established in eternity". And a short while before that, he had outlined his purpose as follows: "to unfold the hidden truths of theological investigations".

So, from the foregoing reflections, it is evident what are the material, formal, final, and efficient causes of the Book of the Sentences.

"The Big Question"[1]
Alan Webster

In June 1974 THE YORKSHIRE POST declared that "religious television programmes were towards two extremes: the awfully worthy, which tend to be dull, and the frightfully trivial, which try to be entertaining". They found one exception: the programme entitled "The Big Question" analysing serious issues confronting society. This series of ten minute discussions was televised by Anglia TV from Norwich most Wednesday nights for ten years at 10 p.m. deliberately intended to catch people talking for the last half hour before closing time at the pub or in the evening at home when conversation can flag. The last recording was January 31, 1984.

At the heart of the conversations was Eric, always in a Franciscan garb always quirky, funny and very alert, listening to the questions, not dogmatic or authoritarian. He was loyal, liberal and strikingly likeable. With him were three others, a Free Church Minister, myself then Dean of Norwich, afterwards from 1978 Dean of St Paul's Cathedral, London, and a question master chosen with great skill by Anglia TV guided by their Religious Director, Canon Freeman.

The programmes were recorded eight at a time and were never rehearsed and only once censored—a discussion of Irish politics. Anglia regarded "The Big Question" as of such importance that during a railway strike they flew us from London by private plane to Norwich. After 30 years people still come up to talk to me about them and Father Eric is always specially remembered with a smile, though there are fewer Roman Catholics in this part of England than elsewhere. They say: "Such a lovely man—he made Christianity attractive".

Viewers over the years were astonished to see a loyal Catholic in his Franciscan garb so at ease, friendly and able to share the jokes of his non-Catholic colleagues. It was only a generation since Catholic priests had been forbidden to say the Lord's Prayer (even after the Blitz raids) with Protestant

---

[1] Original contribution published with permission. Alan Webster is a former Dean of St. Paul's Cathedral, London.

colleagues in public. Eric brought ecumenism alive week after week in about 400 interviews.

Our Free Church colleague, Edmund Banyard and Eric accepted my invitation to preach a three-some sermon in St Paul's. "Three men in a boat" Eric said. Encouraged by Eric's example I joined one inter-church visit to Central America, took part in the Lenten Via Pacis march in Nicaragua and enabled a Jesuit from El Salvador to preach and participate in the Eucharist at St Paul's. Eric took risks in order to act out the spirit of Vatican II and of Liberation Theology. Oscar Romero was his hero.

"The Big Question" style of conversation was to use down to earth language. There was no dumbing-down of profound and perplexing theological or social questions—but slowly a realistic terminology was evolved. We remembered that the homes and pubs would be taking their own decisions about worship, family planning, the cold war or conservatism and socialism. We banned such words as 'eschatology' or 'infallibility' but were concerned with what was at stake. Here Eric was a genius. The Irish, Methodist, Liberation and Franciscan strands in his personality gave him a special knack of making links with our audiences—as well as with the camera men and Anglia staff. He loved the dramatic: once in his Franciscan garb holding up the Norwich traffic.

As the years passed we asked if we could leave the studio in Norwich and do the programmes where the problems were for real. We broadcast from a ward for paraplegics at Stoke Mandeville hospital, from Norwich jail and from a nuclear bomber air base in Lincolnshire.

Eric never once hinted that the Catholic Church had the answers—only that we were searching together with the vulnerable God who had been through it all in Christ. We were given conscience not dogmatic solutions.

Eric also shone when "The Big Question" was transmitted on the national network with David Self as question master. The Cambridge papers said of Eric that "he was the best all round performer working in TV today. . . .This man is an original, a non-pareil: after they made him they broke the mould". With David he made school radio programmes explaining to secular audiences what it means to say "I believe".

Though not always a good time keeper and addicted to cigarettes, he was sought after until his final illness. His sense of wonder, his mischievous humour and his intellectual curiosity were all a delight. Two days before his death he rang up David Self. "David, I'm going". "Going where? To the States?" "No, no. I don't know where. I just wanted to say Goodbye". He was always introducing new dimensions of honest vision.

Journalist's Report on "The Big Question"[2]

Late at night, when all are asleep. Anglia. "The Big Question". At last—David Self introduces Eric, a monk, but more than a monk. A man, but more than a man. Each Wednesday Fr. Eric, Alan Webster (the Dean of St. Paul's) and a Free Church Minister discuss affairs of the spirit. Eric, to be plain, is quite simply the best all-round performer working in television today. Every gesture, every ejaculation of the arms and legs, every considered rubbing of the fingers, every gasping catch for breath, every accent and cadence bespeaks the full and noble soul of a dedicated Thomist[3] and born entertainer. Like the genius he is, he cannot bear to be off-screen for a moment. A planned 'one-shot' of Webster suddenly finds itself embracing part of Eric's knee and Eric's brilliantly expressive fore-arm and wrist. Like a grisaille by Giotto, Eric is quite simply too big for the frame, and parts of him will burst animatedly out of picture in the committed pursuit of theological absolutes. Eric is, quite simply, the man to follow. The length, breadth and width of his discourse, if the dimensions of his body-language are a reliable index, is quite simply colossal. I quite simply demand that you do not fail to join me, and thousands of like-minded fans, in watching Eric's saltatorial displays each Wednesday night. This man is an original, a non-pareil; before they made him, they broke the mould. Quite simply.

---

[2] Editors' note: Every attempt was made, each one unsuccessful, to locate the source of this lively report (1981).

[3] Editors' note: From the collection of Doyle's writings on St. Bonaventure and Blessed John Duns Scotus in this anthology it is clear that Doyle's focus was on the Franciscan intellectual tradition.

Eric Doyle and "The Big Question"[4]
Edmund Banyard

"Would you care to come and take part in a discussion programme, it's an experiment, we haven't any great hopes for it, but think it might be worth a try?" In some such words Peter Freeman issued invitations to a recording session at the Anglia Television Studios in Norwich, where for the first time I met Alan Webster, John Swinfield who was to be our first chairman, and Eric Doyle. that morning we made four programmes and at the end of the session Peter Freeman's verdict was that they could have been worse, and it might be worth making a few more. That was the beginning of "The Big Question". Over fourteen years we made more than 400 programmes together and ran through six chairmen. Long before we made our last recordings in March 1984. Eric and Alan and I had become close friends.

We each enjoyed the freedom of an unscripted broadcast and though we were advised in advance the subjects we would be discussing, no one could predict how the conversations would develop. Eric was immediately at home in this setting with his gift for taking deep theological issues and talking of them in deceptively simple terms. On one occasion when we had been talking about prayer as a two way conversation the chairman suddenly asked Eric, "Does God ever speak to you?", "But of course" was the immediate reply. The chairman persisted, "then what does He say?" Without a moment's hesitation and with great conviction Eric replied, "I love you, I love you". Again an again Eric had the right response for the potentially awkward question and you always felt that this was no mere cleverness, but rather a word simple, but profound, which came straight from the heart.

Most of the programmes we made were epilogues for late night transmission in the Anglia region, recorded in the studio and transmitted as recorded. Over the years however we made some twenty other programmes for use on Sunday evenings across the whole network and these were recorded on location with an audience participating. Usually we would have the

---

[4] Original contribution published with permission. E. Banyard is a Minister and former Moderator of the General Assembly of the United Reformed Church.

opportunity to meet informally with the audience before or after the programme and here Eric was immediately involved in animated conversation whether it was with paraplegic patients at Stoke Mandeville hospital, men serving a sentence in Norwich prison, airman at bomber base in Lincolnshire, magistrates and policemen at Huntingdon or whatever other group it might be.

On one occasion we were asked to mount a Big Question Special as part of an all night youth event in St. Edmundsbury Anglican Cathedral. This we duly did in the early hours of the morning and afterwards, understandably, I felt tiredness creeping up on me, but Eric showed no signs of fatigue and still had young people around him when dawn broke and the event concluded with breakfast being served.

When "The Big Question" was launched it was considered a little daring and somewhat risky to bring representatives of three different Christian traditions together in this way and expect something positive to emerge. Indeed, we were probably a little surprised ourselves to discover how much common ground we shared. In the penultimate programme where we were asked to reflect on our experiences together Eric, amid laugher, said that he had come to our first meeting with some apprehension but went away happier having discovered that the Dean of Norwich was less grand and that I was less of a heretic than he had supposed. We all three testified from the heart that we had ourselves learned much from the experience of exploring such a wide variety of issues together.

Even now, twenty years after our last broadcast together, folks will occasionally stop me and refer to "The Big Question" and always they want to speak of Eric, and if for the moment they can't recall his name, they will probably refer to him as the little Friar. No one who knew him could mistake the fact that Eric's Christian faith was the ground of his being, a faith which embraced and valued all created things. With his deep scholarship went a childlike wonder and openness to new experiences and a delight in simple pleasures which, with his delightful personality, made him a great communicator. It has been one of the great privileges of my life to have known and worked with Eric Doyle and to have been able to call him a friend.

Photo 13

With colleagues
for TV-program,
"The Big
Question"

Photo 14

Speaking at
Canterbury
Cathedral

Photo 15

Singing with
confreres at
Canterbury

Photo 16
With the artist Bernard Coleman OFM
(+1986)

Photo 17
With Kevin Bloggs at
Canterbury

Photo 18
A happy moment at
Canterbury

On Blessed John Duns Scotus

Duns Scotus—A Man for All Time[1]

1. Outline of Scotus' life

When a historian sets out to reconstruct the story of the past, his first objective is to discover the documents relative to that part of the past with which he proposes to deal. Once he finds them, what strikes him immediately is their amazing partiality. In some cases they preserve a man's memory down to the smallest details of his life and achievements; in others, they record barely more than a name. Where it is a question of medieval documents, the historian is faced with a further difficulty. Medieval writers did not have the care and concern for biographical details, such as distinguishes historians of our own day. Often their intention in writing was to edify, and in so doing, they were not overscrupulous if their accounts did not always tally with the facts. Therefore, what they have to say about a man, whether much or little, has to be checked and scrutinized before they can be used with anything like solid reliability.

The documents that have come down to us about Duns Scotus have not been too generous in biographical details. Indeed, so little was known about him at one time, that serious doubt was cast upon his ever having existed at all! However, over the last fifty years or so, research has brought to light sufficient data about him that now make it possible to draw up a fairly accurate, though by no means full, account of his life. An outline of that account is given here.

Birth and Early Days

John Duns Scotus was born in Scotland sometime between December 23rd, 1265, and March 17th, 1266. The exact date is not known, but historians take 1266 as the more probable of the two. Though it is accepted now without question that John was Scottish (there was an opinion at one time that he was

---

[1] *The Seventh Centenary of the Birth of Blessed John Duns Scotus,* Edinburgh: Scotus Academy. Editors' note: Scotus Academy is defunct. Published with permission from the Province of Immaculate Conception, England.

born in Ireland), scholars have not always agreed about the precise place of birth in Scotland. Both Maxton-on-Tweed in Roxburgh and Duns in Berwick have been claimed. From recent research, however, it may be said safely that Duns in Berwick is taken, well-nigh universally as the more likely of the two.

Of his early life we know almost nothing. We are told that his father was Ninian Duns of Littledean, whose family had been benefactors of the Franciscans from the time when these first set foot in Scotland in 1231. His paternal uncle, Elias Duns, was himself a Franciscan. Scotus' early schooling is said to have been at Haddington in East Lothian, where the Franciscans had a Friary. Such close ties with the Franciscan Order must have had their part in sowing the seeds of a vocation in the mind of the young John.

Entry into Franciscan Order

In the year 1278 it was decided that the Scottish Friaries should be no longer subject to the Custody of Newcastle and that a Vicar General be chosen to rule them, as forming a body quite distinct from the Province of England. Accordingly, the Guardians met at Haddington where they chose Elias Duns, Guardian of Dumfries, to be their Vicar General. After his election, Elias returned to Dumfries, taking with him his young nephew, by this time a boy of about twelve or thirteen years. It was at Dumfries that Scotus was received into the Franciscan Order. The age required for reception was fifteen, and so Scotus cannot have entered the Order before 1280. His profession of vows probably took place in 1281.

But more important than the date is the fact of his entry into the Franciscan Order. John was now introduced to a form of life and spirituality that was to be his mainstay throughout the years ahead. St. Francis' burning love of the Crucified, his literal observance of the gospel, his tender concern for all God had created, his loyalty towards the Church—all this became John's own ideal. It is this ideal that gives the key to any understanding of his life and works. Everything he taught, everything he wrote, found its point of departure in his Franciscan vision of the world.

Ordination to the Priesthood

It is not known for certain where Scotus did his early studies in the Order. The chief centre of learning in the North was Newcastle. But in view of the withdrawal of the Scottish Friaries from the jurisdiction of the English Provincial, he may well have remained at Dumfries. In any case, we can be sure that he spent the next eight years in assiduous study of Arts.

In 1290 Duns Scotus was at Oxford. Now, according to the Statutes of the University, no one could begin the study of theology without having completed eight years study of Arts. It was perhaps at the end of these studies that Scotus was sent by his Superiors to Oxford.

On March 17th, 1291, Scotus was ordained priest by Oliver Sutton, Bishop of Lincoln, in the church of St. Andrew at Northampton. After his ordination there began for Scotus a series of coming and goings between England and the Continent, which was to end only with his death.

Further Studies

For about two years Scotus continued his studies at Oxford. In 1293 he was sent to Paris, where he attended lectures on the *Sentences*—a work made up of four books written by Peter Lombard. As he did not have the necessary qualifications to lecture on the *Sentences* himself at Paris, he returned to England in 1297. Settling at Cambridge, he lectured on them there until 1300. During the Summer of that year he went back to Oxford where he began lectures on the *Sentences* in the Autumn.

In 1302 he was nominated by the Minister General to lecture at Paris. He set out once more for the Continent with the intention of completing his lectures by the following Summer. But events so developed that he was forced to bring them to a sudden and dramatic end.

Exile from Paris

For several years during this period Philip the Fair, King of France, and Pope Boniface VIII had been engaged in a struggle, due to Philip's having imposed taxes on Church property, in defiance of immemorial custom. In the early months of 1303 the struggle became greatly intensified. Things came to a head when Philip began to look for support of his anti-papal policy among the clergy. He was determined to appeal to a General Council against the Pope. During the month of June, the higher clergy, followed later by the University of Paris and the Chapter of Notre Dame, openly declared their adhesion to the King. On the 25th, the King's Ministers visited the Franciscan Friary at Paris to ascertain whether the Friars favoured Philip's action or not. Eighty gave their assent to his action, some hundred-and-eighty dissented, among which latter was John Duns Scotus. The dissenters were given three days to leave the Kingdom. Scotus was forced to depart in haste and leave his lectures unfinished. On returning to England he went once more to Oxford, where he continued his lectures throughout the scholastic year 1303-1304.

Master in Theology

In the meantime, Boniface VIII had suspended the power of the University of Paris to grant academic degrees. On his death, in October 1303, he was succeeded by Benedict XI who restored the University's privileges in April of the following year. King Philip did all in his power to bring back Masters and students to Paris. Scotus returned sometime before November, 1304.

Final preparations were now made for Scotus' reception of the Mastership in theology. Luke Wadding has preserved a letter from the Minister General to the Guardian and Masters of Paris, containing the former's recommendation that Scotus be presented. The letter continues: "I authorise to be presented. . .the beloved Father in Christ, John Scotus. I am thoroughly informed, partly from my own experience, and partly from his world-wide reputation, of his praiseworthy life, his outstanding knowledge, his most subtle mind, and his other remarkable qualities".

At Easter of the following year he became Master of Theology, and thus reached the crowning point of his long years of study, begun far back in 1281.

After receiving the Mastership, Scotus commenced a further period of teaching at Paris. But even now, with barely three years to live, he was not to find lasting peace. By the beginning of the scholastic year 1307-8 he had already left Paris, and in the early months of 1308 he was teaching in the Franciscan House of Studies at Cologne. The precise reason for his departure is not known, but the turn of events in France may well provide the explanation.

Historians have drawn attention to the fact that Scotus' departure from Paris took place around the time of the process against the Knights Templar. Philip's action put him once more at enmity with the Pope. This must have made Scotus' position highly precarious. What would be the course of events, should the King demand approval of his action against the Knights from the University? Scotus had been expelled from Paris on a previous occasion; what might happen on this? Moreover, it seems that there was strong opposition to his doctrine on the Immaculate Conception among some members of the University, and precisely from those who supported the King in his action against the Templars. It would not be difficult to take reprisals by accusing him of heresy. It seems, therefore, that the Minister General's decision to send Scotus to Cologne was prompted by prudence for his safety. On receipt of the obedience, Scotus set out for Cologne at once.

Cologne and Last Days

At Cologne he had but one year left to him. He continued lecturing for some time in the Franciscan House of Studies. It was his last scholastic year, for he died on November 8th, 1308, barely forty-three years of age, at the height of his maturity.

After his death, Scotus' reputation for sanctity spread throughout England, France, Germany, Italy, and many other European countries. Veneration for him has continued down the centuries. He is honoured as Blessed in the Franciscan Order, and a canonically approved diocesan cult is paid to him at Nola in Italy. In 1905 a formal petition was made to the Holy See for his canonization. It is the ardent hope of all who love and venerate him that this will be speedily granted.[2] "With him, early achievement counted for long apprenticeship". [Wisdom 4:13]

II. Scotus Past and Present

The Past

Alongside this veneration paid to Scotus, there has also been a very strange and sad misrepresentation. In the history of Catholic thought there are few theologians who have been so neglected and maligned as John Duns Scotus. In no small number of works dealing with the development of Catholic theology his name appears here and there in a couple of footnotes, but beyond that, no mention of him is to be found. In Manuals of Catholic Doctrine he is only brought in occasionally as an adversary or the exponent of an opinion which holds no particular claim on the author. A learned Jesuit, Fr. Bernard Jansen, has written, not without solid foundation: "Rarely has the figure of an eminent personage of the past been defaced, as has that of the Franciscan, John Duns Scotus". Therefore, before dealing with one or two points from the philosophical and theological legacy left to us by Scotus, we should like to give briefly the reasons which explain this extraordinary treatment.

In the first place, he died before having completed the revision of his works. He began the revision during his last period at Paris; we have seen already the circumstances which brought him to leave that city for Cologne. The change and upheaval involved must have had very adverse effects on his studies and academic life. More than that, he had only one year more to live, hardly sufficient to revise his vast and varied corpus of writings. The

---

[2] Editors' note: The Church beatified John Duns Scotus on 20 March 1993.

consequent lack of any clearly defined systematisation in his works, gave rise to very thorny problems in the organized study of his teaching. Scholars, therefore, tended to shy away from his works because of the difficulties they would inevitably meet, in attempting to decipher the development of his thought.

Moreover, works were attributed to him which, we know now, he could not possibly have written. But for people less wise, these offered solid basis for the accusations against him. Besides this, there was no critical edition of his works. He could be made to say anything with no official text to test its truth or falsity. Writers copied one another, repeating centuries-old formulations of his doctrine, which, in fact have little or no foundation in his works.

Then again, the subtlety of his mind did not always help matters. His works contain the deepest erudition and are full of sharp distinctions. His approach to a problem is often very abstract and always ruthlessly objective—not the best for clarity of style and exposition. It requires courage and perseverance to apply oneself to a study of his works. Beraud de Saint Maurice[3] has pointed out that the epithet 'Subtle Doctor' has sometimes proved unfortunate. The ambiguity of the word 'subtle' has led many to resent him. Finally, there came the most devastating and saddest commentary of all; when scholars began to refer to him as the herald of decadence in the history of Scholasticism.

The Present

Our own century, however, has seen commenced the tremendous task of critically editing his works. Much of what was thought to be of Scotus, has now been discarded. As a result, we can be sure we are reading his doctrine and not the fabricated version of some adversary. No longer does he appear as the carping critic who set out to destroy what his predecessors had built up. A deep and prolonged investigation of his doctrine accompanied by a ready sympathy (the latter so necessary to gauge and penetrate his genius) has discovered for us the picture of the real Scotus: a man on fire with the love of God and His Revelation.

Scotus' insistence that the study of theology is a practical matter, leading, in this life, to a union with God, his teaching on Christ as the manifestation of God's love and the Centre of all creation, his emphasis on the primacy of the will, have all gone to prove that love is the keynote to the vast

---

[3] in: *John Duns Scotus, A Teacher for our Times*, St. Bonaventure 1955, 51f.

synthesis of truth that he created. Fr. Gemelli wrote: "His whole philosophy is based on love".

From this it is clear that Scotus stands well and truly in the Franciscan Tradition. He belongs to that current of thought which owes its origin to the spirit of St. Francis of Assisi. Throughout his works there is to be found overwhelming evidence of an extensive knowledge of the great Franciscan Doctors who preceded him, Alexander of Hales, Bonaventure, and many others. To quote Fr. Gemelli again: "Duns Scotus makes concrete the love and will of St. Francis in doctrines that were bold during his own time, but prophetic for our time".

III. Scotus and our Lady

The originality of Scotus' thought is attested, perhaps best of all, by his defence of the Immaculate Conception of Our Lady. Well-nigh six hundred years before the definition of the dogma by Pius IX, Scotus had laid down unassailable arguments in support of this Marian privilege.

The historical circumstances in which he defended this doctrine merit some consideration. For many decades before Duns Scotus' time, the Immaculate Conception had not found favour among theologians. As far back as the mid-twelfth century, St. Bernard had said that the feast had been introduced without any justification. Nearer to Scotus, St. Bonaventure and St. Thomas Aquinas were doubtful on the matter. Even in Scotus' day, the doctrine was not particularly popular at the University of Paris. We have noted above that the Minister General's action in removing Scotus to Cologne, may well have been due, in part at least, to the opposition he encountered to this doctrine. Scotus' defence of the Immaculate Conception of Our Lady, therefore, attests not only his mental acumen, but also his courage and single-mindedness in the face of what might have been very great danger.

The great difficulty for those who preceded Scotus was the apparent impossibility of reconciling this privilege of Mary with the doctrine of the universal necessity of Redemption. Being a daughter of Adam, Mary needed to be redeemed; how could she be included in Christ's Redemption if she had no sin? This was a real difficulty, for it seemed to these theologians that the Immaculate Conception separated Mary from Christ and His saving work. It was not out of any wish to belittle Mary that they questioned this privilege, their doubts sprang from an anxiety to safeguard her relationship to Christ.

Scotus confronted and solved this difficulty. He showed how she was in fact redeemed by being preserved from original sin through the foreseen merits of Christ. Being a child of Adam she indeed needed to be redeemed, but as Scotus explained, she was redeemed, as it were, in the very act of incurring original sin. As a most perfect mediator between God and man, Christ exercised a most perfect mediation in the case of her who was to be His Mother.

For Duns Scotus, this doctrine is seen logically only from the point of view of the Primacy of Christ. Christ was predestined by God to be the Centre of all creation. Because of sin it was decreed that He should come in a human nature capable of suffering in order to redeem mankind. But this in no way affected God's eternal plan, that even if there had been no fall, Christ would still have come as King and Centre of all creation. It was not fitting, therefore, that Mary should be tainted, even for a single instant of her existence, with original sin, since she was to be so intimately associated with Christ as Redeemer and Restorer of all creation.

The vindication of Scotus' teaching did not come at once. For centuries was the Church to meditate on it. But then on December 8th, 1854, Pope Pius IX declared to be of faith the doctrine holding that Mary, through the merits of Christ, was preserved from all stain of original sin from the very first instant of her existence. What Scotus had asserted so long before, was now proclaimed dogmatic truth.

IV. Scotus and our Time

If one were asked to summarise the vast synthesis of truth created by Duns Scotus, the answer would take no more than a few words: a philosophy of love and a theology centred on Christ. But if one were asked further, to draw out all that is contained in such a summary, the answer could not be given so briefly. It would take far more space than is possible here. Besides, such a task would be beyond the scope and purpose of this writing.

For this last section, therefore, two themes from Scotus' teaching have been selected which drive home the relevance of his doctrine for our time, and bring out its paramount importance for the Church and world of the twentieth century. These are headed 1. *The Uniqueness* of the Person; 2. Christ and the World. What Scotus wrote on these points, might have been intended just for us; for what he said seven centuries ago, we are saying now. Indeed, his doctrines were prophetic for our time.

The Uniqueness of the Person

In an age such as ours, when we have become accustomed to thinking in terms of mass psychology, when the tendency has grown up to herd people into groups and categories, it is imperative that we stop to reflect on the value of the individual person. We must bring home to ourselves that it is the individual who gives dignity and purpose to the group, and not the other way round. If we do not, then we will be sworn to look on man as no more than a tiny cog in a vast machine of Impersonal Humanity, in which his individuality is swamped, and apart from which his personal existence has little or no meaning at all.

In this regard, Christian Philosophy has always been marked by a deep concern for the dignity of man. In a special way does it show itself in the Christian Philosophy of Duns Scotus. In his treatment of what is known as the problem of "The Principle of Individuation", he worked out a theory which is of great consequence for a doctrine of the dignity of man.

Scotus tells us that it is "incommunicability" which makes the individual. Now, in terms of human personality, that can best be described, without oversimplifying his thought, as *uniqueness.* There is about every single human person a uniqueness, an originality, which by definition is inimitable. The dignity, therefore, of each and every person comes from the very uniqueness which he possesses. This makes him the object of the knowledge and love of every other person in this world. Though he shares a common humanity, he has it in a way that no other can have. He is then, someone worth knowing, worth loving, because what he is makes all that he does a unique contribution to the great endeavour of transforming humanity into a human family. In his relationships he has something to give that cannot be given by another—and above all in that relationship we call love, for here what he gives, is himself.

When all this is lifted to the level of a man's relationship with God, his uniqueness, and thus dignity, comes out clearest of all. God created each human person utterly and entirely unique. He sent His Son to redeem, not only humanity, but each individual person. In return for His Love, he asks for the unique love of every man in this world. He wants it; only each can give it, no one else can stand in. If this love is refused, it is never given to God.

This uniqueness must not be confused with egocentricity **or** isolationism. It does not close a man in upon himself; rather it brings him into relation with every man. It leads a man to seek others in their uniqueness, and above all that Eternal Other, Whose uniqueness he reflects.

Christ and the World

We know from God's Revelation that the Second Person of the Blessed Trinity became man to bring salvation to the world to redeem it and give it eternal life. He came, as a matter of fact, to destroy sin and the kingdom of Satan. But beyond this, the question may be asked: Is the Redemption the principal motive of the incarnation? In other words: Would God have become man, had Adam not sinned?

This question was asked by many great theologians and doctors before the time of Duns Scotus. Some answered positively, others negatively. When Scotus came to consider the matter, he was not pleased with the formulation of the question. In posing it, he argued, one should prescind from the sin of Adam, and state it as follows: Is Christ the first predestined of all creatures in the mind of God? He then goes on to answer this in the affirmative, showing that Christ, irrespective of Adam's sin, is intended by God, in the first instance, to be the Centre of all creation.

He is led to this Christocentric idea by the following considerations. Sacred Scripture tells us that God is love. Now, first of all, He loves Himself in the most perfect and most sublime manner, because He is God. Secondly, He loves Himself in others who are able to love Him freely and share in the love He bears Himself. His love tends to diffuse itself, one might say to bubble over. Thirdly, God wills to be loved by someone outside Himself who can love Him in the most perfect way. Finally, He foresees the union between Himself and human nature: Christ, Who is capable of loving Him to an infinite degree as He loves Himself. For Scotus, therefore, the principal reason of the incarnation is God's will to have a perfect Man, Who is at the same time perfect God, Who returns to Him the perfect love He has for Himself. Beginning, then, with the love of God, Scotus arrives at Christ as the very Centre of the whole created order.

In willing the existence of Christ, God's foreknowledge of Adam's sin brought about a qualification in His original plan. It was decreed by God that Christ should assume a human nature in order to suffer and die, and so redeem mankind. But the fact of what Christ did, in no way affects the primary motive of His incarnation. This remained still God's will to have a being outside Himself capable of loving Him to an infinite degree.

To become incarnate means to become man. In a certain sense, man is a compendium of the whole universe—in him are united the material and the spiritual. When Christ became man, He united the material and the spiritual to God. Matter, spirit and the union of these form the whole ambit of creation. So, in Jesus Christ, all creation is united to God. In his sublime vision, then, Scotus sees the whole of creation tending towards Christ, in Whom it finds its meeting point and sanctification.

Of all Scotus' teaching, it is the Primacy of Christ that establishes him most firmly in the Franciscan Tradition. It is a logical development of St. Francis' love of creation, expressed so beautifully and so forcefully in his *Canticle of Brother Sun.*

Throughout the history of the Church there have always been two currents of thought about the relationship of the Christian to the world. The one urges him to flee it and keep clear of its dangers. The other invites him to enter into it heart and soul, and sanctify its structures. The former tends to emphasize the *other-worldly* aspect of Christianity and the ephemeral quality of earthly life and its concerns. The latter tends to stress the essential goodness of this world as the object of God's creation and Christ's Redemption; in view of this, it asserts that the Christian can find God in and through the world. Both currents of thought are valid and have their own attraction.

There can be no doubt in any one's mind, however, which of these views holds sway in our time. Physical science has unravelled the secrets of the universe on a scale that is simply overwhelming. Atomic physics has given man a power that no one would have imagined possible. Space travel has opened up vistas that are mentally staggering. Never before has the world appeared so attractive; never before have men been so overawed by its vastness and complexity. Convinced of its goodness and beauty, astounded by its richness and resources, men—both Christian and non-Christian alike—have thrown themselves into it with eagerness and zeal. The Christian, however, will see dangers here, but he cannot run away from them. He must face them, and face them squarely. He must show how and why the world is lawfully an attractive place, and at the same time point out how the dangers in its attraction may be removed.

It is here that Scotus' teaching on the Primacy of Christ would seem to take on its deepest significance for us. The God-Man, Jesus Christ, is the Centre of all creation. In becoming Man, He sanctified the body and soul which He assumed, in the very union of the divine and human natures. In other words, the essential goodness of human nature is brought out by the very fact of the incarnation. Through His Life, Death and Resurrection, Christ first brings holiness to man; of all creation it is man who is to be sanctified. It is only through his holiness that the world can become holy. Now, the sanctification which Christ puts at man's disposal is decreed to come to him by contact with Christ in the Sacraments. The Sacraments are in part constituted by material elements, which are products of this world—water, bread, wine, oil. These things are sanctified, and have their part in man's sanctification. Man in giving glory to God through Christ, uses bricks and mortar to build churches, cloth and cotton to make vestments, metals for sacred vessels, and so on. Therefore, even at the physical level, man sanctifies the world by bringing its elements into contact with God, in his endeavours to deepen evermore his own sanctification.

The Christian must also sanctify his fellow men by bringing them into contact with Christ. It is of the utmost urgency that he enter into the very heart of human culture. He must penetrate the social, intellectual, scientific, political and artistic life of our time, and bring those he finds there into contact with Christ through himself. In entering these spheres he is sanctifying them. He owes a duty to the world in which he lives, and that duty is best fulfilled by going into it in order to bring it to Christ and Christ to it. His devotion, therefore, to the sacred must not mean a contempt for the secular; on the contrary, it must mean a total and dedicated commitment to the needs of the world through all that goes to make up human culture.

Moreover, this world is fast becoming a gigantic community. There is a growing-together that has its origins in modern times, due to the rapid development in communications. It is for the Christian to make clear that this community is meant to be a family in Christ its King and Head, and the more it becomes one family, the nearer does it come to Christ.

The dangers involved in a whole-hearted commitment to this world will be removed if we are always closely united to Christ. While belonging to this world, Christ is, at the same time utterly beyond it. It is in Him that all things will be finally restored. With Christ at the forefront of vision, our efforts to sanctify this world will never lead us to succumb to the temptation of settling down in it. All our strivings and endeavours will never be fully fruitful until He comes at the end. With that coming, there will be a new heaven and new earth, and God will be all in all.

Conclusion

There we end these few pages on Duns Scotus. Firstly, we traced an outline of his life, and then said something about the revival of interest which our times have seen in his life and works.

Following this, we mentioned his originality of thought in connexion with our Lady's Immaculate Conception. Finally, we attempted to show his importance for us by selecting two points from his doctrine: his philosophy of the individual, from which we drew principles on the dignity of the person; his teaching on the Primacy of Christ, which led us to deduce principles that govern the Christian's vocation to sanctify the world. Much more might have been written, other points might have been chosen. What has been said, however, was an attempt to give at least a glimpse of Scotus' vision of the world. A glimpse of a vision is always dissatisfying. A man cannot be content until the vision itself becomes his own.

Man Is Not an Island[1]

The seventh centenary of his birth really brought Duns Scotus out into the limelight. There was a Congress in his honour, articles about him appeared in the press, he was hailed as the first Methodist, and commended by the Pope. Handsome reparations—one may think—for so much neglect: yet many people were left feeling puzzled. Why so much fuss about a medieval scholastic who has been in discredit since the eighteenth century? Then, despite all the attention he got, Scotus still had his defamers. One writer concluded that, because Scotus denied natural knowledge of God's existence, and especially because of his unacceptable teaching on birth control (!), his writings would not make a suitable basis for ecumenical dialogue, whatever the Pope's commendation.

> This was reasonable enough, I suppose, and especially so when it is remembered that Scotus is not well known outside a rather small circle of experts. Where he is known, it is often as no more than the original dunce, or under the not-too-happy title 'Subtle Doctor', which hardly makes for a sympathetic approach. But even so—and however all this may be explained—it is still irritating for serious students of Scotus, who consider him perhaps the greatest thinker ever to have worn the Franciscan habit.

Profound Influence of St. Francis

I think it should be heavily emphasized that he was a Franciscan. The greatest injustice to Scotus, in my opinion, is to have called him 'a Franciscan without love', 'a Franciscan who lost the spirit of St Francis'. By becoming a Franciscan, Scotus was introduced to a spirituality that had a profound influence on all that he wrote. St. Francis's love of Christ, his tender concern for all creation, his vision of the world—all this became Scotus's own ideal. Nowhere does his Franciscan spirit come out more clearly than in his teaching on the Absolute Primacy of Christ, and in his psychology, where the whole

---

[1] THE LISTENER 77.988 (May 4, 1967) pp. 586f. Editors' note: This article was broadcast as a talk on the Third Programme prior to its appearance in: THE LISTENER. Published with permission from the Province of Immaculate Conception, England.

emphasis is on will, freedom, and love. It is not, I think, too much to say of Scotus what Etienne Gilson said of St. Bonaventure, that he conceptualised St. Francis.

If I were asked where it is that Scotus's Franciscanism found its best expression, I would say unhesitatingly, in his teaching on the Primacy of Christ. And it is here that I would place his chief ecumenical significance. What really baffled most people was the Pope's speaking of Scotus in an ecumenical context at all. The key to what the Pope meant, I would say, is to be found above all in Scotus's Christocentric vision of the universe. Begin with what the Scriptures say about the love of God, he comes to Christ as the 'first-born of all creatures', the King of Creation, and in an absolute sense, and not as conditioned by redemption.

This teaching, I am convinced, contains one of the most basic theological principles for the present efforts of Christians to come to meaningful dialogue with the modern world. Christ, the centre of the Cosmos, is the positive evaluation of all earthly realities down to the last atom. I do not think it would be impertinence to say that Scotus's teaching here is the heritage of all Christians, indeed of all men; and that is why he can claim ecumenical significance. Reading the works of Teilhard de Chardin, one understands clearly why Teilhard had such keen interest in Scotus; the medieval scholar and the modern scientist had, in different ways, reached the same conclusions.

Scotus's ecumenical significance

As for the reasons put forward why Scotus would not be ecumenically significant, to say that Scotus taught that we cannot prove the existence of God is false. On the contrary, he states unequivocally that man can come to a natural knowledge of God; and Scotus is extremely rigorous in his definition of demonstrability. As for the startling reference to birth control, is it fair, I wonder, to relate his teaching on marriage to the present issues? Did Scotus, in fact, have any views on control as we know it now, some 700 years later?

But apart from his strictly ecumenical significance I think that Scotus's philosophy is certainly relevant to other areas of modern thought. That is to say, I think that Scotus as a philosopher has a contemporary significance wider than the ecumenical issue. But in the last analysis perhaps these come to the same thing, since ecumenism is based on philosophical principles.

What do people mean when they talk about the 'contemporary significance' of Scotus, or of any past philosopher for that matter? Obviously, not everything that any philosopher writes will last for ever. But given that philosophical inquiry is always concerned with perennial problems, as for instance with man's capacity for knowledge and the nature of that knowledge, every philosopher gets insights into truths and gives solutions to problems which relate him to every other philosopher before and since, precisely because they all grappled with the self-same problems. And in that sense the history of philosophy forms a coherent whole.

In the history of philosophy Scotus is an Augustinian, or perhaps it might even be better to call him 'Augustinian-Franciscan'. He gave his own emphasis to many tenets of the Augustinian tradition, and he did not hesitate to depart from it where he considered truth, as he saw it, to demand this—as he did, for instance, over the question of the primary object of the human intellect. But allowing for the divergences and personal emphasis, we must still, I think, call him 'Augustinian', in that he retained the most fundamental doctrines of the Augustinian Tradition: the knowability of the individual, the primacy of the will—well defined in terms of a self-determining power in regard to the good known by the intellect, not merely as a power to choose this or that—and his concern for the argument of St. Anselm.

No enemy of Aristotle

The author of the article on Scotus in the *Dictionnaire de Théologie Catholique* is mistaken in saying that St. Anselm's argument for the existence of God 'has no value' for Scotus. Scotus maintained that this argument had to be what he calls 'coloured', and though it is not demonstrative in the strict sense for Scotus, it does have persuasive force. By describing Scotus as 'Augustinian' I do not mean to imply that he is 'anti-Aristotelian'. Scotus was no enemy of Aristotle, as he was no enemy of St. Thomas Aquinas. His works show a profound and extensive knowledge of Aristotle. But he was not a disciple of the philosopher; nor was it his prime concern to reconcile Aristotle with Christian teaching.

But what about Scotus and the twentieth century? Consider, for example, the value of Scotus's philosophy in the light of modern existentialism's preoccupation with the uniqueness of the individual. I am not calling Scotus an 'existentialist'. That would be to commit a gross anachronism; and, anyway, for Scotus there is no real distinction in the concrete order between essence and existence. But the point I want to stress is the concreteness of Scotus's philosophy, and its concern with the individual, which is best expressed in Scotus's own words: 'It is the individual that is most truly being and one'.

In so far as existentialists are concerned with man's concrete situation, and the uniqueness of the individual person in that situation, they are driving home a truth about man's dignity as an individual which is sorely in need of emphasis in a world that has grown so accustomed to thinking in terms of the group, in terms of categories. In the same way they express a profound reality when they define man's meaning in freedom. Uniqueness and freedom are the foundation of man's dignity and destiny, and so form the starting point for an integral humanism. In this regard, Sartre's preoccupation with man's situation and his freedom can only have our deepest respect. But what frightens me, when I read Sartre, is his pessimism and hopelessness. The loneliness of man's situation, the apparent pointlessness of freedom, the destruction of love, I find terrifying. And with love destroyed, how can existence be anything but isolation?

Yet one cannot deny that Sartre is posing very real problems. The answers to those problems are contained, for me at least, in Scotus. For Scotus the precise and formal reason why this individual is this individual is *haecceitas*—thisness—which is the ultimate act that restricts the form of a species to the singularity of its individuals. Individuation does not come through matter and it does not come through form. Bertrand Russell is therefore wrong when he says in his *History of Western Philosophy* that form is the principle of individuation for Scotus; Scotus explicitly denies this. 'Thisness' is a characteristic of every created nature, and the reason why every created nature is individualized in concrete existence. The concrete significance of 'thisness' has perhaps been brought out best by the Jesuit poet Gerard Manley Hopkins, who saw 'thisness' as identical with 'inscape' or the distinctiveness of things. *Haecceitas,* then, gives the ultimate reality of being, encloses a man within ultimate solitude.

The possession of self in uniqueness

Scotus defines personality as incommunicability, which excludes all actual and aptitudinal dependence: that is to say, the possession of self in uniqueness. So 'thisness', ultimate solitude, is uniqueness, the originality which each possesses, the category 'unique' of Kierkegaard; that whereby each individual is himself and no other. It seems to me that Scotus here has accounted well for my uniqueness in every and any concrete situation.

But uniqueness, ultimate solitude, is not isolation. Scotus's emphasis on freedom and love excludes any such interpretation. Love for Scotus does not exhaust itself in self-seeking. There is imperfect love, which Scotus calls 'love of concupiscence', which is imperfect because it seeks the other for advantage. But there is also perfect love—and surely experience bears him out here—which he calls 'love of friendship'—*amor amicitiae*—which seeks out the other for the other's sake. Ultimate solitude, then, for Scotus, does not close a man in upon himself, rather it opens him out to every other, drives him to seek out every other, and above all the Eternal Other, whose uniqueness, thisness, he reflects. For Scotus, man is not an island. Scotus could never, I think, subscribe to Sartre's *'L'enfer, c'est les autres'*. Hell is not other people: according to Scotus, authentic existence is discovered in the relations of unique to unique.

I would argue that there is some affinity between Scotus and modern psychology in a broad sense, and perhaps in particular with Jung. Not that he presages modern psychology, and indeed we must not confuse Scotus's notion of individuation with Jung's use of the term. But when Jung speaks of collective unconsciousness, I would think this is very near Scotus's teaching on common nature as possessing a unity less than numerical, but which is real in the individual person and which is universalised according to Scotus's realism. This must of course go hand in hand with his emphasis on memory, which Scotus as a good Augustinian emphasizes.

An interesting remark on Scotus was made by the American philosopher, C.S. Peirce:

> The works of Duns Scotus have strongly influenced me. . .if his logic and metaphysics, not slavishly worshipped, but torn away from its medievalism, be adapted to modern culture. . . .I am convinced that it will go far towards supplying the philosophy which is most suited to harmonize with physical science. . . .

This becomes all the more interesting when one recalls that Peirce described his own philosophy as 'the attempt of a physicist to make such conjecture about the constitution of the universe as the methods of science permit, with the aid of all that has been done by previous philosophers'. And, as he tells us himself, Peirce was aided by Scotus. It is not merely the fact that Scotus forbids any unwarranted interference by philosophy in physical science that led Peirce to speak of Scotus as he did, but rather the fact that he found acceptable, and even went beyond, Scotus's metaphysical realism.

Peirce states the problem of what realism sets out to solve in this way: 'whether laws and general types are figments of the mind or are real'. Put in another way, realism answers the problem of the particular and the general. In fact only individuals, particulars, exist. If the universal concept—for instance, humanity—is a mere figment of the mind, then as far as the philosopher at least is concerned, science will not have an object, it will not be dealing with reality, since it is not dealing with the individual but with the universal. Scotus's realism, which Peirce accepted, is based on the formal distinction in the individual thing between common nature and 'thisness'. So he is not concerned with mere logical universals here. But, on the other hand, Scotus does not say that universals are real things.

Common nature and 'thisness' are not separate as thing and thing. They are distinct as formalities, that is to say they are metaphysically really distinct, but not physically really distinct. All formalities are contracted by 'thisness', and so Scotus is a moderate realist. The distinction is not made by the mind, it is prior to the intellectual act, and through the intelligible species in the agent intellect, common nature is given a unity that is numerical, and so it is made predicable of the many.

A 'Scotist Realist'

Peirce accepted Scotus's realism to the extent that he called himself a 'Scotist realist'. But he went beyond it, in that he would not admit the contraction by 'thisness'. That is why he felt that Scotus was too 'nominalistic', and so he went on to describe his own position as an extreme form of scholastic realism. Whatever merits there may be in Peirce's interpretation of Scotus's realism, what strikes me most forcibly is Peirce's remark about the harmony possible between Scotus's philosophy and modern science. This comes as all the more welcome when one thinks of the severe criticisms of metaphysicians made by Whittaker. Peirce used the word 'harmonize', and to harmonize is not too far from getting a unitary vision. If Scotus can help in that, then I will not blush to call myself a Scotist realist.

It is in connection with the formal distinction and Scotus's realism that the American Scotist, Allan Wolter, has made the most interesting comparison I have read: he compares Scotus with Wittgenstein. His point is that if we accept epistemological realism, and grant the scholastic assumption that our ideas and the reality they express are in some way isomorphic, then the possibility of conceiving one formality without the other—for instance, common nature, humanity, in man without 'thisness', or the individuating difference—would seem to demand some distinction on the part of the thing itself, prior to the intellectual act. What Scotus is saying about the formal distinction is, according to Wolter, very near what Wittgenstein is saying in the *Tractatus*: 'If things can occur in atomic facts, the possibility must already be in them'. Wolter has even gone so far as to say that Scotus's realism, according to which common nature is known through the intelligible species, becomes much clearer in view of Russell's and Wittgenstein's early attempts to express the metaphysical structure of the world in thought and language, in what they call 'logical form'.

I am not too sure that I know the full extent of this comparison, but it is certainly clear that Scotus is attempting to express the metaphysical structure of the external world in common nature as universal and intelligible. Perhaps they are saying the same thing. If they are, I do not think Wittgenstein would mind. In the preface to the *Tractatus*, Wittgenstein says: 'How far my efforts agree with other philosophers, I will not decide'. Wittgenstein meant, I suppose, that he left that to others.

Duns Scotus and Ecumenism[1]

In the Apostolic Letter of Pope Paul VI to the Hierarchies of England and Wales and Scotland in connexion with this Scholastic Congress[2], the most interesting paragraph is the one which suggests that the teachings of Duns Scotus might form a suitable basis for ecumenical dialogue between Catholics and other Christian denominations[3]. This suggestion has been welcomed by students of Scotus for whom it requires no apology.

As it turned out, however, the suggestion left a lot of people very puzzled, Catholics as well as others[4]. What could be the possible relevance of

---

[1] *Problemata Teologica*, Romae: Commissio Scotistica 1968, Vol. 3 of *De Doctrina Ioannis Duns Scoti*, 4 vols. 1968, pp. 633-652. Published with permission.

[2] Paul VI, *Epist. apost. Alma parens*, in: ACTA APOSTOLIACE SEDIS 58 (1966) pp. 609-614. English Version: *Apostolic Letter. . .on the occasion of the Second Scholastic Congress held at Oxford and Edinburgh on the Seventh Centenary of the Birth of John Duns Scotus*, Typis Polyglottis Vaticanis, 1966; see also L'OSSERVATORE ROMANO (July 24, 1966) p. l.

[3] Ibid., p. 613: *Ad contexenda eiusmodi serena colloquia inter Ecciesiam catholicam et Communionem Anglicanam aliasque Magnae Britanniae christianas Communitates, Scoti doctrina aurea fortasse potent ministrare subtegmina.*

[4] It was reported in THE TIMES (July 26, 1966) p. 12, that "one prominent member of the Anglican Communion was convinced that the Pope had got the wrong man" because "Duns's philosophy was uncompromisingly Roman Catholic". Mr. Christopher Hollis in THE TIMES (July 30, 1966) p. 10, felt that it had to be confessed that the Pope's letter did not make it clear why Scotus is particularly fitted for this task. He writes: "Duns Scotus is not at all easy to disentangle. . . .We cannot, he thinks, prove the existence of God. We cannot prove the doctrines of the Church. The best that reason can provide for us is certain suasions which make them appear plausible. But in the end we accept because the church teaches and we cannot accept for any other reason. That is an edifying and logical position for one who has already accepted the authority of the Church. It is not very easy to see what special value it has in an ecumenical dialogue between men who by definition are not sure whether they have first principles in common and are seeking to discover". Mr. Hollis concludes that the Pope's suggestion shows a readiness to welcome flexibility and to recognize the importance of freedom and diversity. The Pope's words are intelligible and laudable in that Scotus is a good alternative to St. Thomas. Mr. St. John-Stevas in the CATHOLIC HEROLD (August 5, 1966) p. 3, stated that his knowledge of Scotus did not make him think that he would be an ideal writer for this role. To support this he said that Scotus taught that we can prove neither the existence of God nor the doctrines of the Church. As a final reason he gave Scotus's teaching on birth control: "Scotus' views on birth control are even less promising. He held that the purpose of procreation was to populate heaven in general and fill the places left by the fallen angels in particular".

It is of course entirely false to say that Scotus taught that we cannot prove the existence of God. He states quite unequivocally that man can come to know the existence of God "ex a medieval scholastic to so modern a movement as Ecumenism? The reaction is, I think, very reasonable, especially when it is remembered that Scotus is not too well known outside a relatively small number of experts. Where he is known, it is often as no more than the original dunce, or under the not-too-happy title 'Subtle Doctor' which hardly makes for a sympathetic approach.[5]

Because of the confused reaction to the Pope's words here at home I decided to change my original topic. In the programme I am listed to speak on: *The importance of Scotistic thought in Great Britain in pre-Reformation times*[6]. I am well aware of the value such a study would have for Scotistic scholarship. But in the circumstances I judged it would be a greater contribution to the work of this Congress to treat of Scotus from a more modern aspect, and in particular, from that very modern and urgent aspect, the ecumenical. All ages are great ages. There is one, however, greater than them all, one's own. In view of it are graces given and the power to cooperate with them and follow them through to the end.

In this paper, then, I want to show in what way Scotus seems to me to have ecumenical significance. That, I suppose, is the same as saying I want to show that the Pope was justified in making his suggestion. Many, I am sure, found his words difficult to understand because they have never known or even heard of the real Scotus. If I succeed in showing that Scotus has something of lasting value to contribute to our ecumenical efforts I will be more than pleased that I changed my topic.

The paper is divided into three sections. In the first I will make some reflections on ecumenical dialogue and Christian unity. In the second and third

---

naturalibus", by the natural power of reason. It would be tiresome to give the references to the *Opus Oxoniense*, the *Reportata Parisiensia* and the *De Primo Principio*. Both Mr. Hollis and Mr. St. John-Stevas would seem to be repeating biassed Manuals and outmoded or misinformed Encyclopedias. Th. Merton, *The seven Storey Mountain*, New York 1948, p. 94, affirms that Scotus's proof for the existence of God is the most perfect, complete and thorough proof that has ever been worked out by any man. For a recent and very clear presentation of Scotus's proof, see C. Balic, *Duns Scoto antidoto contro l'ateismo*, in: L'OSSERVATORE ROMANO (August 27, 1966) p. 5. - As to what Scotus taught about proving the doctrines of the Church, it is very misleading to relate "existence of God" and "doctrines of the Church" to the same verb "prove" without explanation. It is a doctrine of the Church that God is Three-in-One. This cannot be proved in the same sense as can the existence of God. Mr. St. John-Stevas's reference to Scotus's views on birth control is very puzzling. Whatever Scotus may have held about the purpose of marriage (and he was only one among so many who held the opinion Mr. John-Stevas mentions), is it fair to relate them to the present issues? Did Scotus, in fact, have any views on birth control such as we understand it now, some seven hundred years later?

[5] "Duns" is the etymon of "dunce" (a dullard, one slow in learning). The epithet "Subtle Doctor" is unfortunate, the ambiguity of the word "subtle" tends to arouse suspicion.

[6] *Duns Scotus Congress. Secundus Congressus Scholasticus Internationalis*, Romae 1966, p. 18.

I will treat of the aspects of his teaching which strike me as the most relevant to the ecumenical movement.

I. Ecumenical Dialogue and Christian Unity

There is little need to stress the indispensable part that dialogue takes in the efforts of Christians towards unity. But perhaps the following remarks will not be superfluous. The climate of charity is now all but universally established. In certain circumstances Christians pray with one another, always and everywhere, it is to be hoped, for one another. Besides this they get together for discussion and there have been notable exchanges of visits. Christians have learned a little more about one another and something of what unites them already and what divides them still.

The chief result of efforts thus far made is a steadily increasing awareness among Christians of the primary issues that face Christianity in the modern world. This has come as a grace of the Holy Spirit on whom all ecumenical endeavour depends. On the one hand, these issues centre around the meaning of man, his dignity as a person, his freedom, and his responsibility for the decisions and choices he makes; on the other, they are concerned with the value of the world and all earthly realities, both in themselves and in relation to man[7]. As evidence of this awareness one has only to consult the four volumes of essays published this year for the World Council of Churches[8]. The theme of the Conference of the World Council of Churches which met at Geneva in July this year was Church and Society. Within the framework of that theme the emphasis was placed on the need to interpret the World to the Church and not the other way round. The meaning of man and the evaluation of earthly realities were major topics in the Vatican

---

[7] In using the words *world* and *earthly realities* I mean the whole social, economic, artistic, educational, political, cultural structure all round us, which now, as a matter of fact is not concerned with a future life at all, but devoted to making this one better at the family, local, national and international levels. This stands even though the principles on which that structure is based are Christian principles, whether these are recognized as such or not, or even denied.

[8] The four volumes were published in 1966 for the World Council of Churches by the Association Press, New York, and by the S.C.M. Press London. They are entitled: *Christian Social Ethics in a Changing World* (ed. by J.C. Bennett), *Responsible Government in a revolutionary Age* (ed. by Z.K. Matthews), *Economic Growth in World Perspective* (ed. by D. Munby), *Man in Community* (ed. by E. De Vries).

Council[9]. The relation between Church and World formed the subject of Pope Paul's first Encyclical Letter[10].

They are live issues. Humanism has made them its own and has mapped out systems of thought and lines of action wherein these play major roles. In order to cooperate to the full with the grace of awareness they have received, Christians are coming more and more to make these issues the subject of dialogue at every level. Indeed, it would seem that discussion on them is demanded by the very nature of the Christian mission in the modern world. There is unity in awareness; there must be unity of attitude. It is necessary now more than ever before that Christians speak to the world with one voice according to principles which are universally valid because they are really Christian and eminently human. Dialogue, I am convinced, will bring that unity because in the midst of those who take part in it will be the perfect Lover of our world, the God-Man Jesus Christ.

This awareness has brought with it the realization that the Christian Unity Movement is not purely, or even primarily, an ecclesiastical matter. In does not belong to the sacristy. Christ came that the world might believe. Because it is a *Christian* Movement it concerns everyman and is bound up with the present movement of world history towards unity. It is in relation to the above-mentioned issues that I see the ecumenical significance of Duns Scotus. My intention is to suggest two points of departure for discussion. The first is taken from his philosophy of the individual[11]; the second from his doctrine of

---

[9] See the *Pastoral Constitution on the Church in the Modern World (Gaudium et Spes)* in: *The Documents of Vatican II,* ed. by W.M. Abbott, London-Dublin 1966, pp. 199-308.

[10] Paul VI, *Ecclesiam suam* in: ACTA APOSTOLICAE SEDIS 56 (1964) pp. 609-659.

[11] I should like to take this opportunity to mention the importance of philosophy for ecumenical dialogue; see C.J. Curtis, *Philosophy and Ecumenical Dialogue* in: THE ECUMENIST 4 (1966) pp. 76-78. There are philosophical problems both in natural theology and of an epistemological kind which confront Christian thinkers in the modern world. I would suggest in this connexion that Scotus's philosophy has more to offer than what is indicated in this paper. His proof of the existence of God has been mentioned in brief already (see note 4 above). The thorough and very rigorous notion of proof in Scotus would be acceptable, I think, to modern philosophy. On the question of the relation of philosophy to science C.S. Peirce maintained that Scotus's metaphysics and logic, once stripped of medievalism, "will go far towards supplying the philosophy which is best suited to harmonize with physical science" (cf. *Collected Papers of Charles Sanders Peirce,* ed. by C. Hartshorne and P. Weiss, Cambridge MA, 1931, p. 6). Peirce's Statement is all the more interesting as philosophy becomes existential and takes on the relation to theology which is that of the empirical human sciences (cf. B.J.F. Lonergan, *Insight. A Study of Human Understanding* [revised Student edition], Longmans 1958, p. 743). Perhaps the harmony between Scotus's logic and metaphysics and science lies in the existential character of his philosophy, see B. De Saint-Maurice, *Existential Import in the Philosophy of Duns Scotus* in: FRANCISCAN STUDIES 9 (1949) pp. 274-313.

the absolute primacy of Christ. To speak of Scotus's ecumenical significance is to say that he has contemporary significance. This does not mean that he has answers for all the problems of the present time. But all great men get insights into truth which assure them a place in every age. I believe the points I have chosen are insights of this kind. They bring Scotus into the modern world and are proof that there is a unity in the historical dimension of man's discovery of truth. I have selected them not merely because they are the inheritance of Franciscans, but above all because they are the heritage of all men.

Finally here I think it ought to borne in mind that Scotus was a Franciscan. This may be his best claim to ecumenical significance. The greatest injustice ever done to Scotus is to have called him a Franciscan without love, a Franciscan who lost the spirit of St. Francis[12]. In becoming a Franciscan he was introduced to a way of life that influenced profoundly all that he wrote. His Franciscan *Weltanschauung* is to be found all through his works. Nowhere does it appear more plainly than in his teaching on the primacy of Christ, and in his psychology, where the whole emphasis is on will, freedom and love. It is not too much to say of Scotus what Gilson said of St. Bonaventure, that he conceptualised St. Francis[13].

II. Duns Scotus and the Dignity of the Individual

A. The uniqueness and value of things

The concrete character of Scotus's philosophy finds its most telling evidence in his metaphysics of the individual. Individuality gives reality to things in the full sense. It is the individual that is most truly being and one[14]. His awareness of the existing individual is the reason one writer gives for calling Scotus the ablest exponent of the phenomenological method[15]. If phenomenologists are concerned with the complexity of phenomena, then

---

[12] B. Landry, *La Philosophie de Duns Scot*, Paris 1922, p. 245.

[13] E. Gilson, *The Philosophy of St. Bonaventure*, London 1940, p. 66.

[14] In Metaph. VII q. 13 n. 17 (ed. Vivés, VII 417ab): *Notandum quod individuum, sive unum numero, dicitur illud quod non est divisibile in multa et distinguitur ab omni alio secundum numerum. Prima pars sie intelligitur, quod sibi repugnat divisio in partes subiectivas. Haec repugnantia non potest esse nisi per aliquid quod est in individuo. . . .Item, Individuum est verissime ens et unum. . . .*

[15] Cf. D. Nicholl, *Recent Thought in Focus*, London 1952, p. 91; see also pp. 37f.

Nicholl is amply justified in including Scotus in this category of philosophers.[16]

The principle of individuation is concerned with the formal and precise reason why an individual in the real order is fundamentally incapable of multiplication. That is to say, with the precise reason why *this* individual is *this* individual and not another[17]. For Scotus this precise reason is the determining factor "haecceitas", *thisness,* which differs from the common nature as such of the individual[18]. The principle of individuation for Scotus is neither matter nor form[19], but "the ultimate act which restricts the form of a species to the singularity of its individuals"[20]. Common nature is contracted by *thisness so* that the individual is the only representative of itself[21]. *Thisness* brings intrinsic perfection to a thing and is the reason why each thing is individualized in concrete existence. "Haecceitas" is not a new form, nor is it distinct from common nature as "res" from "res"; it is a reality of the thing formally distinct

---

[16] Nicholl, op.cit., pp. 91-92, draws some very interesting parallels between Scotus and Heidegger. M. Heidegger's first published work was on Scotus: Die Kategorien- und Bedeutungslehre des Duns Scotus, Tübingen 1916. In another place Nicholl states: "There is much to be said for treating Heidegger's philosophy as secularized Scotism" (see I.M. Bochenski, *Contemporary European Philosophy*, trans. from German by D. Nicholl and K. Aschenbrenner, Berkeley and Los Angeles 1956, p. 155, translator's note). On Scotus and phenomenology, see also A. Fliche, V. Martin, *Histoire de l'Eglise, XIII. Le mouvement doctrinaldu XI au XIV siecle*, pp. 337-338. – "Haecceitas as applied to persons would seem to be the same as Heidegger's *Gemeinigkeit.*"

[17] See A.B. Wolter, *The Transcendentals and their Function in the Metaphysics of Duns Scotus*, St. Bonaventure, N.Y. 1946, pp. 103-107.

[18] Ibid., p. 105. The word haecceitas does not appear in Scotus's principal work, the *Ordinatio*, but he uses it in the Rep. II d. 12 q. 5 n. l. 8. 12. 14 (ed. Vivés XXIII 25. 29. 31. 32). The coining of terms such as *haecceitas* and *ultima solitudo* makes a further point of comparison for Nicholl, op.cit., p. 91, between Soctus and Heidegger. Vocabulary is not rich enough for subtle complications and elusive refinements of reality.

[19] Ord. II d. 3 q. 6 n. 15 (ed. Vivés XII, 144a): *Et sicut compositum non includit suam entitatem qua est hoc in quantum natura, ita nec materia in quantum natura includit suam entitatem, qua est haec materia, nee forma in quantum natura includit suam; ergo ista entitas non est materia vel forma nee compositum, in quantum quodlibet istorum est natura, sed est ultima realitas entis, quod est materia vel quod est forma vel quod est compositum.*

[20] E. Gilson, History of Christian Philosophy in the Middle Ages, London 1955, p. 462.

[21] Ord. II d. 3 q. l n. 7 (ed. Vivés XII 48b-49a): *Et sicut secundum illud 'esse' non est natura de se universalis, sed quasi universalitas accidit illi naturae secundum primam rationem eius, secundum quam est obiectum, ita etiam in re extra, ubi natura est cum singularitate, non est natura illa de se terminata ad singularitatem, sed est prior naturaliter illa ratione contrahente ipsam ad singularitatem illam; et in quantum est prior naturaliter ipso contrahente, non repugnat sibi esse sine illo contrahente.*
Cf. E. Bettoni, Duns Scotus. *The Basic Principles of his Philosophy*, trans. and ed. by B. Bonansea, Washington D.C. 1961, p. 61.

from the nature[22]. It is, therefore, the "ultima realitas entis", the "ultima solitudo" of every individual. Scotus's philosophic reflections here are confirmed by experience. We never know one thing as we know another. I can know John, Mark and Andrew; I know them as men through humanity, common nature. But John is known to me as John through his *thisness* or *Johnness;* he is so individualized that I do not know him, and cannot know him, as Mark or Andrew.

The concrete nature of *thisness* may best be described without oversimplifying Scotus's thought, as *uniqueness, originality*[23]. The uniqueness, the unrepeatable something of all things, is what gives them their intrinsic and eternal value. There is about everything, every person, an originality that gives a new insight into reality, another aspect that has never been seen before. Each person enters into a new enriching relationship of knowledge and love with every new person met, with every new thing encountered.

Scotus's principle of individuation strongly attracted and deeply influenced the English Jesuit poet. Gerard Manley Hopkins. Hopkins gives very beautiful expression to the principle in his poetry. *Thisness* becomes *inscape* or the distinctiveness of things[24]. From a study of Hopkins's poetry one is led to conclude that the attraction was founded on Scotus's awareness of the complexity of reality[25]. In their different ways poet and philosopher reached the same insights.

His preoccupation with the distinctiveness of things is one of the principal marks of Scotus's Franciscan vision of the world. If St. Francis was no philosopher he was certainly a poet. Like Hopkins he used another word for the uniqueness of things. Instead of *thisness* he said *brother* and *sister.* St. Francis did not love creation but every creature: his Brother Sun, his Sister Moon, his Brother Fire, his Sister Water. If Assisi embraces Paris in St.

---

[22] Ord. II d. 3 q. 6 n. 15 (ed. Vivés XII 144b): . . .*nec possunt istae duae realitates esse res et res, sicut possunt esse realitas unde' accipitur genus et realitas unde accipitur differentia, ex quibus realitas specifica accipitur, sed semper in eodem, sive parte sive toto, sunt realitates eiusdem rei formaliter distinctae.*

[23] Ibid. n. 12 (p. 135a): *Ista autem entitas individui est primo diversa ab omni entitate quiditativa.*

[24] See W.A.M. Peters, *Gerard Manley Hopkins. A Critical Essay Towards the Understanding of his Poetry*, Oxford 1948, pp. 21-28; W.H. Gardner, *Gerard Manley Hopkins (1844-1889). A Study of Poetic Idiosyncracy in Relation to Poetic Tradition*, London 1954, pp. 21-28; *Poems and Prose of Gerard Manley Hopkins* (selected with an introduction and notes by W.H. Gardner), Penguin Books, XXII-XXIV, pp. 224-226.

[25] Hopkins calls Scotus: "of realty the rarest-veined unraveller" (cf. his poem *Duns Scotus' Oxford in: Poems and Prose*, Gardner, op.cit., p. 40).

Bonaventure[26], most assuredly it embraces Oxford in Duns Scotus. St. Francis lived „haecceitas". Before all else, however, for Brother Francis, before Brother Sun or Sister Moon, was Brother Leo, Brother Peter, Brother Bernard. The uniqueness of living persons was what St. Francis first knew and loved. We must now turn to the uniqueness of individual persons to grasp the meaning of "haecceitas" in all its depth.

B. Thisness and the dignity of man

We have been horrified in our own time by the evils of a system whose philosophy makes the individual person subservient to the State conceived of as an ideal. Most of us are appalled by any system which sacrifices the dignity of the individual for the future of humanity. But for all this, it is not certain that we are safe from the danger of falling into what we condemn. When it has become commonplace to think and talk in terms of mass psychology, when the tendency has grown up to herd people into groups and deal with them according to statistics, when racialism befogs the minds of civilized men, it is an urgent duty that we stop to reflect on the dignity and value of the individual person, whatever his colour, race or creed. It is the individual who gives meaning and purpose to the group, and not the other way round. This is not to maintain that the individual good is to be preferred to the common good; the common good is the individual good *par excellence.* But it is to maintain that people cannot be treated as numbers on sheets if we really believe that the individual person is something more than a tiny cog in a vast political, economic, or industrial machine, in which all individuality is swamped, and apart from which personal existence has little or no meaning at all.

Modern existentialism, in so far as it is pre-occupied with man's concrete situation and the oneness of the individual in that situation, is driving home a truth about personal dignity that is sorely in need of emphasis. Likewise, it expresses a profound truth when it defines man in terms of freedom. In uniqueness and freedom is the foundation of man's dignity and destiny, and the basis, therefore, of an integral humanism. In this context Sartre's concern for man's situation and his freedom demands respect and examination. He is posing very real problems. But the frightening thing about his plays is their pessimism and hopelessness. The loneliness of man's

---

[26] E. Gilson, *The Philosophy of St. Bonaventure*, p. 494.

Situation, the apparent pointlessness of freedom, the destruction of love is terrifying[27]. With love destroyed how can existence be but isolation?

A view of the world, a philosophy of life must be judged finally on its view of the dignity of man and its principles of integral humanism. As I see it, that dignity and those principles are to be found in "haecceitas" as applied to individual persons. I am not calling Scotus an existentialist; that would be to commit a gross anachronism[28]. I do think, however, that his philosophy of the individual and his metaphysics of the person explain satisfactorily man's uniqueness in the concrete Situation of real existence.

Personality is described by Scotus as ultimate solitude, which excludes all actual and aptitudinal dependence[29]. Person is that which does not depend on another "suppositum" in act, and does not have any natural tendency to depend on another "suppositum", but a natural tendency to subsist of itself. Incommunicability is of the nature of personality, which is to say, personality is the possession of self in one's own uniqueness[30]. His uniqueness makes a person the object of the knowledge and love of every other. Though he possesses a common humanity, he has it in a way that no other can have. He is no mere instance of the universal. He is someone worth knowing, worth loving, because what he is, makes all that he does a unique contribution to the tremendous task of transforming humanity into one human family. In his relations with others he has something to give which cannot be given by another. This above all in that relation of freedom which is love, for here what he gives is himself. His "ultima realitas" is his uniqueness; his "ultima solitudo" the mystery of his identity.

Ultimate solitude, therefore, is not isolation. Scotus insists on the primacy of the will as a self-determining power in regard to the good known,

---

[27] See in particular the dialogues between Johanna and Franz in Altona J.P. Sartre, *The Flies*, trans. by S. Gilbert, Penguin Plays, 1965, p. 311. The freedom which Orestes has is only a curse: "What have I to do with you or you with me? We shall glide past each other, like ships in a river, without touching. You are God, and I am free; each of us is alone, and our anguish is akin". Cf. also R. Mehl, *Images of Man*, trans. by J.H. Farley, London 1966, pp. 24-41.

[28] Nicholl, *Recent thought*, p. 77, notes that Scotus, among others, has been called an 'existentialist'.

[29] Ord. III d. 1 q. 1 n. 9 (ed. Vivés XIV 26b): . . .*ita ista negatio, scilicet non-dependentia, non quidem actualis tantum, sed etiam actualis et aptitudinalis, talis complet rationem personae in natura intellectuali, et suppositi in alia natura creata*; n. 10 (p. 27a): *Iste conceptus 'incommunicabilis', qui negat communicationem actualem et aptitudinalem, univocus est Deo et creaturae, personae divinae et creatae*; n. 17 (p. 45a): *Ad personalitatem requiritur ultima solitudo, sive negatio dependentiae actualis et aptitudinalis ad personam alterius naturae*.

[30] Ord. III d. 2 q. 2 n. 3 (ed. Vivés XIV 128b): *De ratione personae est incommunicabilitas*.

whence follows his emphasis on freedom and love[31]. Love may be imperfect, which he calls "amor concupiscentiae", which seeks the other for personal advantage. But there is perfect love, which he calls "amor amicitiae", which loves the other for the other's sake[32]. Uniqueness does not close a man in upon himself. Rather it opens him out to every other, drives him to seek out every other, and above all the eternal Other whose uniqueness he reflects.

At the level of personal relationship with God man looses nothing of his uniqueness. He does not become lost in the Other. On the contrary, he comes to possess himself more firmly. God created freely, endowing human persons with freedom. In its every unique instance freedom is an Image of the infinite diversity of the freedom of God. He gave to the world the perfect image of himself to bring life, salvation, integrity and fulfilment to every man, In Christ man has the possibility of a unique personal relation with God. That possibility can only be realized in freedom. Because of the uniqueness which each person possesses and is, freedom and love are stamped with a uniqueness by definition unrepeatable. It is this love that God seeks out. He is no tyrant. He compels no one to give. He created man's uniqueness and he respects it forever[33]. It is only in the self-giving that springs from the perfect freedom of love that personal uniqueness attains its fullest realization. That is to say, that authentic existence is only discovered in relation of unique to Unique.

III. Duns Scotus and the Primacy of Christ

A. The approach of Scotus

The Scotistic doctrine of the absolute and unconditioned primacy of Christ does not begin from the purely hypothetical question: "If Adam had not sinned, would Christ have become incarnate?" His doctrine, however, is often presented in this way by manuals of theology[34], and the purely hypothetical

---

[31] Ord. II d. 25 q. un. n. 16 (ed. Vivés XIII 210a): *Ratio autem formalior voluntatis est magis libera quam ratio appetitus; quare est ratio recipiendi in quantum libera, sicut ratio libertatis est magis ratio constituendi.* See also Ord. IV d. 49 q. lat. n. 10-21 (ed. Vivés XXI 123-164): *Utra potentia sit nobilior, intellectus an voluntas.*

[32] Ord. IV d. 49 q. 5 n. 1-2 (ed. Vivés XXI 171-182); III d. 28 q. un. n. 2-3 (ed. Vivés XV 378f).

[33] Nicholl, *Recent thought*, 91, expresses this well when he says: "Scotus, for instance, describes the human person as 'incommunicable existence' as 'ultimate loneliness', for there is a fine point of the person whose privacy God himself respects".

[34] For example: *Sacrae theologiae summa*, III, I. Solang, *De Verbo incarnato*, Biblioteca de autores cristianos 62, Matriti 1956, pp. 13-17; A. Tanouerey, *Synopsis theologiae dogmaticae* II, *De Verbo incarnato et redemptore*, Parisiis 1950, pp. 789-795.

approach has a long history behind it[35]. Scotus does not juggle with any hypothesis about what God would have done if there had been no sin, nor does he prescind from the actual order of things as created and worked out in the present economy of salvation. Even where he does mention the hypothesis of Adam not sinning, it is to be understood in terms of, and as coming as a conclusion from, what he says about the predestination of Christ. In any case, such a purely hypothetical approach can find no satisfactory solution. Scotus presents a doctrinal *thesis* which gives deeper meaning both to the Pauline texts on Christ's primacy and to the Christian belief in the Kingship of Christ[36].

The question of the motive of the incarnation had been raised by many Schoolmen before Scotus[37]. As early as the seventh century Isaac of Ninive had written that the incarnation would have taken place independently of the sin of Adam[38]. It is of particular interest to Franciscans that Robert Grosseteste taught the doctrine at Oxford[39]. But prior to Scotus the question had been framed almost exclusively in terms of the hypothesis mentioned above. Scotus did not accept this as a satisfactory presentation of the state of the question[40]. He re-examined it, and concluded from his own approach that Christ is willed absolutely by God.

Given the scriptural teaching that God is love and the doctrine of the incarnation, Scotus takes as his starting point the predestination of Christ. He

---

[35] For a very clear and concise introduction to the question see: *Christ and the Cosmos*, trans. and ed. from the original work of J.F. Bonnefoy, *La primaute du Christ selon l'Ecriture et la Tradition*, by M. Meilach, Paterson N.J 1965, pp. 3-16.

[36] Colossians 1:2-20; Ephesians 1:3-14, and the exegesis of these texts in Christ and the Cosmos, pp. 133-246. *On the Kingship of Christ* see Pius XI, *Quas primas* in: ACTA APOSTOLICAE SEDIS 17 (1925) pp. 593-610.

[37] E. Longpré, *La Royauté de Jésus Christ chez S. Bonaventure et le B. Duns Scot*, Montreal 1927, pp. 17f.

[38] See the treatise *De perfectione religiosa* ed. by P. Bedjan, Paris 1909, pp. 583-586; cf. also I. Hausherr, *Un précurseur de la theorie scotiste. sur la fin de l'Incarnation: Isaac de Ninive*, in: RECHERCHES DE SCIENCE RELIGIEUSE 22 (1932) pp. 316-320; R. North, *Teilhard and the Problem of Creation* in: THEOLOGICAL STUDIES 24 (1963) p. 596.

[39] It is to be found in the work *De cessatione legalium*; cf. D.J. Unger, *Robert Grosseteste Bishop of Lincoln (1235-1253) On the Reasons for the Incarnation* in: FRANCISCAN STUDIES 16 (1956) pp. 1-36. For an exposition of Grosseteste's doctrine on the motives of the Incarnation see C. Urrutiéhéty, *Christus alpha et omega, seu de Christi universali regno*, Lille 1910, pp. 12-21. On the cf. B. Smalley, *The Biblical Scholar* in: *Robert Grosseteste Scholar and Bishop. Essays in Commemoration of the Seventh Centenary of his death*, ed. by D.A. Callus, Oxford 1955, pp. 80-82. For the mss. of the *De cessatione legalium see* S. Harrison Thomson, *The Writings of Robert Grosseteste, Bishop of Lincoln 1235-1253*, Cambridge 1940, pp. 121f.

[40] E. Longpré, *La Royauté de Jésus Christ*, 18 ; B. de Saint-Maurice, *John Duns Scotus. A Teacher for Our Times* (trans. by C. Duffy), St. Bonaventure N.Y. 1955, p. 250.

asks: *Utrum Christus praedestinatus fuerit esse Filius Dei?*[41] From the love that God is he concludes that Christ is the first predestined by God as the *summum opus Dei*. The predestination of Christ is absolute and unconditioned; it is not caused or occasioned by sin. If the fall were the cause of Christ's predestination, then we should have to admit that in the event of no sin, the most perfect creation of God would never have taken place, which, Scotus remarks tersely, appears extremely irrational. The reason is, that if Adam had not sinned, the greatest love would never have been given to God because the less than perfect love of all men—which never can reach the intensity of Christ's love of God—had not been refused. That God should brush aside the greatest and most perfect love of Christ for the lesser love of men (in the sense explained), Scotus cannot accept[42]. Because of the infinite perfection of His love Christ has the primacy of excellence and finality in the Divine intention. He is absolutely and unconditionally prior to every created being.

In God, of course, there is no chronology, no past, no future. He is pure and unique Act. He is the eternal Now. In view of this it might appear extremely hazardous to speak of priorities in the mind of God. But it presents no greater difficulty here than it does in the remainder of theology. If we would speak of God at all, we must use terms and ideas drawn from human experience, or remain forever silent about him. Because Christ is the most perfect work of God he is the first intended by God in the plan of creation. Scotus bases this on the reasoning that rational creatures first intend the end and then the means to achieve this[43]. In an analogous way, but in one act, God "rationabilissime" and "ordinatissime volens"[44] intends Christ before all other creatures because of the supreme perfection of his love. It is for Christ and in Christ that all creation is willed by God.

---

[41] Ord. III d. 7 q. 3 (ed. Vivés XIV 348): Rep. III d. 7 Q. 4 (ed. Vivés XXIII 301): *Utrum Christus sit praedestinatus esse Filius Dei?*

[42] Rep. III d. 7 q. 4 n. 4 (ed. Vivés XXIII 303ab): *Si lapsus esset causa praedestinationis Christi, sequeretur quod summum opus Dei esset occasionatum tantum, quia gloria omnium non erit tanta intensive quanta erit Christi; et quod tantum opus demisisset Deus propter bonum factum Adae, puta, si non peaccasset, videtur valde irrationabile.*

[43] Ord. III d. 32 q. l n. 6 (ed. Vivés XV 433a): *Omnis rationabiliter volens, vult primo finem, et secundo illud quod immediate attingit finem, et tertio alia quae remotius sunt ordinata ad attingendum finem.*

[44] Ibid.: *Cum igitur Deus rationabilissime velit, licet non diversis actibus, sed tantum uno, in quantum illo diversimode tendit super obiecta ordinate, primo vult finem, et in hoc est actus suus perfectus et voluntas eius beata*; Rep. II d. 20 q. 2 n. 2 (ed. VIVES XXIII 98a): *Omnis Ordinate volens, prius vult quod est immediatum fini; sed Deus est ordinatissime volens, et immediate post dilectionem sui vult beatitudinem illis qui eam habeant.*

Scotus arrives at his Christocentric vision of the universe in this way. God is love[45]. That must be grasped first of all. Love is its own reason, and God's love is the reason of all else,[46] though love tends to diffuse itself, to bubble over. Thirdly, it is God's God; through love we learn that mystery is something we never cease to understand the better. Now, in the first place God loves himself in the most perfect manner. He is love. Secondly, he loves himself and Christ, who loves him to the infinite degree in which his love tends to diffuse itself, to bubble over. Thirdly, it is God's will to be loved by Someone outside himself who can love him in the most perfect way. Finally, he foresees the union between himself and Christ, who loves him to the infinite degree in which he loves himself[47]. Beginning, therefore, with the love of God, Scotus arrives at Christ as the Centre of the whole created order.

It would be to go too far to say that St. Francis believed the primacy of Christ in the way that it is exposed by Scotus. Francis was no theologian. But he remains the inspiration of the doctrine which is but a logical development of his Christocentric mysticism. Francis saw with a clarity, never perhaps equalled, that the incarnation means Christ has become our elder Brother and God our common Father[48]. From the love of Christ he was led on to love all creatures, which followed as a natural consequence. Creation reflected for Francis the infinite variety of God. The meaning of that variety he expressed in a poem—as only a poet can do—the *Canticle of Brother Sun*. Because the world was God's creation, it had not been left untouched by Christ's redemption[49]. The whole structure of Scotus's theology of Christ has its foundation in the love of God. In this it is closest of all to St. Francis. The

---

[45] I 10.4,16; Ord. I d. 17 n. 173 (Vivés 222): [*Deus est*] *formaliter caritas et dilectio, non tantum effective.*

[46] Rep. III d. 32 q. un. n. 10 (ed. Vivés XXIII 507b): *In Deo est unus actus diligendi omnia, quia est unum obiectum, quod est ratio diligibilitatis sui et ratio diligendi omnia, quocumque modo diligibilia sunt.*

[47] Ibid. d. 7 q. 4 n. 5 (p. 303b): *Dico igitur sic: primo Deus diligit se; secundo diligit se aliis, et iste est amor castus; tertio vult se diligi ab alio qui potest eum summe diligere, loquendo de amore alicuius extrinseci; et quarto praevidit unionem illius naturae quae debet eum summe diligere, etsi nullus cecidisset.*

[48] S. Franciscus Assisiensis, *Epistola I* (*Opuscula Sancti Patris Francisci Assisiensis*, ad Claras Aquas 1941, p. 94): *O quam gloriosum et sanctum et magnum habere in caelis Patrem. . . .O quam sanctum et quam dilectum, beneplacitum et humile, pacificum et dulce et amabile et super omnia desiderabile habere talem fratrem, qui posuit animam suam pro ovibus suis.*

[49] S. Franciscus Assisiensis, *Epistola II* (Opuscula, pp.100f.): *Deprecor itaque omnes vos, fratres, eum osculo pedum et ea caritate qua possum, ut omnem reverentiam et omnem honorem, quantumcumque poteritis, exhibeatis sanctissimo corpori et sangumi Domini nostri Iesu Christi, in quo quae in caelis et quae in terris sunt, pacificata sunt et reconciliata omnipotenti Deo.*

Franciscan message to the world is the love of God lived out in the holy life of Francis of Assisi.

B. The consequences of Scotus's doctrine

Throughout Church history we find recurring two lines of thought and action on the relation of the Christian to the world. These may be described as "flight" and "involvement". The former tends to stress the *otherworldly* aspect of Christianity and the ephemeral quality of earthly life and its concerns. The latter, believing that God can be found in and through the world, tends to emphasize its essential goodness as the object of God's creation and Christ's redemption.

There is, and there must be an otherworldly aspect to Christianity, and there will always be those who feel themselves called to witness to the life that is to come. But otherworldliness is very far from that kind of dualism which divorces the "sacred" from the "profane". This may take many forms—science from religion, reason from faith, weekdays from Sunday—but in the end they all come to the same thing: Christianity divorced from the world and its concerns. Christianity has all too often been presented as disinterested in *this* world, and as really only concerned with man's passage to the *next*. Frequently one meets the belief that a life of holiness and integrity can only be achieved by concentrating all effort on "Churchliness". This derives ultimately from the idea that a perfect Christian life demands "being-out-of-the-world", or "getting-out-of-the-world", and that a life of devotion to this world is but a poor second best to a life lived in a monastery or more or less exclusively given to the sacred ministry.

The world of the twentieth Century to which the Christian message is to be proclaimed, cannot but reject such a presentation. In August 1966 the Archbishop of York, Dr. Coggan, voiced this very sentiment: "We have presented a God too small for this space age, a God who would seem to be a sort of oversized ecclesiastic, interested in little else than ecclesiastical matters. We have all too often failed to present a Christ magnificent in the greatness of his love, vast in the scope of his redemption"[50].

Science has revealed to us staggering secrets about the universe. Technology has provided us with powers that baffle the Imagination. Space travel has opened out vistas which not so long ago made good material for science fiction. Geology and palaeontology speak to us about our earth in terms of millions of years. Never before has the world and all that it contains

---

[50] Quoted in The Daily Telegraph (August 29, 1966).

appeared so attractive. There are, it is true, appalling evils. There is war, hunger, suffering, and the threat of mass destruction. Despite all this, there is a growing optimism. Assured of the beauty and goodness of the universe, astounded by its riches and resources, Christians and non-Christians alike have thrown themselves into it with eagerness and zeal. When we look out at the world of the modern city we see the image of man reflected back to us. It is easy, perhaps, to see God in a range of mountains; it not so easy to see him in a line of skyscrapers. The modern world is man's world, it is proof of his power and intelligence.

We must now return to the Scotistic doctrine of the primacy of Christ. Incarnation means to become man, to become part of the human Situation. Man is a compendium of the universe where matter and spirit unite. In becoming man Christ united forever the material and spiritual reality that this world is to God. In him all creation and every creature has been brought into the unity that is the incarnation. Water found its true meaning when he stood in it, the dust when he wrote in it, the wood when he was nailed to it. All these and the world itself were found worthy enough to be brought into contact with God-made-Man. For Scotus the incarnation is absolute and unconditioned. Matter as we know it was intended from all eternity in the simple and unique act of God's predestination to be made one with God in Christ. The atoms and the sub-atomic particles of Christ's Body were forever the object of God's love. They were intended from all eternity to be part and parcel of that sublime outpouring of love that is the incarnation.

This would not be the place to go into the details of the similarity between Scotus and Teilhard de Chardin. But the point cannot pass without mention. It has been noted with emphasis that, whatever the similarities are, their world visions differ enormously as static and dynamic[51]. Indeed, it is to be expected that Scotus could never have conceived a dynamic and evolving universe in Teilhard's sense. Since his time man has made tremendous leaps forward; he has had seven hundred and more years to grapple with life and penetrate deeper into the meaning of truth. Man goes on understanding himself and the cosmos. This would hardly surprise Scotus. He says himself: *In processu generationis humanae semper crevit notitia veritatis*[52].

Despite the enormous difference between the two thinkers, there is the very important similarity, not to say identity: the place of Christ in the universe.

---

[51] N.M. Wildiers, *Teilhard de Chardin*, Editions Universitaires, Paris 1960, pp. 94-99; C.F. Mooney, *Teilhard de Chardin and the Mystery of Christ*, London 1966, pp. 121f.

[52] Ord. IV d. 1 q. 3 n. 8 (ed. Vivés XVI 136a).

For Scotus creation is inconceivable without Christ. Christ is its crowning point and completion. Wildiers finds it "curieux" that the texts which Teilhard cites to confirm his view of Christ are the very texts which are quoted by the subscribers to the Scotistic thesis on the primacy[53]. This is understandable in so far as Teilhard seems to have been only vaguely acquainted with the Scotistic view[54]. But in itself it is not at all remarkable that they should cite the same Pauline texts. The subscribers to the Scotistic thesis maintain that the absolute primacy of Christ best explains the Pauline teaching on the primacy[55]. Likewise Teilhard believes that his vision of evolution tending towards Christ in whom it has its fulfilment is a deeper insight into the meaning of the Pauline texts. Moreover, the primacy of Christ as taught by Scotus remains even in the context of a dynamic world view. As I see it, the Teilhardian view is a development at another level of both St. Paul and Scotus. St. Paul knew nothing of evolution as understood by Teilhard; not all the implications of his doctrine on the primacy were known to Scotus. This detracts nothing from St. Paul or Scotus. The Pauline texts are God's Word. Both Scotus and Teilhard found in them their visions of the world. From totally different world views and from totally different points of departure the theologian and scientist reached the same conclusion: Christ is the centre of the universe.

The primacy of Christ is the affirmation of the goodness of the world. Christ is the positive evaluation of all creation. The world and its concerns are not stumbling blocks but instruments of our sanctification. It is the Christian mission to be in the world and of it. Christians must penetrate the social, economic, scientific, cultural, artistic life of the world. To strive for the betterment of the world and mankind is to serve Christ. What he said so long ago about clothing the naked and feeding the hungry: "You did it to me"[56], applies equally now. "When you built spacecraft, you did it to me". "When you worked for peace in the world, you did it to me". "When you prayed for unity, you did it to me". No limit can be set to those words of Christ because the just did not know that they had served him[57]. The primacy of Christ means that we

---

[53] Wildiers, *Teilhard de Chardin*, pp. 94f.: "Il est curieux de noter ici que les textes de l'Ecriture, sur lesquels Teilhard se fonde afin de confirmer son opinion, sont exactement les memes que ceux cites par les tenants de la conception scotiste".

[54] Ibid., p. 94, n. 4: "Teilhard de Chardin se refere parfois explicitement a la these scotiste (voir: *Esquisse d'une dialectique de l'esprit*, 1946, p. 10), qu'il semble cependant ne connaitre qu'assez vaguement".

[55] That is to say the absolute primacy of Christ "ut hic homo".

[56] Matthew 25:35-40.

[57] Matthew 25:37: "Lord, when did we see you hungry and feed you?"

are serving him at every point and every level as we work for a better world. There can be no dichotomy, therefore, between Christ and the world. He is found, loved, and served in and through the world. Science needs religion and religion needs science; reason needs faith and faith needs reason; weekdays need Sunday and Sunday needs weekdays; the world needs Christ and Christ needs the world.

There are Christians who see dangers in so optimistic a view of the world, and who feel the need of detachment-in-commitment. In setting one's heart on the world, it is not difficult to forget Christ for creation, they argue; it does not take too much to make a god out of man. While there is a holy harmony and unity between Christ and the world, there is also a clear distinction. The natures of Christ though inseparable, are united "inconfuse"[58].

No doubt a wholehearted commitment to the world requires a constant reminder of the new heaven and the new earth, of the world that is to come. That constant reminder is the Eucharist. St. Paul tells us: "As often as you eat this bread and drink the cup, you proclaim the Lord's death *until he comes*"[59]. When Christians gather to celebrate the Eucharist they are reminded that the Lord is coming back. He may come tomorrow, he may come in a thousand years. It matters little, he *is* coming back. Then he will transform the world and take up into that transformation every effort made to build a better world. At the Eucharist we are reminded that the world, as well as being ours, is also Christ's, and Christ is God's. To forget that is to loose sight of what Christ has done for the world, of what he has taught us about it. To loose sight of what Christ has done is to turn involvement into idolatry. We need to be detached; our detachment is the Eucharist.

The Eucharist is from bread and wine taken out of our world. The long process that begins with sowing the wheat and planting the vine is contained in the bread baked and the wine matured. Christ teaches us the value of bread and wine by choosing them to be made into his Body and Blood until he comes. Through creation itself he reminds us that he will return. But at the same time it is through the Eucharist that we receive our strength to go back to the world and make it better still even if only by bringing in the harvest or caring for the vines.

---

[58] Cf. the definition of Chalcedon on the two natures of Christ: *[Docemus] unum eundemque Christum Filium Dominum unigenitum, in duabus naturis inconfuse, immutabiliter indivise, inseparabiliter agnoscendum, nusquam sublata differentia naturarum* (Denzinger, *Enchiridion Symbolorum*, Barcinone 1965, n. 302).

[59] 1 Corinthians 11:26f.

Conclusion

There is an awareness among Christians of the issues that confront Christianity in the modern world. These, the meaning and dignity of man and the value of earthly realities are ecumenical in the strictest sense. Two points from Scotus's writings have been examined in connexion with these issues. Firstly, we took the Scotistic principle of individuation and drew out its consequences for the dignity of things in general and the human person in particular. Then we followed Scotus's teaching on the primacy of Christ from which we concluded the value of earthly realities and the necessity of Christian commitment to the task of building a better world. Both points contain principles which are universally valid because they are really Christian and eminently human. In this lies the chief ecumenical significance of Duns Scotus.

John Duns Scotus and the Place of Christ[1]

On the occasion of the celebration in 1966 of the seventh centenary of the birth of Duns Scotus, Pope Paul VI published an Apostolic Letter, *Alma Parens*, in which he emphasised the importance of Scotus' teaching and picked out in particular his ecumenical significance.[2] We are not concerned here with the content of the Pope's Letter, but with some interesting reactions it provoked. *The Times*, for example reported on 26 July 1966, p.12, that "one prominent member of the Anglican Communion was convinced that the Pope had got the wrong man", because "Duns Scotus' philosophy was uncompromisingly Roman Catholic"(!). Mr. St. John-Stevas stated in the CATHOLIC HERALD, 5 August 1966, p. 3, that from his knowledge of Scotus he did not think him an ideal writer for this role. He went on to give his reasons for this, among which he asserted that Scotus held that we cannot prove the existence of God.

It would be unfair, I suppose, to say that Scotus is not known to students of theology. Those familiar with Thomist-inspired manuals of scholastic philosophy and theology will recall his name from the occasional footnote and will remember that he often figured prominently in the laundry lists of adversaries. He is known as the "Subtle Doctor" (a title sufficient of itself to arouse the gravest suspicion) who taught the questionable formal distinction, coined the odd term "thisness" (*haecceitas*), peddled the strange doctrine of the *forma corporeitatis* and who blandly suggested that the Word of God would have been made man even if Adam had not sinned. By the unwary, repeating the errors of the handbooks and dictionaries whose authors, one suspects, never so much as opened a page of Scotus' works, he is solemnly pronounced the Father of Nominalism and is accused of denying reason's power to discover the existence of God—two of the more outrageous misrepresentations of his teaching. The latter is particularly offensive when one finds that Scotus states quite unequivocally in innumerable places that we can

[1] CLERGY REVIEW 57 (Sept. 1972) pp. 667-675; (Oct. 1972) pp. 774-785; (Nov. 1972) pp. 860-868. Published with permission.
[2] *Epistola Apostolica Alma Parens*, in: ACTA APOSTOLICAE SEDIS 58 (1966) pp. 609-614.

come to a knowledge of God's existence.[3] One popular snippet of information which has damaged Scotus' image is that his forename "Duns" is the etymon of the English word "dunce" and that the pointed hood of the Franciscans is possibly the original model of the dunce's cap! A good deal of the misrepresentation and misunderstanding can be traced back to the 1500s. Scotus and his followers were subjected to a vicious attack by the humanists and Reformers of that century. It is ironical to recall that here in England the frenzied celebration of the "funus Scoti et Scotistarum" had been preceded some years previously by St. John Fisher's proscribing the text of Scotus for St. John's College, Cambridge. Nearer our own time Scotus has been accused of Semi-Pelagianism by Scheeben on the Catholic side and by Harnack among the Protestants. The Ancient British Church, of course, bears the honour of having produced Pelagius, the father of that so British heresy of whom St. Jerome said: "Scottorum pultibus praegravatus". Scotus, British though he was, never fell into the errors of Pelagianism or Semi-Pelagianism; the accusation is based on a misunderstanding of *meritum de congruo* in his works, by which, in fact, Scotus means nothing more than is intended by the adage: *facienti quod in se est, Deus non denegat gratiam.*[4]

There can be no doubt, then, that Scotus is known; but how he is known and what masquerades for truth about him needs very severe pruning indeed. One wonders at times whether the blessed shroud of anonymity and oblivion which history draws over some of its more cherished figures might not have been better treatment for the Subtle and Marian Doctor.

Any serious study of Scotus, as of all the great Scholastics, leads the students to the conviction that we cannot ignore the Middle Ages except to our peril. It is sheer folly to imagine that we can leap from late Antiquity to the mid-fifteenth century and so by-pass what is dubbed the obscurantism and superstition of that most glorious period of Western Civilisation, without the profoundest damage to our thought and understanding. The writings of the Scholastics are a treasure of sublime wisdom and common sense with so much to teach us at present. Their wisdom makes manifest that there are principles and facets of religion and spirituality which are neither up-to-date nor out-of-date, neither progressive nor conservative, but simply timeless. Their common

---

[3] See e.g. F. Alluntis, *Demonstrability and Demonstration of the Existence of God in John Duns Scotus, 1265-1965. Studies in Philosophy and the History of Philosophy* 3, ed. by J.K. Ryan and B.M. Bonansea OFM, Washington D.C. 1965, pp. 133-170.

[4] A. Bertoni OFM, *Le Bienhereux Jean Duns Scotus*, Levanto 1917, pp 237-43; H.A. Oberman, *Duns Scotus, Nominalism and the Council of Trent* in: *Studies in Philosophy*, pp. 311-344.

sense proves that in doctrine and life we belong to a living tradition which has inherent authority, which can admit of no absolutely new starting point, which creates originality and gives ever fresher insights, which we did not fashion but into which we are inserted to contribute our part in preserving, strengthening and increasing it, as it makes its way inexorably to the future. Following from this, the Scholastics point out our need of a much wider awareness and greater familiarity with the writings of the Fathers of the Church. They take us beyond themselves to those spiritual giants of the early Church who, for their place in the living tradition, will never be superseded, however long the course of history may yet have to run. Who were ever more conscious of the strength and weakness of their own civilisation and culture, on the one hand, and more thoroughly schooled and formed by the Living Word of God, on the other, than the Fathers of the church? We need them now if for no other reason than to remind us that through the message of the gospel in the living tradition, we can also judge and discern the values and dangers of our own time and history.

This article is concerned with one aspect of Scotus' Christology, namely, the Predestination of Christ or, as is described with less accuracy, the Motive for the incarnation and with some of its implications for theology today. As an introduction to this some few biographical details will be given and a brief remark made on his place in Scholasticism.

Outline of Life of Scotus

John Duns Scotus was born in Scotland at Duns in Berwickshire some time between 23 December 1265 and 17 March 1266. There was an opinion, traceable to Luke Wadding OFM, the famous Irish historian, that Scotus hailed from Ireland. This is now totally discarded, as is the opinion that he was born near Maxton-on-Tweed, Roxburghshire.[5] He entered the Franciscan Order before 1280 and most probably made his profession of vows in 1281. He was ordained priest on 17 March 1291 at Northampton. For the next two years he continued his studies at Oxford, after which he was sent to Paris in 1293, where he attended lectures on the *Sentences*. As he was not yet qualified to lecture on the Lombard in Paris, he returned to England in 1297 where he lectured on the *Sentences* in Cambridge and Oxford. He was nominated by the Minister General of the Franciscan Order in 1302 to lecture at Paris. His stay in Paris on

---

[5] C. Balic OFM, *John Duns Scotus, Some Reflections on the Occasion of the Seventh Centenary of his Birth*, Rome, 1966, pp 5-10, 16-29; H. Docherty OFM, *The Brockie Forgeries* in: THE INNES REVIEW 16 (1965) pp. 79-127.

this occasion, however, was brief. Due to the anti-papal policies of Philip the Fair, the struggle between the Pope and the King became intensified in the early months of 1303. Scotus was among those at the Franciscan friary in Paris who refused to sign the King's petition against Boniface VIII. As a result, Scotus was forced to leave Paris and return once more to England where he continued his lectures at Oxford. After the death of Boniface VIII, Benedict XI restored the University's privileges and Scotus went back to lecture in Paris some time before November 1304. He became *magister* in theology at Easter 1305. By the beginning of the Scholastic Year 1307/8 he had already left Paris and in the early months of 1308 we find him lecturing in the Franciscan *studium* in Cologne. The precise reason for his departure is not known.[6] In any case, on receiving the obedience from the General, it is recorded, he broke off conversation with his brethren, and, after asking the way, set out forthwith for Cologne. He died on 8 November 1308 in Cologne where he lies buried in the Minoritenkirche, barely five minutes walk from Cologne main station.

There is ample evidence of his reputation for sanctity even while still alive. He is honoured today in the Franciscan Order as Blessed, a devotion fully consonant with the decrees of Pope Urban VIII. A canonically approved diocesan cult is paid to him at Nola in Italy. In Franciscan friaries on Saturdays, the *Tota Pulchra* is chanted and at the end of it the following petition is made to God: "Sancta Trinitas ut Beatum Joannem Scotum, Immaculatae Conceptionis Beatissimae Virginis Mariae Adsertorem, glorificare digneris, Te rogamus audi nos". In 1905 a petition was made to the Holy See for his canonisation. This resulted in a formal approval by the Congregation of Rites for the *cultus* paid to him. His canonization, it seems, must await the final volume of the critical edition of his works. It is noteworthy that as the edition has gone apace, eleven of the works attributed to him in the Wadding-Vivès edition have been proved entirely spurious, among which is the *De rerum principio*, a chief source of misrepresentation in the past. Scotus' orthodoxy is beyond question and his writings show him to have been a learned and a holy man worthy enough, I dare to suggest, to be declared a Doctor of the Church. In the meantime, it would seem a most fitting gesture to introduce his cult into all the dioceses of Scotland, for he is, after all, one of Scotland's finest sons.[7]

---

[6] E.M. Giusto OFM, *Vita del B. Giovanni Duns Scoto*, S. Maria degli Angeli 1921, pp. 143-148.

[7] Since these pages were written the Minister General of the Order of Friars Minor, Constantine Koser OFM has officially informed the Order that the Sacred Congregation for

To understand Scotus' place in Scholasticism it needs to be remembered that he came after the condemnations by Stephen Tempier in 1277 and that he flourished in the period of rehabilitation of the moderate Aristotelianism of the followers of St. Thomas. He may be described, I think, as an Augustinian-Aristotelian. Unlike the great Franciscan Masters before him, especially St. Bonaventure, he did not regard Aristotle as no more than a pagan philosopher with little or nothing to offer in our search for the wisdom that beatifies. *Scientia* and *sapientia* were not at such opposite ends of the spectrum for Scotus as they were for some of his Franciscan brethren such as St. Bonaventure and Matthew of Aquasparta. In fact, it is true to say, as the eminent Scotist scholar, Efrem Bettoni OFM, has written,[8] that the originality of the Scotist synthesis is seen best of all in his treatment of the primary object of the human intellect, where he attempted to reconcile the best elements of the Augustinian-Platonic illumination theory with those of Aristotelian empiricism. But at heart he remained above all an Augustinian.

The Motive of the Incarnation

Among the many disputed questions in theology one of the best known is that of the final motive of the incarnation, which gave rise to the controversy between the Thomists and the Scotists. In the manuals of theology we learn that the Thomists hold that the redemption of the human race, in virtue of the actual decree, is the sole principal reason why God became man. Thus, if Adam had not sinned, the Word would not have become incarnate. On the other hand, we learn that the Scotists hold that, since God wills and accomplishes everything on account of love, the incarnation of the Word of God is willed in order that God may be infinitely glorified through Christ's love. Therefore, in virtue of the present divine decree, if Adam had not sinned, the Word would nevertheless have become man.[9] This is a fair, if somewhat brief presentation of the two opinions. Since Thomist manuals were generally used in seminaries and houses of study, it is not surprising that most students of theology learned that the Thomist opinion is the more common and more probable in theology.

---

the Causes of Saints, in a decree issued 4th May 1972, confirmed by Pope Paul VI, has approved the writings and teachings of John Duns Scotus. The greatest obstacle to his canonisation and being declared a Doctor of the Church has now been removed.

[8] E. Bettoni OFM, *The Originality of the Scotistic Synthesis,* in: *Studies in Philosophy*, pp 28-44.

[9] A. Tanquery, *Synopsis Theologiae Dogmaticae* 2, editio vigesima sexta, Desclee et Socii, 1950, pp. 789-794; *Sacrae Theologiae Summa* III, Solano, *De Verbo Incarnato*, Bibliotheca de Auctores Cristianos, Matriti MCMLVI, pp. 13-22.

The controversy between Thomists and Scotists, while demonstrating a laudable freedom of opinion in the schools, seems in the end rather fruitless. What is the point of spending time in speculation on a purely hypothetical question? Given the simple affirmative proposition of the Creed "qui propter nos homines et propter nostram salutem descendit de coelis et incarnatus est", all further search for the motive of the incarnation of the Word appears barren and the difference of opinion seems altogether unrelated to reality. However, neither St. Thomas nor Duns Scotus can be held responsible for the way in which the question has been presented and treated. That rests on the shoulders of their followers, especially the Scotists, who should never have pursued the argument in purely hypothetical terms. It must be remarked, however, that the controversy centres on the question whether in terms of God's *present* decree and the *actual* divine plan, the redemption of the human race is the adequate and principal reason of the incarnation, without excluding necessarily other intended reasons. From this question follows the second: whether the Word of God would have been made man, even if Adam had not sinned. As will be clear, the answer to this depends on the answer given to the first question. But, in any event, the second question can only answered in more or less probable terms, as St. Bonaventure pointed out.[10] The Angelic Doctor, after examining the purely hypothetical question, came down on the negative side and quoted Augustine as his authority.[11] His remarks in his *Commentary* on 1 Timothy that the question is of no great moment since we do not know what God would have decided if he had not foreseen sin.[12] Duns Scotus himself, as we shall see, did not begin with the purely hypothetical question at all.

The question of the principal motive of the incarnation had been treated by a substantial number of theologians before the time of Scotus. The tradition behind his teaching must be mentioned here, however briefly, in order to show that Scotus is no more than a moment, albeit of the greatest importance, in the development of a doctrine which has assumed such significance today. As early as the seventh century, Isaac of Nineveh (+c. 680) had asserted that the incarnation of the Word would have taken place independently of the sin of Adam. Fr. Dominic Unger OFM Cap has argued strongly that Isaac made explicit what had been already implicitly insisted on by St. Irenaeus, St. Gregory of Nyssa, St. Athanasius, St. Cyril of Alexandria, St. Maximus, Anastasius of Sinai and Didymus the Blind. He points out that

---

[10] *Doctoris Serpahici S. Bonaventurae. . . .*In 3, d.I, a.2, q.2, Tomus III, Ad Claras Aquas 1887, pp. 21-28.

[11] *Summa Theologica* III, q.I, a.3, Vivès, vol. 4, p. 596.

[12] *Comment. in Epistolam I ad Timotheum*, c.1, lec. IV, Vivès. vol. 24, p. 459.

Isaac of Nineve was the first to have discussed both sides of the problem and to have rejected the view that God became man primarily because of sin.[13] In the West St. Augustine touches on the hypothetical question in *Sermo 174* and *Sermo 175* where he comes down heavily on the negative side.[14] Later on, in reaction to St. Anselm's *Cur Deus Homo*, both Rupert of Deutz and Honorius of Autun felt that redemption from sin could not be the adequate reason for the Word's becoming man. Rupert of Deutz (+1135), after asking the purely hypothetical question, answered that the redemption of the human race is not the only nor the chief reason for the incarnation. Sin is not a necessary cause of the coming of the Head and King of all the elect, angels and humankind.[15] Honorius of Autun (+1150) treats of the question in dialogue form. The disciple asks the master: Would Christ have become incarnate had man not sinned? The reason behind the question is that the entire Scriptures proclaim that Christ came in the flesh to redeem humankind. For if humankind had remained in paradise and Christ had not come, then it has to be said that sin is the cause of the coming of Christ and, therefore, that sin is a good and desirable thing and not an evil at all. Honorius replies that sin is the greatest evil and is not the cause of the coming of Christ. The cause of the incarnation of the Word is the predestination of humankind to divinisation by grace in the eternal plan of God.[16] In the Franciscan School, Alexander of Hales held that the incarnation would have been fitting even if Adam had not sinned, though it must be admitted that this is not the question at issue. His pupil, St. Bonaventure, after a relatively prolonged treatment of the question, reached the same conclusion as St. Thomas.[17] St. Albert the Great, on the other hand, agreed that Christ would have been made man, even in the event of there being no sin.[18] It is very interesting that Bishop Robert Grosseteste, who lectured to the Franciscans in Oxford,[19] in his treatment of the question in *De*

---

[13] D.J. Unger OFM Cap, *The Love of God the Primary Reason for the Incarnation according to Isaac of Nineve* in: FRANCISCAN STUDIES 9 (1949) pp. 148-155.

[14] Sermo CLXXIV, PL 38, 940; Sermo CLXXV, ibid., p. 945: *Nulla causa fuit inveniendi Christo Domino, nisi peccatores salvos facere. Tolle morbos, tolle vulnera, et nulla causa est medicinae.*

[15] Ruperti Tuitensis, Com. in: *Opus De Gloria et Honore Filii Hominis super Mathaeum, lib.* 13, PL 138, 1624-1629.

[16] *Honorii Augustodunensis Libellus Octo Quaestionum de Angelis et Homine,* c II: Utrum Christus incarneretur si homo in paradiso perstitisset, PL 172, 1187f.

[17] In 3, d. 1, a.2, q.2. Ad Claras Aquas 1887, pp 21-28.

[18] Alberti Magni In III Sent., d. 20. a.5; cf. Tanquerey, *Synoposis* II, p. 792; Solano, *De Verbo Incarnato*, p. 16.

[19] Cf. *Thomas of Eccleston's De Adventu Fratrum Minorum in Angliam* in: Fr. Cuthbert, *The Friars and How They Came to England*, London 1903, p. 186.

Cessatione Legalium, concluded that Christ would have become man if Adam had not sinned.[20]

From this short survey it will be clear that the question of the motive for the incarnation did not have its origin in the thirteenth century, nor was it confined to the Thomists and the Scotists.

The Absolute Predestination of Christ

The most unjust criticism ever made of John Duns Scotus was Bernard Landry's description of him as a Franciscan who lost the sense of love. This extraordinary conclusion is so far from the truth that one wonders if Landry was really writing about Scotus at all. The remark is contradicted time and again in Scotus' writings, but nowhere more completely than in his *Commentary* on the third book of the *Sentences.* For example, while analysing the question about the grace conferred on Christ, he gives us a profound insight into his own spirituality: "In speaking of Christ I would rather err by praising him too much than by praising him too little, if it should happen that through ignorance I were to fall into one error or the other":[22] Like all the great Scholastics, Scotus was not only a very learned man, but also a mystic, "that is, he experienced what he was talking about as a personal experience. That is what mysticism originally meant in the realm of Scholasticism. There was no opposition between mysticism and scholasticism. Mysticism was the experience of the scholastic message. The basis of the dogma was unity with the divine in devotion, prayer, contemplation and ascetic practices".[23] Scotus' awareness of the divine Presence and love of the divine Will, his ardent devotion to Christ and his delicate spiritual sensitivity, are woven into the text of well-nigh every work. The sublime prayers with which he begins and concludes his great work on the existence of God *De primo rerum omnium principio* carry the reader to the highest levels of contemplation.[24] Beyond doubt, however, it is his teaching on the predestination of Christ—the quintessence of Scotus—which shows him above all as a mystic and true son of St. Francis.

---

[20] D.J. Unger OFM Cap, *Robert Grosseteste, Bishop of Lincoln [1235-1253] On the Reasons for the Incarnation* in: FRANCISCAN STUDIES 16 (1956) pp. 1-36.

[21] *La Philosophie de Duns Scot,* Librairie Alean, *Collection des Grands Philosophes,* Paris, 1922, p. 245: "... le Subtil... a complètement oublié ce qui fait le beauté de François, l'amour des hommes et de la nature... Duns Scot est un franciscain qui a perdu le sens de l'amour."

[22] *Ordinatio* III, d.13, q.4, n.9, Vivès XIV, 463b.

[23] P. Tillich, *A History of Christian Thought,* ed. by C.A. Braaten SCM, London, 1968, p. 136.

[24] See Vivès IV, 721-799.

The teaching of Scotus on the predestination of Christ does not begin with the hypothetical question: "If Adam had not sinned would the Word have been made man?" There is no question in his works bearing this title. He does mention the hypothesis of Adam's not sinning; but it is clear that this is to be understood in terms of, and as coming as a conclusion from, his teaching on the love of God and the predestination of Christ. His analysis does not centre on the mere hypothesis about what might have happened had there been no sin, nor does he prescind from the actual order of the divine economy. He presents a doctrinal thesis which gives deeper meaning both to the Pauline texts on the Primacy of Christ in Colossians and Ephesians and to the Church's teaching on the Universal Kingship of Christ.

Scotus' doctrine on the predestination of Christ is to be found in the *Ordinatio* III, d.7, q.3, (Vivès ed., XIV, 348-9, 354-5) and in the *Reportata Parisiensia* III, d.7, q.4, (Vivès ed., XXIII, 301-4). In both cases the title of the question concerns the predestination of Christ.[25] The conclusion of these texts is that Christ is not merely occasioned by sin, but that he takes his place in creation before the foreseeing of sin. It is also evident that for Scotus the Redemption is only part of the total drama of the incarnation of the Word of God. Thus, presuming the Scriptural teaching that God is love and his own earlier reflections on that teaching, Scotus treats of the Word's becoming man in the context of the absolute predestination of Christ. From the love that God is, he concludes that Christ is first predestined in the mind of God as *Summum Opus Dei*, God's Masterpiece.

In the first section of the question Scotus begins his response by quoting the text of Romans 1:4 from the Vulgate, a version which he took as it stood. The word *praedestinatus* of that text is, as is known, an inaccurate rendering of the Greek *horistheutos*, which does not mean predestined, but designated, marked out, established, set-up or declared. Christ was thus declared or proclaimed to be the Son of God by the resurrection. Romans 1:4, therefore, is not all about predestination in the sense in which the Scholastics understood it. Nevertheless, this correction of the text in no way subtracts from the value of Scotus' reflections. He defined predestination as the preordaining of a rational creature firstly to glory and then to the means to attain it.[26] After examining the altogether unique predestination of Christ to personal union in

---

[25] *Ordinatio* III: *Utrum Christus praedestinatus fuerit esse filius Dei?; Reportata Parisiensia: Utrum Christus sit praedestinatus esse Filius Dei?*
[26] *Ordinatio* I, d.40, q. unica, Vivès X, 680b.

the Word, Scotus then turns to consider the place of Christ's predestination in the mind of God.

He remarks that the fall of man is held by a number of theologians to be the necessary reason for Christ's predestination, so that if Adam had not sinned , the incarnation would not have taken place. He goes on to assert that the fall of man was not the cause of the predestination of Christ because, if that were the case, we should be forced to admit that in the event of no sin, the most perfect creation of God (the Incarnate Word) would never have existed which, Scotus adds, seems irrational to say. On this reasoning, if Adam had not sinned, the greatest and most perfect love among creatures, the love of the Sacred Heart, would never have been given to God, because the far less than perfect love of all other rational creatures on earth had not been refused. Scotus, therefore, cannot accept that God would abandon the most perfect love of Christ for the less than perfect love of all humankind which in fact would have been given unreservedly by us all had there been no sin. Because of the infinite perfection of his love Christ has the primacy of excellence and finality in the Divine Intention. He is willed absolutely and unconditionally prior to every other created being.

Since God is Pure Act in an Eternal Now ineffably beyond us, it might seem a little hazardous to be speaking of what is before and after in the Divine Mind. However, it is clear that this presents no more difficulty here than it does in the rest of theology. Nor, in particular, is it more hazardous in this case than in the thesis which makes Redemption the final motive of the incarnation. If we would speak of God at all, we must do so in terms of before and after drawn from our temporal experience, or remain forever silent. And silent about God we may not be, as St. Augustine says: "What does anyone succeed in saying when attempting to speak of you? Yet woe to those who do not speak of you at all, when those who speak must say nothing".[27]

Scotus continues that because Christ is the reason of all else that exists, he is first intended in the divine plan of creation. He established the conclusion on analogy with the experience that rational creatures first intended the end and then the means to achieve it.[28] In an analogous way, but in one sovereign act, God *ordinatissime et rationabilissime volens,*[29] intends Christ before all else and with, in and through him, the whole of creation.

---

[27] *Confessions* I, 4.
[28] *Ordinatio* III, d.32, q.1, n.6, Vivès XV, 433.
[29] *Reportata Parisiensia* II, d.20, q.2, n.2, Vivès XXIII, 98.

We have now arrived at the text which in the opinion of this writer is the most sublime that came from Scotus' pen. It is the cornerstone of his theology and the key to his own grasp of the essence of the Revealed Religion made known in the mystery of the gospel:

> Therefore, I argue as follows: in the first place God loves himself. Secondly, he loves himself in others and this is most pure and holy love. Thirdly, God wills to be loved by another who can love him perfectly and here I am referring to the love of someone outside God. Therefore, fourthly, God foresees the union between the Word and the creature Christ who owes him supreme love, even had there never been the Fall. . . .In the fifth place, he sees Christ as Mediator coming to suffer and redeem his people because of sin.[30]

The starting point of Scotus' Christocentric synthesis is the love of God. The supreme purpose of all God's activity *ad extra* is that God be glorified through love. We may justly conclude from this that there can be no glory of God where there is no love. Therefore, it is not merely by the *fact* of creation or the existence of rational creatures that God is glorified. Rather, God is glorified because the rational creature in transcendence and freedom, having the power to love, is encountered by the Living God and may then glorify God in holiness, by lifting up hands in worship and opening lips in praise, summing up in self the whole of creation. It is only because we possess the power to love, that is, to go out to another for the other's sake, that we are the crowning point of creation. The heavens proclaim the glory of God because they have moved from the beginning towards that moment when the world would have self-reflection in love in the human creature, who found reality not only outside self, but inside and beyond self. God's glory *ad extra* is through love, and Christ is par excellence the Glory of God through the love of his Sacred Heart. In Christ's love is God's supreme glory *ad extra*. Thus, the descending order in God's mind from the union with himself, Christ Jesus, down to the undifferentiated subatomic particles and beyond to the primordial creation, becomes the ascending order of cosmic and human history, through, in and unto Christ to the eternal glory of God. The predestination of Christ, the supernatural order, revelation, creation, redemption are willed and decreed by God in his love, for the will of God is essentially a sovereignly ordered act of love.

---

[30] *Reportat Parisiensia* III, d.7, q.4, n.5, Vivès XXIII, 303b.

Scotus, like St. Bonaventure, described God as an intelligible sphere whose centre is everywhere and whose circumference is nowhere. In humankind, all creation is tending towards that Centre and the principle of this centripetal movement is charity. Now God is formally love, formally charity and not merely the cause of love: "formaliter dilectio et formaliter caritas, non tantum effective".[31] God is love by very essence, not merely because of creation. Love has its own reason in itself, it is always self-explanatory and God's love is the reason of all else.[32]

Because God is formally love, in the first place he necessarily loves himself in the Divine Essence and in this consists infinite beatitude. The Divine Life is sealed in the procession of the Holy Spirit who is Personal Love. The reason of all divine activity is found in the very nature of God's most pure, free and disinterested love, whereby he loves himself forever. Secondly, God loves himself in others and this love is pure and unselfish, since God is the cause of all creatures. The divine love tends to bubble over: *bonum est diffusivum sui*. Thirdly, God wills to be loved by another who can love God perfectly for who God is. God wills that others love the same object as himself, for it is the nature of true love to want the object of its love to be loved by others, since it knows no envy, jealousy or exclusivism. Thus, for God to will others to love the Divine Essence is to will others to have this love in them. It is at this moment in the Divine Intention that Scotus places predestination. Quoting Richard of St. Victor: "perfecte diligens, vult dilectum diligi"[33] Scotus arrives at his most sublime reflection on the generation of divine love: *vult alios diligentes*; God, loving himself in holiness and purity, wills to have co-lovers. Since the final motive of all God's activity outside God is the Glory of God in love, God decrees first the existence of Christ, in whom God is glorified among creatures in the highest possible way. The homage of the Incarnate Word contains the most perfect love and therefore bears within itself radically the love of all rational creatures. The final reason of all God's activity ad extra is the Sacred Heart of Jesus in whom the Creator and creature are united forever. The first intended of the *condiligentes* is Jesus Christ on account of the perfection of his love and consequent on his predestination, the Divine Will intends the entire order of grace and nature. There is creation at all only because there is love.

---

[31] *Ordinatio* I, d.17, n.173, Vivès V, 222.
[32] *Reportata Parisiensis III*, d.32, q. unica, n. 10, Vivès XXIII, 507b: *In Deo est unus actus diligendi omnia, quia est unum obiectum, quod est ratio diligibilitatis sui et ration diligendi omnia, quocumque modo diligbilia sunt.*
[33] *Ordinatio* III, d. 28, q. 1, n. 2, Vivès XV, 378a.

Divine Love is likewise the supreme purpose of Revelation. The truths which have been made known to us are not merely to offer infinite perspectives to our intelligence, but primarily that we should love God with perfect rectitude.[34] There can be no separation between theology and spirituality, nor is there any truth of the purely speculative order in the revealed mystery of the Gospel. Revelation was made to direct the activity of the will to its most noble act: the love of God in the love that God is.

God wills to share the Object of His Love

According to the doctrine of Duns Scotus the incarnation of the Word was already the purpose of God's freedom even apart from the Divine foreknowledge of freely incurred guilt on our part. The reality of Redemption, while fully retained by Scotus, becomes in his view subordinate to the primary purpose of God's will which is communion in sharing the life of love. The predestination of Christ is neither caused nor occasioned by human guilt. The reason for the incarnation is God's free decision from all eternity to share the object of his love with the free and responsible creatures we are created to be. Scotus did not establish his thesis from Scripture, though there can be no doubt about its Scriptural basis. There are many passages in the New Testament, e.g. Colossians 1:13ff., Ephesians 1:1ff., which cannot be restricted in their application to Christ the Logos. Since space will not allow a sustained treatment of the Biblical foundation of the Doctrine of the Absolute Primacy of Christ, we will examine just one of the texts mentioned above.

In Colossians 1:1-20. the subject of the entire passage is Christ, the Word made man. St. Paul asserts that in Christ we gain our freedom, the forgiveness of sin [vv. 13f.]. Now if we ask: "In whom do we have forgiveness of our sin?" we must answer: "In Christ, the Son of God made man, who was born in our history, lived and died for us and then rose from the dead to a new kind of existence". The text continues with a relative clause in verse 15: "Who is the image of the invisible God". Again if we ask: "Who is the image of the invisible God?" we must answer "He, Christ the Son of God made man in whom we have the forgiveness of our sin". St. Paul did not change the subject of the passage at verse 15; he is still speaking of the Incarnate Word. Moreover, he the Incarnate Word, is the firstborn of all creation and in, through and unto him all things were created. He is also firstborn from the dead so that he should be first in every way [v. 18]. The dominant idea of the whole passage is the unconditioned primacy of Christ: as he is the Beginning, so he was the first to

---

[34] *Ordinatio*, Prol. q. 4, n. 32, Vivès VIII, 260a.

be born from the dead. Christ holds the Primacy in every order, in the whole of creation and in the Church, in the material universe and in the entire spiritual order. Since he holds the Primacy in everything, he is first in God's intention. God willed the entire orders of nature and grace through, in and for his most perfect creature, Jesus the Christ.[35]

The Doctrine Since Scotus

Any thorough analysis of the history of the doctrine since Scotus' time would need to include the names of St. Bernadine of Siena, de Cisneros, St. Lawrence of Brindisi (great Capuchin Doctor of the Church), St. Francis de Sales, Suarez, Pope Pius XII (while still a cardinal), Karl Rahner and Teilhard de Chardin. Because it would be beyond the scope of this article to treat of these authors individually, we have chosen three[36] writers who, for different reasons, stand out in the development of this doctrine down to the present. They are St. Francis de Sales, Doctor of the Love of God, and Pierre Teilhard de Chardin, the famous French Jesuit.

St. Lawrence of Brindisi

He was a Franciscan of the Capuchin order. Lawrence believed that God willed Christ and predestined Him primarily because of the supreme communication of divine dignity and glory that would be his through the incarnation. Christ is the most excellent being in the universe embodying all created perfections as well as the uncreated perfections of God Himself. St. Lawrence explains this with the aid of Ephesians 1:10 and Colossians 2:9.

Christ was intended as Mediator of grace and glory for all the elect, the angels included, from the beginning, prior to sin. The pertinent words from St. Lawrence's first sermon on the absolute Primacy are: "He (God) willed and brought about such and so great a mystery to manifest towards the elect His infinite power, goodness, kindness and love. . . ." This goodness of God could benefit them only inasmuch as they received from Him grace and glory through Christ. God willed the incarnation of the eternal word as Mediator of all the elect even prior to His foreknowledge of sin, because of His sheer goodness.

God in fact never willed Christ to be the only being outside Himself. He willed a universe, and a Church of the Elect, Angels and saints. Christ was

---

[35] J.F. Bonnefroy OFM, *Christ and the Cosmos*, Patterson N.J. 1965, pp. 133-246.

[36] Editors' note: We added St. Lawrence of Brindisi from one of Doyle's unpublished lectures. Published with permission from the Province of Immaculate Conception, England.

willed first, then His Mother; all others were willed first through Christ. He was to be Mediator of grace and glory. In other words we need Christ whether there is sin or not.

Christ is the beginning in the sense that He is prior to all others in predestination, and in the sense that He is the principle of their grace and glory. That predestination of all in Christ preceded the divine foreknowledge of sin is clear from St. Lawrence's reasoning that the foreknowledge of sin could not have been prior to the foreknowledge of Christ in Glory, because Christ is first of all the predestined. He states that he cannot see how the divine foreknowledge of sin could be prior to God's foreknowledge of Christ's predestination The foreknowledge of sin presupposes the foreknowledge of grace, for example, as death presupposes life and weakness and illness presuppose strength and health. Original sin was the privation of grace and Christ was the predestined font of all grace and glory [cf. John 1:14-16].

The value of this argument can only be seen if one does not lose sight of the fact that it is not a purely theological reason. It is based on what Lawrence considers an undeniable truth, namely, that Christ is the Source of grace and glory in the present economy, a truth he sees taught by St. Paul. From that it must follow that the prevision of Adam's sin, had to be subsequent to the prevision of Adam's grace and of Christ.

God also willed the incarnation because He desired that Christ the Mediator of the *whole* man—Body and Soul. Man was to be happy by seeing God with his glorified bodily eyes. This was possible only if God would become Man and men could see God-made-man in glory with their eyes. This postulates the incarnation at least as soon as there was a divine decree for glorifying the bodies of the elect, which certainly preceded the foreknowledge of sin.

St. Francis de Sales

His teaching on the Primacy of Christ is contained in the *Treatise on the Love of God,* Book II: *The History of the Generation and Heavenly Birth of Divine Love*, chapters I-V.[37] St. Francis establishes firstly that the Divine Perfections are only a single but infinite perfection. He then passes to consider how in God there is but one act which is his own Divinity: "God is one unique and most uniquely sovereign perfection, and this perfection is one sole most purely simple and most simply pure act, which being for no other thing than the proper divine essence, is consequently ever permanent and eternal".[38] He

---

[37] *Library of St. Francis de Sales II: Treatise on the Love of God*, London, s.a. 6th edition.
[38] *Treatise on the Love of God*, p. 66.

reminds Theotimus that we are compelled to speak of God's actions as though done in great number and variety. This is due to our weakness: "for our speech can but follow our understanding, and our understanding the customary order of things with us".[39] We should not be discouraged by this, however, because the sole most singular, most simple and most eternal divine act is so perfect that it comprehends "the force and virtue of all acts which would seem requisite for the production of all different effects we see".[40]

In the fifth chapter is contained perhaps the most beautiful passage in the whole of the second book:

> And since every well-ordered will which determines itself to love several objects equally present, loves better and above all the rest that which is lovable; it follows that the Sovereign Providence, making his eternal purpose and design of all that he would produce, first willed and preferred by excellence the most amiable object of his love which is our Saviour; and then other creatures in order, according as they more or less belong to the service, honour and glory of him. Thus were all things made for that divine man, who for this cause is called the *firstborn of every creature* [Colossians 1:15].[41]

St. Francis employs the beautiful analogy of the vine and the grape to explain his teaching on the Primacy of Christ: "the principal reason for planting the vine is the fruit, and therefore the fruit is the first thing desired and aimed at, though the leaves and the buds are first produced". On account of the fruit which is Christ, God planted the vine of the universe "and the succession of many generations established, which as leaves or blossoms proceed from it as forerunners and fit preparatives for the production of that grape which the sacred spouse so much praises in the Canticles, and the juice of which rejoices God and men".[42]

According to St. Francis de Sales God destined from all eternity by absolute priority the Sacred Humanity of Jesus Christ to personal union with the Word so that he might enjoy the treasures of God's infinite glory.[43] It is noteworthy also that he quotes Colossians in support of his teaching. With this teaching, the holy Bishop of Geneva placed himself firmly in the tradition of

---

[39] Ibid., pp. 66f.
[40] Ibid., p. 67.
[41] Ibid., pp. 76f.
[42] Ibid., p. 72.
[43] Ibid., p. 74.

Duns Scotus and earned for himself that sublime title, Doctor of Divine Love.[44]

Pierre Teilhard de Chardin

There must be few writers whose works have provoked such different reactions as those of Teilhard de Chardin. He has been declared the herald of a new age and denounced as a traitor of the past. There are some scientists who dismiss his writings, particularly *The Phenomenon of Man,* as little more than nonsense; there are others who find his works scientifically acceptable and maintain that he has compelled the scientist to re-examine methodology. There are some philosophers who contend that he has confused beyond recognition the formal objects of science and philosophy; there are others who hold that he has crossed the no-man's-land between science and religion and, thus, belongs to the category hyperphysicist or scientific phenomenologist. There are some theologians who accuse him of extremely doubtful orthodoxy, if not open heresy; there are others who welcome him for his timely reminder that their task and responsibility is bound up with the problems of the relationship between the God of the Christian gospel and the evolving universe.

For the theologian, the most far reaching of Teilhard's writings concern the place of Christ in his vision of the evolving universe. It is here particularly that some find him seriously defective. It has been maintained that his concern to centre the whole process of evolution on Christ led him to construct a Christology devoid of Soteriology. That this criticism is entirely without substance will be clear to anyone familiar with the twenty essays of the collection *Comment Je Crois,* the tenth volume of Teilhard's works in the French *corpus* and the most recent work to be translated into English under the title *Christianity and Evolution.* The volume treats of the Doctrine of Original Sin and the theology of Redemption in an evolving world.

There is ample evidence in Teilhard's works that his theological understanding of the place of Christ is practically speaking that of Duns Scotus, but expressed in terms of a dynamic and organic relationship with all creation. Teilhard himself mentions the Scotist thesis explicitly only once.[45] He was evidently very well acquainted with it as the recently published account of his conversations with the Franciscan biblical scholar, Padre Gabriel Allegra,

[44] M. Mueller, *St. Francis de Sales,* London, 1936, pp. 27-34.
[45] *Activation of Energy,* Collins, London 1970, p. 150; cf. F. Mooney SJ, *Teilhard de Chardin and the Mystery of Christ,* Collins, London 1966, pp. 121f., 240.

make clear. During one meeting when Padre Allegra was explaining the text of Scotus, Teilhard expressed his profound admiration for the doctrine by exclaiming: "Voilà la théologie cosmique, la théologie de l'avenir!"[47]

It is legitimate to make a distinction in Teilhard's writings between those which may be called hyperphysical and those which are theological. To the former category belongs e.g. *The Phenomenon of Man,* to the latter, *Christianity and Evolution* and *Le Milieu Divin.* This distinction is necessary in order to avoid the error of asserting that Teilhard argues from the phenomenology of evolution to the existence of Christ and his presence in the evolutionary process. This is incorrect. From his scientific phenomenology of evolution he argues to the existence of Omega Point, which ultimately he identifies with the Christ of the gospels. In the opinion of this writer the epilogue to *The Phenomenon of Man* forms the bridge between the two categories of his works mentioned above.

In his writings on Christology, Teilhard was vitally concerned that theologians should speak of the Kingship of Christ not merely in moralistic and juridical terms, but also in organic categories so that Christ's relationship to the physical universe should be presented in all its fullness. According to Teilhard Christ is the Instrument, the Centre and the End of the entire process of continuous creation.[48] This description of Christ reminds one of the text of Colossians 1 whose author he calls: "that most 'cosmic' of sacred writers".[49] St. Paul and the Greek Fathers speak of a cosmic function of Christ; the content of both was certainly known to Teilhard. He makes a significant number of general references to the Greek fathers and mentions explicitly St. Gregory of Nyssa.[50] In order that Christ be seen in his fullest relationship to the universe, Teilhard was convinced that it was necessary to have a renewed Christology:

> Put this question to the rising masses of young Christians, put it to ourselves: we are all looking and waiting, more or less consciously, for a religious efflorescence, a religious impetus—must it not come from a

---

[46] G.M. Allegra OFM, *My Conversations with Teilhard de Chardin on the Primacy of Christ,* Peking 1942-1945, Franciscan Herald Press, Chicago 1970.

[47] Ibid., p. 92.

[48] *The Future of Man,* Collins, Fontana 1969, p. 319.

[49] *Writings in time of War,* Collins, London 1968, p. 58.

[50] *The Future of Man,* p.98; *Human Energy,* Collins, London 1969, pp. 167 etc. He mentions Gregory of Nyssa in *Science and Christ,* Collins, London 1968, p. 76; *Le Milieu Divin,* Collins, Fontana 1966, p. 110.

renewed Christology in which, however fully reparation is retained, it ceases to occupy the foreground (*In ordine naturae*) in the saving operation of the Word. *Primario,* to consummate creation in divine union; and, in order to do so, *secundario,* to annihilate the evil forces of retrogression and dispersion. No longer *first* to expiate, and then in addition to restore; but *first* to create (or super-create) and, in order to do so (inevitably, but incidentally), fight against evil and pay for evil. Is not that the new order in which our faith is now incontrovertibly arranging the age-old factors?[51]

This text is strong evidence that Teilhard did not intend to construct a Christology by ignoring Redemption and human sin. Moreover, it seems clear that he placed himself in a tradition, that associated with the name of John Duns Scotus, which has neither ever been condemned nor even fully exploited. It is Teilhard's merit, I submit, to have discovered the meaning of this tradition for the modern world. It is Catholic doctrine that "by the very circumstances of their having been created, all things are endowed with their own stability, truth, goodness, proper laws and order".[52] Creation has its own intrinsic value and the first evidence of this is that it is created. The Origin, Centre and Purpose of Creation is Christ, who, as he makes mankind more human through union with God, so also makes the world more worldly, the earth more earthly and creation more creaturely by uniting in himself all that has existence in the order of nature and grace.

Implications of the Scotist Doctrine

1. Foundation of Integral Humanism

Humankind is part of nature, linked from our very origins with the entire world over against which we stand. We may not be treated, however, either philosophically or theologically as just one more thing among others; we are not merely there in the world alongside stones and rocks, plants and trees, cats and dogs, computers and spaceships. We are present in the world as the creature whose nature is open and historical, coming from a past and through a present towards an absolute future. We cannot ask questions about humankind in the same way we ask about animals, vegetables and minerals.

---

[51] *Christianity and Evolution*, Collins, London 1971, p. 146.
[52] *Gaudium et Spes*, 36. in *The Documents of Vatican II*, ed. W. M. Abbott SJ, London-Dublin 1966, pp. 233f.

We are the beings in the world who alone can ask the question: What is Man? and in asking that question, our own transcendence is disclosed to us through the mystery of the very possibility of the question in the first place.[53] Once we begin to reflect on the kind of existence we experience in the world and in history, we recognise that we are called in freedom to account for the responsibility we have for our own existence. The primary anthropological significance of the question What is Man? is the mystery of openness and transcendence it reveals to us. To be human is to be mystery in the world.

Though we cannot be said to possess a "nature" in the same sense as the remainder of creation because we are essentially becoming, nevertheless there is a constant element in our being which allows us to utter in uniqueness "I" and "I am". At the centre of our being we discover a point where we recognise that we are at any one moment the product of our own and a total past, looking beyond ourselves to our own and total future. As we pursue our search for the answer to the question about ourselves, we come to recognise at the point of ultimate solitude where we can say "I" that we must answer in freedom to Someone for the responsibility of our own existence.

In our search for the answer to the question about ourselves, we ultimately reach the boundary of our own powers when we arrive at the possibility of Word from God about us. From that moment onwards, we are obliged by fidelity to our historical tradition to seek out the time and place of that Word to us.

The Mystery of the gospel is the Truth of God's journey to us. What it is to be human has been disclosed to us in the grace of God's love and truth which is Jesus the Christ. God meets not merely in visions from afar and voices from on high, but from inside history in the fabric of space and time, in a Word made flesh. The gospels do not merely teach the value and dignity of being human and created, but proclaim in the first place that one Man in our history is God and that every human being is called, in virtue of the divine image we carry by being creature at all, through that one Man to divinisation by sharing God's love and truth now and forever.

The doctrine of the Absolute Primacy of Christ is the doctrine of the Absolute Primacy of Love and Union. There are no afterthoughts in God's mind with regard to the incarnation of the Word. To create means to unite in love; and the supreme paradigm of creaturehood is Jesus Christ, the union in love of God and man. Jesus Christ, as absolutely predestined to union, is God's eternal "Yes" to the value and dignity of creaturehood. He is God's revelation

---

[53] Cf. E. Coreth, *Metaphysics*, Herder & Herder N.Y. 1968, pp. 45-76.

of the most authentic realisation of creaturehood the earth has ever known. As Karl Rahner expressed it: "Radical dependence on God increases in direct, and not inverse, proportion with genuine self-coherence before him".[54] The closer, therefore, we draw to God, the more human and creaturely do we become. Christ is the beginning of Creation. From all eternity God has loved us in Christ and in his face has seen the face of everyone of us from the beginning. As God has loved us from eternity, so in sovereign freedom God desires the love of everyone of us in its uniqueness and originality and therefore God makes our love possible by sharing with us God's love through intimacy. According to the mystery of the gospel to be human is to be a co-lover of God, open in freedom to the eternal Other, who gives us our freedom to choose God for God's own sake. We answer for the responsibility of our existence, therefore, through the love that is in Jesus Christ.

2. Value and Dignity of earthly Realities

The doctrine of the Absolute Primacy is also the assertion of the goodness of matter, the value of work and the meaning of human and cosmic history. This is the reason surely why the Scotist doctrine is so attractive to the Marxists. Roger Garaudy, the famous French Marxist, refers unblushingly to the "Franciscan or Scotist conception" which sees Christ as the crown of the natural world as well as of the supernatural order.[55] According to the Scotist thesis matter, history and the whole of creation could never be viewed as just secondary to spirit, eternity and heavenly existence, or as no more than a background against which we must live out our lives in preparation for eternity. Our life in the world is not something merely to be tolerated, as though it were of no concern to God that we belong to *this* world. Christ is the union of God and Man willed absolutely in God's free and eternal now. The incarnation is the union of the Source of creation with its crowning point. Since we are the microcosm who summarise in ourselves the whole of creation and who make our own future through freedom and responsibility in history, the intrinsic value of earthly realities and human effort is already given in the absolute predestination of Christ.

---

[54] *Theological Investigations I*, Darton, Longman and Todd 1961, p. 162.
[55] *The Meaning of Life and History in Marx and Teilhard de Chardin* in: *Evolution, Marxism and Christianity*, The Garnstone Press, London 1967, p. 66.

3. Original Sin

If Christ is the first intended in the mind of God as the union of Creator and creature, then the human race has its solidarity in him prior to its solidarity in Adam or the first parents of the race. In the actual divine economy the state of "pure nature" has never been realised; spiritual brother/sisterhood is given to the human race in the Absolute Primacy of Christ as an intrinsic element of the free gift of grace and is concomitant with creation itself. On the basis of our unity in Christ, the parent-child relationship (Adam and descendants) takes second place to the Brother-brother/sister relationship (Christ the firstborn of many brethren) to explain both the unity of the human race and the universality of Original Sin.

The existence of freedom in the world and the mystery of individual personality makes sin a free possibility from the beginning. The *mysterium iniquitatis* proceeds from the mystery of our being free creatures in the world. Because our unity *as a race* is already realised in him who taught us at last to say *Our Father*, then our relationship with Christ must be made the starting point of our theological reflection on Original Sin.

All sin is essentially divisive because it is a turning inwards, a turning away from the Other and the others. For this reason even the most personal sin can never be merely individual; it is, as personal, always also communitarian and collective. Sin is destructive of love (unity) which is the going-out to the Other and others for their own sake, in that freedom which is the power of self-determination in the face of the known and acknowledged good. Hence sin is directly and primarily contrary to the unity and solidarity of the human race in Christ. Understood in this way, all sin is christological. Therefore, any sin at the beginning of the race would have the disastrous effect of introducing disunity into our relationships with God and each other, already established and predestined in Christ. This christological understanding of original sin would have validity in a static and evolutionary world view.

With regard to the evolutionary view of the world, the christological presentation of the doctrine of Original Sin offers interesting avenues of research. The brother-sister model as the foundation of the unity and solidarity of the race in Christ puts the question of mono/polygenism in quite a different light. It would be to say too much, perhaps, that the question loses its importance; but, in any case, the brother-sister model makes possible the acceptance of the polygenistic origins of the race without any threat to the Church's teaching on the universality of Original Sin. Nor is this presentation contrary to the teaching of *Humani Generis*.

According to Matthew 25:31-46, it is the explicit teaching of the gospel that the way we treat each other is the way we treat Christ. What we do or refuse to do for each other we do or refuse to do to Christ. It is significant that in this gospel passage ignorance of having served Christ in our brother-sister is not relevant. The *fact* of service is the crucial issue. It is not necessary to know that when we repudiate each other, we repudiate and ignore Christ. If we may use this revealed truth of the gospel for our understanding of Original Sin in an evolving world, then we may safely assert that sin at the beginning of the race would not have required conscious awareness of the supernatural order nor of the unity in Christ. Original Sin, therefore, is the turning away from God at the beginning of the human race (not necessarily the first human act) by the very fact of turning away from brother-sister and, thus, the introduction of disunity into the order of grace and nature. The introduction of disunity into the world of human relationships by freely incurred guilt constitutes the sinful condition of the human race into which we are all born. Through the unity and solidarity we have through Christ with one another, every sin is always an offence against the Personal and Total Christ.

4. The Christ of the Universe

When, some years ago now, the astronauts circled the moon and sent back to us for the first time their view of this earth on which we eat and drink, work and sleep, plan and scheme, curse and pray, kill and cure, are born and die, we also got a glimpse for the first time, one could say of how God sees the earth in all its smallness, significance and absurdity. As I watched TV it struck me with some force that the fundamental datum of the gospel Mystery is that Someone we call God, dwelling in unapproachable light in awful Purity and terrible Holiness, who has been and is now adored, loved, worshipped, cursed and denied by millions, actually entered human history some 2,000 years ago as a tiny baby and grew to mature manhood in a small corner of the planet I was looking at on TV. In a flash I came to the conclusion that the incarnation is a doctrine too fantastic to be false. The argument that God is a projection of the human mind would seem to be neutralised forever once the doctrine of the incarnation is seen in perspective.

Our knowledge of the vastness of the universe makes it a distinct possibility—some would say probability—that there is intelligent life (even carbon based) on worlds in solar systems outside our own.[56] This possibility cannot be ignored by the Christian believer because the gospel claims to say

---

[56] See F. Jackson and P. Moore, *Life in the Universe*, London 1962 pp. 115-121.

something about us and creation and our destiny in Christ. Furthermore, it is obvious that we today no longer think in terms merely of this world, but in terms of a prodigiously expanding universe.

The possibility of the existence of intelligent beings, even intellectually, culturally and spiritually superior to us, does not of itself raise any serious problem with regard to their relationship with God the Creator.[57] The whole of creation owes its origin to the one and only God. With regard to the place of Christ, however, serious questions do arise, especially about the uniqueness of the incarnation. Scripture and Tradition assert that Christ is the Head of all Creation and that he possesses a universal Kingship. Now, it might be argued that the Biblical statements in Colossians and Ephesians, for example, and the teaching of the Church's Tradition, are necessarily restricted in their application to this world. The reason for this would be that "creation" according to the authors of Scripture and the Church's Tradition down to recent times, meant no more than the limited, observable world and the orders of angels. We would have to conclude from this that we do not know anything about Christ's relationship to the rest of creation outside this earth and its immediate environs. This, in its turn, would mean that we only know God's plan for creation for *this* world. On the one hand we would assert the unity of origin in creation of the entire universe and, on the other hand, profess total ignorance of other than a merely partial destiny. It would also mean that we would have little to say to the modern world in its awareness of belonging to an organic, dynamic and, as it appears, unlimited process.

As the record of God's coming to us, the Sacred Scriptures are the Church's book for all time. They have a message for us in twentieth century, just as much as they spoke to believers of the first century, and as they will speak the message of eternal life for all time to come. We read the Scriptures as people of the modern world, conscious of belonging to a universe of vast proportions. The universe as we know it is not something extrinsic to us, but an inner element of our human existence in the modern world. No matter how much we may protest to the contrary, our understanding of what we read in Scripture is affected and even altered by our knowledge of the world and universe as we know and experience these now. We belong to a world which we know is only one small planet in a universe of gigantic spatial and temporal

---

[57] See C. Davis, *The Study of Theology*, Sheed & Ward London & NY 1962, pp. 177-190; W. Burnet Easton, *Life on Other Planets* in: SCIENCE AND RELIGION. NEW PERSPECTIVES ON THE DIALOGUE, ed. I. Arbour, SAM Press, London 1968, pp. 318-323.

dimensions which has come from the hands of the one and only God, the Creator.

When we use the word "creation", as in the assertion "Christ the Head of all Creation", we are referring to the entire universe as we know it, with all the possibilities it may contain. Because there is no problem for us in relating all creation in this sense to the one God the Creator, and because this one God has encountered us in the part of creation we call earth, we are compelled to question what exactly we mean when we assert with Scripture and Tradition that Christ is the Head of all creation.

To answer this question we must take the Absolute Primacy of Christ as our starting point and not the necessity of Redemption. For this reason we cannot agree with the view expressed by Fr. Paul Curtin of Boston College: "The only theology I know or can know is that of a revealed God in relationship to the children of Adam. If there are beings on another planet, then they must be the object of another Providence. They are not the children of Adam and so are not part of our salvation history which is that of a fallen and redeemed race".[58] If, however we begin with the Absolute Primacy of Christ, we can assert, firstly, that all creation (the entire universe) has a unity of origin in Christ. Secondly, presupposing the existence of intelligent beings on other planets, we can also assert that all incarnate spirits (irrespective of their physical form) in the universe have a solidarity with Christ, based on the brother-sister relationship, which is not affected by distance in space or separation in time. Through our unity in Christ we on this planet have a relationship of brother-sisterhood with intelligent beings elsewhere and far removed from us in space, just as we have a relationship of brother-sisterhood with all who have lived before us on this planet, though far removed from us in time. Solidarity in Christ means unity of origin and destiny in him. This follows from the definitive revelation of God's plan to unite all things in Christ. Thus we can admit that intelligent beings on another planet may well be the object of a different relative Providence (the mode of Christ's presence there), but we cannot agree that they are the object of another absolute Providence. The divine plan for all creation is union with God through love in Christ.

Jesus Christ, the first intended in the mind of God is, as the union of matter and spirit with the Word of God, the revelation of God's purpose to us in our history and our world. As present in history, Jesus Christ was present in time as such; as present in the world, he was present in space as such. As the

---

[58] *Life on other Planets* in: TIME MAGAZINE (24 January 1969) p. 53.

origin and crowning point of the natural order, he has taken up into himself all matter, life, spirit and history. What was realised in him, was realised once and for all for the whole of creation. Since his Primacy extends to angels, it appears most fitting to assume that God revealed to the angels the place of Christ in the plan of creation. It would seem fitting also to assume that God would reveal the plan of creation to all possible intelligent beings elsewhere in the universe. This does not necessitate a multiplicity of incarnations, but it does point to a pluriformity of presences of Christ. Whatever hypothesis we may suggest about the moral condition of these intelligent beings (the presence or absence of freely incurred guilt), Christ and the plan of God could be revealed to them openly and publicly through the sacramentality of creation.

Conclusion

The doctrine of Duns Scotus on the absolute Primacy of Christ forms the basis of an integral and authentic Christian humanism. At the present time we are much preoccupied with ourselves and our world, and theology too is devoting a great deal of time and attention to humankind and the meaning of existence in the world. In these circumstances it seems that it ought to be now the concern of Christian humanism to speak not only of human grandeur but also of human humility. The value and dignity of human existence, matter, work, time and history have their unconditioned and intrinsic affirmation in the incarnation of Jesus Christ, absolutely predestined in the love of God. What humanism could be more thorough-going than this which asserts that the Eternal God was made part of human history? On the other hand, it must be emphasised that we need the humility to recognise that we are not first but second, not last, but penultimate. There is Another who is Alpha and Omega, thus constituted by the freely shared love of God. In the acceptance of that love is revealed the true meaning of being fully human, fully alive.

John Duns Scotus and the Primacy of Christ[1]

It would be very unfair to say that Duns Scotus is unknown to students of theology. Those familiar with Thomist-inspired manuals of scholastic philosophy and theology will recall his name from an occasional footnote and will remember that he often figured prominently in the laundry lists of adversaries. He is known as the "Subtle Doctor" (a title sufficient of itself to arouse the gravest suspicion), who taught the questionable formal distinction, coined the odd term 'thisness' (*haecceitas*), peddled the strange doctrine of the *forma corporeitatis* and who blandly asserted that the Word of God would have been made man even if Adam had not sinned.

By the unwary, repeating the errors of dictionaries and handbooks whose authors, one suspects, never so much as opened the works of Scotus, he is solemnly pronounced the Father of Nominalism and is accused of denying reason's power to discover the existence of God—two of the more outrageous misrepresentations of his teaching. The latter is particularly offensive when one finds that Scotus states unequivocally that man can come to a natural knowledge of God. There are some scholars who even know that his forename 'Duns' is the etymon of the English word 'dunce' and that the pointed hood of the Franciscans is most likely the model of the original dunce's cap.

A good deal of the misrepresentation can be traced back, of course, to the early 1500s. Scotus and his followers were subjected to a vicious attack by the humanists of that century who, in their discovery of classical man, fell into that unbridled and most pernicious arrogance which makes man the measure of all things. They imagined in their folly that they could leap from Late Antiquity to the mid-fifteenth century and so bypass what they dubbed the obscurantism and superstition of the Middle Ages. There can be no doubt, then, that Scotus is known; but how he is known and what masquerades for truth about him needs very severe pruning indeed. One wonders sometimes whether the blessed shroud of anonymity and oblivion which history draws over its more cherished figures, might not have been better treatment for the Subtle and Marian Doctor.

---

[1] THE OSCOTIAN 6TH SERIES (1971-1972) pp. 9f. Published with permission.

I will treat here briefly of one of the important doctrines of Duns Scotus: the Predestination of Christ or, as it is described with less accuracy, the Motive of the incarnation. As an introduction to this some biographical details will be given and a brief reflection on Scotus' place in Scholasticism.

His Life

John Duns Scotus was born in Scotland at Duns in Berwickshire between 23 December 1265 and 17 March 1266. There was an opinion at one time that he was born in Ireland. This is now totally discarded as indeed is the view that he was born in Maxton-on-Tweed, Roxburgh. He entered the Franciscan Order before 1280 and most probably made his profession of vows in 1281. On 17 March 1291, he was ordained priest at Northampton. After studying at Oxford he went to Paris in 1293. Because he was not yet qualified to lecture at Paris he returned to England where he lectured on the *Sentences* at Cambridge and Oxford. In 1302 he was nominated by the Minister General of the Franciscan Order to lecture at Paris. In the struggle caused by the anti-papal policies of Philip the Fair, he was expelled from Paris in 1303, whence he returned to England. After the death of Boniface VIII, Pope Benedict XI restored the University's privileges and Scotus returned to lecture at Paris in 1304. By the beginning of the scholastic year 1307/8 he had already left Paris and in the early months of 1308 we find him lecturing in the 'Studium' of the Franciscan Order at Cologne.

The precise reason for his departure is not known, but it is thought that it had some connection with Philip's decision on the Templars and Scotus' defence of the doctrine of the Immaculate Conception. He died on 8 November 1308 at Cologne, where he lies buried in the *Minoritenkirche*, barely five minutes walk from Cologne main station. He is honoured as Blessed in the Franciscan Order and a canonically approved diocesan cult is paid to him at Nola in Italy. In 1905 a formal petition for his canonization was made to the Holy See.

Augustinian Thinker

In the history of Scholasticism, Scotus is an Augustinian. Unlike St. Bonaventure before him, however, he did not regard Aristotle as no more than a pagan philosopher with little to offer in the search for the wisdom that beatifies. In fact it is true to say, as the eminent Scotist scholar, Fr. Efrem Bettoni has written, that the originality of the Scotist synthesis lies in his attempt to reconcile the Augustinian-Platonic illumination theory with Aristotelian empiricism. But at heart he remained an Augustinian.

The teaching of Duns Scotus on the Primacy of Christ does not begin from the purely hypothetical question: "If Adam had not sinned, would Christ have become incarnate?" That this is the more popular presentation of his teaching is obvious from the manuals of theology. Scotus does not, in fact, juggle with any mere hypothesis about what would have happened had there been no sin, nor does he prescind from the actual order of the divine economy. He presents a doctrinal thesis which gives deeper meaning both to the Pauline texts on the Primacy of Christ in Colossians and Ephesians and to the Church's teaching on the universal Kingship of Christ.

"Cur Deus Homo"

The question of the motive of the incarnation had been treated by a number of theologians before Scotus. As early as the seventh century Isaac of Nineveh had written that the incarnation would have taken place independently of the sin of Adam. Among Scholastics prior to St. Thomas, St. Anselm stated in the 'Cur Deus homo' that the reason of the incarnation was the redemption of sinful man. But both Rupert of Deutz and Honorius of Autun felt that sin could not be the adequate reason of the incarnation. Rupert asserts without hesitation that the redemption of the human race is neither the only nor the chief reason of the Word's becoming man. For Honorius the cause of the incarnation of the Word was the predestination of human divinization in the eternal plan of God.

It is very interesting to note that Robert Grosseteste, who taught the Franciscans at Oxford, held that the Word would have become man had Adam not sinned. The Angelic Doctor, after examining the purely hypothetical question came down on the negative side and quoted St. Augustine as his authority. In any case, he concluded, the question is of no great importance since we do not know what God would have done if He had not foreseen sin.

'Hypothetical Question?'

The controversy between the Thomists and the Scotists, while demonstrating a laudable freedom of opinion in the Schools, seems in the end rather fruitless. For what is the point of spending time in speculation on a purely hypothetical question? Given the simple affirmative proposition of the Creed: *qui propter nos homines et propter nostram salutem descendit de coelis et incarnatus est*, all further search for the motive of the Word's becoming man appears barren and the difference of opinion in the Schools altogether unrelated to reality. Such reaction, one feels, is justified. But neither St. Thomas nor Blessed Duns Scotus can be held responsible for the way in which the question was presented and treated. That rests on the shoulders of their followers!

The teaching of Scotus is found in the *Ordinatio* where he asserts that man's fall was not a *conditio sine qua non* of the incarnation. In the *Opus Oxoniense* (a disciple's continuation of the *Ordinatio* based on his lectures of 1302) Christ takes his place in creation before the foreseeing of sin; then, in the *Reportata Parisiensia* (a disciple's account of his Paris lectures, c. 1307), Christ is said not to be merely occasioned by sin. Given the scriptural teaching that God is Love, Scotus takes as his starting point the predestination of Christ. He does not pose the purely hypothetical question at all. He asks: *Utrum Christus praedestinatus fuerit esse Filius Dei?* From the love that God is, Scotus concludes that Christ is predestined by God as the *Summum Opus*, His Masterpiece.

He arrives at his Christocentric doctrine of creation as follows: God is formally love: *Deus est formaliter caritas et dilectio, non tantum effective.* Love has its own reason in itself, it is its own explanation and God's love is the reason of all else. On analogy with human experience, is it not true to say that once the words "I love you" have been uttered, nothing is ever quite the same again? This is very close to what happened when God predestined Christ: there was creation. Now in the first place, God loves Himself perfectly, for He is love. Secondly, God loves Himself in others and this love is most ordered and holy. The love of God tends to share, to diffuse itself, tends to bubble over: *bonum est diffusivum sui*. True love has an intrinsic tendency to share, for it knows no envy, jealousy or exclusivism. In the third place, God wills to be loved by Another Who can love him in the most perfect way and here Scotus is speaking of a love outside God's inner life.

Therefore, finally, He foresees the union between Himself and the creature Christ, Who must love Him to the infinite degree He loves Himself. At the end of this reasoning Scotus adds that this is the case *etsi nullus cecidisset*. This, however, is a conclusion from his reasoning on the Generation of divine love and is not its starting point; it should be noted also that he says: *praevidit unionem illius naturae quae debet eum summe diligere, etsi nullus cecidisset.* Thus, according to Scotus the predestination of Christ is absolute and unconditioned. If the fall of man were the cause of the predestination of Christ, this would mean that God's Masterpiece would be no more than occasioned. Because of the infinite perfection of His love, Christ has the primacy of excellence and finality in the Divine Intention and is willed absolutely and unconditionally prior to every other creature.

Priorities

Since God is Pure Act in an eternal now, it might seem a little hazardous to speak of priorities in the mind of God. But the truth is that it presents no more difficulty here than it does in the rest of theology. If we would speak about God at all we must do so in terms of before and after or remain forever silent about Him. Because Christ is the most perfect creature of God, He is first intended by God in the plan of creation. Scotus bases this on the experience that rational creatures first intend the end and then all the means to it. In an analogous way, but in one sovereign act, God as *rationabilissime et ordinatissime volens* intends Christ before all else, and in, with, and through Him, all creation.

Space forbids us to pursue the history of the doctrine as it has been developed in the writings of St. Bernadine of Siena, de Cisneros, St. Laurence of Brindisi, St. Francis de Sales, Suarez, Pius XII (while still a Cardinal), L. Bello (Minister General of the Order of Friars Minor), Karl Rahner and Teilhard de Chardin. As regards Teilhard, I am convinced that in his theological writings on Christ's place in creation he is saying, in an evolutionary view of the world, no more and no less than John Duns Scotus. Nor can we here investigate the scriptural basis of the Scotistic thesis. We may note in passing, however, that Colossians 1:3ff. appears to be a clear assertion of the Absolute Primacy of Christ. The subject of the whole passage is the Incarnate Christ: in Him we have redemption from our sins and in Him, through Him and unto Him are all things created. It should be noted in particular that verse 15 is a relative clause: *hos estin*.

The doctrine of the Absolute Primacy of Christ is a doctrine we have never needed more than we do now. With our over-emphasis on man, matter and activity we need desperately to check the dangers of humanism by pointing to Him in Whose Face God saw from all eternity our own faces, every creature and all matter, and loved what He saw. What humanism could ever say so much about the inherent value of man and his activity?

ERIC DOYLE OFM 1938-1984[1]
Michael Meilach OFM

The death of Fr. Eric Doyle OFM at the age of 46, on August 25, 1984, at Guildford, England, deprived the English-speaking Franciscan world of one of its most promising young historians and theologians. His colleagues at The Franciscan Institute of St. Bonaventure University received the typescript of the *Life and Works* of William Woodford and his edition of the *Responsiones contra Wiclevum et Lollardos* just two weeks before his death. For many it was a personal loss since Fr. Eric had taught in St. Bonaventure University's Graduate Theology Department from 1970 to 1982 and had formed many friendships in the academic and civic community. In 1983 he had dedicated his translation of St. Bonaventure's sermons on St. Francis, *The Disciple and the Master* to this Institute.

Fr. Eric was born William Martin Doyle, son of Patrick Doyle and Josephine Reynolds, at Bolton in the Catholic diocese of Salford, July 13, 1938, and was educated there, first at St. Joseph's Primary School, and then at Thornleigh Salesian College. He was invested as a novice, September 8, 1954, in the English province of the Friars Minor, solemnly professed, July 14, 1959, the feast of St. Bonaventure, and ordained a priest, July 16, 1961. He took his doctorate in ecclesiastical history at the Pontificium Athenaeum Antonianum in Rome *summa cum laude* and returned to his province as lecturer in ecclesiastical history at the House of Studies in East Bergholt. Later he was one of the founders of the Franciscan International Study Centre at Canterbury and taught medieval ecclesiastical history at the University of Kent.

In England Fr. Eric was best known as a popular spokesman for the Catholic point of view on more than five hundred radio and television programs. Erudite, lucid, sincere, and irrepressibly witty, he was equally at home addressing the Teilhard de Chardin Society or discussing with a lad the possibilities of catching fish in the Stour as it flowed beneath the ancient Greyfriars in Canterbury. He served by appointment of the Holy See as a member of the Anglican-Roman Catholic Working Group on the *Ordination of*

---

[1] The Editorial in: Franciscan Studies 43/44n (1983/4). Published with permission from The Franciscan Institute, St. Bonaventure University, New York.

Women in Assisi in 1975, and as a member of the Anglican-Roman Catholic *Consultation on the Ordination of Women* at Versailles in 1978. He served his Franciscan province as Definitor on more than one occasion, having been elected again to that office just a month before his death.

In the legacy of over a hundred printed articles and books which Fr. Eric left, the most important scholarly work is contained in his six articles on William Woodford, the last of which is published in this issue of the *Studies*. Particularly noteworthy among his other works are *St. Francis and The Song of Brotherhood* (1981), a plea for realisation of that universal brotherhood of all creatures implied in St. Francis' *Canticle of Brother Sun*, and *The Disciple and the Master*. Francis of Assisi, the Franciscan School, and issues affecting faith and the Church in the modern world were the principal subjects of his literary endeavours. As a mark of gratitude and esteem, Fr. Eric's confreres and colleagues at The Franciscan Institute dedicate this issue to his memory.

Requiescat in Pace: Father Eric Doyle OFM
25th August 1984[1]
Ninian Arbuckle OFM

A great many people will have been saddened by the sudden and premature death of Father Eric Doyle OFM. He died on 25th August at Mount Alvernia Nursing Home in Guildford where he was nursed with loving care by the sisters of the Franciscan Missionaries of the Divine Motherhood. Few of his brethren were aware of how ill he must have been when we celebrated our Provincial Chapter a month earlier, in which Eric himself took a leading and inspiring part. It was soon after the Chapter that he began to feel ill and a recurrence of the melanoma, for which he had undergone surgery seven years earlier, was diagnosed as terminal. His condition deteriorated rapidly till he lost consciousness a few days before he died at the age of forty-six.

Eric (baptised William Martin) was born and reared in Bolton, where he was educated, first at St. Joseph's Primary School and then at Thornleigh Salesian College. He joined the Friars Minor in 1954 and was ordained at the age of twenty-three in July 1961. After studying ecclesiastical history at the Pontificium Atheneum Antonianum in Rome, where he received his doctorate *summa cum laude* having gained the maximum marks possible, he returned to the Franciscan House of Studies at East Bergholt as lecturer in ecclesiastical history. This was to be his principal activity throughout his life. Eric was one of the pioneers and "founding fathers" of the Franciscan International Study Centre in Canterbury.

After his return from Rome he was soon engaged in many activities as preacher, lecturer, counsellor, writer and broadcaster. From 1970 till 1982 he was a member of the Department of Graduate Theology, summer Session, at St. Bonaventure's University in the United States. He taught medieval ecclesiastical history at the University of Kent in Canterbury. As a member of the Teilhard de Chardin Society he contributed papers both at national and international level. He was appointed by Rome as a member of the

---

[1] THE TABLET vol. 238, 1984 p. 844.

Anglican/Roman Catholic Working Group on the Ordination of Women which met in Assisi in 1975, and again as a member of the Anglican/Roman Catholic Consultation on the Ordination of Women held at Versailles in 1978. Eric contributed articles to many religious periodicals both learned and popular including the TROUBADOUR, mainly on matters pertaining to Franciscan spirituality. His main publications were *St. Francis and the Song of Brotherhood* and *The Disciple and the Master.* He was working on a book on Christology at the time of his death.

It will be as a broadcaster that Eric will be remembered by many both within and outside the Catholic Church. He took part in more than five hundred radio and television programmes ranging from learned talks to the devotional and encouraging "Prayer for the Day". He will be best remembered for his part in Anglia Television's "The Big Question" which was broadcast weekly, almost without interruption, from March 1971 till March 1984. His sincerity, clarity of mind and, above all, his irrepressible character won him many friends and admirers among the viewers.

"Irrepressible" is the best word to describe Eric. Very many of his students, his fellow friars, the clergy both regular and secular throughout Britain and in many countries abroad, will remember with affection and gratitude the talks and conferences that he gave them. Eric's talks were not only learned and inspiring; they were also very entertaining.

Eric read voraciously and widely, and once humbly confessed that he could remember most of what he read. It was this wonderful memory and the ability to call the right thing to mind at the right time, married to a great appetite for, and methodology in study, that made him such a good debater and welcome speaker. There was no one too grand or too little for his attention. One day he could address an international gathering on Teilhard de Chardin, and the next day celebrate Mass for the under-sevens of the parish whom he had seated around the altar completely enthralled as he spoke to them of the wonder and the peace of Rat and Mole on the river as they encounter Pan. *The Wind and the Willows* was one of Eric's favourite books.

Eric had a great love for the Incarnate Christ, "the first friar", and for St. Francis, and it was this love that lay at the basis of his great energy in studying and spreading the Franciscan message. It also prompted him to search for answers to such human and contemporary issues as ecology, liberation theology, ecumenism and the place of women in the Church. Much of Eric's work will pass unrecorded, known only to the many people from all walks of life to whom he gave counsel, encouragement and spiritual guidance.

For us, his brethren, our life was enriched by Eric's love of the brethren, his community spirit, his great zeal and leadership in our struggles for renewal.

Eric died peacefully. In welcoming Sister Death "from whose embrace no mortal can escape", Eric followed in death, as in life, St. Francis of Assisi.

On Teilhard de Chardin

Teilhard and Theology[1]

Nobody, I suppose, who has studied the works of Teilhard de Chardin would call him a scientist, a philosopher, or a theologian without some qualifications.[2] It may well be desirable for clarity's sake to classify Teilhard according to one or other of the triad: science, philosophy, theology—depending on the line of study adopted. However, it is fair to point out, I think, that any attempt to fit him exclusively, according to pre-conceived ideas, into any one of the triad is a basically wrong approach to his writings. What ought to guide the scientist, the philosopher and the theologian in their study of Teilhard is an openness to his insights into their respective disciplines and a vigilance for the horizons he opens out.

Teilhard is not easily categorized. This is due in large part to the mystical element running through his writings, which is probably the source of all his insights and intuitions. If Teilhard can be fitted into any category at all it is that of Christian mystic. Rahner and Vorgrimler have described Christian mysticism as follows: "Because Christ redeemed all creation in his love, with mankind, genuinely Christian mysticism is neither a denial of the world nor a meeting with the Infinite All, but a taking of the world with one to a loving encounter with the Personal God".[3] For Teilhard the world is taken at Point Omega with, in and through mankind in self-transcendence to a loving encounter with the Personal God, who will be all in all.[4] In this connection it is important to note that Teilhard stresses that at the critical point of speculation towards which the human phylum is moving, union differentiates. There is no

---

[1] THE TEILHARD REVIEW AND JOURNAL OF CREATIVE EVOLUTION 20.1 (Spring 1985) pp. 2-11. This article was originally published in the IRISH THEOLOGICAL QUARTERLY, vol. 38 no. 2 (April 1971). Published with permission.

[2] I refer here to the works which have become the most widely known since his death in 1955. I exclude, therefore, his purely scientific works on geology and palaeontology published during his lifetime.

[3] K. Rahner, H. Vorgrimler, *Concise Theological Dictionary*, ed. by C. Ernst OP, trans. by R. Strachan, Herder, Freiburg, Burns and Oates, London 1965, p. 302.

[4] See *Science and Christ*, trans. by R. Hague, Collins, London, Harper and Row, New York 1968, p. 85; *The Future of Man*, trans. by N. Denny, Collins Fontana Books, London 1969, pp. 321-323.

loss of identity; union with others in the Eternal Other is the condition and guarantee of enduring personal identity[5] To anyone well acquainted with Teilhard's thought it is a little frustrating to hear him dismissed as 'a mystic'. If he can be dismissed in this way, then so can St. Francis of Assisi, St. Teresa of Jesus and many another famous name in Christian history. One gets the impression that mysticism is here being associated with the results of Aldous Huxley's experiments with mescalin. In fact, Teilhard's mysticism has nothing in common with the effects of mescalin. He is no purely 'natural' mystic. His essay *The Mystical Milieu* and his writings on Christ, the Church, and the Eucharist ought to be enough to dispel any doubts on that score.[6] Teilhard was a Christian mystic. As such he sought to communicate consistency, knowledge, being, love, unity, interiority, through a personal and personalising Centre, and through reverence for everything that goes to make up this vast mysterious macrocosm we call the universe, shot through with the presence of God. "The great mystery of Christianity, he says, is not exactly the appearance, but the transparency of God in the universe".[7]

---

[5] *The Future of Man*, p. 316; *The Phenomenon of Man,* with an introduction by Sir Julian Huxley, Collins Fontana Books, London 1966, p. 288: "In any domain—whether it be the cells of a body, the members of a society or the elements of a spiritual synthesis—*union differentiates.* In every organized whole, the parts perfect themselves and fulfil themselves. Through neglect of this universal rule many a system of pantheism has led us astray to the cult of a great All in which individuals were supposed to be merged like a drop in the ocean or like a dissolving grain of salt. Applied to the case of the summation of consciousnesses, the law of union rids us of this perilous and recurrent illusion. No, following the confluent orbits of their centres, the grains of consciousness do not tend to lose their outlines and blend, but, on the contrary, to accentuate the depth and incommunicability of their *egos.* The more 'other' they become in conjunction, the more they find themselves as 'self' ".

[6] *Writings in Time of War*, trans. by R. Hague, Collins, London, Harper and Row, New York 1968, pp. 115-149; cf. also *Creative Union*, op.cit., pp. 151-176, *Forma Christi*, op.cit., 249-269; *Science and Christ*, esp.: *Note on the Universal Christ*, pp. 14-20, *Science and Christ* or *Analyst's and Synthesis*, pp. 21-36, *Super-Humanity, Super Christ, Super-Charity*, pp. 151-173; *Le Milieu Divin. An Essay on the Interior Life*, Collins Fontana Books, London 1966.

[7] *Le Milieu Divin*, p. 131. What Teilhard writes about the transparence of God in the universe (see also op.cit., p. 134; *Writings in Time of War*, pp. 122,125), takes on added interest and importance in view of the section entitled *The Transparence of God* in: T. Boman, *Hebrew Thought Compared with Greek*, The Westminster Press, Philadelphia 1960, pp. 190-192. Boman points out that God's overall relation to the world is designated neither clearly nor exhaustively by the two concepts: transcendence and immanence. He continues: "What has been lacking up until now in the doctrine of God's relation to the world is a third term or relationship or a third dimension in the relation. God is not only above the world and in the world, but he is also *through* the world; as the Apostle has already said: "Who is Lord of all, works through all and is in all" [Ephesians 4:6]. God's being through the world is a separate category which expresses what is most characteristic of God's relation to the world in Greek as well as Israelite terms. . . . God's transparence thus asserts that God is known through the world as the one who really is. . . . We have found, therefore, that the overall relationship between God and the world is three-

His own unceasing search for consistency in things gave him an insight into the "suprareal unity diffused throughout the immensity of the world".[8] Fr. Bernard Lonergan says that insight "goes beyond what is merely given to sense or to empirical consciousness. . .it adds to the merely given an explanatory unification or organisation. . .every insight unifies and organises".[9] Teilhard's whole life may be summed up by saying that he wanted others to see and share the secret of the world: "The secret of the world lies wherever we can discern the transparency of the universe".[10] His vocation was to make others see and share his unifying insight. It is not too fanciful to compare Teilhard's 'seeing' with 'seeing with the heart' which the fox confided as his secret to the Little Prince.[11] The purpose of the following pages is to examine Teilhard's central insight into theology through which he resolved the tension in himself between his love of God and his devotion to the world.

The Task of Theology

On his way to China in 1923 Teilhard reflected: "Professors of Theology would do well to have a spell of what I am doing now. I am beginning to think that there is a certain aspect of the real world as closed to some believers as the world of faith is to unbelievers. . . ."[12] Later on, in 1926,

---

sided, or perhaps better, it is triadic, which is precisely what we should have expected in a trinitarian religion. Perhaps this throws some light on the doctrine of the Trinity and particularly Christology, for as the First Person of the Trinity corresponds to the transcendence and the Third Person to the immanence, so the Second Person of the Trinity corresponds to the transparence". It is a source of ever new surprises to find how deeply so many of Teilhard's insights are rooted in the best traditions of Western culture. He writes in *Le Milieu Divin*, p. 134: "When the time had come when God resolved to realize his incarnation before our eyes, he had first of all to raise up in the world a virtue capable of drawing him as far as ourselves. He needed a mother who would engender him in the human sphere. What did he do? He created the Virgin Mary, that is to say he called forth on earth a purity so great that, within this transparency he would concentrate himself to the point of appearing as a child". This concept of transparency may well be of wider application. It could be argued that one of the distinguishing features of all ecclesial forms and institutions ought to be their transparence. The eternal dimension should always appear through them, otherwise they lose their mediating role and become ends in themselves.

[8] *Writings in Time of War*, p. 123.
[9] *Insight: A Study of Human Understanding* (Revised Students' Edition) London 1965, X-XI.
[10] *Letters from a Traveller 1923-1955*, Collins Fontana Books, London 1967, p. 28; *The Phenomenon of Man*, p. 35.
[11] Antoine de Saint-Exupéry, *The Little Prince*, trans. by K. Woods, W. Heinemann Ltd., London 1958, p. 68.
[12] *Letters from a Traveller*, p. 28.

after hearing a lecture given by a Harvard Professor on the dawn of thought in the animal kingdom, he wrote:

> I couldn't help thinking of the abyss that divides the intellectual world I was in and whose language I knew, from the theological world of Rome with whose idiom I am also familiar. At first it was something of a shock to realise that the latter could be, and indeed must be, just as real as the former; and then I told myself that now perhaps I was capable of so using the first language as to make it fairly express what the other contains but puts into words that most people can no longer understand. However far-fetched the notion might appear at first, I realised in the end that, *hic et nunc,* Christ was not irrelevant to the problems that interest Professor Parker.[13]

Theology has grown out of the Revelation of the Word of God. God has spoken in time. He has had, in the most literal sense, the last Word with a Son to speak for him. The Word of God has spoken to us firstly and primarily about God himself. The Good News in the first place is the gospel of God. Intimately related to this, the Word of God has spoken to us about man and about his world. Because of this the Word of God is the starting point for loving and understanding both God and the entire universe. Moreover, because God became Man (the most basic statement of Christian Revelation), our grasp of what is human has been made the gauge of our grasp of what is divine. The human situation which came to be in Jesus Christ reveals that as deep as are our insights into the meaning of what is authentically human, just so deep and no deeper will be our insights into the meaning of what is really divine.

The definition of theology as a science correlates the two elements: God and the universe. It treats of God and the universe (material, vital, human and Christic) in relation to God. In so far as this denotes the task of theology, Teilhard could have had little complaint with it. Even the manuals with which he would have been familiar express this in their definitions of theology. His complaint was that a certain aspect of the real world was closed to some believers, and from what he wrote subsequently about Christology, it is clear that he was thinking primarily of theologians. From experience he knew that the language of theology is beyond comprehension to the majority of people. It is not over-critical to say that the manuals of theology provide ample grounds for his complaints. They give the impression that theology is for academicians only who speculate within the confines of a closed system on notions of

---

[13] Ibid., p. 85.

substance and accident, essence and existence, nature and person, cause and effect, time, eternity, aeviternity. There is so little about life, about the intrinsic value and dignity of earthly realities, about history, about the value of work and effort, about anxiety, suffering and death, about unity, love and the practical knowledge of God that is mysticism. The perfunctory way in which those who disagree with a stated thesis are labelled *Adversarii* (when they constitute in some way the *Ecclesia quaerens!*) only serves to antagonise further. There is nothing to indicate that all thought is one, that every thinker always grasps an aspect of the one and only Truth.

That Word, in whom the Eternal becomes temporal, where he who is is made he who becomes, is himself the heart of theology. Here is theology in a human life, a human situation, a human history, where *Theos* finds fullest expression in the universe. The Good News that is the New Testament does not of itself give rise to the impression that the world and man's efforts to conquer it are of no significance for man's ultimate fulfilment and destiny. The most glaring contradiction of any such impression is the simple fact of the very presence among men in history of the New Testament's central figure. Theology has its living source and spirit in the life and teaching of Christ: in his parables, especially the Pharisee and the Publican, the Talents (is the one talent life itself?), the Good Samaritan; in the episode of the man born blind whose blindness was for the glory of God; in the sufferings in Gethsemani, in the Cross raised on high, in the Resurrection of him who descended and ascended to the highest heaven, filling the universe with the power and energy of a new life; in the teaching of St. Paul that all things are in, through and unto Christ; in the sublime doctrine that whatever we are about we must do in the name of Christ; in the teaching of St. John that we cannot love God if we do not love our brother.

Love of God and Love of the World

Teilhard experienced a tension in himself between his love of the earth and his longing for heaven. He was a scientist who through science had learned to love the earth passionately. He was also a fully convinced and totally committed Christian, a priest and a member of the Jesuit Order. The man and the vision belong inseparably together. Neither science nor Christ can be ignored in his vision.[14] To leave out of account the one or the other is, equally

---

[14] A strong case could be made for the view that Teilhard's spirituality (as found, for example, in *Le Milieu Divin*) is a full flowering of the spirituality of St. Ignatius and the first generation of

disastrous for the synthesis he constructed, because the result in either case is, in the end, the same: a devaluation of earthly realities. Teilhard yearned, on the one hand, to live fully in the universe he loved; he needed, on the other, something more than an equal to cherish, he needed a God to adore.[15]

For the Christian believer the givenness of an Almighty Creator and the reality of an existing universe constitute the central problem for theology, that, namely, of the relation between them. Teilhard's complete and uncompromising acceptance of the universe as a dynamic, evolving reality and his total commitment to the Christian faith, together formed the source of the tension he experienced. We find this already in that remarkable essay of 1916, *Cosmic Life*. In the very first paragraph he writes:

> What follows springs from an exuberance of life and a yearning to live: it is written to express an impassioned vision of the earth, and in an attempt to find a solution for the doubts that beset my action—because I love the universe, its energies, its secrets, and its hopes, and because at the same time I am dedicated to God, the only Origin, the only Issue and the only Term.[16]

The sentiment of this passage occurs as a theme again and again in his writings. The doubts he mentions are those which every serious minded Christian must have had at some time in his life: What is the significance of terrestrial realities? What is the meaning of existence in an historical universe? What do our efforts, our work, our anxiety, our joys, sorrows, aspirations finally stand for? What is there in the universe to live for, and, far more serious, what is there to die for? Is the universe no more than just one of innumerable possible creations God chose for man to prove himself, before leaving it for a better one? Teilhard set himself to discover "how. . .we can reconcile and provide mutual nourishment for the love of God and the healthy love of the world".[17] He concluded that a reconciliation must be possible "between cosmic love of the world and heavenly love of God. . .between the cult of progress and the passion for the glory of God".[18]

---

the Society. Their emphasis on activity and finding God in works, so distinguishing a feature of the Counter-Reformation, finds new expression in Teilhard de Chardin.

[15] *Le Milieu Divin*, p. 127.
[16] *Writings in Time of War*, p. 14.
[17] *Le Milieu Divin*, p. 53.
[18] *Writings in Time of War*, p. 57.

Christ and the Evolving Universe

The theological problem of the relationship between God and the universe had its solution for Teilhard in the Jesus of history and the Christ of faith. He writes in *Le Milieu Divin*:

> The immense enchantment of the divine *milieu* owes all its value in the long run to the human-divine contact which was revealed at the Epiphany of Jesus. If you suppress the historical reality of Christ, the divine omnipresence which intoxicates us becomes, like all the other dreams of metaphysics, uncertain, vague, conventional—lacking the decisive experimental verification by which to impose itself on our minds, and without the moral authority to assimilate our lives into it. . . .The mystical Christ, the universal Christ of St. Paul, has neither meaning nor value in our eyes except as an expansion of the Christ who was born of Mary and who died on the cross. The former essentially draws his fundamental quality of undeniability and concreteness from the latter. However far we may be drawn into the divine spaces opened up to us by christian mysticism, we never depart from the Jesus of the gospels.[19]

He claims further that "this universal Christ is the Christ presented to us in the gospels, and more particularly by St. Paul and St. John. It is the Christ by whom the great mystics lived: but nevertheless not the Christ with whom theology has been most concerned".[20] The tension between the love of God and the love of the world is, in principle, resolved by the incarnation.[21] Christ is the element common to both terms of the problem of the relationship between God and the world. In Teilhard's synthesis theology becomes pre-eminently Christology: *Christos* is the Revealer of *Theos*. The Christ who immersed himself in the world at the heart of the most developed sphere of evolution, that of mind, "animates and gathers up all the biological and spiritual energies developed in the universe".[22] As the Organic Centre of the entire universe Christ draws all things to himself in a prodigious biological operation. The Kingship of Christ is not, therefore, to be understood in merely moralistic

---

[19] *Le Milieu Divin*, p. 117.
[20] *Science and Christ*, p. 14.
[21] *The Future of Man*, pp. 272-282. In the diagram on p. 282 the tension between faith in God and faith in the world is resolved in Christ.
[22] *Science and Christ*, p. 167. Teilhard's theology is primarily a 'theology of economy' (*oikonomia*, theology of the mystery of Christ), in contrast to *theologia simplex*. See E. Schillebeeckx OP, *Revelation and Theology*, trans. by N.D. Smith, Sheed and Ward, London 1967, pp. 97f.

terms; Christ's rule and sway extends to the natural, physical and biological spheres of the universe. For this reason Christ is Evolver and evolution is holy. In a dynamic, evolving universe it ought to become as customary for us to speak of Christ the Evolver as it was in a static world to speak of Christ the King.[23]

Christ, Omega and Centre of the Universe

Over the thousands of millions of years of the earth's history Teilhard saw operative a process of complexification from the most rudimentary forms of matter to the neuro-cerebral system of *homo sapiens*. According to the Law of Complexity-Consciousness, along with the steady increase in complexity of anatomical structure, there has gone a corresponding increase in consciousness, unity, interiority. Consciousness is understood as embracing a vast spectrum stretching from the most elemental power of matter to unite, to self-reflective consciousness of *homo sapiens*. Man is the spearhead of evolution. Millions of years of development have reached their reason and purpose in him, and with man there has come a thinking sphere, a layer of thought round the earth.

At this point he asks: "After the long series of transformations leading to man, has the world stopped?"[24] Teilhard cannot accept on rational grounds that it has. The whole process of evolution is rendered absurd if the operation of the Law of Complexity-Consciousness has now ceased. From his knowledge of the past Teilhard extrapolated into the future: evolution continues in man and its driving force is love. The energies of the total past have converged in man who is what he is through matter, and this furnishes one of the most basic reasons why matter is sacred. He affirms in *Le Milieu Divin*: "All reality, even material reality, around each one of us, exists for our souls".[25] Our souls cannot be souls without matter. He has not, therefore, introduced the body-soul dichotomy as this has been understood traditionally in theology. Evolution is creative union

---

[23] *Science and Christ*, p. 14: "By the Universal Christ, I mean Christ the organic centre of the entire universe. Organic centre: that is to say the centre on which every even natural development is ultimately physically dependent. . . .Of the entire universe, again, that is to say, the centre not only of moral and religious effort, but also of all that that effort implies—in other words of all physical and spiritual growth".

Ibid., pp. 165f.: "In spite of the repeated assertions of St. Paul and the Greek Fathers, Christ's universal power over Creation has hitherto been considered by theologians primarily in an extrinsic and juridical aspect. 'Christ is King of the world, because his Father *declared* him to be King. He is master of all because all has been given to him'. That is about as far as the teachers in Israel went, or were prepared to venture, in their explanations of the dogma. Except in regard to the mysterious 'sanctifying grace', the organic side of the Incarnation, and in consequence its physical presuppositions or conditions, were relegated to the background".

[24] *The Phenomenon of Man*, p. 256.

[25] *Le Milieu Divin*, p. 56.

and active self-transcendence dependent on divine *concursus* immanent in the process itself.[26]

The noosphere is tending towards a point of convergence, which Teilhard designates as Omega Point. This appears to be the only acceptable, rational hypothesis for a process that has continued over millions of years. The alternative is the absurdity of total death. The attraction of this centripetal movement is love: it is a process of *amorization*. In the process of super-centration every individual, loving, reflecting monad is drawn into association and union with all other centres. Through amorization all things are made loveable and loving in the evolving universe. Around Omega Point is being formed the hyperpersonal organism which does not dissolve the individual centres of consciousness, but guarantees their enduring differentiation.[27] Considered in its total ontological reality love is a property of all life. Though not perceptible in the lower forms of life nor at the level of pre-life, it is present in the 'within of things' as the capacity for ever greater union. With the appearance of man love discloses a universal sense, a sense of the all which, on analysis, is seen to have its source in man's capacity to centre everything on himself partially.[28] Point Omega therefore has a universal and cosmic function: to centre on itself all the reflective particles of the world. In order to be operative now in the thinking layer of the world as a point of attraction and convergence, Omega must be loveable and loving at this moment. For love to be possible it must be co-existent since man cannot give himself to an abstract idea or an anonymous number.[29] Thus, in the process of noogenesis the necessary point of convergence has four indispensable qualities: 1. *autonomy:* it is the Centre of centres grasped in man's universal sense; 2. *actuality:* it is operative now in order to be loveable at this moment; 3. *irreversibility:*

---

[26] Teilhard understands evolution as continuing creation in which the power of God is immanent. Thus understood, it is not necessary that God 'break into' the process at the creation of the soul in such a way that it matters little at what point of development or arrangement of matter he so intervenes. God's creative power as immanent in the process respects the dynamism of evolution, so that it is according to the development of a particular group of vertebrates, a particular group of mammals and a particular group of primates that man appears. Cf. on this B. Towers, *Concerning Teilhard and Other Writings on Science and Religion*, Collins, London 1969, pp. 40-42.

[27] *The Phenomenon of Man*, p. 288.

[28] Ibid., pp. 286-294.

[29] Ibid., pp. 295f.: "But how could it exercise this action were it not in some sort loving and lovable at this very moment?. . . .With love, as with every other sort of energy, it is within the existing datum that the lines of force must at every instant come together. Neither an ideal centre, nor a potential centre could possibly suffice. A present and real noosphere goes with a real and present centre. To be supremely attractive, Omega must be supremely present".

'independent of the collapse of the forces with which evolution is woven'; 4. *transcendence:* as the last term of the series of developments and transformations, it is also outside all series.[30]

The Christian Phenomenon

Towards the end of *The Phenomenon of Man* Teilhard argues that the Christian *phenomenon* provides evidence for the existence of Omega Point. It must be emphasised that Teilhard speaks of the Christian *phenomenon* in this context and not of Christian Revelation.[31] To understand what he writes in the epilogue to *The Phenomenon of Man* does not at all require divine faith but only the ability and openness to *see* one phenomenon among others. Nor do his words at the end of the first section of the epilogue militate against this: "Doubtless I should never have ventured to envisage the latter (Omega Point) or formulate the hypothesis rationally if, in my consciousness as a believer, I had not found not only its speculative model I but also its living reality".[32] The operative words are: 'formulate the hypothesis rationally'. The epilogue to *The Phenomenon of Man* forms the bridge between Teilhard's scientific phenomenology or hyperphysics and his other writings which treat of specifically Christian topics in the light of Christian faith, for example: *Science and Christ* and *Le Milieu Divin*. In the epilogue it appears to be Teilhard's purpose to lead the reader through a phenomenological consideration of the axes of belief of Christianity (affirmation of a Personal God who is Providence and Revealer), of its existence value (no mere ideology), of its power of growth (the cosmic awareness of modern man shows Christianity as more vigorous and more necessary than ever before) to an examination of whether or not after all "some excess of personal extra-human energy should be perceptible to us if we look carefully, and should reveal to us the great Presence".[33] One may, of course, refuse to accept the identity of Omega and maintain that it remains no more than an unknown quantity; in any case, I doubt if the identity can be made

---

[30] Ibid., p. 297: "The radial function of the tangential: a pyramid whose apex is supported from that is what we see during the course of the process. And it is in the very same way that Omega itself is discovered by us at the end of the whole process, in as much as in it the movement of synthesis culminates. Yet we must be careful to note that under this evolutive fact Omega still only reveals half of itself. While being the last term of its series, it is also *outside all series*. Not only does it crown, but it closes. Otherwise the sum would fall short of itself, in organic contradiction with the whole operation".

[31] Ibid., p. 320: "The Christian fact stands before us. It has its place among the other realities of the world".

[32] Ibid., p. 322.

[33] Ibid., pp. 320-327.

with anything more than merely notional assent, without the Christian faith. What Teilhard is asking for here is a phenomenological analysis of the Christian fact as containing the realisation of the most authentic human need: a point of union. In this his methodology resembles in some respects that of the early Christian apologists. Their aim was not simply to demand legal status for the Christians, but to present Christianity as the authentic heir to Greco-Roman civilisation and even as the sole realisation of its ideal.[34]

If what Teilhard de Chardin presents here about the identity of Omega Point is unacceptable it does not follow that the believer and the non-believer must part company when they reach the end of *The Phenomenon of Man*. Given that they both accept the universe as an evolving, dynamic reality, Omega Point (whatever about its precise identity) follows as a logical corollary.[35] Omega unites the believer and the non-believer through the hope it gives of a continuing development towards the hyperpersonal and through the assurance that the end is not absurdity and nihilism. This hope carries with it the responsibility, which must be shared by all, of building the earth. There is, of course, the enormous difference that the believer, can, in humility, claim to know the present and ultimate identity of Omega.[36] But because of the mutual acceptance of Omega as Point of convergence by the believer and the non-believer, they both have the same duty to the past, the same task in the present, and both bear the same responsibility for the future: to contribute to the progress of evolution by uniting mankind in love and thus to create a more human community. Mankind, in fact, has reached a point in its history at which it is no longer possible for the believer to ignore the non-believer, or the non-believer to ignore the believer. Unity in the noosphere forbids one reflexive centre to ignore another. Moreover, both have the duty to strive together for the greater unity of mankind if they are to remain integrally human.

---

[34] Teilhard is not an apologist of Christianity in the traditional sense. On the early apologists here see: J. Danielou, *Message Evangélique et Culture Hellénistique aux IIe et IIIe siècles*, Bibliotheque de Théologie, Histoire des Doctrines Chrétiennes avant Nicée, Desclée & Cie, Tournai 1961, pp. 11-39.

[35] For the unbeliever Omega is the universal cosmic centre; for the believer (Christian), Omega is the universal Christic centre.

[36] The Christian cannot deny Christ without in fact denying the meaning and value of the world. Christ is God made Man, that is to say, made part of the world.

Teilhard's Christology

Teilhard's insight into theology centres on Christ. This would not be the place to discuss at length his Christology; nevertheless, some remarks are called for. The universe cannot centre itself apart from Christ. From a strictly theological point of view, for Teilhard de Chardin Christ cannot be subsequent in God's mind to human guilt. In fact, creation is inconceivable without Christ. He is the Instrument, the Centre and the End of the entire process of continuous creation. Teilhard was convinced that his teaching on the centrality of Christ in the natural as in the supernatural order was a development, in dynamic terms, of the teaching of the New Testament, especially of St. Paul, on the place of Christ in creation.[37] His threefold description of Christ as Instrument, Centre and End clearly has its source in the three prepositions of Colossians 1:17-18: *en, dia* and *eis*.[38] St. Paul states unequivocally: "In him were created all things" (Centre); "All things were created through him and unto him" (Instrument, End). We must bear in mind that the subject of verses 15-20 of Colossians 1 is the same as that of verse 14. St. Paul is speaking of the Word made flesh.[39] The Pauline teaching on Christ's cosmic role was developed later by the Greek Fathers, the content of whose writings on the Cosmic Christ was well known to Teilhard.[40]

A renewed Christology in Teilhard's view requires that redemption from sin (while integrally retained) should pass to the second place in the order of priorities, and union in the love of God communicating himself should take first place. The saving work of the Incarnate Word would then be: "*Primario* to lead creation to its fulfilment in union with God, and for this purpose

---

[37] *Writings in Time of War*, p. 58: "The Incarnation is a making new, a restoration, of all the universe's forces and powers; Christ is the Instrument, the Centre, the End, of the *whole* of animate and material creation: through Him, *everything* is created, sanctified, and vivified. This is the constant and general teaching of St. John and St. Paul (that most 'cosmic' of sacred writers), and it has passed into the most solemn formulas of the Liturgy: and yet we repeat it, and generations to come will go on repeating it, without ever being able to grasp or appreciate its profound and mysterious significance, bound up as it is with understanding of the universe".

[38] See the exegesis of this text and that of Ephesians 1:3-14 in: J.F. Bonnefroy, *Christ and the Cosmos*, trans. and ed. from the original work of J.F. Bonnefroy, *La Primauté du Christ selon l'Ecriture et la Tradition*, by M. Meilach, Paterson N.J. 1965, pp. 133-246. Teilhard quotes Colossians 1 in: *Science and Christ*, p. 15.

[39] Cf. Bonnefroy, *Christ and the Cosmos*, pp. 138-142.

[40] He makes a number of general references to the Greek Fathers: *Science and Christ*, pp. 122, 166, 189; *The Future of Man*, p. 98; *Le Milieu Divin*, p. 110; *Human Energy*, trans. by J.M. Cohen, Collins, London 1969, p. 167. He makes specific mention of Gregory of Nyssa in *Le Milieu Divin*, p. 110; *Science and Christ*, p. 76.

secundario to conquer the forces of evil, regression and dispersion".[41] It is here that Teilhard comes closest to the Scotistic position on the motive of the incarnation. According to the Franciscan tradition in the Scotist School, the hypostatic union has absolute priority in the mind of God. Christ as this man is first predestined to grace and glory as the primary intention of God's will to create.[42] incarnation and Redemption are two moments to be distinguished in God's will to have *condiligentes*.[43] It must be emphasised that the Scotistic thesis, not hypothesis,[44] has never been condemned by the Church and it is fully consonant with Catholic teaching to hold that the incarnation is the goal and purpose of the divine plan of creation, towards which everything tends as to its point of union.

Teilhard's Christology requires theologians to re-examine in depth the philosophical and sociological presuppositions of their science on which their interpretation of the faith depends. His reflections on the relationship of Christianity to the evolutionary view of the world raise the whole question of the development of doctrine. This is particularly the case in his insisting on the involvement of all reality in biological space-time and the reversal of priorities in the purpose of the incarnation. Faith is never to be confused with theology; the philosophical and sociological presuppositions of the latter are subject to radical change once a new dimension, for example, the cosmic dimension, becomes part of man's thinking and culture. It would be arrogant to imagine that we have already exhausted the whole meaning of any aspect of divine revelation. This we can never do. Each new dimension that man acquires as he moves through history furnishes another starting point for a deeper and fresher understanding of the nature and significance of revealed truth.

---

[41] *Le Christ évoluteur,* 1942, pp. 6f., quoted in C.F. Mooney SJ, *Teilhard de Chardin and the Mystery of Christ,* Collins, London 1966, pp. 105f.

[42] I. Duns Scoti, *Reportata Parisiensia* II, d. 20, q. 2, n. 2, (Vivés, XXIII, 98a): *Omnis ordinate volens, prius vult quod est immediatum fini; sed Deus est ordinatissime volens, et immediate post dilectionem sui vult beatitudinem illis qui eam habeant.* Ibid., III, d. 7, q. 4, n. 5, (Vivés, XXIII, 303b): *Primo Deus diligit se; secundo diligit se aliis, et iste est amor castus; tertio vult se diligi ab alio que potest eum summe diligere, loquendo de amore alicuius extrinseci; et quarto praevidit unionem illius naturae quae debet eum summe diligere, etsi nullus cecidisset.*

[43] I. Duns Scoti, *Opus Oxoniense* III, d. 32, q. 1, n. 6 (Vivés, XV, 433a): *Que enim amat se primo ordinate, et per consequens non inordinate zelando, vel invidendo isto modo, secundo vult habere alios diligentes, et hoc est velle allos habere amorem suum in se, et hoc est praedestinare eos, si velit eis hoc bonum finaliter.*

[44] Scotus does not treat of the purely hypothetical question: "If Adam had not sinned, would Christ have become incarnate?"His point of departure is the predestination of Christ: *Utrum Christus praedestinatus fuerit esse Filius Dei? Cf. Opus Oxoniense* III, d. 7, q. 3: *Reportata Parisiensia* Ill, d. 7, q. 4.

Conclusion

Teilhard de Chardin has reminded us that one of the chief purposes of the science of theology is to establish clearly the nature of the relationship between God and the universe. To fulfil this purpose it is its task:

1. To penetrate deeper into the meaning of the Incomprehensible, All-Holy Mystery we call God.

2. To grapple with the significance of this Mystery as made known to us in the human life of him who is the *Kurios Christos,* and who came because God loved the world.

3. To show us "that everything is the sum of the past and that nothing is comprehensible except through its history".[45]

4. To keep us clear of all selfish longings for the past, which turn us away from the present and destroy our care for the future.

5. To teach us that the Gospel is for now: the world of science and technology, of desire for peace and war on want, of political unrest and economic uncertainty.

6. To impress upon us our responsibility for the future and our sacred duty to build the earth.

7. To show us the way to union with others through him in whom "union differentiates" and where we find ourselves realised fully.

8. To make us see that God is everywhere, and that nothing we do because of what we are is irrelevant, unimportant, or ever lost, but that it all contributes to building a better world, a more human brotherhood until

> he has gathered everything together and transformed everything, he will close in upon himself and his conquests, thereby rejoining, in a final gesture, the divine focus he has never left. Then, as St. Paul tells us, *God shall be in all.* This is indeed a superior form of 'pantheism' without trace of the poison of adulteration or annihilation: the expectation of perfect unity, steeped in which each element will reach its consummation at the same time as the universe.[46]

---

[45] *The Future of Man*, p. 13.
[46] *The Phenomenon of Man*, p. 322.

Building the Earth[1]

1. The Final Stage of Man

The heightening of consciousness has taken place in what I call period 'X'; I was very interested to hear Dr. Glynn Faithfull place this date in the 17th century. I've always believed that modern times began in the 1680's—one evening after supper even, and then, that they ended in 1945 and a new era was ushered in 1945, which I have described as period 'X', which I can't say too much about because we are far too near it. But, nevertheless, it seems to me the words to describe this new experience that the Fly saw, *Homo sapiens sapiens*, as distinct from *Homo sapiens neanderthalensis*, now must also be qualified even further. Nothing can be dispensed with, nothing can be said to be secondary that has preceded us, but I believe it must be *Homo sapiens amans*—and then it will become *Homo sapiens amans-orans*, that is to say, not only the human who has knowledge but the human who is defined by *Love* itself and then by *prayer*. So that the final stage in this vision as I see it, that Humanity will itself become a prayer; as long long ago Thomas of Celano said of St. Francis when he prayed, "when this man prayed he was not so much praying as having become himself a prayer". *Homo-orans—non tam orans quam oratio factus*—he's made into a prayer and I consider that form of prayer the highest wisdom and the greatest form of self acceptance that there is,—but I'll return to that. . . .

2. Mystery

A mystery in this sense seems to me to be the inability to say the final word about anything—the inability to do this—and positively therefore, always to find more to be said and more and more and more yet still. And that seems to me to apply from theology down or up—I don't mind which way—or across laterally say from theology to, let us say, elementary particles, where, as you know we now have the quark and no one knew there was a quark waiting until the quark seen as it were metaphorically by the light of the

---

[1] THE TEILHARD REVIEW AND JOURNAL OF CREATIVE EVOLUTION 20.1 (Spring 1985) pp. 21-23. Published with permission. The excerpts are taken from Doyle's talk at the First Transdisciplinary Forum held at Kensington Square on 12th February, 1983.

electron. So we have this fact of experience that we are unable apparently to say the final word about anything. Now that applies, supereminently, to the human being, it applies to everything else but for my purposes, the human being. You will know of course that we have great knowledge of the human being through the genetic code, the D.N.A. and there are indeed genes for writing and speaking and falling in love, but there are no genes for self-consciousness—there aren't any and there are no genes for why Tom falls in love with Mary and no genes for Shakespeare's Sonnets or Macbeth as was quoted earlier. There are no genes for this. So that we are as it were in the presence of a certain ex-quantity that seems to have about it an 'nth' quantity. We can't say the last word but apparently we can't stop saying more things or thinking more things or discovering more things. So the atom is a mystery, the Forget-me-not is a mystery in whose petals the sky reflects its own colour, the human-being is a mystery as she or he looks out and one sees the bright light of human intelligence. Something not quite right; now this of course is so riddled with myth and is so depicted by profound pictures that one has to be very very careful as to what is right and what is not right. My own view is that we have trivialised evil by making it too frequent and too apparent. I find it disgusting to do that and I find it loathsome on the part of the Church to continue perpetuating it. Nevertheless, in some strange way there is a factor in our Universe that seems to be clearly present which Teilhard described as that 'struggle against the multiple'.—*Contre le multitude.* There is some sort of struggle—some sort of power that will drag us into disintegration—whether it is altogether inside us, somewhere outside us, it is not easy to say. It must never be made synonymous with aggression, it is not synonymous with libido or sexuality, it is not synonymous with striving to exist and be better, that is to say ambition, they are all factors necessary to become a mature human being in my opinion but ALL of them have been as it were dragged under this umbrella by—I wish to say in humility—unthinking people, (if I may be permitted to do that). Well now, the recognition of this, first of all—this mystery, raises questions, and for me, the question across planet Earth for all human beings is the question about the question.

3. Wisdom

All the religions have sought to search why we should ask questions about ME. Why we should ask questions about intelligibility—in a word also why we should ask questions about truth and therefore about the holy God. Why we should do that? In so far as they attempt to give some kind of explanation of meaning then they introduce us to wisdom, and wisdom it seems to me, is in essence, the recognition that knowledge is of itself leading to its own transcendence; it must be transcended. All knowledge must be transcended and only the wise man knows this. By that I mean it passes to the level of the heart. We find it for example beautifully described in St. Bonaventure's meditation on St. Francis on Mt. Alverna, where he says the intellect having reached a level, fell asleep and the will passed over into the holy mystery of God. And thus, this man, who as far as we know, certainly never read anything other than the Bible and probably a few bawdy songs in his youth, St. Francis is presented as the epitome of wisdom.

4. A Vision for the Future

Which brings me to the final point—the future. Today, here is sense of the heightened conscience or conscientisation of the human layer on planet Earth. It is a sense of a future that has never before been had. Now I don't mean by that to say, that say Pythagoras didn't know there would be tomorrow or that Plato didn't reflect upon the years to come, but they didn't think about it in the sense of being responsible for it because you are creating it. You see, and at a time when the human race has never known more about its cosmic and human past—biological past—at this point we have the greatest awareness of the future. And so, matters such as—without entering the question of the deterrent—matters such as 'what do you do' with radio-active waste which may stay radio-active for thousands of years just to keep our fridges going and keep us warm, what might happen in two thousand years if the vitrification of this waste proves to be an unsound technology. Now that's just one tiny example. We have therefore along with this awareness a certain *angst*—there's an anxiety in people, I find, it is not necessarily destructive, but there is an anxiety upon the earth, where one goes; some people get pessimistic, I'm sorry to say, although I sympathise with that and some people manage to stay optimistic about that. Well, what can we do? Well you see we've begun: you see, it was lovely to hear the—I am so glad the morphogenetic field was introduced by Brian Scott McCarthy, I was so pleased—I had forgotten about that for the minute and I suddenly remembered what he said—as he said the morphogenetic field means these monkeys spread around what they've learnt. Now, with rats, we find that the experiments showed that the knack that rats in another place—lets say rats in New York had learned to get through a maze in a certain period of time to where the food was—well doing the same thing with rats in London, they did it quicker, the same sort of strain of rats and the rats out in Brisbane—they did it quicker still—thus as it were, the picture of the morphogenetic field. Now you see, when Donne said 'No man is an island' and when a Buddhist says 'I will remember you' or the Muslim tells me 'l will pray for you'—there is the morphogenetic field and I find it is happening more and more. I know people who live in America are suddenly aware of what someone's thinking in London. I know somebody in America very dear to me who seems to know when I have certain thoughts—which was a little frightening at first—I was beginning to wonder if my head was made of a piece of glass, rather than whatever it is. I find furthermore that people are aware if someone else is either suffering tension or is in a moment of elation. Now you see, I've often thought in my naivety I suppose, if everybody on earth stopped for a minute to love everybody else into existence, whether the planet would suddenly burst open and they find something so beautiful inside it. Loving people, you see, are praying people into existence or loving people into existence. So there is what you might call a little theological vision.

Evangelisation in the New Age[1]

When I first received the title I thought: 'What must I do to begin such a vast subject?' And I returned to the volume *Christianity and Evolution,* which seems to me to contain the quintessence of Teilhard de Chardin's vision of the world. I came across the two essays again: *Christianity and Evolution,* (Suggestions for a New Theology, which are pages 173 to pages 176) which had never been published which was written in 1945, and then the second, *What the World is Looking For from the Church of God at This Moment,* (which are pages 212 to 220 of that same volume) which again wasn't published and which he wrote in New York in 1952. So I started from those two essays and I suppose what I have to say is contained, in nucleus at least, in them. But before I do that I have to say something about the title. There are two elements in it, Evangelisation and the New Age. So I will begin, by way of introduction, with the New Age.

I take this to mean that if we accept the threefold distinction of Western history—I know it's not satisfactory—but if we accept for the argument's sake that Western history is divided into Ancient, Mediaeval and Modern, then the contention here being made is that the Modern era has ended and therefore that we have come upon a fourth. Therefore if we have to speak now in terms of what we learnt at school, western history must now be divided into four parts and not three parts as once we were taught to do. That will mean that such countries for example as the United States of America, (I understand perfectly clearly that America is much older than this) but from the point of view of States, would emerge in the Modern era. It probably means something like the sixth period I should imagine for China and perhaps the eighth or the ninth for India and other parts of the Middle and Far East. However, the contention being made is we have entered a fourth period and I think it is somewhere to be dated around the 1940's, probably around 1945. That means I am contending that the Modern era, which began in the 1680's—one evening after supper—and there grew a climate and the climate was first of all the superiority

[1] THE TEILHARD REVIEW AND JOURNAL OF CREATIVE EVOLUTION 20.1 (Spring 1985) pp. 12-20. Published with permission. Talk at the Wantage Conference 1984.

(of course) of reason. That you must *'dare* to know' is what Kant told the whole of the modern world: dare to know, don't be put off by these awful priests and other strange subhuman beings crawling round the world. Don't be put off by them, don't let them do anything to you, you must go out and *dare* to know. So there was created this vast edifice of reason which becomes autonomous reason, one of the greatest aberrations, in my opinion, of the history of the West. Autonomous reason, it is loathsome, absolutely loathsome, and I shall try to say in a little while, why.

Secondly, there arose what we came to call the empirical method which is that method that derives knowledge from observation by the senses and then tests what is observed and this gets the real name, knowledge. Anything else then becomes either the meanderings of mad men or what they call faith with some dishonour and relegated to the subjective. It was at this time that the Holy Church (I'll speak now just for the Roman Catholic, that's the one I know the best)—it was at this time that the Holy Church ran away into a little corner and built a great wall around herself, while a world was created in which for the first time really in Western history, she had little or no part to play. Anyway, it happened that something greater than human beings was excluded from the human scene and there grew then a vision of the world, that the world was getting better, and that we were progressing towards the evermore perfect and that we would eventually conquer everything: indeed that we would go to the moon, probably get out of the galaxy. The first one happened, the second one didn't but we're all waiting for the great breakthrough when we set foot upon the hydroponic farm and off we go with Dr. Who in the Time machine, off into the furthest regions of space, which we gather is somewhere in the region of twenty-five billion light years, take a few thousand million one side or the other and you've got this size of the observable universe which if we wanted to know its miles, we would have to multiply $60 \times 60 \times 24 \times 365.4 \times 186{,}000 \times 25$ billion and there you would have the miles of the observable universe. How splendid! But then in this magnificent development we came to the point where getting better and better, there was little need for reason to invoke anything outside itself and so reason gradually fell into a kind of obsession with itself and from this obsession there came that modern phenomenon, highly modern and very strictly phenomenon of course, that is called atheism which has now reached its nadir in agnosticism and the agnosticism, as no doubt you know, in the western world, is in fact no more than a veneer and if you scratch it you'll find that it conceals a very deep religious hunger. In this time of course, the so-called scientific vision of the world built up an edifice that destroyed all the images that we had inherited from an earlier time, particularly from Ptolemy's universe—it was exploded and it looked as if in the abolition of the images, the baby so to speak had gone down with the bath water, whereas the truth of the matter appears now to be that the baby is at the bottom of the tub, crying its little eyes out and aimlessly stroking the air with its flaccid limbs, longing to be picked up again and given a little cuddle. Now, let us see what we can *do!* We then came into this century and we reached in our evolution and our perfectioning and our ever better status the worst war we have ever ever confronted, the worst; and not twenty years later the second. Then of course after experiments in Arizona and subsequently through the application of all that the great and holy Einstein had left to us, we have harnessed and then used atomic power and done something I believe about which Teilhard de Chardin is quite correct—that what happened with atomic power is comparable to what happened with the discovery of fire. I believe he is quite right. Something changed; but this change is the new era, the new post-modern, post critical era and this new era has certain characteristics that we can speak about. It is not easy to speak of contemporary history but there are some indications which have emerged which can be instanced as symbols of it anyway. Firstly I believe it is realistic, I believe we are more realistic than the modern era, more realistic about ourselves and more realistic about what we, as let us suppose,—anyway—if I may at least hold this, whatever we have evolved from, at least we at the moment are in someway responsible for what is called unity and our efforts as you know, have been paltry. Whether we're speaking of church or whether we're speaking of the world, that side leaves an awful lot to be desired. But, there is I believe a realism—in some places its bordering on pessimism—about the human condition, some people are already saying that the Western civilisation is now in its death throes. I believe when I received the text of Bishop Newbiggins book prior to its publication—it was sent to thirty of us I think and we were asked to give comments on it and I was one of them—and I noted in there he seemed to be of the opinion that we were now in the death throes of a civilisation. I personally think that was too extreme and too pessimistic and I said so, with respect to the Bishop. I think rather, there is a sign of a sickness but it is not necessarily unto death and the tragedy is that there are the means of doing something about it—there really are, but if we let them go by then one indeed does tremble to think what might happen to our ancient and Holy Mother the Earth, the *Mater Teluris*. I tremble to think about that. But nevertheless there is a realism.

Secondly, I agree totally with Teilhard de Chardin in that first essay *Christianity and Evolution*—there is more religious, a more religious time than the previous one, the modern era. Not so churchly, but then that doesn't matter altogether, because in the word religion for me at this moment, will really mean holiness, really holiness is what we ought to talk about on this earth. Holiness—and there are a lot of very holy people—very holy people. All over the place and encountered on the Underground for example, between Victoria and Blackfriars. Often you may encounter a very holy person—they're there— it's shining out. Now first of all, I think the believers are more religious—the believers are more religious I think, firstly because we have learnt that it is not our business to be mealy-mouthed moralisers; we have the name for it and it is loathsome in our ears. Loathsome. We are moralisers. We are adept apparently at telling people what to *do* but not too competent in showing them how to *be,* which is quite another question. If Teilhard de Chardin is metaphysically absolutely right, to identify 'being' with 'unity', then I am talking about 'how to be and to be related', for 'to be' really is 'to be related'. Well, we're waking up to it. If you go out, let us say, among the *Hoi Poloi*, and say Roman Catholic; you'll probably hear, oh dear, 'fish on Fridays' is it, or something about Rome, the Pope, or the Vatican? Then Anglican—Let me see, is that King Henry VIII and six wives or something, St. Paul's? Methodist? Don't like drink, eh? Presbyterian, Mmmmm. . .don't like dancing. Terribly strict on Sundays! and so on—you go through the long list. Orthodox—oh yes, those great big duvets they wear, teacosy's or something; in other words nobody ever identified us by the only thing that matters which is that we believe someone is alive and is alive in a way that nobody before has ever been alive. It's called the Resurrection: but nobody ever says 'there are those people', and we go on our way: 'thank you very much, thank you, thank you'. Nobody ever says that about us, which strikes me as decidedly odd because its the only thing that matters. So we've gone wonky somewhere along the line, you see. So that is how, I would think, we are supposed to be defined. It's merging, thanks be to God. But then even the irreligious, so to speak, if indeed there are any—but let us accept their assessment—they're getting more religious. Isn't it extraordinary that at a time of the greatest sophistication, and I think we are the most sophisticated the world has ever known looking at the broad spectrum of achievements, at *this* time there has never been greater interest in the stars, not astronomically but astrologically. I would consider myself for example a relatively intelligent person, (said he in abject humility), but I always take a peep at the Stars to see what it says about me, I always do that. Tripping along, I think, oh now, you'll fall over a blonde on the stairs and I go away and giggle but the fact of the matter is that I *looked.* There has never been more interest in what we may call the unconscious or the subconscious. That well, that well that is in us. I myself follow the Jungian analysis, I know nothing really about it but I do think, I find it highly congenial to think, that there are these great archetypal ideas rooted in me—nothing will ever get rid of them—I've got to come to terms with them. It's magnificent, to think of that. Look at the interest in it. Then dreams, oh dreams, the interest in dreams! And then we may instance the beauties of Yoga and all that Yoga achieves with regard to inner peace, and then other, what one might describe as, esoteric and even bizarre developments. But all of them point to this, the crisis of the West is the crisis of the imagination and not a crisis of reason. Its our imagination that is starved and where it's not starved, it's being fed the most awful food, that it is sick, sick to death. When one thinks what is produced, let us suppose on some of the little bit of television that I have seen, which is highly infrequent but I consider that to be a very great virtue indeed. But it's sick, all these areas indicate what? That which cannot be controlled by reason. That's the point. Cannot be controlled by reason. It's a protest from the depths and it's *very, very* religious. Then there is concern for world peace, there is concern for world justice, we heard it in the bidding prayers this morning, and there is concern for the environment, which stretches out to the furthest stars. As St. Francis said, 'My Sisters the stars' and he laid the foundation of an inter-galactic fraternity. They were his sisters and his brothers—the stars—so in principle if there is intelligent life in the next or some other galaxy, in principle they are already our brothers and sisters, according to the poor, humble St. Francis of Assisi. That concern—which the Church isn't too bothered about I am very very sorry to say, is the most deeply religious issue on planet Earth today—the most, because it's concerned with the vice-Regents of God, not the Masters of Creation, which we are not. It's rarely about Almighty God's love of the whole of the created order. Whether his Name comes into it or not or whether He is invoked or not, they are speaking the Name and the Word of the silent mystery. It is all around us, the nameless silent mystery, that is God.

Finally, there is a concern about the future. This is unknown prior to us. Not that people didn't know there would be tomorrow but the concern of what we are doing and the repercussions of it, in some instances with regard to radio-active waste, possibly ten thousand million years, possibly, but certainly a very long time, so that we can keep our fridges and we can keep warm, we don't give two hoots about the future. That is emerging as a deep deep concern and I think it is a form of a greater love no one has. So there is the New Age that I believe is in some ways upon us. So I've lived through, so to say, an age something like St. Augustine, who saw the passing of the Ancient world and the emergence of the New that we came to call Medieval times.

Now, Evangelisation. By this I mean simply to share the insights received from whatever source and I suppose in my case from the Holy gospel and the Holy Tradition into the meaning of this world and the meaning, as a problem unfolds itself as origin, the problem of where do we come from? The problem of purpose; what is our value? and the third, the problem of destiny, where are we going? And to these three questions, all philosophical questions may ultimately be reduced and that is the problem of meaning. The insights given from the sources of my experience and thus let us say, the Church's experience and believer's experience into the problem of meaning which is the question, and the question which makes us ask another question, namely why did the question arise? For it shouldn't do. Why should anyone ask: 'Why is there not nothing?' Why should anyone ask: 'What does it all mean?' Why should anyone ask: 'Where do we come from?' Why should anyone ask: 'Where are we going?' Why should anyone ask: 'What is the purpose?'. Say: 'Get on and have your dinner. You've got to eat your sausages, get your sausages eaten and don't be worrying about that'. But strange to say they persist in these questions and so with Heidegger we are brought to the real question, the question about the question, that is the question. *Die Frage über die Frage das ist die Frage.* 'Why does the question arise dearest', and someone peeps up in this Tradition and says ah! do you know why? because the answer came before the question 'and so logic is turned upon its head once more!' So let that do for evangelisation, I'm not talking about going out to convert anybody not talking about bullying anybody, I'm telling them what I believe in with all my heart and would love the whole world to believe in, but it must be respected what anyone believes in. We have the freedom to proclaim meaning and if that meaning is found in someone then proclaim it has to be *Proclamandum est* and this person is the person in the end, of our Lord as far as I am concerned, so let us set about the task of Teilhard and Evangelisation.

He says, in the essay quoted first, *Christianity and Evolution—Suggestions for a New Theology:*

> As the title of this essay indicates, I am writing only in the hope of making a personal contribution to the work which is common to the Christian consciousness, and expression of the demands made in my own particular case, by *fides quaerens intellectum* that is to say: 'the demands made by faith seeking understanding'. These are suggestions, not affirmations, not teachings.

Now when I first read those words some years ago, in fact in 1972 to be precise, for I remember them leaping out of the page at me, I realised that they encapsulated, possibly the key, to what he was doing but certainly the Tradition to which, I myself belong and have been brought up, which is the Tradition of the Augustinians, by the greatest teacher of all the Augustinians, St. Bonaventure. I am not a Thomist but I've nothing against St. Thomas, but I am not a Thomist. I have quite a different vision of the universe and I believe I am now going to try to unfold it. The theme of the conference is 'The Spirit in Evolution'. I noticed in the letter I received that we, the speakers, were invited to reflect on the working of the Spirit in the evolutionary process in the light of Teilhard's rational invitation to faith in the universal Christ. Now my belief is that Teilhard de Chardin has to be compared with James Clarke-Maxwell, Albert Einstein and Michael Polanyi, for these three actually set out as fundamental believers and I am also convinced that they saw by an intuition, the meaning of the order of Nature as a reflection of what they believed by faith and then without letting there be any unwarranted intrusion of what they believed by faith into their investigations of the universe, in fact they *tested* their faith, and saw that it was reflected in the order of the world. Let me then just outline that a little.

All of us are the inheritors of the empiricist theory of knowledge. This is the theory that led Locke to draw a sharp distinction between faith and reason or between belief and rational knowledge. Belief then becomes ungrounded persuasion, private opinion and it falls short of knowledge for it is not based on the evidence of the senses. Rational knowledge on the other hand comes from experience and is established through demonstration operating with certain connections visible to our senses; and so, coupled with Newtonian deism, for there was no place for God intervening in Newton's world, oh no, and much less the possibility of an incarnation was *a priori* excluded, for a bucket cannot get inside itself and if it's all a container, then the container can't get into the contained, and so there is no dynamic interaction between God and the world. Well, it became clear, as no doubt you will know, that there can be no advance whatsoever in our knowledge of the world if science as natural science inhibits itself from having anything to do with a reality beyond the observable or from taking into rational account connections that are inherently unobservable. The observationalist subject to object is challenged radically by the need to penetrate behind sense experience, to the invisible object relations and dynamic field structures which give cohesion to states of affairs in nature.

The first example is *Clarke-Maxwell* who was as you will know, a profound believer and had a profound respect for the nature of creation. For him, the whole of Nature is characterised by a flexible structural relatedness. Field theory. Relationship between things actually belongs to them; relationships are not outside things, they actually form part of what it is to be an event or a thing and therefore relation is what is important to know and of course he believed that that is what God is. God is not simply being He is being-related: that is the Christian God. A set of interdependent, dynamic relations, moving through and in one another—not *actio in discans*—but to be is to be related. The intuition can be tested, definitely. Then he begins with the idea of the ALL not the idea of the 'splintered', the idea of the broken, the idea of the infinitesimal particles of which the whole world is constituted, but synthetically rather then analytically, accepting the whole then proceeds to the parts. Consequently his faith in God, while having no direct interfering casuality upon his science is found to be reflected in a universe of dynamic relationships, showing the mechanical model to be highly unsatisfactory.

Albert Einstein. Well I won't say too much about him, but at least I will say this: I don't think I have ever read more beautiful things—well they are among some of the most beautiful things I have read-about the mystery of God who doesn't play dice. And lying somewhere underneath that appreciation of Clarke-Maxwell's 'field theory' the electro-magnetic field, and his belief, even if it was Spinoza's God—that's difficult to say—there lay an awe which said there is an intuition about the universe, objectively about the universe, that comes towards me, namely first that it's there—that's the first act of faith and the second is that it is intelligible, I don't make it so; thirdly, that that intelligibility is open to me. That's an act of faith, it's an assumption, and it's valid and it's logical and rational. There's nothing unobjective or subjective or purely restrictive about that. It's pure rationality as far as Einstein is concerned. That the lawfulness and the harmony and the beauty that springs from the experience of the universe is a given and it has to be accepted. *Credo ut intelligam.* 'I believe in order that I may understand'. 'Transpose it'—St. Anselm said that a long time ago. "I accept, I receive, and then I start to understand".

And finally *Polanyi*. His lovely little phrase: "There is a tacit co-efficient in scientific theory which says there's something going on and it's more than meets the eye and it's more than meets the ear: it's the little extra that nobody can actually get hold of but it's there". The personal co-efficient. Belief or intuitive apprehension is his word. No human reason, he says, however critical can operate outside a context of faith for it is within that context that there arises within us, under the compulsion from the reality of the world we experience a regulative set of convictions or a framework of beliefs, which impels us and guides us in our enquiries. So we have all got a prior intuitive contact with reality and it's probably true that every child, boy or girl, by the age of six, has learnt more physics than all the greatest and most learned physicians and physicists later, will ever be able to put together, by a set of what we may call intuitive contacts with reality. I am placing Teilhard de Chardin in that position. I believe that when he speaks of the phenomenon and is asking people to see, the seeing must not be taken in the sense of taking a look, but rather in coming to terms with how it is that we actually know anything and what it is we are knowing.

Now, is it not true that throughout the pages of the *Phenomenon of Man*, whatever you make of it, and it is in my opinion like a mosaic, you are led all the way through to a point where coming to us there is a force at work that has something to do with bringing us together. The global village, I don't care what you call it but certainly we have some sense that it's wrong that we are not together and that the present economic links of the planet earth are certainly not what Teilhard de Chardin means, they are certainly not what the great religions of the world mean, and they are certainly not what Christianity means by it, for they are too tied up with Mammon to be able to be what these great sources mean by Unity. But something is afoot. He calls it in the end LOVE, one of the most beautiful words he uses. It's not the sloppy meaning of the term we get poured forth on us these days. It's doing what is right coming from the will, knowing by the intellect and our experience what that word is about, and then postulating, quite legitimately, some kind of centre takes you over the bridge in the epilogue of the *Phenomenon of Man*, to say, would you now—and here is what I take rational invitation to mean—look if you have come this far with me, then can you see how I will identify Omega point with Christ as its reflection. If it is a Marxist and the Marxist says no then we will have to agree, fine, we will work for Omega point and I will work for the universal Christ. We needn't part company—most certainly not. He's simply saying 'can you see it?' 'I saw it *a priori* I believe that is true' that is why he is a mystic. He is a mystic as St. Anselm is a mystic. He is a mystic in the same way as Polanyi is a mystic. That we see and grasp conditions—a priori conditions—for knowledge, that we cannot prove and they're never meant to be proved and it's blasphemy to prove them, because we tear our intellects to shreds in doing it or end up, well like cauliflower really. Instead of this great cranium you would take the top off and there would be a cauliflower inside! That's really what we would be doing, instead of accepting that it is part of experience, that it is mystery. That there *is* mystery. That's the first evangelisation I would like to share. That this mysterious thing we call existence, which has got so many levels—so many many levels, even if we go no further from our own selves and have a little look in the mirror. And just see if we can look into our own eyes. That's not bad—could be better, could be worse—but there is the mystery. And what is the mystery? That which lets itself be known. Oh! What the beautiful Wittgenstein has said in the *Tractato logico philosophicus*—they make themselves manifest. The mysteries, they make themselves manifest and then whereof one cannot speak, one must be silent.

Now, having said that, I must turn briefly to this question of his links with Christ. Teilhard de Chardin has revolutionised theology, whether we accept that or not. The consequences have not yet been drawn but the consequences are myriad and they refer to three fundamental areas: Almighty God; the meaning of Evil; and the place of Christ. He has in my opinion, retained everything that the tradition of the Holy Christian church holds but he has asked for a different perspective of it.

The first concerns God, if I may say so, for the gospel is first about God actually and not about us. It's about God first. The mystery of the Godhead and the Pleroma—how often Pleromisation is on the tip of his pen. He states, God is indeed, self-sufficient, yet the universe constitutes something that is vitally necessary to him. That would take you to the end of eternity reflecting on those words; for it makes us now say that if anybody on earth is able to speak about that which is the nameless mystery that we call God, if anybody is able to do that; and then if anyone says in that mystery-God we have our origin, our purpose and our destiny; and then if it is pursued any further and we realise that this mystery never begins to decide anything, that this mystery has no choice but is sublimely free. Choice is nothing to do with the essence of freedom. We think: 'I will have a sausage or I will have an egg' and we call that 'free'-freedom of specification. 'I will go into Oxford' or 'I will not go into Oxford' the freedom of contrariety. Isn't it ridiculous that I should choose to love the daffodil, that I should choose to love the lily of the valley, that I should choose to love the pied wagtail, which has an M.A. from Oxford—the pied wagtail has. Dr. Pied Wagtail. Doctor. Doctor of Philosophy, definitely; I've seen them now so often, I've come to that conclusion. That I should choose them to say that 'I will be kind to you' 'I'll choose it'—it is abominable. I should be drawn out of me towards the good. *Unire* (to unite). The metaphysics of *unire* drawn to the good and falling into it with open arms. That's the freedom in the Godhead. So it doesn't seem to me to be too far off the mark since God doesn't choose anything and he doesn't ever *begin* to do anything—it always is. So, when I look down to poor little old me then I've been around forever in somebody's mind. My father used to say 'in the waistcoat pocket of God'. But it's been a long time. In other words its called the eternal now. He preached that. Is he indifferent to what has arisen from the depths of himself. This is the multiple. This is Teilhard's beautiful symbol for nothingness. I've heard physicists say: 'In the beginning was a formless void of particles'. And then someone said: 'Let there be the photon—and all was well'. And so if you notice in the Book of Genesis it's not so strange when you come to the first verse: 'In the Beginning God created the Heavens and the Earth. The Earth was a formless void and darkness was upon the face of the deep and the Spirit hovered over the darkness and God said: 'Let there be Light'. He didn't say: 'Let there be the Sun'. He didn't say: 'Let there be the Stars'. They don't come till day No. 4. And when you read, for example, St. Augustine's *Commentary on Genesis*, when you've got a few moments before you drop off to sleep, have a look at that. And then turn to the *De Luce* of Robert Grosseteste Bishop of Lincoln, teacher of the Franciscans in Oxford, you'll find that they said that everything was made of Light. Everything. Light entered into the structure of corporeality. Well, I don't think it would be too odd if somebody said, 'well when you think of *let's say*, nobody ever saw it, but there's the oxygen and hydrogen which makes water, I've got the two little oxygen atoms—with the six nuclei, and I've got the hydrogen with its one, and they got together by photons. Thank you! Isn't that nice to think a photon helped to do that?' Light—Our Lord said: 'I am, the Light of the world'—I am delighted as well. It's not so hard you know. The Pleroma—that this called God is desperately concerned—I think that's what Teilhard said—desperately concerned—and we are part of the Pleroma, we really are and the Lord God is not indifferent to that.

Secondly then: God envelopes himself in participated Being and he says, by evolutive unification, which is His word really for Creation. So he wants us to love it. Love creation. It is imperative to love evolution—for me I hear the same word of St. Francis—it is imperative to love creation. That is a way of talking about what seems to be the case in the Universe, Our Earth is four thousand five hundred million years old. We are approaching—about two million years—*Homo Sapiens*—*Homo Sapiens Sapiens*—and we've got organic links with things—so it seems to me to be a pretty acceptable way of talking about the universe from the data that it is at least interlinked to the point that it has evolved. I wouldn't have any problem about that one way or the other. What I would want to say is—it's talking about a dynamic order of things—creation of things, and that's got to be loved and there is no distinction between loving this and loving Almighty God. They are not divorced and if His word itself is to be taken literally then you love your neighbour as yourself. Let me re-write the answer: Who is my neighbour? A man walks out into the countryside and he saw a little fieldmouse and the fieldmouse was going along very very slowly and so he went over to it and looked at it and helped it and he brought it home and he gave it something to eat. That is my neighbour. There I saw the little rosetree—it was obviously getting very very tired—it was obviously very thirsty. So I went over with a little bit of water and a little bit of biscuit and invited it the rose to take a snack. The neighbour. That's what we're talking about—loving. It implies not only ourselves and not this just as a backdrop but the place where we become who we are and where we achieve unity which is of desperate concern to the Pleroma and therefore to Almighty God. It is a way of speaking of the value of the created order.

And finally, concerning our Lord Jesus Christ, what does Teilhard de Chardin ask us to do? In my view what comes out of the Tradition long before him and is concerned with Christ's organic and cosmic relationships derived from Holy Scripture. It is extraordinary that in a period of about thirty years all the great truths—and I speak now in terms of the Christian faith and I am a theologian—that between the year 32 and 56 or 60 AD all the great themes about this figure had already been worked out and more was said of him in those thirty years than was said in the subsequent four hundred—more—and this is somebody who lived down the road and only the other day, remember. As Teilhard always emphasised—I'm talking about the man from Nazareth— I'm not talking about some fantasy or some divine man or some Greek god or some Homeric myth I'm talking about this concrete particular, scandalously particular being rooted in our history. This man was raised from the dead we hear. Then something said about his baptism, something happens during his life. Then something is said about his birth, then something is said about his conception—next you're into the pre-existence. Then the Cosmic Christ. He keeps quoting—*in quo omnia constat*—in whom all things hold together. 'He is the image of the invisible God'—image of the invisible God—'in whom all things were created'. That's what the Holy Scripture says. This is truly the Cosmos in whom all things were created. What are thrones and dominions? What are Principalities and Powers? They were all created for Him and unto Him so that in Him all things shall be held together—that has come down right through the Western Tradition right through to Dun Scotus of my own Order— right through to Lawrence of Brindisi—the Capuchin—and so on to Teilhard de Chardin—he is in a very long Tradition and it is not so strange what he has said, namely, that it is not evil in the first instance that explains the meaning of Jesus Christ but unity and the desire for unity between the Lord, nameless mystery of God, and this creation, and the medium, the instrument, the beginning and the end of it, is this man. That's a long way from making into some little tributary local deity. It's speaking with some audacity about him in the universe, but it allows us to say things with some kind of coherence about other planets, about people living on other planets, about our relationship with people on other planets, and about what shall happen, when we all must, as inexorably we will, die; and what our relationship will be with them. Well now, I must come to an end.

But you see it's to touch a little on one; the new faith atmosphere of the post-modern era, the post-critical era which now, let that be, dare to believe—not dare to know, if I may with great respect turn Kant on his head— I will say *credere aude*—dare to believe, believe in the intelligibility of the Universe, believe in the harmony of it, believe in the beauty of it, and see what impinges upon your intellect when you do that, when you let it be, which is what Love is, isn't it, it's to first 'be', and then to 'be related'. Within that context I've got already, as far as I can see, a kind of a mirror, reflecting what I call the word 'whispering faith' which is this world, by the mystery that is called God. There's a root—it's not so odd to believe in things. Not at all, it's the most honest thing in the world if you love it first especially and it probably is that we need to invert, nothing is known, nothing is loved unless its known invert that—nothing is known unless it's loved. *Nihil, nihil cognitum nisi amatum'—not nihil amatum nisi praecognitum.* No, nothing is known unless it's loved. In that context to speak of the mystery which surrounds us and in which we are enveloped—to understand its call to us which is not indifferent, and isn't waiting to smash everything and to get on perfecting well without it— the mystery has never been without it, it's never been without us, it's never been without the universe and finally in that context to see the assertion of its value, that what we call mystery, in fact became part and parcel of it in the mystery of being, a human being, which I fancy, is probably at the tip of the mysteries as far as we know them, doesn't make us necessarily proud, I hope, but it tells us that the centre of things—lets say the centre of an atom, well what I call Christ is there, and at the centre of the heart which is in us all, I think he's there. That might be something towards how one might approach evangelisation today in the light of this mystic and prophet.

Eric Doyle—A Personal Memory[1]
Bronwen Astor

The death of Eric has left an enormous gap. I first met him in 1967-68 sharing a Teilhardian platform and when we met again some five or six years later he recalled not only what we had said to one another but what we had been given for supper! This total recall of all aspects of life—from whatever he had read, or heard, or seen, was an astonishing characteristic and one that he used with great humility. In spite of his amazing erudition he never made you feel stupid or uninteresting because whatever you had said he would enlarge upon as if you had thought of something original and transport you with one of his favourite phrases "and then, you see. . ." on a cosmic view.

He allowed me on two consecutive years in 1976 and 1977 to attend his lectures on the theology of grace to the seminarians at our local Catholic Seminary. They were not to be missed and students would sometimes gatecrash to get a whiff of the heady air in which he brought all theology into a whole for them and made sense of it all. He did not mention Teilhard de Chardin on these occasions but he was imbued with his perspective. We would all assemble for the lecture and he would enter, pause at my chair and give me a low bow to the great amusement of the students. This was not because I was a fellow Teilhardian but probably because of his deep respect for the feminine Sophia. Proceeding on to the platform he would stand with his back to us and his face up against the wall for a quick prayer to the Holy Spirit and turning round would say "Now we can begin". This ritual was repeated weekly and on several occasions he would, half way through a lecture, dip his hand into his cowl and hand round a bag of boiled sweets!

One of the students many years later, after his own ordination, met Eric in the Westminster Book Shop. "Hallo, Kevin," he said remembering his name of course, and beckoning him over to the corner of the shop, "Are you still angry with God?" The young priest was utterly amazed at this immediate

---

[1] The Teilhard Review and Journal of Creative Evolution 20.1 (Spring 1985) p. 23. Published with permission.

renewal of their last conversation at the Seminary when Eric had charismatically intuited his personal problem with concern and love.

Eric made his many gifts available to everybody whoever they were. He was a Vice President of our Centre. He is irreplaceable. In his last talk at the Wantage Conference he delivered what surely will turn out to be a classic lecture on Teilhard called *Evangelisation in the New Age*. Teilhard, he said, had *revolutionised theology*. Emphasising his favourite theme of the *mystery* in all things and the utter holiness of God, and of the Church, the magnificent scope of the talk is peppered with his wit and humour. Above all he insisted on Jesus as the meaning to everything, Who came, not so much to *make* us one as to demonstrate that we *are* all one. Thank you, Eric.

Fr. Eric Doyle R.I.P.[2]
Michael Le Morvan

The news of Eric's death was a sudden and quite stunning blow. . . .I remember how, about three years ago, he came to talk at Chichester and how he shared with me about the 'chance' finding of the first cancer several years previously which had meant that the Lord gave him several years longer than he might have had if that cancer had gone undetected.

The loss of Eric is one which will be severely felt at the Teilhard Centre for a long time to come. He had been a member of the Centre for many years and latterly was a Vice-President. His frequent appearances at Teilhard Conferences were always sure to attract an audience because his listeners always felt he had something to say and that he would say it in an humorous and ideosyncratic way. He was always a stimulating speaker and his humour kept breaking through even in the most serious topics. He was able to present profound thoughts and ideas in a simple manner because he had made them a part of himself. He was loved by his audiences. His sympathy came through on the radio as clearly as if he were present in the room. I remember listening to him describing on *Thought for the Day* how he consoled a little girl he met on a train and who had just lost her pet dog. She must have felt much happier after talking to him about it. I know I did because I felt his humanity come through so clearly.

How can we assess such a man? It is true to say that his love for Teilhard was so great because they shared the same vision. For all his 'jesuitness' there was a Franciscan love of the world in Teilhard and this, together with his concern for the future, was deeply shared by Eric. Although by his training Eric was first and foremost a Church historian, his grasp of theology was such that listening to him speaking on theology one would never have known that it was not his first specialisation. He wore his immense learning lightly and was concerned that it had relevance for our own day. It was never learning for the sake of it.

[2] THE TEILHARD REVIEW AND JOURNAL OF CREATIVE EVOLUTION 20.1 (Spring 1985) p. 1: an editorial. Published with permission.

Perhaps because he was such a good speaker he devoted comparatively little time to write. . . .Our respect for his memory should lead us to remember what he stood for. In an excerpt from the talk that he gave at the First Transdisciplinary Forum he spoke about his vision for the future leading to a man who would become love and prayer: *Homo sapiens amans et orans* as he described him. Love compels us to act and to be, otherwise it is not love. Prayer is one expression of love. Does this vision enter into our lives? Lives of love building up creation and the earth, bring about the Kingdom of God. Lives devoted to such building can only be sustained by prayer. Perhaps this vision is Eric's gift for us.

Our Dying or
in Memory of Fr. Eric Doyle OFM[3]
Venetia Carse

Our Dying,
as our Birth,
is ineffable Holy Mystery,
both personal to ourselves
and part of the Whole,
part of Creation,
centred on the Infinite,
encompassed by the All.
Even as we are born into awareness of this world of shimmering,
fragmenting, forming, re-forming,
Energy, Matter, Spirit,
so have we been part of the Universe since before Time.
For we have our beginnings in the dust of which stars are made;
and our first beginnings, with our brothers and sisters,
the vast and varied Totality of the Cosmos,
are cradled in the Breath of God.

From the moment we are born
we begin to die.
The Mechanistic Mind,
with logical precision
centred on expediency,
dimly aware of 'something more'
and yet refusing the gift,
the necessity for Faith, Religion,
Myth and Poetry,

---

[3] THE TEILHARD REVIEW AND JOURNAL OF CREATIVE EVOLUTION 20.1 (Spring 1985) p. 28. Published with permission.

encourages the Pragmatic Shelf,
with sad mistaken honesty,
to doubt the mystic Power of Love,
the Redeeming Cross, the Risen Christ,
and to resign to Death of stark finality.

From the moment we are born,
within the concept of Earth's Time
our physical selves begin to die.
And we mourn, because we are human,
and sadly we shall miss Eric Doyle,
that small gowned figure
so full of scholarship and laughter,
generating Courage and Compassion and Humility.
For Brother and Friend to the fieldmouse,
this joyful Franciscan saw his Sister in the stars;
and with heart and mind reaching out
and through toward the deeper Truth,
he found Christ,
Christ in the multitude of Mankind;
in the Poor, the Oppressed,
the Healers, the Peace-seekers,
in the ordinary goodness of men and women
going about their ordinary lives.
For him, Birth, Life and Death were but part of our beginnings;
and in his love of all Creation and the Blessed Trinity,
he helped unfold for us the Holy Mystery.

Photo 19: With friars at Canterbury, 1981

Photo 20: Grave at Chilworth Friary

Photo 21
Editor's collection of Doyle's writings

On Various Themes

The Gospel and the Revelation of God[1]

Jesus Christ is himself the gospel of God and the Revealer of the mystery of God. We must not allow that truth about him to fade from the forefront of our faith. By the elevating light of his human mind, he made known to us something utterly new about the intrinsic nature of the Eternal Godhead.

I

Jesus was conceived and born in a particular place at a particular time and he came from Jewish stock. For long before him his own People had known that God was the God of dialogue and holiness. By the covenant he established with Israel, God addressed the People as such and individual believers in the dialogue. He was called the God of Abraham, Isaac and Jacob.

He summoned Abraham, he spoke with Moses and the Prophets, he listened to their prayers and entreaties. He heard the cry of the poor and he raged in anger in the heavens at the injustice done against widows and orphans. He punished the unfaithful and he allowed his People to be taken into exile. Thus, the Jews recognised him as the God of dialogue from within their own history.

The God of Abraham, Isaac and Jacob was also acknowledged as the God of unfathomable holiness, the God of perfect integrity, knowing no disparity between what it is to be and what it is to will. They recognised his being and willing as one. From the shrouded depths of that holiness God had spoken his unqualified word to his People: "You shall be holy; for I the Lord your God am holy" [Leviticus 19:2]. The Jews knew him therefore also as the God of holiness in history. The pillars of Israel's history were the dialogue and holiness initiated and offered to them by God.

---

[1] Unpublished manuscript found in the provincial archives and published with permission from the Province of Immaculate Conception, England.

II

By the revelation which proceeds from the mind of Jesus Christ under the inspiration of the Holy Spirit, the God of Abraham, Isaac and Jacob becomes the God of our Lord Jesus Christ. As it unfolded, the basic truth of this revelation was thrown into bold relief. The dialogue with the People of Israel, and indeed all other forms of God's speaking to the human race was the historical prolongation of the dialogue that has been taking place on the inside of God for all eternity. It is the dialogue of the Father, Son and Spirit and Jesus gave us a share in it by virtue of his own historical existence. The way into God has been opened for us through the very flesh and spirit of the of the Son of Man. The resurrection of Jesus Christ from the dead is the beginning of a new dawn and a new humanity and that new humanity is inseparably bound to the Triune God.

The dialogue with Israel and with the whole human race has always been part of God's inner dialogue. In the Eternal Word and Image, the Centre of the Godhead, God has rejoiced forever in the reality of creaturehood, his own and ours. God has always loved and known what he decreed to create.

The dialogue inside God is such that the Partners so affirm one another for always, that they all love what they know and know what they love. The Father, the Son, the Spirit, that is, the Origin, the Expression, the Love are equal but not the same. In these distinctions God is what he loves and knows, he wills what he loves and knows, he loves what he wills and knows, he knows what he is and loves. His sublime holiness, his essential integrity, is the perfect communion which holds together the Three most holy forever.

III

By the reality of the incarnation we are taken on to the inside of God's dialogue and holiness. Without the revelation of Christ we should never have known that the dialogue was intrinsic to God, or that holiness is essentially a share in his triform life. The first inkling of this interior dialogue is given in the gospel every time Jesus uses the word *Father* and the second is the beginning of his discourses with *Amen*.

We call the lifting of our nature to such sublime heights the reality of grace. That sounds a somewhat limp description for so great an enhancement of our native powers, that we should share in a dialogue of love which is God's eternal 'Yes' to all that he is and to all that he has made. When we recall, however, that grace is the expression of the divine graciousness towards us, we can accept the mystery in silence and give thanks from the bottom of our heart.

We are not introduced as outsiders. We are invited as honoured guests, indeed, we are made to take our place as sons and daughters in the Son. There we are able to contemplate on the tender words of love which pass from Father to Son to Spirit. Never was there so generous an invitation to such intimacy. By adoption, according to the Father's mysterious designs, we are made exactly by grace what the Son is by nature. We hear the Father's words of love addressed also to us. He loves us both for ourselves and because we love his Son. Indeed, to love his Son is to love him without distinction. And beyond our wildest dreams, we find ourselves making the self-same response of love with the Son in the Spirit.

We become caught up in that movement which the Greeks call *perichoresis* and the Latins, *circumincessio*, a kind of compenetration of the Divine Persons. It may be described as a perfect and dynamic sphere with an infinite number of lines from the centre to the circumference, wherein the Father, Son and Spirit flow into and out of and through one another in an endless, serene and totally beatifying act of divine communion.

IV

Like the Old Testament the gospel teaches a monotheism, that there is but one, true and living God. We would be in error, however, were we to think that we can simply fit the gospel teaching of the revealed unity of God into our understanding of unity or oneness.

The God of our Lord Jesus Christ—no more than the God of Abraham, Isaac and Jacob—is not a mathematical unity, not a monadic oneness, not a static One. God is not a Lone Power or Faceless Energy in the universe. The revealed unity of God involves by its intrinsic structure a diversity. This cannot be simply dovetailed neatly into our metaphysics of unity. God is indeed the *unum*, but in the special sense of a oneness that holds within itself forever the plurality of the many or the Three. As the One, God is a community, a perfect unity-in-diversity. He is, one might say, a perfect brotherhood or sisterhood.

Besides this, however, there is the revealed reality of being. Here again we cannot simply make this co-terminous with our understanding of Being. According to the gospel to be God is to be related, to be God is to be a network of relationships. At the root and origin of all being lies a Being-Related, a set of relationships, Fatherhood, Sonship and Love.

Without revelation we should never have known that unity essentially involves diversity and being intrinsically implies relationships. At the highest and most authentic point of its existence the Church as such and every group within it is a *speculum Trinitatis* a mirror of the very diversity and relationships of God. Part of its apostolic mission is to strive towards an ever greater unity-in-diversity and an ever more closely bonded set of relationships.

Moreover, just as God is in dialogue with himself and with all the free creatures he called into being, so the Church is intended to pursue an internal dialogue between herself and God in worship and prayer, among her members themselves as together they seek the will of God for the Church, and with those outside the Church's visible boundaries.

It has emerged then that the radical newness of the doctrine of God in the gospel has continuity and discontinuity in the teaching of the Old Testament concerning dialogue and holiness. This originality also has continuity and discontinuity in the teaching of the Old Testament and the doctrine of philosophy concerning unity and being.

Too Fantastic To Be False[1]

Lullay, lullay little child, child reste thee a throwe.
Fro heyze hider art thou sent with us to wone lowe;
Pore & litel art tou made, unkut & unknowe. . .
Lullay, lullay litel child, softe slep & faste,
In sorwe endet everi love but thine at the laste.

These are the opening and closing lines of a lullaby to Christ in the crib, contained in a compilation of preaching material made in 1372 by a Franciscan friar, John Grimestone, who may well have hailed from Yorkshire.

I begin with them because they express in the form proper to Christmastide—a carol—the very teaching of the prologue to the fourth gospel: "In the beginning was the Word. . .and the Word was God. . .and the Word became flesh and dwelt among us, full of grace and truth". This is the heart and substance of the Christian message, the article of faith by which the Church stands or falls.

So, we have come once more to the mystery of the silent and holy night. The universe is full of mystery. Light is a mystery and now, after Einstein, even more so than ever; the atom is a mystery; a snowflake, a spider's web, a goldcrest are mysteries. We know so much about these and many things, yet our vast knowledge has done nothing to dispel the mystery of life or the mystery of love. Rather, the truth is, the more we discover in all the sciences, the greater becomes the mystery of the universe.

Mystery means never being able to say the final word on anything; there is always more to discover, always more to say. That itself seems to point to a source beyond the universe, to a beginning that has no beginning, to a meaning which was in the beginning, containing in itself all grace and truth forever.

This understanding of mystery explains why people do things like dancing around a totem pole or genuflecting before a tiny host in a

---

[1] THE TABLET 236 (December 25, 1982) pp. 1292f. Published with permission (www.thetablet.co.uk).

monstrance—things which at first send 'pure' reason reeling and throw logic into chaos. It also lies behind such questions as "What does it all mean?" and "Why are we here?" There is a drive in us towards further intelligibility and deeper reality, towards final meaning and absolute truth. The human mind seeks to answer the question about the question, that is, the question as to why questions about meaning and truth arise. Yes, there seems to be more to the universe than meets the eye, or the ear for that matter, and people celebrate or investigate it.

Religions, certain philosophies and schools of wisdom focus on the mystery of the universe. As a matter of experience people have discovered some of the contours of the mystery which provide answers to fundamental questions and which evidently bring satisfaction and peace. We learn of the Unmoved Mover, the Ideal, the Absolute, the Primal Truth, the Great Architect, the Universal Mind, the Power behind it all; we know of Yahweh, Brahman and Allah.

The Christian Church leads us to the mystery of Christmas, to the Baby Jesus, God's Word made flesh, through whom we have learned to pray "Our Father, who art in heaven". We are not brought to an inspired prophet, however much endowed with the authority of God's Word, but to the enfleshed Word of God. There have been and indeed are many great prophets, holy men and women on whom God's Spirit has descended and to whom God's Word has been entrusted. As St. Athanasius insisted against the Arians: "He became man, and did not come into a man. We must be clear about this, to avoid the notion. . .that the Word dwelt in a man, hallowing him and displaying himself in him, as in earlier times the Word came to each of the saints. In that case there would have been no paradox. . . ." Thus, 'endowed' or 'entrusted' will not do here. We must say 'en-humaned' or 'enfleshed': "The Word became flesh".

Whoever. would have imagined that a little baby would be the real, true presence of God in time and space? Yet this is the realism of the doctrine of the incarnation. It cannot be made respectable, it cannot be explained away, as Theodotus of Byzantium, Paul of Samosata, Sabellius, Arius and a host of others throughout Christian history have tried to do. Nothing less than realism is sufficient, because anything less than that simply fails to meet the experiences recorded in the New Testament, the witness of Tradition and the instinct of faith today.

However did it enter anybody's mind to write: "For to you is born this day in the city of David a Saviour who is Christ the Lord. And this shall be a sign for you: you will find a babe wrapped in swaddling cloths and lying in a manger?" The Mighty and Holy One of Israel is this little child. Here is the revelation, the plan of the mystery hidden for ages in God who created all things. Had we been Mary or Joseph, one of the shepherds or magi, we would have found a baby in swaddling cloths, a baby poor and little, unknown and unrecognised, as Grimstone's lullaby says.

We would have seen the downy hair, the small, toothless mouth, the flaccid limbs stroking the air aimlessly, the tiny nails on the little fingers; we would have heard the cries, the gurgles and the splutters. And in all this the Image of the invisible God, the Word of the Ineffable God; the Firstborn of all creation, the Radiance of divine glory, the Alpha and the Omega. We may recall Jesus's answer to Philip: "He who has seen me, has seen the Father". That was as true at Bethlehem as it was when Jesus spoke to Philip.

The New Testament and all the ecumenical councils from Nicaea to Chalcedon—covering more than four and a half centuries—proclaim the same truth. This baby is, so to speak, on the inside of God. In and through this baby we come to know God in his innermost being. Who God is in himself as Word, is the one incarnate, Jesus the Baby. Here already is the utmost intelligibility, the deepest reality of the universe, final meaning and absolute truth. The truth of the enfleshment of the Word reveals that babyhood and childhood, as well as adulthood, belong equally to God, as God's very own. That is either sheer absurdity or else it is the literal truth. This baby is the Eternal Word made one of us. It is too fantastic to be false.

We are brought then face to face with a baby, not horizontally, but vertically. We have to look downwards. Generally speaking one has to look down to see newly-born babies: their cots or cradles are not usually on high shelves. Till then people spoke of God in the highest heavens, and we still do so in the *Sanctus* at Mass; they were convinced they had to look upwards to get God's direction. But at Bethlehem they had to look down, and that teaches us to proclaim also: 'Hosanna in the lowest' or at least 'Hosanna in the lower'.

To see a baby we have to stoop; we have bend our proud, stiff necks to see the baby Jesus. It is as though God found one sure way to teach us humility. At the other end of Jesus's life the people had to look up, to raise their heads and eyes, to see a broken, naked criminal on the cross. At Mass, when the priest lifts up the host and chalice, we see horizontally the same humility of God's Word in the silence and lowliness of the bread and wine. Bethlehem, Calvary and the Eucharist are the best commentaries to be found on St. Paul's words in Philippians: "Though he was in the form of God (Christ Jesus) did not think equality with God a thing to be grasped".

I have often wondered what is the precise difference between looking down at the Baby Jesus and looking up at the Crucified Lord, on the one hand, and gazing at the host at Mass, on the other. While certain theological nuances have to be made, it seems in the end there are hardly any differences at all. These are variations on the theme of God's humility. The Word of God was helpless as a baby, defenceless as a crucified criminal, and is made so very silent in the bread and wine.

Christmas compels us to ask ourselves what the Baby Jesus reveals about the inner side of God. Once we ask this, we find ourselves using words like love, tenderness, gentleness—in one word, *humanitas*. These blend perfectly with omnipotence, eternity, immutability—in one word, *divinitas*. The first set is just as disclosive or revelatory of God as the second set. God's divinity has to be reckoned with in terms of God's humanity, and vice versa. His love is all powerful, eternal, infinite, immutable; his omnipotence is loving, tender and gentle. The Baby Jesus is the way God's everlasting love begins to overthrow the powers of evil. This is the love, as Grimestone says, that does not finally end in sorrow.

The Cross as Gospel [1]

In the end was the Flesh
and the Flesh reigned over us,
and Humanity was the Flesh.
And the Flesh was made word
and was slain in our midst.
We have seen its horror,
horror as it is in all of us,
full of emptiness and lies.

The first Good Friday

It was afternoon, not quite three o'clock. The sky had turned black and the colours of the earth had fused into a green, threatening grey. Desolation had settled like dust over everything. On a hill outside the city where undesirables and enemies of law and order were got out of the way, stood the hated and terrifying cross. Nailed to it was a man twitching with pain, disfigured and tragic. At short distances soldiers hung about in twos and threes exchanging coarse jokes, callous and indifferent in their blind service of the almighty State. Close to the cross a few women and a young man huddled together, powerless and frantic with grief, not daring even to think the question: 'Why did it have to be like this?' They were staring into the mid-distance or at the ground not looking at one another for fear their eyes should meet and so confirm the hopelessness of it all. Blood, suffering, darkness, shame, indifference, mockery and incomprehension. Is this how love conquers all things?

But the end of the Flesh's hour and the power of darkness was approaching. Unexpectedly an awful cry pierced the numbness of the silence: 'Eloi, Eloi, lama sabachthani?' The question has echoed down the centuries:

[1] *The Scandal of the Cross,* Ed. N. McElwraith, London, Student Christian Movement 1982, pp. 6-19. This is a revised version of a talk given at the SCM assembly *Voice in the Wilderness.* Reproduced from MOVEMENT magazine by permission of the Student Christian Movement.

'My God, my God, why have you forsaken me?', and it received no answer. Is there an answer? Only the day before those same lips had asked Judas: 'Would you betray the Son of man with a kiss?', and that was not answered either. Was it betrayal once more, betrayal by abandonment and death?

The Cry of Desolation

The awful cry 'My God, my God, why have you forsaken me?' is recorded in Mark's gospel [15:34] and in Matthew's [27:46]. These words are the opening verse of Psalm 22 which is both a lament in suffering and a hymn of thanksgiving for deliverance of the individual believer. Some scholars have questioned whether this cry was actually uttered by Jesus, or whether it was put on his lips by the primitive church. But surely there would have been many other ways, far less scandalous and offensive, open to the first preachers of the gospel to show that Jesus was vindicated by God. It is noteworthy that Luke's gospel does not have the cry of abandonment, but a text from Psalm 31: 'Father, into thy hands I commend my spirit'. [23:46] There is no hint of abandonment there. When we come to John's gospel, desolation and abandonment are even more conspicuously absent. Having commended his mother and the disciple he loved to each other, in calm realisation that his mission was achieved, Jesus said: 'It is finished', then bowed his head and gave up his spirit [19:26-30]. The development is striking. It looks as if it became progressively more difficult for the church to reconcile Jesus' cry of desolation or sense of total abandonment with his status as Exalted Lord after the resurrection. As the first believers grasped more profoundly the relationship between Jesus and God, as God's Word incarnate, his experience of being abandoned by God became as much a stumbling block for Christians themselves as it was for the Jews, and at least as inexplicable to them as it was foolish to the Greeks.

There is every reason, then, to accept a firm historical basis for Jesus' cry of desolation. While it may be a little far-fetched to maintain that anybody would have the presence of mind to quote a psalm in the midst of the sufferings of crucifixion, it is no surprise that a man should scream out while undergoing such mental and physical agonies. Jesus died a terrible death. But there was even more than this involved. What passed into the earliest tradition, I would suggest, was a first-hand account of having heard a cry that was not only the result of excruciating sufferings, but also the effect of a sense of total desolation and abandonment by God. Jesus went utterly alone into the dark silence of death. I would argue, therefore, that the first verse of Psalm 22 was put on the lips of Jesus as an expression of total abandonment he experienced and which was witnessed by those present. This has many things to say to us about God.

The Aloneness of Death

There is an aloneness in death which belongs to its intrinsic structure. As we are born alone, so we die alone, just as we suffer alone. No matter how much health and comfort we may receive in our physical sufferings and mental anguish, we cannot really share our sufferings and anguish with others. We bear our sufferings in unutterable solitariness. All sufferings in life are symbols of death which forewarn us of the last aloneness we have to experience. The aloneness of death has to be endured and it cannot be abolished, not even by God, for then death would not be death. Undoubtedly, death can be actively accepted and even positively embraced, but nothing can take away its inner aloneness. When coupled with the sufferings of crucifixion, such aloneness must approach a state of terror. To be human is to have a beginning, to develop and then to die. No human being can be fully human until the experience of death has been endured. Thus the Word of God enfleshed was finally human in the moment of death's aloneness. The Word of God became human in a truly human becoming: conception to death.

In the aloneness of death Jesus cried out to God. He experienced its intrinsic, unalterable aloneness as abandonment. Abandonment was in fact an interpretation, a way of discovering meaning, of finding something intelligible, in what was so awful and absurd. The aloneness, however, was not abandonment by God in the sense that God could have chosen to do otherwise; rather, as I have maintained, it belongs to the structure of death.

The Cross and the Mystery of God's Will

The New Testament contains no mere speculation about God and creation. Creation is never envisaged without Christ. Indeed, the God and Father of our Lord Jesus Christ chose us in Christ before the foundation of the cosmos [cf. Ephesians 1]; Christ is the firstborn of all creation and in Him all things were created [Colossians 1]. God (the Abba, the Father of our Lord Jesus Christ) so loved the world (cosmos, the sum total of created reality) that he gave the only son (Jesus the Christ). The God who loves the cosmos is not alone power, a faceless energy or an eternal monad, but the God of our Lord Jesus Christ, who was related to Jesus in a unique bond of love. This gives the starting point of a specifically Christian doctrine of

God. God is a set of relationships, a holy community, a trinity, whose mysterious will is to share these relationships with us. That sharing was made possible and realised uniquely through the flesh of the Son of Man, through his historical existence. So it is that we discover in relationships, that is, by going beyond ourselves, by self-transcendence in union with Christ, to others.

Jesus the Christ has established the Community of God (Father, Word and Spirit) and the cosmos. God so loved the cosmos, not just the Jews or Roman Catholics, or the Orthodox or the Reformers or the Pentecostals. He so loved everything that he handed over the only Son. Without these relationships the cosmos cannot be cosmos, and it is quite impossible for us to be human in this world or the next. Jesus changed life on this side of death and on the other side of it: 'The Word became flesh' [John 1:14]; 'The Holy Spirit, whom the Father will send in my name, He will teach you all things, and bring you to your remembrance all that I have said to you'. [John 14:26] 'I go to prepare a place for you'. [John 14:2] 'Your father Abraham rejoiced that he was to see my day; he saw it and was glad'. [John 8:56] Christ 'went and preached to the spirits in prison, who formerly did not obey'. [1 Peter 3:19-20] 'For this is why the gospel was preached even to the dead, that though judged in the flesh like men, they might live in the spirit like God'. [1 Peter 4:6] At the death of Christ a set of relationships came to be beyond the grave, through the glorified humanity of Jesus, and that set of relationships is called heaven.

Jesus the Christ is the unconditional affirmation of the cosmos: 'The Word became flesh', God's Yes dwelt amongst us and so the flesh was made word. Through him the cosmos is enabled to be Amen, to utter Amen, which is a lovely way of saying 'yes' with graciousness to God. Jesus Christ is God's Yes; we are God's Amens [cf. 2 Corinthians 1:20].

Nothing can alter God's original purpose and will to share his life with us through Jesus the Christ. Not even the terrible power of evil, whose power rests precisely in its unintelligibility. Evil is not a problem nor a mystery; we solve problems and adore mysteries. Evil is the 'x' quantity in the cosmos, powerful and destructive in its unintelligibility.

We are saved, redeemed from evil, through the love-relationships established in Christ. The love that is salvation and redemption is not different from the love of God's original purpose to share with us his community life. Even if there had been no evil, our sharing in God's own life would have been no evil, our sharing in God's own life would have been no less a pure gift, for there is nothing in us that demands we share in God's own life. The self-same perfecting, divinising, humanising love of the eternal God choosing us in Christ before the foundation of the world, and therefore before sin and evil, is the love that heals and forgives as it transforms us into our true selves; that conquers evil as it diffuses its own unutterable goodness; that whispers truth and meaning where it finds lies and unintelligibility; that brings unity where there is fragmentation and division; that sheds light in the darkness which cannot master it; that gives life where it comes upon death and the powers of hell. Because of our historical condition of sin, evil, selfishness and lack of integrity, God's sanctifying love is of necessity redeeming, liberating and forgiving. To say Redeemer or Saviour is a way of saying Divine Lover.

Salvation so understood is given through the life, death and resurrection of Jesus the Christ. The cross is literally crucial in that process because the sacrifice it involved reveals with utmost clarity the presence of God's love in the cosmos. The cross belongs to the mystery of God's purpose from before the foundation of the cosmos. But we must be careful not to think that we have thereby explained it away. The cross remains a mystery hidden in the depths of God. It remains a mystery in God that his love went to the cross in the person of Jesus the Christ. It is the self-same love that creates, redeems and makes holy. The cross will be a stumbling block to be removed and a folly to be rationalised, until we are prepared to accept with trusting hearts what it says about God. 'Who has known the mind of the Lord or who has been his counsellor?' [Isaiah 40:13; Romans 11:34]; 'The Spirit searches everything, even the depths of God. . .so also no one comprehends the thought of God except the Spirit of God. Now we have received. . .the Spirit which is from God, that we might understand the gifts bestowed on us by God' [1 Corinthians 2:10-12]. The Spirit will lead us into the mystery of the cross.

God Transcendent and God Historical

The life of Jesus of Nazareth was a dialogue between himself and God the Abba. One can only pass over in silence what Jesus experienced when he withdrew to the hills to be alone with the Father. God was in Christ reconciling the cosmos which he loved to himself. The dialogue was between God transcendent and God historical. In the life, mission and death of Jesus, God actually experienced human existence in history. Until the conception and subsequent development of Jesus this had not been the case. What God knows about human existence in the depths of his wisdom is one thing; to experience that existence is quite another.

The relationship between God transcendent (the Father) and God historical (Jesus of Nazareth) reached its zenith in the cry of desolation from the cross. In freely deciding to take human existence to himself in a personal way, God accepted the entire structure of that existence and risked the rejection of his love. But this is not all. God historical actually experienced the rejection of his love and God transcendent was helpless before it. What must it have been like for God transcendent to witness the rejection of the Son he had loved since before the foundation of the world? What happened to the God of all comfort as Jesus suffered the ultimate aloneness in the midst of unimaginable sufferings? For sure he could not have been indifferent, much less have been in waiting for it to placate his anger or avenge his outraged justice. God's great power is his love, made known at first in the humility of a tiny infant, and proved at last in the defencelessness and aloneness of a dying man and the vulnerability of his own goodness.

We must allow God to be truly God and we must allow God to be truly human. I am sure that many of the problems and difficulties raised by believers and non-believers alike about the doctrine of the incarnation or *enhumanment* of the Word, are really symptomatic of a radical refusal by human beings to accept totally their own humanity with all its limitations, finitude, emptiness and desperate need of divine love. In other words, these problems and difficulties are symptoms of a mixture of fear and pride: Why should God want to be like us? Why on earth would the Infinite and Eternal Mystery of God want to immerse himself in an existence that is shot through with pain and anguish, poised precariously between a past that tyrannises over us through memory and a future that fills us with fear, and that ends in the aloneness of death? We can be as God is and we often make gods of ourselves, but God cannot be as we are. We cannot tolerate that. The doctrine of the incarnation not only raises the question about who Jesus is, it compels us to ask questions about who we are. I do not want to give the impression that there are no difficulties for us today about the doctrine of the incarnation, or to maintain that we can answer today's questions with yesterday's answers, for that would be to answer no questions at all. But what I do want to stress is that the God of Jesus Christ accepts and loves humanity and individual human beings more radically and profoundly than we do ourselves!

The Cross and our Understanding of God

The doctrine of the incarnation or enfleshment of the Word challenges every 'purely ration', speculative, philosophical conception of God. It requires of us not to force our preconceived and predefined notions of God as immutable, all-powerful and all-knowing into the Christian experience of God, but to draw out what the incarnation and the cross reveal about the silent Mystery that surrounds our being, grounds the cosmos and is the source of all our questions, our restlessness and our peace.

The mysterious Origin of existence as revealed in the Judaeo-Christian experience seems at the very least to have an immutability which manages to co-exist with change and decay. Is God's omnipotence only preserved if we argue that this is just one of the possible worlds he might have created? Does not the Christian experience of God hint that omnipotence might well be identical with the power to create, that is, to cause to exist what does not and cannot have existence in itself? Is not the infant Jesus the greatest sign of divine omnipotence? Does God have to know 'beforehand' future free decisions by human beings in order to be all-knowing? Can God understand evil? If he could, would there be evil at all? I realise these are questions, but I imagine they may well be good questions. And a good question has already dimly perceived the answer. Perhaps immutability is reason's way of expressing the unchangeable nature of God's love. Omnipotence, reason's astonished response to the fact that there is creation at all; omniscience, reason's clumsy articulation that God is the fount of all truth.

In any case, we are confronted with Bethlehem, Calvary and the Eucharist which reveal the powerlessness, defencelessness and silence of God historical. Have we really learned to believe that God was helpless infant, endangered by the elements and powers of this world? And what of the terrible death on Calvary where God transcendent was silent before the agonising cry: 'Why have you forsaken me?' And the Eucharist, what are we to say of that? There God-made-human, risen and glorified, is so little and so silent.

The experience of Jesus the Christ, witnessed in the New Testament, makes manifest that God loves us. That means he needs us, not only to do things for him, but to be for him. In becoming a human being God so revealed himself, so opened himself to the cosmos, that he penetrated into the depths of creaturely, fragmented, historical existence. Does not that mean, therefore, that god has taken human life, human suffering, our agonies and our death into himself forever?

The Fact of the Cross

In the post-resurrection era we know that the cross was both an end and a beginning. But did it look anything like a beginning on that dark afternoon? We must not permit our pride and comfortable existence as western Christians to beguile us. This really happened to Jesus, he was crucified in human history. The shadow of his cross lies on the Church until the end of history. The cross belongs to the history of Jesus and therefore also to the history of the Church. Without it there is no Church. All our theories and explanations, and even the revelation of hope fulfilled which it expresses, cannot obliterate the terrible and mysterious fact of it. There was the cross, and its shadow is cast across every explanation of its meaning and over the Church's every worldly success. Jesus died on the cross distanced in his loneliness from God transcendent, deserted by his friends, rejected by the priests, mocked by the people and scorned by the representatives of the greatest political power in the world, the Roman Empire.

The cross became the symbol of hope not because the crucifixion was neutralised but because it happened. The fact of the cross evangelises us, it proclaims the gospel to us. Its shadow falling on us highlights our selfishness and hatred and shows up in stark detail our need of love and grace. It is through the cross that the poor, the downtrodden, the hungry, the exploited and the oppressed evangelise us; it is through the cross that the hangman's noose, the gas chamber and the electric chair evangelise us; it is through the cross that the neutron bomb, guided missiles and the weapons of destruction that we have amassed evangelise us: for "when you did it to one of the least of these my brethren, you did it to me" [Matthew 25:40].

The cross stands in history as a fact of final destruction and defeat. Yet, of all the instruments of death humanity has devised, it alone has become a sign of lastingness and victory. No one wears an electric chair or a guillotine on a chain around the neck as a sign of hope or a talisman of good fortune. Perhaps deep down in our hearts we all know that love can never be defeated because not even the cruelty of the cross could destroy God's love for us.

God put his mark on us in the beginning when he created humanity in his own image and likeness. We retaliated by putting our mark on his beloved Son: the holes in the wrists, feet and side, the scars scourging and the wounds from the thorns. Yet God turned these signs of our hatred and selfishness—the stigmata of our Lord Jesus Christ—into the symbol of love and deliverance.

The Cross and the Power of Love

Recent developments in theology have laced timely and welcome emphasis on the Church's resurrection-faith. The resurrection is the sure ground of our hope and we are constrained to celebrate it. Above all, it saves the death of Jesus from futility. But we must remember that the resurrection belongs to the new world of God's reign and—while it is historical in that it brought about in our world a new presence of Christ through the power of Spirit which we experience as the body of Christ, the Church—as an experience of Jesus it cannot be called historical in the way he experienced the crucifixion.

There is a danger of complacency in emphasising the resurrection. As we have become more aware of the unity of the human race and more conscious of the injustice that divides east and west, north and south, our celebration of the resurrection, especially in the Eucharist, has become at least problematic, if not at times without credibility. As long as there is suffering, oppression and injustice in the universal human community, which can be abolished by human effort through a change of heart, there will always be a certain uneasiness in celebrating the resurrection of Jesus Christ. For this reason Christians are obliged to keep the fact of the cross at the forefront of their minds, as well as the truth of the resurrection. This will guarantee that Christians themselves will continue to be evangelised. And one can only pretend to be ignorant of what one as learned.

The crucifixion of Jesus is an event that took place in space-time. It was the last sacrament of God's love in the life and mission of Jesus. God historical lived among us without religious power, intellectual power or economic-political power. It is noteworthy that he was not born in Jerusalem, Athens or Rome. These worldly powers are frightening in their ambiguity.

Religious power unites the believers and separates them from the unbelievers and sinners; intellectual power unites the learned and separates them from the poor and the oppressed; political power unites the citizens of one state and separates them from the others. Jesus came among us as one who serves and, though devoid of these worldly powers, he was, by the humility of divine love, the holiest, the wisest and richest man the world has ever known, and was possessed of an authority unequalled in history.

Though he founded no religion, he showed us how to reach the Father together with one another; though he established no philosophical school, he taught a doctrine of sublime wisdom; though he outlined no economic policy, he left us riches and treasures that not all the money in the world can buy; though he formed no political party, he was himself the cornerstone of the universal human community.

God's Love and Ultimate Meaning

The cross is the proof that God's power is his love, and in God's love shared with us so graciously and abundantly, lies ultimate meaning. The historical experience which the disciples had in their relationship with Jesus brought them to a new knowledge of God which simply cannot be derived from rational reflection on the nature of this world. By their faith in the God of Israel they already knew that God acts in history and out of that faith they came to the awareness that Jesus is God-with-us historically, in person and action, life and death.

The experience of the life and death of Jesus disclosed the ultimate meaning of existence and all reality. The question about meaning enfolds in three problems: that of origin: how did we come to be? That of purpose: what is our value? That of destiny: where are we going?

First, it is revealed in Jesus Christ that we exist by a sovereignly free act of creation by God. We are not the accidents of fate nor the playthings of chance. We are because God wants us to be. We exist because we are loved; love's power created us. Thus by faith in the doctrine of creation we are able to hold together those contraries: that we began to be yet we were willed eternally to exist.

Secondly, our value and purpose lie in our call to be co-lovers of God and through his love brothers and sisters of his Son. Through grace we are made worthy to be partakers of the divine nature, co-heirs with Christ and first-born with him, and temples of the Holy Spirit. The mystery of divine grace is that God, loving us, wants us to love him and that is no pretence or fiction, but God's eternal will, the mystery of his purpose for us. Thus by faith in the doctrine of grace we can hold together those incompatibles: the awareness of our emptiness and the truth of our dignity in being made sharers of God's love of himself and all creation. Thirdly, our destiny is the glory of the kingdom. We are called to share in God's glory for everlasting ages when God will be all in all and where we will be loved and lovers in one. Thus by faith in the doctrine of eternal life we are able to conjoin those opposites: the certainty of death and the pledge of immortality and so live in peace with the tension between anxiety and hope.

The Cross and Meaning

Death, as the greatest of all passivities and diminishments we have to endure, appears as the dissolution of all meaning. Its utter aloneness brings to us who live a fear of final alienation. That fear in its turn gives rise to questions that make the heart go cold. Is there a real reason for our existence? Is there a purpose to our lives? Do we have a definite destiny? The fear of being finally alienated from ourselves, from the cosmos and from God is the result of evil. Evil drives love away and thus inexorably excludes God. The utter unintelligibility of evil caused the crucifixion and it drove a wedge between God transcendent and God historical. At the moment of Jesus' cry of desolation, God was never further from the world, and never more deeply immersed in its evil worldliness. God is to be found, therefore, as much in the ugliness of death's aloneness as he is present in the splendour of life's transformation in the resurrection. Only total surrender to death can preserve ultimate meaning for us.

The sorrow we feel for the sufferings of God historical who is Jesus and the compassion we may truly experience for God transcendent separated from him in the agony of dying and the aloneness of death, bring us face to face with our own humanity.

What does the perpetration of such a deed as the crucifixion say about our humanity? It exposes our selfishness, our fears, our insecurity and our cruelty. It tells us that we are prisoners in self-created cells grasping the little bit we think is ours and warding off every danger, real or imagined, that threatens to take it away from us. It proclaims that we have to sacrifice our very self if we are to be liberated and come to true humanity.

From what the cross reveals to us about our own humanity there follow grave political consequences. When we have examined ourselves under the shadow of the cross we are brought inevitably to consider the vile injustices in our sad world. What kind of humanity do we in the rich countries have, having made gain and consumerism the goals of our existence? What kind of humanity is it that allows us to live in apparent peace and contentment, while millions of people in the poor countries have only enough food to keep them starving till tomorrow? What kind of humanity is it that says colour and race are determinant factors in judging the value and dignity of an individual person? What kind of humanity is it that considers weapons of destruction more important than people? It is not the Marxist analysis of history, not the Manifesto of the Labour Party, not the right or the left, that first brought us face to face with our humanity; it is the cross of Jesus. I do not mean to make politics irrelevant nor to belittle political activity, but there are far graver reasons to work for justice than the teachings of political ideologies.

The Cross and Evangelisation

Because of the cross of Jesus, the poor and the oppressed evangelise us—the spiritually, psychologically and emotionally poor as well as the materially poor; and the oppressed in the First, Second, Third and Fourth Worlds. The cross shows us that the economically prosperous, the spiritually complacent and all oppressors have the greatest need of the gospel of justice and peace. The rich nations of the earth have more need of the proclamation of the word of God than the poor ones. The cross reveals that God still suffers in the brothers and sisters of Jesus the Christ. And this suffering God is helpless without our efforts to establish a just economic order and a world of peace and spiritual wholeness.

Humanity itself was there on the cross in Jesus and its solidarity in the Last Adam is infinitely deeper than that in the First Adam. In the cruel and incomprehensible death of God historical, love was victorious over all the evil and selfishness of human history. The cross of Jesus proved that God transcendent went to the furthest possible limits to reveal that his love cannot be withdrawn from humanity and that there is no power in this world or the next that can overthrow it.

We belong, then, to a fallen-redeemed world. We live under the shadow of the cross and in the light of the glorification of Jesus Christ. The power of God's love will be able to achieve its mighty deeds only to the extent that each of us strives to make it a reality in our lives, in our actions and in our relationships.

In the beginning was the Meaning
And the Meaning was with God,
And God was the Meaning.
And the Meaning became flesh
And dwelt among us.
We have beheld his glory,
Glory as of the only Son from the Father,
Full of grace and truth.

Our Anxious Faith[1]

St. John tells us in his gospel that Jesus made this prayer on the night before he died: "I do not pray for these only, but also for those who believe in me through their word" [17:20]. In that prayer Jesus prayed for all of us who, through no merits of ours, have received the gift of faith in Jesus Christ, the Saviour of the world. And I have a special reason to be grateful that his prayer included me.

I was ordained a priest on 16 July 1961. Two months later I set out for Rome to do doctoral studies in order to return to England to teach our students preparing for the priesthood.

At the college where I was staying in Rome there were about eighty priest-students from many provinces of the Order around the world. As concelebration was not yet customary, we all celebrated mass individually each day in the basilica crypt attached to the college. There were some forty altars in the crypt. We were divided into groups of two and each served the other's mass.

One morning in late November 1961, I had an experience that shattered me. I had just consecrated the host, elevated it and genuflected. As I came up from the genuflection, a voice in my head seemed to say: 'You don't believe that rubbish, do you?' It is not easy to describe the feeling that came over me at that moment. Words like darkness, desolation, emptiness say something of what I felt. The priest who was serving me thought I had taken ill. Anyway, I finished the mass and tried to ignore the whole thing.

But that proved impossible. The feeling of desolation grew, and nothing I could do would take it away. I was haunted by the thought that perhaps the mass might not be what the Church believes it to be. That led to a sense of uneasiness, shame and hypocrisy in me. There I was, barely four months a priest, studying for the doctorate in theology, and in Rome of all places, the centre of the Church, hallowed by the blood of St Peter and St Paul. The sense of uneasiness and shame brought in turn a feeling of resentment. I had always loved the blessed sacrament for as long as I could remember. As a

[1] JESUS CARITAS (Spring 1984) pp. 13-18. Published with permission.

boy I firmly believed that Our Lord had a little house in the tabernacle, and when I served mass I used to try to see inside through all the satin veils, when the priest opened it to get the ciborium to give us communion. It was linked in my head with *The Wind in the Willows* and countryside animals having little houses in the woods and under the hedgerows, little houses that were always snug and warm and welcoming. But now what was I to do? Everything seemed to have been swept away. Why? It was so unfair, I said to myself, so terribly wrong, and why should it happen to me?

The sense of shame also had its insidious effect. I could not confide in anyone or seek advice and direction. That I did not do so, was a grave mistake. But I was too ashamed and I was convinced that my experience would only evoke horror in a listener. So I carried it in my heart. Sometimes I was able to suppress and forget it and act as though all were well. But there was always daily mass.

This state of things continued for some months. Interiorly, I had a miserable Christmas. The experience would come lurking back in all its grimness at the most unexpected times. I remember one evening at a party in the college for the English-speaking friars, we were all invited to do a party-piece. When my turn came round, I got up from my seat and as I began to go to the other side of the room, the desolation came over me and I said to myself: 'They don't know what I'm like. They don't know my faith is in shreds'. But I shrugged it off as best I could and went on to do my party-piece, a sort of comic version of *The Vicar of Bray*.

One evening a few weeks later, it was now about the end of April 1962, I was sitting at my desk preparing a seminar for the next day, and I began to ask myself questions about this desolation, which had now become a constant, nagging, unnerving companion. I wondered what I was going to do. How could I minister in the Church as a priest not believing in the real presence? And then I asked myself: 'Could I be right and the whole Church wrong?' Who was I to challenge the life and belief of millions of people, a host of holy mystics and doctors in the long history of the Church? By what authority did I question the faith of my mother and father, of Cardinal Newman, of St Thomas and St Bonaventure and above all of St Francis himself, who loved the Holy Eucharist because it reveals so gently yet so graphically the humility and the tenderness of God? That evening proved to be a turning point. I resolved there and then that each day at mass I would ask God the Father through Jesus Christ Our Lord in the Holy Spirit, to enlighten me and give me the faith of the Church. Nothing happened suddenly, but somehow I managed to persevere with the prayer.

One morning some weeks later as I was saying the first of what in the Tridentine mass are the priest's communion prayers, these words leapt out at me: *ne respicias peccata mea, sed fidem Ecclesiae tuae*—"look not on my sins, but on THE FAITH OF YOUR CHURCH". That was it, the faith of the Church. That is what I had received, the faith of Christ's Church, and not all my anxieties and difficulties could alter or shake it. The faith is the Church's faith, and that is where we have to be, with the Church, above all when we have doubts and difficulties, problems, questions and anxieties.

Looking back some twenty-two years later on that awful experience, I feel now a sense of gratitude that I went through it. It engendered in me a deep compassion for people who have difficulties with faith or who feel they have lost their faith. But of course, I did not realise that at the time.

My first and now almost instinctive reaction when someone approaches me about difficulties in faith, is to say: 'Please go to mass, and daily, if you can; or, where possible. Come to mass with me'. Listening, explanations, analyses, advice and direction should follow that. We have one Teacher, the Christ [cf. Matthew 23:8], and he teaches interiorly, and nowhere more surely and limpidly than at mass. There the Lord Jesus is with us really, truly and in his very being, by his threefold presence: the mystical (the Church), the verbal (the scriptures), the sacramental (the Eucharist). The point is, to be where the Church in this world realises most truly of all her nature as sacrament of salvation: the mass. At mass, all of us together with the risen Saviour, despite our sins and weaknesses, our difficulties and anxieties about faith, form the Church which is something far beyond the mere sum total of those present. The Church's faith will save and sanctify us in this world and unto eternal life.

I have not used the word 'doubt' in these pages. That is due to theological caution. We use the word far too loosely, I think. While real, sinful doubt is possible in matters concerning the faith, it is extremely rare. In my own case, I really could not say if the experience I had was doubt or not. And since I cannot say it was, then it was not doubt in the strict, theological sense. The whole experience of difficulties and anxieties in faith is far too complex, too intricate and involved, to be investigated technically. And as Cardinal Newman wisely said: "Ten thousand difficulties do not make one doubt".

We ought not to worry that we get difficulties in faith. It is enough to have the difficulties, without worrying about having them! To experience difficulties about faith means that somewhere deep down inside us we are preoccupied with the things of God. This is a version of that experience in prayer when God is present by his absence. Faith is a life and it grows, changes and matures through being purified. It is a relationship with the God of Our Lord Jesus Christ in the Holy Spirit. On our side of that relationship, difficulties and anxieties can co-exist with the Church's faith which we have received.

Julian of Norwich wrote: "God said not 'Thou shalt not be tempested, thou shalt not be afflicted', but 'Thou shalt not be overcome' ". That is another way of saying what Christ said to St Peter and which he whispers to us all at mass: 'I have prayed for you that your faith may not fail' [Luke 22:32]. Not even Christ himself was exempted from temptation and affliction, from difficulties and anxieties, but he was not overcome. In Gethsemani we see all the majesty and power of God revealed in the lowliness and the weakness of our human nature.

We are desperately in need of assurance about ourselves, of hope for our future, of peace in our innermost being. We need God, the Holy One and all his love and mercy in order to accept ourselves and, what is more important, love ourselves with the love with which God loves us. Oftentimes our difficulties with faith arise more from worries about ourselves than from anxieties about God. And it is well worth keeping that in mind when difficulties with faith arise.

St. Peter wrote to the early Christians: 'Without having seen him you love him; though you do not now see him you believe in him and rejoice with unutterable and exalted joy' [1 Peter 1:8]. Most of us, I imagine, could make the early part of this verse our own. We have not seen the Lord, but we love him, or at least we want to love him, or want to want to love him—and this *is to* love him, for no one can desire to love God without the grace of the Holy Spirit. We do not see the Lord, but we believe in him, even if we have to go on repeating 'Help my unbelief'. But what about the latter part of the verse? Most us would be a little hesitant to affirm that 'we rejoice with unutterable and exalted joy'. Very often we believe in him and worry with all too real anxieties and dejected spirits. We try to make our way stumbling in the dark with heavy and anxious hearts. It is precisely because we do love him and believe in him without having seen him, that we worry and are anxious. If we did not believe in him and love him, there would be no difficulties, for sure; but then, there would be no peace and no meaning or purpose either.

Behind all our difficulties and anxieties with faith lies the experience of the psalmist: "O Lord, hear my voice when I call; have mercy and answer. Of you my heart has spoken: 'Seek his face'. It is your face, O Lord, that I seek;

hide not your face" [Psalms 26:7-9]. If we peer hard and long enough into the darkness, and hold on for grim death in the midst of all our difficulties and anxieties about faith, we will eventually see the holy face of Christ Jesus, as St. Therese of Lisieux somewhere says, smiling at us through the tears.

The Resurrection: Event of Faith[1]

On Easter Sunday morning the Pope proclaims before the world, from the central *loggia* of St. Peter's in Rome, the faith of the Holy Catholic Church: *Christus surrexit, Alleluia.* This proclamation is at the heart of the gospel message and is the foundation of the Church's faith. The life of grace, the redemption of mankind, the high moral teaching of the gospel, the hope of eternal life and the final destiny of mankind in the love of God, stand or fall by this fundamental doctrine. Every follower of Christ accepts without question that the Resurrection faith is crucial in this sense, at least, that the death of Jesus was not the end of things—and that the confession 'Jesus is risen' means that 'Jesus now lives'.

When, however, one descends to a detailed examination of what precisely is involved in this proclamation of faith, the plethora of opinions and the spectrum they cover, can be quite bewildering. One is at times driven to doubt the wisdom of building anything on the shifting sands of exegesis. It is not now beyond the bounds of probability that in a generation or so Rudolf Bultmann will have been turned completely on his head, when the search will be for the identity of the Jesus of faith with the Christ of history. A study of biblical literature at home and abroad reveals a puzzling lack of agreement on such important questions as: What is history? What is the relationship between fact and interpretation? (Do we read into or out of?) Is the Resurrection an historical event? Is the Resurrection to be understood solely as a new perspective on life? Was the Resurrection of Jesus an inference from personal faith? What are we to make of the appearances of Christ reported in the New Testament? How relevant is the empty tomb to the Church's Easter faith?

We must point out at once that in the present debate about the Resurrection of Christ, there is no serious theologian or exegete who denies or even calls into question the faith of the Church that Jesus has risen from the dead. The problem centres on the meaning and content of this faith assertion and on the extent to which the Resurrection is linked to historical events. In all scholarly writings on the Resurrection, even those which advocate an extreme

[1] THE TABLET 227 (21 April 1973) pp. 379f. Published with permission (www.thetablet.co.uk)

existential interpretation of the Easter faith, one discerns a profound humility. And humility is as much the mark of true scholarship as it is the proof of true discipleship. We need to emphasise also that the Church's Resurrection faith is never to be identified with how we imagine the Resurrection to have taken place. Moreover, it would be sheer folly to accept and understand the gospel accounts of the Resurrection as these latter were accepted and understood in the days before biblical criticism. No one can ignore, except to his peril, the findings on the nature of the New Testament writings that have resulted from the most painstaking research of the last few decades. The isolated cases one comes across where a speaker avows it his prime intention to shock, while grossly irresponsible—especially when not even a hint is given that there are other scholars (not usually in the audience) who hold equally well-grounded yet diametrically opposite opinions—can in no way neutralise the value of biblical scholarship. We know now, for example, that any attempt to construct a chronology of the events from the first Easter Sunday to the Ascension and beyond, is doomed to failure. We simply do not possess the material for this kind of construction. There are too many contradictions, (when and where, for example, Christ appeared), too many conflicting traditions, too much evidence of embellishment, to write what we mean by history. In any case it is clear that such was never intended by the writers in the first place.

Most people are now aware of the profound influence that the writings of Rudolf Bultmann and Willi Marxsen have had on all theological understanding of the Resurrection. It is perfectly understandable that a believer who accepts completely the views of Bultmann and their philosophical basis, will be thoroughly satisfied with the explanation that faith in the Resurrection is identical with faith in the saving efficacy of the cross. He will be quite happy to assert that the Resurrection took place on Good Friday. Since he holds with Bultmann that the Resurrection is a myth depicted in mythical language, once the process of demythologising is rounded off he will quite logically maintain that the miracle of Easter is not appearances nor an empty tomb, but the faith of the disciples. If, however, another believer accepts neither the views of Bultmann nor their philosophical basis, but maintains rather, from his reading and study of the New Testament documents, that some happening, experience or event must have *produced* the faith of the disciples, he has a very long Tradition on his side. Furthermore, he will find that there are weighty authors to support his point of view. We may mention, for example, Wolfhart Pannenberg and von Campenhausen. At this level of comparison there are at least equally cogent grounds for both views. When we press the point, the question remains whether or not there are equally cogent reasons to maintain on one side that we can know nothing more than the faith assertion: 'Jesus now lives' and, on the other side, that we can know something quite definite about the content of the Easter faith, over and above the simple assertion 'Jesus now lives', and something more than the death of Jesus on the cross. It appears to us that there are not equally cogent reasons for both these positions.

We should note that it is not our view that the empty tomb can prove the Resurrection faith of the Church. From a historico-exegetical standpoint there are sufficient grounds to hold that the tomb was empty. Now, the gardener may have been responsible for this, as the Jews later maintained. In fact it is reported that the Jews in the 2nd century dragged a body round the streets as clear proof that Jesus had not risen from the dead! The Resurrection of Christ is a mystery of faith in which Christ is revealed as the victor over death forever and in which God's total and irrevocable possession of the world is made manifest. We are treating, therefore, of a unique event, the Resurrection of God's Son and Messiah and man's Saviour and King. The empty tomb is not asserted as the ground of our faith in the risen Lord; on the contrary, it is our understanding in faith of the meaning of the Resurrection of the risen Christ that leads us to the assertion that the tomb was empty: To hold in this context that the tomb was empty is not an exterior support for faith (though it has apologetic value) but rather a specification of the content of faith based on our understanding of Christ's Resurrection.

It is not possible to give here even the briefest analysis of the New Testament narratives of the Resurrection of Christ, nor even the most summary account of the present state of exegesis. The following points, however, have been selected as most worthy of notice.

1. It is *a priori* acceptable, legitimate and fully consonant with the historical nature of the Judaeo-Christian revelation to attempt to discern the precise relationship any part of that revelation may have with historical events.

2. The Jewish understanding of resurrection contained the belief of a resuscitation of the corpse. This was not in the sense of a revivification to this life as reported in the gospels of Lazarus, Jairus's daughter and the son of the widow of Naim because, evidently, these died again subsequently. Resurrection-life was understood as an existence of another dimension altogether and, as has been said, it involved the transformation of the dead body. It is in this sense that we take the Resurrection of Christ and indeed must take it, whatever difficulties men of our time may have about molecules and chemical combinations. We are not dealing here with our resurrection, nor with our understanding of 'resurrection' and 'body', but with the unique Resurrection of Christ as made manifest in the Jewish world of the 1st century.

3. 1 Corinthians 5:1-11. It seems that far too much is made of the fact that Paul does not mention the empty tomb. This text, it must be borne in mind, is one form of the tradition. Though it is the most ancient *literary form* of the tradition of the Resurrection faith, we must not allow ourselves to be trapped into thinking that this alters the fact that the gospel accounts, patently later in literary form, contain elements of a stage of the tradition which are much earlier than that of 1 Corinthians 5. To that very early tradition pertains the discovery of the empty tomb. In *The Tradition-History of the Resurrection*[2] Ulrich Wilckens warns us "against allowing our judgement on the whole history of the tradition to be influenced by the history of the literary material".

4. It must be accepted until there is solid and unassailable evidence to the contrary that Paul assumed the transformation of Jesus's body (much more than, though including, the resuscitation of the corpse) and therefore the empty tomb.

5. There are solid reasons to maintain that the verb 'appeared' (*ophthe*) used here by Paul, means that Cephas and the Twelve (v. 5 belongs to the oldest tradition) were conscious of a confrontation with an objective reality. This is not to argue that the risen Lord was, or could have been, 'seen' by all and sundry. 'To see' the risen Christ requires grace and faith. With Wolfhart Pannenberg we may take Paul's experience on the road to Damascus as the norm for understanding all the appearances mentioned in the gospels.

6. The early Church believed in the Resurrection of Christ on the authority and testimony of official witnesses. The faith of the witnesses was the effect of this experience. It is otherwise impossible psychologically to account for the change in attitude of the apostles.

7. The discovery of the empty tomb belongs to the most primitive pre-literary tradition.[3] Women discovered the empty tomb. As women could not be official witnesses, since their word counted for nothing, it is decidedly odd that the later literary tradition did not use the discovery of the empty tomb to the best of its advantage by having the apostles (the official witnesses) discover it. There can be no doubt that we have here an original, preliterary, historical kernel. Of course the New Testament does not invoke the empty tomb as the

---

[2] *The Significance of the Message of the Resurrection for Faith in Jesus Christ,* ed. C.F.D. Moule, SCM Press Ltd. 1970, pp. 56f.
[3] Wilckens, op. cit., p. 73.

foundation of the Easter faith. This, it has been suggested, is precisely because it was found by women.

8. The Resurrection faith could not have been proclaimed in the city of Jerusalem if the tomb had not been empty.

9. As a conclusion from our faith we can legitimately assert with Pannenberg that God removed the body of Jesus from the tomb by a miracle. It is ever God's ways in the economy of salvation to deal with the recipients of his revelation according to their understanding and beliefs.

10. The resuscitation and transformation of the body of Jesus Christ reveals most unambiguously of all that there is a cosmic dimension and significance to Christ's victory over death and corruption. In the Resurrection of Christ the world is taken up radically into God's own life in the glorified body of Christ as a gratuitous act of love by re-creation.

We see, then, no compelling reason at the moment to alter our view that the faith of the Church in the Resurrection of Christ contains an intimate link with historical events, namely, the objective experience of the official witnesses to the risen Lord—an experience which changed their lives—and the empty tomb. These events belong to the faith of the Church in the uniqueness of Christ as Mediator, Lord and Victor over death.

Finally, our faith in the Resurrection of Christ comes to us through the living tradition of the Church. That tradition is found in its fullness only where the followers of Christ gather together with the bishop in communion with all bishops, in union with the Apostolic See of Rome, around the altar to hear the holy Word and receive the blessed Sacrament of Christ's Body and Blood. There in the mystical and eucharistic Body of Christ is made present through grace, power and love the risen and glorified Saviour of the world.

Victory[1]

Several years ago, Charing Cross, one of the stations on the London Underground, had its name changed to Embankment. This was something of a disappointment to me. Only a few months before, while travelling on the Underground from Liverpool Street to Victoria, I was gazing up at the map of the lines opposite, when suddenly the order of the stations from Temple to Victoria made me think of the paschal mystery.

Here was a passing from the Old Covenant (Temple) to the death of Christ (Charing Cross), from there to the holy sepulchre (Westminster—the Abbey church, a fraction strained perhaps?) and the garden of the resurrection (St. James's Park) and so to the exaltation of Christ (Victoria). However, the change to Embankment put paid to that little meditation and ever since I have had to be content with reading the advertisements.

The point I wish to stress is that *Victoria* is an exact and sublime description of the resurrection of Jesus Christ. This is the greatest victory the world will ever know, whether it recognises it or not. All other victories, whether claimed by Greeks or Romans, Jews, Christians or Muslims, Americans or Russians, vaporise into insignificance when set beside the victory of Christ.

The battle with the powers of evil is over and the final victory is accomplished. By his wondrous cross and glorious rising Christ defeated sin and death, so that these, despite any indications to the contrary, cannot have the last word.

The Church carries in her heart the assurance that the world's total situation has been altered because its final consummation has begun. Even though the earth should endure for 10,000 million years more, no darkness will ever overpower the light of Christ, no hatred will ever destroy his love.

The Church's vocation is to become more manifestly the Assembly of the Risen One. To become this, it rests on each of us to achieve in our life and death the victory irrevocably accomplished through the cross and resurrection of Christ. For that we have God's love, the grace and life of Christ and a share

---

[1] THE TABLET (April 21, 1984) pp. 379f. Published with permission (www.thetablet.co.uk).

in the Holy Spirit. There have gone before us countless saints and martyrs from the age of Nero and Domitian to Maximilian Kolbe, Paul VI and Oscar Romero in our time, who testify that the kingdom of this world is ultimately powerless.

The resurrection reveals the unchanging love of God the Almighty Father for all that he has created. God so loved the world that he both gave his only Son and raised him from the dead. The resurrection reveals that the Father totally accepted the life and sacrificial death of his incarnate Son, and there is the reason he could not let his Holy One see corruption. It is the consummation of God's saving and sanctifying activity on behalf of humanity and all creation.

The Crucified rose to the new life of glory in the fullness of his sacred humanity, body, blood and soul, inseparably united with his resplendent divinity. Jesus Christ is alive in a way no one—without him has ever been alive, whether in this world or the next. His resurrection is unique and through it he has brought eternal life into this world and into the next. By his rising he changed life on this side of the grave and he brought new life to those on the other side of the grave, and in that sense he created heaven, indeed he is heaven: 'Abraham rejoiced that he was to see my day; he saw it and was glad' [John 8:56].

This mysterious and salutary event is the ground of our faith, the reason for our hope and the source of our love.

When our memory taunts and oppresses us, we can look back to the dying and rising of Christ and know that our sins were already forgiven even before they were ever committed. Let faith, then, bring us to accept our past and so to forget it.

When our mind is full of anxieties about how we will cope, about what will happen to us, we can look forward to the second, radiant appearance of Christ and know that he is coming towards us out of the future. It will tell us that he will always be there, in his majesty and gentleness, at any crucial or decisive moment in our lives (including our death), just before we get there ourselves. Let hope, then, lead us to commit ourselves to our unknown future and so to wait for it.[2]

When our will with all its weaknesses mocks our efforts to be better and holier people, we can lift up our hearts to the eternal Now, the Today of God, and share in the love of the Sacred Heart of Jesus for his Father, for ourselves and for all creation. Let love, then, guide us to live the sacrament of

---

[2] Editors' note: Doyle wrote this just four months before his death on 25 August 1984.

the present moment and so to rest serenely in the arms of the Beloved whose embrace is irresistible.

Haec est dies quam fecit Dominus: Easter Day is the Day that the Lord has made. It is the Lord's Day par excellence. It is the Day towards which all the years before it were heading and from which all the years after it take their origin. It is the Day that has enfolded all our days and nights, the Day that assures us that out groanings for redemption are not in vain, that our sighs for union are not futile, that out longings for authenticity and the fullness of humanity will not be disappointed.

The victory, then, is accomplished. Jesus Christ is risen and he is with us. He promised: 'Lo, I am with you always, to the close of the age' [Matthew 28:20].

He is with us now in the assembly of his Church just as he stood among his first followers and greeted them: 'Peace be with you'. He is with us in sacred scripture as truly as he proclaimed in the synagogue, after reading the prophet Isaiah: 'Today this scripture has been fulfilled in your hearing' [Luke 4:21]. He is with us in the holy Eucharist, really, truly and in his very being, just as he gave himself at the Last Supper and hung on the cross on Calvary Hill.

He is there in baptism as truly as he stood in the River Jordan to be baptised himself by John the Baptist. He is with us in confirmation as truly as he promised the Paraclete to his disciples. He is there in holy matrimony as truly as he performed his first miracle at Cana for a newly married couple.

He is with us in the sacrament of reconciliation as truly as he pronounced over Mary of Magdala that her sins were forgiven her. He is there in holy orders as truly as he commissioned his Apostles to go out and teach all nations and baptise them in the name of the Triune God. He is there in the anointing of the sick as truly as he healed the blind and the lame and cured Simon Peter's mother-in-law, who then got up and served him at table.

He is with us each day throughout our lives as truly as he visited the house of Zacchaeus, had a meal with the tax collector Levi and walked the highways of Galilee and the narrow streets of Jerusalem. And he is there in holy viaticum as truly as he took Dismas, the thief crucified beside him, into the glory of paradise to be with him for ever. Amen.

Christus surrexit. Alleluia.

The Living Spirit[1]

'Yes' and 'No' are little words, but my goodness, what powers they hold. They have determined the course of history and so often they bring irrevocable changes to our lives. One might consider, for instance, the *Fiat* or 'Yes' of the Blessed Virgin Mary. Their meaning can be communicated in myriad ways, by sounds, through signs or from movements.

The apostolic faith of the Church proclaims that the Word was made flesh, that the Son of the living God submitted himself to the conditions of our life and the laws of our history. By the inscrutable designs of God, the human race and all creation have their origin, purpose and destiny in him whom Karl Barth described irreducibly as the Electing God and the Elected Man.

The Word was made flesh. We may put the question, humbly but legitimately: Which word was made flesh? And St Paul, the teacher of the nations, gives us the answer: The word is 'Yes'. 'For the Son of God, Jesus Christ. . . was not Yes and No; but in him it is always Yes. For all the promises of God find their Yes in him. That is why we utter the Amen through him to the glory of God' [2 Corinthians 1:19f].

Therefore, in the beginning was the Yes and the Yes became flesh and dwelt among us. The life, death and resurrection of Christ reveal that God is faithful, that he is for us, not against us, that he is the Affirming God who whispered his divine Yes into our world and over each one of us.

To hear the Yes of God we must first deny ourselves, say the No to ourselves which grace makes possible: 'If any man would come after me, let him say No to himself and take up his cross and follow me' [Matthew 16:24]. Then we can utter the Amen (a biblical and beautiful way of saying Yes) to God, to ourselves and to the world around us.

Lent is the Church's time of No and the annual reminder that we need to do penance. Prayer, fasting and almsgiving form a traditional triad and the unity among them should, where possible, be preserved.

But we need to be watchful not to let the charitable element in almsgiving obscure or relativise the penitential element in fasting and other forms of mortification. It is utterly right to give to the needy the often

[1] THE TABLET (March 10, 1984) p. 246. Published with permission (www.thetablet.co.uk).

substantial amounts we save by Lenten sacrifices. Still, when we know it will make us feel the pinch, even just a little, there remains a place for giving up sugar or refusing without ostentation that second helping of plum pudding.

There are creative forces and life-giving hopes in us which drive us to search for union with the world of our experience, human and divine, with the world we love and feel and know. As experience shows, however, these drives and hopes so easily run riot and get out of control, that they speedily become death-dealing and destructive. Only by constantly saying No to ourselves can we keep them life-giving and creative. By penance, then, we also observe the law of evangelical charity. To deny ourselves is to love ourselves and our neighbour. To die to self is to live to God and for the others.

People sometimes say "Life is only lent to us". And there is a truth in that. But we can turn the saying round and, having resolved on our penances, put oil upon our heads, washed clean our faces and proclaimed now is the favourable time, this is the day of salvation, with rejoicing exclaim "Lent is truly life to us".

The Essential Unity of the Church—
Some Consequences for Ecumenism[1]

History is a fascinating and dangerous subject—fascinating because it tries to chart developments and dangerous because it gets at facts. It discovers that there are certain constants in human nature, behaviour, and institutions, and it reveals that many things have not always been the same. That is the case with the history of the Christian church. In this article I want to highlight some of the implications for ecumenism when, for example, Roman Catholic theology takes seriously that the church is a *historical* reality. The first part examines what essential unity the church of Christ possesses, and the second draws out briefly the consequences for a more primary meaning of apostolic succession, the validity of orders, and of what is held to be of divine law in Roman Catholic ecclesiology.

Part I

The Resurrection Faith

The basic truth of the Christian faith is the resurrection of Jesus Christ, and the church stands or falls by it. Experience of the Risen Lord in the primitive church revealed to his followers the decisive significance of Jesus' person, life, and mission. They knew he was alive after his death in a way no one before had ever been alive. His significance was proclaimed by accredited witnesses and celebrated in a holy meal. Others who responded to this proclamation were baptised into the death and resurrection of Christ for the forgiveness of sins and a sharing in his risen life. This same resurrection faith is the unique ground of the church's existence today, and every authentic ecclesiology has its starting point in it.

In the hierarchy of Christian beliefs this is the first, and it is professed by all Christ's disciples. Without it no one can claim the name Christian and no group can call itself the church. Furthermore, every doctrine that Christianity professes is derived from that belief, and all church order developed out of it.

[1] JOURNAL OF ECUMENICAL STUDIES 20 (Spring 1983) pp. 245f. Published with permission.

From the Roman Catholic position, for example, the doctrines of the Immaculate Conception and the Assumption of the Virgin Mary, as well as the primacy and infallibility of the pope, are held as contained in the resurrection faith and as consonant with the whole of Christian revelation. Had they not been so judged, they could not have been defined.

Belief in the Risen Christ is a gift of grace. It is neither the result of reasoning nor a conclusion from historical evidence. That belief involves the recognition of Jesus Christ as Lord and brings with it a sharing in the unity of God. The way Jesus Christ is alive relates him to the whole of humanity and to all creation.[2] There is a solidarity *in Christ,* the Risen One, of which the church is the universal sacrament. To profess the lordship of Christ affirms that he is the source of all authority in the church, that he is the primordial sacrament of God's love, from which all other sacraments have their efficacy, and that the actions of the church as his body are the actions of Christ. As St. Augustine puts it: "Peter may baptise, yet it is Christ who baptises; Paul may baptise, yet it is Christ who baptises; Judas may baptise, yet it is Christ who baptises".[3]

The Shared Unity of God

Through the resurrection faith the church shares in the unity of God which is a unity-in-diversity, because it is a sharing in the unity of the Blessed Trinity, that is, the Holy Community of God—Father, Word, and Spirit. Christians believe and proclaim a unique form of monotheism which holds in vital tension a unity and a plurality. The God of our Lord Jesus Christ is not an eternal monad, not a lone power. God is a unity of eternal and essential relationships. For the Christian the Ground of Being is a set of relationships; to be is to-be-related.

To share the unity of God is to be brought into a set of relationships in which personal uniqueness is affirmed and enhanced. The gift of uncreated grace (sharing in the life of Father, Word, and Spirit), from which derives the gift of created grace (the new creature which results from sharing God's trinitarian relations), brings the church into existence. So it was that St. Cyprian described the church as: "a people brought into unity from the unity of

---

[2] See P. Chirico, *Infallibility: The Crossroads of Doctrine,* Sheed Andrews and McMeel Inc., Kansas City 1977, p. 168: "It is the fullness of humanity attained in resurrection that makes Christ the fullness of revelation for us. Because in him all the capacities of humanity are realized, he is capable of expressing his unique divine sonship to every aspect of creation".

[3] *In Iohannis Evangelium* VI, 7 in: PL 35, 1428.

the Father, the Son, and the Holy Spirit".[4] The church's unity is a sharing in God's unity in which the Father is not the Son, the Son is not the Spirit, the Spirit is not the Father. As St. Athanasius explained against the Arians:

> For they are 'one thing' not in the sense of a thing divided into two parts, these being nothing but one thing; nor in the sense of one thing with two names, so that the Son is at one time Father, at another time his own Son. . . .But they are two in that the Father is father and not also son; the Son is son and not also father. . . .thus, since they are one, and the godhead itself is one, the same things are predicated of the Son as of the Father, except the title of 'Father'.[66]

The Unity for which Christ Prayed

This is the unity for which Christ prayed: 'Holy Father keep them in thy name, which thou hast given me, that they may be one even as we are one' [John 17:11]. We do not create this unity, and it cannot be realised by our efforts. It is the result of Christ's prayer. This unity, therefore, is not the aim of the ecumenical movement but is its cause. The ecumenical movement came into being because of it and through it. And, even if there were not different denominations in the church of Christ as we know them today, this shared unity of God would still be both a gift and a task to be achieved. It is a sad fact of our experience that the various denominations are divided within themselves because of the power of evil. Indeed, the evidence is that the divisions within the several denominations of the church are often graver and more scandalous than the divisions among the denominations. Sin exercises its power in every denomination of the church. It weakens and would even destroy our unity with God, and by deceit it convinces one denomination that it is irreparably divided from another.

The gift of God's unity is the source and means of all our efforts to remove what really divides us. It sheds a light that lets us see that unity is not uniformity and that diversity is not division. It brings healing to our memory, both individual and especially communal. Our divided, common memory leads us, for example, if we are Roman Catholics, to consider that the Protestants of the sixteenth century were simply in bad faith, and, if we are Protestants, to

---

[4] *Liber de Oratione Dominica* 23 in: PL 4, 636: *et de unitate Patris et Filii et Spiritus Sancti plebs adunata.*

[5] *Contra Arianos* III, 4 in: PG 26, 327-330. The translation is from H. Bettenson (ed.), *The Early Christian Fathers. A Selection from the Writings of the Fathers from St. Clement of Rome to St. Athanasius,* Oxford University Press, London, Oxford, New York 1969, pp. 286f.

judge that the Roman Catholics had long ceased to be evangelical Christians at all. God's shared unity is the key which unlocks the treasures of diversity and makes clear that most of what we call our divisions are really God-willed and God-blessed diversities. It brings us to recognise that we are often zealous, not for Christian unity, but for an un-Christian uniformity.

Holy, Catholic, Apostolic

As with unity, so also holiness, catholicity, and apostolicity are first gifts of God and then tasks to be achieved. The church is holy because the Holy Spirit was given after the glorification of Christ. By the gifts of wisdom, understanding, counsel, knowledge, courage, holiness, and awe of the Lord, the church bears witness to God as the sublime and adorable Holy Mystery. God's holiness is integrity in which the divine being and will are one. Sharing in that integrity, the church in every member is called to growth in holiness by deeper incorporation into the Risen Christ under the promptings of the Holy Spirit. The church is catholic because it shares in the community life of Father, Word, and Spirit. It participates in the *perichoresis* or co-inherence of God's irreducible diversity. This gift carries with it the task of bringing the various peoples of the earth into communion with God so that their variety and uniqueness are preserved and enhanced, through belonging to a community which is more than the sum total of its several members.

The church is apostolic in the first place because the Son was sent to the world. He is the Apostle sent from the distant nearness of God's triune life to reveal the mystery of the divine purpose to unite all things in the Beloved in whom we were chosen before the foundation of the world. Because the Son was sent, the church is made one; because the church is sent, the world will be made one. The church is apostolic, secondly, because the Holy Spirit was sent. The mission of the Holy Spirit is to bring back to the church's mind all that Christ said. And, because Christ is what he said, the Holy Spirit makes the Risen Christ truly present in our midst. The church is apostolic, thirdly, because it is founded on the Apostles. The Twelve were first a community before they were sent, *Apostoloi*. In the Twelve the church was sent to proclaim Christ in the power of the Spirit. The church is apostolic, fourthly, because each Christian is sent at the end of every Eucharist to share with others what God graciously accomplishes in Christ.

The Easter People

It is a disturbing fact that Christians are not commonly recognised by others as the people who believe in the Risen One, as the people of hope, the people who await Christ coming toward them out of the future. If the resurrection is not our distinguishing feature in the common mind, then what have we done to the gospel?

There are obviously complex reasons for this—sociological and psychological, as well as theological. At the risk of oversimplification, it seems to have a good deal to do with our appearing to be moralisers. We seem adept at telling people what to do; we rarely seem capable of sharing with them how to be. I do not mean to question the sublime moral teaching of Christianity, but that teaching ought to come across for what it truly is: a consequence of the new life of grace and a liberation from the demands of the law. The Christian gospel and mission is first and foremost about meaning, about *Logos,* the meaning of life, suffering, and death, the meaning of history, the meaning of matter, flesh, and spirit. We derive meaning from the truth of the Risen One in our midst, and this is what ought to define us.

If we look at how the various denominations are commonly identified, not only is belief in the Risen Christ not mentioned, but something else is substituted as our distinguishing feature. Roman Catholics, for example, are identified as those who have to go to Mass on Sundays and, until recently, as those who had to eat fish on Fridays. The latter has now become opposition to contraception. I recently heard Methodists described as the Christians who are against drink! Anglicans are known in Britain as the Church of England, and in the United States as Episcopalians. Sometimes the Queen is mentioned as having a connection with the Church of England.

The very titles we have given ourselves say nothing about our belief in the Risen Christ: Roman Catholics, Orthodox, Anglicans, Lutherans, Methodists, United Reformed, Baptists, Calvinists, Presbyterians, and so on. Who thinks of the Risen Saviour, the Exalted Lord of life and death, when they hear these titles? How sadly relevant Paul's words continue to be: 'For while there is jealousy and strife among you, are you not of the flesh, and behaving like ordinary men? For when one says, "I belong to Paul", and another, "I belong to Apollos", are you not merely men?' [1 Corinthians 3:34].

The most urgent ecumenical task for the church of Christ is to become more clearly what it is: the people of God and the assembly of the Risen Lord. This will do more to create unity among the churches and in the world than all our debates about what divides us. In the unity we share in God we have a unity to strive for, namely, the unity of contemplative prayer and the unity of the combined effort to create a just and peaceful world through the unity of intercommunion, that is, of sharing in the Lord's table as the symbol of the unity we share in our belief in the Risen Christ. Agreed common action needs shared communion as its inner dynamic and constant support.

Belief in the resurrection of Jesus Christ and the God-given unity, holiness, catholicity, and apostolicity that are inseparable from it forms the essential unity of the church of Christ. Everything we hold about God, humanity, and the world, all our particular emphases, all our distinguishing practices and specific features are derived from the resurrection faith.

Part II

Apostolic Succession

Once this essential unity is granted, important questions begin to arise, first in regard to the meaning of apostolic succession. Is it not doctrinally sound, theologically acceptable, and historically credible to understand this as "continuity in the faith of the apostolic Church?"[6] This designation emphasises the ecclesial character of succession. In the foundational sense it is the church as the people of God which succeeds to the apostolic church rather than a particular group in it—say, the bishops. This is not to question that the bishops succeed to the apostles in some—though not all—of their functions. But that is the case because the church as such succeeds to the apostolic church.

In this connection the order of the first three chapters of the Constitution on the Church of Vatican II, *Lumen gentium,* is of crucial significance. The document opens with a doctrinal reflection on the mystery of the church, then moves to consider the model of the church as the people of God, and comes only in the third chapter to treat of the hierarchical structure of the church and, in particular, the episcopate.[7] Succession to the apostolic church is discerned and assured by belief in the Risen Christ as truly present and active in the world, for this is succession in the apostolic faith in its most fundamental sense. 'And they devoted themselves to the apostles' teaching' [Acts 2:42]; 'Where two or three are gathered in my name, there I am in the midst of them' [Matthew 18:20]—the oldest community-order of the primitive church.[8] Where the resurrection of Christ is proclaimed, there is the church, and

---

[6] See Hans Küng, ed., *Apostolic Succession. Rethinking a Barrier to Unity,* Concilium 34 (New York: Paulist Press, 1968).

[7] *Sacrosanctum Oecumenicum Concilium Vaticanum II. Constitutiones Decreta Declarationes* (Rome: Typis Polyglottis Vaticanis, 1974), pp. 93-150.

[8] See J. Duss-von Werdt, *What Can the Layman Do Without the Priest?,* in: H. Küng, *Apostolic Succession,* p. 114.

"where the Church is, there is the Spirit of God; and where the Spirit of God is, there is the Church and every kind of grace".[9]

The more specific meaning of apostolic succession held by Roman Catholics, the Orthodox, and a significant section of the Anglican Communion, according to which bishops succeed to the apostles, is derived from the foundational meaning just explained. This derived and secondary meaning is a valid interpretation of and development from the primary meaning. However, it does not and cannot render every other interpretation simply invalid or erroneous. The principal reason for this is that historically there were many expressions and interpretations of fidelity to the apostolic teaching in the New Testament times and varied developments up to and beyond the time of St. Ignatius of Antioch. On the other hand, the church of Christ has never existed without proclaiming the Risen Christ, recognising his lordship, and celebrating his living presence in a holy meal by appointed or elected leaders.

Validity of Orders

The phrase 'validity of orders' is an unhappy one and would be better replaced by 'authenticity of commissioned ministry', which derives from the ecclesial character of a denomination in the church of Christ. According to Roman Catholic ecclesiology, the church of Christ subsists in the Roman Catholic Church "although many elements of sanctification and of truth may be found *(inveniantur)* outside of its visible structure, which, as gifts *belonging to the Church of Christ* (my italics), are forces compelling towards Catholic unity".[10] If we seek what these elements might be, we find them listed in the Decree on Ecumenism of Vatican II:

Moreover, some, even very many, of the most significant elements and endowments which together go to build up and give life *to the Church itself* (my italics), can exist *(exstare possunt)* outside the visible boundaries of the Catholic Church: the written Word of God; the life of grace; faith, hope and charity, with the other interior gifts of the Holy Spirit, as well as visible

---

[9] St. Irenaeus, *Adversus Haereses* III, 24, 1 in PG 7, 966. The translation is from Bettenson, *Early Christian Fathers,* p. 83.

[10] *Lumen gentium* 8 in *Vaticanum II. Constitutiones, p.* 105. The translation is from Edward H. Peters, ed., *De Ecclesia. The Constitution on the Church of Vatican II* (London: Darton, Longman & Todd, 1964), p. 74.

elements. All of these, which come from Christ and lead back to him, belong by right "to the one Church of Christ".[11]

Since the text of the Constitution on the Church uses the subjunctive *inveniantur* (may be found) and the Decree on Ecumenism says *exstare possunt* (can exist), the question arises: Are these elements found outside the visible structure of the Roman Catholic Church? The answer is found in the Decree on Ecumenism itself and from experience. The Decree explains that, despite the many and sometimes serious obstacles to full ecclesiastical communion, "it remains true that all who have been justified by faith in baptism are incorporated into Christ".[12] To be incorporated into Christ by justification means to share through Christ the life of grace, to possess the gifts of faith, hope, and charity, and through the indwelling of the Holy Spirit to have the interior gifts. Justification is precisely that. Experience testifies that believers in Christ proclaim the resurrection and the doctrine of the Trinity; they profess faith, cherish hope, and live charity. Thus the text from the Constitution on the Church of Vatican II is unsatisfactory in having used the subjunctive *inveniantur,* as is the text from the Decree on Ecumenism for having said *exstare possunt.* They ought to have used the indicative, that is, respectively, *inveniuntur* (are found) and *exstant* (exist).

This ecclesiology is of paramount importance in establishing the authenticity of ministry. Because the Roman Catholic Church, according to its own teaching, is not simply identified with the church of Christ, attention has to focus on the latter. As a matter of fact, the church of Christ has diverse visible structures, and it needs to be emphasised that the Decree on Ecumenism mentions 'visible elements', as well as interior graces, outside the Roman Catholic Church. Though the Roman Catholic Church may consider the ecclesial structures outside its visible boundaries to be incomplete, that does not make them false or invalid. Nor indeed could it do so, because every visible structure is derived from the Risen Christ and the gifts of unity, holiness, catholicity, and apostolicity.

Pluriformity in the Primitive Church

From the historical evidence there have always been local Christian communities with leaders as signs of unity and presidents at the Eucharist. That is clear from the primitive church down to the present. Leaders and presidents

---

[11] *Unitatis redintegratio* 3, in: *Vaticanum II. Constitutiones,* pp. 248f. The translation is from Austin Flannery, ed., *Vatican Council II. 7he Conciliar and Post Conciliar Documents* (Tenbury Wells, Worcs.: Fowler Wright Books, 1975), p. 455.
[12] Flannery, *Vatican Council II,* p. 455.

have never simply assumed their role but have always been appointed or commissioned and in one way or another received the consent of the church. Beyond this there were diverse and fluid arrangements of church order in the New Testament churches and varied developments from the last decades of the first century to the middle of the third century.[13]

It is well known that the difference between *presbuteroi and episkopoi* in the New Testament cannot be established. Further, it is not clear how those who presided at the Eucharist were appointed or chosen. There is evidence that the presidents of the Eucharist were not necessarily leaders of the community.[14]

The letters of St. Ignatius of Antioch (c. 110) distinguish the three offices of overseers *(episkopoi),* elders *(presbuteroi),* and deacons *(diakonoi).*[15] He witnessed to a monarchical episcopate at Antioch and in several congregations in Asia Minor, but he was not describing a universal situation. The sources do not permit us to say how this development took place, but what data we have indicate that the development was not uniform. A different picture is given, for example, by the *Shepherd of Hermas* (c. 100-155, perhaps 140-155).[16]

It is this very diversity of development which advises the substitution of the phrase 'authenticity of commissioned ministry' for 'validity of orders'. Authenticity is discerned by fundamental historical continuity in the resurrection faith and from experience. It can be maintained, therefore, that all forms of church order in the church of Christ are authentic on the basis of the highest common factor, belief in the Risen Christ.

Divine Law

There is of course an ecumenical problem in regard to what Roman Catholic ecclesiology and canon law hold to be *de iure divino* or of divine law in church order.[17] This could be considered to neutralise the position adopted in this article. However, it is evident on historical grounds that there must be a

---

[13] See R.E. Brown, *Priest and Bishop: Biblical Reflections* (London, Dublin, Melbourne: Chapman, 1971), pp. 34-345.

[14] See ibid. and G. d'Ercole, *The Presbyteral Colleges in the Early Church* in *Historical Investigations,* ed. by R. Aubert, CONCILIUM 17 (New York: Paulist Press, 1966) pp. 20-33.

[15] See e.g. *S. Ignatii Epis., ad Philadelphenses,* 4 in: PG 5, 700; *ad Magnesios, 6, 1* in: PG 5, *668; ad Smyrnaeos, 8,* 1 in: PG 5, 713.

[16] See *Visio* II, iv, 2-3 in: PG 2, 899; *Visio* III, v, 1 in: PG 2, 903; *Similitudo* IX, xxvii, 2 in: PG 2, 900.

[17] See A. Dulles, *Ius Divinum as an Ecumenical Problem* in: THEOLOGICAL STUDIES *38* (1977) pp. 681-708.

hierarchy of elements of divine institution in the church of Christ on an analogy with the hierarchy of truths as explained in the Decree on Ecumenism:

> When comparing doctrines with one another, they (Catholic theologians) should remember that in Catholic doctrines there exists an order or 'hierarchy' of truths since they vary in their relation to the foundation of the Christian faith.[18]

At the basis of this hierarchy of elements *de iure divino* are belief in the Risen Christ and sharing the life of the Trinity, the proclamation of these at first by accredited witnesses and later by appointed leaders, initiation by baptism into the death and resurrection of Christ for the forgiveness of sins, and the celebration of this in the Eucharist under the leadership of appointed or ordained presidents or ministers. Because of his wide influence, I would like to examine a profound and in some ways intriguing reflection on divine law in Roman Catholic thought by Karl Rahner.[19] It is intriguing because it does not appear to be as convincing as it is profound. The key idea is that of history. He writes: "The historical development of a historical structure is not necessarily reversible simply because the development in question is a state which did not always exist".[20] Though he gives no specific examples of this, the development of the papacy and the monarchical episcopate may be instanced. These are forms of the Church's authority and leadership under Christ which are the outcome of a historical development. They have not always had the same form as they have now. Rahner continues:

> It is certainly true that one will only really be able to explain the phenomena of the Church and of her life in history if one is able to conceive at the same time of the identity of nature throughout the historical variation of its form and the difference of form in spite of the same nature (of the divine law).[21]

With regard to the relationship of nature and form, it should be stressed that nature always has some form, for no historical nature can exist above the level of history. Therefore, primary and secondary forms have to be distinguished, and I would argue that the latter derive from the former. The primary forms of church order are primitive in that they existed from the

---

[18] Flannery, *Vatican Council II*, p. 462.
[19] *Reflection on the Concept of 'Ius Divinum' in Catholic Thought. Theological Investigations V.- Later Writings*, trans. by K.-H. Krüger (Baltimore: Helicon Press; London: Darton Longman & Todd, 1965) pp. 219-243.
[20] Ibid., p. 226.
[21] Ibid., p. 222.

beginning. Because they are primary they must be constant and therefore present now where the authority and leadership of the Risen Christ are acknowledged. Thus, in regard to the historical forms of the papacy and monarchical episcopate, the nature is the authority and leadership of Christ and the primary form the sharing in and exercise of these as realised in the primitive church. Rahner argues further:

> There are processes within a historically existing reality which at least can be recognised as legitimate by the nature of this existing reality, even though they spring from a free decision and even though these processes and decisions cannot be proved to be the only possible ones, and hence cannot be proved to be the only obligatory means for the nature of the historically evolving reality.[22]

This reflection, I would maintain, is the very reason that allows one to conclude that a valid interpretation does not render other interpretations invalid, not even where another interpretation is introduced subsequently, provided it was derived at an earlier time from the primitive form. Examples of this would be the Orthodox, Anglican, Presbyterian, and Methodist interpretations of church order.

> From the Roman Catholic side, given the concept of primary form, these interpretations can only be judged incomplete: they lack a form which the Roman Catholic Church judges to be of divine law. They cannot, however, be invalid. For that to be the case, a sharing in the authority and leadership of Christ would have to be rejected. On the other hand, churches and ecclesial communities outside the visible limits of the Roman Catholic Church are obliged, I would submit, to concede that the ecclesiological and canonical positions regarding the papacy and episcopate are legitimate developments within the historical process of the church's existence and are thus of divine law, without being obliged to embrace them in their present historical form.

The Relationship of Nature and Form

Rahner then introduces biological analogies and analogies with the spiritual development of individuals which weakens his Argument considerably. One needs to be cautious about using these analogies in relation to historical development. He writes: "It is possible to conceive of such a historical decision—a decision in conformity with nature even though not

---

[22] Ibid., p. 228.

necessary by nature—which is both of a juridical nature and itself creative of law (in the sense of proposition 1), and irreversible".[23]

This, I think, must be conceded. He continues: "In itself, it is quite possible to conceive that such an irreversible juridical decision and establishment is also of the necessity of nature".[24]

Of course, it is true that the mere fact of something developing later in time does not prove it is not of the necessity of nature, but neither does it prove that it is. He argues further:

> It is certainly possible, for instance, to characterise the faculty of sight, the capacity to laugh or the capacity to make contact with the surrounding world by free decisions, etc., as being of the necessity of nature or as belonging with absolute necessity to the nature of man. And yet one will not be able to say that these necessities of nature are present in the embryonic stage of a human being in the same way as later on, nor will it be possible to say that what is added in this way later on must no longer be designated as being 'necessary to the nature'.[25]

These elements of human existence which Rahner instances are known to us *a priori* from our experience; we know what characteristics a human being ought to have. It was not known *a priori* what forms the church's order would or should take. A human being sees, laughs, and makes contact with the surrounding world by free decisions. A human being devoid of these characteristics would be psychologically and socially defective. One does not choose to see, to possess the mark of risibility, or to have the capacity to make free decisions. These are endowments of human nature. But one can choose what one looks at; there are very diverse senses of humour; and there are as many free decisions in making contact with the surrounding world as there are free persons. The forms which these endowments of human nature take are very diverse. The analogy, therefore, if it is to be used at all, should highlight the comparison between diversity of forms of church order and, for example, the variety of senses of humour. No one knows *a priori* what will be humorous to one person and what to another.

These endowments cannot be compared with historical decisions by the church to embrace forms which are undoubtedly in conformity with nature,

---

[23] Ibid., p. 229.
[24] Ibid., p. 229f.
[25] Ibid., p. 230. Dulles, in *Ius Divinum*, p. 702, also employs biological analogies. It would apply the criticisms of Rahner also to Dulles on this point.

in order to argue that they are also of the necessity of nature. One cannot compare, say, the capacity to see with the free decision to have a monarchical episcopate, or the absence of the capacity with the rejection of the episcopate in favour of a *collegial presbyterium*.

While the papacy and monarchical episcopate are held to be of divine law and they may be described as secondary forms in the hierarchy of elements of divine law—I cannot see how one could conclude that they are necessary to the church's nature simply because they developed. The most that one could say is that, having developed, they are in conformity with the church's nature. Despite his earlier argument, Rahner himself seems to recognise this problem:

> Since, however, the sheer beginning and basis of a reality cannot be attained directly in itself. . .it is not so easy to judge as to whether something which is historically established later on belongs necessarily to the nature or is merely in conformity with the nature and as such (for this or that reason) irreversible.[26]

Conclusion

The basic elements which give the church of Christ its essential unity are the necessary and sufficient conditions for an official sanctioning of intercommunion. The Eucharist is a sign of the unity we share, not only as so many diverse denominations but also as the one church of Christ. It is likewise the cause of closer unity with God and of increasing our unity with one another. At its most fundamental, the Eucharist everywhere proclaims the death and glorification of Christ; testifies to his real, living, and life-giving presence; and gives a pledge of future glory.

The essential unity of the church of Christ is not organisational but organic. Hence, we should be working toward a service or act of reconciliation among the various denominations. This liturgy could be celebrated in local communities throughout the world and would be one of mutual forgiveness for all the uncharitableness committed against one another, for our sins of misunderstanding and mockery which are terrible obstacles to our common witness to the love and mercy of God. The service would include the kiss of peace and culminate in a common celebration of the Eucharist. In this way we

---

[26] Rahner, *Reflection*, p. 230.

would express our organic unity as the church of Christ. What might follow in institutional forms could be left serenely to the Holy Spirit.

Spiritual Law[1]

To speak of spiritual law introduces a dimension of existence which we cannot ignore in our efforts for the peace and freedom of mankind. It brings us to the reality of self-awareness in the universe. Man belongs to the earth. He is made up of different combinations of the same chemical elements as the food he eats, the air he breathes and the ground he walks on. But he is also something more. He is spirit. In him the evolving earth reached the point of self-consciousness, in him the earth became *spiritualised*.

When we have said this, however, the question arises: Does development continue in the sphere of spirit? On the answer to that depends the ultimate significance of knowledge, being and death. For if there is no spiritual development then man has nothing more to know for, nothing more to be for and, what is worst of all, nothing more to die for.

The "Within" of Man

Spiritual law concerns the "within" of man. It turns our attention to the interiority of the pentadactyl plantigrade who discovers reality in the inner depths of his own being. It is about that fine point at the core of his existence which compels a man to cry out in anguish and joy: "I am"; the point where he finds himself plunged into the flow of existence winding its way inexorably to a term, an end, that will be a beginning; a beginning that will last forever; a beginning that will transform death into the supreme moment of living. It dwells upon that aspect of human life which convinces a man that it is against the truth to say: "You don't miss what you've never had". It focuses attention on the power in man, as Teilhard de Chardin says, to centre all reality on himself partially.[2]

Spiritual law touches upon that area wherein a man finds himself the product—now of everything he has achieved, experienced, suffered, omitted and longed for in life; that area wherein he realises he is not an isolated monad

[1] *Foundations of Peace and Freedom. The Ecology of a Peace World,* Ed. T. Dunn, Christopher Davies, Swansea 1975, pp. 60-70. Published with permission.
[2] P.T. de Chardin, *The Phenomenon of Man,* with an introduction by Sir Julian Huxley, Collins Fontana Books, 1966, p. 284.

but a being-in-the-world, a being-with-others, a being-for-others. In a word, it is about the self-awareness of the human spirit which has in its very structure an openness to others, to the world and to Mystery and Transcendence, the Mystery of ultimate meaning and the Transcendence of greater than self that we call God: the incomprehensible, all-holy, all-embracing, ever-present, adorable Someone Who is the Primal Origin of all that is.

Inner Freedom and Peace

The question of spiritual development (increase in consciousness), cannot be ignored because it is dependent on inner freedom and peace. There will be no lasting peace and no true freedom on a planetary scale unless individuals acquire that inner peace which surpasses all understanding, and that inner freedom which, while allowing a man to remain himself, takes him out of himself towards the other. Inner peace comes from self-knowledge and all knowledge is at the service of being—we know more to be more—which recognises self as it is. Self-knowledge must not be confused with morbid introspection; it is knowledge of *this* self situated in the world, *this* self in its relationships. Thus, through humility and truth comes inner peace bringing self-possession in self-realisation. Inner freedom is the power of self-determination in the face of the good. It drives a person to seek out the other for the other's sake, destroying egoism which is ultimately self-destructive. It is therefore an error to imagine that world freedom and peace lie exclusively in the hands of governments and in the decisions of heads of state. They lie in the hands and decisions of all of us together, as our consciousness of belonging to an ever-greater unifying whole increases. The more we are at peace with ourselves, just so much more is the world at peace; the more we are united with others in the freedom of love, just so much more is it a world freedom.

A World of Science and Technology

When we speak of man's self-awareness through inner freedom and peace as being-in-the-world, we do not understand "world" in some abstract sense. We mean it as in this world as it is now, developing from its past into the future. The lunar landing in July 1969 is perhaps the best evidence that we belong to a world of science and technology. To achieve what at first had seemed incredible, we assembled bits of earth and hurled them at the moon as Apollo 11. The moon used to be called the mother of lunatics and to them all she had given her name. Now she has become the symbol of the most breath-taking achievements of *homo sapiens,* and she has given us a new name—lunerant. It is said that soon we will be able to take a holiday on the moon.

Accommodation will be provided in an enormous plastic bag filled with fresh air—a lunar hotel. And all this, journey and holiday, for the price of a transatlantic air ticket. There is talk of space stations, hydroponic farms, hibernation in space, of leaving the solar system and of reaching Proxima Centauri. Meanwhile, here on earth, machines and Computers do the work of hundreds of pairs of hands. Through science leisure is increasing; and leisure will be a problem in the future. The day is fast approaching when salaries will be earned for going down twice a week to the local museum to dust a Greco-Roman vase or the skeleton of a dinosaur. We'll come home for our tablets and glass of air (that will be lunch), then float off to the next room to chat with relatives in Brisbane about topics of purely local interest, like what's happening in the Galaxy of Andromeda. Despite the advances that have brought us more comfort, speedier travel and longer lives, we still live in a world of political, social and religious unrest. It is a world sick for peace. The last twenty years have been years of hot wars, cold wars and rumours of wars. There is widespread pessimism about the powers in the hands of *homo sapiens* as a result of his exploitation of nature. Some would argue that the very word *sapiens* has been proved a misnomer. Others are extremely doubtful whether we will have enough time to lay even the foundations of a Planetary Economic Community.

Grounds for Hope

Whatever may be felt about the achievements of science and technology, the undeniable fact is that they have unified the globe. The media of communication have brought a knowledge and information explosion through which we can be actively and passively present on the furthest continents and even in outer space. It is as though a vast brain had been constructed around the earth. Man's self-awareness is of belonging, not merely to a family, a class, a nation, or a continent, but to the world: Planet Earth, and to the entire universe. His environment is no longer circumscribed by the boundaries of nations, but only by the outer reaches of space.

To dismiss as groundless the pessimism mentioned earlier would be, of course, to play the ostrich. Future development lies in the hands of men and so depends on the right use of freedom. Moreover, the paradox is that though science has unified the globe, there is by no means universal awareness or recognition of the intrinsic unity of mankind. Yet there are grounds for hope based on a significant development in the sphere of spirit on the earth. These may be listed as follows: increasing awareness of the unity of mankind;

searching questions about man and his future; widespread interest in meditation.

1. Increasing awareness of the unity of mankind

Over the past twenty years or so there has grown up imperceptibly a greater awareness of the intrinsic unity of mankind, More and more people have come to see the simple truth, which no distinction of race, colour, creed or culture can possibly alter, that to be man is to be brother. This is not at all as extensive as it ought to be. But the fact is that it exists and is increasing. Qualitatively speaking it gives reason for hope. Its chief cause is undoubtedly the scientific and technological advances that have unified the earth. The scientific revolution contained from the beginning the seeds of a deeper humanisation. This has manifested itself during recent decades. Almost two hundred years have passed since the French Revolution proclaimed the principles of freedom, equality and brotherhood. But it is only over the span of the last generation that there has been any appreciable awareness of the responsibility of establishing those principles on a universal scale.

Against this background the *Universal Declaration of Human Rights* adopted and proclaimed by the General Assembly of the United Nations in 1948, marks a turning point in history. There has been much criticism of the United Nations, and no doubt the last twenty years provide ready material for the cynic, and are more than enough to temper even the most moderate of optimists. However, the *Declaration* stands and no one can claim inculpable ignorance of its articles. Whatever open contradictions of world unity exist, whatever crises man may still have to encounter, the plain and irreversible truth that there is an increasing awareness that mankind is one. It should be noted in this context that the Christian Unity Movement cannot be understood as an isolated event. It is bound up with the present movements of world history towards unity.

2. Searching questions about man and his future

These are inseparably linked to the growing awareness of human unity. They take a variety of forms which may be reduced to the following: Where are we going? What does it all mean? Can we look forward to the future? Are we really any better off for all our scientific discoveries? To ask questions means problems have been recognised which opens the way to solutions. Now, these questions show a concern about man and his future which has led to *dialogue* among individuals and groups of the most varying beliefs and divergent ideologies. Here we may note particularly the Christian Marxist

Dialogue and the study groups of the Teilhard de Chardin Association. The Teilhard de Chardin Association has as its object to make people increasingly aware of their responsibility for directing the future. Dialogue at every level, which is crucial for the future, proves that passive resignation, pessimism, despair and cynicism are not the only reactions possible to the state of the world and the future of mankind.

Science was once believed to have the key to the riddle of existence and the meaning of life. This, however, proved to be a chimera. Science *in itself* does not bring satisfaction to the mind and heart. As a source of knowledge, it is subservient to being. Questions about the value of scientific advances indicate that there is a growing realisation of this. Scientific advances are gains in so far as they contribute to the convergent tendencies of evolution in the sphere of spirit. However, we must be on our guard not to allow the misuse of science to lead us into condemning science itself. That would be like condemning the washing machine because it can provide opportunities for laziness. Where science is misused we can condemn only ourselves.

3. Widespread interest in meditation

This, in the present writer's opinion, is one of the most important phenomena of recent years. Only those who are unacquainted with its results can dismiss it as an esoteric pursuit of a few cranks. Meditation heightens self-awareness, increases inner freedom and peace and discloses to the mind the truth of human unity. One of its most important aspects is the effect it has on the individual's time outside the periods of formal meditation. It gives an all-embracing calm and deepens the sense of responsibility for others.

The International Spiritual Regeneration Movement has established centres in every country of the world. The purpose of the *Movement* is to teach a method of transcendental meditation in order to conquer the world with love. It is a direct way of reaching the peace in all men. Equally important here at home is *The Fellowship of Meditation*. More and more people are drawing spiritual comfort and inner peace from the simple method explained in the pamphlet published by the *Fellowship* under the title: *Inner Peace.*

The *sine qua non* condition for meditation is, of course, silence and goodness knows we need it! It is a reason for the greatest joy that we have begun once more to discover the positive value of silence in a world where noise breaks in on us from all sides.

Teilhard de Chardin and Spiritual Development

We began these reflections on spiritual law by noticing that the evolving earth reached the point of self-consciousness in man. We then submitted that, as a result of the humanising influence of science there is some evidence of spiritual development in the increase of self-awareness of belonging to a unified and unifying whole. To draw together all that has been said thus far, we turn now to Teilhard de Chardin's phenomenology of evolution which, based on a scientific examination of the whole phenomenon of man, establishes that evolution continues in the sphere of spirit and that man's total environment leads in fact to the reality of love in the universe.

1. Scientific Phenomenology

Teilhard develops a scientific phenomenology of the universe in which the whole phenomenon of man (the 'within' as well as the 'without') is central. Scientific phenomenology or hyperphysics is "a branch of science which reflects on its own results in order to find their true import—a science which learns the total lesson of its discoveries".[3] In his explanation of evolution Teilhard made one his love of God and his love of the world by relating the discoveries of science to man's spiritual and religious experiences. He has shown that religion (and specifically, the Christian religion) does not alienate man from the world, but gives a greater love-energy in the sphere of spirit, impelling towards human unity. Thus, Teilhard crossed the no-man's-land between science and religion which have gone their respective ways for centuries in mutual distrust and isolation. It was his strongest conviction that all truth is one and that light from one source cannot extinguish light from another.

2. Complexity—Consciousness

For Teilhard de Chardin the universe is an essentially dynamic, organic, evolving reality. He speaks always, not of cosmos, but of *cosmogenesis:* a universe in process. Over the millions of years of cosmic evolution he saw operative a process of complexification extending from the subatomic particles of hydrogen to the neuro-cerebral system of man. Along with the increasing complexity of anatomical structure there has gone a corresponding increase in consciousness, unity, interiority. Consciousness is

---

[3] Oliver Rabut, *Dialogue with Teilhard de Chardin,* Sheed and Ward, London and Director of the Centre for the Analysis of Conflict, London and Sydney 1961.

understood as a vast spectrum stretching from the most primitive power of matter to unite to the unifying self-consciousness in *homo sapiens.*

With the appearance of man millions of years of dynamic development reached their purpose. Thought had come and evolution attained its most important stage. Teilhard now draws our attention to the fact that man, confronted with space-time, experiences a certain anxiety: "After the long series of transformations leading to man, has the world stopped?"[4] He cannot accept that it has. Meditating on the total past it would be irrational and to render the whole process absurd to imagine that the operation of the Law of Complexity Consciousness suddenly ceased. His scientific phenomenology will not permit so unscientific a conclusion! Not only are there not reasons to say it has ceased, there are positive indications it is actually continuing. Some of these, we would submit, are the growth in awareness of human unity, the desire to create a United States of the World, questions about the future of man and interest in meditation.

3. Creative Evolution

The evolution of man is unique in showing the dominance of convergence over divergence. The sphere of mind (noosphere) is progressing to higher levels of hominization: it is a *noogenesis.* The future of the noosphere lies in the development of persons through inter-personal relationships. Thus with the appearance of man, evolution becomes the growth of humanity as a whole. The individual is becoming more conscious of his belonging to a whole, and this because of the threefold property possessed by every conscious being:

1. "of centring *everything* partially upon itself;
2. of being able to centre itself upon itself *constantly;*
3. of being brought *more* by this very super-centration into association with *all the other centres* surrounding it".[5]

Socialisation depends on the free giving of love over the whole earth. Thus, the process of continuing evolution is one of *amorization.* That is to say, everything now depends on love: the reaching out towards the other for the other's sake, in order to discover oneself. Love means communicating to the other what is deepest and most interior in oneself. It means unity and consistence which belongs to its very dynamism.

---

[4] Teilhard de Chardin, *The Phenomenon,* p. 256.
[5] Ibid., p. 284.

4. Omega Point

Creative evolution in the noosphere is tending towards a centre which Teilhard calls 'Omega Point'. The individual centres of consciousness are not destroyed because Omega is a point of convergence, not of submergence. Spiritual synthesis, or the union of persons can only be achieved on the basis of enduring personal identity and uniqueness. Union does not mean being dissolved into the 'All'. Here the principle is: "In any domain—whether it be the cells of a body, the members of a society or the elements of a spiritual synthesis—union differentiates. In every organised whole the parts perfect and fulfil themselves".[6]

Teilhard goes on to identify Omega Point, which is loving and loveable at this moment, with the Risen Christ. I am not directly concerned here with this aspect of his teaching since my terms of reference are natural spiritual law. It may be noted, however, that the identity is made because of the central Christian truth that God is Love.

5. Love on the Earth

What is clear from Teilhard's teaching is that there can be no heightening of self-awareness in isolation, there can be no increase in spiritualization without love. In a pluralistic world, unity will be achieved only through the love and good will of all men. Love alone will break down the centrifugal forces of individualism, nationalism, racialism, collectivism and class consciousness; love alone will convince us that war is not necessary; love alone will show us that we are Earthmen and that our task is to build the Earth. As Teilhard says: "Love is a sacred reserve of energy, and the very blood stream of spiritual evolution; that is the first discovery we make from the Sense of Earth".[7]

Knowledge and the Future of the World

There is no doubt that the future development of freedom and peace in the world and increase in self-awareness of belonging to the Earth are inextricably linked with progress in knowledge in every sphere. Self-knowledge, knowledge of mankind and of the world will bring us to a greater degree of being. Knowledge destroys fear because it dispels ignorance. With fear removed man becomes free to love.

---

[6] Ibid., p. 288.
[6] P.T. de Chardin, *Building the Earth,* Geoffrey Chapman, London-Dublin 1965, p. 40.

To conclude these reflections on spiritual law I want to give some practical suggestions in the spirit of Article 26 §2 on Education of the *Universal Declaration of Human Rights*. I would suggest that it ought to be considered basic to education and formation at every stage:

1. To inculcate an ever deeper appreciation of the uniqueness and dignity of every person. Each individual person has an originality, an incommunicability (what the medieval philosopher John Duns Scotus called *haecceitas*, "thisness") which is the source of his irreplaceable value in the world. Literature, art, science, theology, philosophy, offer ample opportunities for this.

2. To show that no individual can be fully a person without others. Man is by Definition a being-with-others. The only true foundation of interpersonal relationships is love which takes a person out of himself to the other for the other's sake.

3. To communicate that man belongs to the human family and that his home, in the first place, is the Earth.

4. To demonstrate the intrinsic meaning of history and to introduce as early as possible the study of Universal History. Nothing is intelligible without its history, least of all man and the world.

5. From a knowledge of the past man understands himself in the present, and prepares himself for the future. As the *magistra vitae*, history teaches us that we have a duty to the past, a task in the present and a responsibility for the future.

6. To teach by shared experience that unity is not uniformity, diversity is not division.

7. To instruct the students in the history and methods of meditation of the East and West. This would include a thorough knowledge of the great mystics of East and West. Methods and techniques found suitable and attractive would be taught to those wishing to learn them.

8. To instil an awareness of the constructive value of silence. Could not the possibility and advisability be investigated of introducing periods of silence into school curriculas?

9. To teach respect for the sacredness of matter and of life in all its forms. This could be done in the most graphic way, for example, by familiarising the students with the mysticism of St. Francis of Assisi who called the sun, the moon, the stars, water, fire, the birds, the wolf, his brothers and sisters; or with the teachings and practices of the Jains; or with the life and writings of

Mahatma Gandhi. This would be a most positive way of teaching the horrors of violence in all its forms.

The Blessed Virgin Mary
and Dialogue with Evangelicals[1]

It would be unpardonable pessimism and contrary to the virtue of hope to describe the Marian doctrines as insurmountable barriers blocking the way to full unity of the Church of Christ. So much has been achieved during the past ten years in the field of ecumenism, that one needs to be cautious about negative predictions. In many areas once considered to contain totally irreconcilable differences, not only has the unthinkable been thought, it has been done.

There remain of course wide areas of difference and disagreement which render ecumenical encounters often sensitive and delicate and at times even explosive, but never hopeless or without fruit. To these areas belong the Marian doctrines. There can be no doubt that they create enormous problems for dialogue, especially between Roman Catholics and Evangelicals. With the exception of the doctrines of papal primacy and infallibility, probably no topic is more calculated to rouse feelings of anger and fear in both parties to the dialogue, than the place of Mary in the life and piety of the Church.

For a time the attitude was one of discreet silence. Better to ignore what might open old wounds. This attitude is obviously unsatisfactory and perhaps even a little dishonest, precisely because Mary has such an important place in the life of the Roman Catholic Church and because that place is considered to be unscriptural by a large majority of those who belong to the tradition of Reformed Christianity. It is clear now that these issues have to be faced as calmly and charitably as possible. Dialogue has begun and great credit for this is due to the Ecumenical Society of the Blessed Virgin Mary.

The Wider Context of This Dialogue

It has to be admitted that this is no easy subject for the Roman Catholic theologian in the dialogue. The Marian doctrines belong to a wider doctrinal and theological context which the Roman Catholic cannot ignore. In the first place, the question of Mary's place in the Church is for Roman Catholics as

[1] CLERGY REVIEW 64 (Oct. 1979) pp. 347-357. Published with permission (www.priestsandpeople.co.uk).

much a matter of the heart as of the head. And it is notoriously difficult to transfer matters of the heart into clear and distinct propositions. Secondly, there is the vast extent of literature on Mary. Bibliographies list literally thousands of entries covering every aspect of Marian studies: biblical, patristic, historical, theological, ecclesiological, ecumenical and devotional.[2] Faced with so much material one needs a discerning and shrewdly selective eye. Thirdly, the theology of Mary is linked to the rest of theology and indeed is unintelligible if separated from it. The doctrines of creation, incarnation, the Holy Spirit, grace and justification, the Church and eschatology, are so intimately bound up with the Marian doctrines, that any study of Mary's place in the economy of salvation is in fact a variation on one or other of these themes.

There are, moreover, great differences in our theological understanding of a number of the basic doctrines of the Church. We may note as especially relevant here: justification, man's freedom and the sovereignty of grace, the relation between scripture and Tradition, the nature of the teaching authority of the Church. In almost every Mariological question it soon becomes clear that what is being discussed is one or other of the fundamental issues that have divided us since the sixteenth century. For this reason a good case could be made for the view that there is no specifically Mariological problem at all for ecumenists to tackle. For behind every ecumenical discussion about Mary stand the as yet unresolved problems created by our differences concerning the authority of scripture and the development of doctrine. Fourthly, there are still grave misunderstandings about our respective attitudes to Mary and these lead inevitably to misrepresentation. They are the product of ignorance and prejudice on all sides and have a history of more than four hundred years behind them. For this reason we have to listen between the lines in the dialogue. What ecumenism needs more than anything is a theology of listening—listening to the Holy Spirit and to one another in the Holy Spirit.

What I want to do in this article is, firstly, to make some general remarks on ecumenical dialogue concerning the Virgin Mary and to describe the character of a theology of Mary as a Roman Catholic theologian would see it today. Secondly, I will consider in some detail the question concerning the relationship to scripture of the doctrines of the perpetual virginity, the immaculate conception and the assumption. Thirdly, I will attempt to construct the skeleton of a theological approach to Mary which might form the basis of

---

[2] See, for example, G. Besutti OSM, *Bibliografia Mariana 1967-1972*, Ed. MARIANUM, Roma 1974.

ecumenical discussion. Finally, I will make some suggestions about topics which, because of their importance, should have a place in all dialogue about the Virgin Mary.

Mary and Ecumenical Dialogue

It should be emphasised at the outset that ecumenical discussion on the Virgin Mary must begin with those aspects on which there is agreement between us. I have found these nowhere expressed more succinctly than in an article by J.M. Haire, formerly Professor of Systematic Theology and Apologetics at the Presbyterian College, Belfast. Professor Haire writes:

> We can, therefore, sum up first our basic agreement. Mary is for Matthew, Luke and John as an example of faith and obedience to be regarded and praised in the Church. She is also the highly favoured one to whom was given the wholly wonderful task and privilege of being the human mother of the Son of God. If it was true of another woman that wherever the gospel was preached, her faith would be recalled, it is more so of Mary. As with all great Christians we rightly stand at a distance and feel awe, respect and affection.[3]

No one, I think, would want to question any of the statements made here by Professor Haire. While the paragraph does not contain the full Roman Catholic doctrine about the Virgin Mary, nevertheless, any Roman Catholic could subscribe to its contents as expressing the basic minimum of his belief about her place in God's plan. What Professor Haire has written could well be the starting point of any dialogue between Roman Catholics and Evangelicals.

Ecumenical discussion on Mary involving Roman Catholics should confine itself at the beginning to what the Roman Catholic Church teaches *explicitly* to be *of faith* concerning the Virgin Mary. This means, for example, that the doctrines of the immaculate conception and the assumption have to be treated and that the titles such as Mediatrix and Co-redemptrix may be left out of account for the time being. This is not to say that they can simply be dismissed. There is patristic evidence for the content of these titles.[4] Furthermore, if we can pray for one another and fill up what is lacking in the sufferings of Christ, and if the Church herself is Mediatrix and Co-redemptrix, and Mary is her Image, then it may not be so strange to call Mary Mediatrix and Co-redemptrix. However, these are not declared doctrines of the Roman

---

[3] J.M. Haire, *Born of the Virgin Mary* in: Doctrine and Life 26 (1976) p. 561.
[4] O. Semmelroth SJ, *Mary Archetype of the Church,* trans. by M.V. Eroes and J. Devlin, Gill and Son, Dublin 1964.

Catholic Church. It is significant that over the past few years these titles have in the main been set on one side. This is without doubt due to the Second Vatican Council itself. In its Constitution on the Church, *Lumen Gentium,* the eighth chapter, which treats explicitly of the Virgin Mary, points out that the titles 'Advocate', 'Helper', 'Benefactress' and 'Mediatrix' must be so understood as neither to take anything from nor add anything to the dignity and efficacy of Christ the one Mediator.[5]

The theology of Mary has undergone important developments since the Second Vatican Council. Whatever excesses there may have been in the past, Mary has been brought back from a position of isolation and restored to her unique position in the Church. It can be stated now quite unambiguously that Mariology is the study of the modality of Mary's justification by the sovereign grace of God and of her place in saving history. There has been a shift from considering her in purely individualistic terms, to seeing her as a member of the Church and included among the redeemed. In other words, a study of the Virgin Mary is a study of the meaning of salvation and of the Church in history. It is about a concrete person in whom God's grace was beautifully victorious. It is crucial to hold this in order to avoid removing Mary artificially away from the Church of which she is pre-eminent member and model. If we do not begin with this understanding, we will have no satisfactory perspective in which to place the doctrines of the immaculate conception, the perpetual virginity, the assumption and, for that matter, the divine motherhood.

Perpetual Virginity, Immaculate Conception and Assumption

In dialogue with Evangelicals the relationship has to be considered between these doctrines and scripture. And it has to be stressed once more that we have different approaches in our understanding of how scripture exercises its authority in the Church. From the Roman Catholic point of view scripture and Church are so intimately bound up with one another, that it is impossible to conceive of them apart. Scripture has as its most venerable function to preserve the purity of the Word of God which cannot be simply identified in a literalistic manner with scripture. This understanding opens up at once the question about the formation of the canon. How are we to interpret this as an act of the believing Church? What principle lay behind the decision that certain

---

[5] *Dogmatic Constitution on the Church,* 62, in: *Vatican Council II. The Conciliar and Post Conciliar Documents,* ed. by A. Flannery OP, Fowler Wright Books Ltd., Tenbury Wells, Worcs. 1975, p. 419. But see, however, M. O'Carroll CSsP, *Vatican II and Our Lady's Mediation,* in: THE IRISH THEOLOGICAL QUARTERLY 37 (1970) pp. 24-55.

writings were to be included in the canon and others excluded? Furthermore, how are we to conceive, for example, the relationship between the original Aramaic version of Matthew and the vernacular versions we use today, all of which have had a complex history? Should we not rather speak of the 'Holy Library' than the 'Holy Bible'? These are questions which have a direct bearing on any discussion of Mary's place in the Church.

It is not my intention in this section to enter into detailed exegesis of the biblical texts, nor is that necessary. What I want to do is to indicate lines of investigation.

1. Perpetual Virginity

This is a doctrine of the Roman Catholic Church. The important question in regard to it is this: What basis is there in scripture for it? Any examination of the question reveals at once an astonishing variety of opinions among exegetes. Of course the problems for theology raised by exegesis are well known. But the question I am concerned with here is what effect does this pluriformity of opinion have on the faith of an Evangelical Christian? It seems to me that there are these alternatives open: either to ignore this pluriformity altogether in favour of what is believed, which would be surely, in some way, to invoke an authority connected with, though not reducible to the material text of scripture; or to embrace a state of calm agnosticism in regard to the historicity of the virginal conception of Jesus, though not necessarily in regard to its symbolic meaning.

Division of opinion about the scriptural basis of the virginal conception cuts across the confessional barriers. There are Roman Catholic and Protestant scholars who deny this basis and there are Roman Catholic and Protestant scholars who affirm it. Among Protestants, for example, Heikki Räisänen defends the virginal conception of Jesus very strongly. Mary's virginity is the presupposition for the miracle of the virginal conception.[6] On the other hand, the famous Wolfhart Pannenberg denies it. He states categorically that 'in the virgin birth we have to do with a legend'.[7]

Among Roman Catholics we may single out Fr. Raymond Brown SS. He concludes his study of the pertinent scriptural texts with the statement that in his judgement 'the totality of the *scientifically controllable* evidence leaves

---

[6] *Die Mutter Jesu im Neuen Testament,* Suomalaisen Tiedeakatemian Toimituksia, ANNALES ACADEMIAE SCIENTIARUM FENNICAE, Series B, p. 158. Helsinki: Suomalainen Tiedeakatemia, 1969.

[7] *The Apostles' Creed in the Light of Today's Questions,* trans. by M. Kohl, SCM Press Ltd., London 1972, pp. 71-77, esp. 73.

an unresolved problem'.[8] In a footnote he goes on to add: "In particular, as a Roman Catholic whose biblical studies have led him to appreciate all the more the importance of a teaching Church, I cannot resolve the problem independently of the question of authority raised in Section II".[9]

Brown's treatment, however, did not satisfy all Roman Catholic scholars. Michael O'Carroll CSsP in an article on Marian theology addressed some important and leading questions to Fr. Brown:

> Why, in the light of Old Testament birth narratives, in which the father has such prominence, why in the light of New Testament insistence on the father as the prime member of domestic society, should Matthew and Luke want, and be able, to eliminate the father of the most important Child in the Bible save under the pressure of reality? Why should Matthew, who showed his consciousness of the paternal role in the genealogies, insisting on this in generation after generation, suddenly present us with a Child conceived without a father?. . . .Why, despite the close parallel between the two annunications (in the Lucan narrative), is there one massive difference: the father, singled out in one case, absent in the other? Why, even if Luke 2 has an independent origin, as Fr. Brown suggests, is the evangelist so careful to feature Joseph only in public acts—the census, the Temple ceremonies—which accord entirely with a legal fatherhood? Why is there no phrase like 'whom he had begotten' about the Child.[10]

All this serves to stress the point being made here: the virginal conception is debated among exegetes and scholars as to its scriptural basis. This introduces the difficult question about the relationship of faith and theology to the shifting sands of exegesis.[11]

Or the matter about the brothers and sisters of Jesus we find again that it is debated and opinions are divided. J. Blinzler, for example, asserts that not one of the brothers and sisters is ever described as a son or daughter of Mary. In fact in most cases they are identified as having another mother.[12] On the

---

[8] *The Virginal Conception and Bodily Resurrection of Jesus,* Geoffrey Chapman, London-Dublin, 1973, pp. 66f.

[9] Ibid., n. 117, pp. 66f.

[10] *Marian Theology: Testing the Foundations* in: THE IRISH THEOLOGICAL QUARTERLY 42 (1975) pp. 216f.

[11] See J.A. Fitzmyer, *The Virginal Conception of Jesus in the New Testament* in: THEOLOGICAL STUDIES 34 (1973) pp. 541-573; A.C. Piepkorn, *The Virgin Birth Controversy: A Lutheran's Reaction* in MARIAN STUDIES 24 (1971) p. 101, suggests that the real question with regard to the virginal conception is whether it is an historical event or only a *theologoumenon.*

[12] *Die Brüder und Schwestern Jesu,* Stuttgart 1967.

other hand S. Benko[13] recognizes no problem at all in the Bible about the brothers and sisters being the sons and daughters of Mary.[14]

It seems therefore that there is no purely scriptural, unambiguous answer to the question: 'Is it, or is it not, necessary to believe that Christ had no human father, in view of his divinity?'[15] This also appears to be the case with the question about the brothers and sisters of Jesus. Thus we arrive at the same difficulty: What does this diversity of opinion mean for the faith of an evangelical Christian?

At the risk of appearing 'unbiblical' I feel bound to point out that there are grave difficulties connected with the Evangelical approach to Christianity. For us today the literal sense of scripture is not identical with its historical content. This was the outlook of the founding Fathers of Protestantism. There are a number of Protestant theologians today who recognise that this is one of the causes of the crisis concerning the foundation of Evangelical theology. A good deal more consideration needs to be given to this question at the ecumenical level, because it lies behind the dialogue about Mary.

---

[13] *Protestants, Catholics and Mary,* Valley Forge 1968.

[14] For the debate on Matthew 1:18-25 the following will be found helpful and interesting: M. Kramer, *Die Menschwerdung Jesu Christi nach Matthäus* (Matthew 1). *Seine Auslegung und sein literarisches Verfahren* in: BIBLICA 45 (1964) pp. 1-50 (Matthew's purpose is not the defence of the virgin birth of Jesus but of his Messiahship); O.A. Piper, *The Virgin Birth. The Meaning of the Gospel Accounts* in: INTERPRETATION 18 (1964) pp. 132-148. Both Matthew and Luke intended to relate the virgin birth as a historical fact; J. Wilkinson, *Apologetic Aspects of the Virgin birth of Christ* in: SCOTTISH JOURNAL OF THEOLOGY 17 (1964) pp. 159-181 (An extremely good presentation of the arguments *pro* and *con);* A. Vögtle, *Mt 1:25 und die Virginitas B.M. Virginis Post Partum* in: THEOLOGISCHE QUARTALSCHRIFT 147 (1967) pp. 28-39. (That Joseph did not know Mary till she brought forth her son is intended to insist on the *virginitas in partu;* it does not deny or affirm *the virginitas post partum);* I. Broer, *Die Bedeutung der "Jungfrauengeburt" im Matthäusevangelium* in: BIBEL UND LEBEN 12 (1971) pp. 248-260. (Matthew is concerned with the conduct of Joseph only up to the time of the birth of Jesus in order to show that the virgin gave birth to her child as foretold by the prophet. Matthew affirms but he does not emphasize the virgin birth); J.M. Germano, *Et non cognoscebat eam donec. . .inquisitio super sensu spirituali seu mystico Matthew 1:25* in: MARIANUM 35 (1973) pp. 184-240 (This text is not only about marital relations between Mary and Joseph; it also has a mystical sense concerning the dignity of Mary. The virginal conception was so great a miracle that it would have been unnecessary and unfitting to assert the absence of marital relations after such a conception); T. Stramare, *Giuseppe, 'uomo giusto' in Matthew 1:18-25* in: REVISTA BIBLICA 21 (1973) pp. 287-300 (The stress is on the mission of Joseph to act as the father of Jesus, not on the virginal conception. Jesus is born of a virgin mother and descends from David through Joseph).

[15] See the review article on the Dutch Catechism by J. Coventry SJ in: THE TABLET (September 23, 1967) p. 991.

For the Roman Catholic, the Church is taken to be the authentic interpreter of scripture and the Roman Catholic Church teaches the doctrine of the perpetual virginity of Mary. And it cannot be asserted categorically by any Christian that this doctrine is unbiblical.

2. Immaculate Conception and Assumption

It has to be admitted by the Roman Catholic partner in the dialogue that these doctrines are not to be found in scripture in a *literal and explicit* form. From this point of view, however, that is not the same as saying that they are not in scripture. The Roman Catholic Church considers these doctrines to have been revealed by God in respect of their having emerged in the Church's consciousness as a result of prayer and reflection on the Word of God, under the guidance of the Holy Spirit.

Roman Catholics have a normative Word of God Christianity. Holy scripture and holy tradition flow from and are subject to the one indivisible source, the Word of God. Scripture is supremely the Word of God when it is proclaimed in the midst of the church gathered to celebrate the Eucharist. Scripture does not exist without the faith of the Church and there is no faith without the Word of God. It does not stand over or above the Church, rather it belongs to it. This is not a purely arbitrary arrangement. When the Church looks back over her history and becomes aware of what it means to have received the Word of God, she knows that this Word is heard from the moment that Jesus Christ was on earth (I am prescinding here from the presence of the Word in creation) and that it has been heard in the Holy Spirit throughout her history right into the present moment. And the Holy Spirit does not give us new doctrines for himself; he speaks what he hears, declares the things that are to come and guides the Church into all the truth [cf. Jn 16:12-14]; he brings to the Church's remembrance all that Christ said [cf. Jn 14:25-26]. Under the guidance of the Holy Spirit the Church canonised the writings contained in scripture as expressions of her faith.

This understanding lies behind the Roman Catholic Church's belief in the Marian doctrines. It is not that she decides arbitrarily to add on a few more doctrines alongside what is contained in scripture. She does not know this kind of distinction.

So we are led directly to the question of the development of doctrine. On this Jaroslav Pelikan has written: "The doctrine of Mary constitutes a very special and difficult case of doctrinal development and as such a case it occupies a special place in the history of the controversy between Roman Catholicism and Protestantism over the propriety of 'new doctrines' ".[16]

The Roman Catholic Church does not consider that she has received these doctrines through a process of historical transmission that can be traced back in an unbroken line to an explicit statement in the New Testament. Her understanding of the development of doctrine is quite other than this. The development takes place under the guidance of the Holy Spirit at work in the Church leading her ever more deeply into the mystery of the Word of God. What is defined in terms of the development is considered to be *the faith of the Church* and is judged consonant with the entire teaching of revelation. Indeed were it not so considered and judged it could not be defined.

With regard to the immaculate conception it was through prayer and reflection on the holiness and sinlessness of Christ that the insight gradually emerged in the Church and came to complete clarity as to how the grace of redemption and holiness gained for us in Christ, applied to the Virgin Mary. In the case of the assumption it was through prayer and reflection on the eschatological victory of Christ over the final enemy death, that the insight gradually emerged in the Church and came to complete clarity, how the grace of Christ is totally victorious in Mary as perfectly redeemed and sanctified.

I do not imagine that such a brief presentation will commend the position of the Roman Catholic Church on the development of doctrine to those who profess the Evangelical position of Reformed Christianity. However, it does serve to indicate that the real issue theologically in respect of the Marian doctrines is the development of doctrine and the teaching authority of the Church. It may also serve to highlight the fact that these doctrines are not arbitrary accretions to the catholic and apostolic faith. They are understood by Roman Catholics to have emerged from the central truths of that faith and to have decisive anthropological, ecclesiological and eschatological significance for the whole of Christian life.[17]

Perhaps it will be of some assistance at this point to draw out a little more fully the meaning of these doctrines. As a prelude to this I would like to make a personal comment about these titles. It seems a pity that we did not arrive at a better English rendering of' them. We have no more than

---

[16] *Development of Christian Doctrine. Some Historical Prolegomena,* New Haven & London, 1969, pp. 96f.

[17] The Marian doctrines do not stand on the same level as the Trinitarian, Christological and Soteriologial doctrines of' the Church. There is clearly a 'hierarchy of truths'. Nevertheless, the formal reason for accepting any revealed doctrine raises difficulties (not insuperable) for the 'hierarchy of truths'.

transliterations from the Latin *immaculata conceptio* and *assumptio*. The *all-gracing of Mary* would be a more beautiful rendering of the first and *Mary's journey to heaven* a more beautiful rendering of the second. For the latter the Germans are more fortunate with *Mariä Himmelfahrt*.

The immaculate conception means that Mary is perfectly redeemed. From the first moment of her existence she was given the divine life of grace through the merits of her Son, Jesus Christ. In no way did she merit it, it was the gift of God's gracious will. God's choice is God's choice. As he chose Abraham, so he chose Mary. And it is precisely because it depended solely on God's will that we honour and revere Mary and in that, worship and adore God.

It can never be stressed enough that it was God's gift whereby a member of our race received the unique privilege of being redeemed by being preserved from sin. For many theologians in the Middle Ages (including St. Thomas) the difficulty about this doctrine was the apparent impossibility of reconciling the privilege with the doctrine of the universal need of redemption. How could Mary be included in redemption if she had no sin? This was a real difficulty for it seemed that the immaculate conception separated Mary from Christ and his saving—liberating and integrating—power.

John Duns Scotus holds an honourable and pivotal place in the solution of this difficulty. He demonstrates how Mary was redeemed by being preserved from sin through the foreseen merits of Christ. In fact I hold that this doctrine can be derived without too much trouble from his doctrine of the absolute primacy of Christ. Being a child of Adam Mary needed to be redeemed, and, as Scotus explains, she was redeemed in the very moment of incurring original sin.[18] As the one perfect mediator between God and man, Christ exercised a most perfect redemption in the case of her who was to be his mother. Thus by the immaculate conception Mary is not excluded from God's plan of redemption nor is she placed outside its framework. On the contrary, she belongs to it most perfectly of all of us. Hence it is that Scotus says: 'Mary needed Christ most of all as redeemer'.[19]

---

[18] The doctrine of original sin has undergone considerable development during the last two decades. This development has important consequences for the interpretation of the immaculate conception, but it does not affect the privilege of the modality of Mary's redemption as preservative.

[19] *Opus Oxoniense III*, d.3, q.1: *Utrum Beata Virgo feurit concepta in originali peccato?* (Vivès, XIV, pp. 59-176). The relevant text is found, ibid., p.171: *quia Maria maxime indiguisset Christo ut redempore; ipsa enim contraxisset originale peccatum ex ratione preparationis communis, nisi fuisset preventa per gratiam Mediatoris.*

The dogmatic definition of the assumption teaches that: the Immaculate Mother of God, Mary ever Virgin, when the course of her earthly life had ended, was taken up body and soul into the glory of heaven.[20]

It is significant that this doctrine is not described as a unique privilege granted to Mary, as is the immaculate conception in the Bull *Ineffabilis Deus.*[21] This implies that we must understand the doctrine of Mary precisely as pre-eminent member of the Church. If we take seriously the fact that Mary belonged to the New Israel on earth and that she is now model and image of the Church, then we may hold legitimately that what is defined of her may well be of wider application.[22] It should be noted that the text of the dogmatic formula uses a circumlocution for death: 'when the course of her earthly life had ended'. This leaves us free to hold that she died or that she did not die. As I understand it, to hold that she died seems more consonant with the remainder of revelation.

Suggestions for an Ecumenical-Theological Approach to Mary

I want to present now a theological approach to Mary which may be of some assistance in working out an ecumenical theology of Mary. My reflections are arranged under the following headings: 1. Mary the woman. 2. Mary the woman perfectly redeemed and image of the Church. 3. Mary the Mother of Jesus the Lord. 4. Mary the Woman of faith. 5. Mary the disciple of the Lord.

1. Mary the woman

An ecumenical theology of Mary should begin with the fact that she is a woman. Faith teaches us first of all that she is woman. This is fundamental about Mary. She was the woman chosen by God to be the mother of his incarnate Son. Thus her place in God's plan is formally as a woman who became a mother. Her womanhood, her being-a-women-in-the-world, her motherhood, her being-a-mother-in-the-world, give the key to any understanding of her significance and it also wards off the danger of

---

[20] *Constitutio apostolica. Munificentissimus, Deus*, 1 November 1960 in: DS 3903.

[21] 8 December 1954 in: DS 2803: *Definimus, doctrinam, quae tenet, beatissimam Virginem Mariam in primo instanti suae conceptionis fuisse singulari omnipotentis Dei gratia et privilegio, intuitu meritorum Christi Jesu Salvatoris humani generis, ab omni originalis culpae labe praeservatam immunem.* . . .

[22] On this see the splendid article by J.P. Kenny SJ, *The Assumption of Mary: Its Relevance for Us Today* in: THE CLERGY REVIEW (Augsut 1978) p. 287-294; on the definability of the assumption see B. Lonergan SJ, *The Assumption and Theology* in: *Collection*, papers by B. Lonergan SJ, ed. by F.E. Crowe SJ, Darton, Longman & Todd, London 1967, pp. 68-93.

transforming her into a goddess to counterbalance the exclusively masculine Trinity. God is the source of both masculine and feminine.[23] This will also contribute to a more thoroughly Christian anthropology of woman.

In his Apostolic exhortation *Marialis cultus* February 1974, Paul VI took, care to emphasise the active and responsible role of the Virgin Mary in the mystery of salvation and to stress how specifically in her activity, rather than in her passivity and submissiveness, she is the model of' modern woman.[24] However, it is not only her relationship to women that the Pope is concerned with in this Exhortation. Mary is also a model for men: 'the Blessed Virgin does not disillusion any of the profound expectations of the men and women of our time but offers them the perfect model of the disciple of the Lord'.[25]

2. Mary the woman perfectly redeemed and image of the Church

This aspect of an ecumenical theology of Mary will emphasise that Mary is the most beautiful realisation of the theology of grace and explain the modality of her redemption and sanctification. All the Marian doctrines are specific expressions of the doctrine of grace, and each Marian doctrine has an ecclesiological and anthropological character.

The basic principle of this approach will be Mary understood as archetype of the Church, which draws the four chief Marian doctrines into a fine unity. In her immaculate conception Mary is image of the holy Church. In her the community of the redeemed is already God's holy people. From the beginning in Mary the Church is without spot and wrinkle.

Mary became the mother of God through a free decision made possible by the totally necessary and utterly gratuitous grace of God. This does not necessarily involve us in the question about whether God so chose to depend on her, that had she not consented, the entire plan would have been frustrated. Free decisions in grace are the result of grace. The blessed in heaven, for example, love God and can do none other, yet they remain absolutely free. Freedom must never be reduced simply to a matter of choice to do this or not to do it, to do this or to do that. Freedom is the power of self-determination when confronted with the known good.

---

[23] See E. Doyle, *God and the Feminine* in: Clergy Review 56 (Nov. 1971) pp. 866-877. Editors' note: This article is reprinted in this anthology: pp. 557 ff.

[24] *To honour Mary. Apostolic Exhortation 'Marialis cultis of his Holiness Paul VI.'*, Typis Polyglottis Vaticanis 1974 (CTS Do 462) p. 63.

[25] Ibid., p. 64.

The Roman Catholic Church understands Mary's *fiat* as an event in the history of salvation, that is, an event which is part of God's plan to save, sanctify and liberate the world. It was not merely a private concern of hers. It was a public and official response for which Mary received the grace of God to co-operate freely with His will. This *fiat* was as public—in fact more public than Abraham's response to his call from God. Mary is placed by Luke on the dividing line between the Old and New Testaments. As Abraham is at the beginning of the Old Israel, so Mary stands at the beginning of the New.

Redemption comes to us through an active reception of the Word of God: "Blessed are those who hear the word of God and keep it" [Luke 11:28]. As Mary heard the Word of God, kept it and brought it forth, so also at baptism the Church hears the Word of God, keeps it and brings it forth at the font. And each member of the Church is called to bring the Word forth by a life of holiness and peace. "We are mothers to him", writes St. Francis, "when we enthrone him in our hearts and souls by love with a pure and sincere conscience, and give him birth by doing good".[26]

The virginal conception reveals to anyone who comes to know Christ Jesus that he is the absolutely free gift of God to us. He is *the* grace to humanity. But Christ must be known first. Christ as gift is the key to the meaning of the virginal conception. In the conception of Jesus the new humanity—the Second Adam—had its origin in the grace of God's loving kindness towards us. Nothing demanded him, not even the beautiful process of human generation; he came not by the holy urge of the flesh, not by the free will of man but by the free decision of God. The process of evolution did not demand him, though it is indeed wonderful how as gift he crowns and perfects that process. As the virginal bride of Christ, the Church is the gift of God, proceeding from the side of the Crucified One, whence flowed blood and water. Mary is ever-virgin because her vocation is centred exclusively on Christ and his redeeming work. As such she is also image of the Church, because the Church's all-consuming concern must be to serve Christ wheresoever he may be found in the world and to follow him wheresoever he may lead her.[27]

In her assumption Mary is image of the Church as totally redeemed, risen and glorified. What took place for Mary when the end of her earthly life came, is the model of what happens to every person in death. Once Mary is

---

[26] *Letter to All the Faithful* in: *The Writitigs of St. Francis Of Aissisi,* trans. by B. Fahy OFM, with introduction and notes by P. Hermann OFM, Burns & Oates, London 1963, p. 96.
[27] See K. Rahner SJ, *Mary Mother of the Lord. Theological Meditations,* Herder and Herder 1964, pp. 69f.

understood as model and pre-eminent member of the Church, it speedily becomes clear that in reflecting on her, one is considering the Church as such. This is the thrust of Roman Catholic theology today concerning the Virgin Mary.

3. Mary, the Mother of Jesus the Lord

In the first chapter of Luke's gospel we read that the angel said to Mary: 'The Holy Spirit will come upon you' [1:35]. In the Acts of the Apostles it is recorded: 'All these with one accord devoted themselves to prayer, together with the women and Mary the mother of Jesus, and with his brethren' [1:14]; and a little later: 'When the day of Pentecost had come, they were all together in one place. . . .And they were all filled with the Holy Spirit' [2:1, 4]. We are dealing here as it were with two infancy narratives: that of Jesus—the physical Christ, that of the Church—the mystical Christ. Mary is involved in both. These texts form the starting point for a fruitful understanding of Mary's relation to the Church as mother, in respect of her being the mother of Jesus Christ, the first born from the dead and brother of us all.

4. Mary, the Woman of Faith

In the eighth chapter of *Lumen Gentium* Mary is presented as the woman of faith:

> In the course of her Son's preaching she received the words whereby, in extolling a kingdom beyond the concerns and ties of flesh and blood, he declared blessed those who heard and kept the word of God [cf. Mark 3:35; par. Luke 11:27f.] as she was faithfully doing [cf. Luke 2:19, 51]. Thus the Blessed Virgin advanced in her pilgrimage of faith, and faithfully persevered in her union with her Son unto the cross.[28]

We must not forget that Mary lived by faith as we live by faith and she trusted in God absolutely. Nothing was any easier for her than it is for us. I have often wondered what is the precise difference between looking down at a little child in a crib and believing him to be the Messiah of God, and seeing the bread and wine on the altar and believing it to be the Body and the Blood. Mary had that faith for which Christ prayed on the night before he died; the kind of faith that goes on believing, hoping and trusting come what may; that goes on

---

[28] *Dogmatic Constitution on the Church* 58 in: *Vatican Council II*, p. 417.

proclaiming God's fidelity no matter what indications there may be to the contrary; that moves mountains, above all the on one called Calvary and sees through and beyond to the resurrection.

5. Mary the disciple of the Lord

Our knowledge about the historical life of Mary is practically non-existent. For this reason it does not seem to me that 'a new quest for the historical Mary'[29] would yield much fruit. Yet what history failed to furnish, pious fantasy managed to produce and then presented for our imitation. One thing, however, that seems to emerge clearly enough from the New Testament about Mary's life is that she was a disciple of her Son.[30] As pre-eminent member of the Church in whom God's grace is totally victorious, Mary is also pre-eminent among the followers of Christ and in this sense she is the perfect Christian. We need not only stand at a distance, as professor Haire suggested. We can draw close by imitating her life of faithful service, and in this way give to our devotion to her its most authentic expression. "She is worthy of imitation", writes Paul VI "because she was the first and the most perfect of Christ's disciples".[31]

These five considerations could furnish the basis for a most construction dialogue on the Virgin Mary between Roman Catholics and Evangelicals. They cannot pretend to be exhaustive and they may well prove not altogether satisfactory in the long run. But if they can help us to grow into a deeper understanding of why so many of Christ's followers today honour and revere his mother they will have served a useful purpose.

Concluding Remarks

To draw the article to a close I want to mention some topics which have considerable relevance in any dialogue about the place of Mary in the life of the Church.

---

[29] As suggested by C. Bernas OCSO in his review of Heikki Räisanen, *Die Mutter Jesu im Neuen Testament* in: THE CATHOLIC BIBLICAL QUARTERLY 31 (1969) p. 601: "With the help of its (the book's) description of what might be termed 'Mary of faith' we may even now be ready for a 'new quest of the historical Mary' ".

[30] See R.L. Brown SS, *The Meaning of Modern New Testament Studies for an Ecumenical Understanding of Mary* in: BIBLICAL REFLECTIONS ON CRISES FACING THE CHURCH, Darton, Longman & Todd, London 1975, pp. 90f., 103f.

[31] *Marialis Cultus,* p. 61.

1. Prayer through Mary

A very large sector of the Church not only prays through the intercession of Mary the Mother of God, but also believes totally in the efficacy of this prayer, which is always in, through and with Christ. Those who constitute this sector—Roman Catholics, Orthodox and a considerable part of the Anglican Communion—do not consider Mary to be a goddess nor that she takes the place of Christ before God, if we ask one another on this earth to pray for us (and there is good biblical foundation for that) is it so strange to implore the blessed in heaven, and especially Mary, to do likewise?

2. Mary and Islam

This introduces the wider ecumenism. Mary the mother of Jesus has a relatively important place in Islam. It is worthy of reflection that Muhammad was so influenced by Christian sources concerning Mary that he included her in the Koran. This should inspire us to increase our efforts to reach a better mutual understanding of the place of Mary in the Christian scheme of things.[32]

3. Jung and the Assumption

Carl Gustav Jung considered the assumption to be the most important religious event since the Reformation.[33] He demonstrated how congenial the definition is to the psychological mind, being based on a belief stretching back for more than a thousand years. And indeed it should be emphasised that this belief was not excogitated by Pius XII in 1950. Jung saw the definition as an event of great significance and in terms of it he made a trenchant criticism of Protestantism, saying that it is left with the odium of being nothing more than a man's religion. Jung himself, I think, fell into the excess of viewing Mary as well-nigh divine. However, it is obvious in respect of his reflections that the definition responds to deep psychological needs in us, and in this way proves graphically the truth of the ancient saying that grace perfects nature.[34]

4. The Virgin-conception and Anthropology

Anthropologists have shown an amount of interest in this doctrine ever since Edmund Leach published his controversial work on the subject in 1966.[35]

---

[32] F.J. McCarthy SJ, *Mary in Islam*, n. 13 in the series MOTHER OF JESUS, publ. by the Ecumenical Society of the Blessed Virgin Mary, 1971.

[33] *Answer to Job*, Routledge & Kegan Paul, London 1954, pp. 165-178, esp. 169f.

[34] See Doyle, *God and the Feminine*, pp. 867-870. Editors' note: This article is reprinted in this anthology: pp. 557 ff.

[35] E. Leach, *Virgin Birth* in: PROCEEDINGS OF THE ROYAL ANTHROPOLOGICAL INSTITUTE OF GREAT BRITAIN AND IRELAND FOR 1966, pp. 34-49; see also M.E. Spiro, *Virgin Birth, Parthenogenesis and Physiological Paternity. An Essay in Cultural Interpretation* in: MAN 3

The reflections of anthropologists have a good deal to contribute to our understanding of the social functions and symbols of the doctrine.[36]

5. Mary and iconography

The place and influence of Mary in the life and doctrine of the Church has had phenomenal influence on this most rich and beautiful section of the history of art. As belonging to aesthetic categories, icons disclose that truth is beauty and beauty is truth, and where there is truth there is always being. Icons of the Virgin Mary communicate as much as theological reflection on the place of Mary in the Christian understanding of the world and of God's relationship to it.

It must surely be counted among the mighty works of God in our time that dialogue between Roman Catholics and Evangelicals has begun to consider the Virgin Mary and to discuss in openness and honesty topics that have been barriers and bones of contention for so long. We must now strive and pray that the good work, begun will come to its fruitful end.

To conclude I reproduce a Litany I wrote some years ago for Our Lady's shrine at Walsingham.[37]

Litany of our Lady of Walsingham

Mary,	pray to the Lord for us
Mary all-graced by God,	pray to the Lord for us
Mary mother of the Lord,	pray to the Lord for us
Mary ever a virgin,	pray to the Lord for us
Mary taken to heaven,	pray to the Lord for us
Mary at Bethlehem,	pray for all mothers
Mary at Nazareth,	pray for all families
Mary at Cana,	pray for all married couples
Mary at the cross,	pray for all who suffer

(1968) pp. 242-261; J.D.M. Derrett, *Virgin Birth in the Gospels* in: MAN 6 (1971) pp. 289-293; S. Montague, *Trobiand Kinship and the Virgin Birth Controversy* in: MAN 6 (1971) pp. 353-368.

[36] See the most instructive article by J.A. Saliba SJ, *The Virgin-birth Debate in Anthropological Literature. A Critical Assessment* in Theological Studies 36 (1975) pp. 428-454.

[37] I gratefully acknowledge permission from the Administrator of the Slipper Chapel to publish this text. Permission to publish was originally obtained from Bishop Alan Clark. I have modified some of the original phrases and I have added one line: "Mary examplar of humanity, pray for all of us".

Mary in the upper room,   pray for all who wait
Mary model of womanhood,   pray for all women
Mary exemplar of' humanity,   pray for all of us

Woman of faith,   keep us in mind
Woman of hope,   keep us in mind
Woman of love,   keep us in mind
Woman of suffering,   keep us in mind
Woman of anxiety,   keep us in mind
Woman of humility,   keep us in mind.
Woman of poverty,   keep us in mind
Woman of obedience,   keep us in mind
Woman of integrity,   keep us in mind

Woman who wondered,   remember us to God
Woman who listened,   remember us to God
Woman who followed Christ,   remember us to God
Woman who longed for Christ, remember us to God
Woman who loved Christ,   remember us to God

Mother of God,   be our mother always
Mother of the Church,   be our mother always
Mother of humanity,   be our mother always
Mother of the earth,   be our mother always
Mother we need,   be our mother always

Mary who went on believing, we thank God for you
Mary who never lost hope,   we thank God for you
Mary who loved to the end,   we thank God for you

All holy and immortal God,
in giving us Jesus Christ as our redeemer and brother,
you gave us Mary his mother to be our mother also;
grant us, we implore You,
to live lives worthy of so great a brother and so dear a mother,
that we may come at last to you the Father of us all.
Amen.

Some Thoughts on *Mysterium Ecclesiae*[1]

After reading the *Declaration* from the Congregation for the Doctrine of the Faith and reflecting on the issues which so clearly lie behind its publication, I was reminded in a vague way of the controversy, in early third-century Rome between Pope St. Zephyrinus (199-217) and St. Hippolytus on the reality of our Lord's divinity. In the midst of all the philosophical wrangling that surrounded him, St. Zephyrinus, bombarded by the subtle reasonings, high learning and hot temper of Hippolytus, steadfastly refused to do other than repeat what had been the received tradition: "I know only one God, Christ Jesus, and none other, who was born and suffered; it was not the Father who died, but the Son". Like the Congregation for the Doctrine of the Faith, Zephyrinus made assertions but gave no arguments!

This rather loose historical analogy (the *Declaration* comes from a Congregation, not directly from the Pope) may be taken as a starting point in assessing the importance and the content of the *Declaration* in the present development of Ecclesiology. It must be emphasised that this *Declaration* emanates from the Congregation for the Doctrine of the *Faith* of the Catholic Church, not for the doctrine of *theology*. It is a doctrinal statement. This does not, of course, place the *Declaration* outside the bounds of critical assessment, but it does determine the spirit in which it is to be received. Now, I am fully aware that I might well be accused here of begging the question and riding slipshod over the delicate problem of the relationship between faith and theology. It must be readily admitted that the *Declaration* opens up many questions which still require study and analysis, for example: the meaning of the development of doctrine, the nature of the Magisterium of the Church, the historical nature of the Church, the relationship between Revelation and the faith and practice of the Church as realised historically, and so on. These are and will remain open questions, though they involve doctrinal and irrevocable principles. Of course it would not be fitting for the Congregation to enter into public controversy. It is a pity, all the same, that the *Declaration* did not

---

[1] CLERGY REVIEW 58 (Dec. 1973) pp. 944-949. Doyle is discussing here the questions Hans Küng had evoked by his book *Infallible?* and the Roman Curia's reaction in form of a *declaratio*. Published with permission (www.priestsandpeople.co.uk).

recognise in a positive manner the results of theological research on the very questions it treats.

However, in the final analysis, faith is not theology. They are inextricably bound together, they can never be simply identified. Theology is a service in the Church; she is not the queen of the sciences but the *ancilla verbi*. The faith of the Church is given and lived long before it becomes an object of reflection. The truths of the faith cannot depend on theological acumen, for if they did, there would be very few believers indeed. Consequently, one can understand the content of the concluding paragraphs: it was not the *Declaration's* intention to prove by way of study that divine revelation is entrusted to the Church. For this reason also one feels that Professor Küng's remarks in his interview with *Herder Korrespondenz* were overcritical and intolerant.[2]

Nine years have now passed since the promulgation of the Dogmatic Constitution on the Church, *Lumen Gentium*. That Constitution marked a crucial stage in the development of ecclesiology which stretches back through the work of theologians, the teaching of the Popes (especially Pius XII and Leo XIII) and the definitions of the First Vatican Council to the unique contributions to a renewed understanding of the Church made by the Tübingen school in the writing of Drey, Sailer and, above all, Johann Adam Möhler in the early nineteenth century. A study of this fascinating story vindicates the judgement of Henri de Lubac that, as far as the development of dogma is concerned, the twentieth century is destined to be the century of the Church. Now, once more it is Tübingen that has our attention and no one can deny that Professor Küng has played an indispensable and significant (if sometimes stormy and truculent) part in this development. It is important for us both doctrinally and theologically to see *Lumen Gentium* not as the end of a process, but as a crucial stage in the Church's understanding of her own nature. Christian sanity forbids us to absolutize the present or relativize the past to the point of meaninglessness. Firstly, it is important doctrinally, because *Lumen Gentium* presents us with a deeper understanding of the Church as a mystery and a mystery is a truth we never cease to grasp better, for we can never comprehend a mystery. Secondly, it is important theologically because it enunciates principles which will guide and allow theological endeavour to discover and draw out the implications of the faith for the Catholic Church in

---

[2] THE TABLET (September 1, 1973) p. 835.

her self-understanding and in her relationships with other Christians, the World Religions, atheism and the structures of the world as such.

The *Declaration* is to be placed and assessed in the context of this development. Theology has its freedom, but it is pursued in all its scientific rigour within the community of believers. (It is the word that makes theology possible.) However, given this proviso, it is a fact of experience that theologians are an indispensable factor in the development of dogma. The Holy Spirit inspires men to put the highest faculties of the human spirit at the service of the Word and of the Church. But the teaching of theology and the views of theologians are not the Magisterium of the Church. The theologian cannot place himself outside or above the Magisterium. At times it is absolutely necessary that the Magisterium draw attention to and reiterate the truths of the faith which cannot be called into doubt. One may well debate the mode in which this is done and the methods used and certainly there has been too much 'cloak-and-dagger' atmosphere in the Roman Congregations' dealings with theologians. That it must be done, however, is obvious. It seems to me that both the attitude of Professor Küng (which is so sadly anti-Roman) and certain statements made in his books on infallibility and the ministerial priesthood, demanded a statement of the Catholic Faith. This does not mean that the *Declaration* has said the last word or that Professor Küng should be silenced. But we do need to hear how he reconciles certain of his views with some pivotal dogmas of the Catholic Faith. This is not the place to analyse his works, but if I may be permitted a personal comment, I would say that his views always seem to me to offer too easy a solution to what are without doubt great problems. In attempting to solve problems and answer questions of this magnitude, all sides and every principle must be accounted for.

The *Declaration* is made up of an introduction, six sections and a short conclusion. At a first reading it appears to be little more than a catena of texts from the Council. The mode of presentation, however, makes the document a very positive one and leaves open the road to further development.

The first section concerns the unity of the Church. It asserts that the Church of Christ is one and this Church is then identified according to par. 8 of *Lumen Gentium.* The oneness of the Church is God's gift in Christ and, as far as the Catholic Faith is concerned, it would be to blaspheme the Triune God, whose unity itself makes the Church what it is, to hold otherwise. There is, then, a *Church* of Christ, not an Amalgam of Christ or a Collection of Churches and Ecclesial Communities of Christ. This, of course, introduces the very difficult question of what is the precise, formal nature of the relationship between the Catholic Church and the Churches and Ecclesial Communities outside her visible structure. It is a pity that nothing is said on this question in the *Declaration*. After all, the Church has already declared that many of the significant elements that go to build up the Church can exist outside the visible boundaries of the Catholic Church. How this is the case needs explanation in terms of the faith. The Congregation would have done incalculable good had it given some authentic guidelines here. Ecclesiology, in any case, must now turn its resources to a protracted examination and analysis of those far-reaching statements of *Lumen Gentium*, par. 8, and *Unitatis Redintegratio*, par. 3. The unity of the Church is itself a gift, a grace from which flows the unity of faith and worship, life and work, but not uniformity.

The second section concerns the infallibility of the universal Church. It should be noted that this section precedes the one on the infallibility of the Church's Magisterium. The context, therefore, in which we must place the infallibility of the Magisterium is the "certain shared infallibility, which is restricted to matters of faith and morals, which is present when the whole People of God unhesitatingly holds a point of doctrine pertaining to these matters". One might compare this with the very important order of the early chapters of *Lumen Gentium* where that on the People of God precedes the one on the Hierarchical Structure of the Church. It is in the light of this order that we should understand the teaching of the First Vatican Council. The Pope enjoys that infallibility which Christ intended his Church to have. The *Declaration* asserts once more the truth of the Catholic Faith that by divine institution it is the exclusive task of the pastors alone, the successors of Peter and the other Apostles, to teach the faithful authentically. This task belongs to the gift of hierarchical communion. But even this task must be set in the context of the infallibility of the universal Church. Here, then, without question the *Declaration* has made a significant contribution to the development of Ecclesiology.

The fourth and fifth sections may be taken together. These touch on the very foundation of the Catholic Faith and I cannot myself see how certain positions held by Professor Küng in his book *Infallible? An Enquiry* can be reconciled with the teaching of the Faith. The *Declaration* does not explain how the truth of Revelation is discerned and expressed. Yet it does admit the historical relativity of dogmatic propositions and even Professor Küng admits that this is an important concession to modern theology. However, the *meaning* of dogmatic propositions remains ever true and constant. It is difficult to understand how Professor Küng's view, which holds that the meaning and content of dogmatic propositions can change, can be reconciled with the doctrine of the Catholic Faith. Surely any sound epistemology admits a distinction between meaning and the proposition. A dogmatic proposition contains an 'open structure' which allows the believer to make precisely this distinction between meaning and formula—a practice engaged in by preachers every Sunday morning at Mass. The *Declaration* has reiterated here the Catholic Faith that there are irrevocably true propositions of the faith which endure.

The sixth section treats of the universal and ministerial priesthood of the Church. The ministerial priesthood is placed in the context of the Church as a priestly people. The bishop and priest are set apart, though not separated, from the Church or mankind—they are precisely *priestly* men, not clerical men. Moreover, ordination confers on priests a permanent designation by Christ or a character and the enduring nature of the priestly character throughout life pertains to the teaching of the faith. The *Declaration* here responds directly to Professor Küng's book on the priesthood (though he is not mentioned by name). There is much evidence in the New Testament for considering priests as set apart and permanently designated in their ministry. The assertion of the development of the Church's understanding of the priesthood is significant and will be welcomed by theologians.

One notes a certain biblical naivety in this section. Some explanation ought to have been given of the meaning of "apostolic succession" based on the evidence provided by New Testament exegesis and historical research into the immediate sub-apostolic era. This evidence in no way detracts from the Church's faith in the necessity of the episcopacy. The use of it in so important a document as this would have had far-reaching repercussions for Ecumenism, especially in regard to non-Episcopal Churches and Ecclesial Communities.

The Future of the Papacy[1]

The death of Paul VI, the election, brief pastorate and death of John Paul I, and the election of the remarkable John Paul II, turned the attention of the world towards Rome and the papacy. The space allotted to these events in the press and the time given over to them on radio and television were extensive. But this is hardly surprising. There is a mystique attached to the papacy which always evokes a reaction, whether positive or negative. Its long history, the many great and often fascinating personalities who have held the office, the very nature of the petrine claims, make indifference to the papacy almost impossible. For most people 'the greatest religious office in the world'[2] remains intriguing, attractive and strangely alluring. Many a hard-headed cynic has been known to fall under its spell at a papal audience and to be carried away by the extraordinary yet indefinable atmosphere these audiences spontaneously create.

A salutary and edifying consequence of those events, noted by many a parish priest, was an increase in Mass attendance on the Sundays immediately following them. That even popes must die is a sombre and particularly acute reminder of our mortality. That a new one is elected sooner or later, to come forth from the mysterious secrecy of the Sistine Chapel, like a child coming from the womb, or springs of fresh water from the dark earth, is a sign that death gives way to a new kind of life. The papal deaths and elections were powerful and effective means of grace to the Church and world.

Declaration of Criteria

In the interval between the death of Pope Paul VI and the election of his successor, ten theologians published a declaration containing six criteria for the kind of pope today's Church needs, namely: 1. a man open to the world; 2. a spiritual leader; 3. an authentic pastor; 4. a true fellow bishop; 5. an ecumenical mediator; 6. a genuine Christian.[3] These are decisive criteria which

---

[1]   DOCTRINE AND LIFE (Dec. 1978) pp. 612-629. Published with permission.
[2]   Thus did Peter Nichols describe the papacy in an article in THE TIMES, Monday August 28th 1978, p. 1.
[3]   The full text of the declaration was published in DOCTRINE AND LIFE (October, 1978) pp. 531-534.

have emerged out of the spirit of the times under the guidance of the Holy Spirit.

Over the last few decades the papacy has enjoyed a moral authority unequalled at any previous period in its long and complex history, including the reigns of St. Gregory VII (1073-1085) and Innocent III (1198-1216). In recent years, however, that moral authority has waned a little. The recognition and use of these criteria in the declaration will not only bring reforms to the institution of the papacy, but will also re-establish completely the papacy's moral authority and prestige in the world, and restore its credibility as an institution believed by Roman Catholics to be crucial to the life and future of the human race.

We have no means of course of knowing whether this declaration had any direct influence on the choice of John Paul I or John Paul II. It is significant, however, that John Paul I decided to be known as Supreme Pastor rather than Supreme Pontiff, and not to be crowned with the tiara. These decisions made it clear that he wished to emphasise to the whole world the primarily spiritual and pastoral character of the papal office. We shall never know how he would have developed his understanding of the pastoral role of the papacy. He may well have come to take a more direct and active part in the affairs and daily life of the Roman diocese, rather than fulfil this aspect of his episcopal office almost exclusively through a vicar. There are some people who would warmly welcome such a development. In this connection it has been suggested that the pope should take up residence at the Lateran. All this would make it clearer to the Church that the pope is a true fellow bishop. However, a word of caution needs to be added here. Due in large measure to the media, the international importance of the papacy has grown enormously. This cannot be separated now from his universal role in the church. The pope cannot ignore or neglect this element in his office except to the detriment of the papacy. It is for this reason that John Paul I's friendly and open attitude to the journalists must be counted among the noteworthy and indicative features of his short pastoral ministry.[4] He was at home and at ease with the media, and he could use them with evident skill. In an important area of modern life he showed himself open to the world.

The pope, then, ought not to develop his involvement with the Roman diocese at the cost of curtailing his global ministry as a spiritual leader. For

---

[4] See his address to the journalists on September 1st 1978 in L'OSSERVATORE ROMANO (1 Ottobre 1978) p. 9. Ronald Singleton reported in THE UNIVERSE (September 8, 1978) p. 20, that the pope had said in an aside that had he not become a priest he would have been a journalist.

example, it would be a great mistake to reduce general audiences for any reason. These furnish tremendous opportunities for the pope to make contact with people from all over the world. Bound up with his universal pastoral role is the responsibility to help us all to rise above the constricting limits of nationalism and narrowness and to teach us by word and example that we are first of all terrestrians. There is no one in the world better suited, with greater claim or more competence to fulfil this responsibility than the pope.

What influence the above criteria may have had on the election of John Paul II and on the pope himself we shall mention briefly later in the article.

Theology of the Papacy

There are difficulties with regard to the papacy from an ecumenical point of view. Paul VI himself expressed this succinctly in 1967 when he said that the pope is beyond doubt the gravest obstacle in the path of ecumenism[5] However, it is not only outside the visible boundaries of the Roman Catholic Church that there are difficulties about the papacy. These are now encountered inside the Roman Catholic Church itself and they are by no means confined to the ranks of the theologians. No one of course who professes the beliefs of this Church and is in communion with its Supreme Pastor would want to ignore the papacy or so diminish its importance as to render it effete. This is why the declaration of criteria for electing a pope manifests not only the belief of its signatories in the papacy, but also their firm conviction about the importance of its role. And indeed it is true that the papacy has never been more necessary and more relevant than now.

There is dissatisfaction in the Church concerning the papacy because of factors which militate against its relevance and role, and which prohibit it from exercising its mission to the maximum degree and to the widest dimensions in the world. There are the powerful entrenched vestiges of eighteenth century absolutism which are totally uncongenial and even repellent today; there is the bureaucratic machinery of the Curia which tends to obscure the evangelical character of the papal office; there is the legalistic and uninspiring terms in which the pope's place in the Church is described and expounded.

---

[5] Allocution to the Secretariat for Unity, April 28th 1967 in: ACTA APOSTOLICAE SEDIS LIX (June 28, 1967) p. 498: "Le Pape, Nous le savons bien, est sans doute l'obstacle le plus grave sur la route de l'oecumenisme".

During the great papal events this year I found myself again and again thinking about the theology of the papacy and reflecting on what kind of theological approach to it would be most suitable and attractive in the church and world of today. This article is the result of those thoughts and reflections.

A theology of the papacy which hopes to have meaning today and be attractive to people of our time and especially to the young in age and heart, must studiously avoid beginning with the primacy of jurisdiction, or with the doctrine of infallibility. To take these as starting points betrays an excessively legalistic approach to an office which is primarily and fundamentally pastoral and spiritual. Only when theology has studied and presented the spiritual and pastoral character of the papacy may it turn confidently and serenely to the primacy of jurisdiction and papal infallibility. And we must never forget that the pope's primacy of jurisdiction is episcopal.[6] Hence it is to be distinguished from all earthly power and authority and there is no totally satisfactory political analogue for it. There is an apposite text in the declaration of criteria which is found in the explanation of the sixth criterion, 'a genuine Christian':

> (The pope) should be a Christian in the genuine sense of the term, mainly a man who in thought, word and deed is guided by the gospel of Jesus Christ as the decisive norm of his life. . . .He should preside over the Church in an attitude of calm patience and confidence, ever aware that the Church is not a bureaucratic organisation, not a business enterprise, and not a political party, but rather the encompassing community of believers.[7]

This text serves to remind us that the pope is not an emperor, not a monarch, not a president. Theological reflection on the papacy, therefore, has to begin with the Church's faith in the revealing word of God.

It is not particularly helpful now either to begin a theological inquiry into the nature of the papal office by explaining the distinction between the defined primacy of jurisdiction and what is known as the primacy of honour. Such a starting point proves sterile. It only leads down the familiar alley where one stresses the difference between the position of the pope as possessing a primacy of jurisdiction and the position of the patriarch of Constantinople or the archbishop of Canterbury as having only a primacy of honour. And this alley always turns out to be a *cul-de-sac*. What a theology of the papacy for today must do is first of all eschew this well-worn distinction as a starting

---

[6] *Constitutio dogmatica I de Ecclesia Christi*, c. 3: *De vi et ratione primatus Romani Pontificis*, DS 3060.

[7] DOCTRINE AND LIFE (October, 1978) pp. 533f.

point, establish another and then aim to create the right context in which the primary of jurisdiction and the doctrine of infallibility can be understood as significant and applicable. Such a theology of the papacy will begin with and develop from two spiritual and eirenic considerations:

1.   the pope as the sign and centre of unity, and
2.   the evangelical primacy of the papacy.

The Sign and Centre of Unity

The constitution on the Church, *Lumen gentium,* begins by proclaiming that the Church is a mystery. It is a mystery because it is "a people brought into unity from the unity of the Father, the Son and the Holy Spirit".[8] The unity of the Church is the gift of God, who shares with us the inner unity of his triune life. The unity, therefore, which the Church possesses, is the unity which she is. This mark of the Church is derived directly from that grace of God which we designate as *church.* The Church is one because God is one. The Church is a gift, a grace, flowing from the superabundance of the divine life. The other three marks of the Church: holiness, catholicity and apostolicity are likewise derived directly from God's own being. The Church is Catholic because God is three-in-one. He is not a lone power, but a unity-in-diversity. The Church is holy because God is integral, that is, utter identity of being and will, having therefore a most authentic existence. The Church is apostolic because the Son was sent from the Father and the Holy Spirit was sent by the Father and the Son after Christ's glorification. Before there are Twelve Apostles there are already Two Apostles with crucial missions to the world.

The papacy expresses the Church's unity in the midst of a vast catholicity of rites, languages, colours, cultures, discipline and customs. By the nature of his mission the pope has to think and speak in international and transcultural terms. We, of what may be called the Western Church, for far too long have confused unity with uniformity. And paradoxical though it seems, uniformity is calculated to render the papacy ever more superfluous and finally unnecessary. A centre of unity is only indispensable and crucial where diversity flourishes. When uniformity prevails, creative tension ceases, originality is neutralised, and soon there is only dullness and monotony. But what is more serious is that uniformity is contrary to the Church's intrinsic being. In origin—

---

[8]   Dogmatic Constitution on the Church, *Lumen gentium* 4 in: *Vatican Council II. The Conciliar and Post-Conciliar Documents,* ed. by A. Flannery OP, Dominican Publications Dublin, p. 352.

God's grace—the Church is constituted catholic, diverse, pluriform. The inner logic of uniformity in the Church leads ultimately to a denial of God's own triune fife.

A centre of unity keeps diversity from degenerating into division. In the dialectic diversity safeguards unity from congealing into uniformity. The papacy then is meant to signify and preserve the Church's unity, the universal episcopate to signify and encourage its diversity. The more diversity grows and develops according to the principles of collegiality and coresponsibility, the greater becomes the need of the papacy in the Church.

These reflections on unity-in-diversity can be summarised in the following schema:

THE TRIUNE LIFE OF GOD

THE MYSTERY OF THE CHURCH OF CHRIST[9]

ONE	CATHOLIC
POPE	BISHOPS
UNITY	DIVERSITY
NOT UNIFORMITY	NOT DIVISION

The Evangelical Primacy

In an important reflection in THE TABLET last Easter Fr. Gerald O'Collins SJ presented a view of the petrine ministry according to which the pope is understood to succeed to Peter in his role as fundamental witness to the resurrection of Jesus Christ.[10] By stressing Peter's function among the Twelve as primary witness to Christ's resurrection, Fr. O'Collins locates the key to a new understanding of the papacy in the primacy of witness to the paschal mystery.[11]

The importance of this theological approach to the papacy cannot be overstated. One passage in particular discloses the author's concern that we have the right priorities in our theology of the papacy: "Undoubtedly, the fundamental witness to the Lord's resurrection must also responsibly guide, govern and teach the Church. But it would be inverting the sequence of

---

[9] Prior to all models we might employ, we must profess that the Church is a mystery whose origin is veiled in God's inscrutable wisdom and goodness to share with us his own inmost life.

[10] *The Easter Witness* in: THE TABLET (March 25, April 1, 1978) pp. 297f.

[11] Ibid., p. 297: "The key becomes primacy of witness to the paschal mystery. . . ."

importance to insist first on jurisdiction and public authority and then perhaps add something about testimony to the resurrection".[12]

Fr. O'Collins has done us an enormous service in publishing this instructive and inspiring reflection. It will not be considered peevish of me, I hope, if I express some reservations concerning the content of his approach.

Firstly, there are certain functions which pertain uniquely to the Apostles and to which there is no succession in the Church. The Apostles' function as *the foundation* of the Church and their function as *witness* to the resurrection of Jesus Christ, are not part of the apostolic succession. The pope and the bishops do not, and indeed cannot, succeed to these functions of the Twelve Apostles. The pope, therefore, does not succeed to Peter as first witness to the risen Christ. In no sense pertaining to public, official, saving history in the world, can it be said that the Risen Lord has appeared to John Paul II. Hence it is not to Peter's primacy as witness that the pope succeeds, but rather to his primacy as proclaimer of the Risen Lord. We will return to this shortly.

Secondly, while the primacy of proclaiming the resurrection forms a constitutive element of papal primacy, there are other constitutive elements also based on the New Testament, which need to be mentioned if we are to have a comprehensively new approach to the pope's primacy. These further elements are: the primacy of proclaiming the divine sonship of Jesus Christ, the primacy of witness to unconditional love of Christ and the primacy of service of church and world. Together these elements may be taken as forming what we have described as the evangelical primacy of the pope. This primacy can now be presented schematically as follows:

Constitutive Elements of the Evangelical Primacy of the Papacy

1. The primacy of proclamation of the incarnation [Matthew 16:16]; resurrection [Acts 2:14-36; 10:34-43].

2. The primacy of witness to unconditional love of Christ [John 21:15-17].

3. The primacy of service [John 21:15-17; Luke 22:31-33; Acts 3:1-9] of church and world.

---

[12] Ibid., p. 298.

The Primacy of Proclamation

This centres on the unique and fundamental truths of the gospel: the incarnation of God's only Son, our Lord Jesus Christ and his resurrection from the dead. On these truths rests the whole edifice of the Christian religion for they are the heart of revelation.

In answer to Jesus's question: "But who do you say that I am?", Simon Peter made this confession: "You are the Christ, the Son of the living God" [Matthew 16:15f]. This confession was made not by Peter's own wit nor from his own resources, but in virtue of a revelation from God the Father: "Blessed are you, Simon Bar-Jona! For flesh and blood has not revealed this to you, but my Father who is in heaven. And I tell you, you are Peter, and on this rock I will build my church, and the powers of death shall not prevail against it. I will give you the keys of the kingdom of heaven" [16:17-19].[13] Immediately prior to this question Jesus had asked the disciples: "Who do men say that the Son of man is?" There was evidently a variety of opinions among the people: John the Baptist, Elijah, Jeremiah or one of the prophets. Peter's unambiguous and unhesitating answer put speculation at an end and excluded all uncertainties, at least as far as the immediate disciples were concerned.[14]

We are familiar with the use of the texts concerning the keys of the kingdom of heaven and the authority to bind and loose, to support the primacy of petrine jurisdiction.[15] What I want to emphasise in this passage is the primacy of confession—the *primatum confessionis* as St. Ambrose calls it[16]— from which I derive the pope's primacy of proclamation of this truth. This is based on the clear evidence that Peter exercised definite leadership in the Jerusalem church and on the belief that his leadership continues in the Roman bishop.[17]

---

[13] Peter undoubtedly has a special place. To all the disciples it is said: "Whatever you bind on earth shall be bound in heaven, and whatever you loose on earth shall be loosed in heaven" [Matthew 18:18; cf. 16:19]. But to Peter alone: "I will give you the keys of the kingdom of heaven".

[14] Cf. *Peter in the New Testament. A Collaborative Assessment by Protestant and Roman Catholic Scholars,* ed. by R.A. Brown, K.P. Donfried and J. Reumann, Augsburg Publishing House MN, Paulist Press N.Y., Paramus, Toronto 1973, pp. 83-101, 105-107.

[15] *Constitutio dogmatica I de Ecclesia Christi,* c. 1: *De apostolici primatus In beato Petro institutione,* DS 3053; I. Salaverri SJ, *De Ecclesia Christi* in: *Sacrae Theologiae Summa I Theologia Fundamentalis,* BIBLIOTECA DE AUTORES CRISTIANOS, Madrid 1958, pp. 558-573.

[16] *De Incarnationis Dominicae Sacramento* 4, 32 in: PL 16, 826: *His ergo ante reticebat, ut doceret nos quod impiorum nec verbum debeamus iterare: hic, inquam, ubi audivit: 'Vos autem quid me dicitis?'* [Matthew 16:15] *statim loci non immemor sui primatum egit: primatum confessionis utique, non honoris; primatum fidei, non ordinis.*

[17] See Oscar Cullman, *Peter, Disciple—Apostle—Martyr. A Historical and Theological Study.* Trans. from German by F. V. Wilson, SCM Press Ltd., London 1953, pp. 33-40; O. Karrer,

The Church has to proclaim Jesus because in him what the world and mankind mean to God has been revealed with total clarity. But who do people today say Jesus is? Who do they think he is? Is he a divine man? A superman? A social reformer? A revolutionary? A teacher of good private and social ethics? He can indeed be all these, but none of them have priority. For unless he is first confessed as Son of the living God, it is of little significance that he may also have been and remains still to us a social reformer or a revolutionary.

The incarnation of the Son of God has provided the Christian Church with the most profound anthropology ever conceived in human history. Jesus discloses to us in the reality of his own humanity (not through it) what God is like and this is expressed in its most original form by the words *Father* and *Forgiving Love.* He reveals to us also what it means to be human: the being in this world who is called in the innermost depths of his historical existence to surrender himself unconditionally to the will of God, as to his ultimate destiny in faith, hope and love. By the doctrine of the incarnation of God's Son the Church has come to know that God himself is the guarantee of our humanity. To surrender to God is to arrive at one's true and full humanity. Through the incarnation the Church knows in her very being that when she speaks of God, she automatically says something about humanity; that when she speaks of humanity, of men and women in history, she proclaims also a word about God.

According to what may well be the oldest Christian text [1 Corinthians 15:3-5] the Risen Lord appeared first to Peter: 'For I delivered to you as of first importance what I also received, that Christ died for our sins in accordance with the scriptures, that he was buried, that he was raised on the third day in accordance with the scriptures, and that he appeared to Cephas, then to the twelve'. It is certain that Paul here has given a chronological enumeration of the appearances. It is instructive in this context to refer to Matthew 5:18—the call of Peter and Andrew, and to Matthew 10:2: 'The names of the twelve apostles are these: first, Simon, who is called Peter. . . .'

The formula in Luke 24:34: 'The Lord has risen indeed, and has appeared to Simon' comes from the same tradition as that which lies behind 1 Corinthians 15:5. However, we know nothing of the actual circumstances of the Lord's appearance to Simon Peter. It has been suggested that it may have taken place in Galilee and may have been described in the now lost conclusion of St. Mark's gospel'.[18]

Peter and the Church. An Examination of Cullman's Thesis, Herder, Freiburg, Nelson Edinburgh-London 1963.
[18] See Cullman, *Peter,* pp. 58-63.

After the coming of the Holy Spirit at the first Pentecost, Peter 'standing with the eleven, lifted up his voice' and proclaimed the resurrection: 'Men of Israel, hear these words. . .this Jesus, delivered up according to the definite plan and foreknowledge of God, you crucified and killed by the hands of lawless men. But God raised him up, having loosed the pangs of death, because it was not possible for him to be held by it' [Acts 2:22-24]; 'This Jesus God raised up, and of that we all are witnesses' [Acts 2:32]. It is Peter who speaks on behalf of all the accredited witnesses of the resurrection of Jesus Christ. In this passage we have almost a blueprint for the specific collegiality of the pope and bishops: Peter stood with the eleven, proclaimed the resurrection and testified that all the eleven with him were witnesses of it.

Jesus promised that the Holy Spirit would be given after he had been glorified: 'These things I have spoken to you while I am still with you. But the Counsellor, the Holy Spirit, whom the Father will send in my name, he will teach you all things, and bring to your remembrance all that I have said to you' [John 14:25]. Because Jesus Christ is what he said to his disciples,[19] the Holy Spirit brings to the Church's remembrance not merely words about Jesus Christ, but the Word that he is: the Risen and Glorified Saviour. "(Jesus) does not announce that something will happen. His proclamation is itself an event. What he declares takes place in the moment of its proclamation".[20] As I wrote on another occasion:

Proclamation of the good news was carried out by the apostles under the command of Christ. He commissioned those he had chosen to proclaim him to the world. Christ himself is the centre of the apostolic preaching. This preaching was no mere instruction about Jesus Christ and the facts of his life, as though the content of what was proclaimed could be obtained from private reading or study. This apostolic *kerugma* is the Word of the Exalted Lord in their proclamation. Through the Holy Spirit Christ speaks in those commissioned by him as human instruments of the divine Word. The Word of God is made words in the preacher. . . .[21]

In the very proclaiming of the resurrection the Risen and Exalted Lord is there in our midst.

---

[19] Cf. Luke 4:21: "And he began to say to them, 'Today this scripture has been fulfilled in your hearing' ".
[20] *Encyclopedia of Biblical Theology,* ed. by J.B. Bauer, vol. 2, p. 689.
[21] *Reflections on the Theology of Preaching* in: NEWSLETTER ON SEMINARY EDUCATION 12 (May 1971) p. 9.

The first constitutive element, then, in the evangelical primacy of the papacy is the mission and responsibility to proclaim to the Church and world that Jesus Christ is the Son of the living God and that he has risen from the dead. It is no mere pious practice that the pope gives a message to the world at Christmas or that he speaks *urbi et orbi* on Easter Sunday from the central *loggia* of St Peter's Basilica in Rome, announcing the joy of the resurrection. On these occasions he is fulfilling his mandate to preach the good news to humanity.

The Primacy of Love

The second constitutive element of the pope's evangelical primacy is the primacy of witness to unconditional love of Christ. In answering Christ's questions related in John 21:15-17, Peter professes an absolute love of him. The person who loves Jesus is assuredly loved by the Father, for the Father loves that we love Jesus: 'for the Father himself loves you, because you have loved me and have believed that I came from the Father' [John 16:27]. And love of course is always its own reason, is always self-explanatory; that is why God is love. The threefold question and answer of John 21 has been connected by some scholars with Peter's threefold denial of knowledge of Christ. The threefold profession of love is considered by them to be the cancelling of the denial and the complete rehabilitation of Peter.[22] From then on the motive of everything Peter did was the love of Christ, from proclaiming the resurrection to giving his life for him at the end.

It is the pope's duty to lead the Church in giving concrete witness to unconditional love of Christ. We must love Christ without compromise. The Church throughout the world must love Christ above all else and follow him wherever he may go, whether it be again to the mount of the transfiguration or the hill of the crucifixion. Absolute love of Christ requires the church to be a socio-critical Church in different ways and at different levels in various parts of the world.[23] This love demands that the pope give the lead in condemning every form of injustice and exploitation, in proclaiming liberty, equality and brotherhood and by encouraging every effort wherever and by whomsoever made, to establish harmony and peace on earth.

This element of the pope's primacy may be expressed by saying that he has to make the See of Rome ever more what St. Ignatius of Antioch said of

---

[22] Cf. Cullman, *Peter,* p. 183; B. Lindars, *The Gospel of John,* New Century Bible, Oliphant's London 1972, p. 633.

[23] Karl Rahner, *The Shape of the Church to Come,* trans. with an introduction by E. Quinn, SPCK, London 1974, pp. 123-132.

it in the early second century: "the Church. . .worthy of God, worthy of honour, worthy of consolation, worthy of praise, worthy of success, worthy in purity, having the chief place in love, keeping Christ's law, bearing the Father's name".[24]

The Primacy of Service

After his profession of love Peter was commissioned to feed Christ's lambs, tend his sheep, feed his sheep. He is appointed to take care of Christ's sheep. The sheep are Christ's, not Peter's. The one qualification for being given this responsibility was love of Christ and Peter was endowed with it admirably: 'Lord, you know everything; you know that I love you' [John 21:17]. The example he must follow in tending Christ's flock is that of the Chief Shepherd, the Good Shepherd, Christ Jesus himself, who goes before the sheep and they follow him because they know his voice [John 10:4], 'who lays down his life for the sheep' [John 10:11]. Peter is endowed with the primacy of service and to this the pope succeeds as indeed the servant of all God's servants.[25]

Not by his own merits but through Christ's prayer for him it is granted to Peter that his faith will not fail. And by his unswerving adherence to Christ Jesus he will strengthen and confirm his brethren in the Church [cf. Luke 22:31-33]. To the lame man who was carried each day to the Beautiful Gate, Peter gave what he had received from Christ: 'I have no silver and gold, but I give you what I have; in the name of Jesus of Nazareth, walk' [Acts 3:6]. In succeeding to Peter, the pope has the primacy of service to strengthen us in our commitment to Christ and to heal us, to help us to walk along the Way, by the power he has himself received from Christ.

Jesus of Nazareth came among us 'as one who serves' [Luke 22:27]. He washed the feet of his disciples and taught us that we 'ought to wash one another's feet' [John 13:14]. By washing the feet of his disciples Jesus gave the most beautiful example the world will ever see of love without power yet full of authority. One who serves others with love is a person of very great authority indeed.

---

[24] *To the Romans,* opening in *The Early Christian Fathers. A Selection from the Writings of the Fathers from St. Clement of Rome to St. Athanasius,* ed. and trans. by H. Bettenson, Oxford University Press, London, Oxford, New York 1969, p. 45, but note the original: *prokatheméne tes agápes (universo caritatis coetui praesidens)* K 25.

[25] The description *servus servorum Dei* was first used by Pope St. Gregory the Great (590-604); see *Dictionnaire d'Archéologie Chrétienne et de Liturgie* XV P. 1, pp. 1360-1363.

Karl Rahner has written that the Church should be a Church concerned with serving. He points out:

> We are not merely uttering pious platitudes, fit only for Sunday sermons, when we say that the Church must not be concerned with serving others merely for the sake of proving her own claims and that she must stand by the side of the poor, the oppressed, life's failures. But does the reality correspond to this sacred principle, the principle that the Church has to be there for all and therefore also for the others, that she must serve even those who attach no importance to her and regard her as a relic from a vanished age? Is this form of the 'folly of the cross' very much in evidence among us? Is enough love applied in the Church, is there enough courage for stubborn confrontation, and are enough power, time, and money given to unselfish service for others, without calculating the advantages to the Church herself?[26]

The model of the Church as servant is important and attractive, and it may well be the most effective and influential for a long time to come. This certainly has more appeal for people today than other familiar models, for instance, institution, mystical communion, sacrament, herald.[27] I do not mean to advocate that these models can be eliminated. They must simply take a second place. Perhaps they can be understood better through the model of Church as servant, just as the model of Christ as Suffering Servant endows the model of Christ as Sacrament with a very special content.

The modern understanding of the Church as servant is not exactly co-terminous with the New Testament notion of the Church's *diakonia*. Avery Dulles SJ explains that this modern sense, while having no direct basis in the scriptures, may be said to have an 'indirect foundation' in the Servant Songs in Isaiah.[28] I wonder, however, if it can be said to have something more than an indirect basis in Christ's miracles of healing and in Matthew 25:31-46, where it is shown that the righteous did not know that they had served Christ and the unrighteous did not know that they had refused him service. What counted in the one case was what had actually been done and in the other what had not actually been done.

In recent times and specifically since John XXIII, the popes on certain occasions and in some of their documents have addressed themselves not only

---

[26] *The Shape of the Church to Come*, pp. 62f.
[27] A. Dulles SJ, *Models of the Church,* Doubleday & Company Inc., Garden City N.Y. 1974, pp. 31-82.
[28] Ibid., pp. 93f.

to the Church, but also to all people of good will. To proclaim to the world the demands of justice, to exhort humanity to strive for peace, to warn against the dangers of dehumanisation, to speak words of consolation, strength and encouragement across the earth, to announce again and again the new understanding of man made known in the life, death and glorification of Christ, are graphic and powerful expressions of the pope's primacy of service of the world. One of the most impressive acts of service of the world by the papacy in our time was Paul VI's address to the United Nations General Assembly on October 4th 1965. Among the most noteworthy elements of his splendid speech I would emphasise the following:

> In fact We have nothing to ask, no question to raise; at the most a desire to formulate, a permission to ask: that is to serve you, as far as in Us lies, disinterestedly, humbly, lovingly. . . .Our message is first of all a moral ratification, a solemn approbation of this eminent Institution: it comes from Our experience of history. It is as an expert in humanity that We bring to this Organisation the approval of Our immediate Predecessors, that of all the Catholic episcopate and of Ourself, convinced as We are that this is the path that modern civilisation and world peace must follow.[29]

His address was an exercise of the primacy of service with the avowed intention of making the world a better place. It belongs to the pope's primacy of service of the world to lead the whole Church in cooperating with international organizations and national institutions devoted to establishing a more just and peaceful world order. Such cooperation of course must never be allowed to obscure the Church's belief in her own eschatological character. Nor must she become so introspective as to forget that she is part of this world. The Church in fact can only live rightly in history through awareness of the tension that must be present between the incarnational and eschatological aspects of her nature.

These various elements of the pope's evangelical primacy establish the right and, in my view, only context in which to understand the primacy of jurisdiction and papal infallibility. The pope's universal episcopal authority as 'Bishop of the Catholic Church'[30] and his being kept from teaching error by the grace of that infallibility, with which the Divine Redeemer willed his church to be endowed, in this approach have their meaning determined directly from the gospel. This evangelical context has not only considerable ecumenical

---

[29] *The Pope's Appeal for Peace*, London: Catholic Truth Society, 1965, pp. 2f.
[30] Thus does the pope's signature occur after each of the conciliar documents.

implications in respect of the papacy, it also makes the papacy's place in the Church more intelligible and significant, and shows its relation to the faith and life of believers, and to the longings and aspirations of humanity.

John Paul II

In his first message after his election John Paul II drew our attention to the theology of the Church and the teaching on the collegiality of the bishops. The Church is the universal sacrament of salvation and of unity for the human race. Collegiality links the bishops to the pope and to one another, and so they carry out their pastoral office. What is involved in all this, the pope stressed, is still in need of much reflection. Having set the context—ecclesiology and collegiality—the pope then turned his attention to the petrine ministry:

> We must always keep intact the deposit of faith, mindful of the special mandate of Christ who, making Simon the 'Rock' on which He built the Church, gave him the keys of the Kingdom of Heaven. He commanded him to strengthen his brothers and to feed the sheep and lambs of his flock as a witness of love. We are completely convinced that all modern inquiry into the 'Petrine ministry' must be based on these three hinges of the Gospel. What is proper and peculiar to it becomes clearer day by day. We are dealing here with the individual facets of the office which are connected with the very nature of the Church to preserve its internal unity and to guarantee its spiritual mission. This has been entrusted not only to Peter but also to his legitimate successor. We are convinced also that this most singular mission must be done always in love. Love is the source which nourishes and the climate in which one grows. It is the necessary response to the question of Jesus: 'Do you love me?'[31]

In his address to members of diplomatic missions accredited to the Holy See, John Paul II reiterated his view of the papacy as a ministry of love: "As a Christian, and still more as Pope, we shall be the witness of divine love".[32]

He began his homily at the inaugural Mass with the text: 'You are the Christ, the Son of the living God' [Matthew 16:16]. He pointed out that this confession did not have its origin in Peter but was given to him by grace. John Paul II then went on to proclaim his faith in the incarnation of the Son of God before the whole world: "On this day and in this place these same words must

---

[31] Off. Vatican Translation prov. by Reuters, in: The Times (October 18, 1978) p. 7.
[32] The Times, Saturday October 21st 1978, p. 4.

again be uttered and listened to: 'You are the Christ, the Son of the living God' ".[33]

In these reflections John Paul II has given us in seminal form a splendid and profoundly attractive theology of the papacy. One hopes that he will turn his attention to it again in the future to treat it at greater length. His openly evangelical approach may well prove to be of far greater significance for the foreseeable future, to the place of the papacy in the Church and world, than the definitions of the primacy of jurisdiction and infallibility.

As regards the criteria for a pope the Church needs today, John Paul II appears to fulfil them eminently: He is *1. A man open to the world:* consider his background and very varied experience, his studies, his knowledge of Marxism, his preference for dialogue, his courage, his knowledge of languages. *2. A spiritual leader:* he is patently a man of great personal and charismatic authority who has already made a deep impression on the human race. *3. An authentic pastor:* above all else he is this as his years as Archbishop of Cracow show. *4. A true fellow bishop:* he has a profound grasp of collegiality and is thoroughly committed to making it a greater reality in the Church. *5. An ecumenical mediator:* in his first message to the Church and world he announced:

> At this point, we cannot forget our brothers of other churches and Christian confessions. The ecumenical cause is actually so great and delicate that we cannot let it go unmentioned. . . .We intend, therefore, to proceed along the way already begun, by favouring those steps which serve to remove obstacles. Hopefully, then, thanks to a common effort, we might arrive finally at full communion[34]

6. A genuine Christian: in proclaiming his intention 'to work for the consolidation of spiritual supports on which human society can build', John Paul II promised to seek timely and unprejudiced action 'inspired by the gospel'.[35] Let us listen again to his words to the diplomats: "As a Christian, and still more as Pope, we shall be the witness of divine love".[36]

Conclusion

With the election of John Paul II a new era has been ushered in for the Church as she journeys towards the beginning of the third millennium of her

---

[33] THE TIMES, Monday October 23rd 1978, p. 5.
[34] THE TIMES, Wednesday October 18th 1978, p. 7.
[35] Ibid., p. 7.
[36] THE TIMES, Saturday October 21st 1978, p. 4.

history on earth. Humanity has been sighing and longing for a figure of the present pope's stature, spirituality and strength, for quite some time. By God's grace we now possess one. John Paul II has captivated the world. He is obviously a spiritual leader. And it looks as though he is destined to be endowed, by the willing and free assent of more and more people, with an ever greater primacy of spiritual leadership across the globe, by people who are not Roman Catholics, and not in fact Christians. This will place an increasing responsibility on his shoulders. If it is not impertinence I would like to make two suggestions as to how the pope might meet at once this growing responsibility. First, at the earliest opportunity, the pope should speak to humanity about the mystery of human death. In many parts of the world at the moment there is a very ambiguous attitude towards death. And our attitude to death is a fairly good gauge of our attitude to life. His statement would need to touch on how Christ's free death affected and altered our death, on preparation for death, life after death, prayers for the dead, the meaning of purgatory as purifying love, and the communion of saints. A text should be produced that could be used by study groups anywhere in the world, and especially by those seeking how to come to terms with death's utter inevitability. Above all this text should be written in terms that any editor could announce across the front page of his paper: 'Pope declares the meaning of human death'.

Secondly, it would be a venture of tremendous significance if the pope were to invite the youth of the world to come to Rome to spend, say, three days with him reflecting and praying on the theme 'Prayer and the Future of Humanity'.[37] John Paul II has fired the imagination of a large sector of the world's youth. We should not be sceptical about a suggestion like this. For many young people from all over the world make their way each year to Taizé. Were the pope to issue this invitation there would be an overwhelming response. Accommodation would present no problem as tents could be erected in St. Peter's Square, and the basilica and the new audience hall could be used as dormitories. (There were bars in St. Peter's during the Vatican Council!). And in any case, the whole venture could be repeated, for instance, four times over a two year period. The papal nunciatures and delegations around the globe could act as liaison offices with the Vatican to determine the numbers from different nations on any one occasion. The international character of the whole experience would be crucial to its success. The programme of the three days

---

[37] Editors' note: This suggestion became a reality on 20 December 1985 when Pope John Paul II announced the institution of 'World Youth Day', with the first international gathering in 1987.

would need to include a short address each day, preferably mid-morning, from the pope to the whole assembly, proclaiming what the Christian gospel teaches about the nature of human beings: their origin, purpose and destiny. During the afternoons and evenings the pope could speak to various groups and pray with them. On the final evening the pope would celebrate the Eucharist in St. Peter's Square, during which he would commission all present to return to their various countries to spread the good news about justice and peace, to help others to pray and so gradually to transform the face of the earth. This venture would proclaim most graphically to the whole world that the pope is the minister of love and the servant of all the servants of God.

The Church in Us[1]

On the kitchen wall at East Bergholt there's a plaque bearing a poem headed *My Kitchen Prayer* which begins: "Bless my little kitchen, Lord/ I love its every nook/ And bless me as I do my work/ Wash pots and pans and cook". As I sat down to write these notes on renewal of the Church, I realised in a confused kind of way that everything I wanted to say was somehow in that simple poem. Perhaps when I've finished you'll see what I mean.

The first and chief aim of the Second Vatican Council was renewal of the Church. Everything the Council said, all the documents it published, lead back to that basic aim of renewing the Church and the Christian life in the modern world. To grasp what the Council meant by renewal we need first of all to look at what it said about the Church.

The Council restored to the Church its most beautiful title: *The People of God*. In doing this the Council wanted us all to know that the visible society made up of various groups is not the whole picture of the Church. That visible society is an outward sign of an invisible but very intimate communion made so by God Himself. The life of God is given to each member of the Church by the Father, through the Son and in the Holy Spirit. God's very life is what makes the individual members into one People. And that People—Christ's Church—is proof of what God has done in the world, and will do yet. It was to the whole People of God that the Council addressed its urgent appeal for renewal. No one was exempted, no one excused, from the most recent member to the Pope himself. It is up to each one in the Church to renew the Church in himself in the most fruitful way, in every situation and in every place.

I have been asked often by lay people: "How does all this renewal affect me?" In answer to that I wonder if sufficient effort has been made to realise better what it means to be baptised and confirmed? By baptism and confirmation we have been made *full* members of God's People. No matter who we are or what we achieve in life, there is nothing that can ever equal what happened to us at our baptism and confirmation. We were consecrated and made holy forever. We became brothers and sisters of Christ, our Elder Brother,

---

[1] THE NEW FRANCISCAN I,7 (January 1968) pp. 12-14. Published with permission from the Province of Immaculate Conception, England.

and so, sons and daughters of a Father in heaven. We were given a share in Christ's own role as Priest, Prophet, and King. That is, we were given a *mission:* to make holy *all* that is part and parcel of our daily lives (from washing nappies to taking a drink), and offer it all to the Father at Mass; a mission to proclaim the holy Word of God in our own words, but above all in our deeds. Think of how husband and wife make God known to one another and to their children. We were given a mission to spread God's kingdom of love, justice and peace in a world that is good, but which needs Christ to make it better.

The life of lay people in the world must, never be looked on as second best to a life in a monastery or a convent. The holiness of work and recreation in the world is bound up with the meaning of the incarnation of our Lord. The most basic doctrine of our faith is that God became man. And He became man because He loved the world. A man himself is a little world in which are to be found the same material elements as are in the soil, in wood, in the table we sit at, in the food we eat. All those elements are united to spirit, which together go to make a man what he is. In Jesus Christ all this was united to God forever. We have been saved, restored and made holy by God-made-man—the God Who lay in straw, the God Who learnt a carpenter's trade and got splinters down His finger nails, the God Who was nailed to the Cross, the God Who rose from the dead.

To encounter Him now and be united with Him, we need water, oil, human love, human sorrow, and above all, bread and wine For the Holy Eucharist is bread and wine taken from our world and consecrated God's Body and Blood, bread that grew in our fields, wine from grapes crushed and matured. When we go to church and gather around the altar, we are made one People in Christ through elements taken from the world. There at the altar we draw our strength—strength to go back to the world and make it better and holier, by giving to it the Christ Who came to us in the form of bread and wine. If God, then, has made us holy through the world, can we dare consider it second best to love and serve Him in and through it? Christ has to be brought to the world more and more. That is the mission of the consecrated People we call the Laity. So God has to be brought to the pots and pans and the washing-up. This, I suppose, is what the poem on our kitchen wall is all about.

Pluralism in Theology and
Search for Meaning[1]

In the year 1277 Stephen Tempier, bishop of Paris condemned 219 propositions culled from a variety of sources, including the works of Thomas Aquinas. The initial investigation was instigated by Pope John XXI and though he himself issued no condemnation, it is beyond question that Tempier's action had papal approval.

The condemnation was endorsed by the Dominican Archbishop of Canterbury Robert Kilwardby and by his successor in that see, the Franciscan, John Pecham. The Franciscans, I must own with some embarrassment, had more than a minor part in this sad, if understandable, episode. The condemnation resulted in a victory, temporary though it was, for the conservative theologians, that is, those who adhered strictly to the Augustinian tradition and were opposed to the relatively recent Aristotelianism. Thomas Aquinas had entered into dialogue with the thought of his time, but this did not impress the opponents. Eventually, of course, the Dominican Order rallied to his defence and this was greatly strengthened by his canonisation in 1323. Six centuries later Pope Leo XIII issued an encyclical which gave St Thomas an unparalleled place in schools of Catholic theology and Aquinas is the only theologian to get honourable mention in the Code Canon Law.

I do not mean to begin a discussion on the intricacies of these controversies, nor do I think they had much influence beyond scholastic circles. Few outside the academy would have worried about the orthodoxy of the question whether God can move the heavens in a straight line because then there would be a vacuum! There were, I realise, graver matters, but these are not to my point either.

Pluralism in history

What this episode serves to illustrate is that pluralism of theologies is a datum of Church history, the diversity of theological approaches to the one faith is not unique to our time. Diversity of theological expression is not new. The present pluralism has clearly a quite unprecedented character and I will

[1] THE SOWER 4.1 (Lent-Easter 1980) pp. 21-25. Published with permission.

return to it shortly. But as for the pluralism itself there is a definitive feeling of *déjà vu* in anyone familiar with the rich history of Christian thought. We may instance the schools of Antioch and Alexandria in the ancient church which had very different approaches to the mystery of Christ; there were Augustinians and Aristotelians in the middle ages to which I referred briefly at the beginning; in early modern times the Jesuits and Dominicans were locked in controversy about grace which has never been resolved.

The life, death and glorification of Jesus Christ have revealed the intrinsic value of human existence and the ultimate purpose of creation. Our lives are not absurd and pointless, the world is not an illusion nor the plaything of chance which one day will no longer have the whim to appear to us. Our origin lies in the eternally free love of God. We exist because God loves us. Our purpose is to be co-lovers of the Father with Christ in the fellowship of the Holy Spirit and to fashion through God's grace a community where the dignity and uniqueness of everyone is reverenced without discrimination. Our destiny is to share God's own eternal glory when each will be lover and loved in one.

God's revelation and the response to it that is faith do not exist in a sacrosanct, untouchable region of the mind nor are they above and beyond the vicissitudes of history. The Word of God is believed by men and women of flesh, blood and spirit who, convinced of its crucial significance, strive to unravel for their own time, place and culture, its message about God, humanity and the world. God's Word enfleshed discloses life's meaning and every honest effort to make that meaning clearer, is an act of worship of God through the drive and complexity of human intelligence. That is theology's mission, task and adventure.

The New Testament itself contains a variety of theologies and there have been believers who maintained that St. Paul's betrayed the original, simple message of Jesus! In elaborating the theologies of the New Testament the first disciples did not hesitate to describe Jesus Christ as 'the Last Adam'. For in him not only had the history of Israel reached its culminating point, not only had the destiny of world history attained its initial fulfilment, but also the human race had begun all over again. Christ is the Last Adam, that is, the first-born of all creation, the first-born from the dead. Never, I believe, has such a claim been made for any other historical figure before or since. And when one says 'first' one may logically look for a second, a third and so on. Yet in the city of the living God all will be first-born [cf. Hebrews 12:22ff].

In their encounter with the sophisticated world of the Greeks, Christian writers from the second century did not blush to present this crucified criminal, the risen and glorified *tekton*—carpenter or worker in stone—as the very wisdom the Greeks themselves had sought. Not only had Abraham rejoiced to see his day but evidently Plato, Aristotle, Heraclitus and the rest had attained their deep wisdom and knowledge in the light of the Truth he is.

Today's Challenge

The challenges which face the Christian believer and theologian today are unequalled since the early centuries of Christian history. Believers then were part of a world of cultures which had not been formed by Christianity. The Jewish, Greek and Roman cultures were already formed and in possession when the apostles began their preaching of the gospel. How Jesus Christ gave to these cultures their essential and ultimate meaning was the apostles' primary task in preaching Jesus Christ crucified and risen from the dead. After the fall of the Roman Empire the Christian Church succeeded eventually in forming a homogeneous culture which flowered as medieval Christendom. Its fundamental unity made the pluralism of medieval theologies radically different from what we have now. Theologians then were trained in the same background, they all had fundamentally the same culture, formation and outlook. Thomists and Scotists might differ, but each knew exactly what the other was arguing about and understood the reasons for the disagreements. They were part of a uniform world.

Today the Christian theologian belongs to a world vastly different from that of the Middle Ages. Its origins go back to the late eighteenth century. With the mentality created by the advent of modern science and through the wide influence of the Enlightenment, a culture came into existence in whose formation the Church had no significant part. In fact, the Church withdrew into a shell while a world of thought-forms, outlooks and attitudes was born which she did not understand and, apparently, did not want to understand. Then she became alienated from the world.

The modern world made promises and held out hopes which have simply not materialised. The heady optimism which captivated our nineteenth century forbears has evaporated. Indeed, the modern world has come to an end and we have entered a new era which may be called chronologically 'post-modern', it is too early to give it more precise designation. The unattained promises and unfulfilled hopes led to certain disillusionment and engendered a stark realism, but this has not brought crowds flocking to the churches. And still the search goes on for ultimate meaning and values that last.

There is no basic philosophy today and no fundamentally uniform way of viewing the world. A vast spectrum of cults, religions, and ideologies is there for the interested, non-committed seeker, spanning everything from astrology and the occult, through eastern religions and mysticism, Christianity and humanism, to bland agnosticism.

The world has grown smaller because of easy travel and advanced means of communication; it has become insignificant through the knowledge that the extent of the observable universe is twenty-five billion light years. And while cultures intermingle on the earth and their histories and glories are opened up to us, we realise daily that western civilisation is not the best of all possible worlds.

Historical research has taught us the relative character of our customs, laws and institutions. Languages develop and words change their meaning. This has important consequences for Christian faith which has to be expressed in words as well as lived in actions. Consider, for example, the understanding of the word 'person' in the fifth or thirteenth century and the understanding of that word today.

New problems have arisen for which theology was not prepared, though there are theologies which have begun to face them. Among the more grave may be mentioned: the Third World, the ecological crisis, the discovery of nuclear power, the manufacture of nuclear weapons. What has theology to say of importance about space travel or the silicon chip, for that matter?

Neo-scholastic theology, even at its best, was neither suitable nor competent to face the challenges of our time. The realisation of this was one of the motive causes behind the convoking of the Second Vatican Council. Among its major documents is the *Pastoral Constitution on the Church in the World of Our Time,* for it was clearly recognised that the Church must first understand the form and character of the cultures and societies to which she is sent, before the message of Jesus Christ can be proclaimed with any hope of success.

Dialogue with a Pluralistic World

The resolve to understand and enter into dialogue with a world whose distinguishing feature is pluralism, has issued in a diversity of theologies. The majority of these have no genetic link with scholasticism. It is simply not possible to reduce this diversity to a uniform system. The starting points are totally different and there is no common philosophical basis. The task to which these various theologies are committed is what it has always been: to communicate the ultimate meaning for humanity and the world revealed in

Jesus Christ. Upon this alone the Christian faith is founded. But the data they employ and the methods they follow are vastly diverse and irreducible. For example, there are theologies which expound the unity of God and man in Jesus Christ and his unique and decisive significance for world history and human destiny without using the Chalcedon formula, while professing the truth it teaches.

Through the encounter between faith and modern thought and experience, a plurality of theologies has appeared and new theologies are emerging. African Christianity is producing a new theology that is very different from anything we know. Liberation theology in Latin America has developed out of the experience of believers in that subcontinent. Theologians there have read their national histories from the point of view of the losers. They know that the universal meaning of Christ's life, death and resurrection can have no credibility in the face of flagrant injustice and economic oppression. There are ecumenical theologies for which authenticity not validity is a primary category. Following this they arrive at very different assessments of ministry and priesthood in other denominations than those we are accustomed to from scholastic theology. There are theologies for the environment which are passionately concerned with the rights of animals, flowers, the air, the rivers and the seas as creatures of a Loving Creator who saw all that he had made as very good. None of these theologies can be reduced to preconceived, uniform patterns.

Küng & Schillebeeckx

In Western Europe I would like to single out for some comment the theologies of Hans Küng and the Dominican Edward Schillebeeckx. I choose these because they are well known as theologians striving to dialogue with people of our time.

Matters of faith and questions of theology are discussed today in the market place. The mass media have an interest in theological topics that is little short of astounding. What lies behind this, I am convinced, is the search for ultimate meaning. How that should make us rejoice and redouble our efforts to share what we have so generously received. Hans Küng and to a lesser extent Edward Schillebeeckx, have demonstrated that theology is not a science of conundrums, not an heirloom from a bygone age now lost in the twilight of fantasy, but a vital effort to come to grips with the meaning of life in the light of God's Word revealed in Christ. I know people who have become better Christians for reading Küng and I know an agnostic who is studying *On Being a Christian* and Schillebeeckx's book *Jesus.* In works such as these which are dialogic in character there are points in need of further elucidation. Authorities in the Church have the duty to safeguard the truth of God's revelation to humanity because if we get it wrong about this, then we get it wrong about everything. But it has to be recognised that these works are dialogic writings, they are tentative and experimental, speaking to the doubtful, the disillusioned and the wary. We have to remember too that there is always a theology behind even the most sacred doctrinal formulae. The words employed are not simply co-terminous with the truth expressed.

Continuing and Patient Dialogue

What the 'case' of Hans Küng and that of Edward Schillebeeckx prove is that there is need for patient dialogue among the diverse theologies of the Catholic Church and not only across the confessional barriers. It seems to me that it would be an enormous contribution towards removing suspicion on all sides, if the Congregation for the Doctrine of the Faith were to sponsor a continuing dialogue among some of the many theologies co-existing in the Church, for example, between Roman Theology, Liberation theology, what can be called 'Dutch' theology and of course 'Tübingen' theology. This would lead at least to a better reciprocal understanding of the presuppositions, methodology and goals of these diverse theologies.

On Praying and Being Human:
Reflections on the Anthropological Value of Prayer[1]

This article contains reflections on the activity we call prayer in terms of its anthropological value. Such an approach is possible because of the prior anthropological character of revelation, faith, and theology. Since there are two key concepts involved in these reflections, namely, anthropology and prayer, the article has been divided into two major parts. The reason for presenting these reflections in a review intended principally for religious will be clear from the content of the first part of the article.

I

Christology and Anthropology

The christological doctrine of the Church, if correctly understood, is the most radical and authentic anthropology the world has ever known. In the historical event which is the life, death, and glorification of the Man, Jesus of Nazareth, the Church has the source and centre of everything that she knows and can ever know about God and man. Because He is the Incarnate Son of the Eternal God, Jesus of Nazareth discloses to us in the very reality of His own humanity who God is, what God is like; and this is expressed in its most original form by the words 'Father' and 'Forgiving Love'. In the same way He reveals what it means to be man: the being in the world who is called in the innermost depths of his historical existence to surrender himself unconditionally to the will of God, as to his destiny, in faith, hope, and love. This is not to argue that the Church has nothing to learn about man from the historical, positive, and natural sciences or that she can ignore the teachings of psychology, psychotherapy, and sociology. What we are asserting here is that the Church has a point of reference for all that can be known about man and that point of reference is Christ who allows her to grasp the ultimate depth of meaning of anything that may be discovered about man. From this source and

---

[1] REVIEW FOR RELIGIOUS 33 (Nov. 1974) pp. 1276-1300. Published with permission.

truth namely, that God Himself is the guarantee of man's humanity. To centre there is one truth which the Church knows with infallible certitude, the surrender oneself to God is to arrive at one's own unique humanity. The process of growth in the relationship with God—a relationship established by grace which divinizes and therefore humanises man in his historical existence—is a process of drawing ever closer to the Origin of humanity itself and thus of becoming more authentically human. When the Church speaks of God, in virtue of the very word she utters, she says something about man; when she speaks of man in the light of the grace she has received in her Saviour and Lord, she proclaims also a word about God.

The Church's Doctrine of Man

This essentially anthropological and authentically human orientation of the word she proclaims is the primary reason why the Church has a right to address herself to the world of today and to the men of our time. Above all, it is the foundation of her right to establish educational institutes of every kind and at every level—primary, secondary, and tertiary and of the right to present herself ready before the authorities of State and religiously "neutral" universities and other higher institutes of education, to form theological faculties. She possesses a doctrine about man which has the courage to speak about his multi-dimensional nature and this doctrine is worthy of a hearing wherever and whenever men come together to pool their resources in order to grapple with the question of what it means to be human.

It is true, of course, that this anthropological character of her word, her faith, and her theology has not always been apparent. Moreover, many people share the conviction that believers in God and especially theologians, are desperately concerned with some ideal world far removed from the stark realities of day-to-day life. Indeed, one still stumbles across the vulgar prejudice that theologians as a breed pass their time hair-splitting and juggling with ideas, oblivious of the world going on around them and even indifferent to its concerns. How far this idea corresponds to reality is, I suppose, a matter for some debate. In any case that it is now a figment of misinformed minds and has been for a good number of years as will be obvious to anyone familiar with the development of theology in our times. It is incumbent upon us all who believe in the universality of the revelation of God in Jesus Christ who is Lord, to do all in our power to dispel these false notions and gross misunderstandings by the quality of our lives, the extent of our concerns, and the intellectual honesty, rigor, integrity, and high calibre of our theology.

Christian Anthropology and Dialogue with the World

The radically historical character of the Church's faith, in virtue of which she constantly returns to the life of the Man, Jesus of Nazareth, formally distinguishes the content of the Christian gospel from all mythological worldviews and explanations of the meaning of man. The doctrine of the historical incarnation of the Son must have a paramount place in all dialogue with atheists, anonymous Christians, and implicit believers. If we prescind for the moment from the source of the Church's belief in this doctrine, namely the gratuitous love of the Immortal God for mankind and concentrate on the content of the assertion as de facto held by committed Christian believers, we can make it our point of departure in the dialogue that we for our part are paying the highest possible tribute to human dignity. The content of this assertion is that the being whom the human race calls God, the Supreme Being, is held to be present to and united with this Man who lived out a human life like other men and who reached His destiny in total fidelity to His own humanity and this in such a way that His humanity was not impaired or in any way abolished, but on the contrary was radically realised as itself in its own true and authentic nature. The implications of this assertion for an understanding of man demand analysis precisely because of the influence that the content of this assertion has on the lives, outlook, and activity of a significant number of people today who own the name Christian, because of the history of the Church's understanding of this assertion, and because it is an essential element of the assertion that Jesus is most truly a man. The assertion cannot be dismissed simply by the shabby argument of 'projectionism' firstly because of the historically conditioned existence of this man and secondly because the assertion holds in its dialectic that by the very fact that God is here, Jesus of Nazareth is the realisation of what it means to be human.

Revelation and Christological Anthropology

This anthropological orientation of Christology must have priority also among Christian believers. This is the case not only that they may be able to present an intelligible account of the meaning of their faith to a largely sceptical and unbelieving world, but because it is part of the revelation itself. God's word and His grace are the foundation of authentic and integral humanity so that without Him we cannot be truly human at all. The anthropological orientation of Christology, therefore, is in no way a betrayal of the specifically supernatural character of Christian revelation nor can it be suspected of reducing this revelation to a subtle form of humanism. Theological science is not committed to answering riddles or solving problems in the manner of the positive and natural sciences. Its purpose in every age is to strive to understand man as he is and as he is becoming, in his finitude and openness as the being made in the image of God and called by God to share the divine life. This is an ongoing process which is always new and never exhausted. No matter how much more knowledge may be accumulated by man in the future, no matter how many more secrets may be wrested from nature, man will be always the being in history who is open to God and capable of receiving the treasures of divine grace. This would still be the case even in the condition of the world where the vast majority of mankind had ceased to have any belief in God at all. Leaving aside what might be said about such a state of affairs from a purely phenomenological standpoint, we would still have to proclaim that we have Christ's word in hope that He will be with us to the end. Though this word gives no guarantee about numerical quantity—and at present it does seem that the number of explicit believers is growing less—it is the sure basis that the Church will not disappear from the face of the earth and that the remnant will remain on behalf of the nations.

Renewal in the Church

What is written in these pages about prayer applies to every Christian believer and, for that matter, to any man who prays, as distinct from someone who merely uses a method or follows a system in order to arrive at inner equilibrium. My reflections, however, are addressed specifically to religious in the Church and this for a number of important reasons. It is my belief that the renewal of the religious life is only now beginning to move out of its preparatory stages. This is also true of the Church in general. The last ten years since the final session of the Second Vatican Council have been a time of re-assessment, of preparing the ground, of hammering out principles, and of establishing priorities. Much has been achieved, but there is quite an amount left to be done. Let us take one example: developments in ecclesiology. The Church has come to a deeper awareness of her own nature as a community of believers in the world. This community is founded on the gift of God's grace of unity which is logically prior to its every expression in faith, worship, life, and order. This awareness of the Church's nature as a community has had repercussions in every area of the Church's life. It has raised questions at the practical level which are by no means yet answered. For example: What do we mean by 'community' when applied to the Church in general and when we use it of a local group in the Church? What is the relationship between a territorial parish as realised at present and the theology of the local community in terms of a constantly shifting population? How does liturgical celebration reflect and foster the presence of community? Should diocesan priests be scattered over a multiplicity of parishes in a town or area of a city where they are compelled to live alone or in groups of no more than two or three or should they work to establish a form of community life that is specifically priestly and not just a limp copy of religious life? If they were to live a much more realistic community life, how would they serve and retain contact with the people of those areas where once a priest was resident? What are the consequences for eschatology of this awareness of the Church as community? In what sense is 'heaven' heaven before the *Parousia* of Christ? What is the relationship between a local parochial community and the community of a religious order in the parish? These are some of the questions that require us to reflect again on what may have appeared to us once as unchangeable structures and beliefs. A similar list might be drawn up with direct reference to the religious life. Enough has been said, however, to demonstrate that we ought not to allow ourselves to be lulled into thinking that the renewal is achieved and that we can now slacken our efforts.

Religious and Spiritual Direction

Religious life[2] is an indispensable (not to say essential!) element in the life of the Church. If I read the signs of the times aright, then it seems to me that in the future members of religious orders and congregations of men and women (I prescind here altogether from the question of the ordination of women, though it is by no means irrelevant to the point under discussion) are destined in the providence of God to assume an ever greater if not the maximum responsibility for spiritual direction. This will be one of the finest fruits of the renewal of the religious life in the Church. It is already the case that people approach religious (and let us admit it quite simply and candidly that they approach us precisely as religious, that is, as those in the Church who publicly profess the evangelical counsels, however unthematic and even hazy their expression of this may be) with their questions or problems or mysteries and they rightly expect us to bring a spiritual dimension into the situation they present to us. They have the right to expect this of us for the simple reason that we are presumed to know something about the workings of divine grace in human life. After all, we have behind us the years we have spent in religious life with all the experiences of reflection and prayer that these years have provided—and we must not forget that it is the Church and God's grace, more

---

[2] *Reflections on the Theology of Religious Life* in: REVIEW FOR RELIGIOUS 33 (Nov. 1973) pp. 1238-1263. Editors' note: This article is reprinted in this anthology: pp. 504 ff.

than ourselves, that have made this possible. Moreover, we were called by God to the religious life for the sake of the Church.

Psychotherapy and Spiritual Direction

In emphasising the importance of spiritual direction I am not denying nor even playing down the place of psychotherapy. Carl Jung has furnished us with more than enough evidence of how dangerous and uninformed such an outlook is. Indeed, every religious, but especially those engaged in any form of apostolic work ought to read his profound and, in some ways, disturbing essay *Psychotherapists or the Clergy*. Much of what he has to say about the attitude of the doctor may be applied without qualification to spiritual directors. One passage will suffice to demonstrate this. Speaking of the requirements in a doctor who wants to offer guidance to another he writes:

> We can get in touch with another person only by an attitude of unprejudiced objectivity. . . .It is a human quality—a kind of deep respect for facts and events and for the person who suffers from them—a respect for the secret of such a human life. The truly religious person has this attitude. He knows that God has brought all sorts of strange and inconceivable things to pass, and seeks in the most curious ways to enter a man's heart. He therefore senses in everything the unseen presence of the divine will. This is what I mean by 'unprejudiced objectivity'. It is a moral achievement on the part of the doctor, who ought not to let himself be repelled by illness and corruption. We cannot change anything unless we accept it. Condemnation does not liberate, it oppresses. I am the oppressor of the person I condemn not his friend and fellow-sufferer. I do not in the least mean to say that we must never pass judgement in the cases of persons whom we desire to help and improve. But if the doctor wishes to help a human being he must be able to accept him as he is. And he can do this in reality only when he has already seen and accepted himself as he is.[3]

These words reminded me of a passage in the *Rule* of St. Francis of Assisi which, for all practical purposes, says exactly the same: "And they (the Ministers) must take care not to be angry or agitated on account of anyone's sin because anger and agitation hinder charity in themselves and in others".[4]

---

[3] C.G. Jung, *Psychotherapists or the Clergy* in: *Modern Man in Search of a Soul*, trans. by W.S. Dell and C.F. Baynes, New York: Harcourt, Brace and World 1933, pp. 234f.

[4] *Rule of St. Francis*, ch. 5.

The spirit and the psyche are intimately connected and any religious who bears the responsibility now or will do so in years to come would be well advised to acquire a basic knowledge of the principles and methods of psychotherapy. What I am anxious to stress in this context, however, is that spiritual direction exists in its own right and to imagine that it can be simply replaced by psychotherapy is patent nonsense. It would be as foolish to reduce spiritual direction to psychotherapy as it would be to hold that a glandular extract will cure a neurosis.[5]

New Forms of Prayer

The new forms of community prayer, the sharing of experiences of God, the openness and sympathy in communicating joys and sorrows, emptiness and fullness, darkness and light experienced in the spiritual life are also providential in regard to this matter of religious and spiritual direction. It is a well-known fact that religious, especially in the United States of America and, to a much lesser extent, elsewhere, are leaders in these new forms of common prayer and this highly desirable openness in sharing with others one's experiences of God. All this has served to bring home to many religious the fundamental reason why they came to religious life, namely, to love and praise the Living God, His Son, and the Holy Spirit and to love and serve the brethren of that Son throughout their entire lives. The actual sharing of these experiences teaches, as no book can, how God intervenes in a person's life, how His blessed grace renews people in the hidden depths of their being, how the Holy Spirit of God guides and enlightens people in the midst of the most humdrum and monotonous daily lives. I know from my own experience that listening to another person speaking about God's presence in daily life can actually become an experience of the presence of God for the listener.

Religious and Theological Formation

The mushroom growth in the numbers of religious who are pursuing theological studies is also providential and here again the United States has the lead. So many of these religious are involved in education and formation at various levels and there are many of these who belong to the Charismatic Renewal Movement. One must be careful, therefore, not to brand this Movement generally as anti-intellectual. Of course the beast of anti-intellectualism shows its ugly head periodically in the history of the Church and these are areas where it is raising its head at the moment. Experience itself

---

[5] See Jung, *Psychotherapists*, pp. 223-229.

teaches unequivocally, however, that a solid theological formation is an essential requisite for spiritual direction. Indeed, I would go so far as to say as a general rule, that without a protracted period of theological formation no one should dare to assume the responsibility of spiritual direction at all. By theological formation I mean a formation that is firmly rooted in the Church's Tradition of theological reflection and not confused with 'fashion-theology' which arrogates to itself the titles 'existential' and 'personal', shifts its point of reference with every 'new' issue and is as ephemeral as it is superficial. This awareness among so many religious of the necessity of a theological formation is born of the sound intuition that pietism, fundamentalism, emotionalism, and comforting platitudes just will not suffice for the apostolate of spiritual direction. All theological endeavour is subservient to the faith and the Word of God and can never be an end in itself. In accord with the signs of the times, as they appear at least to me, we may say more specifically that the current widespread pursuit of theological formation among religious is directed towards achieving a greater competence in spiritual direction the responsibility for which, as we have already said, religious will assume increasingly at every level of the Church's life and, for that matter, outside the body of committed Christian believers.

The Experience of God

It is obvious also that religious will have to be more prepared and willing to speak to those who come to them for this kind of direction and counsel about the experience of God in their lives and this without embarrassment, but with courage and humility. Such openness is desirable and necessary not only because it will aid committed believers to recognise God's presence in their own lives, but also because of its witness value and the salutary effect it has on non-believers, sceptics, and the doubtful. Just as a solid theological formation furnishes the believer with the means of presenting an intelligible account of the faith and of giving reasons for accepting the Christian revelation which forbid the non-believer to dismiss the Christian as a hoodwinked fool—even when no 'proof' is forthcoming for what is believed—so also the readiness to speak in humility and honesty of the workings of God's grace and the experience of His presence in one's life, demonstrates that the believer is not someone merely committed to repeating intellectual propositions and to presenting the 'party line', but a person made more human by the grace of God, which forbids the non-believer to brush religion aside as having no relation to concrete human existence.

What has been suggested above about the increasing responsibility for spiritual direction on the part of religious takes on added seriousness in the light of the following passage from Jung's essay already mentioned above. It should be emphasised that what he writes is the result of his own research:

> I should like to call attention to the following facts. During the past thirty years, people from all the civilised countries of the earth have consulted me. I have treated many hundreds of patients, the larger number being Protestants, a smaller number of Jews, and not more than five or six believing Catholics. Among all my patients in the second half of life—that is to say, over thirty-five—there has not been one whose problem in the last resort was not that of finding a religious outlook on life. It is safe to say that every one of them fell ill because he had lost that which the living religions of every age have given to their followers, and none of them has been really healed who did not regain his religious outlook. This of course has nothing whatever to do with a particular creed or membership of a church.[6]

With the principle of the anthropological character of the Christian revelation briefly established, we may now turn to the anthropological value of prayer. Jung pointed out, as we have already quoted, that a doctor can only accept a human being as he is "when he has already seen and accepted himself as he is".[7] We noted that this may be applied without qualification to spiritual directors. What we have to say from here onward can be taken as a commentary on this text as applied to the spiritual director. Our reflections belong, of course, to another dimension where science ends, but it is a dimension of human existence brought to be by the grace and the love of God. To direct and counsel another human being in the ways of God requires experience, personal prayer, theological formation, and some knowledge of the teaching of the classical authors of spiritual theology. We are concerned here with one aspect of one of these requisites, namely, the humanising power of prayer. By prayer one learns to accept oneself before God. The spiritual director must have already seen himself as he is before God and accepted what he has seen.

---

[6] Ibid., p. 229.
[7] Ibid., p. 235.

II

Praying and Being

Thomas of Celano, the most famous biographer of St. Francis of Assisi, describing the Saint at prayer, tells us that "all his attention and affection he directed with his whole being to the one thing he was asking of the Lord, not so much praying, as becoming himself a prayer".[8] This description serves to emphasise the principal point of these reflections: that prayer is not primarily saying something but being someone in virtue of a relationship with God Who is ever-present everywhere in the totality of His Being. The purpose of all prayer, be it liturgical, public, corporate, personal, vocal, or silent, is to deepen our union with God. It is essentially a relationship of union with God, made possible by God Himself who, in absolute freedom and pure loving kindness, bridges the infinite gulf that separates us in our creaturehood from Him the Sovereign Lord and Creator of the universe. In this relationship we draw ever nearer to Him and the nearer we are to Him, the more do we become like Him. The more we become like Him, the more are we made truly ourselves. We already have some faint notion of this on the ordinary principles of the Creator/creature relationship. In every man there is a desire, a longing—however it may be expressed—to reach the Source whence he came and to which he must inevitably return. Our certainty in the matter, however, is given uniquely in the doctrine of the incarnation. Jesus Christ is the truest man, the most authentically human man who ever walked our earth.

Jesus Christ the Man

There has been great emphasis in recent times on the humanity of Christ and we have been advised frequently to throw off the shackles of the fear of Arianism. While this is a most desirable development in Christology, we need to be on our guard constantly against any form of reductionism that would make Him no more than a particularly good man among men in the world. Nor should we forget that for Arianism not only was Jesus not God, he was not really man either, since the Logos (understood to be the first, the highest, and the noblest of God's creatures) was made flesh by taking the place of the soul in the man Jesus. What we need to stress now is that because Jesus Christ is God-made-man, he is more *human than* any man. In His humanity Jesus is set apart in His aloneness (not to be confused with loneliness), though He is not

---

[8] Thomas of Celano, *Vita Secunda S. Francisci,* 95 in: ANALECTA FRANCISCANA 5.10 (Florence 1941) p. 187.

separated from us, precisely because He is so truly, so radically, so authentically, and so devastatingly human.

Prayer and Human Life

There is nothing that can make a man more himself than the constant effort to deepen his relationship with God by loving the divine will and living in the divine presence. The kind of response a man makes to the divinely-given awareness of the Blessed Mystery who is God, who penetrates every fibre of our existence, radically determines the type of person he is. Prayer is not some optional extra in our lives, not some purely peripheral activity out on the fringe of the real business of our concrete, practical monotonous day-to-day occupations, not a luxury for those with time to spare. Prayer is an indispensable element in our relationship with God springing from the transcendent dimension of human existence, without which nothing in our lives can ultimately have any lasting value or validity. This is the chief reason why those who hold that it is not necessary to pray if one works generously and devotedly for others, support a fundamentally anti-human doctrine. We know, of course, that there is a true sense in which to work is to pray, dependent on consciously attending to the things of God. But as anyone knows who has spent protracted periods in the active apostolate, work sooner or later begins to lose its attraction and becomes a boring burden. It is then that one understands the power and value of prayer. Without prayer there is soon no work at all.

Man is the being in the world who is becoming. He finds himself plunged into the flow of existence that is steadily making its way to a term. When he comes to ask himself the questions What is man? and Who am I? he discovers he is limited and finite, on the one hand and always something more, something beyond what he has thus far experienced, on the other. If the Source and Centre of all existence is not somehow a factor in his becoming, then a man will never be human or really himself at all. There is an area of mystery in every man at the core of which is an openness to God, the All-Holy One, who calls out to him from His own blessed eternity *homo sapiens,* the being who finds truth and reality not only outside himself but in the inner depths of his own being must also be *homo orans.* If he is not the latter, then he will also slip back into being no more then *homo sciens*—and knowledge only puffs up, wisdom it is that builds up. Man must progress from *homo sapiens* to *homo amans* by being *homo orans,* that is to say, by praying a man becomes himself a prayer.

Belief and the Existence of God

The Eternal God is the Absolute Other. He is ineffable in His being, uncontainable, incomprehensible, inconceivable, incomparable, inimitable, indescribable, without beginning and without end; He is the Immortal One. For the believer the existence of God is the most obvious thing in the world. God and His grace exist more truly than the world of sense objects and experience that surrounds us and makes us what we are. The believer knows that God exists more really than he does himself. Many people would claim that these are smug and arrogant assertions; others would listen wistfully, thinking to themselves: "How fortunate believers are to know with such certainty that there is after all something to cling to, something to give meaning to life; how blessed they are to feel that life is not in the end empty, pointless, and absurd". These reactions fail to appreciate all that is involved in belief in God. For it is only when God is accepted totally in faith that the real problems confront the believer and these are infinitely greater than the question of His existence. These problems arise from man's existence who as a believer finds himself faced with the absolute demands of God's existence. For once a man believes in God and lives by his faith in union with Him, he becomes aware sooner or later that this God is the Holy God. Unlike goodness, power, mercy, justice, beauty, truth, unity, and peace, holiness is a quality which is not immediately part of our experience. Holiness is a reality of another order altogether. In the faith encounter with God a man becomes aware that he is known in the inmost depths of his being. This encounter with God as the Holy One reveals the seriousness of existence and the responsibility a man bears for his existence in the world. From this arises the concomitant awareness of creaturehood which can cause a man to cry out to God in anguish: "What moved You in the depths of Your own eternal blessedness to bring my existence out of nothing?" In the anguish is the answer: "Love eternal called you out from nothingness" and in this answer a man knows that the source of his anguish is Love itself.

The Holiness of God

God is holy and He bears a holy Name [Exodus 3:1-6; Josua 24:19-20; Isaiah 6:1-3; Ezechiel 36:16-36]. The almost impossible truth is that He demands of us that we be holy as He is holy: "Be holy for I, Yahweh your God, am holy" [Leviticus 19:4]; "Yes it is I, Yahweh, who brought you out of Egypt to be your God: you therefore must be holy because I am holy" [Leviticus 11:45]; "Be holy in all you do since it is the Holy One who has called you, and scripture says 'Be holy for I am holy' " [1Peter 1:15]. The holiness of God comes from His innermost Being which is separated from and utterly beyond everything that is finite and creaturely. God's holiness is not in the first place the opposite of sinfulness, immorality, and self-seeking—though it includes the notion of moral holiness; it is rather the contrary of all that is not God Himself. God's holiness is the perfection of His Being which ineffably transcends everything created. In the fullness of His Being God is absolute identity between His Will and His Being. God is, simply and supremely. There can be no disparity, no contradiction between God's Being and God's Will: God is what He wills, He wills what He is. In His holiness lies the mystery of His Being, that is, the Mystery of what it is simply to be. God, then, is the Holy Mystery: Holy Source, Holy Wisdom, Holy Love—Holy Father, Holy Son and Holy Spirit. God is the Mystery of the Thrice Holy One.

God the *Mysterium Tremendum et Fascinans*

The absolute identity of the Being of God evokes feelings of awe and reverence which go beyond the categories of the purely rational. Our utter creaturehood is revealed to us in the awareness of God's holiness and this revelation occurs in the deepest recesses of the soul.

In His holiness, God is both terrible and attractive, the *Mysterium* at once *tremendum and fascinans* as Rudolf Otto has profoundly analysed and described it.[9] In the presence of the Holy God man is both afraid and not afraid at one and the same time as Rat explained to Mole in *The Wind in the Willows:*

> Then suddenly the Mole felt a great Awe fall upon him. "Rat!" he found breath to whisper, shaking, "Are you afraid?" "Afraid?" murmured the Rat, his eyes shining with unutterable love. "Afraid! of *Him?* O, never, never! And yet—and yet—O, Mole, I am afraid!" Then the two animals, crouching to the earth, bowed their heads and did worship.[10]

God is the *Rex tremendae maiestatis* who is revealed to us as the one who is and, as such He is made known as utterly beyond us. As Pure Being He is so utterly other that when He is encountered in His holiness He inspires awe and reverential fear of necessity because as the Holy One He is unknown and precisely as holy is totally outside all previous experience. Were it not for Him we should not be able to sustain the awareness of Pure Being.

---

[9] R. Otto, *The Idea of the Holy: An Inquiry into the Non-rational Factor in the Idea of the Divine and Its Relation to the Rational*, trans. by J.W. Harvey, Oxford: Oxford University 1923.
[10] K. Graham, *The Wind in the Willows*, London: Methuen Children's Books 1972.

Man experiences himself as divided and disorientated in his existence: there is always tension between his being and his willing, disparity and open contradiction between what he is and what he wills. His being is fragmented and dissipated in its finitude and creatureliness. Yet God draws near to man, though He dwells in light inaccessible, He approaches man and reveals Himself as Holy Mystery and Divine Majesty. It is because He draws so close to us that we know Him to be totally other and utterly beyond us. A man is confronted with the truth of Pure Being and Total Unity and he is filled with awe and fear in the presence of such unambiguous simplicity.

At the same time, however, this revelation of the holiness of God makes known to us that we are in some way like unto God. The meaning of having been created in the image of God is disclosed in all its wonder. Because He is One, the pure identity of being and willing, God is experienced as attractive, alluring and fascinating. In the absolute simplicity of His holy existence God is the fullness of reality. Man strives by the law of his being to be and to be more; he searches out and is drawn towards that which is to be most of all, most authentically and simply to be: the One who is the Holy Other and who lives forever.

The Fidelity of the Holy God

God the Holy One is revealed in the covenant wherein He pledges Himself to man forever. Despite man's finitude, sinfulness, and ingratitude the covenant remains forever: "I will punish their sins with the rod and their crimes with the whip, but never withdraw my love from him or fail in my faithfulness. I will not break my covenant, I will not revoke my given word; I have sworn on my holiness, once for all, and cannot turn liar to David" [Psalms 89:32-35]. The fidelity of the Holy God evokes a personal attitude on the part of man which issues in adoration and establishes the foundation of true humility. In the presence of the Holy God man is made aware of who and what he is, not primarily of what he has done or has not done. God's holiness evokes an ontological attitude, one of *being,* not merely a moral or aesthetical attitude, which is brought about by the very presence of Pure Being and Simple Truth. The knowledge of God's holiness is what allows the man who arrives at it to integrate into his relationship with God the fact that he is a creature.

The experience of the All-Holy God as the *Mysterium tremendum et fascinans* involves also an awareness of the absolute fidelity of God and of His total acceptance of a man as he is. This leads to self-acceptance as a creature and marks the beginning of the transformation into a new creature. The realisation comes that a man is known in the inmost depths of his being and this liberates him from the ambiguity of creaturely existence.

Jesus Christ the Model of Prayer

The unfathomable mystery of God the Holy One has been made known and drawn close to us in the human life of the Man Jesus of Nazareth. Jesus Christ is the Father's Love which He will never take back; He is the Word that will never be revoked; He is the Covenant that will never be broken. In sending Jesus Christ to the world God has already accepted man and has already answered every prayer that might ever arise from a human heart. Since Christ is the foundation and centre of the Christian life, it is only in contemplating Him that we can come to know what prayer means. We must now turn to Him whose life was itself an unbroken prayer to the Father.

The prayer of Christ is a favourite theme of the gospel of St. Luke. He tells us that while Christ was praying after His baptism the Holy Spirit came down upon Him as a dove and a voice was heard from heaven: "You are my Son, the Beloved" [Luke 3:21]. Again it was while at prayer that He was transfigured and a voice from heaven proclaimed: "This is my Son, the Chosen One" [Luke 9:28-9]. The foundation of Christ's prayer is the already established relationship with His Father, from which flow the desires of His will and the affections of His heart.

Apart from the episodes where it is related that Christ went off to pray alone, St. Luke also tells us that Christ prayed in the presence of His disciples. This experience was one of the most treasured memories of the early Church: "Now one day when he was praying alone in the presence of his disciples he put this question to them 'Who do the crowds say I am' " [Luke 9:18-9]; "Now once he was in a certain place praying and when he had finished one of his disciples said, 'Lord teach us to pray just as John taught his disciples.' He said to them, 'Say this when you pray: Father, may your name be held holy' " [Luke 11:1-2]. This must have been a frequent occurrence in the disciples' experience, and it was one they remembered in their preaching and one which the Church preserved for us in the Holy Scripture. There must have been something truly remarkable and unforgettable about the sight of Jesus at prayer. In the episode which records that He taught them the Our Father, the Evangelist states quite simply: He was in a certain place praying. It is not said that he was in ecstasy but simply that He was praying. It was evidently the sight of Jesus at prayer that moved them to ask Him to teach them to do the same. What can have moved them to ask Him to teach them to pray? After all they were Jews and therefore familiar with prayer.[11] The daily life of the pious Jew was filled with a round of prayer. Yet all this had not taught them what the simple act of this man at prayer had called forth from the inner depths of their being. One can try to picture the sight of Jesus praying in the midst of His disciples and try to discover what made them ask Him to teach them to pray. Perhaps it was His serenity, the entire composure of His being; perhaps they wanted to get at what was going on in His heart and mind that made Him the kind of man He was. If we reflect a little on the passage in Luke 11:1ff., the answer will be seen to lie in what He told them to pray: "Say this, when you pray: Father, may your name be held holy. . . ." He told them to say 'Father'. It was this that came to His lips without hesitation, quite simply and in utter confidence. Perhaps this was the very word He had been using when they saw Him at prayer. In any case, the word 'Father' tells us almost everything we need to know about Jesus and it is the clue to what caused His disciples to ask Him to teach them how to pray.

He taught them to say 'Father'. This familiar little word, which no contemporary Jew would have dared to use of God, Jesus made the heart and soul of all prayer forever. The Sublime Mystery of God, the Sovereign Creator of the universe, is addressed by this Man in a term so familiar that it can only be translated 'Daddy'. God is our 'Abba'. What the disciples experienced, therefore, was not so much a man saying something as being someone. They saw Jesus the Son, that is Jesus being totally Himself in the presence of the Most High God.

In teaching the disciples His own prayer which expresses the intimate relationship He had with God, Jesus revealed to us well-nigh everything about God: His kindness, His love, His tenderness, His mercy, His desire that we approach Him on the same intimate and familiar terms as did Jesus Himself. We will never be able to grasp what it means to address God as Father because this is one of the most staggering mysteries of the entire revelation we have received in Jesus Christ. We say this prayer very often in liturgical worship and in public and personal prayer. We must always be on our guard not to allow it to become no more than a mere jingle of words. The Church has always treasured this prayer of her Lord and she always will. It is a matter for some sadness that the translations of the Mass have rendered the introduction to the Our Father *Praeceptis salutaribus moniti et divina institutione formati audemus dicere* by the limp invitation *Let us pray with confidence to the*

---

[11] Joachim Jeremias, *The Prayers of Jesus,* London: SCM, 1969.

Father. This rendering fails abysmally to express the sense of privilege and utter distinctiveness that *audemus dicere* contains. In this prayer we are using the very words of Christ and we are allowed to do this for no other reason than that He taught us to address God in His words and He drew us into His relationship with the Sovereign Lord of life and death. This sense of privilege has been beautifully retained in the translations of the Divine Liturgy of St. John Chrysostom: "And make us worthy, Master, to dare with confidence and without condemnation to call You Father, O God of heaven, and to say: Our Father".[12]

By divine grace, which is the life and love of God Himself, we are truly made God's sons and daughters. Now in human adoption there is necessarily required a likeness of nature—the mother and father must adopt a human being. There is, however, no likeness of nature between God and man. God brings it about by His own most holy grace and we become like Him and are thus His sons and daughters. Human adoption is purely external, dependent only on the will of the adopter. In divine adoption there is realised an internal change so that we are rightly said to be born of God. Finally, in human adoption in order to succeed to the goods of the adopter, the latter must die. In divine adoption God the Adopter is always the Living God and we receive the riches of His love and eternal life in the very act of adoption.

In coming to the awareness of God's holiness we arrive also at the knowledge of our own creaturehood—we come to acknowledge who and what we are. The incarnation of the Son discloses to us that we are accepted by the Holy God to the degree that He makes us His sons and daughters and, therefore, that we are a new creation in Christ Jesus our Lord. With these two fundamental principles before our mind we can now turn to their practical implications for the life of prayer.

Prayer and Becoming Ourselves

The Creator/creature relationship has been transformed and elevated by God's grace to the Father/Son relationship of an entirely new order. In His revealing Word God has made Himself known to us as He is and it is through His Word that all prayer is possible. There have been many definitions of prayer, the best known being *the raising of the mind and heart to God.* Yet every one of them proceeds from and is intelligible only in terms of this

---

[12] *The Divine and Holy Liturgy of Our Father among the Saints: John Chrysostom, Byzantine Daily Worship,* Alleluia Press 1969, p. 288; see also *The Divine and Holy Liturgy of Our Father among the Saints: Basil the Great,* ibid., p. 336. See also K. Rahner, *On Prayer,* New York: Paulist 1968, p. 20.

fundamental relationship with God the Father, through Jesus Christ, in the Holy Spirit. The purpose of prayer, in all its modalities, is to lead us to conscious awareness and ever clearer recognition of the grace of being a son of God the Father. This grace is not an entity added to our natural being as spiritual creatures, but a radical assumption of our entire being by the love of God. It is a dimension of our human existence which God has brought into being. Prayer increases our awareness of divine adoption-that is, of being this person before God the Father by reducing to conscious reflection this fundamental condition of our human existence.

When we place ourselves in God's presence we are before the One who is at once our Creator and our Father. We are able to do this because He has loved us from before the foundation of the world. We are not the result of fate nor the plaything of chance, but unique, original persons called into existence by the creative act of God's most sovereignly free love. We were willed into existence by the love of God; we exist because God wants us, as ourselves, to exist. The Father saw us from all eternity in the face of His Christ and He always loved what He saw. The simple truths that God created us and allows us to address Him as Father, disclose to us that God is Love, not only in Himself, but also to us. In this most radical, most basic sense God has already accepted us even before we are able to approach Him and it is this acceptance that makes any relationship with Him possible. We must be careful, therefore, not to think of God as changing His "mood" towards us; He does not, because He cannot, grow hot and cold in our regard. We must not project our own changeability onto Him. God does not *spy* on us, He does not try to "catch" us. On the contrary, He gazes at us in His sovereign holiness from His blessed eternity and by this gaze conserves us in being. Through prayer we deepen the awareness of who and what we are in the very structure of our being and this is the primary reason why prayer is indispensable in self-development.

Prayer and Self-acceptance

The awareness of who and what we are before God also reveals to us the dark side of our spiritual nature. This is not a purely psychological phenomenon; it has its origin in the mystery of iniquity. The refusal to admit this dark side of our being and the tendency to reduce the awful reality of sin to psychological disorders and cultural conditioning are among the chief causes of the spiritual sickness of our time. From the dark and sinful side of our nature proceeds the strange power which drives us to seek ourselves and to assert ourselves. Yet instead of bringing us to a unified selfhood, this self-seeking and self-assertion have the contrary effect of splintering our being in multiplicity, and of driving us into loneliness in the midst of the crowd. This dark and sinful side of our being must be acknowledged. We have all experienced the divided self; denial of it is itself a further proof of the division in ourselves. We wear so many masks and it is worth comment that the very word *person* which describes our uniqueness is derived from the Greek *prosopon* which originally meant a mask. Yes, we act, we play so many parts, we assume such varying roles according to the circumstances of persons, times, and places. In truth we are pretenders and hypocrites. And while we wear so many masks we are hiding from ourselves. In the midst of this frightening multiplicity we are unable to answer the question "Who am I?" So we run away from ourselves, we try to forget what we were yesterday and to convince ourselves that we really are ourselves today. We are disgusted because we are counterfeit and we try to lose ourselves in the feverish activities of our life of masquerade, while being driven further into the desert of loneliness, so that we dare not be alone.

Emergence of the Real Self

When we place ourselves in God's presence—and this means that all pretence ceases—we see ourselves in the light of God's Primordial Unity behind the—masks that hide us. We recognise the multiplicity of our being. We see ourselves in the midst of all our pretence, hypocrisy, and acting. Yet the miracle is that we do not go mad, we do not commit suicide. In prayer the real self begins to emerge and with it and through it the deeper knowledge and conscious awareness that we are loved already and accepted; that is to say, we know God as Father and Forgiving Love. He has not condemned us, we are not oppressed. By the power and grace of His acceptance we are able to accept ourselves; we no longer turn from ourselves in nausea and disgust. From the moment of self-acceptance the process of unification of our being has begun. Furthermore, this grace of self-acceptance begins to make itself felt outside the formal moments of prayer. The real self begins to appear in our relationships with others so that we are no longer the victims of our changing environment. The masks begin to drop away to reveal the much more delightful, loveable, and authentic someone who was hidden under the rubble of hypocrisy and pretence for so long. Self-acceptance, however, must not be thought to be recapitulation before our sinfulness nor passive resignation in the face of our divided being. It is the realisation of ourselves as creatures of a Loving Creator and sons of a Tender Father which defines our inmost being and which allows the absolutely unique, never-to-be-repeated, utterly original someone who we are to emerge from the depths of our being. With this comes the concomitant awareness of the uniqueness of others. Even in the act of speaking to another person we become more and more aware of the love of God and we are no longer afraid to let another look into our eyes.

Self-acceptance through prayer brings recognition of one's dignity as creature and son of God. As creature we realise we owe to God our adoration, thanksgiving, praise, worship, and honour; as sons we know we owe Him our love. To love God with all our heart, our mind, our soul, and our strength—this is our dignity in the world as sons of God.

Once we have learned this self-acceptance we will never be lonely again. Rather, we become conscious of our aloneness in the world which is part of our uniqueness. This brings with it a longing to be alone whenever life will allow us in the midst of all our duties, responsibilities, and work. These moments alone will be amongst the most blessed in our life, for they will be spent in the presence of our Creator and Father before whom, with Whom, and in whom we will be most truly ourselves.

Prayer and True Self-love

Self-acceptance through prayer leads gradually to a true self-love. After a time God reveals to the man who prays that He does really want the love of the human heart. This brings us, of course, to the centre of the mystery of Divine Love. How is it possible that the Eternal God in the self-sufficiency of His Triune Blessedness should want the love of the human heart? And yet this is the simple and staggering truth of God's will for man. The knowledge of this truth reveals to us our dignity and worth before Him. God wants the love of my heart. If I refuse it, then He will never have it, because no one can stand for another or take another's place in loving God. God's love of our love for Him brings us to a love of self which is born of the awareness of our uniqueness. Self-love, thus understood, will preserve a person from the frightful stupidity of wishing he were someone else. When one examines the implications of this stupidity, which is the worst form of envy, it becomes apparent that it is the most awful act of ingratitude to God. For He has given every one of us at least one talent of being ourselves. If we have two or five talents besides, all to the good. But let us not ignore the one that is the most precious of all—ourselves. If we hide this talent or bury it under pretence and hypocrisy, if we while away our time in daydreams, wishing we were someone else, then we are ignoring not merely what we have, but actually who we are and there will be no interest at all on the day of reckoning! Moreover, if we recognise this one talent and love it as a gift from God, then we will avoid all odious comparisons. For which is the fuller, a glass filled with water or a bucket filled with water? The fact that the bucket has more water than the glass is neither here nor there as far as the glass is concerned! Finally, true self-love brings with it the desire to be like God, that is, the longing for holiness. We do not mean a desire for the effects of holiness, but for unity of our being and our will. It is a longing for integrity, a longing to rid ourselves of the disparity between who we are and what we will and it is one of the most precious graces God grants to us. Integrity is not achieved at once, of course; it is the fruit of long effort and the constant practice of virtue. It demands a rooting out of all self-seeking which is hidden in the depths of our being. We will come back to this in a later section.

Prayer and Listening

It is not easy to be a listener. We often wait for what we want to hear, sometimes we do not listen at all. So often we imagine that our own words are far more important than anything we may hear. In conversations we find ourselves waiting for the other to stop talking so that we can cast forth our pearls and give voice to our wisdom! How sad all this is; for we probably say far more in the silence of really listening than by all the words that pour out when we talk.

It is no fancy to describe prayer as listening. Not that this means hearing voices or having words whispered in our ear. Prayer is a listening to God, listening for the word which says "I love you". For sooner or later God utters this word to us in prayer and once He does, nothing is ever quite the same again. In human relationships when one person says to another "I love you", a sacred word is heard, the world is changed, history is made, time stands still and nothing is ever quite the same again. This is the reason why these words may never be said lightly nor ought they to fall carelessly from human lips. The very utterance is a self-disclosure in which the speaker and listener become truly themselves in union of mind, heart, and word with each other. All this is the case at the level of human love.

If this word is sacred when uttered by men on earth, it is thrice sacred when spoken by God in prayer. It is a self-disclosure of God who is known then as the One who is. This word of His makes it possible for us to whisper back to Him "I love You". At that moment we are really ourselves because we are lost in union with God. But one has to learn to listen, to wait on God in silence, to seek His face and to know His will. To practice listening in prayer eventually has its influence on how we listen to others. One begins to discover gradually that so much more is always being said in human words than the words themselves contain. The Bible also, especially in the liturgy but also in private reading, takes on an added dimension which brings the fundamental certitude that its every word is addressed directly to the listener and that it is saying only one Word: God.

The Guidance of the Holy Spirit

The practice of listening in prayer, which is synonymous with being quietly in God's presence, leads one to the certain assurance that the Holy Spirit is always with us directing and inspiring us in all our ways. Whatever the Holy Spirit inspires has to be done—this may be taken as a self-evident principle. Sometimes, of course, we have to consult learned and prudent people about the content of the inspiration, for we cannot always discern it of ourselves. Above all, when the inspiration deeply involves the lives of others, for example, the desire to embrace a new form of the apostolate by certain members in a religious community, then there is an obligation to consult a spiritual director. It would be presumption to act on one's own inspiration alone in a matter of such gravity. There are, however, certain rules which we can apply ourselves. When we are inspired to increase the amount of time we spend in prayer and this can be done without detriment to the duties of our state; when we are inspired to practice some small form of asceticism that does not impair our-health nor interfere with our work, then we must act on the inspiration. This applies to the minutest details of daily life. If we are moved to make a visit to the chapel, to stop in the midst of our work and for a moment allow the mind and heart to rest in God, to kiss the crucifix in our room, to kneel down in adoration of the Most Holy Trinity on getting out of bed in the morning, to refuse quietly and without fuss a second helping of our favourite dessert, to write pronouns used of God with a capital letter, to recall Christ's death when we cross our "t's" while writing an essay—then all this has to be done. If we do not follow what the Holy Spirit inspires in tiny things, then we cannot complain that we find prayer hard and at times a burden. Fidelity to God in these small matters is the only guarantee we have that we will be faithful to Him in important and serious matters. All that can be advised is the word Our Lady gave to the waiter at Cana: "Do whatever He tells you".

Efforts to be faithful to the inspirations of the Holy Spirit will add conviction and honesty to our words of counsel and advice. Mere will be many times when the spiritual director will discern that what is missing in a person's life is precisely this fidelity. There can be no inner peace without it. If the word of counsel has grown out of one's own experience in striving to be faithful to the grace of the Holy Spirit, then the word of counsel will have a power and a strength far beyond the content of the words. Furthermore, efforts in this regard bring profound humility. The awareness that one is an instrument being used by God grows in the heart of the faithful man and this begins to make itself felt above all in the actual encounter with another person. One becomes aware of the presence of the Holy Spirit in such a way that one can listen to the other person talking and at the same time listen to the Holy Spirit.

The extraordinary result is that one knows exactly what has to be said by the time the person has finished speaking. I have come across so many examples of this. One begins with a feeling of incompetence and inadequacy, even of fear in the face of one's ignorance and sinfulness, yet at the moment one has to speak it is given in that hour what has to be said.

Fidelity to the grace of the Holy Spirit produces many small miracles of this kind. I would like to single out two. Firstly, it heightens spiritual sensitivity so that one begins to have a "sixth sense" about the presence of Christ in others, about the workings of grace in their lives, and about the crosses they carry. Secondly, it brings a certitude that is unshakeable about the existence of God. One is on the verge of being able to say "I know God exists". This is an experience that cannot be communicated, but there can be no doubt that it is a God-given grace.

Confession and the Life of Prayer

The question about the role in the spiritual life of private confession of sins is usually bedevilled by the relatively unimportant and certainly secondary issue about frequency of confession. This ought to be the final consideration for there are essential theological and anthropological questions to be settled first. Obviously we cannot enter into a discussion of these questions here. But something has to be said about the place of confession of sins in relation to prayer understood as an essential element in growth of selfhood.

No one would disagree about the totally unsatisfactory experience of "laundry list" confession especially religious who have been obliged by rule or constitutions to weekly confession. For a long time now there have been serious doubts among religious not only about the manner in which the obligation of weekly confession has been fulfilled (and certainly it has left much to be, desired), but also about the precise place it should have in their spiritual lives. This is in no way to call in question the necessity and advisability of "devotional confession". We are faced here with the power to forgive sins committed given to the Church by Christ in a sacrament in which He is really and truly present as Judge, Saviour, and Sovereign Lord and wherein the grace of God is given as Forgiving Love. This sacrament is anything but superfluous even for those who have only "small" sins to confess.

One frequently hears the remark, expressed with some anguish: "I don't seem to have anything to confess". This cannot be set aside as a baseless worry of the pious nor cynically dismissed as in the story of the wag who advised a lady who told him she had nothing to say in confession "Say three Hail Marys in honour of your Immaculate Conception". I am convinced that the remark is a cry from the heart for more than a routine weekly confession can provide. It contains the unspoken wish for direction and it is an expression of a basic awareness of the need for the forgiving love of God. Now I do not wish to get bogged down here in the question of whether the spiritual director and the confessor should be the same person (and this introduces once more the question of the ordination of women to the priesthood). What I am concerned about here is the place of confession in the life of prayer.

The confession of grave sins presents no difficulty at all as it is patently clear they need Absolution. In regard to "devotional confession" I am convinced that the majority of people who practice it or are obliged to it are really in need of direction and not just Absolution. This requires time, of course, but it is time well spent; it also demands a degree of seriousness in the confessor which will forbid him from ever dismissing what *seem* small things, for example, a question about giving up smoking for spiritual reasons. Less frequent confession and more opportunity to discuss the spiritual life would be far more beneficial in these cases.

Growth in selfhood through prayer brings with it, as we have indicated already, a sense of our sinful condition before God. All our selfishness and self-seeking have their root in this condition. It demands that we meet Christ Jesus as the Crucified One who died for our sins in order to receive God's grace in its formal aspect as forgiving love. To confess sins of uncharitableness, lying, vanity, pride, envy, and the rest is an attempt to give expression to the awareness of our still sinful condition. As a practical guide it may be suggested that we set aside one day each month or every two months to be devoted to a consideration of the mercy and forgiving love of God. Some personal penance should be undertaken and the day should include the Stations of the Cross or some other meditation on the Passion and Resurrection of Christ. This should be the day for confession. We should not present a list of our "small" sins, but rather concentrate on one particular defect and explain it briefly as it is in simplicity and truth. For example, it is far more helpful and truthful to say: "I deliberately refused, out of envy, to rejoice at another's success" or "I spent ages looking at myself in the mirror thinking 'umm, not too bad!' " rather than "I have been uncharitable" or "I have been vain". The confession of these sins gives expression to the sinful condition of our lives which is the reason why we are still so far from perfect love of God and man. Apart from increasing our spiritual sensitivity and helping us to come to terms with the dark side of our being, a practice such as this will add conviction to our words when we have to advise another person to go to confession.

Difficulties and Trials in the Life of Prayer

The spiritual life knows a development or a growth in union with God which is attested by Sacred Scripture. The classical division of this development is threefold: purgative, illuminative, and unitive ways, corresponding to purification of self, illumination by divine grace, and union with God. This division has been traced back to Origen, Evagrius Pontus, and others, but it is most closely associated with the Pseudo-Dionysius through whom it exercised its greatest influence.

While it is necessary to make this distinction in order to understand the nature of spiritual development and while it does correspond to experience in the spiritual life, we should not seek to apply it too rigidly. Tanquerey points out that there can be nothing absolute or mathematical in the distinction.[13] Father Bouyer emphasizes that all the authorities agree in saying that there is no peak in the spiritual life here on earth so high that it cannot be transcended. He continues: "Conversely, God can, without doubt, in certain more or less exceptional cases, raise a soul from sin to a high degree of sanctity without any very apparent period of transition. . . .In truth the distinction in question here is rather one of predominant aspects in the spiritual life during one or another of its phases than of rigorously successive forms".[14]

Each of these ways knows periods of deep peace and periods of great trial, both of which are periods of grace. There is not space here to treat each one in the detail it would require. Therefore, we have restricted our reflections to some general remarks about trials and suffering experienced in the life of prayer.

Firstly, we should remember that all difficulties in prayer which do not proceed from sinfulness, dissipation, or laziness, have the purpose of bringing us to the realisation that all prayer is primarily for the honour and glory of God and not for what we may get out of it. The highest form of prayer, which is mystical union with God, is also the purest form of human existence. In the ecstasy of union a person is most truly himself, lost in contemplation of the Divine Being; in ecstasy prayer and existence are identified. Mystical union

---

[13] A. Tanquerey, *The Spiritual Life: A Treatise on Ascetical and Mystical Theology,* trans. by H. Branderis, Tournai: Desclée 1950, p. 301.
[14] L. Bouyer, *Introduction to Spirituality,* New York: Desclée 1961, p. 245.

with God does not come quickly. We must be prepared to resign ourselves to this no matter how unwelcome it may be. We live in a world obsessed with speed. At the turn of a switch we get our entertainment and favourite music; pre-cooked food can be heated in a matter of minutes, if there is time to eat it warmed; we can have tea, coffee, milk, and chicken soup in a couple of seconds from a machine; we can cross the *world* in a matter of hours. All this and much besides has had the disastrous effect on our generation of making us 'speed-fiends'. One wonders at times if the widespread tragedy of drug addiction is just another example of our obsession with speed in the form of an attempt to arrive at the peace and serenity of contemplative union with God. The sad truth is that nobody ever had a mystical experience of God by taking drugs. Mystical union with God through prayer is the result of long and courageous fidelity to the divine will and constant practice of virtue. It involves also a stripping away of everything that is of sin in our being.

The process of arriving at union with God has periods of light and darkness. There can be deep feelings of consolation followed by an almost unsupportable aridity; total control of one's being, followed by the most frightful temptations against chastity and faith; a profound sense of peace and joy in the service of the Lord, followed by a feeling of absolute frustration accompanied with the idea that one has done nothing worthwhile, achieved nothing up to the present and that everything seems pointless and absurd. There can be times when one is almost convinced that God does not exist or that one has lost the faith completely. Any of these experiences can endure for a good length of time—even years. All this is quite normal and to be expected, for it is part of the process of spiritual growth which requires the rooting out of all self-seeking and selfishness from the depths of our being. It requires delicate handling, however, by a prudent spiritual director learned in the ways of grace. One cannot deal with it oneself because no one is a judge of his own case. Moreover, the attempt to come through it alone will only cause one to flounder and then to drift. None of it is to be confused with a neurosis; above all, none of it must be considered an indication of God's displeasure.

Secondly, the sense of longing coupled with a sense of emptiness is frequently encountered in people who seek the advice of a spiritual director. This longing is a desire for God born of His presence in us. It is the only case I know of where desire is actual possession. If we take seriously the condemnation of the Pelagian heresy, then we may not hold that this desire comes from ourselves. To maintain that it is the product only of our own cold hearts is heresy. It comes from the Holy Spirit who dwells in us as in a temple. The condemnation of the Semi-Pelagian heresy is one of the greatest consolations for the man who prays. It means quite simply that to want to desire to love God with all one's being and yet at the same time to feel empty and unworthy of it is actually to possess the holy grace of God.

Thirdly, there is a particular form of suffering and a specific kind of cross that comes to some religious which, though a little delicate to treat in the written word, demands some remarks in the context of a reflection on the anthropological value of prayer. I am referring here to the suffering and cross which results from the experience of falling in love. The first remark to be made about this experience is that it is a grace from God. There can be no love worthy of the name without God. If all delusion is studiously avoided, we may assert what follows without fear of contradiction. When this experience is cherished as a grace, that is, when it is integrated into prayer and there is no rebellion against the will of God who has the prior claim on the heart in virtue of the call that was accepted, it will foster growth in one's love of God and lead one to accept and believe in oneself precisely as a man or a woman in the world. Moreover, if it is integrated into the specific way of loving that is proper to religious, springing from the profession of evangelical chastity,[15] it will become a most potent factor in the development of one's spiritual life as a religious.

The suffering and the pain will most likely always be present in varying degrees of intensity, for the sacrifice involved is no light matter. For all the pain, there is a most beautiful side to the sacrifice. Fidelity to God, to whom was promised one's entire being and whole life, is the only guarantee one has of fidelity to the loved one. Furthermore, the sacrifice brings great compassion, one of its loveliest and most desirable fruits. Finally, in making the sacrifice with all one's heart and mind for the sake of our Lord, the highest possible compliment is paid to the one loved because it is a proclamation that the only one who claims priority is no other human being, but the Almighty God Himself. Abandonment, then, to His holy providence will increase the longing for His kingdom in the heart and the expectation of that day when we will all be united in love with the Three Most Holy forever.

Conclusion

The central theme of these pages has been that God is alone the guarantee of man's humanity and that Jesus Christ is the most human man the world will ever know. In the light of this fundamental principle we have examined from various aspects the anthropological value and humanising

---

[15] Eric Doyle, *Reflections*, p. 1253.

power of prayer. Our reflections have been related specifically to spiritual direction for which, in our conviction at least, religious in the Church will have an ever increasing responsibility in the future.

We end with a quotation from Karl Rahner which summarises all we have tried to say: "Radical dependence upon him (God) increases in direct, and not in inverse proportion, with genuine self-coherence before him".[16]

---

[16] *Theological Investigations*, v. 1, London: Darton, Longman and Todd 1961, p. 162.

Confirmation for Commitment to Mission[1]

In a discussion recently about the sacraments of initiation a minister of the United Reformed Church told me that he often gets requests from young people for believer's baptism. I should point out that he is minister to a Union Church and is authorised to administer baptism to Baptists.

Some of these young people informed him that they had not been baptised, had received no previous Christian formation and that for most of their lives had had little if any interest in the Church. Others volunteered that they had been baptised as infants, but felt that this meant nothing to them now. Among these one of two admitted that they had been baptised as Catholics, but had lapsed after leaving school and then drifted for a couple of years. Having made friends later with openly committed Christians, they resolved to become committed themselves and to ask for believer's baptism. It has to be granted, I submit, that there is something very attractive and deeply symbolic about the baptism of an adult by total immersion.

It is not my purpose in relating this experience to embark on an examination of the relative merits of infant and adult baptism, much less to re-open the Donatist controversy! The ancient and unbroken practice of infant baptism in the Catholic Church cannot in principle be questioned, and the teaching on the necessity and unrepeatability of the sacrament belongs to the faith of the Church. The doctrine of sacramental character is the proclamation of God's covenantal fidelity in Christ. He does not take back the gifts he confers, no matter how unfaithful, lax or half-hearted we may become. To re-administer the sacrament would be an act of ungraciousness to God. The sacramental character is therefore a christological reality and it has to be understood in the light of the incarnation of the Word, as the historically irreversible crowning point of God's free self-communication to the world.

My intention, though more modest, is of pastoral importance, namely, to highlight a problem. What provision do we have in the Catholic Church for young people (let us say the 15-24 age bracket) to make a public avowal of their discipleship of Christ and a public commitment to spreading the message

[1] CLERGY REVIEW 67 (May 1982) pp. 162-165.
Published with permission (www.priestsandpeople.co.uk).

of the gospel? The problem concerns not only young people who lapse and then seek to be committed, but also the process of initiating all young people into the missionary task of the Church.

Any attempt to deal with the problem introduces at once the sacrament of confirmation. Theological analysis of the significance of this sacrament provides a solution to the problem. It is not satisfactory, I am convinced, simply to direct lapsed young people to the sacrament of reconciliation as a fresh start in their Christian lives. This approach does not meet the zeal and enthusiasm of these young people, and is therefore psychologically unsound, spiritually poor and pastorally unsatisfactory. Besides this, even for those young people who do not lapse, much more ought to be made of their initiation into the Church's mission.

I

In the Apostolic Constitution on confirmation *Divinae consortium naturae,* published in 1971 by Paul VI,[2] there is an assumption which is contradicted by our pastoral practice. The document assumes an order, which is of course traditional, in the sacraments of initiation. Speaking of the similarity between the life of grace and natural life, the pope says: "The faithful are born anew by baptism, strengthened by the sacrament of confirmation, and finally are sustained by the food of eternal life in the Eucharist".[3] Then later in the text: "Finally, confirmation is so closely linked with the holy Eucharist that the faithful, after being signed by holy baptism and confirmation, are incorporated fully into the body of Christ by participation in the Eucharist".[4] Our pastoral practice today, where infant baptism is administered, inverts the order of the last two. Infants are baptised, then at about the age of seven they make their first confession and receive their first communion, and sometime subsequently are confirmed. Up to about the twelfth century it was customary to administer infant baptism, infant confirmation and infant communion, and this is still the practice in the East. The change occurred in the thirteenth century when both confirmation and Eucharist began to be postponed to a later age.

The Code of Canon Law stipulated "that confirmation could be postponed until about the age of seven years (c.788). During the course of this century the Congregation of the Sacraments has made a number of statements

---

[2] *Pontificale Romanum. . .auctoritate Pauli PP. VI promulgatum. Ordo Confirmationis,* editio typica, Typis Polyglottis Vaticanis, 1973.
[3] *Confirmation. The Rite,* CTS 1976, p. 1.
[4] Ibid., p. 3.

which clearly favour the view that confirmation should precede the Eucharist".[5] However, these have been ignored for the most part and this has proved a good example of creative disobedience.

The introduction to the new *Ordo Confirmationis* clearly recognises a certain pluriformity in the matter:

> With regard to children, in the Latin Church the administration of confirmation is generally postponed until about the seventh year. For pastoral reasons, however, especially to strengthen the faithful in complete obedience to Christ the Lord and in loyal testimony to him, episcopal conferences may choose an age which seems more appropriate, so that the sacrament is given at a more mature age after appropriate formation.[6]

I do not wish to take up the controversial question about what age children should be introduced to the sacrament of reconciliation, though experience seems to advise a later rather than an earlier age. Nor am I concerned here to defend the practice of infant communion,[7] though there is much to commend it on the understanding that new life needs nourishment. What I am maintaining is that where it is a case of infant baptism, the order of the sacraments of initiation: baptism, Eucharist, confirmation, is sensible, desirable and preferable. And I would advocate strongly as a matter of principle that the sacrament of confirmation be postponed until at least the mid-teens.

It can be argued that the Apostolic Constitution favours this position, for throughout the text confirmation is really presented as an adult sacrament. This is clear from the examples given which are all adults. Firstly, Christ himself: "The New Testament shows how the Holy Spirit assisted Christ in fulfilling his messianic mission. . . .He was impelled by the Spirit to undertake his public ministry as the Messiah, relying on the Spirit's presence and assistance".[8] Secondly, Mary, the apostles and disciples:

> He later promised his disciples that the Holy Spirit would help them also to bear witness to their faith even before persecutors. . . .And in fact, on the day of the feast of Pentecost, the Holy Spirit came down in

---

[5] ACTA APOSTOLICAE SEDIS 24 (1932) pp. 271-272; 27 (1935) p. 15; 38 (1946) p. 350.
[6] *Confirmation. The Rite*, p. 11.
[7] See the interesting article by C. Crawford, *Infant Communion: Past Tradition and Present Practice* in: THEOLOGICAL STUDIES 31 (1970) pp. 523-536.
[8] *Confirmation. The Rite*, CTS 1976, p. 2.

an extraordinary way on the Apostles as they were gathered with Mary the mother of Jesus and the group of disciples.[9]

Confirmation, then, I would argue, is an adult sacrament intimately connected with the Church's missionary activity. To share in this task demands Christian maturity, a close familiarity with the Word of God, a sound knowledge of the faith and a deep love of the crucified and exalted Lord.

II

The Church is a sublime mystery and no one model nor all the models taken together can totally unravel its nature. It is a mystery in its origin, existence and destiny. The Church Universal is "a People brought into unity from the unity of the Father, the Son and the Holy Spirit".[10] The Church is essentially a holy people made one and a missionary people. She bears the marks of unity and holiness because God is one and holy; she has the mark of catholicity because God is Three-in-One, and the mark of apostolicity because God sent the Son and the Spirit into the world.

We enter into the mystery of this unity by the sacrament of baptism whereby we are made holy, consecrated and appointed to worship God. The new life God gives us is nourished at the tables of the word and Eucharist. In this way we grow in holiness as God is holy and become ever more united as God is one, and this for the building up of the body of Christ "until we all attain to the unity of the faith and of the knowledge of the Son of God, to mature manhood, to the measure of the stature of the fullness of Christ; so that we may no longer be children, tossed to and fro and carried about with every wind of doctrine, by the cunning of men, by their craftiness in deceitful wiles" [Ephesians 4:13-14].

Baptism is the sacrament of justification and by it we are taken into the paschal mystery.

"The Church on earth is by its very nature missionary, since, according to the plan of the Father it has its origin in the mission of the Son and the Holy Spirit".[11] The apostolic character of the Church is thus derived directly from God himself. The people of God is an apostolic people firstly, because God sent the Apostle Jesus Christ, the Word made flesh among us. He came that we might have life, have it abundantly and his very words are life [cf. John 10:10; 6:63]. Secondly, this people is apostolic because after the glorification of Jesus

---

[9] Ibid., p. 2.
[10] Dogmatic Constitution on the Church, *Lumen gentium* 4, Flannery Edition, p. 352.
[11] Decree on the Church's Missionary Activity, *Ad gentes* 1, Flannery Edition, p. 814.

the Father sent in his name the Apostle the Holy Spirit, God's Love made power in us. He came to abide with us always, to teach us all things and to bring to our minds all that Jesus said. He bears witness to Jesus and makes us witnesses of Jesus [cf. John 14:16, 26; 15:26f.]. Because Jesus is what he said, namely life and truth, the Spirit does not merely bring back words about Jesus, he brings to us the living and life-giving presence of Jesus, the Risen Lord. Participation in the Church's mission of preaching the gospel is not some optional extra, it is required by the very nature of Christian discipleship. Confirmation is the sacrament of mission and by it we are taken into the pentecostal mystery.

Pope Paul's Apostolic Constitution asserts that confirmation is primarily concerned with mission:

> Through the sacrament of confirmation, those who have been born anew in baptism receive the inexpressible Gift, the Holy Spirit himself, by which 'they are endowed. . .with special strength'. Moreover, having received the character of this sacrament, they are 'bound more intimately to the Church' and 'they are more strictly obliged to spread and defend the faith both by word and by deed as true witnesses of Christ. . . .'[12]

The Holy Spirit knows the deep things of God and among those revealed to us is the Father's love of the Son and how he loves us for loving the Son [cf. John 16:27; 1 Corinthians 2:10]. The knowledge and the reality of that love have to be shared and this sharing is the mission of the Church.

III

Instruction of children in the faith and Christian life should be directed towards the sacrament of confirmation, as a full commitment to the Church's missionary task. It is the goal to which the young believer is moving. The reception of this sacrament is not something that should happen automatically just because the bishop is coming on visitation. The boys and girls should be led to appreciate that they can be confirmed only out of a free decision on their part.

They should be brought gradually to realise the seriousness of being a follower of Christ and the responsibility confirmation entails for spreading the gospel by word and deed. God has been so generous to us in Christ that his love obliges us to share what we have received. The call of Jesus to his followers to

---

[12] *Confirmation. The Rite,* 3.

proclaim the mystery of God's purpose demands a response. Confirmation is the unqualified 'Yes' to his call.

As a possible structure for the administering of this sacrament, I would like to suggest the following. Each diocese would arrange for confirmation to be administered by the bishop and his assistants in the cathedral every Pentecost Sunday. If it seems that numbers would be too unwieldy, then the same arrangement could hold for the deanery churches. There the dean, as representing the bishop and officially announced as such, assisted by local parish priests, would administer the sacrament. But where possible the confirmands should go to the cathedral. The sacrament involves an apostolic commission and the bishop belongs to the college which succeeds in the Church to the apostles.[13]

At about the age of sixteen and generally no earlier, young Catholics would be invited to make a request in writing for confirmation to the parish priest. They would already know the procedure from their earlier catechetical instruction, and would be expected to have discussed the matter with parents, priest and teachers. The invitation would be made from the pulpit on two or three Sundays after the Epiphany, say on the feast of the baptism of the Lord and the first and second Sundays of ordinary time. It might be objected here that many would not make the request. That being the case, it would have to be accepted that they do not wish to take on the responsibility of the Church's missionary task. There would always be the opportunity for them to make their commitment when they felt ready.

The confirmands would then follow a weekly course of reflections/seminars/discussions on baptism, the Eucharist and the Church, for the whole of Lent in preparation for the public renewal of their baptismal promises at the Easter Vigil. The renewal of these promises could then be omitted from the confirmation ceremony in accordance with the provisions of nn. 16-18 of the *Ordo Confirmationis* concerning adaptations of the rite.[14]

Then from Low Week to Ascension Thursday they would follow a further weekly course on confirmation, the meaning of mission and the Acts of the Apostles in preparation for their confirmation on Pentecost Sunday.

This rite, which ordinarily takes place within Mass, would be celebrated with the greatest solemnity.[15] Again in accordance with nn. 16-18 of the *Ordo,* it would be highly desirable and eminently fitting if a text were

---

[13] See the introduction to the new rite, n.7 in: *Confirmation. The Rite,* pp. 9f.
[14] Ibid., pp. 13f.
[15] Ibid., n.4, p. 9.

added to the rite, after the anointing and before the peace greeting, whereby the bishop would formally commission those just confirmed to the Church's missionary task and this were followed by a brief response in their own words accepting the commission by the newly confirmed.

By such a procedure, I believe, the place and importance of confirmation in the Church's consciousness would be considerably enhanced and it would provide a splendid opportunity for young people who, after lapsing for a period of time, resolve to commit themselves to the Church's mission. It would also realise more satisfactorily the wish of the Second Vatican Council: "The rite of confirmation is to be revised also so that the intimate connection of this sacrament with the whole of the Christian initiation may more clearly appear".[16]

While I have been emphasising that the sacrament of confirmation is a commitment to mission, I would not wish to give the impression that the personal dimension of the sacrament may be ignored. According to the doctrine of grace God the Absolute freely communicates himself to the finite creature. Grace is not merely a matter of created gifts. In his gracious love God turns towards us his creatures and establishes personal relationships with himself which we designate uncreated grace. By a formal (or, as it is said, quasi-formal) causality we are related to the Father as sons and daughters, to the Son as brothers and sisters and to the holy Spirit as temples in which he dwells.

St. Paul asks the Corinthians: "Do you not know that you are God's temple and that God's Spirit dwells in you?" and he reminds them that the body "is a temple of the Holy Spirit within you, which you have from God". [1 Corinthians 3:16; 6:19]. The Holy Spirit dwells in the community as a whole and through the community is given to each individual believer. To the individual the Holy Spirit grants his sevenfold gifts: wisdom, understanding, counsel, courage, knowledge, piety and awe of the Lord. These flow one into the other in a circular movement in such a way that the beginning of wisdom is awe of the Lord. By these gifts we are enabled to respond with alacrity and promptitude to his inspirations.

The Temple in Israel was the focal point of God's presence, the place where he dwelled. In the Temple was the Holy of Holies, the inner sanctuary, into which only the high priest entered once a year on the Day of Atonement. The temple of God that each of us has become, also has its holy of holies: it is

---

[16] The Constitution on the Sacred Liturgy, *Sacrosanctum Concilium* 71, Flannery Edition, p. 22.

the heart. The Holy Spirit opens the way into the sanctuary of our heart, [cf. Hebrews 9:8] so that Christ "the high priest of the good things that have come", and "minister in the sanctuary" [Hebrews 9:11; 8:2] may preside there to offer spiritual sacrifices of love, praise and thanksgiving to the Eternal Father.

Reflections on the Theology of Religious Life[1]

Proem: Rublev's "Trinity"

In these reflections on the theology of the religious life, we will be considering in fact, from a specific vantage point, the mystery of grace in the Church—that mystery of God's own free, absolute decision to communicate Himself to us as He is in the eternal blessedness of His inner life. We need to emphasise at the outset that the religious life belongs to the charismatic form of the Church in order to avoid the error of identifying in any exclusive sense the charismatic with the *sensational* or the *pentecostal* as these latter are experienced and understood at present in the Church.

Besides being reflections on uncreated and created grace, these are also considerations from a particular aspect of the theological virtues of faith, hope, and charity which are given in the baptismal grace. By justification a man is renewed in his inner life *(remissio peccatorum/ interna renovatio),* whereby he is made a sharer in the divine life, becomes God's adopted son, is constituted before God a co-heir with Christ and whereby the Holy Trinity comes to dwell in him as in a temple. The indwelling of the Blessed Trinity is attributed by the venerable Tradition of the Church to the Holy Spirit, an attribution based on the order of the divine processions in God and on the divine missions in the economy of salvation. We need not here debate the various explanations of this appropriation—whether it be by exemplary or quasi-formal causality. It is enough to point out that uncreated grace involves a special relationship with the Holy Spirit as well. In the grace of justification, therefore, a personal relationship is established with the Father, the Son, and the Holy Spirit.

Now because I intend to show, in the first place, that the religious life, wherever it finds expression in community, is an image of the Triune life of God, I would like to begin with a brief meditative reflection on Rublev's Icon of the Trinity.

[1] REVIEW FOR RELIGIOUS 33 (Nov. 1973) pp. 1238-1263. Published with permission. The text given below is that of a talk given March 14, 1973, in Liverpool, England, at the Annual General Meeting of Major Religious Superiors (Men's Section).

A study of iconography gradually leads its devotees to an awareness that they are in fact students of theology and that as well as a verbal theology, there is also a visual theology in the Church: the icon. Christ is the *Eikon* of the God we cannot see, as He is the Logos of the God we cannot express. As the Word, Christ is the source and reason of all words; as the Icon, He is the source and reason of all art. Indeed, it can be said that without Him as the Icon of God, all art must be, in the final analysis, meaningless. Once a person has learned to love icons and has thus penetrated a little into their rich world of mystery, has understood their theology of presence, and grasped the doctrine of God's image in creation, he will then know that all doctrine and theology can be communicated, best of all perhaps, through the medium of the icon.

The Realisation of Perfect Community

This icon of icons—as Professor Evdokimov has described it—*The Holy Trinity,* was painted in the early fifteenth century by the Russian monk, Andrei Rublev.[2] It was inspired by the story in Genesis of the apparition at Mamre: "He looked up and there he saw three men standing near him. As soon as he saw them, he ran from the entrance of the tent to meet them, and bowed to the ground" [Genesis 18:2-3]. In this account many of the fathers of the Church saw a vague adumbration of the doctrine of the Holy Trinity, because although he saw three, Abraham made only one act of homage and he addressed his visitors in the singular.

Gazing at the icon we cannot fail to be mastered in mind and heart by its peace, movement, serenity; its unity, diversity, and even humility. The perfection and completion of the icon are to be seen above all in the circle that contains the three figures, as Professor Evdokimov has noted. The movement of the icon, he explains,

> begins from the left foot of the angel on the right, follows the inclination of the head, passes to the centre angel—carrying irresistibly with it the cosmos, rock and tree—resolving itself in the upright position of the left angel, in whom it comes to rest, almost as in a container. Beside this circular movement, whose fulfilment commands all the rest as eternity commands time, the verticals of the temple and the sceptres express the longing of the earthly for the heavenly where the élan finds its term.[3]

---

[2] P. Evdokimov, *Interpretation of Rublev's Icon of the Trinity. One in Christ,* v. 3 (1967) pp. 304-310.
[3] Ibid., p. 305.

Rublev's icon is a symbol of the Triune life of God. We are gazing at a perfect community gathered round a table: the three figures distinct in their unique personalities, forming a unity-in-equality, thus symbolising the perfection of community which is unity-in-diversity, diversity-in-unity. As the onlooker continues to gaze he cannot resist the icon's compelling invitation to enter and become part of the group. The sheer simplicity and majesty of the figures draws the onlooker into their company where he feels entirely at home and utterly at peace, for in all its perfection and completion, there is nothing exclusive or forbidding about the group of figures. The invitation it holds out is unqualified: "Come, we will refresh you".

We are shown, then, in this icon, the realisation of perfect Community and we are offered an invitation to Community. Our God-given task and calling as religious in community is to strive for the perfection of unity-in-diversity which is surely the quintessence of community life. The true unity we strive to build will prevent our diversity from degenerating into division; the diversity we strive to preserve and foster will prevent our unity from congealing into uniformity. The focal point of all our desires and strivings to build our community is, of course, the Holy Mass. When we gather around the table of the Lord in that most blessed sacrificial meal, we are made one in the Eucharistic Body and the Mystical Body of Christ and we become more truly ourselves in the grace of God's love, which is given to each one of us as uniquely our own. It is our vocation as religious to make our communities here on earth real images of that Blessed Community, which is the one, undivided, Triune God, Father, Son, and Holy Spirit.

Introduction: "They Also Serve Who Resolve to Go on. . ."

It has become fashionable in some quarters to deny the possibility, even the desirability, of making a lifelong promise to God in the religious life. This would be sad enough were its provenance only those who decide, for whatever reason, to leave the religious life. One might then conclude that this were no more than a good example of the invalid illation of arguing from the particular to the general: it is not possible for me to continue to the end of my life as a religious; therefore, it is not possible at all, nor desirable, for anyone to make a promise to live always the life of the gospel counsels. It is not my desire to make any criticism of those who leave the religious life. That would be to arrogate the prerogatives that belong exclusively to the most merciful Judge. Beyond doubt, there are cases where it is clearly the better choice to leave the religious life, even by those who have made life profession of the evangelical counsels. Experience shows that people do make mistakes and wrong decisions about freely chosen states of life. There are men and women who would have been severely impaired physically, psychologically, and spiritually, had they remained in the religious life. Manifestly also, each case has to be considered on its own merits, for the simple reason that every person is endowed with a uniqueness that forbids generalities in certain areas, however well intentioned these may be.

However, it must be emphasised that there is a spiritual life. This life of the spirit, although it is most intimately bound up with the bodily and psychic life of the person, owns, nevertheless, laws proper to itself. People undergo purely spiritual crises which must be treated according to the laws of the spiritual life. It is one of the sadder errors of our time in the Church to imagine that spiritual crises can be treated and controlled by purely psychological methods. When people are sick in body or mind, it is most natural that they should consult a doctor or a psychiatrist; it is also natural and most reasonable that a spiritual crisis should be presented to a spiritual director. We have every right to expect such treatment from prudent and learned men trained in the ways of the spiritual life. It is a matter for the gravest concern that many religious who have left never even considered the necessity of consulting a spiritual director about the state of their soul on its journey to union with God.

The tragedy is, however, that the view which maintains the impossibility of a life commitment to God by profession of the evangelical counsels, is peddled among religious themselves. Here and there one comes across religious men and women who hold that it is a distinct possibility that one day they may well awaken to the realisation that it is now time for them to move on to another way of life. There are some who maintain that such a situation should be expected to arise. In this way, commitment is shorn of its absolute quality and is reduced to the present moment: "I am fulfilled today; who knows what I may feel tomorrow?" "Up to the present my existential commitment has brought me self-realisation and self-satisfaction; these may well disappear later". Many religious men and women, bombarded by such views and this kind of "existential" reasoning—if reasoning it can be called— a re reduced to the condition of wondering whether they are themselves too immature to hold such views, of thinking that they are the failures for staying on in the religious life, and of questioning whether it is they themselves who have just not got the courage of their brethren who leave, to pack up likewise and find real fulfilment outside the religious life. I am not directly concerned here with this state of affairs. My principal purpose is to share these theological reflections on the nature, value, adventure, and desirability of the religious life with those who have resolved, not through their own strength, but trusting in the all-powerful grace of God, who is faithful forever, to go on to their dying day in their profession of the evangelical counsels and then to live out that profession for one day at a time. What I have to say, therefore, is addressed to those religious who know by reflection or intuitively, even in the midst of the present confusion, that the Church cherishes the religious life as a most precious treasure and who also understand why it is loved and admired by thousands of people who own no obvious allegiance to God or to any religion in the world.

The Community of God

Let us begin at the very beginning. The Eternal God—the heart of the mystery proclaimed in the gospel message—is a Community. There in the depths of the divine life from everlasting to everlasting has been a Community, a Family, one might say: the Holy Father, Origin without origin; the Holy Son, indescribable Wisdom and perfect Image of the Father; the Holy Spirit, eternal Love and inexpressible Sweetness between the Father and the Son. There forever has been the perfect unity of absolute diversity and perfect diversity in absolute unity. The problem of the one and the many was solved even before we ever discovered the problem at all!

The Son came to us, sent by the Father, to bring us all to share the richness, peace, serenity, and blessed vitality of His Community for endless ages. He came on a long journey to be our Way, our Road to His Father; He lived our life and endured our death to become our Life; He bore our lies, was rejected and despised, to become our Truth; He was thirsty on the Cross to become our Living Water; He was cold in the tomb, to become our burning fire of love.

He did not merely take to Himself the human condition as the Jesus of history and then become later the Christ of faith in His risen life. He crossed the unbridgeable abyss between the Creator and the creature as the man Jesus of Nazareth among the Jewish people, that people chosen by God on behalf of the nations, that people who lived in history by faith in the Holy One of Israel. He came, therefore, into a believing people, Yahweh's own people, whom Yahweh Himself had forged into unity. Of course, it was a weak faith, a misunderstood faith, a faith often filled with illusions and false expectancy. But it was a faith and that Man came as the Jesus of faith who was the Christ in history.

He chose the Twelve who were the Twelve before they were sent. In them was constituted together with and under Christ, the New Israel, in the line of the Twelve Tribes and the Twelve Patriarchs. It was as the Twelve that they were sent, the Twelve were made *Apostoloi*. By His rising from the dead and glorification, Christ purified the faith of Israel and inaugurated the final age wherein the third Member of His own eternal Community was sent into the world, the Blessed Spirit, whose mission it is to make us one people on earth by transforming us into images of Christ, the Son of the Living God and Icon of the Father who dwells in unapproachable light. Through these two missions, one might say through the first two Apostles, mankind is brought into the life of God Himself. By the grace of the Triune God the Church is made evermore one in the unity of the Father, the Son, and the Holy Spirit. This unity will never be perfect here on earth; its perfection is reserved for the eschatological kingdom where God will be all in all. In the meantime it is our God-given duty to bear witness to this unity and to work to make it ever more perfect until all history has run its course.

The Religious Community

The Church is made up of people from every race, culture, nation, language, and class, who have been called together in unity by God's most gracious kindness. The unity of the Church is intended to cut through every barrier erected by men to divide one group from another. All men stand before God in their uniqueness and are loved by Him from all eternity; and in that sense all men are equal before Him. A religious community is made up of men or women who have been brought together through the grace of God, which is their calling to the religious life. Their coming together is not founded on natural attractions, common talents, or because the members belong to the same class or social stratum. A religious community is made up of individual persons whom God has called together through the grace of brotherhood in Christ. By God's most holy grace and through His most generous love, there comes to be a community of unique persons where there is unity-in-diversity and diversity-in-unity.

Precedence of Community

As I see it, it is the primary vocation of each member of a religious community to build up the community so that it becomes daily an ever more perfect image of the mystery of God's own triune life. This aspect of the religious vocation takes precedence over all external activities, including apostolic work. What I mean to stress here is the absolute priority of 'being' over 'doing'. The public profession of the evangelical counsels lived out in community life (thus manifesting the religious life as a *state* in the Church) has a value of itself, is an apostolate and mission in itself, namely, a public witness to and proclamation of the acceptance of God's grace. Nobody can profess the evangelical counsels without a special grace from God. The presence of this state as such in the Church, anterior to all apostolic work, of even the most active orders, is the apostolate of proclaiming the victory of God's grace over man's finitude and sinfulness. The religious life justifies itself prior to all apostolic activity. In this sense we can understand the words of the Second Vatican Council:

> The profession of the evangelical counsels, then, appears as a sign which can and ought to attract all the members of the Church to an effective and prompt fulfilment of their Christian vocation. The People of God has no lasting city here below, but looks forward to one which is to come. This being so, the religious state by giving its members greater freedom from earthly cares more adequately manifests to all believers the presence of heavenly goods already possessed here below.[4]

Of course, there is no question here of denying the value and indispensable place of apostolic work by religious for the establishment of God's kingdom; the issue involved is the principle which specifies our way of life as religious in the Church. As religious we must define ourselves in terms of community: we are communities of brothers and sisters in which should reign the justice, love, and peace of God Himself and from which should spring our apostolates as from a centre and point of cohesion. The primary vocation of each religious community is to make the Church of Christ ever more present at this local level and, so understood, the theology of the religious community is a variation on the theme of the theology of the local church.

The Need for Self-Giving

In view of what has been said thus far about this primary vocation of a religious in the Church, it is clear that this duty and responsibility must involve as indispensable an element of self-denial, self-sacrifice, self-humiliation—in a word—an amount of self-giving which is demanded by this form of Christian discipleship. There is, obviously, a renunciation involved in the profession of the evangelical counsels, but I am not referring to this at the moment. We shall return to that point later. In the world outside the influence

---

[4] *Lumen Gentium* 44.

of the Church there is a great concern about the meaning and reality of community. Many people (and not only the young) are opting out of what they describe as the rat-race. There are some, no doubt, who are selfish in this, refusing to accept the responsibilities that go with the decision to embrace any way of life that has structures or an occupation which involves accountability. But this is not the whole story. There is also great generosity and much serious heart-searching among those who opt out of society at present. In my view these people are looking for leaders, men and women of integrity, with the courage of their convictions, who are prepared to be signs of contradiction and to give fish instead of snakes, eggs instead of scorpions, and bread instead of stones to those who are searching for peace, justice, equality, and brotherhood in a truly human community. Is it not a sad fact that they do not find authentic community life in the religious orders? Over the past fifteen years or so, but especially since the end of the Council, the religious orders ought to have made themselves centres of true renewal in the Church by concentrating above all on the quality and reality of community life and all that this implies, especially with regard to the interior life and the life of prayer of each member. In my opinion that renewal was not possible because too many of us were seeking ourselves, looking to our own fulfilment and our own satisfaction. We have forgotten the meaning of self-sacrifice for something greater than ourselves and in this we are all guilty.

Excessive Individualism

There is, of course, much talk of community in the Church at the moment. Yet, I think it is true to say, that there has never been more nauseating individualism and more self-assertion than at present. This, again, is not restricted to any age group or to any ideology, be this dubbed 'progressive' or 'conservative'. It is found to an alarming degree in the religious orders. Now, obviously, I am not advocating a stunting of personal growth or a childish dependence on others in the religious life. This kind of excess and of narrowness has led to our undoing in the past. Certainly, no one can offer incense at the shrine of what-things-used-to-be.

The Gospel and the Signs of the Times

Now that the dust has begun to settle a little after the changes, adaptations, and upheavals of the last decade or so, we are able to discern a little better what came from the inspiration of the Holy Spirit and what was the product of human negligence and folly. The source of our discernment is the teaching of the gospel and the signs of the times. In the gospel, there is not a great deal about self-fulfilment or maximum self-satisfaction; the emphasis is rather on self-denial, self-sacrifice, saying "no" to oneself and on following out relentlessly the will of the Father up to and including death itself. In terms of this emphasis it is the sacred duty of us all in the religious orders to examine our conscience to discover whether we are seeking primarily ourselves or the good of the community; and where there is no self-sacrifice for the good of the whole, there can be only selfishness. We cannot come to maturity until we rid ourselves of selfish individualism and we can only rid ourselves of this by self-sacrifice.

In trying to read the signs of the times in the light of the unchanging message of the gospel, it seems clear now that in stressing the value of the individual (a legitimate reaction to an almost obsessive emphasis on structures and "the good of the order" in the past) we have erred by excess. It cannot be denied that there is a type of doctrine which appears to advocate no commitment to other than the present moment of self-fulfilment. It seems to me that very many religious have tended to align themselves with this kind of philosophy of life, which is really a 'spiritualized' play-boy philosophy. At best it re-echoes the liberalism of the 18th and 19th centuries. This, however, seems to have nothing in common with the gospel. The desire for peace justice, brotherhood, the awareness of responsibility for the future, the longing for creative silence, the desire for prayer, the disenchantment with consumer society, are more truly signs of the presence of God's Holy Spirit in our time than all the emphasis on what can only be described as liberalistic individualism and the fulfilment of individual values. It is with these former signs that we ought to align ourselves by manifesting a willingness to sacrifice ourselves for the sake of building true communities and thus contradict the individualism and selfishness now rife in society and to a large extent in the Church. There is a profound lesson for all of us in the universal admiration for Mother Teresa and her order; in the midst of all their good works, their life of prayer and daily program of devotion put our most rigorous timetables of the past completely in the shade.

The Danger of Professionalism

It is, of course, a most desirable development that individual religious should obtain professional standards in their work. The time has gone when everyone in an order did everything in the same way, when superiors had experienced every type of work the order had embraced, so that they were always in a position to show others how it ought to be done. Because of the necessary specialisations it is impossible for any one man or woman to know even superficially every kind of work and apostolate. We need experts in every field of our work. However, there is a great danger in this desirable diversity of individual pursuits in the religious life. I do not for one moment even hint that we should forbid or exclude the acquiring of professional standards over a wide range of work and commitments, but I do beg us all to be aware of the dangers to be avoided. We can so easily turn our religious communities into nothing more than residential centres, training institutes, and glorified lodging-houses for individual people working over a wide range of totally unrelated professions linked by little more than a front door key possessed by all. It must be our prime concern to make our religious houses real communities of prayer and peace where the members are at home, where they do love one another and need one another, where the test of concern for the poverty and horrors of the third and fourth worlds can be made by how we treat those who are physically closest to us of all. One cannot take seriously a concern for the poor of Calcutta or the deprived of Latin America in someone who cannot spend even a fraction of his or her time, insights, and person with another member of the community.

The present emphasis on legitimate personal fulfilment requires a corresponding emphasis on community life where individual people can find real love and concern for them as they are, where people are wanted and loved in Christ just as they are. This requires that we be prepared to take responsibility for our community life with as much interest, seriousness, concern, and devotion as we are prepared to give to our external commitments. The liturgy of the community, its prayer life, its relaxation, its needs and desires—as well as its external works—must really be made our own.

All that has been said is based, of course, on a vision of faith. The only way in which one can be pledged to values which utterly transcend the immediate situation is by faith in the eternally faithful, transcendent, all-holy God, by commitment to Him in hope and by devotion to Him in total and irrevocable self-giving. These form the necessary, indispensable, a priori condition for true and authentic community life in any religious order.

The Bi-polarity of the Church

There is, fundamentally, only one holiness in the Church and one spirituality: union with God the Father through Jesus Christ His Word and Son, in the Holy Spirit who is God's Love poured into our hearts. Every member of the Church is called to bring to perfection their baptismal consecration to be holy as God is holy.

We are concerned here, however, with those in the Church who have freely chosen to actualise their baptismal consecration in a life based on the public profession of the evangelical counsels. We have pointed out that the Church, living by the sacred *paradosis* she has received from the holy Apostles, cherishes this form of the consecrated life. The life based on the profession of the evangelical counsels traces back its history from the rich diversity of congregations and institutes of men and women founded since the Reformation, through the great orders of friars, canons, moniales, and canonesses of the Middle Ages, through the Cistercians, the Carthusians, the reforms of Benedictinism by St. Romuald and St. Peter Damian, through the Cluniac reform and St. Benedict of Aniane to the holy patriarch of monasticism in the West, St. Benedict of Nursia; through Celtic monasticism to the episcopal monasteries of Gaul and from these to the East through St. Basil the Great, to Schenoudi, Pachomius, St. Anthony, St. Paul of Thebes, and so to the early fathers of the desert. The life of these early fathers was itself both the chronological and ideological heir of the age of the martyrs wherein men and women followed Christ perfectly in making the supreme and ultimate sacrifice of their lives for the glory of God's Name and thus proclaimed the indefectibility of truth in the Church and nourished with their blood the seeds of holiness for the future. What the Church cherishes, therefore, is a very precious treasure whose origins stretch back through a most varied and complex history and experience to the very earliest period of her existence in the world.

The Church in the world has a bi-polarity which is incarnational and eschatological. She is in and of this world and, at the same time, she seeks and strives for a world that is to come. Because the Church has this bi-polarity by her very nature, so every state of life and every individual in the Church has to a greater or less extent this same bi-polar character and the tension which of necessity goes with it. The tension between the incarnational and eschatological aspects of the Church in the world has its origin in the revelation or self-communication of God given in the gospel. The world has its own value and goodness and proper laws; yet it bears within itself an obediential potency for that which is beyond itself; to become really 'world' it needs that which it cannot of itself achieve: divinization through grace which, while perfecting it in its inner structure and essence, remains always, nonetheless, a totally gratuitous and unmerited gift.

The Church's Incarnational Character

By virtue of the incarnational character she possesses, the Church bears eloquent and unfailing testimony to the goodness and inherent value of creation which comes from God's most pure and sovereignly free love. Her task and mission of testifying to the world's goodness and the value of earthly realities (however ambiguous these may at times appear) she fulfils par excellence through the sacrament and state of holy matrimony. In the consecrated love of husband and wife is contained the image of God's love of the world and Christ's union with the Church in history. As a husband loves his wife, so Christ loves the Church; as a wife loves her husband, so the Church loves Christ her Spouse. As a husband kisses his wife, caresses her, and takes her to himself, so God has kissed the world, caressed it, and taken it to Himself in the blessed mystery of the incarnation.

The Church's Eschatological Character

The Church also possesses an eschatological character: she points to the aeon that is to come. She proclaims by her very presence in history that there is another world, a transformed creation, a new heaven and a new earth where God will be all in all. Her task and mission of bearing witness to the eschatological kingdom of God is fulfilled primarily by the public profession in the Church of the evangelical counsels of poverty, chastity, and obedience. This actualisation of faith, hope, and charity given in the baptismal consecration is realised through a divine gift whereby God is proclaimed the Infinite Treasure of our lives (poverty), the Pure Love of our hearts demanding undivided and single-minded devotion (chastity), and the Absolute and Sovereign Lord of our freedom (obedience). As such, the profession of the evangelical counsels is a sign that the Church is ever reaching out for a goal beyond this world and our history—the kingdom of God where Christ will hand over everything to the Father. The religious state, then, serves to remind the Church constantly that no matter how lovely and attractive this world may be, it is not the final goal of our efforts. There is an eschatological kingdom to which all of us as pilgrims in this world are on our way.

This twofold testimony to the Church's bi-polarity is essential and indispensable to the Church's life and mission and each is complementary to the other. The married state, as the sign of the goodness of the form of this world, proclaims to religious who publicly profess the evangelical counsels, that they must be on their guard never to allow their renunciation to degenerate into a denunciation and thus into a denial of God's love of the world. On the other hand, the religious state, as a sign of the eschatological kingdom, proclaims to married men and women, that because there is another world, they must never allow their love of this world to degenerate into idolatry which would erect idols in the place of the one, sovereign Lord of life, death, time, and history.

Thus, while religious men and women do indeed and of necessity belong to the world and though they must also by their life and work bear witness to the incarnational pole of the Church's presence in history, nevertheless, the principal and defining element of the public profession of the evangelical counsels is its testimony to the eschatological kingdom of God. By professing the evangelical counsels publicly in a visible structure or state, religious proclaim the ultimate victory of God's grace over the world.

Consecration in Christ

I would now like to recall the sentiments of generosity, freedom, and openness to God's Spirit, the virtues of faith, hope, and charity, with which we all started out on our day of profession to live the life of the evangelical counsels. I take the liberty of including what follows because I think it should be continually brought to mind (perhaps even daily) and always be put before those who ask to leave the religious life and, indeed, put before them in the first place, gently and firmly, even though it does not ultimately win the day. After all, our solemn profession is a promise we make to God and however badly through malice, weakness or negligence we may have failed to observe our promise, we cannot really be excused from continually beginning again. On our profession day, after thought, prayer, advice, and mature deliberation stretching over many more years than the vast majority of married couples spend considering their mutual final commitment, we consecrated ourselves to God in imitation of the poor, chaste, and obedient Christ in a religious order which the Church, as the guardian and discerner of gospel holiness, approved as consonant with the teaching of Christ. The order we joined specified a particular aspect of Christ's mission and work which we also freely accepted. For example, we took it upon ourselves through the grace of God to follow Christ the Preacher, or Christ the Healer, or Christ the Contemplative and so on, according to the particular way of life we embraced. Furthermore, we committed into the hands of God our entire self and our total future. By this profession we realised in a specific, concrete way the virtues of faith, hope, and charity given to us in our baptismal consecration, ratified at our confirmation, and renewed at every Mass in which we have ever participated.

The Moment of Our Profession

Everyone of us, in one form or another, pronounced on our profession day:

> I. . ., today, in the presence of God's People here assembled, by the power of God the Father, in the wisdom of God the Son, through the love of God the Spirit, do most freely consecrate myself forever to the poor, chaste, and obedient Christ (the Teacher, Healer, Contemplative, Preacher) in the order and way of life of (St. Francis, the Christian Brothers, the Most Holy Redeemer), and I most willingly embrace the renunciation of possessions, marriage, and power which this consecration involves; furthermore, I most trustfully commit into the hands of God my entire self and my total unknown future, fully recognising that fidelity to this consecration and commitment, will give me eternal life here on earth and bring me at last to the peace and glory of God's own blessed eternity. In the name of the Father and of the Son and of the Holy Spirit. Amen.

At the moment of our profession we trusted God and He, as He always does, took us at our word. And so the years have rolled by and, our word of promise remaining—since it was made in, with, and through the Eternal Word who remains forever—we have continued to the present through all the trials, crosses, successes, failures, miseries, disappointments, sins, consolations, and ups-and-downs of everyday life. When we look back over our lives, is it not true that all the crosses and trials we have borne and experienced always came from the least expected quarter and in the least expected way? Whoever would have imagined that prayer could prove at times to be the source of such suffering and worry? Whoever would have believed on the day of profession that doubts one day would come even about the value of the religious life? Whoever would have thought that involvement with other people would at times bring us almost to the point of regretting that sacrifice we made of ourselves to God? Whoever would have imagined that such little things in our lives could take on such overwhelming significance? Whoever would have believed that community life could turn out at times to be so utterly unbearable? Whoever would have thought it possible to drift for months, even years on end, without noticing it? Whoever would have imagined it even conceivable to nibble away slowly at what was promised once so unconditionally?

Recovering the Beginning

However, this is what we accepted—yes, even all this—in advance when we committed into God's hands our entire future. The only thing to be done when we come to wonder about the value of our lives as religious, when we see before us the string of infidelities running through our lives, when we turn away from ourselves in sadness, nausea, and disgust, is to try to recapture the generosity that was there at the beginning. For when all is said and done, the fact of the matter is that we have come through to the present and therefore the grace of vocation remains in possession. However scarred and bruised we may be, however bad our co-operation may have been up to the present, however much we may have ignored God and slipped slyly passed Him, even if we have got through to this point only by struggling on our hands and knees in the mire or crawling on our elbows, the fact remains that we are still here and that fact shows that we have never rejected totally the grace of our vocation. What we need at this moment in the religious life is a renewal of the theological virtue of hope in all of us: young, middle-aged, old; novices, temporarily professed, finally professed. That means we must tighten our grip of the pierced and glorified hand of Christ and resolve, no matter what happens, never to let go.

Gratitude and Faith

We have remained then until now. Let us accept this generously before God and thank Him for it. He deserves our thanks, for there He remains from all eternity gazing at us in unspeakable love and tender mercy, knowing in the depths of His Divine Being that what we professed, we professed for His sake. Remembering this, we need only ask ourselves: where, in the end, is my heart? If, in the midst of all our sins, infidelities, negligences, imperfections, tepidity, indifference, our work, achievements, successes and failures, we can answer in honesty: "It is with God and I want to love Him totally", then we may rest assured that our heart is with God and that we are on the way of salvation. For the desire to love God, the longing for Him, comes not from ourselves, but from His Holy Spirit. This is, I think, the only case where desire is, in fact, possession. Holy Scripture assures us: God gives the will and the way. Any other view would be Pelagianism or at least Semi-Pelagianism and who would want to subscribe to that ghastly doctrine which leads in the end to the most terrifying loneliness?

At this time of the rediscovery of the God of Exodus who has called the Church out on a journey, the profession of the evangelical counsels ought to be a sublime act of faith. The Church may well have to wander in the desert of doubt and confusion for forty years, not always knowing the way ahead, settling sometimes here, sometimes there. We must never lose sight of the promise, however, that though the way is not always clear, the destination is certain. The Church is making a journey to the eschatological kingdom, whatever indications there may seem to the contrary. Of that eschatological kingdom the public profession of the evangelical counsels is the supreme witness. We need to keep on praying in hope and love to the unchanging, ever-present, all-holy transcendent God for an always stronger faith to see through the veil to the value and meaning of our lives.

The Unity of the Vows

It is unsatisfactory to present the religious life solely in terms of a profession of the three vows or merely in terms of three promises "we take". This presentation tends to reify and atomise the religious life. The religious life is a specific form of Christian discipleship in the Church whose unity is founded on a well-defined relationship to Christ and to the Trinitarian life of God. It is a way of life based on imitation of the gospel Christ in His distinct characteristics as the poor, chaste, and obedient Servant of the world. It is also a way of life lived out publicly in community, reflecting to a greater or less extent the Community Life of the Eternal Godhead. The unity of the religious life, then, proceeds from a relationship with Christ who is followed in certain specific aspects of His own life for the sake of the kingdom of God. The profession of the evangelical counsels is a distinct way of being related to Christ in the Church which comes about by the grace of God. The formula of profession of the evangelical counsels which we gave above serves to emphasise the unity of our consecration to God. The formula refers precisely to the poor, chaste, and obedient Christ rather than to the vows of poverty, chastity, and obedience. Our profession is a consecration in, through, and with Someone: the Living Christ, known and loved as poor, chaste, and obedient. The formula stresses a relationship which is meant to go on growing throughout our lives. Therefore, we ought to get into the habit of speaking of our consecration to God through profession of the evangelical counsels and put aside all talk of "taking vows".

The Vows and the Trinity

If we pursue the relationship with the Trinitarian life of God, we can relate each counsel to one of the Persons of the Trinity. Poverty may be described as the total giving of all that a person is and has. It is the openness of total giving. Now, in the life of the Godhead, the Father gives everything He is to the Son, so that the Son is the Son because He has received *ab aeterno* all that He is from the Father. By our profession of following the Poor Christ, we are related to the Father because by grace we become images of His total giving. Obedience may be described as a complete receptivity to every person, circumstance, and event of everyday life. Obedience is the openness of total receiving. In the life of the Blessed Trinity the Son receives all that He is from the Father. By our profession of following the Obedient Christ, we are related to the Son, because by grace we become images of His perfect and total receptivity. Chastity may be described as a specific way of loving through the gift of universal love from God. Now, in the life of the Triune God there proceeds and is engendered *ab aeterno* from the total reciprocal giving and receiving of the Father and the Son, the love between them which is the Holy Spirit. By our profession of following the Chaste Christ, we are related to the Holy Spirit because by grace we share in the love He is, which receives its specific form from the way in which we follow the poor and obedient Christ.

Religious Life and Three Aspects of Christ's Life

In the context of this fundamental unity of the profession of the evangelical counsels, I want now to turn to an analysis of the three aspects of Christ's life which form the basis of the religious life in the Church.

It must be emphasised at the outset that the threefold aspect of religious consecration has a negative and a positive side. The negative side is the renunciation of three God-given gifts for the sake of a higher good. In a specific threefold way the world is renounced: we offer back to God the right to possess part of the world, the right to seek power and have authority legitimately in the world, the right to be joined to another person in that love which issues in a community established by free, human choice. This threefold renunciation is made in faith on account of a higher good: God Himself as Infinite Treasure, Almighty in power, and Pure Love. The higher good is possessed in hope, and from this comes a specific form of the virtue of charity.

Through the higher good which is God Himself each counsel is endowed with a rich positive side to be considered at some length.

Chastity as a Unique Form of Loving

Firstly, our following of the chaste Christ, the profession of evangelical chastity. This is the profession of a way of loving which has its own unique character. As a husband and wife love each other in a way that is unique and totally different from the way they love their parents, their children, and their brothers and sisters, so also is the love of a consecrated religious a specific and totally unique form of loving. Married love proceeds from the total giving of man and wife to each other, suffused and elevated by the grace of God; and it is born of the unique experience of this particular couple. Evangelical chastity proceeds from the total giving of a person to God and to the brethren of Christ, suffused by the grace of God—indeed, made possible only by that grace—and is born of the unique experience of this individual living in community. The love that comes about as a result of the profession of evangelical chastity is given from on high. It is given in the form of universal love. It may not be particularised by bodily sexuality because this would be to attempt a consummation of a love that the consecrated religious does not possess, since the love given by the profession of evangelical chastity is of another order altogether. Such attempt at consummation would have the malice of lying. It would be not only a violation of what we have promised God, but also a sin against faith and hope and thus a corruption of our particular exercise of the virtue of charity. The love that is given by God in the profession of evangelical chastity is a very great gift to the Church, given precisely to make manifest that bodily sexuality is a sacrament of an inner reality and, like all the sacraments, it belongs to the form of this world which will pass away. Bodily sexuality is an outward sign manifesting a love that will endure forever. Consecrated chastity is the concrete testimony that there is love—true and real love—which is spiritual and that without spiritual love there can be no love at all.

The gift of universal brotherly love which is given in the profession of this evangelical counsel proceeds from the baptismal consecration and is redemptive love. Because it is a specific form of God's gratuitous love given for the sake of the world, it contains the power of loving all people, all things, and the entire world. It is a way of loving given by God that knows from the beginning the value of the world and its dignity as a sacrament of God. It is an authentic, human, Christ-like love which allows the world of persons and things to be themselves. By consecrated chastity one is led to conclude that if the world can be so attractive and so beautiful, if another person can send the mind spinning and cause the heart to miss a beat, then what must He be like who is the Source and Origin of it all? St. Augustine gives perfect expression to this in his commentary on the eighty-fourth Psalm:

> All these beautiful things which you see, which you love, He made. If these are beautiful, what is He Himself? If these are great, how great must He be? Therefore, from those things which we love here, let us the more long for Him, that by that very love we may purify our hearts

by faith and his vision, when it comes, may find our hearts purified
(no. 9).

Poverty as Sign of Utter Dependence

Secondly, our following of the poor Christ, our profession of
evangelical poverty. We have all become familiar over the past few years with
the Biblical meaning of poverty. Our understanding of the beatitudes in the
charter of the Messianic kingdom, our deeper insights into the meaning of the
anawim—the poor of Yahweh—personified so perfectly in the *Magnificat* of
our Lady, have taught us that external poverty freely embraced is a sign of an
inner reality. It is not, and it cannot be, an end in itself. The following quotation
from A. Gelin deserves much thought:

> Does this mean that we must believe that Jesus "beatified a social
> class?" Has the gospel any of the manifestations of a social manifesto?
> It canonises no sociological state, nor places it in direct relation with
> the kingdom. A spiritual gift can be suitably received only in a spiritual
> situation. Only trusting faith can open man to God's grace. It is this
> openness to God that is called spiritual poverty. It is certain and the
> gospel says it plainly, that real poverty is a privileged path towards
> poverty of soul; it is the soil where the latter can more easily flourish;
> it is a state so precious that it is well worth the trouble of accepting it,
> even of seeking it, just as the mountain climber locates the best path for
> a difficult ascent.[5]

The profession of evangelical poverty raises serious problems today.
Any solution which advocates without discussion an 'absolute' poverty (which
is always relative!) must be viewed with suspicion as either too superficial or
as imposing a particular form of poverty on all other orders or congregations.
There are many forms of poverty and many ways and levels of professing it.

The profession of poverty is meant to be a sign of our utter dependence
on God. We profess *religious* poverty, as distinct from *real* poverty. Though we
possess nothing, we lack nothing and we are secure. Since, then, in concrete
practice, there is no element of *real* poverty in our lives, we are left wondering
what is the sign value of our religious poverty in the Church and the world
today? *The Decree on the Religious Life* of the Second Vatican Council,
Perfectae caritatis 13, draws to our attention:

---

[5] A. Gelin, *The Poor of Yahweh,* trans. by K. Sullivan, Liturgical Press, Collegeville 1963, p.
108.

Poverty voluntarily embraced in imitation of Christ provides a witness which is highly esteemed, especially today. Let religious painstakingly cultivate such poverty and give it new expressions if need be. By it a man shares in poverty of Christ, who became poor for our sakes when before he had been rich, that we might be enriched by his poverty.

While we can give unhesitatingly notional assent to these words of the Council, it must be admitted that the Council is not very helpful in his exhortation to us. The Son of God, rich beyond measure in the life of the Blessed Trinity, assumed the nature of a slave in our sinful condition. But is this poverty? It is surely rather a supreme example of humility, which may well be the same as spiritual poverty, but this is not the point at issue. A rich man can be humble and he can be saved even in the midst of his riches. Moreover, without entering into the old chestnut about the absolute poverty of Christ—which tore asunder the Franciscan Order—can it be asserted without question that Jesus Christ renounced all earthly possessions?

We must admit that people are impressed when it is explained to them what our profession of poverty involves for us at the individual level and they do admire the undoubted hardships that it often entails. But the question remains, is this enough? Is it satisfactory that we should have to explain our poverty at all? Ought not our poverty to be so apparent that we would need only to explain why we profess it and not how?

Aspects to Be Considered with Regard to Poverty

There are a number of aspects on this difficult question that need to be considered:

1. The generally accepted meaning of *poverty.* People in general do not understand poverty as inner poverty, nor as openness and receptivity to God. It is taken to mean by the vast majority of people a lack of material goods, squalor, even degradation and destitution, whatever the causes of this may be.

2. Both the Church and the world are determined to abolish this kind of poverty. It is the mission of the Church and the desire of all men of good will to establish an order of equity and justice on this earth from which peace will ensue. Indeed, it is conceivable that there will come a time when material poverty will be well-nigh conquered on our planet.

3. Religious poverty can never be the poverty we have mentioned above in the first point, no matter how little of this world's goods an individual religious or a particular order may possess. The reason for this is that religious

embrace poverty freely. The poor of the third world are born into it; the homeless and destitute of our society are either born into it or reduced to it and they would get out of it at once if they were able. What for religious is an act of liberation and therefore a fulfilment, is for the real poor a constriction, destruction, and degradation of their humanity.

4. The work and apostolates we carry out and to which we are necessarily committed, must be factors in our discussion of poverty. Modern techniques, it appears, are indispensable for the competent and fruitful execution of the apostolate in the modern world.

5. Poverty does not mean the same thing for all religious orders. Thus, for example, poverty as understood by a Franciscan cannot be what a Jesuit or a Dominican means by it.

If we are to continue to speak about poverty in the religious life we will have to give it some real, material, external expression. It is entirely unsatisfactory to use a word that has no obvious content as ordinarily understood. This will involve a great deal of hard thinking about standards of living and types of work. It may even involve sacrificing certain apostolates and placing a curb on the present wave of acquiring professional standards. I am not sure that the substitution of large buildings by smaller, neat, semi-detached or detached houses, with a good average car parked outside the garden gate is any better an expression of our poverty! This is not to deny the value of small communities for growth in personal maturity and responsibility. But that is not the point at issue here.

A Personal Suggestion

My own solution to this difficult problem would be as follows. If we cannot give any real content to the poverty we profess in the religious life, because of the commitments we have to the apostolate and the kind of involvement and qualifications professional standards require, then I suggest that we abolish the word 'poverty' altogether from the vocabulary of the religious life. Perhaps the word 'detachment' might be introduced in its place. If we keep before our minds the one total consecration we make of our lives to God, we may then present the religious life as a school of self-sacrifice involving total detachment from possessions for the sake of the kingdom of God. It would be part of formation programs to teach and show by example the meaning of detachment on the one hand, and, on the other, to inspire those who come to join our way of life how to contribute towards destroying real poverty and injustice in the world. There are a number of areas in which our detachment could be manifested in the concrete, for example, a concerted effort to be a sign of contradiction to consumer society. In honesty, however, I must admit that I do not think all this can be applied without further analysis to the Franciscan Order. Its charism concerns material poverty in a very real way. But this is a very specific question which it would be out of place to deal with here. This point serves, however, to emphasise precisely that not all Orders should be expected to profess what St. Francis of Assisi meant by poverty.

Obedience as Responsibility for a Way of Life

Finally, our following of the obedient Christ, our profession of evangelical obedience. This is, in the first place, the free acceptance of a way of life which the Church has approved as fully consonant with the teaching of the gospel. Religious obedience, as Karl Rahner has stressed, cannot be specified by the word "familial", for the obvious reason that there comes a time when a person is totally emancipated from parental authority in a family. The relationships of the religious life cannot be understood analogously to those of a family. The religious life is a brotherhood or sisterhood, which is a unique type of community. Moreover, religious obedience cannot be specified by good order or devotion to the *horarium;* any group of people living together needs order and timetables to avoid chaos. It cannot even be specified by the commands of the superior understood as manifesting the will of God, because, firstly, the Holy Spirit speaks to us all in a thousand ways each day and, secondly, it is clear that the mind of the Church now is that religious life should be lived out according to the principles of collegiality and co-responsibility. This is in no way to deny the necessity of true authority in a community; in fact, it has never been more necessary than at present to have a central point of unity and cohesion in religious communities. The superior in a community must have both juridical and spiritual authority; these must never be separated, for the latter authenticates and justifies the former. The superior, then, is not at the tip of a pyramid, but rather the hub of a wheel where the spokes are united. Both spokes and hub are equally necessary if the wheel is to go on turning smoothly.

Religious obedience is the free acceptance of a responsibility for a way of life, and this responsibility is to be exercised according to the collegial principle. The spiritual, liturgical, apostolic, recreational, and financial aspects of community life are the concern of every member of the community. It must be pointed out also, however, that the profession of evangelical obedience means that a person freely accepts as his or her own a way of life which is already in existence. Those who join a religious order take it upon themselves to follow the way of life of that order and to pursue the work that way of life involves. It is beyond question that one of the sacred duties of every superior is to ensure that each one carries out the responsibilities freely taken on for the growth of the community as a whole.

Religious Life and the Church's Holiness

In this final section I want to make a few remarks about the relationship of the religious life to the structure of the Church. There can be no doubt that the spirit of the evangelical counsels is an essential part of Christian discipleship and gospel holiness. Every person baptised into the death and resurrection of Christ must in some way be poor, chaste, and obedient. This is a very general statement, of course, and it is for each one in the Church to live out the gospel spirit in the circumstances of his calling. But this in no way detracts from the importance of the statement. The interior meaning of gospel poverty as openness to God and total receptivity to His grace, of gospel virginity as companionship with God in this life, of gospel obedience as fidelity to His holy will in this world, must all be factors in the following of Christ, even by married people. The evangelical counsels are very near the centre of the charter of the Messianic kingdom. We cannot close our eyes to Christ's teaching on the blessedness of the poor, whose humility and meekness are signs of the kingdom; we cannot ignore His evident commendation of those who make themselves eunuchs for the sake of the kingdom of God; we cannot bypass His unambiguous statements on our duty to submit to lawful authority. Moreover, the Founder of Christianity Himself lived a life of perfect chastity or virginity, He came into the world to do the will of His Father in perfect obedience, and, whatever may be our views about His material poverty as a sign of His unquestionable total dependence on God, there is no evidence in the New Testament that will allow us to number Him among the rich men of this world.

None of this is to pretend that those who profess publicly the evangelical counsels in the religious life are somehow 'better' than those who do not, nor is it to maintain that religious are assured of their salvation. My principal intention is only to establish the context, as I see it, in which the question of the relationship of the religious life to the structure of the Church should be examined. We are not dealing with a matter of secondary importance or with something only peripheral to the Church's life; the profession of the evangelical counsels is based upon the example and teaching of Christ Himself.

Religious Life and the Essence of the Church

We must emphasise also that in asking this question, we are asking a doctrinal and theological question, not merely a canonical one. If we keep this firmly fixed in our minds, then we will not be too eager to answer the question with a simple negative. To say without hesitation that the religious life does not pertain to the essence of the Church is to fail to do full justice to all that is entailed in the question. Certainly we can agree that the religious life does not pertain to the essence of the Church as does the episcopal hierarchy or the sacraments. However, it is not only in the context of comparison with the hierarchy that this question can be asked. We may compare the public profession of the evangelical counsels with other manifestations of God's gifts in the Church's history. We may ask legitimately, for example: Does God's free choice of the Virgin Mary and the *fact* of her virginity pertain to the essence of the Church? Or again: Does martyrdom pertain to the essence of the Church? Neither our Lady nor the holy martyrs *qua* martyrs, pertained to the hierarchical structure of the Church, yet, beyond doubt, they belong to her charismatic essence. Mary's *fiat*, made possible through the gift of God's grace, and at the same time most freely her *fiat,* belongs to the official, public, saving history of God's dealings with mankind. The suffering and death of the martyrs, endured for the sake of the truth of the holy gospel, made possible by the free gift of God's grace, is a public testimony to the indefectibility of the Church's faith.

The Hierarchical and the Charismatic

Thus the structure of the Church is both hierarchical and charismatic. Without the hierarchy the Church most certainly could not continue. It is likewise true that without the special charisms of the Holy Spirit the Church would be infinitely poorer and seriously defective. The public profession of the evangelical counsels in imitation of the poor, chaste, and obedient Christ is numbered among the special charisms of the Holy Spirit to the Church. This profession has no a priori structure, of course, since it owes its origins to the Holy Spirit who breaks into the Church's life in quite unique and unannounced ways. This particular gift—the public profession of the evangelical counsels—manifests the indefectibility of the holiness of the Church, proclaiming that God in Himself is the Infinite Treasure, the Sovereign Lord, and the Pure Love of man's existence in the world, chosen on account of Himself alone, in which lies the essence of true holiness.

Profession of the Counsels and the Charismatic

No particular order or congregation organised in a stable and institutionalised manner belongs to the essence of the Church, for the manifest reason that orders are founded, flourish, and pass away; they may even be suppressed, as happened sadly to the Jesuit Order in the eighteenth century. However, the public profession of the evangelical counsels either by individuals or groups (prescinding, for the moment, from any stable organisation controlled by canon law) does pertain to the charismatic structure of the Church, as does the *fiat* of the Blessed Virgin Mary and the testimony to the truth that is martyrdom. These are special gifts to the Church, given by the Holy Spirit of God Who is the 'soul' of the Mystical Body. It would be a rash, even temerarious, opinion to hold that the Church could forbid the public profession of the evangelical counsels or abolish at one stroke religious life in the Church. She could no more do this than forbid martyrdom in the Church.

The actual form of the public profession of the evangelical counsels by the many and diverse orders in the Church can, of course, change according to historical circumstances and can be changed by the authority of the Church. But even here, it would be hazardous to maintain that the Church could dispense with these orders—as they are now—without the direct effects to her life and mission in the world. Insofar as the essence of the religious life is the public profession of the evangelical counsels, what has been said above applies equally here.

My reasons for touching on this question at all have been primarily to emphasise that the religious life is not just an accidental accretion to the life of the Church, like the froth on beer. Moreover, I wanted to lift the question out of the loaded context of comparison with the episcopate *vis-à-vis* the structure of the Church. This comparison is by no means the only way in which the question can be approached.

The public profession of the evangelical counsels has a long history in the Church. The Church's life and mission in the world would have been seriously impaired and defective without the orders of men and women who, through the gift of God's grace, embraced a life in imitation of the gospel Christ for the sake of the kingdom of God. We see no reason to doubt—despite the crises of the past decade—that the religious life will continue in the Church in the future and to the end of time. Religious have exercised and exercise now an essential and indispensable role in the Church. We are not and we never will be in a position to dispense with their role of manifesting the overriding demands of God's kingdom. That role bears eloquent testimony to an aspect of Christ Himself, the Cornerstone of the Church, which is able, only through the variety of her members, to show Him in His inexhaustible fullness to the world.

Towards the Future

Though we see no reason even to question the future of religious life in the Church, we will all have to accustom ourselves to the fact that our numbers will be heavily reduced for some time to come. Many have left the ranks of the orders, and this exodus has compelled us to do a great deal of thinking and replanning. But this is not what I am referring to here. I have in mind the number of aspirants to the religious life. Now this is not entirely a matter for regret. The emphasis on the role of the laity in the Church's life and mission is undoubtedly one of the reasons why there has been and continues to be a slackening off in the numbers of those aspiring to the religious life. As one reason why the numbers are down, this should be cause for rejoicing. The Church needs many more lay apostles burning with zeal for the gospel message who will be witnesses to Christ from within the structures of the world. Unfortunately, however, there are other reasons for the decline in numbers which give grounds for deep sadness and concern. A materialism and a most insidious humanism have so infected the minds and hearts of many young Catholic men and women that they are not prepared to make the sacrifices that the religious life demands. Further, one hears of cases of Catholic parents threatening to disown a son or daughter who has announced a desire to become a priest or join a religious order. That Catholics should have lost the sense of the great blessing that such a vocation brings upon their home is a state bordering on the diabolical. Then—and perhaps saddest of all—one comes across members of religious orders who have turned sour and cynical and in whose lives the profession of the evangelical counsels appears as an intolerable burden, not as a liberating adventure. These give the impression that religious life is a gradual process of dehumanisation—hardly an attraction to follow the gospel Christ. There are others who openly confess that they positively discourage aspirants to the religious life. Among these are many good men and women who are disillusioned at the changes which have taken place in the Church. They seem to have lost the sense of holy hope. All of us need to examine our consciences, of course, on what kind of advertisement our lives are for the worthwhileness of professing the evangelical counsels. Insofar as we are ourselves responsible for the decline in numbers of those aspiring to the religious life, there is surely much we can do by will power and with a little effort to remove the obstacles that prevent people from recognising the presence of God's grace in the religious life. The only means we have at our disposal to combat the materialism and humanism around us, is to be men and women of detachment and prayer.

Attracting Vocations and Selection Criteria

On the question of attracting vocations to the religious life, the surest way is to allow those who show interest in the religious life to come and share our community life of liturgy, prayer, meals, and relaxation, saving always the compatibility of such a practice with the vocation and objectives of the order involved. This kind of experience will show people how community life is possible and what value it has and do more to bring people to our way of life than all the propaganda we do by preaching and the use of the press.

Moreover, we ought not to be overcautious in selection. While it is obviously necessary that certain signs be present (and I think these can be reduced to four: good health, average intelligence, a sense of humour, and the desire to become a religious), we should not be looking for perfection in any sphere. If we are to look for perfection at all, it should be at the end of the formation process, not at its beginning! We should also have a little more confidence in our renewed formation programs as a means of growth in maturity and responsibility. This brings us to the thorny problem about the age of entry into the religious life. My own view is that the widespread practice (and the theory on which it is based) of refusing admission to young people in their late teens needs radical reappraisal. Are people on average more mature in their mid-twenties than in their late teens? Perhaps they are. My experience, however, is that, as a group, those who used to be called "late vocations" (let us say 25+) do not show themselves any more mature and responsible than those who come to the orders in their late teens (say 18 or 19). I would think it advisable, therefore, that we tone down considerably our frightful preoccupation (bordering at times on obsession) that our aspirants should have "experienced the world" (whatever this may mean) and already have acquired professional skills and qualifications. Given the openness built into our reformed and renewed training programs, it is very unlikely that those in formation will become hothouse plants. It seems to me to be a ridiculous policy to advise a young person with qualifications to enter a university or to follow a course of training in some professional skill, who asks to join an order, to go away, finish his studies or training, and then come back us three or four years later to join the order. What is there, all things being equal, against receiving such a person into an order and then sending him, after temporary profession, to pursue studies or training? The commitment to the gospel Christ will be an aid, not an obstacle, to the maturing process in the midst of secular life with all its variety of experiences and the trials, temptations, and crosses it inevitably involves. It will also assist to preserve the vocation, which can be lost.

Considerations with Regard to Formation

With regard to formation itself, this should take place as far as possible in the context of community life. Separatism should be avoided at all costs. From the very beginning those who join a religious order should share in community life as the primary formative principle.

On the spiritual and intellectual aspects of formation, programs should include the following subjects as indispensable:

1. A thorough course in Church history. History is the *magistra vitae*. No subject is more calculated to bring home to a believer the divinity of the Catholic Church, than a critical, objective, and honest study of her history through the centuries. I am convinced that if more people in the Church had been familiar with her extraordinary career through the last two thousand years, the present crisis of confidence would have been considerably less.

2. A solid training in spiritual theology. Religious should be acquainted with the approved doctrine of the mystical and ascetical writers of the Church. They should be familiar with the various stages of the spiritual life and with the genesis of the soul's relationship with God. People in the Church—clerical and lay—seek and need guidance in the spiritual life. This type of work is going to fall more and more on the shoulders of religious men and women; and people have a right to expect it from religious who ought to be the 'professionals' in this area. Had more of us been familiar with the Church's rich heritage of mystical doctrine and with the teaching of her doctors on contemplation, fewer people would have set out for the East to search for what they had not received in the West. Above all, those in formation must be given a sound theology of prayer and taught by example its necessity. They need good directors to guide them on the way to contemplative union with God where prayer becomes a silent, wordless, unbroken relationship with that Someone who is the holy and adorable Mystery. Likewise, those in formation should be well-grounded in the spirituality proper to the order they have joined, not merely by imbibing it in daily life and experience, but by a systematic study of what is proper and unique to the order and its way of life.

3. A clear presentation of the social doctrine of the Church. This means a basic knowledge of the social encyclicals from Leo XIII's great charter *Rerum novarum*, through Pius XI's *Quadragesimo anno*, to the social teaching

of John XXIII: *Mater et Magistra* and *Pacem in terris* and Paul VI: *Populorum progressio* and *Octogesima adveniens.* As a group, we religious are notoriously ignorant of the great riches of the Church's social teaching over the last eighty years. A study of this doctrine will demonstrate that the Church's teaching on social morality is unsurpassed. It will also give those in formation a concern for the less fortunate and inspire them to make sacrifices.

Centres of Spiritual Renewal

Finally, religious communities the world over should strive to make themselves centres of a deep spiritual renewal in the Church. It is our primary vocation to make our religious communities real centres of prayer, totally dedicated to God, completely open to the world, yet signs of contradiction of its materialism and idolatry.

As a summary of all that has been said we conclude these reflections with a text on the religious life from Hans Urs von Balthasar:

> To the end of time the religious life in the Church will remain the guardian of the wholeness of the gospel; and in each age the Church will be only as live as her active and contemplative Orders are alive in her.[6]

---

[6] *Die grossen Orden,* Cologne 1948, p. 17.

Response to the Word
and the Mystery of Consecrated Obedience[1]

Religious life shares in the Church's nature as mystery. It belongs to the mystery of the Church in such a way that it may be described itself as a mystery, for it has its origin in the mystery of grace and it is sustained in its existence by grace. In common speech the word 'mystery' can suggest something eerie like spectres and phantoms, even the macabre. We are accustomed to refer to detective stories as 'mysteries', when in fact we mean problems or puzzles to be solved by spotting all the clues. Sophisticated unbelievers tend to dismiss all use of the word 'mystery' in religious discourse either as mystification or as an easy escape route from such logical difficulties as are involved, for instance, in the statement: *God is three-in-one*.

The Meaning of Mystery

These ways of understanding mystery must be set aside completely when the word is used in reference to realities of faith. For these realities are not difficulties or problems, mystifications or questions to be solved, unravelled or worked out. They are disclosures about existence and its meaning, to be accepted in humility and love. This does not mean of course that we cannot have difficulties and problems about the mysteries of religion. Experience is manifestly to the contrary. But these do not reduce the mysteries themselves to the level of difficulties and problems.

In the context of faith a mystery is not only a truth we would never have discovered had it not been disclosed, or one which, even when disclosed, we cannot comprehend. A mystery in religion is a truth about reality which we never cease to grasp more fully, to penetrate more deeply, to enter into more intimately. The mysteries of faith are truths disclosed to us in God's free self-communication to man which we call uncreated grace. This gracious self-giving by God reveals to us that God is absolute mystery, and also that human beings themselves are mysteries, that creation as a whole and in all its intricate parts, is mystery. In Catholic theology it is axiomatic that grace perfects nature.

---

[1] Supplement to Doctrine and Life 17 (Sept.-Oct. 1977) pp. 67-75. Published with permission.

As mystery, grace perfects the mystery of created existence by rendering its mystery ever greater; it perfects the mystery of meaning by endowing it with meaning profounder still.

The Religious Life as Mystery

When we refer to the Church as mystery, we are speaking of it precisely as the gift of God's free grace. The Church is that portion of mankind in the world which has conscious awareness of having been taken up with Christ into the very life of God, where Father, Son and Spirit so interpenetrate one another, that they are dynamically and unalterably one. Thus individual persons and scattered communities become a people made one in the unity of the Father, Son and Spirit.

The renewed sense of the Church as mystery, which is so distinguishing a feature of modern theology, has had far-reaching repercussions on all sections of theology. Any theology of religious life which claims to be a theology for today must be guided and sustained in its reflections by the sure principle that religious life is a mystery within the mystery of the Church. To understand the religious life as a mystery of grace is to know that we can never say the final word about it, whether we are speaking of it in general or as concretised in particular orders or congregations. As the effect of grace it remains a mystery. Our appreciation of religious life will deepen in direct proportion to the development in our understanding of it as a mystery.

Mystery and Renewal

I am convinced that this awareness of religious life as a mystery of God's grace is what brought to the surface our dissatisfaction with the legalism that stifled us for so long. Good laws, which are a sure safeguard of freedom, had been turned into codes of constriction and made ends in themselves. We came to see that religious life cannot be enshrined in neat definitions, nor contained within the narrow limits of detailed laws. Our efforts over the past decade to renew constitutions and statutes have not been directed towards establishing new sets of rules to replace the old ones, so that we might still have a yardstick to gauge our fidelity to what we promised, and to judge who is and who is not a "good religious".

What we were attempting to do under the guidance of the Holy Spirit was to express, partly in principles, partly in guidelines, our insights into the meaning of the mystery of religious life. We were not drawing up for ourselves new laws of the Medes and Persians to remain in force till the next 'renewal';

rather we were framing spiritual documents wherein the supreme law of grace was given concrete form in the specific charism and unique genius of our own order or congregation.

The evangelical counsels take us into the mystery of the Church and lead ultimately into the life of the Triune God. It is when we begin to reflect on the counsels in the context of the religious life, understood as a specific realisation of the mystery of grace in the Church, that we see most clearly the barrenness of the predominantly legal approach of the past. Because the element of mystery was absent, it was thought that the counsels could be defined and presented in legal terms of obligation. The utter inadequacy of this outlook was then compounded by the one-sided emphasis on renunciation and negativity. Therefore instead of being pathways to freedom and personal transformation, the counsels were reduced to little more than 'holy' burdens accepted for the sake of eternal life. Religious life itself was a sort of school of asceticism wherein the 'more perfect' strove for ever-greater mastery over self. Nothing in religious life was more deeply infected with, or more strangely warped by, this legal-negative attitude, than the understanding of obedience. What alone was perpetrated and suffered in the name of the 'will of God' would provide ample material for many a horror story and none of it would be fiction!

The renewed appreciation of religious life as a mystery of grace will help us to rid ourselves completely of this legal approach to it. For the future, our point of departure will always have to be the theology of religious life, and not general or particular laws. This is not to suggest that law has no relevance to our lives as religious, but it is to maintain that it must never again be given first place. For when this happens law becomes an end in itself and then an oppressor.

A theology of religious obedience has its proper origin in a consideration of the mystery of obedience. For this reason it is said advisedly in the title: the *mystery of consecrated obedience*. The obedience promised by religious in the Church is intimately connected with a theology of the Word. The relationship of this obedience to the Word is precisely the reason why obedience is a mystery.

Word is defined by the Oxford Dictionary in the first place as any sound or combination of sounds (or its written or printed symbol), recognised as a part of speech conveying an idea. It can also mean speech (say a good word for me), news, intelligence, a message (word came that he was home), a promise, assurance, responsible statement (I give you my word), command, order, password. It can mean the Son of God (the Word was made flesh).

The word 'obedience' is derived directly from the Latin *oboedire* (post classical: *obaudire),* which means especially to obey, yield obedience to, to be subject to, to serve. It can also mean in general to give ear, hearken, or to listen to.[2] This latter meaning has particular interest in the present context because it relates obedience explicitly to the notion of the word. To give ear, hearken and to listen to, suppose sounds with meaning and spoken words belong among these. Likewise, to obey, yield obedience to, to be subject to and to serve, suppose words that have been heard.

When we listen attentively we hear sounds and words. If while listening we hear a word addressed to ourselves, we answer it, we respond to it, because we find in ourselves a responsibility to respond to it. We discover that we are answerable to the Word.

From all eternity there has been a Word; the inner Word of God, the everlasting utterance of the Father. He is the Word of divine self-expression. The Son as Word expresses the whole mystery of the Father. Through that Word all things came to be. The first outer word which God uttered was creation. Creation can be understood as a spoken word, and so we have the sounds of creation, and as a written word, and so we have the book of creation. The spoken word is a sound with a meaning; the written word is a symbol (or image) of a spoken word.[3] Creation contains the outer words about God which he uttered in and through the inner Word, his Son.

The man Jesus of Nazareth is the final outer Word of God. He is the Word made flesh, the union of uncreated inner Word with that created word which is full humanity. So he is the incarnate Word of God. Jesus Christ is that which came to be when the eternal, inner mystery of sonship in God was expressed exteriorly in creation. Perhaps we can understand this a little better by reflecting on what happens when we speak to others.

The human being is spirit-in-the-world. Spirit is that which is present to itself in self-knowledge, being that is aware of itself. A human being begets an inner word which is knowledge of itself or of another, either person or thing. Through the medium of sound (the spoken word) the inner word (idea, *logos)* while remaining in the speaker, is transferred to the hearer, in whom it becomes also inner word. In this way the word binds into a unity the speaker, the hearer and what is spoken. The inner word is incarnated in sound. Yet it remains what it is, an inner word, and as such it does not leave the mind of the speaker in the

[2] C.T. Lewis, C. Scott, *A Latin Dictionary. . .,* Oxford 1975, s.v. 1239.
[3] B. Lonergan SJ, *The Concept of 'Verbum' in the Writings of St. Thomas Aquinas* in: THEOLOGICAL STUDIES VII (1946) pp. 350-352; see also *Verbum: Word and Idea in Aquinas,* Darton, Longman & Todd, London 1968.

act of being spoken. It has another form when it is embodied in a sound. Analogously, we may say that the man Jesus of Nazareth is what took place when the Word was uttered among us, yet the Word did not leave the bosom of the Father.

From the beginning the Word has been uttered and symbolised (written) in varying degrees of intensity and clarity. It was uttered with utmost intensity in the Word made flesh and symbolised with total clarity in the humanity of Jesus Christ. This is the Son of God in whose humanity the Word is uttered and on whose face appears the image of the unseen God.

The word *word* occurs often in scripture and the Son of God is there explicitly referred to as the Word: "In the beginning was the Word, and the Word was with God, and the Word was God. . . .And the Word became flesh and dwelt among us" [John 1:1,14]. After the readings at Mass we say: "This is the Word of the Lord" *(Verbum Domini)*, that is, "This is the Son of the Father". God has given us his Word, that is, he has given us his very self in his Son. The Scriptures, then, are not merely words about Jesus Christ, they are *the* Word, the Son who speaks to us when they are read in our midst.

Jesus Christ is the Word made flesh and this Word is the Yes of God. He is the Yes made flesh, through whom we make our Yes to God: "For all the promises of God find their Yes in him. That is why we utter the Amen through him, to the glory of God" [2 Corinthians 1:20].

Authority and the Word

The Church lives under the supreme authority of Christ, to whom God has given all authority in heaven and on earth. The Holy Spirit empowers us to confess that Jesus is Lord and God is Abba. By this confession individual believers are drawn into a unity, a community, which is something more than the mere sum total of individuals. The community is made one in the unity of the Father, Son and Spirit.

The Holy Spirit brings back to our minds everything Christ said "he will teach you all things, and bring to your remembrance all that I have said to you" [John 14:26]. Because Christ is what he said, the Holy Spirit brings back to us not just a word about Christ, but the Word that Christ is, namely, the Word of God uttered in the incarnation. To live, act and speak the Word of God is to be obedient to the authority and supreme lordship of Christ. This Word demands absolute obedience and total adherence to itself. From it flows all further legitimate authority in the Church of Christ. Authority is legitimate when it is at the service of the Word of God and the lordship of Christ.

Freedom and Obedience to the Word

Human freedom in its most radical form is the power of self-determination through the recognised and accepted good. It is multi-levelled, stretching from surface-freedom to centre-freedom. Centre-freedom is located at that point of our being where we say "I", the area of that strange restlessness (which co-exists with peace and serenity) where we find ourselves always waiting, always looking beyond our own horizon. It is the point of transcendence. Our centre-freedom has the radical ability to answer the call, the summons, of the Transcendent Word and so to achieve self-realisation by self-determination in response to the Word. Centre-freedom contains the power to make oneself more a person, to create through grace one's own personhood.

We have grown accustomed to using the word 'vocation' only for the priesthood and religious life. This is a pity because every believer in fact has a vocation, a call from the Word of God, which requires a response in humility, truth and love. Vocation is the call to be and to live in Christ. It is to have heard and answered the Word with fidelity and devotion up to the present moment in one's life, and to be going on now listening for the Word and responding to it. To answer the Word is to open oneself completely to it in an act of trusting and loving faith: "Blessed. . .are those who hear the word of God and keep it" [Luke 11:28]; "let it be to me according to your word" [Luke 1:38]; "and the Word became flesh and dwelt among us" [John 1:14].

God's Word, then, through whom all things have come to be, is present and active in the world, and each person is called in so many different ways to answer and serve it. To be obedient to the Word of God is to be responding continually to its mysterious summons, as it leads us on to ever more authentic existence.

One distinct form of obedience is the profession of it in the religious life. This obedience does not entail the sacrifice of freedom, nor is it the blind acceptance of another's will. It requires of those Who profess it the positive and free acceptance of full responsibility for a specific way of life. Each member of a community consecrates heart, soul, mind and strength to the tasks of listening attentively to the Word of God and fulfilling its demands, in order to increase the unity-in-diversity of the community's life, and to help each individual member to grow more and more as a free and unique person.

Consecrated Obedience

It is therefore principally in terms of a theology of the Word of God, which calls, summons, obliges and enlightens everyone in the world, that the obedience professed in religious life can be understood to have meaning and purpose.

The mystery of consecrated obedience originates in an act of self-surrender to the Word of God, which is an act of love without limits or conditions. By it a person lays self completely open before the eternal mystery of God. Consecrated obedience is our personal response to the Word of God as it has come into our lives and touched our minds and hearts. As an ongoing process it defines our relationship with God and our discipleship of the Lord Jesus through the particular way of life to which we belong. Besides this personal element, consecrated obedience has a prophetic and apostolic character. To profess obedience publicly in the Church means first of all, that one bears witness that the Word of God is present in the world, that God has spoken in nature and by grace to humankind. Secondly, it proclaims the absolute sovereignty of God's Word, which. demands total adherence and complete obedience to itself. Thirdly, it means that one has accepted the serious obligation of listening to the Word of God in all the ways it may make itself heard and of fulfilling with alacrity and joy whatever it may demand, and this without respect to personal cost.

Consecrated obedience requires of us to listen to the word of God spoken in other persons, in ourselves and in the whole of creation. There is a word of God in the mystery of other persons, in the mystery of self and in the mystery of the cosmos.

1. The mystery of other persons. In each human person God has uttered a word about himself. Every creature is a word in the Word. By grace each person discloses a new aspect of Christ in virtue of a uniqueness that is by definition unrepeatable. In virtue of the vow of obedience we profess to listen attentively to the word God has spoken about himself in the graced creatures we call human beings. The name of each person we know and love has to become a word of mystery, whereby we are taken into union with the love transcendent found at the heart of everything.

2. The mystery of self. The profession of obedience requires each one of us to strive towards total acceptance of self as unique, as loved by God and as being an original word uttering a truth about God which cannot be found elsewhere. It demands, in fact, that I accept myself as myself, with my mind and heart, my sexuality, my gifts, my limitations, my achievements, my failures, my hopes and my joys.

3. The mystery of the cosmos. The world around us, nature and environment man has created for himself, speak words about God. To hear what they are saying we have to listen carefully. And we can only listen carefully when we respect the world around us as created like ourselves.

Obedience as Listening Together

As *communio* (the church realised locally, the community), we are responsible to the Word of God. By obedience we are obliged to seek out together the will of God for the community. We are answerable to the Word together. We share a common responsibility for our way of life in all its diversity and for all its constituent elements. In virtue of obedience each member of a community bears responsibility for the community's life, faith, worship and work. No one can knowingly evade this responsibility without selfishness.

Our common responsibility for community life is exercised and fulfilled in regular meetings of the community, especially the eucharistic liturgy and house chapters. At the celebration of Mass the three real and true presences of the Risen and Exalted Lord are united by the power of the Holy Spirit: the *mystical* presence (community, local church); the *verbal* presence (readings from scripture and the homily); the *eucharistic* presence (the pre-eminent sacrament in which we receive what we are: the body of Christ). In this threefold presence we hear the Word of God, respond to it and receive the power to fulfil whatever it may demand of us as a community and as individual persons.

Community meetings (house chapters) should always begin by calling upon the Spirit of God. After this there should follow a period of silence, during which each one should centre his or her whole attention on the one Spirit who dwells in each of us as in a temple. In this way the Spirit will bring back to our minds the Word of God, will enlighten us and strengthen us by his gifts. By the vow of obedience we oblige ourselves to remain open to the Spirit in order to fulfil our responsibilities to the Word and to await further inspiration for the direction of our common life. This requires that we listen, really listen, to one another at community meetings.

By the vow of obedience, understood as an attending to the Word of God, the community is responsible for : (a) the faith, hope and charity of all members of the community. This responsibility is carried out in discussion of matters concerning the spiritual life, the exercise of the spiritual works of mercy within the community, and by the authenticity and depth of the interior life of each member; (b) the working of the grace of reconciliation and peace among all the members of the community; (c) the observance of the principle of subsidiarity. Those who exercise particular functions and offices must have the necessary freedom and autonomy to exercise them effectively and competently. The one body has many parts and none can dispense with the others.

Conclusion

I have been outlining a theology of religious obedience which has its origin in the Word of God and which takes cognisance of personal freedom and co-responsibility. Such an approach excludes from the outset, any notion of authority that would claim to be an individual and exclusive 'hot-line' to God. This approach, however, does not neutralise legitimate authority. Authority exists by the previous consent of others and it addresses itself directly to freedom. It is itself subservient to the Word of God and is committed to the discernment of its message and demands. It is, therefore, something entirely other than power or coercion. Authority discerns, co-ordinates and persuades. Its purpose is to ensure the unity of the community and to safeguard its diversity.

Poverty and Credibility[1]

Some years ago in an article on the theology of religious life I touched on a few of the problems involved in professing evangelical poverty.[2] Among them it was noted that people in the main do not understand poverty in a spiritual sense, but take it rather as the description of a bad material state, as a lack of the basic necessities of life and, in certain circumstances, as homelessness and destitution.

The words we use to describe ourselves and how we relate to reality are highly significant. They enflesh in sounds and symbols our interior beliefs and attitudes, our world view and our authenticity. That we use a word to denote an aspect of our life (in which, we must admit, we are comfortable and have security into old age and to death itself), which is also used to describe the starving of India and the oppressed of Latin America, is at best ridiculous and at worst a strain to breaking point on our credibility. To a certain extent of course within our own well-defined universe of discourse we know what we mean by the word 'poverty'. It has a canonical connotation entailing obligations and rights and it is enhanced with a spiritual meaning.

My experience, however, is of an increasing dissatisfaction with this word even among religious themselves, but especially among candidates who aspire to join them. In discussion about this dissatisfaction during various courses I have given on the theology of religious life, two alternatives generally emerge: (1) that we should do everything to make the word credible both to ourselves and to the world in general even to the point of destitution which would mean an abandonment of our security and a severe curtailing of our apostolates; or (2) that we should abandon the word altogether.

Real, Material Poverty an Option?

The first, though seemingly desirable and apparently the better, is quite unrealistic. It is not just a question, for instance, of getting rid of grandiose and imposing buildings. We are often glad to be rid of them, for they are

---

[1] *Religious Life Review* 1.88 (January 1981) pp. 16-30. Published with permission.
[2] *Reflections on the Theology of Religious Life* in: REVIEW FOR RELIGIOUS 32 (1973) pp. 1254-1257. Editors' note: This article is reprinted in this anthology: pp. 504 ff.

uneconomical to maintain and usually burdensome heirlooms from a bygone age. Moving into smaller houses does not usually mean a lowering of standards of living, but in fact in most cases quite the reverse. I am not making adverse criticism of this. What I am arguing is that concern with the size of buildings does not necessarily involve poverty at all. A smaller property in suburbia can be very beneficial for growth in personal relationships and for a higher quality of community life, but it does nothing to make poverty in any real sense more credible.

Furthermore, in any case, it is not possible for an entire institute to change over to a radically new form of life. Not everyone will agree with the changes and there are practical problems in respect of care for the sick and elderly to which we are obliged by charity and justice. Then the apostolic commitments which an institute has taken on can be of inestimable value. There are increasing needs such as spiritual direction, pastoral counselling and the desire to know the path of interior peace which religious are beginning to meet. It would be grave irresponsibility at this juncture to abandon them. People have to be trained for these apostolates and that requires funds.

Besides all this there are problems in regard to the profession of poverty itself. What on earth are we professing? Material poverty and destitution are no more biblical or Christian virtues than is oppression. Throughout the history of religious life only very few individuals have lived a life of material poverty and then either as a means to an end or as a sign of something else. Even these chose it freely as a means of liberation. They were usually neither born into it nor reduced to it against their will. St Francis of Assisi, for example, had the luxury of being able to reject riches, ambition and security. The real poor have nothing to reject but their poverty.

The material poverty of the real poor is a scourge which has to be eliminated. Quite evidently this is not the kind of poverty to which religious oblige themselves. In some parts of the world, such as India or Latin America, it is undoubtedly required of religious to profess and live a poverty which identifies them as far as possible with the real poor. But this is not, nor can it ever be, because the lot of the poor is a blessed one. This kind of identification is rather a means to an end and the end is twofold. First, so that the Church through the witness of these religious may be completely dissociated and seen to be such, from the powers of evil which cause poverty, injustice and oppression through political and economic structures. Secondly, in order that by their presence among the poor and oppressed, religious may work to destroy the hopelessness that material poverty always spawns and to build the assurance that something can be done about world poverty both by the poor themselves and by the rich nations of the earth.

It is true, of course, that religious could lead simpler lives and there is nothing to justify any of us accepting the shallow values of the consumer society. But even this is possible only to a limited extent because of the complex economic structure of the planet. It is just not possible for anyone to opt out of it entirely. I heard recently about some renewed Franciscans in southern Italy who have embraced a life of material poverty to the point of going barefoot. This, however, did not prevent one of them from arriving in London to learn English, having hitch-hiked his way the length of Italy. I wonder did it ever cross his mind that someone had paid for the cars he rode in and for the petrol that kept them moving? Many of those who gave him lifts may well have been saving for a year to give their family an annual holiday!

Even in the case where a religious of an established institute embraces a life of real material poverty in the First World as a witness to higher values, there is always the security of the institute to fall back on in a crisis. All in all, then, it appears to be little more than a dream that real poverty can or will be embraced in any significant sense by religious in the Church.

Equality Rather Than Poverty?

The second alternative is that we should abandon the word 'poverty' altogether. There is a good deal to commend this suggestion in terms of credibility. For the purpose of this article I propose that we accept this second alternative. To do so, however, does not mean that we can simply resign ourselves to the *status quo* in respect of what we call 'poverty'. On the contrary, it will oblige us, I think, to strive to make our life-style more credible expressions of our discipleship of the gospel Christ.

As a substitute I suggest the word 'equality'. The idea came to me one evening while thinking about the relationship between democracy and religious life. One conclusion I reached was that the principles of modern democracy: liberty, equality and fraternity (which are derived ultimately from the Christian gospel), could, without too much difficulty, be used satisfactorily to express the meaning of obedience, poverty and chastity.

The vow of obedience is a declaration of gospel freedom. The Truth, which is the Word of God, sets the believer free. Obedience is intended to lead one to that ever more perfect form of listening which issues in an ever more ready response to God's Word in creation and revelation.

The vow of poverty is a declaration of gospel equality. We all have our origin in a sovereignly free act of God's creative love. The one talent of our own being and personhood we have received as gift, and by God's will we are meant to bring it to ever more perfect and lovely expression in our historical existence through the gift of grace in Jesus Christ. To achieve this each person needs the appropriate means, nutritional, medical, educational, physical, psychological, intellectual and spiritual

The vow of chastity is a declaration of gospel fraternity. This is expressed as sisterhood or brotherhood. Christ is the first of many brethren and in him we have all become brothers and sisters of one another. We profess and live out a love that is in essence fraternal and in scope universal. By this love our local communities are meant to become sacraments of the unity and fraternity of humanity itself.

It must be emphasised that I am speaking of evangelical equality, not sameness. There are real differences among us as individual members of the same institute, between one local community and another, between one institute and the next. Within the institute there are those in formation whose needs are quite different from those of the finally professed. There are professed members who have needs which others do not have. There are some, for example, who need to change from their present apostolic work to another and this for reasons that are utterly unique and personal. Mature recognition and unselfish acceptance of these differences will protect us from the insidious mentality which demands and bullies, in the name of equality, that we should all have the same.

Evangelical Equality

I propose, then, that evangelical equality replace evangelical poverty. By evangelical equality I mean that new condition of existence which results from being in Christ and living under the reign of God. In Jesus Christ, the Last Adam, a new creation has come to be, so that we are not only creatures of the Sovereign Creator, but sons and daughters of the Eternal Father, brothers and sisters of the Lord Jesus Christ and dwelling places of their Holy Spirit: "If anyone is in Christ, he is a new creation; the old has passed away, behold the new has come" [2 Corinthians 5:17]; "There is neither Jew nor Greek, there is neither slave nor free, there is neither male nor female; for you are all one in Christ Jesus" [Galatians 3:28].

The primary and all-consuming preoccupation of Jesus' mission was the proclamation of God's kingdom or reign in the world. All else was subordinate to that. As the gospels testify unambiguously, God's reign was actually inaugurated in the person and ministry of Jesus. Of course that reign will not be perfect until God is all things in everything. Nevertheless, as seminal reality which will flourish hereafter, the reign of God has established "the assembly of the first- born who are enrolled in heaven" [Hebrews 12:23] or, as the Jerusalem Bible has it: "the whole Church in which everyone is a 'first-born son' and a citizen of heaven". Where it is a question of God's reign there are no second places, each one is first. There is no more fitting a blueprint for the life of religious communities than that description of 'God's reign'. Though its realisation is eschatological, this does not excuse us from striving to give it ever more perfect expressions where and as we can until the Day of the Lord comes. The elements involved in the profession of evangelical equality by religious are: *surrender* (prayer, total openness to God, the search for his will), *self-denial* (fasting, penance, the resolve to follow in the footsteps of Christ) and *sharing* (almsgiving, common life, generosity towards one's neighbour). For any sympathetic understanding of the proposal being made here, it is necessary to set aside what we accepted and practised in the past as 'the observance of poverty'. In particular we should dissociate ourselves from all past notions of poverty which reduced it almost exclusively to preoccupations with financial minutiae and from the equally absurd idea that the granting of permission automatically rendered some particular action or project an observance of poverty and thereby absolved the petitioner from all further responsibility.

The Persons of the Godhead

My point of departure to examine the meaning of evangelical equality is the doctrine of the Trinity of God which discloses as nowhere else the utter difference between equality and sameness.

The three Persons of the Godhead are constituted by subsistent relationships. A 'subsistent relationship' is a relationship which is itself a person. To be persons is to be related. Each Divine Person is equally, but not identically, the absolute perfection of being God. The Father is God as Father, the Son is God as Son and the Spirit is God as Spirit. What is true of the Father is true also of the Son and the Spirit, except only the Father is Father. The Father is Father by being related eternally to the Son. Their mutual love, the Holy Spirit, is eternally related to them both and they to the Holy Spirit. It is crucial to stress that the Father *as the Father* loves the Son, the Son *as the Son* loves the Father, and the Holy Spirit *as the Holy Spirit* loves the Son and the Father, and so on. They know and love one another as Persons of the one identical Godhead and thus for instance the Holy Spirit loves the Father in a way that is different from the Son. Their love is equal but not the same. The Personhood of the Three is constituted by eternal relations in such a way that

God could not be God without these relations. In the Godhead, therefore, there is equality, not sameness; unity, not uniformity; diversity, but not division.

The Godhead is evidently not a thing to be grasped even in the Godhead itself. In an eternal openness, which is a mysterious outpouring of love, is begotten an Equal to the Father, his Son, who is Another; and in a mysterious inpouring of love from the total receptivity and corresponding openness of the Son to the Father, proceeds an Equal to the Father and the Son, the Holy Spirit, who is yet Another. All reality therefore has its origin in an eternal giving and receiving in love and an eternal giving back and receiving back in love which is the circumincession or *perichoresis* of the Three Divine Persons.

The Enhumanment of the Word

Christ Jesus "though he was in the form of God, did not count equality with God a thing to be grasped, but emptied himself, taking the form of a servant, being born in the likeness of men. And being found in human form he humbled himself and became obedient unto death, even death on a cross. Therefore God has highly exalted him" [Philippians 2:6-9].

As the historical figure Jesus of Nazareth, the Word of God became other than he is. He identified himself with a new mode of being and in so doing became one of us. We proclaim in the Church that he was made like us in all things except sin. That is to say, he became equal with us but not precisely the same, for he is more radically human than we are. Sin is a dark power, utterly inhuman and totally unintelligible. It renders human beings less human and can finally destroy our very humanity. Being-without-sin does not detract from our humanity; on the contrary it is the condition of humanity's developing to its fullness.

The sinlessness of Jesus, however, must not be thought to have made his historical, worldly existence less ambiguous than it is for us, nor devoid of anxiety. The sinful worldliness of human existence—as distinct from its God-willed worldliness—had its effect on him, indeed, it brought him to a tragic and cruel death. The sinlessness of Jesus among us lies in the fact that he never confirmed in himself the sinful worldliness of human existence by free action.

The Son of God who exists in subsistent relations with the Father and. the Holy Spirit became a real human being. Sharing our humanity he is equal with us, being God's Son sharing our existence he is different from us.

Our personhood is constituted by relations with other persons. We each share humanity in an equal though different and unique way. How our intelligence forms and applies the conception of a class of particulars, we will most likely never know. Yet by what Michael Polanyi has called 'tacit integration',[3] we know humanity and we know particular human beings, and in this we discover at once both our equality and difference before God the Creator.

Our individual nature which is intrinsically historical is actualised or unfolded progressively through all that we experience in the course of our lives. When we enter into a love relationship with another person, for example, in discovering a new friend, we bring to this relationship all the richness we already enjoy with other friends and loved ones. In the new relationship the friends are brought reciprocally into the network of relations to which each already belongs.

In the incarnation Jesus brought us all into the relationship he has as Son with the Father and the Spirit. We share equally with him, though not in the same way, his relationships in the Godhead. By becoming other than he is, which of necessity is to become less than he is, Christ Jesus made us rich by sharing with us, in and through his real, historical existence, his own relationships of knowledge and love which bind him eternally to the Father and the Spirit. So it is that Paul could write those profound and lovely words: "For you know the grace of our Lord Jesus Christ, that though he was rich, yet for your sake he became poor, so that by his poverty you might become rich" [2 Corinthians 8:9]. His becoming poor, being less than he is, was the means of making us rich, that is, more than we are and thus our true selves. He who is Eternal Word subjected himself to the process of historical development in order to share with us his own eternal blessedness. By his equality with us which is the divine poverty, we became rich by being made equal with him.

Jesus in History

The Word of God entered this world, like all of us, as a helpless child. He was born in the poverty of the stable and he died naked and defenceless nailed to a cross. He grew up with his family at Nazareth where he learned a trade: "Is not this the carpenter, the Son of Mary and brother of James?" [Mark 6:3]. The word *tekton* here apparently covers a wide range of occupations: builder in stone, architect, worker in wood or metal. Though he can hardly be considered to have been among the influential, economically or socially, of this world, as a worker Jesus seems to have enjoyed economic security for the greater part of his life.

---

[3] M. Polanyi, H. Prosch, *Meaning,* The University of Chicago Press, Chicago and London 1975, p. 52.

During his public ministry he lived as an itinerant preacher, but there is no evidence to suggest he was either destitute or that he practised begging. The group which gathered round him shared a common money box: "Some thought that, because Judas had the money box, Jesus was telling him, 'Buy what we need for the feast'; or that he should give something to the poor" [John 13:29]. It seems, therefore, that no one in the group was in need and that it was a custom of Jesus to give money to the poor.

Jesus evidently had the luxury of being able to choose the life of an itinerant preacher: "And Jesus said to him, 'Foxes have holes, and birds of the air have nests; but the Son of man has nowhere to lay his head' " [Matthew 8:20]. Yet the fact is, he had left his own home by free choice in order to preach the reign of God. The symbolic rather than the literal meaning of this text is to be preferred: only the true Messiah, the Son of man, is not at home in Israel; there is no place for him, he is not accepted. He came unto his own and his own received him not. As he had 'left' the glory of the Godhead in order to share his divine life with us, so he left the stability of home life to proclaim the reign of God on earth.

The poverty of his birth and his nakedness and desolation in death must be understood, I submit, as proofs of God's unlimited love for all humanity. But neither these nor his free choice of an itinerant's life can be considered ends in themselves. They manifest that sacrifices are necessary in order to share with others what has been received as pure gift. From all eternity the Son receives his entire being from the Father and in his historical existence all that Jesus was by being and by grace was received as gift.

The Recorded Teaching of Jesus

In his teaching Jesus makes particular mention of the poor, the sick, the afflicted and the oppressed. The gospel of God's reign is preached to them not simply because having no power of their own in any worldly sense they are more likely to trust in God, but rather because the reign of God means the presence of God's love and therefore of his justice and peace. With the advent of God 's reign the poor and less fortunate of the world can rightly expect the rich to share their possessions so that no one will be in need. God has done his part by sharing his life and love with the brothers and sisters of his Son. The reign of God proclaims the equality of human beings before God without discrimination and their equal dignity as first-born with Jesus. This demands as its necessary corollary that those with influence and possessions do all in their power to make God's justice a reality in the social and economic structures of the world. God's reign does not make material poverty into a virtue, it requires its elimination.

Therefore because God's reign has begun, oppression has to cease, poverty has to be destroyed, the illiterate have to be educated and the sick have to be taken care of and provided with all the means at our disposal to bring them comfort and healing. How can God's reign be anything more than nominal when the governments of the world spend £435,000 every minute on arms and weapons of destruction?

In the Lucan account of the beatitudes Jesus declares the poor to be blessed. This is not because their oppressed state or destitution is a blessed and desirable human condition. They are blessed rather because their poverty will be wiped away if all who hear the gospel of God's reign act in accordance with God's justice. In Matthew's gospel the poor in spirit are declared blessed. The poor in spirit, be they economically prosperous or materially destitute, are blessed in their openness to God. This openness is the fruit of humility by which we recognise that we are finite creatures and in desperate need of God's grace. Through poverty of spirit God's reign begins in our heart and his justice leads the rich to share what they have with the poor and protects them both from falling into avarice and making idols and false gods of possessions.

It is important to note that in the Old Testament there was a shift in meaning of the term *anawim* from being primarily the description of a deprived social condition to a state of spirit before God.[4] Our understanding of the work 'poor' in an exclusive sense of economic and social conditions, makes it extremely difficult, if not altogether impossible, to appreciate its having a religious and spiritual connotation in the bible. We may note this usage especially in the Psalms: cf. 10:17; 18:28; 37:11; 86:1 ff. These are Yahweh's poor and if many of them are pious, hard-working folk, there is nothing to suggest that they must be materially poor to be blessed. The paradigm of the poor of Yahweh is Jesus himself as meek and humble of heart, and as we have

---

4 See R.E. Murphy O Carm, *Psalms* in: *The Jerome Biblical Commentary* 35:11, p. 573: "Long before the fundamental study of A. Rahlfs (1892) the difference between *'ani* and *'anaw* was being debated. Rahlfs's study indicated that *'ani* was one who was oppressed by misery and distress in this life; the *'anaw* was one who was humbled himself before the Lord (hence the *'anawim,* the "faithful"). With R. Kittel a still greater spiritualization of terms denoting social distress took place (*'ebyon* "poor"), and in recent times many adopt the thesis of A. Gelin that the vocabulary relative to poverty, although originally sociological, came to carry an intense spiritual meaning. The influence of the prophets (as early as Zephaniah; cf. 3:12) and of the Exile are invoked to explain this development. . . .In view of the wide range of opinion, it seems that the term "poor" can have both a sociological and religious sense, and the dominant idea must be derived from the context".

seen, there is no evidence that he was materially deprived or destitute, at least not prior to the crucifixion.

Nevertheless, the condition of the rich is precarious. Possessions can so easily become idols in the place of the true God. Salvation for them through God's reign does not consist in making themselves destitute, but in opening their heart to God's grace and in sharing what they have with the poor. We are all less human as long as any of our brethren are suffering poverty, oppression or sickness. If those who are fortunate enough to have possessions and the means of alleviating others in need, yet turn away from them, they lose both God and their own humanity.

It is instructive in this regard that the rich young man lacked only one thing in order to inherit the kingdom: "Go, sell what you have and give to the poor, and you will have treasure in heaven; and come follow me" [Mark 10:21]. In this dialogue the reign of God was approaching this young man. He was by all accounts a religious man and Jesus loved him. But he was not in the kingdom. The obstacle to his entry was that he could not accept the justice that God's reign ineluctably involves. There is no hint that acceptance of God's reign would reduce him to destitution; on the contrary, he would have been liberated and have received the security of living in Jesus' company and sharing the common money box. But there was a rival god, money, and God's reign is powerless before it.

The Primitive Church

It would be romanticism to consider the life of the primitive Church to have been without problems and idyllic in all respects. Indeed the Acts of the Apostles plainly shows this to be false. Yet there is one text which indicates that the reign of God came, at least for a time, like a fire-fly in the evening darkness, close to full realisation: "And all who believed were together and had all things in common; and they sold their possessions and goods and distributed them to all, as any had need" [Acts 2:44f.]. Nobody evidently was made destitute or became materially poor. All were equal in that no one suffered need. Again we may note there is no teaching that material poverty or need is a virtue. It is rather a scourge to be eliminated wherever God's reign becomes a reality.

This very point is made by St. Paul in the text of 2 Corinthians which has already been mentioned. His words may be taken as a fair summary of the idea of evangelical equality being urged here: "I do not mean that others should be eased and you burdened, but that as a matter of equality your abundance at the present time should supply their want, so that their abundance may supply your want, that there may be equality. As it is written, 'He who gathered much had nothing over, and he who gathered little had no lack' " [2 Corinthians 8:13-15]. The Corinthians are being asked to deprive themselves for the sake of others. Deprivation is not an end in itself nor is there virtue in the negative state of non-possession of goods. It is a means of alleviating human need and a positive action to eliminate poverty.

The Profession of Evangelical Equality

The proposal earlier in the article was that we substitute the term evangelical equality for evangelical poverty. The theological meaning of equality will now be clear from the foregoing reflections. It should be recalled once more that the understanding of it is intimately bound up with Jesus' teaching on the advent of God's reign.

We may now turn to the elements of evangelical equality and the consequences that follow from them. These elements were listed as three: surrender, self-denial and sharing; and each was coupled with one of the traditional triad: prayer, fasting and almsgiving, which are themselves structural to growth in Christian life.

Surrender to God

First of all, surrender. I take this to mean total openness to God and thus to incorporate the life of prayer and the spiritual meaning of poverty as found in the Psalms and the Matthean form of the first beatitude: "Blessed are the poor in spirit, for theirs is the kingdom of heaven" [5:3]. My analysis of surrender is based upon the doctrine of creation and the primary data of Christian anthropology.

According to the doctrine of creation we believe that God is the Sovereign Lord of life and death, that he is the origin, centre and goal of all reality. We have our existence because God wills it. The ultimate reason, therefore, of our being is found not in ourselves but in God's free and all-powerful love. The recognition of God as Creator is an act of sublime humility and profound rationality. As creatures of the one God all human beings are equal in his sight.

Christian reflection on human existence reveals it to be finite and under the powers of evil. Our condition of finitude, our very creaturehood, means that we are beings-unto-death. Out of our finitude grows anxiety about human existence: as we did not always exist, so we might not continue to be. Anxiety, in its turn, gives rise to the temptation to refuse to accept our humanity with its intrinsic limitations, radical emptiness and simultaneous longing for fullness, indeed, for infinity. To succumb to the temptation is to erect idols in place of the true God and even to make gods of ourselves. Such refusal of our humanity is the result of the dark power of evil whose hold on the world can be broken only by the reign of God.

Surrender to God is made possible through the mysterious union of human freedom and divine initiative we call co-operation with grace. In other words, surrender to God is itself his gift. It is the result of divine enlightenment whereby we recognise ourselves as creatures intrinsically limited yet open to God and as sinners unintelligibly selfish yet yearning to love, serve, worship and adore.

Belief in God the Creator of all things tells us that our being is his gift and the only gracious response to a gift is to accept it and give thanks. And thanks to God for creation as a whole and for our own being in particular is made best of all at the Eucharist where Jesus Christ is at once God's gift to us and our gratitude to him. Moreover, by the gift of the gospel we believe that God is Liberator and Sanctifier who accepted our humanity unconditionally in the incarnation and by the sending of the Spirit, and thus set us free from the powers of evil and made us whole. In virtue of God's unqualified 'Yes' to our humanity in the incarnation we are enabled to accept ourselves and to have faith where there was doubt, hope where there was anxiety and love where there was selfishness, and by these gifts to answer 'Amen' to our humanity re-created and re-fashioned in Christ. With Christ we become co-heirs and co-lovers and therefore equal as first-born with him.

The profession of evangelical equality proclaims that all is gift and it constitutes every religious community a community of affirmation, adoration and thanksgiving. Affirmation, because it accepts creaturehood and finitude with serenity and peace; adoration, because it thanks God for being God; thanksgiving, because it thanks him for his grace in Christ Jesus.

Self-denial

Secondly, self-denial. This second element follows directly from surrender to God and is intimately connected with the third, sharing.

The paradox is that we have to say 'No' to ourselves in order to hear God's 'Yes' to our existence and respond with the 'Amen' of total affirmation. God's reign in us has to do battle with the constant threat of our refusing to accept our human nature and recognise its meaning is in God. Self-denial therefore is the negation of a negation. Evangelical equality requires of us as individuals and communities to say 'No' to ourselves, to take up our cross, in our discipleship of Jesus.

This personal and spiritual aspect of self-denial must not be separated from its social aspect. Self-denial is not spiritual athleticism nor cultivation of the 'spirit beautiful' for its own sake. God's reign in the world has not produced its intended results. There is too much poverty, injustice and oppression to allow any such starry-eyed notion. The sad truth is that in countries of the First, Second or Third Worlds where the gospel has been preached for many centuries, the justice of God's reign is absent, if not positively excluded. In Christian countries of the Third World there is terrible poverty and horrible oppression. In formerly Christian countries of the Second World there is still oppression and flagrant inhumanity.

The rich nations of the First World have set up Mammon in the holy place and the gross materialism that characterises them is symptomatic of their well-nigh complete loss of meaning. The false gods of the First World are proof that we do not accept our humanity and this leads inevitably to the conclusion that our belief in the incarnation is hardly much more than nominal. We are alienated from God, from ourselves and from the world and the disorientation that accompanies our alienation has driven us to seek a focus for life in the world that is not only unworthy but disastrous.

If those who profess to live publicly in accordance with the absolute demands of God's reign limply accept the standards dictated by consumer society, not only do they contradict by their actions what they proclaim with their lips, but also tacitly confirm that life has no real meaning. Consumer society has created 'needs' which are not needs at all. The truth is that our basic needs are really very few and most of us in religious life could probably get on quite well with about two-thirds less of what we think is necessary for life.

There is, furthermore, an ecological need for self-denial. What industry and technology have done to this planet over the last two hundred years must be among the greatest crimes against nature in the history of the race. Greed, unwarranted belief in progress and irrational optimism have deceived us into thinking we were gods and the fruits show that we are false gods.

It must be said that riches, in the present condition of the human race, are an obstacle to God's reign. This is not because possessions in themselves are evil and material poverty preferable. Humanity has become conscious of its basic unity and therefore while there are still members of the race suffering deprivations which can be remedied by concerted human effort, the proclamation of God's reign will be ineffectual. We are members of one another and therefore by God's justice those who can are bound to meet the needs of others.

There are many religious in the world. If every community were to reduce its 'needs' to the point at least of contradicting the standards of consumer society this would render the preaching of God's reign more credible and would also, I am convinced, have considerable effect eventually on the consciences of the rich nations. I do not mean to advocate that we should reduce ourselves to destitution nor sacrifice apostolates without discrimination. What I am advocating is that we give credible signs of our belief in the equality of all peoples.

By the profession of evangelical equality then, every religious community obliges itself to be a community of penance for the sake of the reign of God.

Sharing

Thirdly, sharing. In respect of the daily life of a religious community it seems to me that the Acts of the Apostles has laid down the essentials: "And all who believed were together and had all things in common" [2:44]; "And they devoted themselves to the apostles' teaching and fellowship, to the breaking of bread and the prayers" [2:42]. By the profession of evangelical equality we freely accept to share our person and life and the fruits of our work with the community to which we belong. By having all things in common no one in a religious community suffers material needs. There are, however, other needs which have to be met if people are to grow as people in our communities. These are spiritual, emotional, psychological and intellectual and they can only be met by our sharing with one another our time, insights and talents; our joys and sorrows, our crosses and exaltations, our successes and failures, our weaknesses and strengths and the fruits of our prayer. Because we celebrate the Eucharist together and share equally in the Body and Blood of Christ, we are obliged to make our communities places of fellowship where each is loved and wanted as co-heir and co-lover with Christ. To continue in the apostles' teaching is to strive to make God's reign with all its consequences ever more a reality in our midst. In this way the religious community becomes a symbol of the unity and fraternity of the human race and concrete proof that God's reign is not merely a romantic ideal reserved for some utopia.

The element of sharing will have its effect on the external relations of the community. Those who come to the community will be received with openness and kindness and their needs met as far as possible. Any who seek material help should be given what they ask. And does it really matter if sometimes we are deceived? Is it not better to err on the side of excess in this matter in order to escape the judgement implied in the words of James: "If a brother or sister is ill-clad and in lack of daily food, and one of you say to them, 'Go in peace, be warmed and filled', without giving them the things needed for the body, what does it profit? So faith by itself, if it has no works, is dead" [2:15-17].

What we have left over once our material needs are met should be given to those still in need, again, as far as this is possible. In the vicinity of every religious community there are people suffering deprivation. This applies also to spiritual need, for instance the needs of the lonely, with whom we can share our time. Above all, whenever we do penance, such as fasting in Lent or depriving ourselves of legitimate recreation, we should always give what we have saved to those in need. Self-denial and sharing (fasting and almsgiving) always go together .

By the profession of evangelical equality, therefore, every religious community is meant to be a community of generosity as a witness of God's generosity to us in Christ Jesus.

Conclusion

Religious life is one way of following in the footsteps of Jesus Christ. Those who embrace it do so because it expresses for them the ultimate meaning of life. I have been arguing that religious should profess evangelical equality rather than evangelical poverty. This substitution, I maintain, would render this form of the gospel life more credible to religious themselves, to the Church and to the world at large.

God and the Feminine[1]

Over the last fifty years women have taken an ever greater and more active part in public life and administration at both the national and the international levels. A few years ago it was calculated that some fifty per cent of the women of this country had accepted and espoused what is called "the feminine revolution". The anniversary of the emancipation of women celebrated in 1968 saw the cause of women's equality much advanced since Mrs. Pankhurst's days and indeed so much so, that the movement for the equality of women is counted among the signs of the times. As a result of the movement it was to be expected that sooner or later speculation would begin about the possibility of women priests. During the past few years the question of women and holy orders has received close attention and quite an amount of publicity.

This is an important question which cannot be brushed aside as no more than an esoteric pursuit of a few cranks. It merits consideration not only because of the seriousness with which it has been discussed and presented,[2] but also, so it seems to us, because of a theological issue which is intimately connected with it—that, namely, of the source of the feminine in God. Arguments and evidence arising from sociological, psychological, anthropological and historical studies are, of course, of profound significance here because of the theological implications they may carry. However, the theological question of the source of the feminine in God is also relevant to the question of women and holy orders, insofar as it constitutes the starting point for a theology of womanhood. In the following pages we shall examine whether there are reasons for asserting that the feminine has its source in God, the Primal Origin of all things. If there are reasons, then these will serve to remind us of the essential equality of the sexes before God and, above all, will

---

[1] CLERGY REVIEW 56 (Nov. 1971) pp. 866-877. Published with permission (www.priestsandpeople.co.uk).
[2] See for example: V.E. Hannon, *The Question of Women and the Priesthood. Can Women be admitted to Holy Orders?*, Chapman, London 1967. *Women in Holy Orders. Being the Report of a Commission appointed by the Archbishops of Canterbury and York*, Church Information Office, London 1966.

safeguard us from rhapsodizing woman away under those lovely but often doubtfully applied attributes: receptivity and passivity.

Jung and the Assumption

It is well known that Jung considered the definition of the dogma of the Assumption to be the most important religious event since the Reformation.[3] In a most interesting and now famous argument based on his lifelong investigations into the psychology of religion, he demonstrated how congenial the definition was to the psychological mind. The following quotation may be taken as a fair summary of his argument: "The method which the Pope uses in order to demonstrate the truth of the dogma makes sense to the psychological mind, because it bases itself firstly on the necessary prefigurations, and secondly on a tradition of religious assertions reaching back for more than a thousand years".[4]

There is much in the argument that is very welcome from a Roman Catholic's point of view, especially that it serves to illustrate how revelation dovetails with our natural aspirations. Moreover, the theological significance of Jung's reasoning cannot be ignored in ecumenical dialogue on the place of Mary in the Church. There are, however, two passages in the chapter which leave one with a feeling of uneasiness. The first appears early in the chapter: "One could have known for a long time that there was a deep longing in the masses for an intercessor and mediatrix who would at last take her place alongside the Holy Trinity and be received as the 'Queen of Heaven and Bride at the heavenly court' ".[5]

The second is one of the many passages in which Jung expresses severe criticism of Protestantism:

> The logic of the papal declaration cannot be surpassed, and it leaves Protestantism with the odium of being nothing more but *a man's religion* which *allows* no metaphysical representation of woman. In this respect it is similar to Mithraism, and Mithraism found this prejudice very much to its detriment. Protestantism has obviously not given sufficient attention to the signs of the times which point to the equality of women. But this equality requires to be metaphysically anchored in the figure of a 'divine' woman, the bride of Christ. Just as the person

---

[3] C.G. Jung, *Answer to Job,* Routledge & Kegan Paul: London 1954, pp. 165-178, esp. pp. 169ff.

[4] Ibid., p. 170.

[5] Ibid., p. 166.

of Christ cannot be replaced by an organisation, so the bride cannot be replaced by the Church. The feminine, like the masculine, demands an equally personal representation.[6]

The feeling of uneasiness arises most of all at the words in the first quotation: "Who would at last take her place alongside the Holy Trinity" and, in the second quotation, at the reference to "the figure of a 'divine' woman" and at the statement: "The feminine, like the masculine, demands an equally personal representation", which makes Mary the personalized feminine, just as Christ is the personalized masculine. Jung does point out, of course, that the doctrine of the Assumption according to the dogmatic view does not mean that Mary has attained the status of a goddess. Nevertheless, he adds: "As mistress of heaven. . .and mediatrix, she is functionally on a par with Christ, the king and mediator".[7] One concludes here that Mary is being exalted to the position of 'divine' woman and personalized feminine alongside the Trinity, by way of compensation for an over-masculinized Godhead. It would seem, however, that the equality of women is not radically enhanced in the present context by being metaphysically anchored in the figure of a 'divine' woman in the person of Mary. To be taken really seriously from the religious point of view, the equality of women requires to be anchored in God. However intelligible it may be on the psychological side to assert that Mary is functionally on a par with Christ, it appears to be theologically unacceptable and ultimately psychologically unsatisfactory, precisely because Mary is not divine: "For no creature could ever be classed with the Incarnate Word and Redeemer".[8] Furthermore, the titles "Advocate, Auxiliatrix, Adjutrix, and Mediatrix. . .are to be so understood that they neither take away from nor add anything to the dignity and efficacy of Christ the one Mediator".[9] What has been said here of Jung's statements about the Assumption applies also to the remarks of Teilhard de Chardin to Pere Leroy in 1950: "I am too conscious of the biopsychological necessity of the 'Marian' (to counterbalance the

---

[6] Ibid., pp. 170f.

[7] Ibid., p. 171.

[8] Dogmatic Constitution on the Church *Lumen Gentium* of the Second Vatican Council in: *The Documents of Vatican II,* ed. by W.M. Abbott SJ, Chapman: London-Dublin 1966, par. 62, p. 92.

[9] Ibid. par. 62, pp. 91f.

[10] Quoted in Henri de Lubac SJ, *The Eternal Feminine,* Collins: London 1971, p. 125. Cf. also p. 235. Teilhard speaks of "the need to correct 'a dreadfully masculinized conception of the Godhead' ", cf. ibid., p. 126.

'masculinity' of Yahweh) not to feel the profound need of this gesture".[10] He was speaking here of the definition of the Assumption.

At a pivotal point in the history of God's dealings with mankind stands the woman Mary and she is a Mother. When we turn to contemplate her place in the mystery of divine economy, we must be clear in our minds that we turn our gaze on her in faith, which is God's gracious gift to us. Without faith guiding us all the while, Mary becomes just another woman on whom we hardly need look twice. But in faith we realize precisely what she is: just a woman. In the Christian faith that is fundamental about Mary. Faith protects us from the blasphemous absurdity of ranking her with the Godhead. Her place in the mystery of God's plan is precisely and formally as a woman—the holiest, the most feminine, the most womanly woman, but only a woman and creature of God. To grasp this through the light of faith prepares the ground for a more thorough understanding of her role in God's designs as Type and Image of the Church. The Council's emphasis on Mary as Type of the Church, crystallizing modern mariological insights, has had the result of bringing our Lady closer to us than ever before. Her womanhood, her being-a-woman-in-the-world, has to be stressed in order to avoid the danger of transforming her into a 'divine' woman to counterbalance the exclusively masculine Trinity. If there is a lack of balance in our imagery, conceptualizations and categorizing of God, it is surely most unsatisfactory to seek to redress the balance by mariology, precisely because this evades the point at issue.

That a woman stood at the most crucial point in salvation history, that her fiat belongs to official, public, saving history in the economy of God, that she is depicted by the most venerable and ancient Christian writers as Archetype of the Church—all this provides weighty grounds for inquiring into the question of whether Mary, as a woman who is a mother, reveals an aspect of God's life and nature; that is to say, whether womanhood and motherhood have their source in God.

On the occasion of the definition of the Assumption, Fr. Victor White OP wrote:

Perhaps it (the definition) will lead the Church to closer consideration and ultimate formulation of the deep mystery of the 'Motherhood of God'. For by the Assumption Mary returns to her own eternal source, and not she, but God himself is the ultimate prototype of Motherhood, womanhood—even materiality. . . .As Christ, ascending to heaven leads the way to God our Eternal Father, perhaps Mary, assumed into heaven, will lead us to a deeper knowledge and love of God, our Eternal Mother.[11]

Mary's significance is, therefore, that she makes us look beyond herself for the source of what she is by nature and grace.

The Mystery of God and the Image of God

In the Scriptures God is referred to as "He" and not as "She". The heart of the Christian mystery is that God became a man, not that God became a woman. The Eternal Logos became a member of our race in the male sex. Jesus Christ revealed to us that God is Father, his Father and our Father, not that God is Mother. It is from God the Father that all fatherhood in heaven and on earth is named. Moreover, it is the Son who proceeds from the Father from all eternity, so that we must profess God the Son, not God the Daughter. When Christ promised the Advocate, "the Spirit of truth who issues from the Father", it is He, we say, not She, who will be Christ's witness; it is He who will show the world how wrong it was about sin and about who was in the right and about judgement.[12]

The Scriptures tell us that God dwells in light inaccessible. As the invisible, indescribable, ineffable and incomprehensible Mystery, God is beyond every category, every word and every thought. He is, in fact, above all we can affirm or deny of him. To God belongs super-essential existence, and he is of superdivine divinity.[13] Yet in our obviously necessary "God-talk" we assert that God is Pure Spirit. This must be understood as differentiating God not only from matter but also from all finite spirit, angelic or human. In reality God is no "closer" to finite, limited spirit than he is to matter.[14] Whatever definition we would ultimately give to "Pure Spirit", it would be agreed that it is intended to exclude sex from God. God is neither male nor female. Consequently, the terms "Father" and "Son" indicate that the perfections of fatherhood and sonship are to be found pre-eminently in God. Fr.McKenzie draws attention to the fact that for the Jews God is masculine: "We have already noticed that in the Mesopotamian myths sex was as primeval as nature itself. The Hebrews could not accept this view for there was no sex in the God they worshipped. God is, of course, masculine, but not in the sense of sexual

---

[11] *The Scandal of the Assumption* in: *Life of the Spirit*, vol. V, 1950, nn. 53-54, pp. 211-12
[12] John 16:8-9.
[13] Pseudo-Dionysius, *De divinis nominibus,* c. ii, 4, PG 3, col. 641; cf. also c. i, i, ibid. col. 588, c. i, 6, ibid. col. 596.
[14] See Karl Rahner, *Hominisation. The Evolutionary Origin of Man as a Theological Problem,* Herder, Freiburg; Burns & Oates, London 1965, pp. 50-52.

distinction".[15] While we can readily understand the reasons why the Hebrews considered God masculine, nevertheless, given the understanding of Pure Spirit in theology, can God be said to be masculine any more than feminine? If we may rightly refer to the Primordial Mystery as "He", is it so unthinkable to say "She"? Would it not be as true to say: "God is, of course, feminine, but not in the sense of sexual distinction?" Such a designation of God may well be emotionally unacceptable, but this does not necessarily render it theologically unsound.

When we reflect on the image of God in man and woman there is no intention here of playing down the psychic and social importance of sexual difference. Man and woman are different both physically (much wider than reproductive organs: blood, skeletal structure, etc.) and psychologically. Nevertheless, it has to be remembered that there is a real complementarity between them based on equality.

The creation of mankind in the book of Genesis is introduced with great solemnity: "Let us make man". Man appears as the crown and purpose of the whole created order. God created man (adam) in the image of himself, in the image of God he created him, male and female he created them [1:27]. In his commentary on this text G. von Rad writes:

> Sexual distinction is also created. The plural in verse 27 ("he created them") is intentionally contrasted with the singular ("him") and prevents one from assuming the creation of an originally androgynous man. . . .The idea of man according to P, finds its full meaning not in the male alone but in man and woman.[16]

Mankind is created in the image of God and mankind is male and female. The image of God cannot be restricted to man's spiritual nature exclusively because "soul" does not define what we mean when we say "man". It would be much nearer the truth to describe man as "spatter" or "mirit", "spody" or "boul". G. von Rad notes that "the marvel of man's bodily appearance is not at all to be excepted from the realm of God's image".[17] Man is not a spirit-in-a-body, nor a soul-encaged-in-flesh, but a unity, a real unity, that is at once material and spiritual. God created mankind in the divine image. The masculine and the feminine only together express fully what is human, what is mankind. Consequently, both trace back their origin to the image of

---

[15] *The Two-Edged Sword. An Interpretation of the Old Testament,* Chapman, London 1955, pp. 93f.

[16] *Genesis-A Commentary,* trans. by J.H. Marks, S.C.M. Press Ltd. 1961, p. 58.

[17] Ibid., p. 56.

God. Man as masculine is created in God's image and God is the source of what is precisely masculine; woman as feminine is created in God's image and God is the source of what is precisely feminine. Sexuality is an essential part of what it is to be human, whether man or woman; thus, the two sexes contain the image of God, since man and woman constitute what is human in its complete sense.

Jung assures us that in every man there is a complementary feminine element and in every woman a complementary masculine element. These he calls *anima* and *animus* respectively In man *animus* predominates, but there is also *anima;* in woman *anima* predominates, but there is also *animus.*[18] Each of the sexes, therefore, possesses qualities and elements which are characteristic of the other. Mankind as realized in man and woman, created in the image of God, allows us again to trace back to God the source of what is masculine and the source of what is feminine.

It is no disrespect, but an honour surely, to insist that there was and remains this complementary feminine element in Jesus Christ. Jung tells us that "a collective image of woman exists in a man's unconsciousness with the help of which he apprehends the nature of woman".[19] It is, however, only woman in general that man apprehends in this way, because the collective image is an archetype. This image only becomes conscious and tangible through actual contacts with woman that a man makes during his life. The first and most important experience comes to him through his mother and is the most powerful in shaping him.[20] This provides food for thought on the vital role our Lady played in this respect in the life and formation of Jesus Christ. It was through his relationship with Mary his Mother that our Lord was able to have such mature friendships with Martha and Mary and with the other women mentioned in the gospel of St. Luke.

Motherhood in God

When we begin to contemplate the Word of Revelation we put ourselves in the presence of the God of our faith. That is to say, we unite ourselves with the God of undiscoverable majesty who has willed in infinite wisdom and love to reveal his inner life to mankind through Jesus Christ. We are not therefore concerned with the arguments which philosophy furnishes to establish the existence of a Supreme Being or First Cause of the universe.

---

[18] See Frieda Fordham, *An Introduction to Jung's Psychology,* Penguin Books 1964, pp. 52-58.

[19] *Two Essays on Analytical Psychology,* trans. by R.F.C. Hull, Routledge & Kegan Paul, London 1953, p. 188.

[20] Fordham, *An Introduction,* pp. 52f.

Admiration and gratitude are surely born in us when we consider the achievements, for example, of the Greek philosophers who have demonstrated to us the powers and the openness of the human mind. Perhaps the longings and strivings of Plato and Aristotle are in us all when we meditate on the holy mystery of the gospel. Nevertheless, the God of philosophy is an impersonal-personal God. We do not wish to undermine the importance of reason's search for meaning in creation. Man is compelled by the very laws of his mind to seek out an explanation of being-in-space-and-time and thus to discover the Ground and Reason of all that is. However, the knowledge of God which reason discovers does not satisfy because the mind and heart cannot rest in what has been discovered. The knowledge which human reason arrives at in virtue of its own powers does not bring beatitude.

The God of light inaccessible has been revealed to us in the blinding light of faith. Jesus Christ reveals to us new knowledge of God and new knowledge of man. What is made known to us in revelation about God brings us knowledge of man and what is revealed about man gives us knowledge of God. This is the reason why every authentic anthropology must, in fact, be Christology and why theology must always take Christ as its starting point. Had we been left to ourselves, we should have known only the "impersonal" God of Nature and the cold Prime Mover of philosophy. We should never have known that "begetting and birth, fatherhood and sonship are realities existing in him".[21] Through God's gracious mercy we profess in the Creed our belief "in one Lord Jesus Christ, the only-begotten Son of God, born of the Father before time began". This formula of the Creed brings to mind the texts of Proverbs 8:24 and Psalm 109:3, which are interpreted by the Fathers of the Church and theologians as applying to the Eternal Logos. We profess, therefore, that the only-begotten Son is born of the Father. The Athanasian Creed warns us that we may not say of the Son *factus* or *creatus;* the Son is *genitus* of the Father. Our knowledge and experience in this world, however, know only of birth from woman. Yet the Creed is emphatic: the Son is born of the Father. This is, of course, an analogy and analogy is proportion, similarity, a process of reasoning from parallel cases; it is based on like and unlike in the comparison. Now since God is the pre-eminent source of all perfections in the created order, he must be the source of motherhood, the supreme feminine perfection. One might feel

---

[21] Yves Congar, *The Revelation of God,* London and New York 1968, p. 84.

a little reluctant in stating this, were it not for a very instructive reflexion on the Motherhood of God by Clement of Alexandria in the *Quis dives salvetur* He actually says God became a woman in the divine life itself through the eternal generation of the Son:

> God is himself Love, and it is because of love that we pursue him. In his ineffable majesty he is our Father, but in the comfort he extends to us he has become our mother. Yes, the Father in his love became a woman, and the Son whom he brought forth from himself is strong proof of this.[22]

The eternal birth of the Son from the Father makes God the Eternal Mother. According to Donald Nicholl St Ephraem the Syrian (c. 306-373) refers to the Holy Spirit as "Mother in God", the "eternal woman in God".[23]

The Motherhood of God is a theme familiar in Western spirituality. St Anselm, for example, addresses Jesus as mother : *Sed et tu Iesu, bone domine, nonne et tu mater? An non est mater, qui tamquam gallina congregat sub alas pullos suos? Vere, domine, et tu mater.*[24] But, beyond doubt, this theme has its best known and most beautiful expression in the *Revelations* of Julian of Norwich. Speaking of the divine operations in every soul, she writes:

> And thus in our making, God, Almighty, is our kindly Father; and God, All-Wisdom, is our kindly Mother; with the Love and the Goodness of the Holy Ghost: which is all one God, one Lord.[25]

The Trinity possesses three properties: Fatherhood, Motherhood and Lordhood.[26] Motherhood is attributed specifically to the Second Person who is our Mother in nature and grace:

> and the second Person of the Trinity is our Mother in kind, in making of our Substance, in whom we are grounded and rooted. And he is our Mother in Mercy, in our Sensuality taking. And thus our Mother is to us in diverse manners working: in whom our parts are kept undisparted.[27]

---

[22] PG 9, col. 641-44, quoted and translated in: The Way 4.2 (April 1964) p. 146.

[23] *Recent Thought in Focus,* Sheed and Ward 1952, p. 90.

[24] *S Anselmi Cantuariensis Archiepiscopi Opera Omnia,* vol. III. . . .Ad fidem Codicum recensuit Franciscus Salesius Schmitt, Monachus Grissoviensis OSB (Apud Thomam Nelson et Filios, Edinburgi MDCCCCXLVI), *Oratio* 10, pp. 4041; PL 158, *Oratio LXV, col.* 982.

[25] *Revelations of Divine Love,* ed. from the MSS. by Dom Roger Hudleston, monk of Downside Abbey, Burns Oates, London 1952, chap. 58, p. 119.

[26] Ibid., p. 119

[27] Ibid., p. 120.

What is most attractive in these pages of the Lady Julian's *Revelations* is the unaffected way in which she attributes feminine qualities to God. It is surely to God our Mother that we trace back that loving concern of the All-Merciful Lord for each one of us, as we strive in this world to reach the holiness to which we have been called from all eternity.

Concluding Remarks

Any attempt to establish a theology of femininity must take its origin from God. Womanhood and motherhood, it would seem, do have their eternal source in the Triune God. Our Lady, therefore, in her Assumption, must be said to return to the Primal Origin of her own womanhood and motherhood in God. Now, if we can take seriously that God is the source of femininity, then it is legitimate to ask what is the *theological* reason behind the assertion of Canon 968, par. I of the Code of Canon Law:

Sacram ordinationem valide recipit solus vir baptizatusa? Fr. Francis Sola SJ holds that the proposition: *Femina est incapax sacramenti ordinis* seems to be *doctrina de fide catholica.*[28] A. Tanquerey maintains it is *iure divino* that only men can validly receive orders.[29] We cannot, of course, ignore that St. Irenaeus, St. Epiphanius and St. Augustine considered the Pepuzians, the Marcosians and the Collyridians as heretics for having women bishops and priests. However, is this reaction not to be explained by the somewhat over-literal and too restrictive exegesis of certain texts in Scripture, especially Genesis 2-3 and some passages in the Pauline corpus: 1 Corinthians 11:3-16, 14:34f.; 1 Timothy 2:12? In any case it is clear that the question cannot be decided merely by the repetition of texts from Scripture. Given the present state of exegesis, there would seem to be no textual argument from Scripture against the ordination of women. It is at least open to discussion that only men by divine law can receive sacred orders.

Finally, since there are some grounds for tracing back womanhood and motherhood to God, it would seem desirable and fitting that these aspects of the divine life be manifested in the priestly ministry of the Church. As a preparation for this and by way of experiment, subject to the approval of the Church, serious consideration should be given to introducing altar girls without distinction and to ordaining nuns so willing, to the diaconate, especially in

---

[28] *Sacrae Theologiae Summa IV, De Sacramentis. De Noaissimism,* Bibliotheca de Autores Cristianos, Matriti, MCMLVI, p. 701.

[29] *Synopsis Theologiae Dogmaticae.* Tomus Tertius, editio vigesima sexta (Desclee et Socii, 1950) pp. 735f.

boarding schools, who could preach, give spiritual direction and distribute holy communion.

Reflections on the Theology of Preaching[1]

Any theologian who applies himself to a study of the proclamation of the Word of God in order to establish a theology of preaching, must take it as his basic premise that there is theology at all only because firstly, God has spoken His Word at a particular point in human history and secondly, because the Church—the People of the Word—is commissioned to proclaim God's Word today. This is to say that it is because there is preaching that there is theology. The grace and office of being a theologian in the Church is possible, justified and intelligible precisely because there are ministers of God preaching His Word from the pulpits of our churches every Sunday and missionaries carrying it to the furthest corners of the earth. Every seminary professor knows that his lectures and the notes he distributes from those on philosophy to those on mystical theology receive their intrinsic orientation as instruments in the service of the Word from the proclamation of the gospel message. The theologian is a theologian because he has received and continues to receive his nourishment from the Word of God. However deep his learning may be, whatever talents he may possess, he too must listen in openness, receptivity and humility to the words proclaiming the Word of God. It is not his business to subject the proclaimed Word to critical analysis as though he could stand aside to judge what is proclaimed. He must allow the faltering and hesitant words of the poorest preacher to enter into and penetrate his entire being in order that his faith may be strengthened for the reception of the most penetrating words of all: "This is my Body, this is my Blood", through which there comes to him what has been proclaimed. Thus, like all others, the theologian must listen to the Word of God, not analyse it; he must be judged by it, not submit it to his judgement; he must receive all that is offered by the Word, not choose from it. For if he does not practise his science on the fundamental principle that preaching precedes theology, that theology is the *ancilla Verbi*, then he cuts himself off from the chief source of his science and makes of theology an arid intellectualism which inevitably turns sour and deadly.

---

[1] NEWSLETTER ON SEMINARY EDUCATION 12 (May 1971) pp. 4-15. Published with permission.

The Apostolic Origin of the Church

There is proclamation or preaching (*kerugma*) in the world because there is a Word and there is a Word (for us) because the Holy One spoke for God [Hebrews 1:1-4]. The Holy One, Who is Jesus of Nazareth, the Crucified and Exalted Lord, established the Church on earth as the eschatological community commissioned by divine authority to implant the reign of God in the hearts of men. The reign of God is the reign of the One-in-Three. The perfect unity of perfect diversity in God expresses the specific Christian doctrine of the Godhead, namely, that God is not alone, He is no mere face-less Energy or Lone Power in the universe. God is plurality in unity; God is a Family Whose names are Father, Son and Holy Spirit. The perfection of unity-in-diversity has its intrinsic being in the dynamism of the divine life itself. From all eternity the Son proceeds from the Father Who is the Origin-without-origin of the divine life. The Logos-Son is the perfect utterance and expression of the Father; between them and from them is the Spirit-Love Who seals the perfect diversity of these subsistent relationships in perfect unity. These three are absolutely united, completely one, knowing and loving one another always. God is God because God is community. The trinitarian teaching of the New Testament is the answer to the perennial human problem of the one and the many and, as historically revealed to us in the divine economy, is the most comforting and most beatifying of all divine truths. In the very inner life of the Godhead we find the source and cause of the unity of the Church: a People made one in the unity of the Father, the Son and the Holy Spirit. Through the unity of the Godhead the Church is constituted the community on earth. In the Church alone can a man be entirely himself in his own incommunicable originality by being in complete union with others whereby he becomes ever more truly himself.

The essential note of the Church's apostolicity traces back its origin to the mystery of God's inmost life. God's dynamic unity-in-diversity is the source of the Church's apostolicity.

Because the Son proceeds from the Father by logical priority in the trinitarian life, so it is the Son Who is first sent into the world. Thus, the Church is apostolic in the first place because her Founder is the Apostle, Jesus Christ, sent from the Father, Who is the Source of all that is. Christ's being sent into the world must not be thought of as posterior to human sin in the order of God's will; it does scant justice to Holy Scripture to consider Christ an after-thought in the mind of God or a mere *bonum occasionatum*: "For in him were created all things in heaven and on earth" [Colossians 1:16].

The Son is predestined from all eternity to be sent into the world that we may be made one. In the Apostle Jesus Christ our unity is already radically given and established. Because He is sent, the Church becomes one; because the Church is sent, the world will be made one.

The Church is apostolic, in the second place, because the Spirit of the thrice-holy God is sent to her by the Father and the exalted Lord after his glorification. The mission or sending of the Holy Spirit, Who seals us as unique persons in the community of the Church by the holiness of God Himself, is to bring back to our minds all that Christ said (that is, all that Christ is), to make us priests, prophets and kings and, thus, to fashion us as images of Him Who is the *eikon* of the God we cannot see.

The Church is apostolic, thirdly, because she is built on the Twelve (who became the Twelve because Christ was sent), who were sent into the world in the name of Christ through the power of the Holy Spirit. In them the Church received her mission to preach in season and out of season that the kingdom of God has come, that God is our Father, that Christ is our Risen Saviour and Brother, the Conqueror of sin and death, the Hope of life and holiness, that the Spirit assures us we are the sons of God. In the Apostolic College the Church was authorised to proclaim that God is First and man is second, that God is Last and man penultimate and to preach that every work and every effort must be ultimately traced back to a specific event in human history; the life, death and glorification of Jesus Christ.

The Church is apostolic, finally, because the People of the Word are sent into the world at the end of every Mass. At that moment Christ the Head commissions His Body, the Church, to take and proclaim what it has so generously been given. From our lips others must hear something of the mercy and unutterable holiness of God; in our eyes others must see something of the kindness and charity of Christ; in our actions others must find something of the inspiration and grace of the Holy Spirit. At each Mass we encounter the Risen and Exalted Lord in Word and Event in order to draw ever new strength to persevere to the end in proclaiming all that has been accomplished in the wonderful works of God.

The Proclamation of the Word

The final unity of the Church which will mark the culmination of God's saving work has its source in the Apostolic Word of God.[2] Because the Word of God has been uttered in time for the salvation of mankind, it must be

---

[2] *Presbyterium Ordinis*, p. 4.

proclaimed by the Church until all history shall have reached its appointed end. The Council teaches in the most explicit terms: "The Catholic Church has been commissioned by the Lord Christ to bring salvation to every man, and is consequently bound to proclaim the gospel".[3] We are concerned here with preaching as the public and divinely authorised proclamation of the gospel message by the consecrated and officially commissioned ministers of the Church[4].

It is commonly known that there are various terms in the New Testament to express the saving message of Christianity. We may distinguish three: *kerugma, marturion* and *didakhe*. Here we are principally concerned with *kerugma*. This is translated proclamation or preaching. The *kerugma* of the New Testament is the public, official proclamation of the saving event, Jesus Christ. As such it is distinct from *marturion*, which is the testimony borne by the Apostles to what they themselves had experienced; from *didakhe* and *katekkesis*, which draw out at length the meaning and implications both doctrinal and moral, contained in the *kerugma*; from *didaskalia*, which is a more profound form of religious instruction. It should be noted that the preaching of the Christian moral ideal is never a mere presentation of rules of behaviour; this always bears witness to Christ and to His saving work.

There is abundant evidence in the New Testament writings that the word *kerugma* may be used to designate the earliest form of the preaching of the Christian mystery. Robert Koch, however, has drawn attention to the relative use of the three words *kerugma, kerux* and the verb *kerussein* in the New Testament. The first, *kerugma*, occurs eight times; the second, *kerux*, (herald) occurs three times and the third, *kerussein* (to proclaim) occurs sixty-one times. The frequent use of this verb, he points out "may well be indicating the enormous importance of the *kerugma* since it is, in the last analysis, God or Christ who speaks by means of the herald"[5]. The rare use of *kerux*[6] which, incidentally, never describes the person of the preacher, indicates that "the only bearer of the proclaimed word is either God himself or Christ".[7] The verb *kerussein* implies the solemn and official announcement of an event made in the name of God or Christ. Its frequent use emphasizes, that it is not so much

---

[3] *Inter mirifica*, S3, *Documents of Vatican* II, Chapman, p. 320.
[4] Romans 10:15; 2 Timothy 1:2; 1 Timothy 5:22; *Lumen Gentium*, SS 24-25, 28, *Presbyterorum Ordinis*, S 4, *Christus Dominus*, S 30.
[5] *Encyclopedia of Biblical Theology*, ed. by J.B. Bauer, vol. 2, p. 687.
[6] Ibid., p. 686; cf. 1 Timothy 2:7; 2 Timothy 1:11; 2 Peter 2:5.
[7] *Encyclopedia of Biblical Theology*, p. 686.

the bearer of the message, nor even the message itself that is central, but the act of proclaiming the message, which is brought about by the Spirit of God.[8]

With the preaching of Jesus, who is the Apostolic Word made flesh, proclamation in its most authentic form was realised in history. Jesus not only proclaims a message; He is the very content of what He proclaims. In this He is fundamentally different from all the prophets of the Old Testament and from John the Baptist.[9] By the very proclamation of the message of salvation He realises the good news of the kingdom of God and calls men to repentance. "(Jesus) does not announce that something will happen. His proclamation is itself an event. What he declares takes place in the moment of its proclamation".[10]

Since Christ is Himself the event He proclaimed, we have the reason why the apostolic *kerugma* in the post-Resurrection period was based not only on the apostles' immediate experience of the Risen and Exalted *Kurios*, but also on their direct and personal experience of the pre-Easter Jesus: they were vitally concerned to be accurate in all the details about Jesus [Acts 18:25]. Jesus, as the revelation of God was the proclamation of the good news from the moment he entered the world to his glorification and exaltation at the resurrection. The historical Jesus is, therefore, indispensable to the apostolic *kerugma*. The preaching of the apostles was effected through the power of the Holy Spirit Whom Christ had promised would be sent after His glorification [cf. John 7:30]. The mission of the Holy Spirit is to bring back to the apostles and the Church everything that Christ said, which is, as we have already pointed out, to bring back all that Christ is, Christ being what He proclaimed. The Holy Spirit was given, therefore, so that the apostles could proclaim the total mystery of Christ. The continuity between the Jesus of history and the Christ of faith is central in the post-Resurrection *kerugma*.

The extreme existentialist interpretation of the *kerugma* is questionable, therefore, not merely because it leaves one with the nagging doubt whether faith is anything more than subjective delusion, but also because it destroys the fullness of proclamation by truncating its content. The apostolic *kerugma* of the post-Resurrection period is made possible because Jesus of Nazareth is Himself the proclamation He proclaimed.

Proclamation of the good news was carried out by the apostles under the command of Christ. He commissioned those He had chosen to proclaim

---

[8] Ibid., p. 688.
[9] Ibid., p. 689; cf. Acts 13:24.
[10] *Encyclopedia of Biblical Theology*, p. 689.

Him to the world [Matthew 28:18-20; Mark 16:15; Luke 24:47]. Christ Himself is the centre of the apostolic preaching. This preaching was no mere instruction about Jesus Christ and the facts of His life, as though the content of what was proclaimed could be obtained from private reading or study. The apostolic *kerugma* is the Word of the Exalted Lord in their proclamation. Through the Holy Spirit Christ speaks in those commissioned by Him as human instruments of the divine Word [2 Corinthians 5:20; Romans 6:25]. The Word of God is made words in the preacher and is heard and encountered in those words just as in a similar way the Word was made flesh and was heard and encountered in the man Jesus of Nazareth.

The apostolic Tradition remains normative for all proclamation in the Church until the Exalted Lord is made manifest in His glory at the end of time. As normative, the apostolic Tradition is endowed with a unique character. The apostolic proclamation is preserved for us in the apostolic Tradition which includes among its constituent elements the proclamation of the saving event in the life, death and glorification of Jesus Christ, the personal and immediate testimony of the apostles, united with the testimony of the Holy Spirit [Hebrews 2:3f] to the life, death and resurrection of Christ (the apostolic *marturion*) and their sound teaching (the apostolic *didakhe*, *didaskalia* and *katekkesis*). The apostolic Tradition embraces in fact the period from the birth of Jesus Christ to the death of the last apostle. In this Tradition the Church's proclamation has its origin and permanent norm.

The Church's Proclamation

In continuity with the apostolic age and subject to it as to its norm, the Church commissioned to proclaim forever the saving event that is Christ. In the Church's proclamation today Christ Himself speaks through the Holy Spirit. The Holy Spirit preserves in the memory of the Church all that Christ is by bringing back to her continually all that Christ said. Proclamation is always an official and public act of the Church which requires from the Church a mission in the name of Christ.[11] It is addressed today to both non-believers and believers. To non-believers the proclamation brings the grace of faith which is the beginning of salvation.[12] When addressed to believers, its object is an encounter with Christ through an increase of faith, hope and charity, a change of mind and heart and an inner renewal of life in preparation for the fullness of the saving event in the Holy Eucharist. The New Testament makes it clear that

---

[11] D 643 - 644, 687, 853.
[12] D 801: *fides est humanae salutis initium.*

proclamation was not addressed exclusively to non-believers and heathens [cf. Romans 16:25; 1 Corinthians 1:21; 1 Corinthians 15:14; Acts 14:27]. Those who have received the gift of salvation in Christ must continually nourish their life of faith on the Word of God and nourishment comes principally from the proclamation of the Word at the event which is the Blessed Eucharist. There is an intrinsic link between the preacher and the listeners which is the Holy Spirit Who, in the act of proclaiming-listening inspires him who proclaims and gives grace of openness and receptivity to those who listen. Proclamation is never merely one-sided activity. In view of this it may be asked here in passing whether 'dialogue-sermons' should take place during the celebration of the holy mystery of the Eucharist. This would seem not to be the occasion for discussion of what is proclaimed (provided, of course, that what is said is proclamation of the Word of God which has been prepared by study and prayer). It would seem more correct and more fitting that the proclamation of God's Word be received in silence, leaving dialogue for other occasions. From silence comes that complete openness to real listening, so necessary for the preacher's words to have their full effect.

The Mystery of Preaching

Proclamation is a mystery. Though it is governed by the laws of rhetoric and though practical techniques of speech-training, voice-production and even histrionics have their part to play in its effectiveness, nevertheless, preaching can never be reduced to any other form of human discourse, no matter how sublime. It remains a mystery in its origin, its performance, its object, its effectiveness and its ultimate purpose.

Its Origin

The proclamation of the Word of God begins in eternity with God's decision to create all things in Christ. That decision, made known to us in saving revelation, is an act of pure graciousness on God's part to us, so that without it we should never have had the blessed knowledge that leads to life everlasting. Only through grace and faith do we know that the Word was made flesh. The Word made flesh in the fullness of divine authority commissioned the apostles to pass on the Word to all mankind [Matthew 28:18ff.].

Its Performance

When the minister of the Word opens his lips to proclaim the mighty works of God, true conversion of heart and inner renewal of life, he speaks from his own faith in the Word entrusted to him by the Holy Spirit. He is obliged, of course, to give the Word his own personal expression. The preacher must make the content of his preaching what is contained in formal homiletics, he must speak a language that his hearers can understand and he must always "apply the perennial truth of the gospel to the concrete circumstances of life".[13] But it must be remembered at the same time that the words he speaks are neither purely his own nor merely about Christ. Preaching is Christ being proclaimed. Thus the preacher must be possessed entirely by the Living Word, he must be a lover of the Truth and a disciple of the Way. In the very performance of the office of preaching, the preacher is saved or judged. He must be continually on his guard never to preach what is out of harmony with the gospel or the spirit of Christ. Above all, the preacher must be ever vigilant not to propagate what are merely his own ideas and to guard the truth which has been entrusted to him.[14]

Its Object

Though the preacher must obviously know how to speak in public and must search for the best and most beautiful words to convey his message, the object of preaching is in no way to entertain or give aesthetic enjoyment.[259] Its object is to bring the message and grace of salvation to the hearers. While good voice production (in the aesthetic sense), the correct use of words and fine gestures may all contribute to the efficacy of preaching, they are, in the final analysis, dispensable. The only absolutely necessary requisites are prayer, knowledge of Christ, holiness of life, fulfilment of duty, study and a voice that can be heard.

Its Effectiveness

This depends on the preparation made by the preacher and on the grace of God in him and in his hearers. It does not depend on the learning or feelings of the hearers but on their wills strengthened by grace and the consequent openness to receive what is offered by the Holy Spirit in the words of the preacher.

Its Ultimate Purpose

Preaching is for eternal life because it contains the Word of eternal life: "Whoever listens to my words, and believes in the one who sent me, has eternal

---

[13] *Presbyterorum Ordinis*, S4, *Documents of Vatican* II, Chapman, p. 540.
[14] 2 Timothy 1:13, Titus 1:9, *Sacrosanctum Concilium*, S 35, *Dei Verbum*, S 7.
[15] See Ernst Haensli, *Preaching* in: SACRAMENTUM MUNDI 5, p. 87.

life" [John 5:24]. The Church teaches explicitly that there are no more and no less than seven sacraments. These are actions of the Glorified Christ in which salvation is not dependent on the moral dispositions of the minister; the sacraments are *opera operata*[16]. Hence preaching may not be called a sacrament. However,

> most Catholic theologians today attribute a certain sacramental structure to the word of God in the sense of being an observable sign through which the God of grace works our salvation. It is true that that happening of grace is less assured and more linked with the person of the minister than in the sacraments strictly so-called where Christ alone operates.[17]

The instrumental cause of our justification is the sacrament of baptism which is the sacrament of faith[18] and, indeed, all the sacraments presuppose faith[19]. Faith comes from preaching [Romans 10:17]. Non-believers must receive the Word of truth which comes to them through preaching before they can be baptised. Moreover, the preaching of the word of God in the Christian assembly itself "is needed for the very administration of the sacraments".[20] Through the audible sign of the preacher's words grace comes to those who hear. But, as we have noted, this effect is linked to the person of the preacher. So much depends on him which is not the case with the sacraments. If, for a moment, we separate the sacraments from the preaching of the Word of God, we know that for their valid administration the minister need only have the *intentio faciendi quod facit Ecclesia*.[21] However, when preaching and sacraments are seen in their intrinsic unity, we realize that this intention can never be more than the absolute minimum. Preaching requires the *intentio praedicandi quod praedicat Christus* which the preacher cannot have unless he has made his very own the mind of Christ. This he acquires through prayer, the study of Scripture and the knowledge and love of the Church's teaching and tradition. When he has the mind of Christ the preacher is a man of the Church. Since preaching the Word of God is directed to and consummated in the celebration of the sacraments, preparation for preaching the Word of God is *ipso facto* preparation for the celebration of the divine mysteries, above all the

---

[16] D 844, 855.
[17] Yves Congar OP, *Sacramental Worship and Preaching* in: CONCILIUM 3.4 (March 1968) p. 27.
[18] D 799.
[19] *Presbyterorum Ordinis*, p. 4; Congar, *Sacramental Worship and Preaching*, p. 29.
[20] *Presbyterorum Ordinis*, S 4, *Documents of Vatican* II, Chaprnan, 538f.
[21] D. 672, 695, 854, 1318, 2304.

Holy Eucharist. The more devoted the preacher is in preparing to preach the Word of God, the more deep and personal will be his involvement in the mysteries he celebrates. Preaching the Word of God should nourish and increase his own life of faith in what he preaches and what he does. With a faith that embraces his whole life his preaching will be all the more effective to strengthen the faith of those who hear him.

Concluding Remarks

All reflection on the mystery of preaching always leads eventually to a consideration of the priesthood. Though the latter does not fall strictly within our terms of reference, one or two remarks may be made by way of conclusion. Just as the Church is the People of the Word, constituted as such in, through and with the Word, so also is the priest primarily the minister of the Word, in through and with the Word. As the Conciliar document *Presbyterorum Ordinis* has expressed it: "The People of God finds its unity first of all through the Word of the living God, which is quite properly sought from the lips of priests. Since no one can be saved who has not first believed, priests, as co-workers with their bishops, have as their primary duty the proclamation of the gospel of God to all".[22] The priest, by sharing in the priesthood of Christ in an altogether unique way, is made above all a servant of the Word of God. The extent of his service will depend on his fidelity to the Word. His fidelity must be uncompromising, and life-long. The priest has been called by the mercy of God to be a co-worker with Christ. It is God's holy will which allows him to share in Christ's work for the salvation of mankind [cf. Hebrews 5:4]. It should be the first duty of every priest each morning to bow down in humble adoration before the mystery of God's will which permits him to open his mouth and raise his hands in proclamation and worship of the eternal and thrice-blessed God. His second task should be to implore the grace always to proclaim God's mighty deeds and never to adulterate the divine word by preaching himself.

The priest's service is unending and life-long. For this reason any theory of purely temporary service should be abandoned. God has called the priest to proclaim His Word and to co-operate in the sanctification of others until his dying day. On his ordination day God says to every priest what once He said long ago to His prophet Jeremiah: "There! I am putting my words into your mouth" [Hebrews 1:9]. On that day every priest commits his entire and unknown future into the hands of God. From that moment, as a minister of the Word, every word the priest speaks and reads must be drawn into the service

---

[22] *Presbyterorum Ordinis*, S 4, Chapman, pp. 538f.

which remains forever. In particular, his private reading and study of the Scriptures is a proximate preparation for the Liturgy of the Word at Mass and especially for the proclamation of the gospel and the breaking of the bread of the Word which is the homily. The homily is the means of grace-whereby the faith of the community is increased and strengthened to hear and receive again the most blessed and most terrifying Word that any man was ever commissioned to proclaim: "This is my Body; this is my Blood". Through these words the people and priest receive in event what was proclaimed in word. Thus strengthened God's People are sent back to the world by the Word of Christ on the lips of the priest. The priest himself returns to that sacred round of service of the Word of God which always leads him back to that point where the Word of eternity meets the words of time: the Holy Mass where he is most surely of all leader, preacher, servant and priest.

Peaceful Reflections
on the Renewal of Moral Theology[1]

Theology today is grappling with a host of problems which have arisen from three basic questions: the development of doctrine, the approach to morality and the use of religious language and symbols. These are not purely academic questions. They are also pastoral questions concerning faith, morals and worship in the Church. My concern here is with matters arising from the question about the approach to morality. In many ways this could be treated as a specific instance of the question about the development of doctrine. Developments are taking place in the approach to morality which may well turn out to be the most far-reaching the Church has ever known.

My reflections were occasioned by two features in THE CLERGY REVIEW last year: the article by Fr. Henry Allard SCJ *Recent Work in Moral Theology: In Defence of Objective Morality*[2] and the discussion contributed by Fr. James McManus CSsR with the assistance of Fr. Sean O'Riordan CSsR and Fr. Henry Stratton on *The Declaration on Certain Questions Concerning Sexual Ethics*[3]. The first section of my article presents the difficulties and questions which came to mind while reading these contributions to THE CLERGY REVIEW. I must emphasise at the outset that I am concerned directly with matters arising from these contributions and therefore no more than indirectly with the *Declaration* itself. The second section outlines an approach to morality which attempts to do justice to the specific contribution Christian revelation makes to moral understanding and to combine this with a truly personalist moral theology.

I

There are weaknesses in the manualist approach to moral theology which are the source of dissatisfaction at the level of pastoral experience. In the first place, this moral theology operates with a concept of human nature that is altogether static. This is taken as applicable from the foetus to the aged person

---

[1] THE CLERGY REVIEW 62 (Oct. 1977) pp. 393-401.
Published with permission (www.priestsandpeople.co.uk).
[2] Ibid. (May 1976) pp. 111-195.
[3] Ibid. (June 1976) pp. 231-237.

and to all peoples of all times everywhere. Its exclusive concern with nature makes it impersonal in character. As a result of this it is directly and primarily preoccupied with the individual acts of the person rather than with the person. Secondly, for all practical purposes, historical understanding has no place in the manualist approach to morality. Thus it cannot take seriously the essentially historical dimension of human existence. A corollary of this defect is the manualist's assumption that everything can be known by a process of deduction from metaphysical first principles. Actual experience can have no place in this understanding and interpretation of human nature.

Moral and Pastoral Theology

The most serious difficulties for an exclusively nature-based moral theology, which is concerned primarily to establish abstract, detailed, immutable and universally applicable norms, arise from the open conflict between most of the principles of this moral theology and the findings of the behavioural sciences, the pastoral experience of priests, Christian counsellors and social workers and the daily experience of a rapidly increasing number of believers in the Church. The conflict is caused chiefly because the principles of this nature-based morality deal with 'ideal', not with real people, with 'ideal' not with real situations, and because it offers no help whatever in the concrete circumstances of life in the Church and world.

The conflict is solved by so eminent a representative of the manualist tradition as Fr. Visser CSsR by invoking the principles of pastoral theology, the precise science for pastoral ministry. His procedure, as reported by Fr. O'Riordan, while most charitable and commendable, raises very grave doubts about the *raison d'etre* of moral theology as he understands it.

As Fr. O'Riordan remarks: "If moral theology is concerned with principles and pastoral theology is concerned with persons we may ask what real place has moral theology in the Christian life".[4] For many people in the Church today—and these include a high percentage of priests who were trained in the manualist tradition—the answer is quite simply, for all practical purposes, none at all. The inherent logic of Fr. Visser's position leads one to conclude that both his moral theology and moral theologians of his persuasion, are irrelevant to the daily life of the Church. On his procedure one could argue, for example, that the *pros* and *cons* of a particular case of sterilization are to be decided by the doctor and the pastoral theologian; that as to whether a homosexual enter into a steady partnership or not, is for the psychologist and

---

[4] Ibid., p. 233.

pastoral theologian to decide. The moral theologian need not come into these cases at all.

Fr. Visser maintains that it can be recommended in certain circumstances that a homosexual seek a steady partnership and at the same time he maintains that homosexual acts are always intrinsically evil.[5] In terms of his moral theology, therefore, he holds that homosexual acts are intrinsically evil; in terms of pastoral theology he advises that in certain circumstances homosexuals may seek steady partnerships in which, presumably, they are permitted to express their love for each other by homosexual acts. This is indeed a compassionate procedure. But there is little new in advocating compassion or in counselling the lesser of two evils—or the lesser of two goods. All this is demanded by the law of charity.

The problem with Fr. Visser's procedure, in terms of my understanding of person-based morality, is to discover how he makes the transition in what appears to be an obvious example of 'double-think'. One wonders if he has considered what possibilities there may be to bridge the incredible gap between theory and practice. There are definite and clear circumstances for him where pastoral theology advocates a solution that is diametrically opposed to the formal principles of his moral theology. In his moral theology Fr. Visser appears to ignore circumstances; in his pastoral practice they are decisive. This approach has led to the disenchantment with the moral theology of the manualists. It would be interesting to learn Fr. Visser's views on the case of two homosexuals who expressed the wish to enter a steady partnership where the 'circumstance' is solely that they love one another.

The *Good Pastor* of Yesterday and Today

After a description of Fr. Visser's understanding, merciful and tolerant attitude, Fr. McManus asks: "So, in a sense, the good theologian of the traditional school is doing in pastoral theology and pastoral practice what the personalist theologian is doing in moral theology?" Fr. O'Riordan replies: "You have defined it exactly. Again and again the personalist type of moral theology is only working out in a theoretical way what the good pastors have always instinctively known and done".[6]

---

[5] Ibid.: Fr. Visser's own pastoral approach to homosexuality is illuminating. As a moral theologian he has no doubt in categorically stating that homosexuality is intrinsically immoral. . . .But when he comes to deal with the person who is a homosexual, Fr. Visser's one concern is to help the person to live as stable a Christian life as possible in his situation.

[6] Ibid., p. 234.

These are important reflections. As no doubt both Fr. McManus and Fr. O'Riordan would agree, where a moral theology appears which is born of and in conformity with pastoral practice, resulting from reflection on experience, then the kind of moral theology pursued by Fr. Visser is rendered completely redundant. In practice this moral theology is gradually being ousted and its place is being taken by a personalist moral theology.

But there is more to be said about these reflections. We need to point out the considerable difference that exists between the *good pastor* of days gone by and the new type of *good pastor* which has emerged in the Church over recent years—a type not restricted by any means to those ordained since Vatican II. For the most part the old type of *good pastor*, while acting with understanding and compassion at the pastoral level, held in theory all the abstract principles of the manualist moral theology. But the new type of *good pastor* adheres to a very different theoretical framework. Proceeding from an intuited personalist theology and philosophy (and that is the order: from theology to philosophy, not *vice versa*), the *good pastor* today has serious objections to the validity and truth of an exclusively nature-based morality as the foundation and expression of Christian morality, he finds it irrelevant and frequently he rejects it outright.

We cannot sweep all this under the carpet and pretend it is not there. Nor can we neutralize this new approach by dismissing those who hold it as 'contextualists', purveyors of 'situation ethics' or secularists in the Church who have sold the pass to a world bent on its own moral destruction. The new theoretical attitude in the approach to morality demands serious study precisely because it is held by so many intelligent people deeply committed to the pastoral ministry of the Church. The experiences from which it has sprung constitute a theological *locus* of prime importance.

Over the past ten years I have given many retreats to priests and I have taken part frequently in courses of theological renewal for priests. In reflecting on the many hours of discussion and dialogue in groups and with individuals that this work has entailed, I find the word intuition comes constantly to mind. So many priests are acting—and have been acting for some time—on intuition in the matter of morality. Intuition jumps the logical process of reasoning and goes directly to the conclusion which is grasped as correct. It is not just a matter of a compassionate attitude at the pastoral level. Nor is it simply a question in all cases of the theology of the limited situation or of limited responsibility. It concerns the very principles and theoretical attitudes which lie behind their pastoral practice and which are at variance with the principles of an exclusively nature-based morality.

In discussion with priests about this intuition, one assertion and a cluster of questions occur again and again in relation to various moral issues. The assertion is: experience proves the manualist approach to morality to be at best irrelevant, and at worst an obstacle to responsible and free decisions and a cause of anxiety, scrupulosity and fear. The questions are: Is such and such a moral principle really identical with the immutable will of God for mankind? Is such and such an activity forbidden by God or contrary to the natural law? What does it mean to speak in general and abstract terms of 'living in a state of sin'? Is it the case that every gravely evil act is automatically a rejection of the holy God? Is the essential purpose of a specific act sufficient to determine its morality? From these follow more fundamental questions still: What exactly do we mean by 'human nature'? How do we know what is 'of nature'? When we have arrived at some kind of satisfactory answer to these questions, there comes the question about responsibility: What responsibility does man have for his own nature? What is the relation between freedom, responsibility and morality? These questions were not asked by the manualists. Yet so many of them have already been answered at the pastoral level for individual cases in terms of the intuition just mentioned and full responsibility before God is taken for the decisions that have been made.

I am not sure that all personalist theologians would simply agree with Fr. O'Riordan's statement: "A personalistic theology of sexuality looks on pre-marital sex, masturbation and homosexuality as deviations from true morality".[7] A fair number would want to place certain qualifications and ask several questions before subscribing to this as it stands. In any debate on the renewal of moral theology, the statement begs the question: What is true morality? In its turn this question itself evokes other questions to which as yet there are no straight and universally agreed answers: What is the relation of nature and person, norm and uniqueness, in morality? What precisely has Christian revelation disclosed about the structures of human existence that applies always, everywhere and to all? How far do the findings of the behavioural sciences enter into the actual construction of a moral theology? In what way is morality culturally and socially determined? To what extent and in what areas is morality relative? With respect, I would submit to Fr. O'Riordan that there is much involved and far more at stake in the difference between nature-based morality and personalist morality, than questions of

---

[7] Ibid., p. 232.

methodology.[8] It is a matter of complete shift of perspective if not indeed a Copernican revolution.

A Renewed Moral Theology

Fr. Allard's important and instructive article on the renewal of moral theology rewards serious study. It commends itself highly to anyone concerned about the kind of moral theology required by and appropriate to the Church's situation in the world. In accordance with the Council's advice to Christians in an age of change and transition, he emphasizes that the problems of moral theology have to be studied in the light of the gospel and human experience.[9] It is noteworthy, first of all, that the Council says "in the light of the Gospel" and not "in accordance with biblical texts". The difference is crucial, all the difference in the world between relevance and archaism. The light of the Word of God shines on every age in the Church's history enabling believers to discover what the Holy Spirit is saying to them in their time. It does not send them backwards over nineteen hundred years to an age that has gone by forever, to seek out texts to apply to each and every new situation. Secondly, moral problems are to be studied in the light of human experience. Man's always new understanding of himself in history is part of human experience at any specific time. Of the structure of human experience are the questions man asks about himself and his world and the solutions he proposes: of the structure of human experience are the images and symbols he employs to grapple with and come to terms with the mystery of his existence in the world. To take account of human experience in this way does not lead to relativism. It emphasizes rather the essentially relational character of human existence: its relation to God, to other human beings, to the world, to time and to history.

Fr. Allard's presentation of the function of pastoral theology does greater justice by far to its place and dignity in the theological enterprise than the understanding which appears to emerge from Fr. Visser's practice. This latter gives the impression of a narrow and limited function. It seems that pastoral theology is concerned primarily and almost exclusively with moral dilemma in the light of theoretical and abstract ideals which are *de facto* not attained. On the other hand for Fr. Allard pastoral theology is a wider field than merely applying the dictates of moral theology. Its primary concern is with caring for people in the light of the Christian faith.[10] The discernment of spirits,

---

[8] Ibid., pp. 232-234.
[9] Ibid. (May 1976) p. 191.
[10] Ibid.

the ministry of healing, spiritual direction, Christian counselling, the discovery of God's provident will in the choice of a state of life, instruction in the practice of contemplative prayer, teaching the demands of social morality in the world—these are also part and parcel of the function and concern of pastoral theology. Therefore when Fr. Allard points out that "pastoral theology. . .will start from where people are", we ought not to forget that "where people are" so often proves to be at the heights of contemplative union with God. The proposals which Fr. Allard makes for the renewal of moral theology,[11] surely mean that he rejects the description of moral theology's function given earlier in the article: "Moral theology deals with the ideal image of the mature adult who is capable of accepting responsibility for his actions".[12]

On his proposals it follows that there must be a specific morality for the various stages of growth and development of the individual person. If this is the case—and I hold that it is—then the notion of limited responsibility, for instance, will be decided in a particular case by comparing an actual adolescent with the *ideal* image of an adolescent. If moral theology is renewed intrinsically by what we are learning from the behavioural sciences, then it will have to incorporate at least as many *ideals* as there are various stages of growth and development.

II

The basis of the reflections contained in the first section of this article is located in the new-fashioned Christian law of love theology, with some natural motivation suggested here and there. This stands at the opposite pole from the old-fashioned natural law theology, with some Christian motivation suggested here and there, which Fr. O'Riordan so justly describes as the theology of the *Declaration*.[13] This new understanding of moral theology is not intended to neutralize the validity of the natural moral law, nor to suggest that this law is separable from the law of Christ. Such intending would ultimately arrive at a denial of the value and consistency of human existence itself. Grace perfects nature and all grace is Christic. The natural moral law exists in its own right and is in form distinguishable in the actual teaching of Christ, while being for the most part materially identified with it. As is manifest, however, there has never been a purely natural order. Historically and existentially nature has

---

[11] Ibid., pp. 192-195.
[12] Ibid., p. 192.
[13] Ibid. (June 1976) p. 234.

always been graced nature. All that is of the structure of human existence has always been assumed by grace and has ever been under the law of grace.

The New Period of History

It cannot be denied, I submit, that humanity has entered a new phase in its history. How it may be reckoned in various parts of the world such as Europe, the United States, Japan, Latin America or Africa, will obviously depend on the length of their historical past and how that past is understood. We in Europe, for instance, are familiar with a tripartite division of our history into ancient, medieval and modern. If, for the sake of argument only, we accept this division (I realize that it is not satisfactory), then it seems clear that we have entered a fourth period which may be termed 'post-modern' or 'period X'. No doubt it will be described with far greater precision by historians, say, in five hundred years' time. But for the time being we will have to be content with designations such as have been suggested.

While it is impossible at present to give anything like an exhaustive list of the characteristics of this period, nevertheless, reflection on developments and currents of thought over the past sixty years, allows us to single out certain factors which characterize 'period X' even in its initial stage. These factors are of paramount importance for a developing theology in general and for moral theology in particular.

The first is man's awareness of the future and his sense of responsibility for it. Man has come to see himself as open to all kinds of possibilities which are in his power to actualise. His distinct awareness of the future carries within itself the certain knowledge that it can be controlled. Involved in this is the consciousness of accountability to the future for the decisions that are made now.

The second factor concerns man's relationship with nature. Man no longer sees at first sight a world of divinely established and unchangeable order, but a world made by himself which can be changed and re-fashioned. In fact, man has changed himself and his environment.

The third is the profound realization of himself as essentially historical. By this realization he has awakened fully to the relative dimension of his own nature, of his institutions and cultures, of his laws and customs.

The emergence of these factors has thrown up all kinds of problems for us. From the point of view of morality these are some of the more significant: Do we really understand what we mean by the distinction between 'natural' and 'artificial'? Is it *a priori* clear what is meant by asserting that man must exist in harmony with nature? Are we not a little too hasty with our use of the verb 'to interfere' when speaking of certain powers of control and change with which advances in science have endowed us? Have we not been a little loose in our application of the notion of ontic or pre-moral evil? These and similar problems can only be solved in terms of man's new understanding of himself in the post-modern world.

The Christian Norm of Morality

In the Christian law of love theology, Jesus Christ is the norm of morality for the Christian believer. As God-made-man he is the most truly human man ever to have lived in the world. By the incarnation the lasting value and final meaning of human existence has been disclosed to us without trace of ambiguity. In him is the divine affirmation of human existence and of all that we call the 'natural' order. He is God's 'Yes' and through him we are able to say 'Amen'.[14] The grace of the incarnation communicates to the world the dignity of all that is natural by revealing the potency in human nature to be thus united with the Word and the fact of the union which took place in Jesus Christ.

As the total realization and complete fulfilment of what it means to be authentically human through relationships of love with God the Father and with his brethren, Jesus Christ is made the norm of Christian morality. Morality receives an utterly new context through grace. It becomes an intricate structure of relationships at the heart of which is the living and Spirit-filled relationship with Jesus Christ, risen and glorified. Natural moral law is thereby incorporated into a structure of relationships which owes its existence to uncreated grace. For instance, the first practical principle, which according to Scotus is: God must be loved,[15] is taken into the grace-relationship established

---

[14] See 2 Corinthians 1:17-22.

[15] *Joannis Duns Scoti. . . Opera, Old. IV,* d.46, q.1, n.10, Parisiis 1894, p. 426; cf. E. Bettoni, OFM, *Duns Scotus: The Basic Principles of His Philosophy,* trans. and ed. by B. Bonansea OFM, Washington D.C. 1961, pp. 160-182; A.B. Wolter OFM, *Native Freedom of the Will as a Key to the Ethics of Scotus* in *Deus et Homo ad mentem I. Duns Scoti,* Acta Tertii Congressus Scotistici Internationalis, Romae 1972, pp. 359-370; see p. 370: "The law of nature, in his system, loses something of its impersonal and inflexible character. . . .The conception of a nature that achieves its end or perfection only gradually and by an internal mechanism that allows for a trial and error method of progression does not seem foreign to or incompatible with the conception of God that Scotus held. Though he stated the principle of evolutionary development *Deus ordinate agens procedit de imperfecta ad perfectum* in reference to God's supernaturally revealed law, there seems no reason why it cannot be extended to his promulgation of the law of

by God's self-communication to the human person whereby he is made a son in the Son, co-heir with Christ and a temple of the Holy Spirit. Therefore Christian morality cannot be merely a matter of fulfilling the demands of the law. Belief in Jesus Christ, love of him, total commitment to him, reveal to his disciple a new way of understanding God, self, humanity and the world. The truth and grace which Jesus Christ is, illumine human values and meaning by manifesting the love of the Triune God for all creation and by revealing God's total acceptance of its intrinsic value by having taken it into the order of grace. To be moral is to love and the highest morality is to love God with every fibre of our being and our brethren as we love ourselves, which we do by the love with which God loves us.

Love creates relationships and it exists and endures by relationships. To love and be loved is of the very structure of the divine life. To love is the law of God's being. It is his will that love be, and become ever more, the law of our being and so it is that love can be commanded, both love of God and love of one another. To love and be loved is the law of being human. This is revealed in the being and life of Jesus Christ. To love is to be human; to love more is to become more human; to love less is to become less human.

As well as a given structure of love-relationships, Christian morality is a process of growth in love-relationships and the norm or law of that process is Christ's love of the Father in the Spirit, and his unfailing love of his brethren. God's love is given so that we may all attain to the measure of the stature of the fullness of Christ.[16]

Christian moral responsibility

Jesus Christ is the Word of God addressed to mankind. He is the Word made flesh, God's 'Yes' made flesh. The grace of God is obedience and response to this Word, for grace makes possible its own response. And at the heart of every grace-response is the great 'Amen'. Once the Word of God is heard, it demands a response and to respond involves us ineluctably in responsibility. So the theme of responsibility is paramount in the new Christian moral theology. Already in creation God revealed words about himself, communicated something about himself. Through sinfulness the human mind was obfuscated and therefore incapable of unambiguous understanding of the inherent meaning, intrinsic value and symbolic character of the world. The

---

as well, viz. to a gradual growth in moral awareness, protracted over a period of centuries or even millenia if you will. *In processu generationis humanae, semper crevit notitia veritatis*".

[16] See Ephesians 4:13.

words of creation were all but illegible, its sounds a cacophony and its symbols were reduced to puzzles. Through the Word made flesh, man's ability was restored to read again the words of creation, to hear its sounds and to interpret its symbols. By the Word of God in the world, man has become capable of understanding creation as valuable in itself, as full of meaning and as symbolic of the transcendent love at the heart of everything. Above all, by the grace of the incarnation it is disclosed that human persons are words in the Word. So the theme of responsibility in the new Christian morality embraces obedience and response to the Word and to the words in the Word. Responsibility belongs to the very structure of love relationships and it has its source in uncreated grace.

Christian moral responsibility, which has personal, social and cosmic dimensions, requires a free individual person to use the resources of discerning love to discover how God's love can best be realized according to its intrinsic demands. In the many varied situations of life, the person is bound by love to discern and then to respond to the demands of love in union with and in imitation of Christ. Discernment can be an arduous task, for it is a process of discovery and growth, and not just the application of abstract objective laws to individual acts and concrete cases. It must be stressed that it is not an arbitrary determination of the demands of love; it is not a matter of 'situationism' or 'contextualism' (if these words can be used now in any general sense at all). It is neither objectivism nor subjectivism. It is a process of discovery within the love relationships of distinct subjectivities or individual persons.

The Process of Discovery

The process of discovery takes place under the guidance of faith and of reason illumined by faith. It is directed by the Word of God and by the light of human experience. Its aim is to discover the demands of God's love in each new situation (personal, social, political) and to seek how best to fulfil these demands and thus to make present God's love in the concrete circumstances of life.

1. The Word of God

The only perduring rule is that one should try to display the most effective and wide-ranging love possible in a given situation.[17]

---

[17] Juan Luis Segundo, *Liberation of Theology*, trans. by J. Drury, Orbis Books, Maryknoll, New York 1975, p. 155; cf. p. 150: "Faith liberates men from a preoccupation with the law so that he can launch out into creative love rather than remain paralyzed by the problem of personal security and individual salvation. The only criterion for the latter things can be the static criterion

It will be clear from what has been said already that the new moral theology does not use the bible, especially the New Testament, as a collection of directives to be applied in individual cases. The source of revelation is not a book, not the magisterium, but Christ, the Word of God, alive and active now in the world. From him scripture and tradition are derived as from their unique evangelical source. To emphasize that Christ himself is the source of revelation does not neutralize the bible. The bible is not set aside, but is received in this moral theology as teaching with the highest authority that the Word of God is revealed in and through history, and as containing the most authentic and archetypal form of the historical realization of the Word of God. It remains normative, therefore, as the primordial exemplar of how the Word of God is realized and operative in a specific historical situation. The New Testament is historically conditioned, and as such it is relative.[18] Revelation did not occur, nor does it operate, in a vacuum above the course of human events. It took place in historical conditions. As history flows on and the world changes, new situations come to be, new questions are asked, new demands are made. These are understood and interpreted, answered and met, not by texts from the bible, but under the light of the Word of God.[19] New questions demand new answers;

---

of the law". The importance of Segundo's theological reflections for theology in general and moral theology in particular (especially in Europe and North America) cannot, in my view, be overestimated. His consistent and thorough-going application of the principle of the hermeneutic circle is the most convincing biblical methodology I have read. He defines the hermeneutic circle as follows: "It is the continuing change in our interpretation of the bible which is dictated by the continuing changes in our present day reality, both individual and societal. 'Hermeneutic' means 'having to do with interpretation'. And the circular nature of this interpretation stems from the fact that each new reality obliges us to interpret the Word of God afresh, to change reality accordingly, and then to go back and re-interpret the word of God again, and so on". (p. 8)

[18] Ibid., p. 181: "Faith does not need to absolutize things which in fact are not absolute and which, once absolutized, conspire against the absolute and transcendent character of faith itself. . . .What, then, is the factor that seems so intent upon absolutizing something that evidently is not absolute? The customary response to that question is not only superficial but also quite out of line with reality. It assumes that the quality of absoluteness, with its attendant notions of universality, certainty, and invulnerability to the ravages of time, is both important and essential for preserving and safeguarding the supreme values of humanity. In the realm of concrete facts and deeds, however, quite the opposite is true. The essential values of man, both as an individual and as a social group, call for an ongoing process of creation in the face of new situations and problems".

[19] V.J. Furnish, *The Love Command in the New Testament*, SCM Press Ltd. 1973, pp. 214f: "The importance of the New Testament for contemporary Christian ethics does not consist in its provision of specific solutions to the ethical problems of every subsequent age. It is clear enough that the moral complexities faced by the earliest Christians belonged to their own time, not to ours. Their answers are not automatically, and sometimes not at all transferable to our situation. Rather, what is most important for us is an understanding of what the theological bases were upon which the earliest church's ethical teaching was founded and the way it went about

new situations call for new responses.[20] Continuity in change is rooted in obedience to Christ's command to realize the gift of divine love in the most effective way in each new historical situation and through each new challenge.

2. The Light of Human Experience

Modern man has been busy creating his modern world, freeing himself from reliance on tradition and authority, working out his own world view, and so re-interpreting the views held in the past. . . .So the Law has been removed from the context of Christian morality and theology and placed in the context of some post-Christian philosophy and attitude to life.[21]

The teaching of personalist philosophies and the findings of the behavioural sciences most relevant to the renewal of moral theology, may be summarized in the following three conclusions:

(a) The human race is a historical reality; each human person is a historical being. An indisputable fact of modern human experience is historical consciousness. Through this consciousness we have come to understand that all human institutions and systems are historical. Morality is historical and therefore there is a development of morality and a development of morals.[22] What is historical is historically conditioned.

(b) Each individual person is endowed with a uniqueness which makes repetition impossible. A person is not just a specific instance of a universal nature.[23] Hence an individual's moral activity can never be understood merely

---

interpreting and applying its gospel in daily life". See also J.T. Sanders, *Ethics in the New Testament, Change and Development,* SCM Ltd. 1975.

[20] For this reason, it is my view that the advocates of a new approach to moral theology and morality are not obliged to reconcile their teaching with particular texts of the bible, nor is it necessary for them to present a 'biblical' justification of their views. This would apply, for example, to homosexuality. While it may be helpful and even necessary, in view of the opposition and prejudice, to treat of the question of scripture and homosexuality, this is not necessary in terms of methodology. See J.J. McNeill SJ, *The Church and the Homosexual,* Darton, Longman & Todd," 1977: c. 2, *Scripture and Homosexuality,* pp. 37-66.

[21] B.J.F. Lonergan SJ, *Method in Theology,* Darton, Longman and Todd 1972, pp. 154-155.

[22] *A Second Collection.* Papers by B.J.F. Lonergan SJ, ed. by W.F.J. Ryan SJ and B.J. Tyrrell SJ, Darton, Longman and Todd 1974, p. 39: "Professor Novak has given a subtly accurate account of my position on philosophic ethics. I quite agree (1) that, as I base metaphysics, so also I base ethics not on logically first propositions but on invariant structures of human knowing and human doing, (2) that this basis leaves room for a history and, indeed a development of morals, (3) that there is a concrete level of intelligibility reached by insight but missed when universal concepts are applied to particular instances, and (4) that such concrete intelligibility is relevant not only to science but also to conduct".

[23] See K. Rahner, *On the Question of a Formal Existential Ethics* in: *Theological Investigations,* H. Darton, Longman and Todd 1963, pp. 215-234.

as an expression of the demands of a universal norm. Moral activity is personal activity and what is personal by definition is unique, original, unrepeatable. There is an irreducible element in all personal moral activity. Morality is inter-subjective and there is, at the same time, an individual morality for each individual person.

(c) Man is a complex reality who lives at many levels. There are manifestly different levels of freedom, stretching from surface freedom to central freedom. Surface freedom is exercised frequently in the freedom of specification and the freedom of contrariety, in the multi-faceted activity of everyday life. Central freedom is exercised rarely. This involves in its exercise the total commitment of the whole person in decision and love. It is here, and here alone, that we locate the area of serious morality. Central freedom is the capacity of the human person to respond to the call of transcendence; it is not merely the faculty of choosing between various objects. At the depths of central freedom lies the basic or fundamental choice, state, attitude, of a person's existence. At this level, being and freedom are one. Individual acts have their meaning only from their relationship to the person's central freedom. Not each and every 'sinful' act discloses a person's fundamental or basic attitude to life, the world, other people and God. Individual acts can manifest or veil, strengthen or weaken, a basic attitude. But a basic attitude cannot be altered except by a decision of central freedom formally altering it. Because man is temporal, developing, in process, the free disposal and commitment of himself cannot be achieved formally in one act prior to death.

The outlook being expressed here requires us to re-examine our traditional categories of mortal and venial sin and to re-consider the meanings we have given them and the consequences we have drawn from them. It also leaves place for a theology of the limited situation. However, we need to be careful about the application of the limited situation. There is a place for it; but we must remember that every situation is to some degree limited. What we describe sometimes as 'limited', is really the result of a human situation which has come about simply as the stage of development reached by the persons involved.

Conclusion

I have been proposing a new approach to moral theology and morality. This approach is consistently christocentric and is derived from the absolute law of love revealed by the Word of God. As a personalist approach to moral theology it bridges the gap between moral theory and practice. It is of inestimable consequence for a healthy pastoral theology and practice. For example, it teaches a much more Christian and human attitude to the divorced who have married again. It excludes the arrogant phrase 'living in sin' and it allows those concerned to approach the sacraments of the Church. All this it does without calling in question the quite sublime doctrine of the indissolubility of marriage.

World Transformed[1]

It is remarkable that St. Paul should designate the risen Christ "the last Adam" [1 Corinthians 15:45], it is truly astonishing that the author of an ancient homily for Holy Saturday (PG 43:439-464) should present him as delivering the first Adam from imprisonment in Hades: "Awake, sleeper, I have not made you to be held a prisoner in the underworld. . . .Rise, let us go hence; for you in me and I in you, together we are one undivided person".[2]

To call Christ "the last Adam" is to intend, in one way or another, that by his rising from the dead, the human race received a fresh start: there came a new dawn for humankind, a re-creation, another beginning, and this time never to go wrong. Their unpredicted and totally unpredictable experience of the risen und glorified Lord, revealed to his first disciples a truth of decisive significance, not only for the history of the people of Israel, but for the destiny of the human race as a whole.

According to the anonymous author of the homily, Christ's descent into hell is a glorious triumph over the powers of evil and a liberation of the first Adam from every form of bondage. The new beginning thus takes up into itself the old beginning, the second Adam is one undivided person with the first. It is no idle fancy to understand by Adam in this homily the whole of mankind, all men and women, that is, from the beginning of human history to its end. These ideas are legitimate developments of 1 Peter 3:19-20, where we are told that Christ "went and preached to the spirits in prison, who formerly did not obey, when God's patience waited in the days of Noah, during the building of the ark": and 4:6: "For this is why the gospel was preached even to the dead, that though judged in the flesh like men, they might live in the spirit like God". As Christ had sanctified the very structures of this world by entering into it and becoming part of it at the incarnation, so he transformed the life of the other world by descending into the abode of the dead. Through his death and then rising to the life of glory, Christ took this world initially in himself into immortality. And so through Him heaven came to be for all of us.

---

[1] THE TABLET 232 (March 5, 1978) pp. 291f.
Published with permission (www.thetablet.co.uk).
[2] *Liturgy of the Hours* in: *Lent and Eastertide*, p. 321.

We should avoid every temptation to restrict or play down the implications of the texts quoted from 1 Peter. They contain the doctrine of universal salvation and disclose in plain terms that God's saving grace reached not only the righteous who had died before Christ, yet had not and could not have known him, but also those "who formerly did not obey". There was salvation evidently beyond the grave. On the basis of what is written in 1 Peter about Christ's preaching to the dead, it seems clear that the teaching of Christ's descent into hell is one of the most significant elements in the creeds of the Church.

The theme of Christ's descent into hell is taken up at the artistic and imaginative level in iconography. It is revealing that in this branch of sacred art Christ's descent into hell is described as his resurrection. In these icons we see the salvation and restoration of Adam depicted in a most graphic way. Christ stands in the centre of the painting, with the gates of hell beneath his feet. In one hand he is clasping the hand of Adam and, quite often, in the other the hand of Eve. The truth of the Lord's resurrection emerges, in my view, with greater clarity and power from icons, than it does from creedal formulae or descriptions in the New Testament. As we contemplate an icon of this mystery, the truth of Christ's resurrection is revealed by illuminating grace working in the order of exemplary causality. Grace floods the imagination and an image is created in us of the mystery we know and love. In fact it can be said, I think, that grace works in us through the medium of an icon, in a way analogous to that in which it works in us through the liturgy, as we celebrate the various mysteries of Christ throughout the year. By the revealing word and the enlightening image, the truth of God's universal salvific will and the truth of Christ's universal saving grace, are made known to us for our consolation and hope.

The wider—what one may call the cosmic and universal—implications of Christ's resurrection were brought home to me some years ago through a remark made by a Marxist friend. When we still lived in East Bergholt he used to call at the friary each Tuesday to discuss with me possible areas of dialogue between Christians and Marxists. I should point out that he professed no belief in God or in an after life. On his second visit I showed him round the friary. As I was telling him in the chapel that we had Mass there and Divine Office he interrupted: "Excuse me, but isn't Christ the Lord and King of the universe in here?" "Yes, Fred", I replied, "he is". "Where is he?" he asked. Pointing to the tabernacle, I explained that the Blessed Sacrament was reserved in it. Then to my utter amazement he got down on the floor and touched the tiles with his forehead. I genuflected and without further comment we came out and Fred went home. At Easter that year he came to the vigil. Afterwards over coffee in the refectory I asked him if he had enjoyed the service. He said he had in a strange kind of way, but that he had not been able to renew the baptismal promises nor to profess belief in the articles of faith. But one thing, he confided, he would like to have done and that was to have gone to communion. "I have never read a sentence in the writings of Marx or Lenin", he told me, "that comes any way near so clear and profound a statement about how good the world is, as a doctrine which teaches that God is a little piece of bread". I thought about his words for a long time afterwards. They apply equally to the doctrine of the resurrection. Can there be any more graphic way to teach the sacredness of matter and spirit and the dignity of the human person, than the doctrine of Christ's resurrection from the dead? It tells us volumes about God's love of the human body, in particular, and of the whole material universe. There is really nothing unholy or profane in the universe God loved enough to create, to restore and to transform for all eternity. The resurrection gives ultimate meaning to all human and earthly reality. In Jesus Christ, moreover, the final destiny of all humanity, the whole world and the entire cosmos has already reached fulfilment.

Jesus Christ is the same yesterday, today, tomorrow and forever. All seasons and all times are in his hands. Time before Christ reached in him its meeting point; time after him took from him its point of departure. Until he existed in our history, all time was time-bound. 'Through him the tyrant time was given a soul and all moments were made capable of eternal significance through wisdom and love. Our own individual times, our totally personal histories are taken up into Christ, are held in his hands. This certain knowledge should inspire us to accept our past and be committed to our future. Through scrupulosity we worry so much about our past; in anxiety we are troubled so often about our future. So by being preoccupied over what we cannot change (our past) and what we cannot control (our future), we make life impossible for ourselves in the present. Because Christ has risen from the dead, he inaugurated a new aeon for us all. We have to learn to accept our past whatever it has been, because it has been taken up into Christ and accepted by God. We have to learn to be committed to our future whatever it will be, because it has already been sanctified in principle by Christ and placed under the providence of God. By accepting our past and being committed to our future, we can be truly ourselves and live in the present, through God's gracious kindness, in serenity and peace.

By the risen Christ, our faith is made firm, our hope established and love assured forever. And in this we are strengthened and consoled: that through Christ Jesus all men are saved, all matter sanctified, all history and all times fulfilled.

St. John's gospel records that on the night before he died Jesus prayed to the Father for his apostles and for us: "I do not pray for these only, but also for those who believe in me through their word" [John 17:20]. We have received the word of the apostolic witnesses to the risen Christ. Let us pray that our faith remain steadfast to the end.

Lord God,
when our clutch of the hem of Christ's garment is not enough,
and we long to feel the grasp of his pierced and glorified hand,
help our unbelief.

Lord God,
when we are not satisfied with the crumbs that fall from your table,
help our unbelief.

Lord God,
when we kneel down to pray
and we think you are absent and darkness surrounds us,
help our unbelief.

Lord God,
when we feel we can stand no more
and that we must surely collapse under the weight of burden we carry,
help our unbelief.

Lord God,
when we can see no way out
and it looks as though we are going round and round in circles,
help our unbelief.

Lord God,
when our work is hard
and it blots you out from our short and very narrow vision,
help our unbelief.

Lord God,
when we are confused and troubled about our past,
help our unbelief.

Lord God,
when we tremble about our unknown future
which we know we should commit to your care,
help our unbelief.

Lord God,
when we wonder about what will happen to us in death,
when we doubt if we will be able to bear its darkness,
and have forgotten that Christ rose from the dead,
help our unbelief.

Lord God,
when we ask for a sign, when we look
and cannot see, when we listen and cannot hear,
when we demand to be sure that you are with us,
help our unbelief,
strengthen us,
say but the word
and
we shall be healed.

Amen.

Fraternal Farewell[1]
Alcuin Coyle OFM

Responding to the mandate of the Plenary Council of the Order of Friars Minor, I was summoned to Rome to assist in the evaluation and renewal of the Antonianum, our Franciscan University. I was appointed President of a commission established by our general leadership. In that capacity, I recommended Eric to serve on the Theological Commission for the renewal and updating of all theological programs, and to serve as one of the twelve members of the Visiting Team for the evaluation.

It was during the last year of this commission's work that I was informed by Fr. Louis Brennan, general council member, that Eric was seriously ill. Eric and I had planned on a summer vacation together, so I knew that I would be seeing him very shortly. When I flew to England, I met Fr. Luke Faupel, the Provincial Minister, who brought me to the noviciate house where Eric was recuperating and receiving medical help at the local clinic. Though very fragile and weak at the time, he hastened to show me the noviciate and the friary where he requested to be buried. I remained with Eric for approximately three days during which time we chatted about many things. From time to time he would return to his desk in an attempt to complete much of his writing. At our fraternal farewell, Eric, with a "stiff upper lip" mixed with his undying Franciscan optimism, promised to meet me in Rome for the final meeting of the Theological Commission in September.

After my visit, the Provincial took me to the airport. On the way, the he assured me that upon medical advice, Eric should try to do whatever he was capable of accomplishing, and hoped he could continue effectively unless the cancer would affect a vital organ. Upon my return to Rome some time later, a friar brought me the shocking news that Eric had been buried the day before. When I called the English Province to offer my sympathy, I discovered that the Province was in total shock. When arrangements were eventually made for a memorial service in September, the General Minister sent me to Canterbury to attend.

---

[1] Original contribution published with permission.

At that time I also had the opportunity to meet Eric's mother and sister. After the memorial service, the Provincial Minister accompanied us to Eric's room where we were greeted by the quiet space of a true historian. It was a room filled with his treasured collection of books, files containing his lectures and sermons, and memorabilia reflecting his life and ministry. As I was reviewing his personal effects and the many unedited manuscripts with his family, I came across some dated brochures, a variety of photographs and a number of his personal reflections regarding the vicissitudes of the time, as well as with the theology program at St. Bonaventure University then in transition. The range of his observations was wide and the remarks were always insightful. Reflecting on the implications of a renewed theological program on campus, he summed it up wisely with the understatement: "The challenge is only beginning. The real work is yet to be done".

On this visit, having been given the leisure time to review the many unedited works on Eric's desk, I encouraged the Provincial to appoint a literary executor in order to preserve the great legacy of Eric's literary works.

Eric was particularly well-known and loved within Holy Name Province and he shared his great esteem and affection for the friars during his many visits "to the colonies". During the late sixties he came to the summer campus of St. Bonaventure University as a professor in the department of Sacred Science. And his irrepressible character won for him many friends and admirers. Though he was a very gentle friar, Eric was a person of great conviction—always searching and exposing his ideas on human and contemporary issues. He generously shared his variety of gifts and talents, particularly well remembered were those of joy and contemplation. These were readily revealed in his learned lectures and inspiring homilies, which were as entertaining as his conversations.

For many of us, our lives were enriched by Eric's great love for St. Francis, the Order and humanity. Under the inspiration of St. Francis' edifying death, of which he wrote so powerfully in his work, *St. Francis and the Song of Brotherhood*, Eric died peacefully, welcoming Sister Death as St. Francis did.

Memorial Mass Homily[1]
Jarlath M. McDonagh OFM Conv

A few years ago the Order of Friars Minor published a Directory in Latin, with biographical details on each of the Order's Friars. One of the entries reads: "Eric William Doyle, son of Patrick Doyle and Josephine Reynolds, born in Bolton 13th July 1938, received the habit of the Order on 8th September 1954. He made First Profession on 9th September 1955 and Solemn Profession on 14th July 1959. Ordained a priest on 16th July 1961. A Friar of the English Province of the Immaculate Conception".

That concludes the entry in the Directory. Now a crucifix over a plot in the Friars' Cemetery at Chilworth reads: "Fr. Eric Doyle died 25th August 1984, aged 46. May he rest in peace". You will have noted that Fr.Eric entered the Order at the early age of 16. This was when he was given his religious name Eric. He had been baptised William Martin. His Solemn Profession as a Franciscan was the day after his 21st birthday, the earliest that this is allowed. His ordination as a priest at 23 required a dispensation of one year.

As we look back to 25th August and the days following Fr. Eric's death I am sure most of us will be able to identify with the two disciples mentioned in the gospel of this Mass. They were on the way to Emmaus. They were stunned at what had happened. The Master had been taken from them. While He was alive they had experienced the great things He had done and they expected even greater. Then He was crucified and their hopes were dashed. Their words sum it all up: Our own hope had been. . . .All seemed lost. It was hard for them to begin to hope once more even when the women came from the tomb, with the suggestion that He might be risen from the dead.

Those of us who had lived with Fr. Eric had experienced the great things he was doing in his own jovial and inimitable way and we had as we thought well-founded hope that he would do even greater things on this earth. Towards the end of July when he fell ill, it took us some time to realise that this

---

[1] Published with permission from the Province of Immaculate Conception, England. Editors' note: This homily was delivered at the Franciscan International Study Centre, Canterbury, 13 October 1984.

was a terminal illness. Then on 25th August he was called away by Sister Death.

In the weeks that followed we have had occasion to ponder what Christ said to the downcast disciples as he joined them on the road: "You foolish people! So slow to believe the full message of the prophets! Was it not ordained that the Christ should suffer and so enter his glory?" All that had happened fell within God's plan. Afterwards Christ revealed Himself to them in the breaking of bread. From this encounter with Christ their hearts burned within them, and they had greater hope than ever.

"Death, where is your victory? Death, where is your sting?" [1 Corinthians 15:55]. Christ is Risen and so we will have a hope that even death doesn't dim. The celebration of the Eucharist—the breaking of bread—bears witness to our belief that death was not the end for Christ. Our celebration this evening bears witness to our belief that death was not the end for Fr. Eric.

In this Mass we thank God for Fr. Eric's life and yes! for his death as well. Did we not hear in the second reading: "The life and death of each of us has its influence on others; if we live, we live for the Lord; and if we die, we die for the Lord, so that alive or dead we belong to the Lord. It is to God that each of us must give an account of himself".

We might think that Fr. Eric had a short life—46 years—but then we remember that Francis of Assisi lived for only 44 or 45 years. In spite of his short life, Francis will be remembered until the end of time. There was much in Francis' short life and Fr. Eric resembled him in this as in many other ways. Ever since I first got to know Fr. Eric I have felt he could be nothing but a Franciscan, a follower of Francis. He had been educated by the Salesians—one of the great teaching Religious Congregations of our Church—at Thornleigh, Bolton. I believe that when he was at the age of 16 he was asked why he would not be entering the Salesians but the Franciscans, he explained that he was not clever enough to be a teacher! He certainly underestimated himself in this. Coming to the Order he was prepared to give everything and so it remained throughout his life a further 30 years. For its part the Franciscan Order provided the right atmosphere and setting for him to develop as a young man, a christian, a priest, a member of community.

In fact, the Lord gave Fr. Eric great intelligence, an inquiring mind and a retentive memory. These gifts he was able to develop as a friar and these he used to the full not for his own glory but in the service of others. There was no one too grand or too little for his attention. The unlettered felt as comfortable in his company as the most highly educated. He saw Christ as the first mother of the Order and all others as his brothers and sisters through Christ. Like

Francis of Assisi he had a great love and respect for the whole of creation and he was concerned that this world should not be destroyed.

In spite of his great learning, Fr. Eric retained his own simple faith and we thank his mother for nurturing that faith from an early age and then providing the Church and the Franciscan Order with so great a young man, a precious gift. His faith was also nourished by his teachers. I mention in particular the primary school teacher whom Eric immortalised, the teacher who taught him his catechism and whom he often affectionately called 'The Great Theologian' or 'The Doctor of the Church', Nolly Conroy. It is good to know that Nolly is still alive. Her great fan has gone ahead of her. Fr. Eric never grew away from his roots and he was grateful to those who helped him become the person and friar he was.

The many enquiries concerning his condition during the final weeks of his life and the number of expressions of sympathy which we received on the occasion of his death give us some indication of the extensive influence which Fr. Eric had at home and abroad. One would not dare attempt to list his works for his Order, for society and for the Church but a few must be mentioned.

Fr. Eric will be remembered for his work for students at East Bergholt and here at the Franciscan Study Centre. Since its foundation as a member of staff he was a wonderful colleague, ever willing to share the teaching load and to contribute to the life of the institute. I remember him not only as a Lecturer in Ecclesiastical History, Franciscan Theology, Franciscan Spirituality and Ecumenism, but also as Spiritual Director and Counsellor to many students. He enjoyed being with the students and with his community; and his sense of humour, his light touch and his irrepressible character were a delight and an encouragement to all. Those of us from the Franciscan Study Centre will always treasure the memory of his party piece at the end of last term: his playful impersonation of J.D. Crichton who had spent the term with us.

Like St. Francis Fr. Eric had a great love and respect for priests. . . .In spite of his many other tasks, he somehow managed to conduct at least one retreat each year in one of the major seminaries at home or abroad. . . .There was also his contribution to the University of Kent at Canterbury as Lecturer in Medieval Ecclesiastical History and more recently in Franciscan Theology. His lectures were not only learned and inspiring but also very entertaining.

Fr. Eric was indeed a great communicator. He took part in some 580 radio and television programmes, ranging from the weekly transmission on Anglia TV "The Big Question" to "Prayer for the Day" on Radio Four.

As a theologian he contributed many articles to several periodicals especially on Religious Life, Franciscan Spirituality and Ecumenism. His main publications were *St. Francis and the Song of Brother* and *The Disciple and the Master*. He took a deep interest in the Ecumenical movement and contributed much to the debate on the ARCIC[2] Documents, especially the Agreed Statement on the Eucharist. At all times he tried to bring to discussion a peace which would aid a meeting of minds in the search for truth. In this he was true to his Franciscan calling: He remembered that Francis of Assisi did not wish to join the Crusaders in using force of arms to reconquer the Holy Lands but went to meet the Sultan with the message of Christ, a message of peace.

Through Fr. Luke, Minister Provincial, I extend our sympathy to the Friars Minor Province and I express our thanks to that Province for having made Fr. Eric available to the Franciscan Study Centre. I know his death seems a great loss to the Province. He had been elected a Definitor as recently as July. But since the Lord never takes back His gifts, we are confident He will fill the gap left through Eric's death. I express our appreciation to the General Curia of the Order being represented here today by Fr. Alcuin who read the gospel. His presence is an indication of the contribution Fr. Eric made to the Order as a whole, particularly through his service on various commissions and study groups.

I commend Eric to your prayers as we ask the Lord to receive him into glory. Eric would not wish us to praise him but to pray for him. And while we feel we would fail if we did not praise him, for in that we are really paying tribute to God for the gifts He gave, and to Eric for the way he accepted and used those gifts, at the same time we do accept his request for prayer.

In this regard we take consolation from the First Reading: "The souls of the virtuous are in the hands of God. Those who are faithful will live with him in love; for grace and mercy await those he has chosen and they are in peace". May Eric's soul and the souls of all the faithful departed through the mercy of God rest in peace.

---

[2] Editors' note: Anglican-Roman Catholic International Commission, initiated by Pope Paul VI and Michael Ramsey, Archbishop of Canterbury, in March 1966.

A Singer and His Song
Father Eric Doyle OFM, 1938-1984[1]
Conrad L. Harkins OFM

Sister Death came to Father Eric Doyle OFM at Guildford in his native England on August 25. He was only 46; she had delayed only one more year than for his spiritual Father and Brother, Saint Francis. He died peacefully, a victim of the melanoma that threatened him for seven years, warned him that already evening was at hand, and urged him to complete his share of the Lord's work while it was still day. Friends of Saint Francis throughout the English-speaking world, to whom perhaps he was most familiar, know that in Eric's *transitus* has departed one of the most vibrant Franciscans of this century.

An historian and a theologian, Eric Doyle was a man deeply in touch with the past, the present, and the future. He loved God's people, knew where they had been, and devoted his life to help them to love the goodness of God, who alone can satisfy them, and who invites them at the end of time to a new heaven and a new earth.

He is best known in North America for his writings in Franciscan spirituality and history, of which the most recent (1983) volume, *The Disciple and the Master*, was the first published English translation of Saint Bonaventure's sermons on Saint Francis. Eric loved Francis and Bonaventure, and his heart was stirred by the history of the venerable English province that had fought so valiantly for the pure observance of the Franciscan *Rule*, produced several of medieval Europe's greatest theologians, and shed blood in witness to its faith. His writings reflect these interests: *The Rule and Testament of St. Francis of Assisi, A Translation and Introduction* (1974), *Canterbury and the Franciscans 1224-1974* (1974), the introduction (co-author) and his articles on the Christology of Saint Clare and of Saint Bernardine in *Franciscan Christology* (1980). But his literary interests went beyond Franciscan topics.

---

[1] The Cord 34.11 (Dec. 1984) pp. 321-324. Published with permission from The Franciscan Institute, St. Bonaventure University, New York.

The list of over twenty articles in this review (on whose editorial board he served), and in such publications as CLERGY REVIEW, JOURNAL OF ECUMENICAL STUDIES, NEW BLACKFRIARS, REVIEW FOR RELIGIOUS, and the London TABLET ranges from ecumenism to ecology, from faith to feminism, and from prayer to moral theology. He was a scholar as well as a popularizer. On August 10, fifteen days before his death, he sent me for publication in Franciscan Studies his completed edition of a fourteenth century Franciscan text on which he had been working for several years, William Woodford's *Replies to Wyclif and the Lollards*. In a shaky hand he asked, "Incidentally, can you give me any idea of when *Responsiones* will be published? Thanking you in anticipation and with every fond and respectful good wish".

Many friars and sisters on this side of the Atlantic came to know Eric personally when in the late 1960s he joined that illustrious faculty of dedicated Franciscan theologians brought together by Fr. Alcuin Coyle in St. Bonaventure University's Department of Sacred Science. Brilliant, erudite, urbane, affable, humane, compassionate, and irrepressibly witty, Eric was loved in America. There was no mistaking that he was very English. He once delivered, with a twinkle in his eye, an impromptu lecture to children in Philadelphia's Independence Hall describing how democracy began with the Magna Charta and grew normally in British parliament and colonial legislature until in 1776, "at that table, boys and girls—the one there with the green tablecloth—delegates from all the colonies signed a paper by which all normal growth was interrupted and an act of treason was committed against his majesty's government". By the following year a tour guide had incorporated the incident into his speech. No one but Eric could preach at St. Bonaventure on Independence Day, and only he could possibly risk wishing Americans "Happy Boom-Boom Day", a reference to our penchant for fireworks. But those Americans who were guided by Eric to see the ancient walls of Greyfriars rising above the Stour, or mounted with him the steps of Canterbury Cathedral, hollowed and hallowed by the steps of long forgotten pilgrims, or prayed with him at the tomb of Canterbury's Franciscan Archbishop, John Pecham, knew that the spirit of Marsh and Bacon, of Faversham and Eccleston, of Hales, and Scotus, and Ockham lived in this friar. I remember him directing me to stand in one spot in the crypt of Canterbury Cathedral because from this vista all remained as it was when the body of the martyred Becket lay guarded by the monks on the last days of 1170. The past inspired Eric to make of the present, the future's glorious past.

The Church in England was well served by Father Eric as a popular spokesman as well as a theologian. For thirteen years he appeared weekly on an ecumenical television presentation, "The Big Question", and in all, he participated in more than 500 television and radio programs. He was a member of the Anglican-Roman Catholic Consultation on the Ordination of Women, and Vice President of the Teilhard de Chardin Society of Great Britain. He served his Franciscan Province as Definitor (Counsellor) for more than one term, and had been elected to this office just a month prior to his death. In recent months he was co-chairman of the international and inter-Franciscan commission for the renewal of the important Franciscan academic centre in Rome, the *Antonianum,* his own alma mater.

Like his spiritual Father, Saint Francis, Father Eric was small of stature, tall in spirit, and every bit alive. "This book is about a singer and his song", he wrote in his most important volume, *St. Francis and the Song of Brotherhood* (1981), his reflections on Saint Francis' most famous *laude, The Canticle of Brother Sun.* For many of us, he brought the singer and the song to life once again. "Under God, the ever-present, sustaining origin of the universe", he wrote,

> all creatures are a brotherhood or sisterhood in Christ. St. Francis left his belief in the brotherhood of creatures as a precious legacy to his followers. Part of the Franciscan calling is to make this belief one's own, to live by it and proclaim it throughout the world. As a Franciscan friar I have tried to make it mine, and though my efforts have not been entirely without fruit, to what precise degree they have been successful it is impossible to say. One thing, however, is certain. The immediate outcome of any serious effort to take the belief to heart is a heightened awareness of creatures other than ourselves. My one purpose in writing the book has been to attempt to show how belief in the universal brotherhood can help us to create a better world.

Thank you, Fr. Eric, for letting the song sound again for us. We are neither *angeli* nor *angli,* but you have spoken our language, and we have listened.

Bibliography
of Doyle's Publications[1]

[1] FRANCISCAN STUDIES 43.XXI (1983-84) pp. 7-16. Published with permission from The Franciscan Institute, St. Bonaventure University, New York. The original plublication of this bibliography was due to the dedication of Eric Doyle's friends, and collaborators at The Franciscan Institute, especially R.A. White SFO, C. Dyczek OFM, H.S. Queja OFM Cap, A. Guam and B.R. Creighton OFM. It is based on the autograph of Eric's list of publications. Editor's note: While preparing this anthology, the bibliography was revised because other articles were discovered or inaccuracies detected.

1965

So Ends the Third Session. . . .Thoughts in Vatican Council II in: THE FRANCISCAN 70.2 (February 1965) pp. 1-4.

Assisi and Ecumenism trans. from Italian *La Porziuncola* of B. Capezzali OFM in: THE FRANCISCAN 70.9 (September 1965) pp. 8f.

God Loves the Cheerful Giver in: THE FRANCISCAN 70.9 (September 1965) pp. 6ff.

1966

Duns Scotus—A Man for All Time. The Seventh Centenary of the Birth of Blessed John Duns Scotus, Edinburgh: Scotus Academy.

The Council Comes to You: Constitutions, Decrees, Declarations in: THE FRANCISCAN 71.4 (April 1966) pp. 12-14.

The Council Comes to You: The Church—the People of God in: THE FRANCISCAN 71.5 (May 1966) pp. 2f.

1967

Man is not an Island in: THE LISTENER 77.9 (4 May 1967) pp. 586f.

St. Francis and the Vatican Council in: THE FRANCISCAN 72.9 (4 September 1967) pp. 192-198.

1968

The Church in Us in: THE NEW FRANCISCAN 1.1 (January 1968) pp. 12-14.

The Order in the World in: THE NEW FRANCISCAN 1.11 (November 1968) pp. 258-261.

Duns Scotus and Ecumenism in: *Problemata Teologica,* Romae: Commissio Scotistica 1968, Vol. 3 of *De Doctrina Ioannis Duns Scoti,* 4 vols., 1968, pp. 633-652.

1969

A Manuscript of William Woodford's 'De Dominio Civili Clericorum' in: ARCHIVUM FRANCISCANUM HISTORICUM 62 (1969) pp. 377-381.

Church History and Ecumenism in: NEWSLETTER ON SEMINARY EDUCATION 8 (October 1969) pp. 6-17.

1970

A Litany of Our Lady of Walsingham in: THE DOVE 10 (Summer 1970) pp. 19f.

St. Francis and a Theology of Creation in: THE FRANCISCAN 12 (13 December 1970) pp. 31-34.

1971

God and the Feminine in: CLERGY REVIEW 56 (November 1971) pp. 866-877.

Reflections on the Theology of Preaching in: NEWSLETTER ON SEMINARY EDUCATION 12 (May 1971) pp. 4-15.

Teilhard and Theology in: IRISH THEOLOGICAL QUARTERLY 38 (April 1971) pp. 103-115.

John Duns Scotus and the Primacy of Christ in: THE OSCOTIAN 6TH SERIES (1971-1972) pp. 9f.

1972

The Anglican/Roman Catholic Statement on the Eucharist: Comment and Discussion in: CLERGY REVIEW 57 (April 1972) pp. 250-257.

Ecology and the Canticle of Brother Sun in: NEW BLACKFRIARS 55 (Sept. 1972) pp. 392-402.

John Duns Scotus and the Place of Christ in: CLERGY REVIEW 57 (Sept. 1972) pp. 667-75; (Oct. 1972) pp. 774-85; (Nov. 1972) pp. 860-68.

1973

Reflections on the Theology of Religious Life in: REVIEW FOR RELIGIOUS 33 (November 1973) pp. 1238-1263.

The Resurrection: Event of Faith in: THE TABLET 227 (April 21, 1973) pp. 379f.

Some Thoughts on MYSTERIUM ECCLESIAE in: CLERGY REVIEW 58 (December 1973) pp. 944-949.

William Woodford's De Domino Civili Clericorum against John Wyclif in: ARCHIVUM FRANCISCANUM HISTORICUM 66 (1973) pp. 49-109.

Postscript on the Mirror of Perfection and the Life of St. Francis by St. Bonaventure in: EVERYMAN'S LIBRARY, J. M. Dent & Sons Ltd. 1973, pp. X-XII. Correction of bibliographical note and additions to the bibliography, pp. XII-XIII.

1974

Canterbury and the Franciscans, 1124-1974. A Commemorative Essay, Guildford, England: Guildford Offset Service, 1974.

On Praying and Being Human: Reflections on the Anthropological Value of Prayer in: REVIEW FOR RELIGIOUS 33 (Nov. 1974) pp. 1276-1300.

The Rule and Testament of Saint Francis of Assisi, Guildford, England: Guildford Offset Service, 1974.

The Seraphic Doctor in: THE TABLET (July 13, 1974) pp. 668-670.

St. Bonaventure on St. Dominic in: SUPPLEMENT TO DOCTRINE AND LIFE 52 (July-Aug. 1974) pp. 26-46.

St. Bonaventure's Prayer for the Seven Gifts of the Holy Spirit, trans. by Eric Doyle in: THE TABLET (July 8, 1974) p. 567.

St. Bonaventure 1274-1974. Some Aspects of His Life and Thought in: THE BULLETIN 37 (July 7, 1974) pp. 16-33.

Saint Bonaventure Seraphic Doctor, 1217-1274 in: THE FRANCISCAN 16 (September 6, 1974) pp. 176-179, 182.

Ecology and the Canticle of the Sun in: NEW BLACKFRIARS 55, n. 652 (September 1974) pp. 392-402.

The Men St. Francis Sent Us in: THE UNIVERSE (September 6, 1974) p. 10.

1975

Book Review: Theological Investigations XI: Confrontations 1. By Karl Rahner in: CLERGY REVIEW (March 1975) pp. 187f.

A Bibliographical List by William Woodford OFM in: FRANCISCAN STUDIES 35 (1975) pp. 93-106.

Spiritual Law. Foundations of Peace and Freedom. The Ecology of a Peace World, Ed. T. Dunn, Christopher Davies, Swansea 1975, pp. 60-70.

1976

Believing: Its Relationship to Scripture and Creeds in: CLERGY REVIEW 61 (May 1976) pp. 78-82.

St. Francis and the Benedictines. A Commemorative Article in: THE AMPLEFORTH JOURNAL 881.3 (Autumn 1976) pp. 18-20.

1977

Peaceful Reflections on the Renewal of Moral Theology in: CLERGY REVIEW 62 (Oct. 1977) pp. 393-401; reprinted in Gaka Publications 175, 1978.

Response to the Word of God and the Mystery of Consecrated Obedience in: SUPPLEMENT TO DOCTRINE AND LIFE 17 (Sept.-Oct. 1977) pp. 67-75.

Seven-hundred-and-fifty Years Later: Reflections on the Franciscan Charism in: REVIEW FOR RELIGIOUS 36 (June 1977) pp. 12-35.

William Woodford OFM and John Wyclif's 'De Religione' in: SPECULUM 52.2 (April 1977) pp. 329-336.

William Woodford on Scripture and Tradition. Studia Historico-Ecclesiastica: Festgabe für Prof. Luchesius G. Spätling OFM, Ed. I. Vázquez OFM, Romae: Pontificium Athenaeum Antonianum 1971, pp. 481-504.

1978

The Future of the Papacy in: DOCTRINE AND LIFE (Dec. 1978) pp. 612-629.

World Transformed: The Risen Christ in: THE TABLET 232 (March 5, 1978) pp. 291f.

Anglican-Roman Catholic Consultation on the Ordination of Women to the Priesthood, co-author and signatory, Lambeth Conference, 1978.

Foreword to Lord Langford, *Francis of Assisi, A Life for All Seasons,* London 1978, pp. XIII-XV.

Christian Viewpoint: A Dynamic Union, the Communion of Saints in: EASTERN EVENING NEWS 29.758 (October 28, 1978) p. 8.

St. Francis and God's Humility in: THE TROUBADOUR 28.1 (Christmas 1978) pp. 8f.

1979

The Blessed Virgin Mary and Dialogue with Evangelicals in: CLERGY REVIEW 64 (Oct. 1979) pp. 347-357.

1980

The Cross as Gospel in: MOVEMENT. THE STUDENT CHRISTIAN JOURNAL 42 (Sept.-Oct. 1980) pp. 3-6.

Franciscan Life and the Evangelical Counsels in: THE CORD 30.5 (1980) pp. 132-141.

Gospel Poverty and St. Francis of Assisi in: THE MONTH (Dec. 1980) no page numbers.

The Image on the Shroud in: THE TABLET 234 (5 April 1980) pp. 342f.

The New Humanity: A Reflection in Word and Image in: THE SOWER 4.3 (Autumn 1980) pp. 3-12.

On Discipleship of Christ in St. Clare's Letters to Blessed Agnes of Prague in: *Franciscan Christology,* Ed. D. McElrath, St. Bonaventure N.Y., Franciscan Institute Publications 1980, pp. 14-39.

On St. Bernardine of Siena and the Devotion to the Name of Jesus in: *Franciscan Christology*, ed. D. McElrath, St. Bonaventure N.Y., Franciscan Institute Publications 1980, pp. 210-220; publ. as extract in commemoration of new friary at Siena College, Albany N.Y. (Sept. 1981) Loudonville N.Y.

On the Christocentric Character of Franciscan Life and Doctrine in: *Franciscan Christology*, Ed. D. McElrath, St. Bonaventure N.Y., Franciscan Institute Publications 1980, pp. 1-13.

Pluralism in Theology and Search for Meaning in: THE SOWER 4.1 (Lent-Easter 1980) pp. 21-25.

Questions and Answers: Devotion to Our Lady and the Doctrine of the Assumption in: CLERGY REVIEW 65 (April 1980) pp. 129f.

How Valuable Is This Survey? in: THE UNIVERSE (February 1, 1980) p. 14; cf. THE TABLET (February 2, 1980) pp. 103f.

St. Francis and the Song of Brotherhood, George Allen and Unwin, London 1980; reprint: *St. Francis and the Song of Brotherhood and Sisterhood*, Franciscan Institute Publications, St. Bonaventure N.Y. 1997; *Francesco e il Cantico delle Creature. Inno della Fratellanza Universale,* trans. into Italian by Anita Sorsaja, Cittadella Editrice, Assisi 1982; *Von der Brüderlichkeit der Schöpfung. Der Sonnengesang des Franziskus,* trans. into German by Maria-Sybille Bienentreu, Benziger Verlag AG, Zürich 1987.

St. Francis, Patron of the Environment in: THE TROUBADOUR 29.4 (Oct. 1980) pp. 56f.; THE ARK (Dec. 1980) pp. 13f.; TAU (Nov. 1980) pp. 114-116.

1981

The Franciscan Order and the Permanent Diaconate, part I in: THE CORD 31.4 (1981) pp. 101-107; part II in: THE CORD 31.5 (1981) pp 132-135.

Poverty and Credibility in: RELIGIOUS LIFE REVIEW 1.88 (January 1981) pp. 16-30.

St. Francis and Franciscan Theology in: Editorial THE CORD 31.8 (1981) pp. 226f.

St. Francis and the Song of Brotherhood, New York: Seabury Press 1981.

St. Francis of Assisi and the Christocentric Character of Franciscan Life and Doctrine in: THE CORD 31.2 (1981) pp. 336-347.

The Witness of Religious Life in: THE SOWER 5.1 (Spring 1981) pp. 31-36.

An Instrument of God's Peace in: THE FRANCISCAN MISSIONARY HERALD 46 (1981) pp. 1-3.

Poverty and Credibility—Reply to Fr. A. Delaney OP in: RELIGIOUS LIFE REVIEW, SUPPLEMENT TO DOCTRINE AND LIFE 20.90 (1981) pp. 160-162.

The Secret Beauty of an Ugly Little Man in: CATHOLIC HERALD (2 October 1981) p. 5; SCOTTISH CATHOLIC OBSERVER (9 Oct. 1981) p. 4.

Select Bibliography on the Life and Message of St. Francis in: CONCILIUM 149 (November 1981) pp. 73-77; *Bollettino bibliografico sulla vita e sul messaggio di S. Francesco* in: CONCILIUM RIVISTA INTERNAZIONALE DI TEOLOGIA pp. 125 - 133 (1469-1477); *Bibliographie choisie sur la vie et le message de Saint Francois* in: CONCILIUM 169 (Spiritualité) Paris: Beauchene, pp. 111-117; *Bibliografia Selecta sobre Francisco de Asis* in: CONCILIUM REVISTA INTERNATIONAL DE TEOLOGIA, 169 (Noviembre 1981) pp. 409-415; *Geselecteerde Bibliographie over bet leven en de boodschap van Sint Franciscus* in: CONCILIUM-INTERNATIONAAL TIJDSCHRIFT VOOR THEOLOGIE (1981) pp. 77-82; *Eine ausgewählte Bibliographie zum Leben und eine Botschaft des heiligen Franziscus* in: CONCILIUM-INTERNATIONAL TIJDSCHRIFT VOOR THEOLOGIE (1981) pp. 747-752; *Assisi Szent Ferenc élete és tanitása i (könyveszeti válogatas)* in: MÉRLEG 82.2 (Herder Kiadó, Bécs) pp. 170-178.

St. Francis of Assisi in: BRENTWOOD DIOCESAN DIRECTORY (1982) pp. 128-130.

1982

Confirmation for Commitment to Mission in: CLERGY REVIEW 67 (May 1982) pp. 162-165.

The Cross as Gospel in: *The Scandal of the Cross,* Ed. N. McElwraith, London, Student Christian Movement 1982, pp. 6-19.

Franciscan Spirituality in: RELIGIOUS LIFE REVIEW 21 (Sept.-Oct. 1982) pp. 250-259.

Francis of Assisi—His Life and Message in: SERVICE INTERNATIONAL DE DOCUMENTATION JUDEO-CHRETIENNE 15.3 (1982) p. 34.

Hasidism in: SERVICE INTERNATIONAL DE DOCUMENTATION JUDEO-CHRETIENNE 15.3 (1982) p. 35.

Religious Life and the Sacred Humanity of Christ in: SIGNUM 10.4 (March 5, 1982) pp.1-12.

St. Bonaventure's Sermons on St. Francis: A Comparison of the Quaracchi Edition with some manuscripts in: ARCHIVUM FRANCISCANUM HISTORICUM 75 (1982) pp. 416-420.

St. Francis and Theology in: THE CORD 32.4 (1982) pp. 108-111.

St. Francis: Contemplation and Hermitages in: MOUNT CARMEL (Winter 1982) pp. 193-199.

Too Fantastic To Be False in: THE TABLET 236 (December 25, 1982) pp. 1292f.

St. Francis and the Papacy in: THE TROUBADOUR (Easter 1982) pp. 24f.

A Saint's Choice of Action in: CATHOLIC HERALD (April 30, 1982) p. 10.

In Search of a Dialogue with Humanity in: CATHOLIC HERALD (May 28, 1982) p. 10.

God's Presence in the World: Redeeming Past and Future in: CATHOLIC HERALD (June 4, 1982) p. 15.

St. Bonaventure's Sermons on St. Francis: A Comparison of the Quaracchi Edition with Some Manuscripts in: *De Francesco Assisiensi Commentarii 1182-1982*, II. Grottaferrata: ARCHIVUM FRANCISCANUM HISTORICUM 75 (1982) pp. 416-420.

Catholic Christianity, the Pope and England and Wales. A Brief Historical Survey in: *Briefing-Watching*, Part F, THE PAPAL VISIT-DOSSIER EIGHT 12.23 (1982) pp. 1-16.

Francis—Fettered or Free? The human Jigsaw, University of Reading: Anglican Chaplaincy 1982.

Saint Francis: Prayer, Brotherhood, Littleness in: SCHOOLS OF PRAYER (1, Autumn 1982) pp. 8-15.

Transcript of Interview on Teilhard de Chardin for the CBC in: *Ideas: Pierre Teilhard de Chardin—Parts I-IV* (broadcasts: 381). Toronto: Canadian Broadcasting Corporation 1982.

St. Francis on Praying and Being a Creature in: PLAN FOR FRANCISCAN LIVING COMMITTEE, Eighth Centenary Project (1982).

Our Sister, Mother Earth in: FARNBOROUGH HILL (1982-1983) pp. 12-18.

1983

The Disciple and the Master—St. Bonaventure's Sermons on St. Francis of Assisi, Chicago: Franciscan Herald Press 1983.

The Essential Unity of the Church: Some Consequences for Ecumenism in: JOURNAL OF ECUMENICAL STUDIES 20 (Spring 1983) pp. 245-256.

The Final Report. Some Theological Reflections in: BRENTWOOD ECUMENICAL NEWSLETTER (July 1983) pp. 2-5; (January 1984) no page numbers.

St. Francis and the Our Father in: SCHOOLS OF PRAYER 2 (Spring 1983) pp. 9-20.

Mission Today in: FOCUS ON THE WORLD (Franciscan Missionaries of Mary) I, I (1983) p. 3.

Liturgy, Gloria in Excelsis Deo in: THE CANADIAN CATHOLIC REVIEW 9.4 (April 1983) p. 30.

Liturgy, The Pater Noster in: THE CANADIAN CATHOLIC REVIEW 1.5 (May 1983) pp. 30f.

St. Francis of Assisi in: A DICTIONARY OF CHRISTIAN SPIRITUALITY, Ed. G. S. Wakefield, London: SCM Press Ltd. 1983, pp. 157f.

Franciscan Spirituality, Franciscans in: A DICTIONARY OF CHRISTIAN SPIRITUALITY, Ed. G.S. Wakefield, London: SCM Press Ltd. 1983, pp. 159f.

The Witness of Saint Clare in: TROUBADOUR 33.1 (Christmas 1983) pp. 8-9.

The Question of Women Priests and the Argument In Persona Christi in: IRISH THEOLOGICAL QUARTERLY 50 (1983-1984) pp. 212-221.

1984

The Living Spirit in: THE TABLET (10 March 1984) p. 246.

Our Anxious Faith in: JESUS CARITAS (Spring 1984) pp. 13-18.

Victory in: THE TABLET (21 April 1984) pp. 379f.

Bringing Forth Christ. Five Feasts of the Child Jesus by St. Bonaventure, Translation and introduction, Fairacres, Oxford, England: SLG Press 1984.

The Rule and Life of the Brothers and Sisters of the Third Order Regular of Saint Francis, trans. for the TOR, Luprimene de la Centrale, Premier Trimestre 1984.

1985

St. Bonaventure: Prologue to the First Book of Sentences in: THE CORD (March 1985) pp. 80f.

Teilhard and Theology in: THE TEILHARD REVIEW AND JOURNAL OF CREATIVE EVOLUTION 20.1 (Spring 1985) pp. 2-11.

Evangelisation in the New Age in: THE TEILHARD REVIEW AND JOURNAL OF CREATIVE EVOLUTION 20.1 (Spring 1985) pp. 12-21.

Building the Earth: four excerpts in: THE TEILHARD REVIEW AND JOURNAL OF CREATIVE EVOLUTION 20.1 (Spring 1985) pp. 21-23.

1986

William Woodford OFM (c. 1330-c. 1400): His Life and Works together with a Study and Edition of his Responsiones contra Wiclevum et Lullardos in: FRANCISCAN STUDIES 43 (1986) pp. 17-187.

With all my good wishes,

Eric.